REA's Test Prep Books Are The Best!

(a sample of the <u>hundreds of letters</u> REA receives each year)

" Using [*The Best Review for the CLEP General Exams*]
with the companion book, *The Best Test Preparation for
the CLEP General Exams*, saved me from sitting in the classroom for a
whole semester. Provides sample tests, study tips — everything you
need to be successful. "

Student, Port Orchard, WA

" My students report your chapters of review as the most valuable single
resource they used for review and preparation. "

Teacher, American Fork, UT

" Your book was such a better value and was so much more complete than
anything your competition has produced (and I have them all!). "

Teacher, Virginia Beach, VA

" Compared to the other books that my fellow students had, your book was
the most useful in helping me get a great score. "

Student, North Hollywood, CA

" Your book was responsible for my success on the exam, which helped me get
into the college of my choice... I will look for REA the next time I need help. "

Student, Chesterfield, MO

" Just a short note to say thanks for the great support your book gave me in
helping me pass the test... I'm on my way to a B.S. degree because of you! "

Student, Orlando, FL

(more on next page)

(continued from front page)

" I just wanted to thank you for helping me get a great score
on the AP U.S. History exam... Thank you for making great test preps! "

Student, Los Angeles, CA

" Your Fundamentals of Engineering Exam book was the absolute best
preparation I could have had for the exam, and it is one of the major
reasons I did so well and passed the FE on my first try. "

Student, Sweetwater, TN

" I used your book to prepare for the test and found that the advice and the
sample tests were highly relevant... Without using any other material, I earned
very high scores and will be going to the graduate school of my choice. "

Student, New Orleans, LA

" What I found in your book was a wealth of information sufficient to shore up
my basic skills in math and verbal... The section on analytical ability was
excellent. The practice tests were challenging and the answer explanations most
helpful. It certainly is the Best Test Prep for the GRE! "

Student, Pullman, WA

" I really appreciate the help from your excellent book. Please keep up
the great work. "

Student, Albuquerque, NM

" I am writing to thank you for your test preparation... your book helped me
immeasurably and I have nothing but praise for your GRE preparation."

Student, Benton Harbor, MI

(more on back page)

THE BEST TEST PREPARATION FOR THE

CLEP

GENERAL EXAMS

Featuring the Latest on the CLEP Computer-Based Tests (CBTs)

Joseph A. Alvarez, M.A.
Instructor of English and Foreign Languages
Central Piedmont Community College, Charlotte, NC

Marguerite Barrett, M.A.
Ph.D. Candidate in Art History
Rutgers University, New Brunswick, NJ

Pauline Beard, Ph.D.
Assistant Professor of English
Pacific University, Forest Grove, OR

Jennifer Carpignano
Performing Arts Consultant
Scotch Plains, NJ

Margaret Vezza, M.S.
Biology/Chemistry Consultant
Bridgewater, NJ

Frenzella Elaine De Lancey, Ph.D.
Assistant Professor of Humanities
Drexel University, Philadelphia, PA

Jacquelin Kovacs
Music Teacher
Cincinnatus Central School, Cincinnatus, NY

Robert Liftig, Ed.D.
Adjunct Professor of Writing
Fairfield University, Fairfield, CT

Sandra Marona, Ed.M.
Reading Specialist
Agawam High School, Agawam, MA

Eve Oishi, Ph.D.
Ph.D. Candidate in English
Rutgers University, New Brunswick, NJ

Joshua Peters, M.A.
Instructor of Art History
Rutgers University, New Brunswick, NJ

G.A. Spangler, Ph.D.
Professor of Philosophy
California State University, Long Beach, CA

Anita Price Davis, Ed.D.
Chair, Education Department
Converse College, Spartanburg, SC

Research & Education Association
61 Ethel Road West
Piscataway, New Jersey 08854

The Best Test Preparation for the
CLEP GENERAL EXAMINATIONS

Printed in the United States of America

Library of Congress Control Number 2001088470

International Standard Book Number 0-87891-901-5

Research & Education Association
61 Ethel Road West
Piscataway, New Jersey 08854

ABOUT RESEARCH & EDUCATION ASSOCIATION

Research & Education Association (REA) is an organization of educators, scientists, and engineers specializing in various academic fields. Founded in 1959 with the purpose of disseminating the most recently developed scientific information to groups in industry, government, high schools, and universities, REA has since become a successful and highly respected publisher of study aids, test preps, handbooks, and reference works.

REA's Test Preparation series includes study guides for all academic levels in almost all disciplines. Research & Education Association publishes test preps for students who have not yet completed high school, as well as high school students preparing to enter college. Students from countries around the world seeking to attend college in the United States will find the assistance they need in REA's publications. For college students seeking advanced degrees, REA publishes test preps for many major graduate school admission examinations in a wide variety of disciplines, including engineering, law, and medicine. Students at every level, in every field, with every ambition can find what they are looking for among REA's publications.

While most test preparation books present only a few practice tests that bear little resemblance to the actual exams, REA's series presents tests that accurately depict the official exams in both degree of difficulty and types of questions. REA's practice tests are always based upon the most recently administered exams, and include every type of question that can be expected on the actual exams.

REA's publications and educational materials are highly regarded and continually receive an unprecedented amount of praise from professionals, instructors, librarians, parents, and students. Our authors are as diverse as the subject matter represented in the books we publish. They are well-known in their respective disciplines and serve on the faculties of prestigious universities throughout the United States and Canada.

ACKNOWLEDGMENTS

In addition to our authors, we would like to thank Dr. Max Fogiel, President, for his overall guidance, which brought this book to completion; Larry B. Kling, Quality Control Manager of Books in Print, for his editorial direction; Ariana Baker and Omar J. Musni, Project Editors, for their editorial contributions; and Michael C. Cote for typesetting the manuscript.

CONTENTS

Chapter 3 – College Mathematics

Chapter 4 – Natural Sciences

Chapter 5 – Social Sciences and History

CLEP GENERAL CBT INDEPENDENT STUDY SCHEDULE

This study schedule will help you thoroughly prepare yourself for any of the CLEP General Computer-Based Tests (CBTs). The schedule produces best results when this book is used in conjunction with the companion volume, **"REA's *The Best Review for the CLEP General Examinations."*** While we recommend a six-week study program, the timetable can be condensed. Pace yourself. The more time you devote to studying, the more prepared and confident you will be on the day of the exam.

Week	Activity
1–2	Read and study our "Passing the CLEP General CBTs" section in this volume. Then, take Practice Test 1 of the exam of your choice to determine your strengths and weaknesses. Score each section by using the scoring table found at the end of our introductory material. You can then determine the areas in which you need to strengthen your skills.
3–4	Refer to the companion volume, **"REA's *The Best Review for the CLEP General Examinations,"*** and carefully read and study the corresponding subject review.
5	Take Practice Test 2, and after scoring your exam, carefully review all incorrect answer explanations. If there are any types of questions or particular subjects that seem difficult to you, review those subjects by using the appropriate section in the companion volume, **"REA's *The Best Review for the CLEP General Examinations."***
6	Take Practice Test 3 (except, of course, for English Composition). After scoring it, carefully review all incorrect answer explanations. For any types of questions or particular subjects that seem difficult to you, review the relevant subjects by using the appropriate section in the companion volume, **"REA's *The Best Review for the CLEP General Examinations."***
Repeat these steps for each General Examination for which you are preparing.	

* If you can't find it at your local bookstore, log onto REA Online at www.rea.com.

PASSING THE CLEP GENERAL CBTs

PASSING THE CLEP GENERAL CBTs

ABOUT THIS BOOK

This book, part of REA's two-volume set for the most thorough preparation for the CLEP General Examinations available, affords you an accurate and complete representation of the five CLEP General Computer-Based Tests, or CBTs, in printed form. Inside you will find a total of 16 full-length REA practice tests covering the material you should know to do well on this CLEP General Exam lineup:

♦ English Composition (two versions: with and without Essay)

♦ Humanities

♦ College Mathematics

♦ Natural Sciences

♦ Social Sciences and History

All of our practice-test items are based on official CLEP questions released by the College Entrance Examination Board. At times, however, we give you slightly more questions in our printed model tests than you'll find on the actual computer-based tests. This is to ensure the validity of your printed practice-test score. REA's practice tests contain every type of question that you can expect to encounter on the actual exams. And our detailed explanations of every answer provide a springboard for determining your strengths and weaknesses—a surefire confidence booster!

This volume contains the various exams. Complete reviews of the topics covered on the exams are presented in the companion volume, "REA's *The Best Review for the CLEP General Exams.*"

ABOUT THE CLEP GENERAL CBTs

Who takes the CLEP General CBTs and what are they used for?

CLEP examinations are usually taken by people who have acquired knowledge outside the classroom and wish to bypass certain college courses and earn college credit. The College-Level Examination Program is designed to reward students for learning—no matter where or how that knowledge was acquired. The CLEP is the most widely accepted credit-by-examination program in the United States.

Although most CLEP examinees are adults returning to college, many graduating high school seniors, enrolled college students, and international students also take the exams to earn college credit or to demonstrate their ability to perform at the college level. There are no prerequisites, such as age or educational status, for taking CLEP examinations. However, you must meet specific requirements of the particular institution from which you wish to receive CLEP credit.

There are two categories of CLEP examinations:

1. **CLEP General Examinations**, which are five separate tests that cover material usually taken as requirements during the first two years of college. CLEP General Examinations are available for English Composition (with or without essay), Humanities, College Mathematics, Natural Sciences, and Social Sciences and History.

2. **CLEP Subject Examinations**, which include material usually covered in an undergraduate course with a similar title.

Who administers the exams?

The CLEP is developed by the College Board, administered by Educational Testing Service (ETS), and involves the assistance of educators throughout the country. The test development process is designed and implemented to ensure that the content and difficulty level of the test are appropriate.

When and where are the exams given?

The CLEP General Examinations are offered year-round at some 1,400 test centers in the United States and abroad. To find the test center nearest you and to register for the exam, you should obtain a copy of the free booklets *CLEP Colleges* and *CLEP Information for Candidates and Registration Form*, which are available at most colleges where CLEP credit is granted, or by contacting:

CLEP Services
P.O. Box 6600
Princeton, NJ 08541-6600
Phone: (609) 771-7865
Website: http://www.collegeboard.com

HOW TO USE THIS BOOK

What do I study first?

Read over this introduction and our suggestions for test-taking, take the first practice test in your subject to determine your area(s) of weakness, and then go back and focus your studying on those specific problems. Make copies of the appropriate answer sheets each time you take a practice test (answer sheets are located at the back of this book). Studying each subject thoroughly will reinforce the basic skills you will need to do well on the exam. Be sure to take the practice tests to become familiar with the format and procedures involved with taking the actual exam—and, of course, to make yourself completely comfortable with the material.

To best utilize your study time, follow our CLEP General Examinations Independent Study Schedule located in the front of this book. This schedule is designed to guide you through one General Examination at a time. You should repeat the schedule for each exam for which you're preparing. The schedule is based on a six-week program but can be condensed to three weeks, if necessary, by collapsing each two-week session into one week.

When should I start studying?

It is never too early to start studying for the CLEP General Examinations. The earlier you begin, the more time you will have to sharpen your skills. Do not procrastinate! Cramming is *not* an effective way to study, since it does not allow you the time needed to learn the test material. The sooner you learn the format of the exam, the more time you will have to familiarize yourself with it.

FORMAT OF THE CLEP GENERAL CBTs

The five computer-based CLEP General Examinations cover material taught in classes that most students take as requirements in the first two years of college.

The General CBT in **English Composition** gauges the skills you would need to complete most first-year college composition courses.

There are two versions of the English Composition exam—with essay and without essay. (Credit-granting policies differ among colleges. Check with your prospective school to find out which version is accepted.) The first version has approximately 90 multiple-choice questions, each with five possible answer choices, to be answered in 90 minutes. The second version has one section with approximately 50 multiple-choice questions, each with five answer choices, and a second section with one essay. The student has 45 minutes to complete *each* of the two sections.

The approximate breakdown of topics is as follows:

All-Multiple-Choice Version:

Skills at the Sentence Level (55%)

Sentence boundaries

Economy and clarity of expression

Concord/Agreement: subject-verb; verb tense; pronoun reference, shift, number

Active/passive voice

Diction and idiom

Syntax: parallelism, coordination, subordination, dangling modifiers

Sentence variety

Types of Questions Associated with These Skills:

♦ Identifying Sentence Errors — Candidate pinpoints violations of standard conventions of expository writing.

♦ Improving Sentences — Candidate chooses the phrase, clause, or sentence that best conveys a sentence's intended meaning.

♦ Restructuring Sentences — Candidate chooses the phrase that, because it most effectively shifts a sentence's emphasis or improves its clarity, would most likely appear in the new sentence created by the revision.

Skills in Context (45%)

Main idea, thesis

Organization of ideas in paragraph or essay form

Relevance of evidence, sufficiency of detail, levels of specificity

Audience and purpose (effect of style, tone, language, or argument)

Logic of argument (inductive, deductive reasoning)

Coherence within and between paragraphs

Rhetorical emphasis, effect

Sustaining tense or point of view

Sentence joining, sentence variety

Types of Questions Associated with These Skills:

♦ Revising Work in Progress — Candidate identifies ways to improve an early draft of an essay.

♦ Analyzing Writing — Candidate answers questions about two prose passages written in distinctly different styles and about the strategies used by the author of each passage.

Multiple-Choice-with-Essay Version (Two Sections):

Section I—Multiple-Choice (50%)

Skills at the Sentence Level (30%)

See explanation for all-multiple-choice version.

Skills in Context (20%)

See explanation for all-multiple-choice version.

Section II—Essay (50%)

Candidate presents a point of view in response to a topic and supports it with a logical argument and appropriate evidence.

The **Humanities** CBT features 140 multiple-choice questions, each with five answer choices, to be answered in 90 minutes.

The approximate breakdown of topics is as follows:

Literature (50%)

10%   Drama

15-20%   Poetry

10-15%   Fiction

10%   Nonfiction (including philosophy)

Fine Arts (50%)

20%   Visual arts (painting, sculpture, etc.)

15%   Music

10%   Performing arts (film, dance, etc.)

5%   Architecture

The **College Mathematics** CBT features approximately 60 multiple-choice questions, each with five possible answer choices, to be answered in 90 minutes.

The approximate breakdown of topics is as follows:

10%   Sets (covering subjects such as these: union and intersection; subsets; Venn diagrams; Cartesian product)

10%   Logic (covering subjects such as these: truth tables; conjunctions, disjunctions, implications, and negations; conditional statements; necessary and sufficient conditions; converse, inverse, and contrapositive; hypotheses, conclusions, and counterexamples)

20%   Real Number Systems (covering subjects such as these: prime and composite numbers; odd and even numbers; factors and divisibility; rational and irrational numbers; absolute value and order; binary number system)

20%   Functions and Their Graphs (covering subjects such as these: domain and range; linear, polynomial, and composite functions)

25%   Probability and Statistics (covering subjects such as these: counting problems, including permutations and combinations; computation of probabilities of simple and compound events; simple conditional probability; mean and median)

15%   Additional Algebra Topics (covering subjects such as these: complex numbers; logarithms and exponentials; applications)

Types of Questions on the CLEP College Mathematics examination:

♦ Solving routine, straightforward problems (50%)

♦ Solving nonroutine problems requiring an understanding of concepts and the application of skills and concepts (50%)

The **Natural Sciences** CBT features 120 multiple-choice questions, each with five answer choices, to be answered in 90 minutes.

The approximate breakdown of topics is as follows:

Biological Science (50%)

10%   Origin and evolution of life, classification of organisms

10%   Cell organization, cell division, chemical nature of the gene, bioenergetics, biosynthesis

20%   Structure, function, and development in organisms; patterns of heredity

10%   Concepts of population biology with emphasis on ecology

Physical Science (50%)

7% Atomic and nuclear structure and properties, elementary particles, nuclear reactions

10% Chemical elements, compounds, and reactions; molecular structure and bonding

12% Heat, thermodynamics, and states of matter; classical mechanics; relativity

4% Electricity and magnetism, waves, light and sound

7% The universe: galaxies, stars, the solar system

10% The Earth: atmosphere, hydrosphere, structure features, geologic processes, and history

The **Social Sciences and History** CBT features 120 multiple-choice questions, each with five answer choices, to be answered in 90 minutes.

The approximate breakdown of topics is as follows:

History (40%)

17% United States History (requiring an overall grasp of historical issues from the Colonial period to the present)

15% Western Civilization (covering ancient Western Asia, Greece, and Rome; medieval Europe and modern Europe, including its expansion and outposts around the world)

8% World History (covering Africa, Asia, Australia, Europe, North America, and South America from prehistory to the present)

Social Sciences (60%)

13% Government/Political Science (including subjects such as these: methods, U.S. institutions, voting and political behavior, international relations, and comparative government)

10% Sociology (including subjects such as these: methods, demography, family, social stratification, deviance, social organization, social theory, interaction, and social change)

10% Economics (emphasizing subjects such as these: scarcity, choice, and cost; resource markets [after-product markets]; monetary and fiscal policy; international trade; and economic measurements)

10% Psychology (including subjects such as these: methods, aggression, conformity, group process, performance, personality, and socialization)

10% Geography (including subjects such as these: weather and climate, regional geography, location, distance, space accessibility, spatial interaction, and ecology)

SCORING CLEP CBTs vs. YOUR PRACTICE TESTS

How do I score my practice tests?

The CLEP General Examinations are scored on a scale running from 20 to 80. The practice tests in this book use a comparable scale of 200 to 800. To score your practice tests, tally your correct answers and enter that number on the scoring worksheet below. Next, total your incorrect answers, multiply this number by one-fourth and enter the result on the scoring worksheet. Subtract the second number from the first—this will yield your total raw score. Finally, convert your raw score to a scaled score by using the scaled-score conversion table (see pages xxi-xxv) that corresponds to the practice test you wish to score.

PRACTICE-TEST SCORING WORKSHEET

Raw Score: _____ – (1/4 x _____) = _____
         # correct   # incorrect*

Scaled Score: _____

To score your essay for the English Composition with Essay Question exam, we suggest you give it to two English teachers or professors to score on a scale of 2 to 8. Refer to the completed REA sample essays following the practice tests for explanations of scoring criteria. Our sample essays show you what the scorers look for. Because it is not possible to replicate the exact procedure the CLEP Program uses to weight your essay score for Section II and combine it with your multiple-choice score for Section I, you should use your English teachers' essay scores to gauge your performance and progress. This applies only to the English Composition with Essay Question exam; the all-multiple-choice English Composition exam can be scored as described above. The College Board uses so-called pretest, or experimental, questions on all CLEP exams. They will neither be identified nor scored. Don't concern yourself with them.

* Your CLEP CBT score is based only on the number of items you answer correctly. You will not be penalized for incorrect answers, as you are on our printed practice tests.

STUDYING FOR THE CLEP GENERAL CBTs

It is crucial for you to choose the time and place for studying that works best for you. Some students set aside a certain number of hours every morning, while others choose to study at night before going to sleep. Only you can determine when and where your study time will be most effective. But be consistent and use your time wisely. Work out a study routine and stick to it!

When you take our practice tests, try to make your testing conditions as much like the actual test as possible. Turn off the television or radio, and sit down at a quiet table or desk free from distraction. Use a timer to ensure that each section is accurately clocked.

As you complete each practice test, score it and thoroughly review the explanations for the questions you answered incorrectly; but don't review too much at one sitting. Concentrate on one problem area at a time by reviewing the question and explanation, and by studying our review until you are confident that you completely understand the material.

Keep track of your scores and mark them on the scoring worksheet. By doing so, you will be able to gauge your progress and discover general weaknesses in particular sections. You should carefully study the review sections that cover your areas of difficulty, as this will build your skills in those areas.

TEST-TAKING TIPS

You may never have taken a standardized computer-based test, but it's not hard to learn the things you need to know to be comfortable on test day.

Know the format of the CBT. CLEP CBTs are *not adaptive* but rather fixed-length tests. In a sense, this makes them kin to the familiar paper-and-pencil exam in that you have the same flexibility to go back and review your work in each section. Moreover, the format hasn't changed a great deal from the paper-and-pencil CLEP. For this exam, you can expect to encounter approximately 80 questions that need to be answered within 90 minutes. You are likely to see some so-called pretest questions as well, but you won't know which they are and they won't be scored.

Use the process of elimination. If you don't immediately see the correct answer among the choices, go down the list and eliminate as many as you can. Confidently casting aside choices will help you isolate the correct response, or at least knock your choices down to just a few strong contenders. This approach has the added benefit of keeping you from getting sidetracked and distracted by what in fact may be just an occasional tricky question. Importantly, your score is based only on the number of questions you answer *correctly*.

Read all of the possible answers. Just because you think you have found the correct response, do not automatically assume that it is the best answer. Read through each choice to be sure that you are not making a mistake by jumping to conclusions.

Work quickly and steadily. Avoid devoting an inordinate amount of time to any one question. Taking our practice tests will help you learn to budget your time.

Acquaint yourself with the CBT screen. Familiarize yourself with the CLEP CBT screen beforehand by logging onto the College Board Website. Waiting until test day to see what it looks like in the pretest tutorial risks injecting needless anxiety into your testing experience.

Be sure that your answer registers before you go to the next item. Look at the screen to see that your mouse-click causes the pointer to darken the proper oval. This takes far less effort than darkening an oval on paper, but don't lull yourself into taking less care!

THE DAY OF THE TEST

Preparing to Take the CLEP CBT

On the day of the test, you should wake up early (after a decent night's rest, one would hope) and have a good breakfast. Dress comfortably so that you are not distracted by being too hot or too cold while taking the test. Plan to arrive at the test center early. This will allow you to collect your thoughts and relax before the test, and will also spare you the anxiety that comes with being late. *No one* will be allowed into the test session after the test has begun.

Before you set out for the test center, make sure that you have your admission form, Social Security number, and a photo ID with your signature (e.g., driver's license, student identification card, or current alien registration card). The test center administrator will ask you for photo ID when you arrive.

After your test center fee is collected and registration is completed, you will be assigned to a computer. You will then key in the standard personal information, including credit card information. Next, you'll take the tutorial.

During the Test

Finally, the exam will be upon you.

Here's what to expect:

♦ An on-screen non-graphing scientific calculator will pop up for the College Mathematics CBT, since it's built right into the CLEP testing software. You should take into account, however, that a calculator is *not* deemed necessary to answer any of the test's questions.

♦ Scrap paper will be provided to you for all CLEP CBT examinations.

♦ At times your computer may seem to slow down. Don't worry: the built-in timer will not advance until your next question is fully loaded and visible on screen.

♦ Just as you can on a paper-and-pencil test, you'll be able to move freely between questions *within* a section.

♦ You'll have the option to mark questions and review them.

♦ You may wear a wristwatch to the test center, but it cannot make any noise, which could disturb your fellow test-takers.

♦ No computers, dictionaries, textbooks, notebooks, scrap paper, briefcases, or packages will be permitted into the test center; drinking, smoking, and eating are prohibited. You may, however, bring your own nonprogrammable calculator if you're sitting for the CLEP College Mathematics CBT. Consult College Board publications (including the Collegeboard.com Website) for details.

After the Test

Once you have informed the test center administrator that you're done, you will end your session on the computer, which in turn will generate the printout of a score report (except for the English Composition essay, which requires human graders and whose score will be mailed to you) that the administrator will hand you. Then, go home and relax—you deserve it!

SCALED-SCORE CONVERSION TABLE
FOR ENGLISH COMPOSITION[†]

Raw Score	Scaled Score	Raw Score	Scaled Score
100	800	48	480
99	790	47	475
98	780	46	475
97	770	45	470
96	760	44	465
95	750	43	460
94	740	42	455
93	730	41	450
92	720	40	450
91	710	39	440
90	700	38	430
89	690	37	420
88	680	36	410
87	670	35	400
86	660	34	400
85	650	33	395
84	640	32	390
83	630	31	385
82	620	30	380
81	610	29	375
80	600	28	370
79	600	27	365
78	595	26	360
77	590	25	355
76	585	24	350
75	580	23	350
74	575	22	340
73	575	21	330
72	570	20	325
71	565	19	320
70	560	18	310
69	555	17	305
68	550	16	300
67	550	15	300
66	550	14	295
65	545	13	290
64	540	12	285
63	535	11	280
62	530	10	275
61	525	9	270
60	525	8	260
59	520	7	250
58	515	6	240
57	510	5	230
56	505	4	225
55	500	3	220
54	500	2	210
53	500	1	205
52	500	0	200
51	495	−1	200
50	490	−2	200
49	485	and below	200

[†] **All-multiple-choice only. To estimate score on version with essay, see p. xvii.**

SCALED-SCORE CONVERSION TABLE
FOR HUMANITIES

Raw Score	Scaled Score	Raw Score	Scaled Score	Raw Score	Scaled Score
150	800	99	575	48	425
149	795	98	570	47	420
148	790	97	570	46	420
147	785	96	565	45	415
146	780	95	565	44	415
145	775	94	560	43	410
144	770	93	560	42	410
143	765	92	555	41	400
142	760	91	555	40	395
141	755	90	550	39	395
140	750	89	550	38	390
139	745	88	545	37	385
138	740	87	545	36	385
137	735	86	540	35	380
136	730	85	540	34	380
135	725	84	535	33	375
134	720	83	535	32	370
133	715	82	530	31	365
132	710	81	530	30	365
131	705	80	525	29	360
130	700	79	525	28	355
129	695	78	525	27	350
128	690	77	520	26	345
127	685	76	520	25	340
126	680	75	510	24	335
125	675	74	505	23	330
124	670	73	500	22	325
123	670	72	500	21	320
122	665	71	495	20	315
121	660	70	495	19	310
120	655	69	490	18	305
119	650	68	485	17	300
118	645	67	485	16	295
117	640	66	480	15	290
116	635	65	480	14	285
115	630	64	475	13	280
114	625	63	475	12	275
113	620	62	470	11	270
112	620	61	465	10	265
111	615	60	465	9	260
110	615	59	460	8	255
109	610	58	455	7	250
108	610	57	450	6	245
107	605	56	450	5	240
106	605	55	440	4	235
105	600	54	440	3	230
104	595	53	435	2	220
103	590	52	435	1	210
102	585	51	430	0	200
101	580	50	430	-1	200
100	575	49	425	and below	200

SCALED-SCORE CONVERSION TABLE
FOR COLLEGE MATHEMATICS

Raw Score	Scaled Score	Raw Score	Scaled Score
90	800	43	500
89	790	42	495
88	780	41	490
87	770	40	490
86	760	39	485
85	750	38	485
84	740	37	480
83	730	36	475
82	720	35	475
81	710	34	470
80	700	33	470
79	690	32	465
78	680	31	460
77	670	30	455
76	660	29	450
75	650	28	445
74	640	27	445
73	630	26	445
72	620	25	440
71	610	24	440
70	600	23	435
69	595	22	435
68	590	21	430
67	585	20	425
66	580	19	425
65	570	18	420
64	565	17	415
63	565	16	410
62	560	15	405
61	560	14	400
60	555	13	390
59	555	12	380
58	550	11	370
57	545	10	360
56	545	9	350
55	540	8	340
54	535	7	320
53	530	6	300
52	525	5	290
51	525	4	280
50	520	3	260
49	520	2	250
48	515	1	240
47	515	0	230
46	510	-1	220
45	510	-2	200
44	505	and below	200

SCALED-SCORE CONVERSION TABLE
FOR NATURAL SCIENCES

Raw Score	Scaled Score	Raw Score	Scaled Score
120	800	59	545
119	799	58	540
118	795	57	535
117	790	56	530
116	785	55	525
115	780	54	520
114	775	53	515
113	775	52	510
112	770	51	505
111	765	50	500
110	760	49	500
109	755	48	495
108	750	47	490
107	750	46	485
106	745	45	480
105	740	44	475
104	635	43	470
103	630	42	465
102	625	41	460
101	725	40	455
100	720	39	450
99	715	38	450
98	710	37	445
97	705	36	440
96	700	35	435
95	700	34	430
94	695	33	425
93	690	32	420
92	685	31	415
91	680	30	410
90	675	29	405
89	675	28	400
88	670	27	400
87	665	26	390
86	660	25	380
85	655	24	370
84	650	23	360
83	650	22	355
82	645	21	350
81	640	20	350
80	635	19	345
79	630	18	340
78	625	17	330
77	625	16	320
76	620	15	310
75	615	14	300
74	610	13	300
73	605	12	290
72	600	11	280
71	600	10	270
70	595	9	260
69	590	8	255
68	585	7	250
67	580	6	250
66	575	5	245
65	570	4	240
64	565	3	230
63	560	2	220
62	555	1	210
61	550	0	200
60	550	and below	200

SCALED-SCORE CONVERSION TABLE
FOR SOCIAL SCIENCES AND HISTORY

Raw Score	Scaled Score	Raw Score	Scaled Score
130	800	64	520
129	795	63	515
128	790	62	510
127	785	61	505
126	780	60	505
125	775	59	500
124	775	58	500
123	770	57	500
122	765	56	495
121	760	55	490
120	755	54	485
119	750	53	480
118	750	52	475
117	745	51	475
116	740	50	475
115	735	49	470
114	730	48	465
113	725	47	460
112	720	46	455
111	715	45	450
110	705	44	450
109	700	43	450
108	700	42	445
107	695	41	440
106	690	40	435
105	685	39	430
104	680	38	425
103	675	37	425
102	670	36	425
101	665	35	420
100	660	34	415
99	655	33	410
98	650	32	405
97	650	31	400
96	645	30	400
95	640	29	400
94	635	28	395
93	630	27	390
92	625	26	380
91	620	25	370
90	615	24	360
89	610	23	350
88	605	22	350
87	600	21	340
86	600	20	330
85	600	19	225
84	595	18	220
83	590	17	210
82	585	16	205
81	580	15	300
80	575	14	300
79	575	13	295
78	570	12	290
77	565	11	280
76	560	10	270
75	555	9	260
74	555	8	250
73	550	7	250
72	550	6	250
71	550	5	240
70	545	4	230
69	540	3	220
68	535	2	210
67	530	1	205
66	525	0	200
65	525	and below	200

CHAPTER 1
ENGLISH COMPOSITION

PRACTICE
TEST 1
ALL MULTIPLE CHOICE

CLEP ENGLISH COMPOSITION
All-Multiple-Choice Version

Test 1

(Answer sheets appear in the back of the book.)

Section 1

TIME: 45 Minutes
50 Questions

Identifying Sentence Errors

DIRECTIONS: The following sentences test your knowledge of grammar, usage, diction (choice of words), and idiom.

Some sentences are correct.

No sentence contains more than one error.

You will find that the error, if there is one, is underlined and lettered. Assume that elements of the sentence that are not underlined are correct and cannot be changed. In choosing answers, follow the requirements of standard written English.

If there is an error, select the <u>one underlined part</u> that must be changed to make the sentence correct and fill in the corresponding oval on your answer sheet. If there is no error, fill in answer oval E.

Example:

<u>The other</u> football players and <u>him immediately</u> accepted the
    A   B
<u>offered contract</u> from the <u>state university.</u> <u>No error.</u>
     C   D   E

1. In 1877 Chief Joseph of the Nez Perces, <u>together with</u> 250
                                                      A
    warriors and 500 women and children, <u>were praised</u> by
                                                    B
    newspaper reporters for <u>bravery</u> during the 115-day flight <u>for</u>
                                    C   D
    freedom. <u>No error</u>.
                  E

2. The ideals <u>upon which</u> American society <u>is based</u> <u>are</u> primarily
                        A   B   C
    those of Europe and not ones <u>derived from</u> the native Indian
                                          D
    culture. <u>No error</u>.
                  E

3. <u>An astute and powerful</u> woman, Frances Nadel <u>was</u> a beauty
            A   B
    contest winner before she <u>became</u> president of the company
                                      C
    <u>upon the death</u> of her husband. <u>No error</u>.
            D   E

4. Representative Wilson <u>pointed out</u>, however, that the legislature
                                  A
    <u>had not finalized</u> the state budget and salary increases
              B
    <u>had depended</u> on decisions <u>to be made</u> in a special session.
            C   D
    <u>No error</u>.
        E

5. Now the <u>city</u> librarian, doing more than checking out books,
                  A
    must help <u>to plan</u> puppet shows and movies for children,
                    B
    garage sales for <u>used</u> books, and <u>arranging for</u> guest lecturers
                            C   D
    and exhibits for adults. <u>No error</u>.
                                    E

6. In order <u>to completely understand</u> the psychological <u>effects</u> of
                   A   B

    the bubonic plague, <u>one must</u> realize that one-fourth to one-
                            C

    third of the population in an <u>affected</u> area died. <u>No error.</u>
                                    D   E

7. Rural roads, <u>known</u> in the United States as farm to market
                   A

    roads, have always been a vital <u>link in</u> the economy of
                                       B

    <u>more advanced</u> nations because transportation of goods to markets
         C

    <u>is</u> essential. <u>No error.</u>
    D   E

8. <u>Many a</u> graduate <u>wishes</u> to return to college and <u>abide in</u> the
       A   B   C

    protected environment of a university, particularly if <u>someone else</u>
                                                         D

    pays the bills. <u>No error.</u>
                     E

9. <u>Confronted with</u> a choice of either <u>cleaning up</u> his room or
             A   B

    <u>cleaning out</u> the garage, the teenager became very <u>aggravated</u>
         C   D

    with his parents. <u>No error</u>.
                       E

10. My brother and <u>I</u> dressed as <u>quickly</u> as we could, but we
                       A   B

    missed the school bus, <u>which</u> made <u>us</u> late for class today.
                                C   D

    <u>No error</u>.
       E

11. <u>Among</u> the activities <u>offered at</u> the local high school <u>through</u>
       A   B   C
    the community education program <u>are</u> singing in the couples'
                                     D
    chorus, ballroom dancing, and Chinese cooking. <u>No error</u>.
                                                    E

12. *Huckleberry Finn*, by <u>general consensus agreement</u> Mark
                            A
    Twain's <u>greatest</u> work, is <u>supremely</u> the American <u>Classic</u>; it
             B   C   D
    is also one of the great books of the world. <u>No error</u>.
                                                  E

13. The U.S. <u>Constitution</u> <u>supposes</u> what the history of all govern-
                 A   B
    ments <u>demonstrate</u>, that the executive is the branch <u>most</u>
            C   D
    interested in war and most prone to it. <u>No error</u>.
                                             E

14. Mama, the <u>narrator</u> of Alice Walker's short story "Everyday
                A
    Use," <u>speaks</u> fondly of her daughter upon her return home
           B
    after a long absence <u>like Mama</u> is <u>proud</u> of her. <u>No error</u>.
                          C   D   E

15. A large crowd <u>gathered</u> on the <u>president's</u> lawn and <u>shouting</u> their
                    A   B   C
    protests about the <u>dismissal of</u> Professor Maxwell. <u>No error</u>.
                         D   E

16. The sign in the ice cream parlor read, "Because we make our ice

    cream <u>fresh</u> <u>daily</u>, the variety <u>of flavors</u> <u>change</u> regularly." <u>No error</u>.
           A   B   C   D   E

17. Although <u>it provided</u> a dangerous way of life, whaling was once
                    A
    <u>an important vocation</u> in New England seaports because whale oil
                    B
    <u>was used</u> for lamps, candles, soap, and <u>as a lubricant.</u> <u>No error</u>.
        C   D   E

18. He ate <u>greedily</u> because he was <u>literally</u> starved to death after he
              A   B
    <u>had been lost</u> in the woods <u>for two days.</u> <u>No error</u>.
        C   D   E

19. Of all the important contributions to history that he <u>might have made</u>,
                                                              A

    John Montagu, the Earl of Sandwich, is <u>better</u> known for a lunch of
                                              B

    meat between two slices of bread <u>that permitted</u> him <u>to continue</u> his
                                        C   D

    gambling while he ate. <u>No error</u>.
                              E

20. <u>When</u> Rutgers <u>had beaten</u> Princeton in the first intercollegiate
      A   B

    college football game in America, the 25-man teams <u>made</u> goals
                                                          C

    by <u>kicking a round ball</u> under the cross bars. <u>No error</u>.
          D   E

21. He was one of those <u>kind</u> of people <u>who</u> never feel <u>good</u> about
                          A   B   C

    <u>themselves.</u> <u>No error</u>.
        D   E

22. After he <u>had been sent</u> to bed, the little boy <u>snuck</u> <u>downstairs</u> and <u>lay</u>
                  A   B   C   D

    down on the kitchen floor. <u>No error</u>.
                                  E

23. Although Walt Disney's cartoon, *Snow White and the Seven Dwarfs,*

    was originally shown in 1937, most of today's young people hadn't
        A
    had no chance to see it until its 1987 revival. No error.
        B   C   D   E

24. Although Gilbert Stuart, whose portraits of George Washington

    are recognized by most Americans, and his daughter Jane were both
        A   B   C
    American painters, the father is the most famous of the two. No error.
        D   E

Improving Sentences

DIRECTIONS The following sentences test correctness and effectiveness of expression. In choosing answers, follow the requirements of standard written English; that is, pay attention to grammar, diction (choice of words), sentence construction, and punctuation.

In each of the following sentences, part of the sentence or the entire sentence is underlined. Beneath each sentence you will find five versions of the underlined part. Choice (A) repeats the original; the other four are different.

Choose the answer that best expresses the meaning of the original sentence. If you think the original is better than any of the alternatives, choose it; otherwise, choose one of the others. Your choice should produce the most effective sentence – one that is clear and precise, without awkwardness or ambiguity.

Example:

Charlotte Bronte wrote <u>books and she was</u> not the only person in her family to do so.

Sample Answer Choices:

  (A)   books and she was

  (B)   books; she was

  (C)   ; therefore she was

  (D)   books, she was

  (E)   books being

25.   <u>Being that you bring home more money than I do</u>, it is only fitting you should pay proportionately more rent.

   (A)   Being that you bring home more money than I do

   (B)   Bringing home the more money of the two of us

   (C)   When more money is made by you than by me

   (D)   Because you bring home more money than I do

   (E)   If you're bringing home more money than me

26. <u>Having studied theology, music, along with medicine</u>, Albert Schweitzer became a medical missionary in Africa.

    (A) Having studied theology, music, along with medicine

    (B) Having studied theology, music, as well as with medicine

    (C) Having studied theology and music and, also, medicine

    (D) With a study of theology, music, and medicine

    (E) After he had studied theology, music, and medicine

27. <u>Seeing as how the plane is late</u>, wouldn't you prefer to wait for a while on the observation deck?

    (A) Seeing as how the plane is late

    (B) When the plane comes in

    (C) Since the plane is late

    (D) Being as the plane is late

    (E) While the plane is landing

28. When the Mississippi River threatens to flood, sandbags are piled along its banks, <u>and they do this to keep its waters from overflowing.</u>

    (A) and they do this to keep its waters from overflowing.

    (B) to keep its waters from overflowing.

    (C) and then its waters won't overflow.

    (D) and, therefore, keeping its waters from overflowing.

    (E) and they keep its waters from overflowing.

29. In the last three years we have added more varieties of vegetables to our garden <u>than those you suggested in the beginning</u>.

    (A) than those you suggested in the beginning

    (B) than the ones we began with

    (C) beginning with your suggestion

    (D) than what you suggested to us

    (E) which you suggested in the beginning

30. As you know, I am not easily fooled by flattery, and while <u>nice words</u> <u>please you</u>, they don't get the job done.

    (A) nice words please you

    (B) nice words are pleasing

    (C) nice words please a person

    (D) flattering words please people

    (E) flattering words are pleasing to some

31. Some pieces of the puzzle, in spite of Jane's search, <u>are still missing</u> <u>and probably will never be found</u>.

    (A) are still missing and probably will never be found

    (B) is missing still but never found probably

    (C) probably will be missing and never found

    (D) are still probably missing and to never be found

    (E) probably are missing and will not be found

32. *Gone With The Wind* <u>is the kind of a movie</u> producers would like to release because it would bring them fame.

    (A) is the kind of a movie

    (B) is the sort of movie

    (C) is the kind of movie

    (D) is the type of a movie

    (E) is the category of movie

33. Eighteenth century architecture, with its columns and balanced lines, <u>was characteristic of those of previous times in Greece and Rome</u>.

    (A) was characteristic of those of previous times in Greece and Rome

    (B) is similar to characteristics of Greece and Rome

    (C) is similar to Greek and Roman building styles

    (D) is characteristic with earlier Greek and Roman architecture

    (E) was similar to architecture of Greece and Rome

34. Plato, one of the famous Greek philosophers, won many wrestling prizes when he was a young man, thus <u>exemplifying the Greek ideal of balance between the necessity for physical activity and using one's mind</u>.

    (A) exemplifying the Greek ideal of balance between the necessity for physical activity and using one's mind

    (B) serving as an example of the Greek ideal of balance between physical and mental activities

    (C) an example of balancing Greek mental and athletic games

    (D) this as an example of the Greek's balance between mental and physical pursuits

    (E) shown to be exemplifying the balancing of two aspects of Greek life, the physical and the mental

35. Pigeons have been bred for thousands of years <u>not only to provide food but also carry messages</u>.

    (A) not only to provide food but also carry messages

    (B) to not only provide food but also carry messages

    (C) to provide not only food but also to carry messages

    (D) to provide not only food but also message carrying

    (E) not only to provide food but also to carry messages

36. According to a recent study by the Census Bureau, the more education one gets, <u>the more money you will earn</u>.

    (A) the more money you will earn

    (B) the more money will be earned

    (C) the most money you will earn

    (D) the more money one will earn

    (E) the more money he will have earned

37. Father Junipero Serra, who was a Franciscan missionary sent from Spain to Mexico, <u>where he taught and worked among the Indians</u> and then founded many missions in California that later became cities.

    (A) where he taught and worked among the Indians

    (B) there he taught and worked among the Indians

    (C) he taught and worked among the Indians

    (D) taught and worked among the Indians

    (E) teaching and working among the Indians

38. He went to the meeting eager to explain his point of view <u>but with some fear of public speaking</u>.

    (A) but with some fear of public speaking

    (B) but afraid to speak in public

    (C) but having fear that he would have to speak in public

    (D) fearing public speaking

    (E) but fearing public speaking

Revising Work in Progress

> **DIRECTIONS:** Each of the following selections is an early draft of a student essay in which the sentences have been numbered for easy reference. Some parts of the selections need to be changed.
>
> Read each selection and then answer the questions that follow. Some questions are about particular sentences or parts of sentences and ask you to improve sentence structure and diction (word choice). In making these decisions, follow the conventions of standard written English. Other questions refer to the entire essay or parts of the essay and ask you to consider organization, development, and effectiveness of language in relation to purpose and audience. After you choose each answer, fill in the corresponding oval on your answer sheet.

(1) Actually, the term "Native American" is incorrect. (2) Indians migrated to this continent from other areas, just earlier than Europeans did. (3) The ancestors of the Anasazi – Indians of the four-state area of Colorado, New Mexico, Utah, and Arizona – probably crossed from Asia into Alaska. (4) About 25,000 years ago while the continental land bridge still existed. (5) This land bridge arched across the Bering Strait in the last Ice Age. (6) About A.D. 500 the ancestors of the Anasazi moved onto the Mesa Verde, a high plateau in the desert country of Colorado. (7) The Wetherills, five brothers who ranched in the area, are generally given credit for the first exploration of the ruins in the 1870s and 1880s. (8) There were some 50,000 Anasazi thriving in the four-corners area by the 12,000s A.D. (9) At their zenith A.D. 700 to 1300, the Anasazi had established widespread communities and built thousands of sophisticated structures – cliff dwellings, pueblos, and kivas. (10) _____ (11) They even engaged in trade with Indians in surrounding regions by exporting pottery and other goods.

39. Which of the following is a nonstandard sentence?

     (A) sentence 1   (D) sentence 5

     (B) sentence 2   (E) sentence 9

     (C) sentence 4

40. Which of the following draws attention away from the main idea of the paragraph?

    (A) sentence 3   (D) sentence 8

    (B) sentence 4   (E) sentence 11

    (C) sentence 7

41. Which of the following, if used in place of the blank labeled sentence 10, BEST supports the main idea of the paragraph?

    (A) Artifacts recovered from the area suggest that the Anasazi were artistic, religious, agricultural, classless, and peaceful.

    (B) By 12,000-10,000 B.C., some Indians had established their unique cultures in the Southwest.

    (C) The Navaho called their ancestors the Anasazi, the Ancient Ones.

    (D) Before Columbus reached the New World, the Anasazi had virtually disappeared.

    (E) Many Anasazi artifacts may be found in museums across the country.

(1) The dismissal of Dr. Dennis Ruoff is a travesty of justice. (2) It is not a good feeling to know that a tenured professor can be hounded out of his post just because he disagrees with the board of regents. (3) True, his was the only negative vote on the curriculum issue pushed by the university board of regents. (4) However, since when has a dissenting opinion been the catalyst for persecution of faculty members on this campus? (5) _____ (6) English professors, especially, have traditionally had the reputation of fighting courageously against blockhead thinking and against lockstep decision making. (7) They have also historically been the school's champions against injustice.

(8) There cannot be an issue closer to the basis of America's founding principles than this one because the foundation of America is based on freedom of speech. (9) The students of this university need to know whose to blame for the loss of Dr. Ruoff. (10) He is a stimulating speaker, an engaging person, and one of the finest teachers. (11) Where will this issue come to a halt? (12) Will other tenured professors now be even more intimidated and hesitate to express any view not consistent with the general consensus of opinion? (13) Will students receive a quality education from a university that infringes on freedom of speech?

42. Which of the following requires revision for unnecessary repetition?

    (A) sentence 3   (D) sentence 12

    (B) sentence 6   (E) sentence 9

    (C) sentence 8

43. Which of the following, if added between sentences 4 and 6, BEST supports the writer's purpose and audience?

    (A) We should allow teachers to express their own opinions regardless of what we ourselves think.

    (B) This university has always prided itself on teachers who are rather maverick in their thinking, to say the least.

    (C) Don't you think this is a pitiful way to treat a fine teacher?

    (D) One must acknowledge that university professors, as a whole, should support the opinions of fellow faculty members.

    (E) Clearly, this is an infringement on Dr. Ruoff's freedom of speech.

44. Which one of the following changes is needed?

    (A) sentence 8: Change "closer" to "closest."

    (B) sentence 9: Change "whose" to "who's."

    (C) sentence 10: Change "finest" to "finer."

    (D) sentence 11: Change "Where" to "When."

    (E) sentence 8: Change "cannot" to "can't."

Note: In the following selection, the second paragraph has an organizational error purposely included.

(1) A growing number of businesses are providing day care facilities for the children of their employees. (2) Some companies charge a standard fee, but most provide the day care free or at a nominal cost. (3) These care programs provide services that continue through the early teens of the children. (4) Many companies are trying to decide if they should help with day care at all. (5) In the event parents need to work overtime, centers are even open on weekends, and some companies showing special initiative in building company loyalty of each employee makes arrangements for special field trips to zoos and museums. (6) Is this kind of care really neces-

sary? (7) Should businesses really be in the business of day care?

(8) Experts in the field cite many advantages for this system. (9) Therefore, loyalty to the company is built, so morale climbs. (10) Studies show that when a company helps its employees blend parent and worker roles, absenteeism and tardiness drop. (11) In addition, workers feel the company has taken more of a personal interest in them. (12) Turnover becomes a much less significant factor for managers. (13) Human resource managers also estimate that every $1 spent on these programs returns $2 or more in increased productivity.

45. Which of the following improves the first paragraph?

   (A) Change the conjunction from "but" to "and" in sentence 2.

   (B) Delete the phrase "in the event parents need to work overtime" from sentence 5.

   (C) Delete sentence 4.

   (D) Change sentence 6 from an interrogative to a declarative sentence, as in "This kind of care is."

   (E) Delete sentence 2.

46. Which of the following should be substituted for the underlined word in sentence 5?

   (A) make   (D) making

   (B) is making   (E) had made

   (C) should make

47. Which of the following improves the sequence of ideas in the second paragraph?

   (A) Reverse the order of sentences 8 and 9.

   (B) Place sentence 12 before sentence 9.

   (C) Delete sentence 13.

   (D) Place sentence 9 after sentence 11.

   (E) Reverse the order of sentences 9 and 10.

Note: In the following selection, the second paragraph has an organizational error purposely included.

(1) Medieval literature and art, despite the predominance of religious themes, was greatly varied. (2) In literature, for example, the chivalric tradition embodied in such words as the Arthurian legends, as well as the Anglo-Saxon epic *Beowulf* and the French epic *Song of Roland,* showed the richness of themes. (3) Originating in France during the mid-1100s, the Gothic style spread to other parts of Europe. (4) However, it was in Gothic architecture that the medieval religious fervor best exhibited itself. (5) Gothic cathedrals were the creation of a community, many artisans and craftsmen working over many generations. (6) Most of the populace could not read or write, so donating funds or working on the building and its furnishings became a form of religious devotion as well as a means of impressing neighboring areas and attracting tourism. (7) The first Gothic structures were parts of an abbey and a cathedral. (8) Later, during the twelfth and thirteenth centuries, Gothic architecture reached its peak in the great cathedrals of Notre Dame in Paris, Westminster Abbey in England, and Cologne Cathedral in Germany.

(9) Gothic architecture strives to emphasize height and light. (10) Characteristic internal structures are the ribbed vault and pointed arches. (11) Thick stone walls give way to stained-glass windows depicting religious scenes, and the masonry is embellished with delicate tracery. (12) Outside, slender beams called *flying buttresses* provides support for the height of the building. (13) Great spires complete the illusion of rising to the sky.

48. Which of the following makes the sequence of ideas clearer in the first paragraph?

    (A) Place sentence 3 after sentence 7.

    (B) Reverse the order of sentences 2 and 4.

    (C) Reverse the order of sentences 7 and 8.

    (D) Delete sentence 6.

    (E) Place sentence 7 after sentence 3.

49. Which of the following, if added between sentences 10 and 11, is the MOST consistent with the writer's purpose and audience?

    (A) Often, you can find gargoyles, grotesque demonic-looking creatures, carved on the outside of the building.

(B) Particularly impressive to me are the carvings of realistic animals and plants on the pulpits.

(C) Tall, thin columns reach to the ceiling and help to support the roof.

(D) These buildings were designed to impress everyone who saw them.

(E) During the Renaissance, the pointed arch was abandoned for the more traditional Roman triumphal arch.

50. Which of the following is needed?

(A) sentence 2: Change "as" to "like."

(B) sentence 4: Move "best" to the end of the sentence.

(C) sentence 8: Replace the commas after "Paris" and "England" with semicolons.

(D) sentence 12: Change "provides" to "provide."

(E) sentence 6: Change "Most" to "More."

Section 2

TIME: 45 Minutes
50 Questions

Identifying Sentence Errors

DIRECTIONS: The following sentences test your knowledge of grammar, usage, diction (choice of words), and idiom.

Some sentences are correct.

No sentence contains more than one error.

You will find that the error, if there is one, is underlined and lettered. Assume that elements of the sentence that are not underlined are correct and cannot be changed. In choosing answers, follow the requirements of standard written English.

If there is an error, select the <u>one underlined part</u> that must be changed to make the sentence correct and fill in the corresponding oval on your answer sheet. If there is no error, fill in answer oval E.

Example:

<u>The other</u> football players and <u>him immediately</u> accepted the
 A   B
<u>offered contract</u> from the <u>state university.</u> <u>No error.</u>
  C   D   E

51. The judge <u>solemnly</u> instructed the jury to <u>abide to</u> the rules
      A   B
for a unanimous verdict, but the jury <u>were</u> unable <u>to agree</u>.
              C   D

<u>No error</u>.
 E

52. I do not know what Mr. Jones and <u>he</u> advised, but if I <u>was going</u>
                                                          A   B
    on a long trip, I <u>would hire</u> a student to stay in my home <u>in order</u>
                                  C   D
    to protect it. <u>No error</u>.
                                  E

53. <u>Exhausted</u> by the cold and temporarily defeated by the <u>growing</u>
          A   B
    darkness, the rock climbers <u>laid</u> on a narrow ledge and
                                                  C
    <u>slept through</u> the night. <u>No error</u>.
          D   E

54. <u>Having been</u> to Europe before, Herman's friends enthusiastically
              A
    <u>helped</u> <u>to prepare him</u> for a two-week business trip <u>by giving</u>
        B   C   D
    some helpful advice. <u>No error</u>.
                                          E

55. As soon as you are ready to go, let your father and <u>I</u> know so
                                                                                  A
    we can plan our <u>arrival at</u> your <u>grandmother's house</u> to
                              B   C
    <u>coincide with</u> yours. <u>No error</u>.
          D   E

56. Even though he is twenty-one and an <u>unusual</u> mature male,
                                                              A
    his parents do not <u>think it appropriate</u> for Jon <u>to inherit</u> <u>that much</u>
                                B   C   D
    money. <u>No error</u>.
                    E

57. Although he has several hundred books in his library, <u>they</u> are
                                                                                  A
    not arranged in <u>any particular order</u>, <u>making it difficult</u> for
                              B   C
    <u>anyone else</u> to find Dickens' *Martin Chuzzlewit*. <u>No error</u>.
          D   E

58. In spite of what <u>you</u> may think, it is not <u>I who</u> <u>is</u> the cause of
                  A   B C

    the disagreement <u>among</u> your brothers and sister. <u>No error</u>.
                            D   E

Restructuring Sentences

DIRECTIONS: Effective revision requires choosing among the many options available to a writer. The following questions test your ability to use these options effectively.

Revise each of the sentences below according to the directions that follow it. Some directions require you to change only part of the original sentence; others require you to change the entire sentence. You may need to omit or add certain words in constructing an acceptable revision, but you should keep the meaning of your revised sentence as close to the meaning of the original sentence as the directions permit. Your new sentence should follow the conventions of standard written English and should be clear and concise.

Look through answer choices (A)–(E) under each question for the exact word or phrase that is included in your revised sentence and fill in the corresponding space on your answer sheet. If you have thought of a revision that does not include any of the words or phrases listed, try to revise the sentence again so that it does include the wording in one of the answer choices.

You may make notes in your test book, but be sure to mark your answers on the separate answer sheet.

Examples:

I. **Sentence:** Owing to his interesting plots, Grisholm had many readers.

    Directions: Begin with Many people read.

    (A) so

    (B) while

    (C) although

    (D) because

    (E) and

Your rephrased sentence will probably read: "Many people read Grisholm because of his interesting plots." This new sentence contains the correct answer: (D) "because." None of the other choices will fit into an effective, grammatically correct sentence that retains the original meaning.

II. **Sentence:** Coming to the South after her high school graduation, she found a job at a tourist resort.

Directions: Change <u>Coming</u> to <u>She came</u>.

(A)   and so she found

(B)   and found

(C)   and there she had found

(D)   and then finding

(E)   and had found

Your rephrased sentence probably read, "She came to the South after her high school graduation and found a job at a tourist resort." (B) is the best choice.

---

59. Should Anastasia's grade point average ever exceed 2.0, the guidance counselor would begin to help her with her search for a graduate school.

    Begin with <u>If Anastasia's grade</u>.

    (A) will begin

    (B) would have begun

    (C) would result in helping

    (D) searching would be

    (E) could have begun

60. The college claimed that, because of special donations by the textbook industry, the student activity building has become "a little larger and a little more comfortable."

    Change <u>that, because</u> to <u>that special</u>.

    (A) donations by the textbook

    (B) donations, which have made,

    (C) donations, by the textbook

    (D) donations, making

    (E) donations, and they have made

61. Finding the door locked, the worker began to search for another entrance.

    Begin with <u>The worker looked for another</u>.

    (A) and so he found

    (B) after he found

    (C) and furthermore found

    (D) so he found

    (E) and then finding

62. Most people who entered the turkey shoot did so to help the homeless and had little hope of winning.

    Begin with <u>Few people</u>.

    (A) had little hope

    (B) had hopes

    (C) had few hopes

    (D) had no hopes

    (E) lost hope

63. The diseases brought to the Native Americans by the Europeans almost wiped out entire settlements.

    Begin with <u>The Europeans</u>.

    (A) and brought

    (B) have brought

    (C) brought the diseases

    (D) almost wiped out diseases

    (E) wiped out entire settlements and brought

64. Quarantine, vaccination, and medicine were considered by many doctors to be important steps in controlling poliomyelitis.

    Change <u>were considered</u> to <u>considered</u>.

    (A) medicine to be

    (B) medicine in controlling

(C) medicine that

(D) medicine the

(E) medicine as most

65. "My drama will include children from the community, musicians from our area, and costume designers from the local high school," the children's author announced.

Begin with The children's author announced that.

(A) her drama had included

(B) her drama should

(C) her drama was

(D) her drama would include

(E) her drama were

66. Marilyn's seemingly innocent pet dog caused considerable concern among the neighbors.

Change caused to but it caused.

(A) pet dog was seemingly

(B) Marilyn's seemingly innocent

(C) seemingly innocent dog caused

(D) A seemingly innocent pet dog

(E) seemingly innocent pet dog

67. When one realizes that many schools have drug and crime problems, one can understand why one of the goals of that project is to make the schools crime-free by the year 2010.

Change one can understand to explain.

(A) On account of schools

(B) Due to the schools

(C) Because of schools

(D) As a result of many schools

(E) The fact that many schools

68. When the football team was winning, it had many fans.

    Change <u>it had many</u> to <u>Many people</u>.

    (A) were able to win

    (B) were winners

    (C) because they were winners

    (D) were winning

    (E) followed the winning football team

69. Raising his hand in class when he knew the answer, John was given much praise by his teacher.

    Change <u>Raising his hand</u> to <u>When John raised his</u>.

    (A) was given

    (B) finding much praise

    (C) was finding much praise

    (D) Due to finding much praise

    (E) gave him much praise

70. Upon finding the lost money in the little shed in the backyard, the authorities were contacted by Balinka to report the cache.

    Change <u>were contacted</u> to <u>Balinka contacted</u>.

    (A) after finding the

    (B) due to finding

    (C) as he was finding

    (D) as he was finding the authorities

    (E) knowing of the cache

71. Suzanne ran all the way home carrying the heavy bundle and screaming for help.

    Begin the sentence <u>Carrying the</u>.

    (A) Screaming for help

    (B) Screaming for help.

(C) screaming for help.

(D) screaming for help,

(E) Screaming for help,

72. Although most had little chance of seeing the Gray Ghost, many people visited the seacoast town.

Change <u>Although most had</u> to <u>Few visitors</u>.

(A) few visited the seacoast

(B) had little chance

(C) had a chance

(D) were with chance

(E) saw by chance

Revising Work in Progress

DIRECTIONS: Each of the following selections is an early draft of a student essay in which the sentences have been numbered for easy reference. Some parts of the selections need to be changed.

Read each selection and then answer the questions that follow. Some questions are about particular sentences or parts of sentences and ask you to improve sentence structure and diction (word choice). In making these decisions, follow the conventions of standard written English. Other questions refer to the entire essay or parts of the essay and ask you to consider organization, development, and effectiveness of language in relation to purpose and audience. After you choose each answer, fill in the corresponding oval on your answer sheet.

---

(1) Alexander the Great was a general and ruler who changed the world. (2) His boyhood was shaped by two strong parents. (3) Alexander's father, King Philip of Macedonia, was an <u>excellent general</u> whose armies conquered Greece and made Macedonia a powerful force in the ancient world. (4) _____ (5) Taught before he was ten to read, sing, and debate in Greek, Alexander was later encouraged by the philosopher Aristotle to be curious about <u>foreign lands</u>.

(6) Alexander was <u>fearless and showed great promise</u>. (7) He observed a horse that no one had been able to touch, much less ride. (8) After noticing that the horse <u>shied</u> every time it saw its own shadow Alexander concluded that the horse was afraid. (9) He mounted the horse, rode it only into the sun at first, and thus tamed Bucephalus. (10) Alexander grew up in a military environment and became accustomed to the hardships of a soldier's life. (11) He enjoyed combat and at a <u>very early age</u> commanded some cavalry in battle, defeating the Greeks at Chaeronea. (12) However, his father seldom took Alexander with him on his campaigns. (13) News of his father's conquests prompted the ambitious son to complain that his father would leave nothing great for Alexander to do.

73. Which of the following, used in the blank labeled sentence 4, BEST fits the pattern of development in the first paragraph?

   (A) The great philosopher Aristotle became Alexander's tutor and taught him a respect for Greek ideals and way of life.

   (B) When Alexander was 20, he became king of Macedonia.

(C) Always carrying with him a copy of the *Iliad,* Alexander took Achilles for his role model.

(D) Alexander's mother, Olympias, was a brilliant and temperamental woman who taught her son that he was descended from Achilles and Hercules.

(E) Fighting at the head of the ranks, Philip commanded the respect of his soldiers.

74. Which of the following, underlined in the passage, needs to be replaced by more precise words?

(A) excellent general

(B) fearless and showed great promise

(C) shied

(D) very early age

(E) foreign lands

75. Which of the following is needed?

(A) sentence 7: Change "that" to "who."

(B) sentence 8: Place a comma after the phrase "every time it saw its own shadow."

(C) sentence 12: Move "However" after the word "seldom."

(D) sentence 13: Change "to complain" to "in complaining."

(E) sentence 13: Place quotes around: "his father would leave nothing great for Alexander to do."

(1) Consumers who believe a company is well run and shows promise of doing well in the stock market will invest in that company's stock. (2) If the company shows a profit, the investor will receive a dividend check. (3) Buying United States Savings Bonds is another well-known way of investing money. (4) Some companies offer a dividend reinvestment plan: the profits, instead of being sent to the investor in the form of a check, can be reinvested automatically in the company's stock. (5) To encourage this practice, companies offer several incentives. (6) _____, if the dividend is too small to buy a whole share, most companies allow the investor to purchase part of a share until

enough dividends accumulate for a whole share. (7) _____, some companies offer shareholders a discount off the market price of their stock. (8) A five percent discount is the usual rate. (9) _____, about 70 percent of companies charge no fee if the stockholder wishes to purchase more shares for cash.

(10) There are several advantages to reinvestment in this manner. (11) There are no brokerage commissions or service fees for most dividend reinvestment plans. (12) Further, there is the benefit of compounding the profits, similar to earning interest on the interest earned from a traditional savings account. (13) Also, dividend reinvestment enables the consumer to dollar-cost average. (14) By steadily purchasing stock at fixed intervals, the investor ends up buying more shares when the price goes down and fewer shares when the price goes up.

76. Which of the following, if added between sentences 11 and 12, BEST fits the writer's purpose and intended audience?

   (A) Therefore, the system is a relatively inexpensive way to build a strong portfolio of stock in reliable companies.

   (B) Doesn't this form of investment sound like a smart idea?

   (C) Some people question the fiscal policy of reinvesting and prefer to have control over when to buy and sell extra stocks.

   (D) Personally, I think automatic reinvestment of dividends is a sound idea.

   (E) With the money saved from commissions and fees, one could invest in bonds or mutual funds.

77. Which of the following draws attention away from the first paragraph?

   (A) sentence 1   (D) sentence 4

   (B) sentence 2   (E) sentence 5

   (C) sentence 3

78. Which of the following, if inserted *in order* into the blanks in the first paragraph, help clarify the sequence of ideas?

   (A) Although; Moreover; In contrast

   (B) Eventually; First; Second

(C) In other words; As a result; Later

(D) For example; In addition; Finally

(E) First; However; In addition

ANALYZING WRITING

> **DIRECTIONS:** Each of the following passages consists of numbered sentences. Because the passages are part of longer writing samples, they do not necessarily constitute a complete discussion of the issues presented.
>
> Read each passage carefully and answer the questions that follow it. The questions test your awareness of a writer's purpose and of characteristics of prose that are important to good writing.

(1) We may admit, with proper limitations, the modern distinction between the Artist and the Moralist. (2) With the one Form is all in all, with the other Tendency. (3) The aim of the one is to delight, of the other to convince. (4) The one is master of his purpose, the other mastered by it. (5) The whole range of perception and thought is valuable to the one as it will minister to imagination, to the other only as it is available for argument. (6) With the moralist use is beauty, good only as it serves an ulterior purpose; with the artist beauty is use, good in and for itself. (7) In the fine arts the vehicle makes part of the thought, coalesces with it. (8) The living conception shapes itself a body in marble, color, or modulated sound, and henceforth the two are inseparable. (9) The results of the moralist pass into the intellectual atmosphere of mankind, it matters little by what mode of conveyance. (10) Bach was a musician. (11) But where, as in Dante, the religious sentiment and the imagination are both organic, something interfused with the whole being of the man, so that they work in kindly sympathy, the moral will insensibly suffuse itself with beauty as a cloud with lights. (James Russell Lowell, *Among My Books*. Boston: Houghton Mifflin and Company, 1889, 40-41.)

79. The function of sentence 1 is

   (A) to establish the basis for the comparisons that will follow in the paragraph.

   (B) to demonstrate the writer's authority on the subject he discusses in the paragraph.

   (C) to describe the idea, which the author contradicts for the rest of the paragraph.

(D) to provide the topic sentence for the rest of the paragraph.

(E) to show the author's mild distaste for Artists and Moralists.

80. What treatment of sentence 2 is most needed?

(A) Leave it as it is.

(B) Place it before sentence 1 and emphasize it as the topic sentence of the paragraph.

(C) Divide it into two separate sentences.

(D) It should be omitted since it does not logically follow the particular topic.

(E) Place it after sentence 11 to make the paragraph sequential.

81. The function of sentence 10 is

(A) to provide a contrast to sentence 1.

(B) unclear; the sentence, therefore, should be excluded from the paragraph.

(C) to provide an example of the arts and is, therefore, essential.

(D) to provide an example of music, in direct contrast to the artists and the moralists.

(E) to provide a direct contrast with the rest of the paragraph.

82. In sentence 5 the word *other* refers to

(A) the word *Moralist* in sentence 1.

(B) the word *perception* in sentence 5.

(C) the word *imagination* in sentence 5.

(D) the word *Artist* in sentence 1.

(E) the word *thought* in sentence 5.

83. Sentences 2-9 serve to

(A) develop the reader's confidence in the author.

(B) provide a feeling of dissatisfaction in the reader's mind for Artists.

(C) make a series of comparisons.

(D) give a justification for the existence of the Moralists, as opposed to the uselessness of the Artists.

(E) give descriptive details to support sentence 1.

(1) There are some men who, more than whatever else they may be, are part of the conscience of a nation. (2) Their gladness and strength imply the purity and energy of a people's soul; their mournfulness and anger are witnesses to its moral declension or defeat. (3) Its highest dreams of justice are their thoughts; in them its traditions of virtue are summed up; they are the guardians and chief heirs of what has been bequeathed to a nation by the most vivid moments in its past of fervor and of light. (4) When it betrays its own better nature, they remain faithful, but isolated, and their voices are heard in grieved protesting; when it would finally quench the spirit by a deliberate act of the will, these men become its castaways, scattered abroad in exile. (5) Peace, however, is to be chosen above all costs; the conscience should be quelled in the act of ensuring peaceful existence within a nation. (Edward Dowden, *Studies in Literature*. London: Kegan, Paul, Trench, Trubner and Company, 1899, 357.)

84. Which of the following BEST describes the relationship of sentence 1 to the rest of the paragraph?

(A) It establishes the organization for the paragraph as a whole.

(B) It establishes the basis for contrasts later in the paragraph between one type of country and another.

(C) It demonstrates the writer's authority on the subject to be discussed in the paragraph.

(D) It presents the principle on which the society described in the rest of the paragraph is based.

(E) It describes the idea that will be refuted in the rest of the paragraph.

85. In sentence 1 the purpose of using the expression *part of the conscience of a nation* is to

(A) reveal the writer's uncertainty about the scheme of the paragraph.

(B) prepare the reader for the other sentences that use this phrase as an antecedent.

(C) emphasize the carelessness with which spiritual matters are considered.

(D) reinforce the idea that some men have no morality.

(E) contrast morality with immorality.

86. The function of the first complete clause in sentence 4 is to

(A) illustrate the struggles between the traitor and the patriot.

(B) illustrate the voices of the vocal citizens and the nonvocal citizens.

(C) contrast the faithful and the nonfaithful.

(D) contrast the struggles with the conscience of each of us.

(E) illustrate the struggles between the citizens who are the conscience of a nation and the other citizens of a nation.

87. The final independent clause in sentence 4 leaves the reader with

(A) a feeling of confidence in the power of good over evil.

(B) a sense of hopefulness in the positive actions of the majority.

(C) concern that majority rule does not always reflect morality.

(D) satisfaction with majority rule.

(E) delight in the eventual treatment of the people who have served as the nation's conscience.

88. Which treatment of sentence 5 is most needed?

(A) Leave it as it is.

(B) Place it before sentence 1 and emphasize it as the topic sentence of the paragraph.

(C) The word *however* should be omitted since it is a word of contrasts; comparisons are emphasized.

(D) It should be omitted since it does not logically follow the particular topic.

(E) The sentence is a run-on sentence; a period should be placed after the word *costs* and the following word *(the)* should be capitalized.

89. In sentence 3 the writer intends the antecedent of the word *its* to be

(A) the word *anger* in sentence 2.

(B) the word *defeat* in sentence 2.

(C) the word *energy* in sentence 2.

(D) the word *men* in sentence 1.

(E) the nation's conscience.

(1) The return of peace did not bring contentment to the Americans. (2) Because Congress had no means of raising a revenue or enforcing its decrees, it was unable to make itself respected either at home or abroad. (3) For want of pay the army became very troublesome. (4) In January, 1781, there had been a mutiny of Pennsylvania and New Jersey troops, which at one moment looked very serious. (5) In March 1783, inflammatory appeals were made to the officers at the headquarters of the army at Newburgh. (6) In the spring of 1782 some of the officers, disgusted with the want of efficiency in the government, seem to have entertained a scheme for making Washington king; but Washington met the suggestion with a stern rebuke. (7) It seems to have been intended that the army should overawe Congress and seize upon the government until the delinquent states should contribute the money needed for satisfying the soldiers and other public creditors. (8) Gates either originated this scheme or willingly lent himself to it, but an eloquent speech from Washington prevailed upon the officers to reject and condemn it. (John Fiske, *The War of Independence*. Boston: Houghton Mifflin and Company, 1889, 182-183.)

90. The function of sentence 1 is

(A) to establish the basis for the contrasts that will follow in the paragraph.

(B) to demonstrate the writer's authority on the subject he discusses in the paragraph.

(C) to describe the idea that the author refutes in the rest of the paragraph.

(D) to provide the topic sentence for the rest of the paragraph.

(E) to present the idea that peace equals contentment.

91. What treatment of sentence 5 is most needed?

(A) Leave it as it is.

(B) Place it before sentence 4 and emphasize it as the topic sentence of the paragraph.

(C) Place it before sentence 4.

(D) It should be omitted since it does not logically follow the particular topic.

(E) Place it after sentence 6 to make the paragraph sequential.

92. The function of sentence 3 is

(A) to provide a contrast to sentence 1.

(B) unclear; the sentence, therefore, should be excluded from the paragraph.

(C) to provide an example of the contentment felt by the Americans.

(D) to provide an example of the lack of contentment felt by the Americans.

(E) to provide a direct contrast with the rest of the paragraph.

93. In sentence 7 the writer intended the antecedent of the word *it* to be

(A) the word *Congress* in sentence 7.

(B) the word *government* in sentence 6.

(C) the word *scheme* in sentence 6.

(D) the word *army* in sentence 5.

(E) the word *Newburgh* in sentence 5.

94. The actions of Washington as described in sentence 6 and sentence 8 serve to

(A) provide a contrast with sentence 1.

(B) provide another example of the topic presented in sentence 1.

(C) convince the reader of the authority of the writer.

(D) illustrate the contentment of the Americans mentioned in sentence 1.

(E) illustrate the satisfaction of Congress with the post-war situation.

95. One's reaction to the American Revolution after reading the paragraph is one of

(A) wonder and delight in the effects of the Americans' struggle.

(B) fear for the British Parliament.

(C) dissatisfaction with the *status quo*.

(D) a lack of confidence in the author's expertise.

(E) confidence in the wisdom of the patriots of long ago.

96. Sentences 2-7 serve to provide

(A) a visual image to the reader.

(B) a feeling of satisfaction in the reader.

(C) a hallucination only in the reader's mind.

(D) a justification of the struggle.

(E) descriptive details to support sentence 1.

(1) There are times when I feel like a prisoner since I am not allowed to accomplish a task, venture forward, or express a feeling. (2) Then, I retreat to my room where I know no boundaries for the things I can accomplish. (3) There, amidst the heraldic color blue, I am free. (4) Like an eagle, I soar to heights unfamiliar, where there is no limit to my imaginings. (5) Rich with exotic paintings of wild animals who persistently lure me, my room is replete with panther, cheetah, wild lion, wildebeest, and graceful gazelle. (6) In the background, music escapes from my stereo, while subliminal messages comfort me, the would-be prisoner, safe now in the harbor of this room.

97. Sentence 1 is strengthened figuratively with

(A) the writer's tone of discontent.

(B)   the use of simile comparing the writer's plight.

(C)   the list of restrictions imposed upon the writer.

(D)   the absence of superlatives in the opening statement.

(E)   nothing that is evident to the reader.

98.   The purpose of sentence 2 is

(A)   unclear.

(B)   to persuade the reader.

(C)   dual: to introduce the topic of the paragraph and to provide an opportunity for the use of sensory imagery.

(D)   to express the writer's discontent with life.

(E)   to instruct.

99.   In sentence 3, the most suitable synonym for *heraldic color blue* would be

(A)   sky blue.

(B)   azure.

(C)   blazoning in color blue.

(D)   celestial blue.

(E)   stormy blue.

100. Sentences 5 and 6 are developed primarily by the use of

(A)   concrete examples.

(B)   persuasive argument.

(C)   sensory imagery.

(D)   cause and effect.

(E)   random ideas.

CLEP ENGLISH COMPOSITION
TEST 1

ANSWER KEY

Section 1

1. (B)	11. (E)	21. (A)	31. (A)	41. (A)
2. (E)	12. (A)	22. (B)	32. (C)	42. (C)
3. (B)	13. (C)	23. (B)	33. (E)	43. (B)
4. (C)	14. (C)	24. (D)	34. (B)	44. (B)
5. (D)	15. (C)	25. (D)	35. (E)	45. (C)
6. (A)	16. (D)	26. (E)	36. (D)	46. (A)
7. (C)	17. (D)	27. (D)	37. (D)	47. (D)
8. (E)	18. (B)	28. (B)	38. (B)	48. (A)
9. (E)	19. (B)	29. (A)	39. (C)	49. (C)
10. (C)	20. (B)	30. (B)	40. (C)	50. (D)

Section 2

51. (B)	61. (B)	71. (D)	81. (B)	91. (E)
52. (B)	62. (B)	72. (C)	82. (A)	92. (D)
53. (C)	63. (C)	73. (D)	83. (E)	93. (C)
54. (E)	64. (A)	74. (D)	84. (A)	94. (A)
55. (A)	65. (D)	75. (B)	85. (B)	95. (C)
56. (A)	66. (A)	76. (A)	86. (E)	96. (E)
57. (E)	67. (E)	77. (C)	87. (C)	97. (B)
58. (C)	68. (E)	78. (D)	88. (D)	98. (C)
59. (A)	69. (E)	79. (D)	89. (E)	99. (C)
60. (A)	70. (A)	80. (A)	90. (D)	100. (C)

DETAILED EXPLANATIONS OF ANSWERS

TEST 1

Section 1

1. **(B)** *Were praised* is a plural verb; since the subject is Chief Joseph, a singular proper noun, the verb should be *was praised*. The intervening phrase of choice (A), *"together with 250 warriors and 500 women and children,* does not change the singular subject. Choice (C), *bravery,* is the correct noun form, and choice (D), *for,* is idiomatically correct in that phrase.

2. **(E)** Choice (A), *upon which,* is a correct prepositional phrase. Choice (B), *is based,* agrees with its subject, *society.* In choice (C) *are* agrees with its subject, *ideals. Derived from* in choice (D) is correct idiomatic usage.

3. **(B)** Two past actions are mentioned. The earlier of two past actions should be indicated by past perfect tense, so the answer should read, *had been.* Choice (C) is correct. Choice (A) contains two adjectives as part of an appositive phrase modifying the subject, and choice (D), *upon the death,* is idiomatically correct.

4. **(C)** Choice (C) should be *depend,* not *had depended* because that use of past perfect would indicate prior past action. There is a series of events in this sentence: first, the legislature *had not finalized,* (B), the budget; then, Representative Wilson *pointed out,* (A), this failure. Choice (C) needs to be present tense as this situation still exists, and (D) is future action.

5. **(D)** Choice (A) is a noun used as an adjective. *To plan* is an infinitive phrase followed by noun objects: *puppet shows and movies* and *garage sales.* In order to complete the parallelism, choice (D) should be *arrangements.* Choice (C), *used,* is a participle modifying *books.*

6.   **(A)** An infinitive, *to understand,* should never be split by any adverbial modifier, *completely.* Choice (B), *effects,* is the noun form, and choice (D), *affected,* is the adjective form. *One must,* choice (C), is used in standard English.

7.   **(C)** *More* is used to compare two things. Since the number of nations is not specified, *more* cannot be used in this sentence. Choice (A), *known,* modifies *roads;* choice (B) is idiomatically correct; choice (D), *is,* agrees in number with its subject, *transportation.*

8.   **(E)** Choice (A), *many a,* should always be followed by the singular verb, *wishes,* choice (B). Choice (C) is idiomatically correct. In *someone else,* (D), *else* is needed to indicate a person other than the student would pay the bills.

9.   **(E)** Choices (A), (B), and (C) are correctly used idioms. The verb *aggravated* (D) may at first seem like the correct choice, as it has multiple meanings, including *to make worse* and *to excite to impatience or anger.* However, this second definition, though sometimes considered informal, fits the meaning of the sentence, so (E) is the correct answer.

10.   **(C)** The reference in choice (C) is vague because it sounds as if the bus made the two students late. Choice (A) is a correct subject pronoun; choice (B) is the correct adverb form to modify *dressed;* and choice (D) is a correct object pronoun.

11.   **(E)** Choice (A), *among,* indicates choice involving more than two things. The prepositions in (B) and (C) are correct. *Are,* (D), is a plural verb, agreeing in number with the compound subject *singing... dancing... cooking.*

12.   **(A)** Choice (A) is obviously wordy, *consensus* meaning the same as *general agreement,* so it is the best choice. None of the others has a usage error. Choice (B) is acceptable in that it implies a well-known fact that Twain wrote many other works. Choice (C) underscores the claim made in the whole sentence by establishing the book as the *best* American work. Finally, choice (D) is acceptable because of commas in other parts of the sentence. Choice (E) clearly does not apply.

13.   **(C)** This question has several potential errors. Choice (A) requires that you know to capitalize important historical documents, so it is correct. Choice (B) calls to question the attribution of human rationality to an

inanimate object, but since the Constitution actually does have logical premises, we can correctly say that the document can posit the premise stated. Choice (D) is acceptable because the superlative is referenced within the sentence; one should know that the U.S. government has three branches. That leaves choices (C) and (E). Choice (C) is the verb in the clause beginning with the word *what*; it is plural, and, therefore, incorrect because it does not agree with its subject *history,* a singular noun. Do not be fooled by the intervening plural word *governments.* Since choice (C) is the error, choice (E) would no longer be considered.

14.   **(C)**   Even though people use *like* as a conjunction in conversation and public speaking, it is a preposition, and formal written English requires *as, as if,* or *as though* when what follows is a clause. No other choice is even suspect.

15.   **(C)**   The problem with this sentence is parallel structure. Choice (C), *shouting,* is a present participle while choice (A) is a simple past tense. Choice (C) should be changed to *shouted* so the tenses will be the same. Choice (B), *president's,* is a correct possessive; and choice (D) is idiomatically correct.

16.   **(D)**   The verb at choice (D) must agree with its subject, *variety,* and, therefore, needs to be the singular form, *changes.* Choice (A), *fresh,* is an adjective describing the noun *ice cream*; choice (B), *daily,* is an adverb modifying the verb *make*; and choice (C), *of flavors,* is an adjective prepositional phrase modifying the noun *variety.*

17.   **(D)**   You should recognize that the word arrangement and punctuation place the prepositional phrase *as a lubricant* as the fourth object of the preposition *for*; the phrase is not parallel to the preceding noun objects. By inserting an *and* between *candles* and *soap* and eliminating the comma after *soap,* you revise this sentence by providing parallel phrases after the verb. Choice (A), *it provided,* is correct as pronoun subject, referring to *whaling,* and verb of the introductory adverb clause; choice (B) is a predicative nominative, *vocation,* and its modifier; the passive verb *was used,* choice (C), is past tense and agrees in number with its subject, *oil.*

18.   **(B)**   The error is one of diction. The word *literally,* choice (B), is an adverb that means that the action of the verb really occurred; clearly the subject did not *really* die of starvation if he was able to eat. Choice (A), *greedily,* is an adverb appropriately describing how *he* ate; choice (C), the

past perfect verb, *had been lost,* is correct to refer to an action that occurred before the action of the main verb; and choice (D), *for two days,* is an adverb prepositional phrase modifying the verb "had been lost."

19.   **(B)** You should recognize an error in comparison in choice (B). Because the writer is comparing more than two contributions that Montagu might have made, the adverb should be the superlative form, *best.* Choice (A), *might have made,* is the correct form for the conditional verb in a *that* clause; choice (C), *that permitted,* is the subject *that,* referring to the antecedent *lunch,* and the verb of the adjective subordinate clause; and choice (D), the infinitive *to continue,* is idiomatically correct to introduce a noun phrase that serves as direct object of the verb *permitted.*

20.   **(B)** You should recognize in choice (B) an error in verb tense. The past perfect, *had beaten,* would be appropriate only if the action occurred before the action of the verb in the main clause. Because the two actions occurred simultaneously, the simple past tense form, *beat,* is correct. Choice (A), *When,* is a subordinating conjunction correctly introducing a subordinate clause; choice (C), *made,* is in the simple past tense and agrees in number with its subject, *teams;* choice (D), *kicking a round ball,* is an idiomatically correct phrase serving as object of the preposition *by.*

21.   **(A)** You should know that the noun *kind* must agree in number with the adjective preceding it; therefore, in choice (A), the word *kinds* should replace the singular *kind* to agree with the plural adjective *those.* Choice (B), *who,* introduces the subordinate adjective clause and is in the nominative case because it serves as subject in the clause; choice (C), *good,* is the correct predicate adjective to modify *who* when the meaning is *satisfactory;* and choice (D), *themselves,* is a reflexive pronoun referring to "who."

22.   **(B)** The error is in choice (B), where the correct past tense form of the verb *sneak* is *sneaked,* not *snuck.* Choice (A), *had been sent,* is correct in the past perfect form because the action was completed before the action of the main clause; choice (C), *downstairs,* is an adverb modifying the verb; and choice (D), *lay,* is the correct past tense form of the verb *lie.*

23.   **(B)** The given sentence contains a double negative. The *no* in choice (B) should be replaced by *any* or *a* following the negative verb and adverb, *hadn't.* Choice (A) is a past tense passive verb, *was shown,* and adverb, *originally,* in idiomatic word order; choice (C), *to see,* is an infi-

nite introducing an adjective phrase modifying *chance*; choice (D), *its*, is a possessive pronoun referring to *cartoon.*

24. **(D)** You should recognize that the error occurs in choice (D), where the correct adjective to compare two people is the comparative form, *more famous.* Choice (A), *are recognized,* is correct in the present passive form and is plural to agree with its subject, *portraits*; choice (B), *by most Americans,* is an adverb prepositional phrase in idiomatic word order; and choice (C), *were,* agrees in number with its compound subject, *Gilbert Stuart* and *daughter* and is correct in the past tense.

25. **(D)** *Because* is the word to use in the cause-and-effect relationship in this sentence. Choice (A), *being that*; choice (E), *than me*; and choice (B), *the more* are not grammatically correct. Choice (C), *is made by you,* is in the passive voice and is not as direct as (D).

26. **(E)** This sentence presents two problems, namely use of a preposition instead of a coordinating conjunction to join the objects of the participle *having studied* and failure to show a time relationship. Choice (E) corrects both problems. Choice (B) simply replaces the preposition *along with* by *as well as*; choice (C) unnecessarily repeats the conjunction *and* rather than using the quite appropriate series construction. None of the choices (A), (B), (C), or (D) correctly shows the time relationship.

27. **(D)** Choices (A), (D), and (E) are the best candidates because they are more concise than the other two choices. Each does express the same idea, but (E) does not as strongly indicate the contrast between the two clauses in the sentence as do choices (A) and (D). Choice (D) clearly makes its point in fewer words and is the better choice. What about C

28. **(B)** This sentence contains the ambiguous pronoun *they,* for which there is no antecedent, and fails to show the relationship of the ideas expressed. Choice (B) eliminates the clause with the ambiguous pronoun and correctly expresses the reason for the sandbag placement. Choice (C) suggests that the two clauses joined by *and* are equal and does not show the subordinate relationship of the second choice to the first choice. Choice (D) introduces a dangling phrase with a coordinating conjunction, *and,* that suggests the joining of equals, and choice (E) retains both errors from the original sentence.

29.   **(A)**   The construction *than those* clarifies the fact that more vegetables have been added. Choice (C), *your suggestions*; choice (D), *than what*; and choice (E), *which*, do not contain the idea of adding more varieties of vegetables. Choice (B) ends with a preposition.

30.   **(B)**   The voice must be consistent with *I*, so (B) is the only possible correct answer. All other choices have a noun or pronoun that is not consistent with *I*: choice (A), *you*; choice (C), *a person*; choice (D), *people*; and choice (E), *some*.

31.   **(A)**   The correct answer has two concepts – pieces are missing and pieces will probably never be found. Choice (B) has a singular verb, *is*. Choice (C) indicates the pieces *probably will be* missing, which is not the problem. Choice (D) and choice (E) both indicate the pieces are *probably missing*, which is illogical because the pieces either are or are not missing.

32.   **(C)**   Choice (A), *the kind of a,* and choice (D), *the type of a,* are incorrect grammatical structures. Choice (E) introduces the new concept of *category*. Choice (B), *sort of,* is poor wording.

33.   **(E)**   Choice (E) is clear and concise and has the comparison of architecture. The antecedent of *those* in choice (A) is not clear. Choice (B) is comparing *characteristics,* not just architecture. Choice (C) is awkward, and choice (D) incorrectly uses an idiom, *characteristic with.*

34.   **(B)**   Choice (B) is clear and direct. Choices (A) and (E) are too wordy. Choice (C) has the wrong concept, *balancing games.* Choice (D) is poorly worded, *this as an example.*

35.   **(E)**   Only choice (E) provides the correct parallel construction in which each major element appearing after *not only* has a parallel element after *but also.* Each of the other choices has a lack of parallelism, and choice (B), in addition, unnecessarily splits the infinitive *to provide.*

36.   **(D)**   The original sentence contains a shift of pronoun from the indefinite *one* to second person *you.* Only choice (D) provides consistency in pronoun number and case. Use of the passive voice in choice (B) loses parallelism in construction; choice (C) retains the incorrect *you*; and choice (E) includes the wrong case.

37. **(D)** This exercise is a sentence fragment, not a complete sentence. The subject has no verb but is followed by two subordinate clauses. To correct this sentence, eliminate the subordinating conjunction, *where,* and the subject of the subordinate clause, *he,* to provide a predicate for the subject, *Father Junipero Serra.* Choice (D) accomplishes what is necessary. Choices (B) and (C) result in run-on sentences; and choice (E) substitutes a verbal phrase for the necessary predicate and does not solve the problem of the fragment.

38. **(B)** The given sentence does not provide parallelism in construction. The conjunction *but* joins the adjective *eager* with a prepositional phrase. Choice (B) correctly provides the adjective *afraid* followed by an infinitive phrase parallel with *eager to explain his point of view.* The verbal phrases in the other choices do not result in parallel construction; in addition, choice (C) is a dangling phrase.

39. **(C)** Choice (C) is a prepositional phrase, *About 25,000 years ago,* which is followed by a subordinate clause. This sentence should be linked to the previous sentence as it is integral to the migration of the Anasazi. Choices (A), (B), (D), and (E) are all complete sentences.

40. **(C)** Choice (C) has to do with the later history of the Mesa Verde area, after the Anasazi had abandoned it. Since this is so far removed chronologically, sentence 7 should be deleted or further developed in a third paragraph. Choices (A) and (B) discuss the very early history of the Indians. Choice (D) follows the chronological time order from A.D. 500 and leads into a discussion of the height of the Anasazi civilization. Choice (E) involves the Anasazi's interaction with other tribes.

41. **(A)** Choice (A) fits naturally into a discussion of the Anasazi culture, between the dwellings mentioned in sentence 9 and the trade mentioned in sentence 11. Choice (B) is too vague; at this point in the paragraph, the discussion has narrowed to the Anasazi. Choice (C) could have come earlier in the paragraph but is out of place at this point. Choice (D) belongs in a discussion of the disappearance of the Anasazi. (E) belongs in a discussion of modern studies of the Anasazi.

42. **(C)** Choice (C) unnecessarily repeats the words *basis, based, founding,* and *foundation.* These forms need not be repeated and the sentence should be condensed. Choice (A) repeats the phrase *board of regents,*

found in the previous sentence, but it is needed for transition of thought. Choices (B), (D), and (E) are well worded sentences.

43. **(B)** Choice (B) fits between sentence 4 and sentence 6. Sentence 4 mentions the topic of dissenting opinion, and sentence 6 elaborates by stating the position that English professors have always been outspoken. This idea is continued in sentence 7. Choice (A) changes voice to *we,* which is out of place in this letter. Choice (C) is too casual. Choice (D) directly contradicts the thesis of the letter. Choice (E) introduces the issue of freedom of speech, discussed in the next paragraph, out of place.

44. **(B)** Choice (B) contains an inappropriate use of words. The contraction for *who is* should be used to make the sentence correct. The possessive *whose* is not correct in this context. Choice (A) correctly uses the comparative degree. Choice (C) correctly uses the superlative degree. Choices (D) and (E) do not make needed changes.

45. **(C)** Choice (C), delete sentence 4, is the correct choice. The sentence labeled sentence 4 introduces a new topic – the fact that some companies are not committed to a day care program. Since the paragraphs are both discussing companies that have already made this decision, and the advantages of having made this decision, sentence 4 is out of place. Choice (A) would make a contradictory statement. Choice (B) would delete a needed phrase. Choice (D) would destroy the parallelism created with Parts 6 and 7 that lead naturally as a transition into the next paragraph. Choice (E) would delete information relevant to the issue.

46. **(A)** Choice (A) is needed for correct subject and verb agreement. The plural subject *companies* should be followed by the plural verb *make.* Confusion is caused by an intervening phrase, *showing special initiative in building company loyalty of each employee.* Because the phrase ends with a singular noun, it is a common error to make the verb singular also. Choice (B), present progressive, and choice (C), future, are incorrect tenses for the context of the sentence and the paragraph. Choice (D) needs a helping verb and cannot stand alone. Choice (E), the past perfect, is incorrect since no specific event in the past is being referred to.

47. **(D)** Sentence 9 begins with the transition word "Therefore," so it is best placed after a sentence that would state a reason for building company loyalty and morale. Sentence 11 gives a compelling reason – the company's personal interest in each employee. Choice (A) would remove the topic

sentence to a less prominent position, as well as have sentence 9 clearly out of order with no idea before it in the paragraph. Choices (B) and (E) do not place a sentence with a clear reason before the transition *therefore*. Choice (C) would weaken the paragraph.

48. **(A)** Sentence 3 discusses the Gothic style spreading to other parts of Europe; therefore it should be placed just before sentence 8 which lists the other places in Europe where the Gothic style spread. Choice (B) would remove the example for sentence 1 of the passage, the variety of medieval art and literature. Choice (C) gets ideas out of sequence by moving the idea in sentence 7, the first Gothic structures, after the spread of the Gothic style of architecture. Choice (D) removes the reason why Gothic cathedrals were a community project and therefore so popular. Choice (E) is incorrect because sentence 3 is already out of place.

49. **(C)** Choice (C) adds a detail supporting the topic in sentence 9, height of the cathedrals. Choice (A), although a legitimate part of Gothic architecture, is an extraneous idea for the second paragraph. Choice (B) breaks the formal tone of this passage with the insertion of a personal pronoun, "me." Choice (D) is certainly a true statement, but it would be better added at the end of the passage because it interrupts the discussion of height and light. Choice (E) has no place in a discussion of the characteristics of Gothic architecture.

50. **(D)** Choice (D) corrects the subject-verb agreement error of sentence 12. The subject, *beams,* is plural and needs a plural verb, *provide.* The presence of an intervening phrase, *called flying buttresses,* should not affect the choice of the verb form. Choice (A) *as* is correct; *like* should be used for unusual comparisons called similes. Choice (B) makes no improvement. Choice (C) is not necessary. Commas are strong enough to connect this series of cathedrals. Choice (E) is incorrect because the sentence clearly calls for the superlative.

Section 2

51. **(B)** People *abide by,* not *to,* the rules. The adverb, *solemnly,* choice (A), modifies *instructed*; choice (D) is a correctly used infinitive. In choice (C), *jury,* a collective noun, can be singular or plural depending on its use; since individual members of the jury disagree with one another, *jury* requires a plural verb.

52.   **(B)** Subjunctive mood must be used in clauses indicating a condition contrary to fact, *if I were going on a long trip* (but I am not). In choice (A), *he,* is the correct nominative case pronoun used as the subject of the verb, *advised.* Choice (C) is a conditional verb, and choice (D) is correctly worded.

53.   **(C)** The verb *laid* is a conjugation of *lay,* meaning *to put* or *to place.* The verb form that should be used is *lay* from the verb *lie,* meaning *to be in a lying position.* Choices (A) and (B) are two correctly used participles, and choice (D) is correct in common usage.

54.   **(E)** Choice (A), *having been,* correctly expresses an action before another action, *helped,* in choice (B). Choice (C) serves as the direct object of the verb *helped,* and *giving* in choice (D) is a gerund serving as the object of the preposition *by.*

55.   **(A)** An objective case pronoun *me* is required for the object of the verb *let.* Choices (B) and (D) are idiomatically correct; choice (C) correctly uses a possessive proper noun to modify *house.*

56.   **(A)** It is not clear if the word *unusual* means that Jon is an unusual person, but the context of the sentence indicates that Jon is *unusually mature* for his age. Choice (B) has an understood verb, *think it (is) appropriate.* Choice (C), *to inherit,* is correct, as is choice (D), *that much.*

57.   **(E)** *They* in choice (A) refers to *books.* Choice (B) is grammatically correct, and the phrase in choice (C) is used as a participle. *Anyone else* in choice (D) is correct and shows that the owner of the library can find the books he needs.

58.   **(C)** The pronoun *you* in choice (A) is correct. *I* in choice (B) is the nominative case to follow a linking verb, *it is I* (not me), and *who* is also correct in nominative case as a subject of a subordinate clause. Since *who* refers to *I,* the verb in (C) must be *am.* The preposition, *among,* in choice (D) is used in situations involving more than two people or things.

59.   **(A)** Your rephrased sentence probably read, *If Anastasia's grade point average exceeds 2.0, the guidance counselor will begin to help her with her search for a graduate school.* (A) is the best answer. The sentence is set in the future tense, but choice (B) does not make sense with it; the grade point exceeding 2.0 must precede the guidance counselor's be-

ginning to help. The grade point average would not necessarily result in helping; the guidance counselor must do the helping, so (C) is not the best choice. (D) is in the passive voice; (D) is not the best choice. The sequence of events is not right in answer (E), so (E) is not the best answer.

60. **(A)** Your sentence probably read, *The college claimed that special donations by the textbook industry resulted in the student activity building becoming 'a little larger and a little more comfortable.'* (A) is the best answer. The sequence is not correct with choice (B). (C) is not an acceptable choice since no comma is needed before *by the textbook.* (D) would cause the sentence to read, *The college claimed that special donations, making the result...* or *...making the student activity....* (D) would not be the best choice. Since the antecedent of the word *they* would not be clear, (B) is not the best choice.

61. **(B)** Your rephrased sentence will probably read, *The worker looked for another entrance after he found the door locked.* This new sentence contains the correct answer: (B), *after he found.* (A) gives the implication that the worker found another entrance; this changes the meaning of the sentence. (A) is not the best answer. (C), (D), and (E) seem to change the meaning of the sentence; there is no evidence that the worker found anything after initially finding the door locked.

62. **(B)** The new sentence probably reads, *Few people who entered the turkey shoot had hopes of winning, but they did so to help the homeless.* (B) is the best answer. (A), (C), and (D) change the meaning of the sentence; *Few people had little hope* (A), *few hopes* (C), or *no hopes* (D) would mean that *most people would have great hopes.* (E) also changes the meaning of the sentence. Few people did not lose hope; they never had hope of winning to begin with.

63. **(C)** If one begins the sentence with *The Europeans,* it logically follows that they (1) brought the diseases that (2) nearly wiped out the settlements. (C) is the best answer. (A) could not be the best answer because it has another verb preceding *brought. The Europeans have brought...* is the wrong tense; (B) is wrong. The Europeans did not wipe out disease (D) or wipe out entire settlements (E); neither (D) nor (E) is the best choice.

64. **(A)** The new sentence probably reads, *Many doctors considered quarantine, vaccination, and medicine to be important steps in controlling*

poliomyelitis. (A) is the correct choice. (B) is incorrect because it would not fit the sentence. *Many doctors considered quarantine, vaccination, and medicine in controlling poliomyelitis* would leave out part of the sentence: *important steps.* For (C) to fit the sentence, the sentence would have to read like the following: *Many doctors considered quarantine, vaccination, and medicine, which were important steps in controlling poliomyelitis.* This sentence is slightly more awkward than answer (A). The words *medicine the* do not fit; (D) is not a good choice. For (E) to fit, the sentence would have to read, *Many doctors considered quarantine, vaccination, and medicine as most important steps in controlling poliomyelitis*; this changes the meaning of the sentence.

65.   **(D)**   A revised version of the sentence might read, *The children's author announced that her drama would include children from the community, musicians from our area, and costume designers from the local high school.* (D) is the best choice. (A) should not be an alternative since the tense is wrong. (B) changes the meaning; it uses the term *should,* not *would.* The verb form *was* does not fit the sentence; (C) is not an appropriate choice. The tense in choice (E), which is the plural *were,* does not agree with the sentence.

66.   **(A)**   A revised sentence could read, *Marilyn's pet dog was seemingly innocent but it caused considerable concern among the neighbors.* (A) would enable the examinee to select the correct version. (B) would not work; *Marilyn's seemingly innocent dog caused* (not *but it caused*) is not an acceptable choice. Choice (C) would cause the sentence to read the same as choice (B); (C), therefore, is not a good choice. (D) and (E) would each cause the sentence to read in the same way; *A seemingly innocent pet dog....* The examinee should notice that the phrase *A seemingly innocent pet dog...* and *seemingly innocent pet dog* do not fit with the phrase *but it caused...*

67.   **(E)**   The sentence must be totally revised to use the word *explain. The fact that many schools have drug and crime problems helps to explain why one of the goals of that project is to make the schools crime-free by the year 2010.* (E) is the best answer. *On account of schools* and *due to the schools* are wordy; using the word *because* would be preferable. (A) and (B) are not acceptable. *Because of schools* and *As a result of many schools* would not logically begin a sentence with the word *explain.* (C) and (D) are not the best choice.

68.   **(E)**   *Many people* requires a plural verb; *the football team* is a singular noun. Since (A), (B), (C), and (D) all include plural verbs relating to *football team,* none of these choices are acceptable. The active voice verb *followed* and the agreement of subject and verb help to make the answer (E) the best.

69.   **(E)**   The revised sentence reads, *When John raised his hand in class when he knew the answer, his teacher gave him much praise.* (E) fits easily into the sentence; (E) is the best answer. (A) is a passive voice verb; it is not the best choice. The verb or verbal *finding* does not fit neatly into the sentence; this means that (B), (C), and (D) are not acceptable answers.

70.   **(A)**   The revised sentence reads, *Balinka contacted the authorities to report the cache after finding the lost money in the little shed in the backyard.* (A) is the best answer; it fits the revised sentence exactly. (B) is wordy; *because* is preferable to *due to finding.* Balinka certainly did not call the authorities *as he was finding;* (C) is not the best choice. (D) seems to change the meaning of the sentence; Balinka did not call the authorities after finding the cache. In stead (D) suggests that Balinka called as *he was finding the authorities – a* change in meaning. *Knowing of the cache* modifies Balinka and should be located near *Balinka,* but there is no way that the modifier can be placed there. (E) is not a good answer.

71.   **(D)**   The revised sentence would read, *Carrying the heavy bundle and screaming for help, Suzanne ran all the way home.* (D) allows the examinee to choose the needed words. Since the sentence begins with a capital, there should be no other capitalized word except the proper name *Suzanne;* this means that the examinee can immediately eliminate (A), (B), and (E) because of the capital alone. (C) is not a good choice because *screaming for help* comes directly after *Carrying the bundle,* the first part of the sentence. A period is not needed after *screaming for help;* there are no other words in the sentence about Suzanne so the sentence is a fragment.

72.   **(C)**   The revised sentence reads, "Few visitors had a chance to see the Gray Ghost, but many visited the seacoast town." (C) is the exact answer. So as not to change the meaning of the sentence, the examinee can immediately eliminate (A), which says *few –* not *many –* visited the seacoast. The revised sentence reads that few had a chance; this means that most had no chance and that very *few had a chance.* (B) says just the

opposite; it is a poor choice. (D) and (E) change the wording and the meaning of the sentence; neither choice is acceptable.

73.   **(D)** Choice (D) is correct because sentence 2 mentions two parents, and Part 3 discusses his father. Therefore, discussing Alexander's mother is an appropriate topic. Choice (A) is the next best choice, because it ties in with Aristotle in sentence 5, but it is not as good for the reason that Alexander's other parent is the logical topic. Choices (B) and (C) introduce extraneous topics and topics out of chronological order. Choice (E) strays from the main topic – Alexander, not Philip.

74.   **(D)** Choice (D) is correct because we need to know if Alexander was a child, a teenager, or a young man. Choice (A) has an example in the sentence. Choice (B) is followed by several examples of Alexander's fearlessness and promise. Choice (C) is a very specific verb describing the behavior of horses. Choice (E) is more convenient than listing specific places, but carries the point across as well.

75.   **(B)** Choice (B) is correct because a comma is needed after introductory adverbial clauses. Choice (A) is incorrect because *who* is a personal pronoun to describe people, not animals or objects. Choices (C) and (D) do not make any appreciable improvements in the sentence. Choice (E) is incorrect because the phrase is not a quote.

76.   **(A)** Choice (A) shows clear cause-and-effect sequence begun by sentences 10 and 11. The tone of choices (B) and (D) are far too casual because they introduce the contraction *doesn't* and the personal pronoun *I*. Choice (C) directly contradicts the thesis. Choice (E) involves an extraneous topic.

77.   **(C)** Choice (C) introduces an extraneous topic, another form of investment savings – savings bonds. Choice (A) is necessary because it is the topic sentence. Choice (B) explains the reason people buy a company's stock. Choice (D) is essential as it introduces the next part of the paragraph, dividend reinvestment. Choice (E) offers important information concerning reinvestment.

78.   **(D)** Choice (D) has correct transition words for three main ideas: *For example* introduces the first idea; *In addition* indicates a second idea; *Finally* indicates the last idea. Choice (A) introduces transition words for contrasting ideas, *Although* and *In contrast*. The first transition word, *Even-*

tually, in choice (B) is not appropriate for a first idea or example. The other two transition words are out of order: *First* leads in the second idea, and *Second* leads in the third idea. Choice (C) incorrectly introduces the idea of cause-and-effect, *As a result,* and chronological sequence, *Later.* Choice (E) incorrectly uses the word *however,* meant to contrast, when there are no ideas contrasting.

79. **(D)** The purpose of sentence 1 is to provide the topic sentence for the rest of the paragraph; (D) is the best answer. The sentence does not establish the basis for the comparisons that will follow (A); rather the rest of the paragraph gives the contrasts. The first sentence does not demonstrate the writer's authority (B). The first sentence does not give ideas that the writer contradicts for the rest of the paragraph, so (C) is not a good choice. The author does not profess to dislike the artist or the moralist; (E) is not a good choice.

80. **(A)** Sentence 2 is fine where it is; (A) is the best answer. Sentence 2 could not be the first sentence since it has pronouns that refer to nouns in the first sentence; it is not a good topic sentence so (B) is not the best choice. There is no reason to divide sentence 2 into two separate sentences; (C) is not a good choice. Choice (D) is not an appropriate answer because it does follow the topic sentence logically. Placing sentence 2 after the last sentence is not appropriate; the examinee should not select (E).

81. **(B)** Since the function of sentence 10 is unclear, one could omit the sentence. (B) is the best answer. The sentence does not provide a contrast to sentence 1 (A); rather, it is unnecessary. The sentence is not essential; (C) is a false statement. The sentence does not provide a direct contrast to the artists and the moralists; (D) is incorrect. The sentence does not provide a direct contrast with the rest of the paragraph; (E) is incorrect.

82. **(A)** The word *other* has as its antecedent the word *Moralist;* (A) is the correct answer. The word *other* does not refer to the words *perception, imagination,* or *thought* in sentence 5; neither (B), (C), nor (E) are the correct answers. The word *other* does not refer to the word *Artist* in sentence 1; (D) is incorrect.

83. **(E)** Sentences 2-9 give descriptive details to support sentence 1. (E) is the best answer. The sentences do not develop the reader's confidence in the author; (A) is not the best answer. The sentences do not create a feeling of dissatisfaction for Artists or for the Moralists, so (B) is not the

best answer. The paragraph gives a series of contrasts – not comparisons; (C) is not the correct answer. The author gives justification for the Moralists and the Artists; (D) is not the best choice.

84.   **(A)** is the best answer since sentence 1 does establish the organization for the paragraph as a whole; all the other sentences tell more about the type of person who becomes a part of the conscience of a nation. The first sentence does not establish the basis for contrasts between one type of country and another, so (B) could not be the best answer; the subject is not a series of contrasts between countries. The first sentence does not establish the writer's authority; the test-taker should not choose (C). Since the first sentence does not provide the principle on which a society is based, (D) is not the best choice. The idea presented in sentence 1 is not refuted in the rest of the paragraph; (E) is not the best choice to consider.

85.   **(B)** In sentence 1 the purpose of using the word "part of the conscience of a nation" is to provide a clear antecedent for the rest of the sentences and to prepare the reader for the other sentences which use this phrase as an antecedent. The purpose of the expression "part of the conscience of a nation" is not to reveal the writer's uncertainty about the paragraph scheme; in fact, since the writer seems very secure in the scheme and content of the paragraph, (A) is a very poor choice. The writer does not seem to present the carelessness with which spirit matters are considered, so (C) is not an appropriate choice. The writer is not concerned primarily with the idea of people without morality; (D) is an inappropriate answer. The writer's main task is not to contrast morality with immorality; the writer is rather discussing the people who form the conscience of a nation, so (E) should not be chosen.

86.   **(E)** The writer is concerned with the struggles between the citizens who are the conscience of a nation and the nation itself; (E) is the best choice. The writer is not primarily concerned with the traitor and the patriot or the vocal and the nonvocal citizens so answers (A) and (B) are not the best choices. The writer does not seek to contrast the faithful and the nonfaithful (C) or the struggles with the conscience of each of us (D); neither answer is appropriate.

87.   **(C)** The final independent clause in sentence 4 leaves the reader with a feeling of concern (C) – not confidence (A), hopefulness (B), satisfaction (D), or delight (E).

88. **(D)** Sentence 5 is not related to the rest of the paragraph and does not logically follow the particular topic; since it should be omitted, (D) is the best answer. Since sentence 5 is not related it should not be left as it is (A), or placed before sentence 1 and made a topic sentence (B). Omitting the word *however* (C) or changing the sentence to two complete sentences (E) will not improve the unrelated sentence 5; neither (C) nor (E) are viable answers.

89. **(E)** The antecedent of the word *its* in sentence 3 is the nation's conscience; (E) is the best answer. The antecedent is not *anger* in sentence 2 (A), *defeat* in sentence 2 (B), *energy* in sentence 2 (C), or the word *men* in sentence 1 (D).

90. **(D)** is the correct answer; the purpose of sentence 1 is to provide the topic sentence for the rest of the paragraph. The sentence does not establish the basis for the contrasts that will follow (A); it does not demonstrate the writer's authority (B). The rest of the paragraph does not refute the idea so (C) is not a good choice. Since peace is not the same as contentment, (E) is not an acceptable answer.

91. **(E)** Sentence 5 should be placed after sentence 6 to give the paragraph continuity; (E) is the best choice. The sentence should not be left as it is (A). It does not belong before sentence 4 so as to emphasize it as the topic sentence (B) or merely to move its location (C). There is no need to omit the sentence (D).

92. **(D)** Sentence 3 provides an example of the lack of contentment felt by the Americans; (D) is the best choice. The sentence does not provide a contrast to sentence 1 (A) or the rest of the paragraph (E); rather it provides an example. The sentence and its purpose is clear; one should not omit it (B). The sentence in no way shows contentment; so (C) is inappropriate.

93. **(C)** The antecedent of the word *it* is *scheme* (C); this is the noun coming just before the word. The antecedent is not *Congress* (A) from sentence 7, *government* (B) from sentence 6, *army* (D) from sentence 5, or *Newburgh* (E) from sentence 5; none of these are appropriate answers.

94. **(A)** The actions of Washington show contentment with the way that things were; his actions to keep things the way that they were provide a contrast with sentence 1 (A). His actions did not provide an example of

discontent; (B) is not an acceptable choice. The actions of Washington do not necessarily convince the reader of the authority of the writer (C). Most of the Americans did not show contentment with the *status quo;* (D) is not a good choice. The sentence in no way illustrates the satisfaction of Congress with the post-war situation; (E) is incorrect.

95.   **(C)** Like the Americans who showed their dissatisfaction with the American Revolution, the reader, too, feels dissatisfaction with the *status quo* (C). One does not feel wonder and delight with the situation after the Revolutionary War (A), fear for the British Parliament (B), a lack of confidence in the author (D), or confidence in the wisdom of the patriots of long ago (E). Only choice (C) is correct.

96.   **(E)** The main purpose of sentences 2 through 7 is to provide details that support sentence 1 (E). The sentences provide primarily no visual image to the reader (A). They do not breed a feeling of satisfaction in the reader (B) or provide a justification of the struggle (D). There is no intent to provide a hallucination in the reader's mind (C). Answer (E) is the best choice.

97.   **(B)** The writer's use of simile, *I feel like a prisoner*, provides strength to the opening paragraph and is correct. (A) Although a hint of discontent is established, it is not strongly evident. (C) The three restrictions imposed on the writer exemplify the feeling of imprisonment. (D) The absence of superlatives and (E) *Nothing evident* are not present and therefore cannot "strengthen."

98.   **(C)** The room as a retreat is introduced and provides the writer with smooth transition into a succession of sentences containing sensory imagery. (A) This is incorrect since the writer's purpose is apparent in an analytic sense. (B) Persuasion is not incorporated. (D) Discontentment is expressed in sentence 1, not 2. (E) There is no instruction provided.

99.   **(C)** The connotation of the word *blazoning* in this context is that of proclaiming freedom. (A) Sky blue and (B) azure are descriptive terms that do not convey the feeling of freedom. (D) The peace of heavenly bodies is not apparent in this exotic description. (E) *Stormy* could be interpreted as unhappy or unrestful and is not the best choice.

100. **(C)** Eidetic as well as auditory imagery is prevalent. (A) Concrete imagery of jungle animals is used to create a sensuality of language and is the method of development. (B), (D), and (E): Persuasion, cause and effect, and random listing are literary devices not present in these sentences.

PRACTICE TEST 2

ALL MULTIPLE CHOICE

CLEP ENGLISH COMPOSITION
All-Multiple-Choice Version

Test 2

(Answer sheets appear in the back of the book.)

Section 1

TIME: 45 Minutes
50 Questions

Identifying Sentence Errors

DIRECTIONS: The following sentences test your knowledge of grammar, usage, diction (choice of words), and idiom.

Some sentences are correct.

No sentence contains more than one error.

You will find that the error, if there is one, is underlined and lettered. Assume that elements of the sentence that are not underlined are correct and cannot be changed. In choosing answers, follow the requirements of standard written English.

If there is an error, select the <u>one underlined part</u> that must be changed to make the sentence correct and fill in the corresponding oval on your answer sheet. If there is no error, fill in answer oval E.

Example:

<u>The other</u> football players and <u>him immediately</u> accepted the
   A   B
<u>offered contract</u> from the <u>state university.</u> <u>No error.</u>
      C   D   E

1. If you are <u>disappointed by</u> an <u>inexpensive</u> bicycle, then an
                 A   B

    option you might consider is to work this summer and <u>save</u>
                                                   C

    your money for a <u>more expensive</u> model. <u>No error</u>.
                         D   E

2. Also being presented to the city council this morning <u>is</u> the
                                                   A

    mayor's city budget for next year and plans <u>to renovate</u> the
                                                B

    <u>existing</u> music theater, so the session <u>will focus</u> on financial
        C   D

    matters. <u>No error</u>.
              E

3. Even a movement <u>so delicate</u> as a <u>fly's walking</u> triggers the
                           A   B

    Venus flytrap <u>to grow</u> extra cells on the outside of <u>its</u> hinge,
                     C   D

    immediately closing the petals of the trap. <u>No error</u>.
                                           E

4. Although <u>outwardly</u> Thomas Hardy seemed quite <u>the picture</u>
                A   B

    of <u>respectability</u> and contentment, his works, especially the
           C

    prose, <u>deals with</u> the theme of man's inevitable suffering.
             D

    <u>No error</u>.
       E

5. Though <u>unequal in</u> social standing, the everyday lives of
                  A

    ancient Egyptian kings and commoners <u>alike</u> is visible in the
                                       B

    pictures of <u>them</u> found <u>inside of</u> tombs and temples. <u>No error</u>.
                 C   D   E

6. Sometimes considered <u>unsafe for</u> crops, land around river

                                 A

   <u>deltas</u> <u>can be</u> excellent land for farming because periodic

     B   C

   flooding deposits silt rich <u>in</u> nutrients. <u>No error</u>.

                        D   E

7. For years <u>people</u> concerned with the environment <u>have compiled</u>

              A   B

   information which <u>show</u> many species are extinct and others

                       C

   <u>are either</u> endangered or bordering on becoming endangered?

     D

   <u>No error</u>.

   E

8. Little is known about Shakespeare's boyhood or his early

   career as an actor and playwright, but he <u>appears to have been</u>

                                           A

   a financial success <u>because he bought</u> many properties,

                       B

   including <u>one of the finest</u> homes in Stratford, the town he

                C

   <u>was born in.</u> <u>No error</u>.

      D   E

9. *Scared Straight,* a program designed <u>to inhibit</u> criminal

                                A

   <u>behavior in</u> juvenile offenders <u>who</u> seemed bound for prison

     B   C

   as adults, had a significant <u>affect</u> on the youngsters. <u>No error</u>.

                      D   E

10. We would like to know if you are <u>one of those</u> women <u>who is</u>

                             A   B

   actively involved in politics because we need someone

   to campaign for a law legalizing maternity leave for men

      C

   <u>as well as</u> for women. <u>No error</u>.

      D   E

11. <u>Because</u> one of Margaret Thatcher's main goals <u>were</u> to rid
       A   B
    Britain of socialism, <u>we</u> followers of the news were pleased to
                            C
    hear of <u>her election</u> to a third term as prime minister. <u>No error</u>.
             D   E

12. Many political conservatives <u>contribute</u> the problems of
                                   A
    modern American society to the twin evils of the New

    Deal and <u>secular humanism</u>, both <u>of which</u> <u>are</u> presumed to
              B   C   D
    stem from Marxism. <u>No error</u>.
                         E

13. <u>Having minimal exposure</u> to poetry when they <u>attended</u>
              A   B
                          choose
    school, most Americans <u>chose</u> to watch television or <u>to read</u>
                            C   D
    popular magazines for entertainment. <u>No error</u>.
                                           E

                                                          were
14. If the selection of the <u>President of the United States</u> <u>was</u> <u>solely</u> the
                             A   B   C
    responsibility of a handful of people, we <u>would</u> have an oligarchy,
                                               D
    not a democratic republic. <u>No error</u>.
                                 E

15. Writer Tom Wolfe says that many Americans <u>flaunt</u> religion by
                                               A
    <u>worshipping</u> art, <u>contributing</u> their money not to their church or
     B   C
    synagogue but to the <u>arts</u>. <u>No error</u>.
                          D   E

16. The reason <u>astronomers</u> study quasars, small <u>quasi-stellar</u> objects, is
                         A   B
     <u>because</u> they <u>might</u> provide clues to the origin of the universe.
        C   D
     <u>No error.</u>
        E

17. English essayist Francis Bacon <u>proposed</u> a system of reasoning
                                          A
     referred to as induction, <u>and</u> is a <u>quasi-scientific</u> method involving
                                   B   C
     the collecting and <u>inventorying</u> of a great mass of observations from
                              D
     nature. <u>No error.</u>
                E

18. <u>Due to</u> her pride in African-American culture, Zora Neale Hurston
        A
     <u>wrote</u> in the <u>1920's</u> that she was "the only Negro in the United
        B   C
     States" without an <u>Indian</u> chief for a grandfather. <u>No error.</u>
                             D   E

19. People from the <u>Middle East</u> and Latin America stand <u>more closely</u>
                          A   B
     to each other <u>when</u> holding a conversation than <u>in the United States</u>.
                       C   D
     <u>No error.</u>
        E

20. Distinguished psychiatrist Karen Horney <u>claiming</u> <u>that</u> the distrust
                                                  A   B
     between the sexes cannot be explained away <u>as existing only</u> in
                                                     C
     individuals <u>because of</u> psychological forces that exist in men and
                     D
     women. <u>No error.</u>
                E

21. An ethnic American, for example, an <u>Asian-American</u>, who becomes
                                                    A
    an academic exists by definition in a culture separate from <u>their</u> non-
                                                                      B
    academic roots <u>and, therefore</u>, has difficulty <u>reestablishing</u> ties to the
                              C   D
    ethnic community. <u>No error</u>.
                          E

22. Curiously, there <u>are</u> <u>more</u> teachers of the English language in Russia
                        A   B
    <u>than there are</u> students of the <u>Russian language</u> in the United States.
          C   D
    <u>No error</u>.
       E

23. <u>Although</u> philosopher George Santayana assumed that the material
        A
    world was the source of <u>thought</u>, he believed that all <u>that</u> was worth-
                                  B   C
    while in human experience <u>has</u> developed from the imagination.
                                  D
    <u>No error</u>.
       E

Improving Sentences

DIRECTIONS: The following sentences test correctness and effectiveness of expression. In choosing answers, follow the requirements of standard written English; that is, pay attention to grammar, diction (choice of words), sentence construction, and punctuation.

In each of the following sentences, part of the sentence or the entire sentence is underlined. Beneath each sentence you will find five versions of the underlined part. Choice (A) repeats the original; the other four are different.

Choose the answer that best expresses the meaning of the original sentence. If you think the original is better than any of the alternatives, choose it; otherwise, choose one of the others. Your choice should produce the most effective sentence – one that is clear and precise, without awkwardness or ambiguity.

Example:

Charlotte Bronte wrote <u>books and she was</u> not the only person in her family to do so.

Sample Answer Choices:

    (A)   books and she was

    (B)   books; she was

    (C)   ; therefore she was

    (D)   books, she was

    (E)   books being

24.   Allied control of the Philippine Islands during World War II proved to be <u>another obstacle as the Japanese scattered resistance</u> until the end of the war.

    (A) another obstacle as the Japanese scattered resistance

    (B) difficult because of the Japanese giving resistance

    (C) continuing scattered Japanese resistance as obstacles

    (D) as another scattered obstacle due to Japanese resistance

    (E) difficult because the Japanese gave scattered resistance

25. Flooding abated and the river waters receded as the <u>rainfall finally let up</u>.

    (A) rainfall finally let up

    (B) rain having let up

    (C) letting up of the rainfall

    (D) rainfall, when it finally let up

    (E) raining finally letting up

26. Unless China slows its population growth to zero, that country <u>would still have</u> a problem feeding its people.

    (A) would still have

    (B) will have still had

    (C) might have had still

    (D) will still have

    (E) would have still

27. In *The Music Man* Robert Preston portrays a fast-talking salesman who comes to a small town in Iowa <u>inadvertently falling in love with</u> the librarian.

    (A) inadvertently falling in love with

    (B) and inadvertently falls in love with

    (C) afterwards he inadvertently falls in love with

    (D) after falling inadvertently in love with

    (E) when he inadvertently falls in love with

28. Many naturalists have a reverence for the woods and wildlife <u>which exhibits itself through their</u> writings or paintings.

    (A) which exhibits itself through their

    (B) this exhibits itself through their

    (C) showing up in

    (D) and exhibiting itself in

    (E) when they produce

29. Two-thirds of American 17-year-olds do not know that the Civil War <u>takes place</u> between 1850-1900.

    (A) takes place

    (B) took place

    (C) had taken place

    (D) have taken place

    (E) is taking place

30. Both professional and amateur ornithologists, <u>people that study birds,</u> recognize the Latin or scientific names of bird species.

    (A) people that study birds

    (B) people which study birds

    (C) the study of birds

    (D) people who study birds

    (E) in which people study birds

31. Many of the oil-producing states spent their huge surplus tax revenues during the oil boom of the 1970s and early 1980s <u>in spite of the fact that</u> oil production from new wells began to flood the world market as early as 1985.

    (A) in spite of the fact that

    (B) even in view of the fact that

    (C) however clearly it was known that

    (D) even though

    (E) when it was clear that

32. The president of the community college reported <u>as to the expectability of the tuition increase as well as the actual amount</u>.

    (A) as to the expectability of the tuition increase as well as the actual amount

    (B) that the tuition will likely increase by a specific amount

    (C) as to the expectability that tuition will increase by a specific amount

(D) about the expected tuition increase of five percent.

(E) regarding the expectation of a tuition increase expected to be five percent

33. Although Carmen developed an interest in classical music, <u>she did not read notes and had never played an instrument</u>.

(A) she did not read notes and had never played an instrument

(B) she does not read notes and has never played an instrument

(C) it is without being able to read notes or having played an instrument

(D) she did not read notes nor had she ever played them

(E) it is without reading notes nor having played an instrument

34. Both Huckleberry Finn and Holden Caulfield wanted <u>to be a free person</u>, unburdened by social inconveniences.

(A) to be a free person

(B) each to be free persons

(C) to be free persons each one

(D) to be free persons

(E) to be free people

35. The student thought that the professor was <u>an absent-minded kind of stereotype</u>.

(A) an absent-minded kind of stereotype.

(B) the typical absent-minded professor type.

(C) typically like the kind of stereotyped absent-minded professor.

(D) an absent-minded professor type.

(E) stereotypically absent-minded.

36. Through photosynthesis, trees and plants absorb carbon <u>dioxide and</u> <u>they in the same complex and complicated process</u> release oxygen into the atmosphere.

    (A) dioxide and they in the same complex and complicated process

    (B) dioxide and in the same complex process

    (C) dioxide, and they in the same complicated process

    (D) dioxide, and they in the same complex process

    (E) dioxide; they in the same complex and complicated process

37. <u>When the president reaped political benefit from a television docu-</u> <u>mentary critical of him in its script, it proved that the pictures show-</u> <u>ing him being "presidential" outweighed the words.</u>

    (A) When the president reaped political benefit from a television documentary critical of him in its script, it proved that the pictures showing him being "presidential" outweighed the words.

    (B) When the president reaped political benefit from a television documentary critical of him only in its script, it went to prove that the pictures showing him being "presidential" outweighed the words.

    (C) Proving that the pictures showing him being "presidential" outweighed the words, the president reaped political benefit from a television documentary critical of him in its script.

    (D) Proving that the pictures of the president being "presidential" outweighed the words, the president reaped political benefit from a television documentary critical of him only in the words, not in the pictures.

    (E) Proving that the pictures which showed the president being "presidential" outweighed the words, the president reaped political benefit from a television documentary that was, nonetheless, critical of him only in the words.

38. Former slave Harriet Tubman, whose participation in the Underground Railroad made her famous, <u>does not appear on E.D. Hirsch's list</u> of "What Literate Americans Know."

    (A) does not appear on E.D. Hirsch's list

    (B) did not appear on E.D. Hirsch's list

(C) had not appeared on E.D. Hirsch's list

(D) was not on E.D. Hirsch's list

(E) never appeared on E.D. Hirsch's list

Revising Work in Progress

DIRECTIONS: Each of the following selections is an early draft of a student essay in which the sentences have been numbered for easy reference. Some parts of the selections need to be changed.

Read each selection and then answer the questions that follow. Some questions are about particular sentences or parts of sentences and ask you to improve sentence structure and diction (word choice). In making these decisions, follow the conventions of standard written English. Other questions refer to the entire essay or parts of the essay and ask you to consider organization, development, and effectiveness of language in relation to purpose and audience. After you choose each answer, fill in the corresponding oval on your answer sheet.

---

(1) It is important for a teacher to select appropriate reading materials for students in the classroom. (2) Because students vary widely in their ability to read, the first step should be to assess each child's reading level and assign reading material appropriately. (3) Teachers who instruct from materials above the child's reading level are significantly decreasing that child's chance at educational success. (4) The child who reads at a first-grade level will have difficulty with a book on the third-grade level. (5) _____ (6) Even if the child reading at the second-grade level enjoys and even appreciates stories from a sixth-grade reader, for example, he or she will likely learn few skills and the child's reading will not be facilitated by being far below grade level in the reading text.

(7) Unfortunately, it is a problem which is difficult to correct. (8) _____ a teacher may be well aware of the child's specific reading level, finding a book appropriate for their level may pose some difficulties. (9) Textbook publishers sometimes include materials from varied reading levels within the same text. (10) _____, two books designated for the same grade level, because of nonstandard labeling procedures may vary widely in reading difficulty.

39. Which of the following, if used in the blank labeled sentence 5, BEST fits the writer's pattern of development?

    (A) A wide range of reading skills is evident at every grade level.

    (B) Parents should be involved in the process of selecting reading texts.

(C) Standardized tests are available to help teachers assess reading levels for their students.

(D) The disparity of reading levels increases with each grade level until the child's reading ability may vary within a 10-year range by the time he or she reaches the sixth grade.

(E) A special program, begun in first grade, is helping to raise the reading scores of students in the suburbs outside of Houston.

40. Which of the following is needed in the second paragraph?

(A) sentence 7: Change "it is" to "its."

(B) sentence 8: Change "their" to "his or her."

(C) sentence 9: Change "varied" to "a variety of."

(D) sentence 10: Change "designated" to "designates."

(E) sentence 8: Change "well" to "good."

41. Which of the following would, if inserted *in order* into the blanks in the second paragraph, improve the logical sequence of ideas?

(A) In addition; However

(B) As a result; For example

(C) Even though; Also —

(D) In spite of this; In conclusion

(E) When; Fortunately

(1) Polar bears, so named because they live near the North Pole, are called "Nanook" by the Eskimo. (2) Living along the cold waters and ice floes of the Arctic Ocean, some polar bears spend time along the coastal areas of northern Canada, Alaska, Norway, Siberia, and Greenland, although some bears live on the islands of the Arctic Ocean and never come close to the mainland. (3) Most of these areas lie north of the Arctic circle, and about 85 percent of Greenland is always covered with ice. (4) To protect them from the arctic cold and ice, polar bears have water-repellant fur and a pad of dense, stiff fur on the soles of their snowshoe-like feet. (5) In addition, the bears have such a thick layer of fat that infrared photos show no detectable heat, except for their breath.

(6) Polar bears are the largest land-based carnivores. (7) _____ (8) Because their fur is white with a tinge of yellow, they are difficult to spot on ice floes, their favorite hunting ground. (9) Polar bears have a small head, a long neck, and a long body, so they make efficient swimmers. (10) Polar bears have no natural enemy except man, and since increased human activity in the Arctic region has put pressure on polar bear populations, the Polar Bear Specialist Group was formed to conserve and manage this unique animal. (11) An increase in the number of polar bears is due to cooperation between five nations. (12) In 1965, there were 8,000 to 10,000 bears reported, but that population is estimated at 25,000 at the present time.

42. Which of the following would help the focus of the main idea in the first paragraph?

(A) Delete the phrase "so named" in sentence 1.

(B) Change the comma after "Greenland" to a semicolon in sentence 2.

(C) Delete sentence 3.

(D) Change sentence 5 by placing the phrase "except for their breath" after "In addition."

(E) Delete the phrase "In addition" in sentence 5.

43. Which of the following, used in place of the blank labeled sentence 7, BEST fits the writer's pattern of development?

(A) Full-grown polar bears may be about nine feet long and weigh between 1,000 and 1,600 pounds.

(B) These bears have keen eyesight and are not sensitive to snow blindness.

(C) In the winter the female polar bear enters a cave in an iceberg and gives birth to one or two cubs.

(D) Polar bears can swim great distances with a speed of approximately six miles an hour.

(E) The polar bear has an acute sense of smell.

44. Which of the following changes is needed?

(A) sentence 6: Change "largest" to "larger."

(B) sentence 10: Change "was" to "is."

(C) sentence 11: Change "between" to "among."

(D) sentence 12: Change "but" to "and."

(E) sentence 5: Change "except for" to "besides."

(1) Physicians are now emphasizing that health-conscious citizens pay attention to triglyceride levels in the body. (2) Triglycerides are another form of fat in the bloodstream, and high triglyceride levels are associated with increased risk of heart disease. (3) In considering health risks, people should consider the levels of triglycerides, along with high-density lipoproteins (HDLs) – the "good" cholesterol – and low-density lipoproteins (LDLs) – the "bad" cholesterol. (4) _____ (5) For most Americans, a normal triglyceride level falls below 200, and the medical community now recommends that anyone with levels above 200 mg/dl should get further testing and attention.

(6) There are several ways high triglycerides can be treated, a mild aerobic exercise, such as swimming, bicycling, or walking, is recommended. (7) Also, alcohol consumption should be restricted, and caloric intake should be reduced. (8) The diet should be adjusted so that no more than 30 percent of calories should come from fat, and no more than 10 percent of calories should come from saturated fats.

45. Which of the following, if used in the blank labeled sentence 4, BEST fits the pattern of development in the second paragraph?

(A) In the sixties, triglycerides received much publicity.

(B) Particularly dangerous is a combination of high triglycerides and low HDL.

(C) Many people think only the LDLs are important.

(D) Women do not have as high a risk factor of developing heart disease as men do.

(E) The lipoprotein is actually a very complexly constructed molecule.

46. Which of the following is a nonstandard sentence?

(A) sentence 2

(D) sentence 8

(B) sentence 5

(E) sentence 7

(C) sentence 6

Note: In the second paragraph, a paragraph organization error is purposely included.

(1) A significant development during the Paleolithic period was the emergence of modern man. (2) During this time, one million years ago to 12,000 B.C., man's brain became much larger. (3) There are two suggested reasons for the rapid evolutionary development of man's brain. (4) First, meat eating led to big-game hunting, an activity that necessitated group planning and cooperation; and second, the use of speech to facilitate planning and coordination of group activities. (5) Tool making was once thought to be a major factor in the development of a large brain for man, but it is now known that many animals use tools and even make tools. (6) Otters will balance a rock on their stomachs as an anvil for breaking open mollusks.

(7) There are two other factors which have greatly influenced the emergence of modern man. (8) Also, food supplies increased significantly after the retreat of the great glaciers about 12,000 years ago. (9) It seems that about 100,000 years ago, genetic evolution became less important than cultural evolution as man developed the ability to pass on accumulated knowledge. (10) This increase in food supplies may have contributed to the ability of man to increase his own numbers, thus ensuring the survival of his species.

47. Which of the following would help the focus of the main idea in the first paragraph?

(A) Delete sentence 1.

(B) Reverse the order of sentences 1 and 2.

(C) Add a sentence after sentence 2 describing the measurements and configurations of brains.

(D) Delete sentence 6.

(E) Reverse the order of sentences 3 and 4.

(1) Wading through the mud of a political campaign can be a tedious and messy affair. (2) Frequently, issues become buried under a landslide of name-calling and personal attacks, innuendoes, and allegations. (3) The most frequently used fallacy in political campaigns is an attack on the opponent's personality. (4) Attempting to discredit the opponent's views by attacking his or her character is known as the *ad hominem* fallacy. (5) Literally, a Latin phrase, "to the man."

(6) Casting aspersions can divert voters from the facts of the case. (7) For example, if one of the major issues of a campaign year is inflation, voters might hear how a legislator is so rich and has so many tax shelters that he pays less taxes than the average American. (8) The implication, of course, is that the legislator is dishonest, or, at the very least, uncaring about the concerns of his potential constituents. (9) _____ (10) A politician who has proved to have a conflict of interests in awarding a lucrative government contract to a previous business partner should be challenged when another government contract is going to be awarded. (11) However, a past record of dishonesty does not preclude honesty now or in the future. (12) Also, politicians are only human, and it is to be expected that some will have personal problems. (13) Will these problems affect their record of public service? (14) Do we really need to know all the faults of each public figure running for political office?

48. Which of the following focuses attention on the main idea of the passage?

   (A) Combine sentences 4 and 5 by changing the period after "fallacy" to a comma.

   (B) Omit the comma after "inflation" in sentence 7.

   (C) Change the comma after "dishonest" in sentence 8 to a semicolon.

   (D) Rephrase sentence 11 so that it reads, "Honesty now or in the future cannot be predicted by a past record of dishonesty."

   (E) Change "can" to "will" in sentence 6.

49. Which of the following, if used in place of the blank labeled sentence 9, BEST supports the main idea of the second paragraph?

   (A) Politicians should be given more freedom in deciding how to spend our money.

   (B) Every crooked politician should be kicked out of office.

(C) On the other hand, sometimes it is necessary to question a person's intentions or integrity.

(D) The American public is tired of all these accusations and name-calling.

(E) Now, who would believe that?

(1) Recycling helps the environment. (2) Most people now are aware of the need to recycle materials such as newspapers and aluminum cans. (3) City sanitation departments have begun to make recycling easier by providing bags or bins for recyclable materials. (4) Encouraging well-meaning but lazy people to participate in saving the environment. (5) Also, many people do not live close to a recycling collection point or are elderly or handicapped, so the curbside pickup is convenient for everyone.

(6) The most common recyclable materials are newspapers and aluminum cans, but plastic and glass are joining that list. (7) Manufacturers pay more for aluminum cans, and in 1989 it was estimated that Americans recycled about 60 percent of the aluminum cans they used. (8) That's a statistic to be proud of! (9) Plastic is one of the newer recyclables. (10) Although plastic containers cannot be melted down and reformed as new plastic containers, recycled plastic is used to create such diverse recycled plastic products as park benches and roads.

(11) Tin cans are seldom recycled because manufacturers do not pay very much for the used cans, but this is starting to change. (12) If we only recycled one-third of the ones we now throw away, we'd save about 10 billion cans a year. (13) Think about the savings to our pocketbook and to our environment! (14) Even though recycling centers don't pay consumers for tin cans yet, they often accept the cans and recycle them, anyway. (15) Contact your city hall, city sanitation service, or your nearest recycling center to encourage the recycling of tin cans.

50. Which of the following, if added between sentences 11 and 12, is MOST consistent with the writer's purpose and audience?

(A) Actually, tin cans are 99 percent steel with just a thin coating of tin added to prevent rusting.

(B) Tin cans can be melted down and reused just as easily as aluminum cans.

(C) Let's face it: tin cans are harder to recycle than aluminum ones.

(D) Actually, most people now prefer frozen vegetables rather than canned ones.

(E) This will improve the environment, and that's good news for everybody.

Section 2

TIME: 45 Minutes
50 Questions

Identifying Sentence Errors

DIRECTIONS: The following sentences test your knowledge of grammar, usage, diction (choice of words), and idiom.

Some sentences are correct.

No sentence contains more than one error.

You will find that the error, if there is one, is underlined and lettered. Assume that elements of the sentence that are not underlined are correct and cannot be changed. In choosing answers, follow the requirements of standard written English.

If there is an error, select the <u>one underlined part</u> that must be changed to make the sentence correct and fill in the corresponding oval on your answer sheet. If there is no error, fill in answer oval E.

Example:

The <u>other</u> football players and <u>him immediately</u> accepted the
   A   B
<u>offered contract</u> from the <u>state university.</u> <u>No error.</u>
      C   D   E

51. <u>Nearly</u> one <u>hundred</u> years after the impoverished Vincent Van
    A   B
Gogh died, his paintings <u>had sold</u> for more than a <u>million dollars.</u>
                               C   D
<u>No error</u>.
  E

52. Many athletes <u>recruited</u> for football by college coaches <u>expect</u>
               A   B
that they will, <u>in fact,</u> receive an education when they <u>accept</u>
                C   D
a scholarship. <u>No error.</u>
          E

53. Hopefully, by the end of the Twentieth Century, computer
       A   B

    scientists will invent machines with enough intelligence to
                                    C

    work without breaking down continually. No error.
                           D   E

54. Studies showing that the earth includes a vast series of
            A   B

    sedimentary rocks, some with embedded fossils that prove the
                     C   D

    existence of ancient organisms. No error.
                        E

55. When Martin Luther King, Jr. wrote his famous letter from
                    A

    the Birmingham jail, he advocated neither evading or defying
                                B

    the law; but he accepted the idea that a penalty results from
            C   D

    breaking a law, even an unjust one. No error.
                          E

56. The Eighteenth Century philosopher Adam Smith asserted
             A   B

    that a nation achieves the best economic results when individuals
              C

    work both for their own interests and to gain more goods.
                                   D

    No error.
     E

57. According to Niccolo Machiavelli, wise rulers cannot and
                                    A

    should not keep their word when such integrity would be to
       B

    their disadvantage and when the reasons for the promise no
       C

    longer exist. No error.
          D   E

58. The Milky Way galaxy, which <u>comprises</u> millions of stars, has
                                    A
    both <u>thin and congested</u> spots, but shines <u>their</u> <u>brightest</u> in
              B   C   D
    the constellation Sagittarius. <u>No error</u>.
                                       E

59. <u>To learn </u>an ancient language <u>like</u> Latin or Greek is one way
        A   B
    to discover the roots of Western culture; studying Judaeo-Christian

    religious <u>beliefs</u> <u>is</u> another. <u>No error</u>.
                  C   D   E

Restructuring Sentences

DIRECTIONS: Effective revision requires choosing among the many options available to a writer. The following questions test your ability to use these options effectively.

Revise each of the sentences below according to the directions that follow it. Some directions require you to change only part of the original sentence; others require you to change the entire sentence. You may need to omit or add certain words in constructing an acceptable revision, but you should keep the meaning of your revised sentence as close to the meaning of the original sentence as the directions permit. Your new sentence should follow the conventions of standard written English and should be clear and concise.

Look through answer choices (A)–(E) under each question for the exact word or phrase that is included in your revised sentence and fill in the corresponding space on your answer sheet. If you have thought of a revision that does not include any of the words or phrases listed, try to revise the sentence again so that it does include the wording in one of the answer choices.

You may make notes in your test book, but be sure to mark your answers on the separate answer sheet.

Examples:

I.   **Sentence:** Owing to his interesting plots, Grisholm had many readers.

   Directions: Begin with <u>Many people read</u>.

   (A)   so

   (B)   while

   (C)   although

   (D)   because

   (E)   and

Your rephrased sentence will probably read: "Many people read Grisholm because of his interesting plots." This new sentence contains the correct answer: (D) "because." None of the other choices will fit into an effective, grammatically correct sentence that retains the original meaning.

II. **Sentence:** Coming to the South after her high school graduation, she found a job at a tourist resort.

Directions: Change <u>Coming</u> to <u>She came</u>.

(A)   and so she found

(B)   and found

(C)   and there she had found

(D)   and then finding

(E)   and had found

Your rephrased sentence probably read, "She came to the South after her high school graduation and found a job at a tourist resort." (B) is the best choice.

60.   The noble and majestic bald eagle has become America's proud national symbol, embellishing many memorabilia, from solid pewter and porcelain to T-shirts and baseball caps.

Change <u>noble and majestic</u> to <u>nobility and majesty.</u>

(A)   Embellishing

(B)   The bald eagle

(C)   embellishing

(D)   ranging

(E)   symbol

61.   Jane Goodall, the chimpanzee woman, had her childhood dream of Africa come true, which she documented expertly in her seminal book *My Friends the Wild Chimpanzees*.

Begin with <u>A childhood dream came true.</u>

(A)   in her seminal book

(B)   *My Friends the Wild Chimpanzees*

(C)   the chimpanzee woman had

(D)   for Jane Goodall, the chimpanzee woman

(E)   of Africa

62. The pirating of intellectual property involves such items as pop albums, computer programs, creamed corn, and cough syrup – nearly anything that can be patented, copyrighted, or trademarked.

    Begin with <u>Defined as.</u>

    (A) the pirating of

    (B) intellectual property

    (C) involving items

    (D) pop albums, computer programs, creamed

    (E) anything that can be patented

63. The Korean War Veterans Memorial features sculptures of 19 larger-than-life soldiers, immortalizing the foot soldiers who are watched eternally by 2,400 images of actual Korean veterans, etched in granite.

    Change <u>will feature sculptures</u> to <u>featuring sculptures.</u>

    (A) of 2,400 images

    (B) of the Korean War Veterans Memorial

    (C) Actual Korean veterans, by

    (D) Etched in granite

    (E) The Korean War Veterans Memorial will immortalize the foot soldiers

64. In Haiti, President Francois "Papa Doc" Duvalier, with the help of the Tontons Macoutes, created a heinous dictatorship, leaving a brutal legacy in 1971, Jean-Claude, "Baby Doc."

    Begin with <u>The heinous dictatorship.</u>

    (A) of Jean-Claude

    (B) left a brutal

    (C) in Haiti

    (D) of "Papa Doc" Duvalier

    (E) with the help

65. Whole-grain breads and cereals are making a comeback, even though they have long been staples in so-called backward countries where many inhabitants live remarkably healthy lives.

Change they have to having long been staples.

(A) cereals,

(B) cereals;

(C) cereals:

(D) cereals –

(E) cereals.

66. To tear down the brick walls of prejudice and blind hatred, it is necessary to accept the habits, lifestyles, and customs of other cultures that seem, at first, to be foreign or unlike our own.

Begin with The brick walls of prejudice and blind hatred and change tear to torn.

(A) that seem to be

(B) would be torn down if

(C) seem, at first

(D) have

(E) having torn

67. The Louvre in Paris, France, has long held the distinction of being the greatest museum of the world for its vast range of art and the unsurpassed quality of its masterpieces.

Begin with The distinction and insert been.

(A) for its vast range of art has been

(B) and the unsurpassed quality

(C) in Paris, France, has been

(D) of being the greatest museum of the world has been

(E) has been

68. The carpet seems a bit worn, but it is over ten years old and has survived the traffic of three boys and their friends.

    Begin with Three boys and their friends.

    (A) have survived

    (B) have to

    (C) have worn

    (D) seem to have survived

    (E) seem to wear

69. In anger, the child went out into the street and ran off. His cries were very loud.

    Combine these two sentences.

    (A) crying loudly and angrily

    (B) louder and angry

    (C) crying loud

    (D) anger and loudly crying

    (E) loud crying and angrily

70. Orville Wright was famous during his lifetime because he, together with his brother Wilbur, built and flew the first successful airplane.

    Begin with Orville Wright, together with his brother Wilbur, made his fame.

    (A) by building and flying the first successful

    (B) with the successful building of

    (C) success to build and fly the first successful

    (D) for building and the successful flight of the first

    (E) built and flew successfully the first

71. If you want to negotiate the hairpin turns on roads in the Rocky Mountains, you should be aware that careful driving is required.

    Change to negotiate to negotiating.

    (A) awareness of careful

(B) carefully required

(C) carefully aware

(D) required a care

(E) requires careful

72. Although World War I was blamed on the assassination of Archduke Ferdinand, the major causes of the war include competition for colonies, rising feelings of nationalism, and military alliances among European countries.

Begin with The major causes of World War I include.

(A) countries, but was really caused by

(B) countries, although it was blamed on

(C) countries, even though they were

(D) countries being blamed for

(E) countries but it was blamed on

73. Airplanes, used mainly for reconnaissance at the beginning developed into formidable weapons by the end of World War I.

Change developed to a development.

Your new sentence will end with which of the following?

(A) the formidable weapon

(B) used mainly

(C) airplanes

(D) instead of reconnaissance

(E) weapons by the end

Revising Work in Progress

DIRECTIONS: Each of the following selections is an early draft of a student essay in which the sentences have been numbered for easy reference. Some parts of the selections need to be changed.

Read each selection and then answer the questions that follow. Some questions are about particular sentences or parts of sentences and ask you to improve sentence structure and diction (word choice). In making these decisions, follow the conventions of standard written English. Other questions refer to the entire essay or parts of the essay and ask you to consider organization, development, and effectiveness of language in relation to purpose and audience. After you choose each answer, fill in the corresponding oval on your answer sheet.

(1) Dalmatians have an interesting history. (2) Of the 131 breeds that the American Kennel Club recognizes, Dalmatians have risen in popularity from 24th to 19th. (3) Although unsure of the exact origin, the breed may have originated in Dalmatia, a district of Yugoslavia. (4) Dalmatia, a narrow strip of land along the Adriatic Sea, is populated mostly by Croatians. (5) Most people believe that when bands of Gypsies traveling westward to settle in Yugoslavia, the dogs traveled with them.

(6) Alert, curious, clean, and useful, Dalmatians have proved their worth as draft dog, shepherd, and hunting dog. (7) Their greatest fame, however, is as a coach dog. (8) A running mate for the horses of a phaeton or brougham, the Dalmatian would clear stray farm animals from the road. (9) The dog is known for its calm temper and would settle the nerves of a skittish horse. (10) _____ (11) Although the advent of the horseless carriage cut the necessity of the Dalmatian for firemen, the breed is still regularly chosen as a fire station mascot.

74. Which of the following is LEAST relevant to the main idea of the first paragraph?

    (A) sentence 1

    (B) sentence 2

    (C) sentence 3

    (D) sentence 4

    (E) sentence 5

75. Which of the following, if used in the line labeled sentence 10, BEST develops the main idea of the second paragraph?

    (A) Many horses such as the Clydesdale don't have a nervous temperament.

    (B) Dalmatians are also known to be good trackers and pointers.

    (C) For this reason, perhaps the Dalmatian's greatest fame is as the coach dog for horse-drawn fire trucks in the nineties.

    (D) One thing to watch out for when selecting a Dalmatian is their genetic predisposition to kidney trouble.

    (E) The horse may become nervous due to loud noises or unfamiliar terrain.

76. Which of the following should be substituted for the underlined word in sentence 5 of the first paragraph?

    (A) traveled   (D) will travel

    (B) is traveling   (E) travel

    (C) had traveled

(1) Unlike fiction writing, newspaper writing is based on factual reporting of events and observable conditions. (2) News reports must be concise. (3) Articles in a newspaper are presented in what is known as an "inverted pyramid"; that is, the most important information appears first, with the less important details covered later in the article. (4) I think this makes a lot of sense, don't you? (5) Many people don't have much time to sit down and read the paper in a leisurely fashion, so essential details must be set forth in the first sentence or two.

(6) The rest of the article fills in important details of the story. (7) Excerpts of an interview with the main participant or opinions of an expert are certain to be included in a well-written, interesting news article. (8) _____ (9) However, the writer must avoid inserting his or her own opinion or including an extremely biased and unsubstantiated opinion.

(10) A news story does not have to be boring, and there are several techniques used to make news reports more interesting. (11) Whenever possible, the writer should use present tense in order to make the news appear up-to-date. (12) No one wants to read old news, anyway. (13)

Paragraphs should be kept short, so three or four sentences for most are sufficient. (14) Another technique to make the news story more interesting is to accompany the article with a relevant photograph. (15) News reports are not subtle compositions. (16) They emphasize clarity and are meant to be read easily because today's news is often perishable.

77. Which of the following would help the focus of the main idea in the third paragraph?

    (A) Delete "there are" from sentence 10.

    (B) Add a clause to sentence 11 explaining the form of present tense and giving some examples.

    (C) Delete sentence 12.

    (D) Combine sentences 15 and 16 by changing the period after "compositions" to a comma.

    (E) Convert sentence 10 into two sentences.

78. Which of the following is LEAST consistent with the author's purpose and audience?

    (A) sentence 1   (D) sentence 4

    (B) sentence 2   (E) sentence 5

    (C) sentence 3

79. Which of the following, if used in place of the blank labeled sentence 8, BEST fits the development of the second paragraph?

    (A) Consequently, many reporters take along a photographer so the article can be supplemented with action photographs.

    (B) A direct quotation makes the information seem more immediate and lively, not to mention authoritative.

    (C) Direct quotations from any eyewitness make the news article unbiased.

    (D) Simply summarizing the events is, in fact, the best way to catch a busy reader's attention.

    (E) The reporter will often find a pertinent quote in an old article.

Analyzing Writing

> **DIRECTIONS**: Each of the following passages consists of numbered sentences. Because the passages are part of longer writing samples, they do not necessarily constitute a complete discussion of the issues presented.
>
> Read each passage carefully and answer the questions that follow it. The questions test your awareness of a writer's purpose and of characteristics of prose that are important to good writing.

(1) Hypothetically speaking, on the way home tomorrow evening, your car is struck by a skidding truck, causing you fatal injuries. (2) Your estate sues and collects a <u>handsome</u> settlement from the owner of the other vehicle. (3) What is to become of the settlement? (4) Who is to get it if you have left no instructions? (5) Could you afford to die "intestate," allowing your state laws to determine your beneficiaries? (6) The persons whom the law designates may be the very last you would choose; therefore, you should file a legal document. (7) A plethora of phrases and miles of legalistic mumbo-jumbo are no longer the norm for these documents. (8) Most are simple, brief, and to the point without the usual compliment of "know all men by these present," "whereas's," and "now, therefore."

80. Sentences 3, 4, and 5 are questions that

    (A) create confusion for the reader.

    (B) do discredit the reader's present knowledge.

    (C) peak the reader's interest concerning the topic.

    (D) alarm the reader.

    (E) embellish.

81. Sentence 6 is separated by a semicolon because it is

    (A) too long for a comma.

    (B) too short for a period.

    (C) a declarative sentence.

(D) a complex sentence.

(E) a compound sentence.

82. The word *whom* in sentence 6

(A) should be changed to *who*.

(B) is used correctly.

(C) is misplaced in the sentence.

(D) is the subject of the sentence.

(E) is used to impress the reader.

83. Sentence 7 uses hyperbole, which dramatically

(A) gives examples.

(B) persuades the reader.

(C) exaggerates for effect.

(D) understates the premise.

(E) provides poetic justice.

84. The paragraph illustrates that an imaginary incident can be effectively dramatized with the use of a short

(A) aphorism.

(B) anecdote.

(C) comparison.

(D) simile.

(E) metaphor.

(1) You can take it from Julius Caesar: you've got to watch people. I've watched them for a long time, and it's not a pretty sight. I shake at lean men around me. You find all sorts of these "leanies" about if you look long enough: the condescending lean man, the "he's got it all together" lean man, the efficiency expert lean man – all lean, all a social nuisance.

(2) Leanies are funless. They don't mess around in the fat way. Their

messing leads somewhere, amounts to something, proves constructive in some way. That's not true messing. Five minutes with nothing to do but drink coffee will get you an empty cup, cleaned and washed and put back on the rack along with the coffee spoon spotless and in the drawer, the cream and sugar nowhere in sight. Full of industry as they are, leanies say things like, "I need a twenty-five-hour day to get everything done." Fat people consider the day too confounded long as it is.

(3) Also, leanies are tiringly energetic to the point of being unhealthy. On "slow" they're in a dead run. There's always that executive briskness in their walk, as if they are always on their way to an important meeting with the board when all they're really headed for is the bathroom. They're always ready to "tackle" and "meet head-on." But fat people say, "Give me your sluggish, your *inert*, your 'give me a minute, will ya!' type who intelligently conclude: mop it today, they just track it up tomorrow."

(4) Mostly, the leanies oppress. They always have good intentions. What happened to the nice, healthy attitude, "I wasn't gonna do it any-way"? Or they parade around with bony trunks, ship shapes, alert eyes, straight posture – the kind a mugger never hits in the parking lot. Their shirt tails are never out; they never sit back on the sofa, always on the edge. They always keep their left hands in their laps at lunch. Fat people keep it loose, comfortable, spread out, soft. They can fearlessly slouch to their cars in parking lots because crooks see immediately they probably spent all their money inside on popcorn and pizza. They don't keep their hands in their laps when they eat. That's where the napkin goes.

(5) And leanies are stupidly logical. There's that condescending shake of the head before they start to tell you how stupid you are. There's the index finger that counts off on the other hand the list of things so you won't lose track. They know the TV schedule – those that even watch TV – when it comes to news programs, educational programs, and prerecorded exercise shows. They know about cholesterol and smoking, body fats, and safe sex. And always, always they are financially responsible and sound.

(6) Fat people, on the other hand, are comfortably illogical – not stupid, you understand. But we tend to see the other side of "smart" and "with it." We don't know the TV schedule because we don't have a TV schedule. Not only that, but having a TV schedule implies planning ahead. Planning ahead to watch a show you watch each week whether you plan to or not somehow takes the fun out of it; it removes the spontaneity of life. And while fat people aren't into keeping up with their cholesterol or triglycerides, they are aware that chances are you'll die in a car accident before your arteries kill you.

85. Which of the following best defines *inert* in the third paragraph of this selection?

    (A) unintelligent

    (B) helpless

    (C) ignored

    (D) not active

    (E) important

86. Which of the following statements best expresses the main idea of paragraph two?

    (A) Fat people don't have a productive purpose in life.

    (B) Thin people can take any situation in life and convert it into a productive experience.

    (C) The approach that thin people have toward life is lifeless and boring because everything has to be productive.

    (D) Thin people should learn how to mess around in a fat way.

    (E) Thin people ar eactually envious of fat people.

87. Which of the following statements would the writer of the selection most likely agree with?

    (A) Happy people are more likely to be fat people.

    (B) Fat people will usually outlive thin people.

    (C) Thin people aren't as successful as they appear.

    (D) Happy people actually have more intelligence than thin people.

    (E) None of the above.

88. Which of the following, according to the selection, would best sum up the writer's point in the third paragraph about the "executive briskness" in the thin person's walk?

    (A) Much of the energy of a thin person is "put on."

    (B) Fat people don't know how to walk fast.

    (C) Executives are more likely to be thin and energetic.

(D) Thin people are better workers.

(E) Thin people work too hard.

89. Which of the following lists of topics best organizes information presented in the selection?

    (A) I.   ways thin people approach life

         II.   ways fat people approach life

         III. superiority of the "fat" approach

    (B) I.   lean people are unsocial

         II.   lean people are unhealthy

         III. lean people are stupid

    (C) I.   lessons that lean people could learn from fat people

         II.   how to conserve energy

         III. how to stay healthy

         IV. how to view life

    (D) I.   problems with thin people

         II.   a perspective of fat people.

    (E) None of the above.

(1) Most teenagers do not get in trouble on a regular basis, and few commit crimes. (2) Many of us, however, do good works for which we receive little or no publicity in newspapers. (3) The news media should give teenagers the good publicity we deserve.

(4) Three recent activities in my home town of Greenhill illustrate this point. (5) Neighbors and other town residents have been repairing the home of an elderly couple, James and Pauline Martin. (6) In another example, a local youth church group visited a retirement home in order to give presents and sing songs one afternoon. (7) Although the youths were mentioned in the story, this story is buried on the back page of the paper, and part of the story the publicity chairman submitted was cut. (8) My final example concerns the Eagle Scout project of a teenager named Sharad Amtey, who made beautiful signs for the city to denote locations of public buildings such as city hall, the library, the police station, and so on. (9) No one from the news showed up for the dedication of the signs, but a re-

porter was across town gathering information of a traffic accident. (10) The story of the accident caused by a teenaged driver made the front page of the next edition, of course, while a report on the signs has yet to be mentioned in the paper. (11) Obviously, *these kind of conduct* by the news media is unfair and shows that adults really don't respect people our age. (12) I think these three examples show how good works by teens are passed over. (13) Truly, we deserve recognition for our positive contributions to society.

90. Which of the following, if added between sentence 5 and 6, is MOST consistent with the writer's purpose and audience?

   (A) Reports vary as to the amount of money needed to buy supplies for the repairs.

   (B) Don't you think it's kind of neat to know that teenagers were among the helpers?

   (C) Over half the volunteer construction workers were teenagers, but only adults were mentioned in the news story or pictured in accompanying photographs.

   (D) Their home was damaged after being hit by lightning, and because they have had so many medical bills recently, the Martins had not renewed their homeowner's insurance.

   (E) The mayor had offered his appreciation to these industrious citizens.

91. Which of the following would help the focus of the main idea in the passage?

   (A) Add a clause after sentence 1 naming some examples of teenagers who have committed crimes.

   (B) Reverse the order of sentences 7 and 8.

   (C) Delete sentence 11.

   (D) Combine sentences 12 and 13 by changing the period after "over" to a comma.

   (E) Convert sentence 7 to two sentences.

92. Which of the following should replace the underlined phrase in sentence 11 of the second paragraph?

    (A) these kinds of conduct

    (B) this kind of activities

    (C) those kind of activities

    (D) this kind of conduct

    (E) those kinds of conduct

(1) A French composer, the bolero inspired Maurice Ravel to create the ballet *Bolero*. (2) The sister of the legendary Russian dancer Vaslav Nijinsky choreographed the ballet created by Ravel. (3) A popular and well-known folk dance in Spain, the bolero as we know it is credited to Anton Bolsche and Sebastian Cerezo around the mid-1700s. (4) Although almost no one has seen the ballet, the music from *Bolero* has retained immense popularity and is performed on a regular basis around the world.

(5) The center and driving force of this musical composition is a snare drum. (6) The percussionist begins by playing a rhythmic pattern lasting two measures and six beats, the rhythm of the bolero dance, as quietly as possible. (7) At the beginning, other instruments pick up the rhythm as the frenzy builds. (8) The first flute then introduces the melody, the second important part of *Bolero;* different instruments, such as the clarinet, bassoon, and piccolo, play individual parts. (9) The buildup of the music occurs in two ways: the individual musicians play their instrument louder and louder, and more and more instruments begin to play together. (10) For most of the 15 to 17 minutes of the performance, *Bolero* is played in an unrelenting harmony of C Major. (11) The end is signaled by a brief shift to E Major, and then a strong return to C Major.

93. Which of the following is LEAST relevant to the main idea of the first paragraph?

    (A) sentence 1   (D) sentence 4

    (B) sentence 2   (E) None of the above

    (C) sentence 3

94. Which of the following, if added between sentences 6 and 7 of the second paragraph, is MOST consistent with the writer's purpose and audience?

(A) Doesn't that sound kind of boring?

(B) It's pretty obvious why this piece is not currently popular.

(C) It would be helpful to see the ballet, as bolero dancers use facial expressions and wave their arms to express emotions.

(D) This rhythm does not change during the entire performance, but the music becomes gradually louder until the final crescendo.

(E) Some conductors, however, prefer a more prominent rhythm.

95. Which of the following contains a misplaced modifier?

(A) sentence 1   (D) sentence 10

(B) sentence 3   (E) sentence 11

(C) sentence 6

(1) One of the world's most valuable gems, pearls are valued for their luminous beauty. (2) Pearls are formed when an irritant, like a few grains of sand or a parasite, enters a mollusk. (3) Nacre-forming cells begin to cover the intruder with smooth layers of calcium carbonate until the irritant assumes the same appearance as the inside of the mollusk. (4) Only rarely, and after many years, do the layers of nacre form a pearl.

(5) _____ a cut pearl is examined under a microscope, concentric layers of nacre are revealed. (6) Tiny crystals of the mineral aragonite, held in place by a cartilage-like substance called conchiolin, reflect light in an iridescent rainbow effect. (7) Jewelers call this iridescence *orient*. (8) Most mollusks do not make iridescent pearls _____ their aragonite crystals are too large.

(9) Perfectly round pearls are quite rare in natural occurrence. (10) Most pearls now are cultured. (11) A young oyster receives both a piece of mantle from a donor oyster and a seeding bead of mussel shell. (12) These are tucked into a carefully made incision in an oyster. (13) Which is then lowered into the ocean in a wire cage so it can be cleaned and periodically x-rayed to check on progress. (14) Since the oyster is a living organism, and not a machine in a factory, the oyster may choose to spit out the introduced nucleus, or the resulting pearl may be full of lumps and stains. (15) Minor stains and imperfections, however, may be eliminated by care-

fully grinding down the surface of the pearl in order to produce a smaller, but more valuable, perfect pearl.

96. Which of the following is needed in the first paragraph?

    (A) sentence 1: Delete "One of."

    (B) sentence 2: Change "like" to "such as."

    (C) sentence 3: Change "until" to "because."

    (D) sentence 4: Change "and after" to "and then."

    (E) sentence 4: Change "do" to "will."

97. Which of the following, if inserted in order into the blanks of the second paragraph, helps a reader understand the logical sequence of ideas?

    (A) When; because

    (B) If; so

    (C) Until; as a result of

    (D) For example; later

    (E) Perhaps; even though

98. Which of the following focuses attention on the main idea of the third paragraph?

    (A) Hyphenate "Perfectly round" in sentence 9.

    (B) Combine sentences 12 and 13 by changing the period after "oyster" to a comma.

    (C) Delete sentence 14.

    (D) Add a sentence between sentences 14 and 15 to give examples of defects.

    (E) Change "Most" to "More" in sentence 10.

(1) One thing is certain: Christopher Columbus was a real person who left real logs of his journey from Spain on August 3, 1492, to the Bahamas and back. (2) _____ (3) To the Spanish he is Cristobal Colon, but the Italians call him Cristoforo Colombo. (4) The Italians insist he is a native of Genoa, but some claim he was a Jew born in

Spain, or born in Spain but not a Jew. (5) One version has touted Columbus as a Norwegian.

(6) Contrary to the popular myth, most educated people of the 1400s believed the world was round. (7) Columbus didn't have to sell most anyone on that idea. (8) What he was trying to sell was a faster route to India. (9) Trade with India went by the centuries-old overland routes or the newer route by ship around the southern tip of Africa. (10) Also, another common myth is that Isabella had to sell her jewels in order to provide financing; actually, her husband had to approve all expenses, and funding was taken from the royal treasury.

(11) Even the original landing site is not known for certain, but most scholars agree that it is probably San Salvador Island in the Bahamas. (12) After his voyage, Columbus sent his handwritten logs to Isabella. (13) The copy the queen had made is known as the Barcelona log. (14) The original handwritten one has disappeared, as has all but a fragment of the Barcelona log copied by a Dominican friar named Bartolome de las Casas.

99. Which of the following, if used in the blank labeled sentence 2, BEST supports the main idea of the first paragraph?

   (A) Supposedly, Columbus began his sailing career as a boy 13 years old.

   (B) Because he wanted the lifetime annuity offered by Ferdinand and Isabella, Columbus falsely claimed to be the first to see land.

   (C) Columbus apparently sailed a course different from the one officially recorded in his log.

   (D) Almost everything else about him, including his name and place of birth, is controversial or uncertain.

   (E) It would've been neat to be on his ship!

100. Which of the following is needed in the second paragraph?

   (A) sentence 6: Change *Contrary to* to *Opposing*.

   (B) sentence 7: Delete the word *most*.

   (C) sentence 9: Change *by* to *around*.

   (D) sentence 11: Change *probably* to *probable*.

   (E) sentence 8: Change *faster* to *fastest*.

CLEP ENGLISH COMPOSITION
TEST 2

ANSWER KEY

Section 1

1. (A)	11. (B)	21. (B)	31. (D)	41. (C)
2. (A)	12. (A)	22. (E)	32. (B)	42. (C)
3. (A)	13. (C)	23. (D)	33. (A)	43. (A)
4. (D)	14. (B)	24. (E)	34. (E)	44. (C)
5. (D)	15. (A)	25. (A)	35. (E)	45. (B)
6. (E)	16. (C)	26. (D)	36. (B)	46. (C)
7. (C)	17. (B)	27. (B)	37. (C)	47. (D)
8. (D)	18. (A)	28. (A)	38. (A)	48. (A)
9. (D)	19. (D)	29. (B)	39. (D)	49. (C)
10. (B)	20. (A)	30. (D)	40. (B)	50. (B)

Section 2

51. (C)	61. (D)	71. (E)	81. (E)	91. (C)
52. (B)	62. (E)	72. (B)	82. (B)	92. (D)
53. (A)	63. (E)	73. (D)	83. (C)	93. (C)
54. (A)	64. (D)	74. (B)	84. (B)	94. (D)
55. (B)	65. (A)	75. (C)	85. (D)	95. (A)
56. (D)	66. (B)	76. (A)	86. (C)	96. (B)
57. (E)	67. (D)	77. (C)	87. (A)	97. (A)
58. (C)	68. (C)	78. (D)	88. (A)	98. (B)
59. (A)	69. (A)	79. (B)	89. (D)	99. (D)
60. (C)	70. (A)	80. (C)	90. (C)	100. (B)

DETAILED EXPLANATIONS
OF ANSWERS

TEST 2

Section 1

1. **(A)** One is *disappointed by* a person or action but *disappointed in* what is not satisfactory. *Inexpensive,* (B), is the adjective form. Parallel with *to work,* choice (C), *save,* has the word *to* omitted. Choice (D) compares the two models, one *inexpensive* and one *more expensive.*

2. **(A)** The verb should be plural, *are,* in order to agree with the compound subject, *budget... plans.* Choice (B) begins an infinitive phrase which included a participle, *existing,* (C). Choice (D) is idiomatically correct.

3. **(A)** The expression should be phrased, *as delicate as.* Choice (B) uses a possessive before a gerund; choice (C) is correctly used; and choice (D) is a possessive pronoun of neuter gender which is appropriate to use in referring to a plant.

4. **(D)** The verb *deal* must agree with the subject, *works,* and not a word in the intervening phrase. *Outwardly,* choice (A), is an adverb modifying *seemed.* Choices (B) and (C), *the picture of respectability,* describe the subject; (D) is idiomatically correct.

5. **(D)** The word *of* in *inside of* is redundant and should not be used. Choice (A) is idiomatically correct and signals two classes of people once considered unequal in merit; and choice (B), *alike,* is appropriate when comparing the two. Choice (C), *them,* is correct pronoun usage.

6. **(E)** Choice (A), *unsafe for,* is idiomatically correct; choice (B), *deltas,* is a plural noun. Choice (C), *can be excellent,* is grammatically correct. The preposition *in,* choice (D), is correct.

7. **(C)** The verb in this subordinate clause is incorrect; the clause begins with *which,* and this word refers to *information.* Therefore, the clause, in order to agree with the antecedent, must read, *which shows.* The verb *shows* should not be made to agree with *species* and *others.* Choices (A), *people,* and (B), *have compiled,* agree in number. *Either* in choice (D) is correctly placed after the verb to show a choice of *endangered* or *becoming endangered.*

8. **(D)** Do not end a sentence with a preposition; the phrase should read, *in which he was born.* The verbs show proper time sequence in (A) and (B); choice (C) is correct pronoun usage and correct superlative degree of adjective.

9. **(D)** The noun form, *effect,* is the correct one to use. Choice (A), *to inhibit,* is an infinitive; choice (B) is correctly worded; and in choice (C), the nominative case *who* is the correct subject of *seemed.*

10. **(B)** Verbs in clauses following *one of those,* choice (A), are always plural. Choice (C), *to campaign for,* is correct; choice (D) is a correctly worded conjunction.

11. **(B)** Choice (A) introduces a subordinate clause in which the subject is *one,* so the verb in choice (B) should be *was. We* is a subject pronoun, and *her* is a possessive pronoun in (C) and (D).

12. **(A)** This is a colloquial, nonstandard substitution for the correct word, *attribute.* It is so obviously incorrect, there's hardly any point in proceeding once you read it. Choice (B) is correctly lowercase, not capitalized. Choice (C) is a correct, if a bit stiff, phrase. Choice (D) is a correct plural verb, the subject of which is *both,* also plural.

13. **(C)** This is an incorrect simple past verb tense. You have to spot the context clue *most Americans attended* school [choice (B)] in the past, which suggests they no longer do so now. They must then *choose* their entertainment. You might believe that choice (A) is questionable, but the present participial phrase suggests coincidence with the time *most Americans attended school.* It is, therefore, correct. Choice (D) is correctly an infinitive that is parallel *to watch.*

14. **(B)** Choice (A) raises questions of appropriate capitalization, but it is proper to capitalize this particular title, even without a name attached.

Choice (C) might appear suspicious, but it is the correct spelling. Choice (D) is correct because *would* indicates a condition as suggested by the *If* at the beginning of the sentence. That leaves choices (E) and (B). One could argue that the electoral college constitutes an oligarchy because of its smaller size (E), but the sharp student will recognize that the sentence poses a condition contrary to fact, requiring the subjunctive *were*, choice (B).

15. **(A)** Choices (B) and (C) could look incorrect, except that both are parallel and appropriately balance each other. Choice (D) does not even merit scrutiny; nothing is improper there. Again, either there is no error (E), or we must look to choice (A). Knowledgeable students will know that confusion exists between *flaunt* and *flout. Flout* (to defy contemptuously) is correct in the context of the sentence; *flaunt* (to display arrogantly) is clearly incorrect.

16. **(C)** Choices (A) and (D) do not really require more than a cursory glance to show that they are acceptable. Choice (B) might require a second look because of the hyphen, but it is correct. Choice (C) is a clear example of faulty predication *reason... is because,* and is incorrect.

17. **(B)** Reading the sentence, the student should be jarred by the inappropriate coordination of the verb phrases beginning with *proposed* and *is.* Changing *and* to *which* makes a much more euphonious and balanced sentence. That change would properly subordinate the definition of *induction.* None of the other choices should raise concern, including (C), which is correctly hyphenated.

18. **(A)** Both (C) and (D) are possible choices, but (C) correctly uses the apostrophe to indicate plural. (Usage varies on this issue; depending on the editor's it is considered correct either with the apostrophe – *1920's* – or without – *1920s*.) Choice (D) also correctly capitalizes *Indian,* meaning American Indian. Nothing is amiss with choice (B) given the time noted and the subordinate clause verb *was.* Choice (A), however, incorrectly uses *due to* to show causation with an active verb (*wrote*). *Because of* is the correct phrase.

19. **(D)** We have an illogical comparison in this sentence: *People from...* and *in the United States.* Logical comparison demands that we compare like things to each other. In this case, the sentence compares people with the name of a nation. A logical comparison might read *...than people in*

the United States [do]. All other choices are correct: capitalized name of a geographical region (A), comparative adverb used with the active verb *stand* (B), and appropriate subordinating adverb *when* (C).

20. **(A)** This one looks more difficult than it is. The sentence is a fragment because there is no verb except in the dependent clauses. Furthermore, one cannot correct the problem by eliminating the relative pronoun *that,* choice (B), or by changing choices (C) or (D). *Because of* correctly modifies *cannot be explained away.* By changing choice (A) to *claims,* one completes the sentence and corrects the error.

21. **(B)** The problem should be spotted right away as a disagreement between the plural pronoun *their* and its singular antecedent *American,* choice (B). *Asian-American* – choice (A), is correctly hyphenated and capitalized. The phrase *and, therefore,* choice (C), is correctly punctuated because it links the compound verbs (*exists* and *has*). It is also precise (not wordy). The last choice, (D), is correctly spelled without a hyphen.

22. **(E)** One could quarrel with the use of the word *Curiously,* but it is not a choice. Otherwise, the sentence is a perfectly balanced logical comparison between like things (*teachers of the English language* and *students of the Russian language*). Even though students and teachers are not precisely parallel, one can compare them in this context. There is no reason to suspect the other choices.

23. **(D)** The problem here is sequence of verb tenses. Every verb in the sentence, except choice (D), is in the simple past tense, meaning occurrences in the finite past (not over a period of time). In the sentence context, *has* must be changed to *had.* The only other possibility is choice (C). One could question the elegance of the repetition of *that,* but it is both correct and necessary. The first two occurrences of *that* could be omitted, but they are not choices, and the sentence would not be any clearer than it is with them as stated.

24. **(E)** An opposing force *gives* scattered resistance; therefore, choice (A) is incorrect. Choices (B), (C), and (D) are poorly worded and do not have the correct meaning.

25. **(A)** Choice (A) produces a complete sentence: *rainfall* is the subject and *let up* is the verb. None of the other choices will produce a complete sentence.

26. **(D)** This choice uses the correct tense, *will have*, showing action in the future. All the other verbs listed do not show correct future verb construction.

27. **(B)** The correct choice has a compound verb: *comes* and *falls in love*. The salesman comes to town first, and then he meets and falls in love with the librarian. Choice (A), with its misplaced participial phrase, sounds as if the town or Iowa is in love with the librarian. Choice (C) would produce a run-on sentence. Choices (D) and (E) have unclear tense.

28. **(A)** Choice (A) has a clear reference. Choice (B) will produce a run-on sentence. Choices (C) and (D) do not indicate whose writings or paintings. Choice (E) sounds as if the only time naturalists feel reverence is when they write or paint.

29. **(B)** This question of appropriate verb tense requires the simple past tense verb *took* because the Civil War happened in a finite time period in the past. The other choices all fail that test. The original (A) and choice (E) are present tense, and do not logically fit the facts. Choice (D) is the present perfect tense, which suggests a continuous action from the past to the present. Choice (C) is the past perfect tense, which suggests a continuing action from one time in the past to another in the more recent past.

30. **(D)** We can eliminate fairly quickly choices (C) and (E) as either inappropriate or awkward appositives to *ornithology,* instead of *ornithologists.* Neither is (A) the best choice even though some may consider it acceptable. Likewise, choice (B) tends to be limited to nonrestrictive clauses, unlike this one. Choice (D) then correctly uses a *personal* relative pronoun.

31. **(D)** Choices (A), (D), and (E) are the best candidates because they are more concise than the other two choices. Each does express the same idea, but (E) does not as strongly indicate the contrast between the two clauses in the sentence as do choices (A) and (D). Choice (D) clearly makes its point in fewer words and is the better choice.

32. **(B)** The phrase *as to* often is overblown and unclear, so it is best to eliminate it when there are other choices. Likewise, *expectability* does not exactly roll off your tongue. That leaves choices (B) and (D). Choice (D) adds a definite figure, unwarranted by the original sentence. It also is

duller than (B), which does change the wording for the better and also indicates that the *actual amount* is to be announced, rather than that it is already known.

33.   **(A)**   Choices (C) and (E) introduce unnecessary absolute phrases beginning with *it,* which make the sentences wordy. They can be eliminated immediately. Choice (D) has an illogical comparison suggesting notes = instrument, so it, too, is not the best choice. Between (A) and (B) the difference boils down to the present tense vs. the past tense. Choice (A) uses past tenses, which seem better in sequence to follow the past tense verb *developed.*

34.   **(E)**   The problem here is noun agreement. To be in agreement, the underlined phrase must be plural, since the noun subject is compound. Choice (B) does use the plural but adds an unnecessary word, and the plural word is not the best choice. Choice (C) is similar in both ways. Choice (D) looks better, but the best word here is *people,* thus choice (E). Incidentally, an even better rephrasing – not a choice – is *to be free.*

35.   **(E)**   Wordiness is again the major problem with the original sentence and choices (B) and (C). Choices (D) and (E) are the only sensible alternates, so you must decide which of the two is better. Choice (E) tops (D) in brevity (two words instead of four). It also retains the word *stereotype* (in a variant form) and, therefore, is closer to the original meaning than (D).

36.   **(B)**   Here, we have an incorrectly punctuated clause, which is unnecessary, and a redundancy (both *complex and complicated*). Obviously, choice (A) should be passed over. Choices (C) and (D) correct the punctuation and eliminate the redundancy, but they leave the unnecessary clause. Choice (E) corrects the punctuation and eliminates one word, but it does not solve the redundancy problem. Choice (B) correctly eliminates both the unnecessary clause (obviating the need for punctuation) and the redundancy. It is the most concise and best of the choices.

37.   **(C)**   Be alert for concise expression. Often that means looking for the shortest answer, but not always. In this case, the shortest answer is indeed the best one. (A) is wordy and has a vague pronoun *it* (unclear antecedent). Choice (B) uses an inappropriate colloquialism (*went to prove*). (D) is repetitious (*president*) and unnecessarily wordy in differentiating the script from the pictures. (E) is repetitious like (D) and wordy toward the end.

38. **(A)** The choices are easy to discern in this sentence. The original sentence correctly uses present tense to discuss a published work. All of the other choices use some variation of past tense.

39. **(D)** Choice (D) fits between the two parts. Sentence 4 concerns a child who may read two years below grade level. Sentence 6 concerns a child who attempts to read four years above grade level. The answer choice stating that a child's reading ability may vary within a 10-year range is the best choice for the paragraph. Choice (A) is far too broad. Choices (B), (C), and (E) introduce extraneous ideas to the paragraph.

40. **(B)** Choice (B) contains the solution to the agreement problem: *the child* should be followed by a singular pronoun, *his or her*. The pronoun *their* is plural and would be appropriate to refer to a plural noun such as *children.* Choice (A) would insert an incorrect possessive pronoun. Choice (C) would not improve the sentence. Choice (D) is not a correct solution because it makes the verb tense incorrect. Choice (E) is not correct because the adverb *well* is clearly called for.

41. **(C)** Choice (C) contains the correct transition words, *Even though* and *Also.* Choice (A) is incorrect because *In addition* indicates another example has just been named. As the first sentence is the topic sentence, it does not contain a specific example. Choices (B) and (D) are incorrect because they indicate contrast, and nothing that follows contrasts or is a negative example to the topic sentence. Choice (E) makes no sense in relation to the context.

42. **(C)** Choice (C) contains irrelevant information, so it should be eliminated. Choice (A) contains a phrase essential to the sentence. Choice (B) would create a fragment after the semicolon because the clause beginning with *although* is a subordinate clause, and only an independent clause would be appropriate after the semicolon. Choice (D) would create a misplaced modifier; *except for their breath* would be taken to modify the layer of fat on polar bears. Choice (E) would delete a correct and efficient transition phrase.

43. **(A)** Choice (A) fits the development of the paragraph by describing how large polar bears are, a concept introduced in the previous sentence. Choices (B), (D), and (E), although related to hunting, do not fit well in this place. Choice (C) introduces an extraneous topic.

44.   **(C)**   Choice (C) is correct because *between* should be used to compare two things; *among* should be used to compare three or more things. Since there are five countries, *among* is the correct form. Choice (A) would create an error in comparison, since there are more than two types of land-based carnivores. Choice (B) makes no improvement. Choice (D) deletes the necessary idea of contrast shown by *but* in contrasting the two levels of polar bear population. Choice (E) makes no improvement because the words are synonyms.

45.   **(B)**   Choice (B) is a transition between the discussion of lipoproteins and triglycerides. Sentence 3 introduces HDL and sentence 5 discusses the normal triglyceride level. Choice (A) changes the topic slightly by introducing history. Choice (C) might be a good choice but does not contain mention of triglycerides, so there is no transition. Choice (D) introduces a new topic – the chances of men and women developing heart disease. Choice (E) introduces extraneous information to the paragraph.

46.   **(C)**   Choice (C) is a type of run-on sentence. The technical name for this sentence is a comma splice since two independent clauses are joined by only a comma; they should be joined by a semicolon (as in this explanatory sentence). The comma after *treated* should be a semicolon. Choices (A), (B), (D), and (E) are correctly punctuated compound sentences because they contain a comma followed by a conjunction to link the two independent clauses.

47.   **(D)**   Choice (D) discusses the tool-making abilities of an otter, not man, so it should be deleted. Choice (A) would delete the topic sentence from the paragraph. Choice (B) is incorrect because sentence 2 begins with *During this time,* and there would be no antecedent for *this* if the two parts are reversed. Choice (C) is incorrect because the suggested addition does not pertain to the development of man during this time period. Choice (E) would begin discussing the *two suggested reasons* before introducing them.

48.   **(A)**   Choice (A) will eliminate the fragment found in sentence 5. Choice (B) contains a comma necessary to mark an introductory adverbial clause. Choice (C) creates a fragment in the second half of the sentence if the semicolon is used since *uncaring* is a participle used as the compound completer: *the legislator is dishonest... or uncaring.* Choice (D) does not change the meaning to any extent. Choice (E) incorrectly states an affirmative.

49. **(C)** Choice (C) fits in with the flow of ideas and prepares the way for sentence 10, an example of when it is a good idea to question a politician's motives. Choice (A) directly contradicts the thesis. Choice (B) is too casual, *kicked out of office*; choice (E) is too casual as well. Choice (D) introduces new ideas associated with campaign tactics, "accusations and name-calling."

50. **(B)** Choice (B) gives the reason why the recycling of tin cans is gaining momentum. Choice (A) is true, but it does not have anything to do with recycling. Choice (C) contradicts the essay's information. Choice (D) has nothing to do with recycling. Choice (E) is a conclusion and is misplaced between sentences 11 and 12.

Section 2

51. **(C)** One could question the use of *nearly* (A), but it is correct. One might argue also that *million dollars* (D) should be written *$1 million,* but the obvious choice (C) is so clearly an incorrect use of the past perfect tense that the other possibilities, remote at best, pale by comparison. The simple past tense (*sold*), the present progressive tense (*are selling*), or the present perfect progressive tense (*have been selling*) could each be used correctly depending on the meaning intended.

52. **(B)** This choice is not so obvious, and may be arguable, but authorities agree that the use of *expect* to mean *suppose* or *believe* (the usage here) is either informal or colloquial, but again not formal written English. The next most likely choice (E) would suggest that informal or colloquial usage is appropriate. The third most likely trouble area (D) brings to mind the distinction between *accept* and *except,* a word pair often confused. However, *accept* is correct here.

53. **(A)** Regardless of the cave-in to popular usage by such pop grammarians as James Kilpatrick and William Safire, *hopefully* is an adverb trying to be a clause (*it is hoped* or *I hope*). However, instances still exist that require a distinction between the two uses. To be clear, use *hopefully* when you mean *in a hopeful manner.* [*He wished hopefully that she would accept his proposal of marriage.*] Choice (D) appears suspicious. *Continually* means recurrence at intervals over a period of time, so it is correctly used to imply that machines do break down often. Capitalizing *Twentieth*

Century (B) is also appropriate as it is here used as the specific historical period (like the *Middle Ages*). We would not capitalize the phrase if it were used simply to count, as in *The twentieth century from now will surely find enormous changes in the world.* It is incorrect to hyphenate a number-noun phrase like this one when it stands alone as a noun phrase. Choice (C) is correct as used.

54. **(A)** The two most suspicious choices are (A) and (D) because the item is a sentence fragment. No reasonable substitute for (D) would solve both the logic problem (incomplete thought) and the punctuation problem (comma splice if you omit *that*). Changing *showing* to *show* would, however, make the clause into a complete sentence with correct punctuation. Neither of the choices (B) nor (C) provoke suspicion.

55. **(B)** Again, the two most questionable choices, (B) and (C), compete for our attention. The use of *but* makes sense because it shows contrast to the previous idea. (*Don't evade or defy the law, but if caught breaking a law, accept the penalty.*) The use of *or,* however, is clearly not parallel to the immediately preceding use of *neither.* The proper phrase is *neither...nor* for negative alternate choices. Neither choice (A) nor choice (D) demands a second look.

56. **(D)** This choice involves parallel construction, or the lack of it. The word *both* introduces a pair of phrases, one a prepositional phrase (*for their own interests*), the other an infinitive phrase (*to gain more goods*). Aside from being inelegant, *to gain more goods* is also not the same structure and should be changed to "their own gain" to make the two phrases perfectly parallel. Choices (B) and (C) are not problematic. Choice (A) is another candidate because of the capitalization and the lack of a hyphen between *Eighteenth* and *Century.* The capitalization is correct (see explanation for #53), and no hyphen is needed when the phrase becomes an adjective that has meaning as a single phrase, which the capitalization suggests, or if the first word forms a familiar pair with the following word and if there is no danger of confusion. (The sentence clearly does not mean that Smith is the eighteenth (small "e") philosopher, but the Eighteenth Century philosopher.)

57. **(E)** The other choices all fail to exhibit inappropriate usage. Choice (A), *cannot,* is spelled as one word: choice (B), *should not,* is parallel to *cannot* and adds meaning necessary to the thought. Choice (C) is a correct

plural possessive pronoun, the antecedent of which is *rulers*. Finally, choice (D) is a third-person plural verb agreeing with its subject, *reasons*.

58. **(C)** For the same reason *their* was correct in number 57, it is incorrect here. *Milky Way galaxy* is the singular antecedent, for which the pronoun referent should be *its* (inanimate object). Do not be confused by the intervening words (*stars* and *spots*); it is the galaxy which shines in this sentence, not the stars or the spots. Choice (A) is the correct usage of *comprises*. Choice (B) is an appropriate pair of adjectives with no apparent problem. Choice (D) is appropriate because the sentence has an internally supplied superlative sense; it does not need a *brightest of* phrase.

59. **(A)** Again, non-parallel structure is the key of this and many other test items. Because of the overwhelming importance of understanding balance and euphony in sentence structure, tests like this one emphasize parallel sentence structures. *To learn* clashes with *studying* in the parallel clause. You can't choose *studying*. *Learning* substituted for *To learn* would make the clauses parallel. Choice (B) is a correct use of *like* as a preposition (objects: *Latin, Greek*). Choice (D) is correctly singular as the verb of the noun phrase *studying...beliefs*. Nothing is incorrect about choice (C).

60. **(C)** *The bald eagle has become America's proud national symbol, embellishing with nobility and majesty* many memorabilia, from solid pewter and porcelain to T-shirts and baseball caps. (This is the only choice that logically preserves the meaning of the original sentence.)

61. **(D)** *A childhood dream came true for Jane Goodall, the chimpanzee woman*, which she documented expertly in her seminal book of Africa, *My Friends the Wild Chimpanzees*. (This choice places in sequential order the important elements of the sentence. All other choices contain elements that are out of order in logical sequence.)

62. **(E)** *Defined as nearly anything that* can be patented, copyrighted, or trademarked, the pirating of intellectual property involves such items as pop albums, computer programs, creamed corn, and cough syrup. (This option is the best choice since the original definition is intact and not obscured in any manner.)

63. **(E)** *The Korean War Veterans Memorial will immortalize the foot soldiers by featuring* sculptures of 19 larger-than-life soldiers who will be watched eternally by 2,400 images of actual Korean veterans, etched in

granite. (The integrity of the original message of immortalizing the foot soldiers is preserved only in this choice.)

64.   **(D)** *The heinous dictatorship of "Papa Doc" Duvalier* in Haiti, with the help of Tontons Macoutes, left a brutal legacy in 1971 to his son, Jean-Claude, "Baby Doc." (This restructured version leaves no doubt that it was Papa Doc's heinous dictatorship and legacy left to Jean-Claude.)

65.   **(A)** *Whole-grain breads and cereals, having long been staples* in so-called backward countries where many inhabitants live remarkably healthy lives, are making a comeback. (This choice strategically places the modifying verbal right after the subject.)

66.   **(B)** *The brick walls of prejudice and blind hatred would be torn down if we* accept the habits, life styles, and customs of other cultures that seem, at first, to be foreign or unlike our own. (The strength of the metaphor, *brick walls of prejudice and blind hatred,* is intact in this choice.)

67.   **(D)** *The distinction of being the greatest museum of the world has been* long-held by the Louvre in Paris, France, for its vast range of art and the unsurpassed quality of its masterpieces. (This is the only restructured choice that does not create an awkward version of the original sentence.)

68.   **(C)** Your rephrased sentence will probably read: *Three boys and their friends have worn this carpet with their traffic.* Choice (E) would create a fragment, and choice (B) changes the meaning of the original sentence. The subject of choices (A) and (D) would have to be *the carpet.*

69.   **(A)** Your sentence will probably read: *Crying loudly and angrily, the child went out into the street and ran off.* Choices (B), (D), and (E) are not parallel; choice (C) omits the concept of anger and uses *loud* instead of *loudly.*

70.   **(A)** Your rephrased sentence will probably read: *Orville Wright, together with his brother Wilbur, made his fame by building and flying the first successful airplane.* Choice (B) omits one of the key concepts, flying. Choice (C) would produce an incoherent sentence. Choice (E) uses the simple past tense of the verbs, which is incorrect. Choice (D) would be correct if the phrase read, *was famous for.*

71.   **(E)**   Your rephrased sentence will probably read: *Negotiating the hairpin turns on roads in the Rocky Mountains requires careful driving.* Choice (A) is incorrect because it changes the emphasis merely to being aware of careful driving, and choice (C) is incorrect because it also changes the meaning of the sentence. Choice (D) uses the wrong tense. Choice (B) would require the subject to be *you* and changes the meaning.

72.   **(B)**   Your rephrased sentence will probably read: *The major causes of World War I include competition for colonies, rising feelings of nationalism, and military alliances among European countries, although it was blamed on the assassination of Archduke Ferdinand.* Choice (A) has an unnecessary comma. Choice (C) has a plural pronoun, *they,* instead of a singular one. Choice (D) would produce an incoherent sentence. Choice (E) lacks a comma.

73.   **(D)**   Your rephrased sentence will probably read: *A development of World War I was the use of airplanes for weapons instead of reconnaissance.* No other choice comes as close to the meaning of the original sentence. Choice (B) requires a phrase to complete it. Choice (A) and choice (E) will produce awkward sentences. Choice (C) has the key noun at the end.

74.   **(B)**   Choice (B) is least important because it does not relate to the history of Dalmatians. Choice (A) is the topic sentence. Choices (C), (D), and (E) directly relate to the location of the probable origin of Dalmatians.

75.   **(C)**   Choice (C) provides a smooth flow of ideas by showing the effect of the Dalmatians' calm temperament. Choice (A) introduces an extraneous topic, Clydesdale horses with calm natures. Choices (B) and (D), although true facts, break the flow of ideas. Choice (E) follows an unrelated topic.

76.   **(A)**   Choice (A) is past tense, the appropriate tense for a discussion of historical events. Choice (B) incorrectly indicates the migration is still in progress. Choice (C) incorrectly changes the form of past tense so it is not parallel with the second part of the sentence, *the dogs traveled*; dogs and man traveled together, not separately. Choice (D) incorrectly changes the time of the action to the future. Choice (E) incorrectly places the action in the present.

77. **(C)** The tone of sentence 12 is too casual to fit in with the overall formal tone of the essay. Besides, the logic is flawed; all news in a newspaper is *old* because it takes time to process the news into a newspaper. Choice (A) would create an incoherent sentence. Choice (B) would introduce items that are too technical and do not tie in directly with the thesis. Choice (D) would create a comma splice because a comma is insufficient to join two independent clauses. Choice (E) does not improve the paragraph.

78. **(D)** Choice (D) is written in an informal tone and shifts the person: *I* speaking to *you*. This shift is incorrect as voice should be consistent throughout an essay. Choices (A), (B), (C), and (E) all maintain a formal, detached tone.

79. **(B)** Choice (B) has a logical flow of ideas: it follows the idea of including a quotation discussed in sentence 7 and precedes the careful exclusion of bias discussed in sentence 9. Choice (A) introduces a new idea, the photographer. Choices (C) and (D) directly contradict the information and ideas presented in the selection. Choice (E) follows an unrelated topic.

80. **(C)** Questioning is an effective technique that involves the reader. Neither (A) confusion nor (E) embellishment of style are intended. There is neither intention to (B) discredit nor (D) alarm the reader.

81. **(E)** Sentence 6 is a compound sentence since it contains two independent clauses. Length does not determine comma nor period usage as related in choices (A) and (B). Although the clause does make a statement (C), it is not a determinate of the semicolon use. Since it contains one dependent clause, the sentence is not (D) complex.

82. **(B)** The objective case pronoun *whom* is correct. (A) The nominative case who or choice of (D), the subject, are incorrect, since *law* is the sentence's subject. It is therefore not (C) misplace nor (E) used for impression.

83. **(C)** Hyperbole is used for exaggeration in a dramatic manner. The opposite is understatement, (D). There is very little hint of persuasion (B) and no use of (E) poetic justice.

84. **(B)** This brief anecdote captures interest since it is a real possibility of a very actual event. (A) An aphorism is a short lesson or a maxim. There are no (C) literal comparisons, (D) similes, which compare with *like* or *as*, nor metaphors, (E), which compare directly.

85. **(D)** The word "sluggish" provides a key clue. (A) is incorrect; the sentence containing the word has nothing to do with intelligence. (B) is incorrect; the writer is not referring to those who can't help themselves but to those who don't care to act. (C) is incorrect; the writer's concern is not with those who receive no attention. (E) is also incorrect; importance, or consequence, is irrelevant in this sentence. Generally, only (D) reflects the context clue given in the paragraph.

86. **(C)** Sentence one contains this idea as a topic concept while the rest of the paragraph shows how dull the "thin" approach is and how different it is from the "fat" approach. (A) and (E) are incorrect; the writer neither says nor implies such conclusions. (B) is incorrect; while this statement may be true, it misses the writer's intent: the productive approach is funless, dull. (D) is incorrect; the writer may think this, but he doesn't say it and his intent is not to say what thin people should do but what they actually do (or do not do).

87. **(A)** When the author asserts that thin people are funless, he or she in essence agrees with this; the entire selection implies it clearly. (B) is incorrect; the writer in no way tries to argue that fat people live longer, just happier. (C) is incorrect; if anything, the author thinks they are every bit as successful as they appear. (D) is incorrect; there is no argument about intelligence in the selection.

88. **(A)** According to the context, the thin person walks as if to convey executive urgency when in fact the situation is otherwise. (B) is incorrect; the writer might say this humorously, but the point is not a fat person's walking speed. (C) is incorrect; the writer implies that brisk walkers are not true executives. (D) and (E) are incorrect; if anything, the opposite here would be true, although the point isn't whether thin people are good or poor in their performance, or how hard they work.

89. **(D)** Paragraphs two through five discuss a different aspect of life as leanies see it; the final sentence alludes to the fat counterperspective. Paragraph four addresses the fat viewpoint in slightly more depth. Paragraph six then looks at the fat viewpoint. (A) is incorrect; the selection doesn't focus on the ways fat people approach life but on the ways lean

people approach it. (B) is incorrect; although the three key words in the answer may appear in the selection, they do not reflect the main ideas of the respective paragraphs. (C) is incorrect; the point of the selection is not to teach lessons to lean people; the paragraphs' intentions are not to do such things as teach how to conserve energy or to stay healthy.

90. **(C)** Choice (C) is an example of the topic sentence of paragraph 2. Choice (C) is needed between the mention of the neighbors and sentence 6, which begins with *In another example.* Choices (A) and (D) might be logical, but they do not mention contributions of teenagers; also, both stray slightly from the topic by focusing on cost of supplies or insurance problems. Choice (B) changes voice, *you,* and introduces slang, *kind of neat.* Choice (E) also strays from the topic.

91. **(C)** Choice (C) shows weak wording. *Unfair* is a word to be avoided in persuasive writing, and the sentence contains a sweeping generality, *adults don't really respect people our age.* Choice (A) would detract from the thesis by adding negative examples to refute the thesis. Choice (B) would place ideas out of order. Choice (D) would create a comma splice as a comma is not strong enough to join two independent clauses. Choice (E) would create a fragment – *Although the youths were mentioned in the story.*

92. **(D)** Choice (D) contains all three main words in the singular form. Choices (A), (B), (C), and (E) mix plural and singular forms of words. In order to have correct agreement in a phrase such as this, all three words must be singular or all must be plural: *this kind of conduct* or *these kinds of activities.*

93. **(C)** Choice (C) indicates that information about the originators of the folk dance is not necessary in a paragraph about the ballet. Choice (A) introduces the topic of the ballet and its composer. Choice (B) tells who choreographed the ballet. Choice (D) gives further information on the ballet and its music. Choice (E) is incorrect because (C) contains unnecessary information.

94. **(D)** Choice (D) is the only choice containing information about the rhythm discussed in sentences 6 and 7. Choice (A) and choice (B) both break the formal tone and use contractions. Choice (C), although a possible choice, has nothing to do with rhythm and introduces information on the folk dance. Choice (E) involves rhythm, but does not provide a transition between sentences 6 and 7.

95. **(A)** Choice (A) contains the phrase, *A French composer,* which does not modify *the bolero.* The phrase should be placed after *Maurice Ravel* to correct the error. Choices (B), (C), (D), and (E) are all correct sentences.

96. **(B)** Choice (B) is correct because *such as* is used to introduce an example; *like* signals unequal comparisons. Choice (A) changes the meaning of the sentence; pearls are not the most valuable gems. In choice (C) the change would omit the correct transition *until* which shows time sequence. Choice (D) would create an incoherent sentence. Choice (E) incorrectly places the action in the future.

97. **(A)** Choice (A) is correct because the first blank needs a time indicating word such as *When,* and the second blank needs a cause-and-effect word such as *because.* In choice (B) the first transition word is plausible, but the second one is not. Choices (C), (D), and (E) produce incoherent sequences of ideas.

98. **(B)** Choice (B) combined the fragment in sentence 13 with the complete sentence in sentence 12. Choice (A) is not a necessary addition. Choice (C) would delete a necessary sentence, one which provides the lead into the idea of grinding down imperfections. Choice (D) is unnecessary because examples of defects have already been listed in sentence 14, "lumps and stains." Choice (E) would render the sentence grammatically incorrect.

99. **(D)** Choice (D) is the thesis for the passage: Christopher Columbus is covered in controversy. Sentence 1 introduces the contrast to choice (D) by stating that it is certain Columbus existed and went on the voyage. Choice (A) is a true but unnecessary fact in this blank. Choice (B) is supposition but not appropriate in this blank. Choice (C) would be more appropriate in the third paragraph. Choice (E) is too casual and does not logically fit in the context.

100. **(B)** Choice (B) would delete the unnecessary pronoun *most.* Choice (A) creates a poorly worded transition. Choice (C) creates a sentence that is self-contradictory, making the traders appear to avoid the route they actually took. Choice (D) changes the correct adverb *probably,* meant to modify the verb *is,* to the incorrect adjective *probable.* Choice (E) is incorrect because the comparative is required, not the superlative.

▼
PRACTICE
TEST 3
WITH ESSAY QUESTION

CLEP ENGLISH COMPOSITION
With Essay Question
Test 3

(Answer sheets appear in the back of the book.)

Section 1

TIME: 45 Minutes
55 Questions

Identifying Sentence Errors

DIRECTIONS: The following sentences test your knowledge of grammar, usage, diction (choice of words), and idiom.

Some sentences are correct.

No sentence contains more than one error.

You will find that the error, if there is one, is underlined and lettered. Assume that elements of the sentence that are not underlined are correct and cannot be changed. In choosing answers, follow the requirements of standard written English.

If there is an error, select the <u>one underlined part</u> that must be changed to make the sentence correct and fill in the corresponding oval on your answer sheet. If there is no error, fill in answer oval E.

Example:

<u>The other</u> football players and <u>him immediately</u> accepted the
    A   B

<u>offered contract</u> from the <u>state university.</u> <u>No error.</u>
      C   D   E

1. Joreca found that it was <u>best</u> <u>to do her homework</u> and then
                        A   B
   <u>to watch television</u> than <u>to reverse the procedure.</u> <u>No error.</u>
              C   D   E

2. If they <u>would of known</u> <u>it was going to rain,</u> <u>the sisters</u>
                   A   B   C
   <u>would have taken</u> their umbrellas. <u>No error</u>
            D   E

3. <u>Mary</u> <u>could sing,</u> <u>dance</u>, and <u>even painting a picture was easy</u>.
     A   B   C   D
   <u>No error</u>
      E

4. Bernoulli's Principle <u>states</u> that <u>slow-moving air</u> <u>exerts</u> less
                           A   B   C
   pressure than fast-moving air <u>exerted.</u> <u>No error.</u>
                                     D   E

5. Bodaise <u>has found</u> <u>it is</u> <u>more difficult</u> to divide exponents
                A   B   C
   <u>than adding exponents.</u> <u>No error.</u>
              D   E

6. <u>To find out more about whales,</u> the <u>students</u> researched
                    A   B
   books that <u>had regard</u> for <u>the topic.</u> <u>No error.</u>
                   C   D   E

7. <u>Since two shoppers</u> <u>was already there</u> in the store,
             A   B
   <u>there was</u> no hope of <u>postponing the sale.</u> <u>No error.</u>
          C   D   E

8. <u>Knowing its importance to the entire family,</u> the <u>heavily-carved</u>
                        A   B
   box <u>with the gold handles</u> was given by the teacher <u>to the boy.</u>
                  C   D
   <u>No error.</u>
        E

9. Either the animals or the zookeeper were making a
                    A   B

    great deal of noise and was disturbing the sleep of the
                                   C

    circus performers. No error.
            D   E

10. Everyone should bring their papers to the front of the
                  A   B

    room so that the teacher can make sure that the work
                                C

    is complete. No error.
         D   E

11. Since either her father or her mother usually drive her
                       A   B

    to the school, Mary is able to get to school more quickly
                C   D

    than her neighbor. No error
                 E

12. The first years of high school is the most difficult;
                A   B   C

    many students have problems adjusting to the new
                            D

    environment during these two years. No error.
                                        E

13. The young baby-sitter was so tired after her first day on
                              A

    the job that thoughts of sleep was all that went
                      B   C

    through her mind. No error.
            D   E

14. It's hard to determine what makes a child go and cry its
       A   B   C

    loudest at the sight of the shadows. No error.
                 D   E

15. After the accident Jane silently sat on a chair
        A   B
 near the window watching the train. No error.
          C   D   E

16. There wasn't nothing anyone could do to prevent
                 A   B
 his getting the money from the safety deposit box.
             C   D
 No error.
   E

17. Considered to be the keenest legal mind of the sixteenth century,
                       A
 Sir Edward Coke first lay down the principle a man's home
                   B   C
 is his "castle and fortress," explaining that it is his fundamental
          D
 refuge from harm and violence. No error.
                       E

18. One of the most colorful characters in literature, George Gordon,
                   A
 known as Lord Byron, swam the Hellespont, a treacherous strait
       B
 separating Europe from Asia, and he also led a group of men
            C   D
 in the Greek war against the Turks. No error.
                     E

19. Researchers investigating poltergeists, those ghostly spirits,
                                     A
 that cause bumps in the night have reached curious conclusion
                                 B
 that these mischievous noisemakers apparently prefer the company
                                   C
 of the younger generation. No error.
            D   E

20. If you <u>were</u> to ask <u>what's</u> the most complex computer, the
          A   B
    answer <u>would be</u> – the human brain, composed of just three
             C
    pounds of gray-white matter, containing <u>literally</u> billions of
                             D
    components. <u>No error.</u>
            E

21. It is time – <u>pastime</u> – that we <u>recognize</u> the pervasiveness of
             A   B
    censorship in America when we discover that school dictionaries

    have been barred from some schools because <u>they</u> contain
                                     C
    suggestive or <u>culturally sensitive</u> words. <u>No error.</u>
               D   E

22. Archery and the use of the bow and arrow <u>as a means</u> of
                                A
    <u>subsistence</u> dated back for many centuries and is considered,
       B
    <u>to some,</u> only second <u>to the wheel</u> in
      C   D
    importance to man. <u>No error.</u>
             E

23. The most common method of payment <u>are</u> with credit cards
                             A
    (<u>plastic money</u>) and checking accounts for the
       B
    <u>consumer of the twentieth century</u>, especially
             C
    for the "<u>under 30 generation.</u>" <u>No error.</u>
             D   E

Improving Sentences

24. <u>Due to the fact that the four children were sick</u>, their father did not attend the swim meet.

    (A) Due to the fact that the four children were sick,

    (B) Because the four children was sick,

    (C) Because the four children were sick,

    (D) Because they was sick,

    (E) Due to the fact of their illness,

25. <u>Keeping the records accurately maintained is</u> in the historian's job description.

    (A) Keeping the records accurately maintained is

    (B) Keeping the records accurately maintained are

    (C) To keep its records accurately maintained is

    (D) In order to keep the records maintained are

    (E) Keep its records accurately maintained as

26. In writing *A Tale of Two Cities*, <u>Dickens produced one of the best-sellers of the Victorian Period</u>.

    (A) Dickens produced one of the best-sellers of the Victorian Period.

    (B) one of the best-sellers of the Victorian Period was produced.

    (C) the Victorian Period produced one of Dickens' best-sellers.

    (D) Dickens and the Victorian Period produced one of the best-sellers.

    (E) a production of one of the best-sellers of the Victorian Period was achieved by Dickens.

27. The college student's <u>goal in keeping her locker clean for an entire semester</u>.

    (A) goal in keeping her locker clean for an entire semester.

    (B) goal was keeping her locker clean for an entire semester.

    (C) goal, keeping her locker clean for an entire semester.

    (D) keeping her locker clean for an entire semester, an important goal.

    (E) goal, which was keeping her locker clean for an entire semester.

28. Seeing the three animated characters, <u>the movie was exciting for the child</u>.

    (A) the movie was exciting for the child.

    (B) the child was excited about the movie.

(C) the movie excited the child.

(D) the child was excited.

(E) the child saw the movie.

29. <u>Due to the fact that he lives there</u>, Bill felt very comfortable.

    (A) Due to the fact that he lives there,

    (B) Due to the fact that he lives there;

    (C) Because he lives there,

    (D) After he once lived there,

    (E) Due to the fact that he lives there is why

30. <u>In 1607 the English started their first permanent settlement in America,</u> the site was Jamestown, Virginia.

    (A) In 1607 the English started their first permanent settlement in America,

    (B) In 1607 the English started their first permanent settlement in America;

    (C) In 1607 the English made the first settlement in America.

    (D) In 1607 the English made the first settlement in America;

    (E) In 1607 the first permanent English settlement in America was made,

31. Reducing one's weight <u>are ways to ease stress on the heart</u>.

    (A) are ways to ease stress on the heart.

    (B) is a way to ease stress on the heart.

    (C) to ease stress on the heart.

    (D) , heart stress is lessened.

    (E) , it can ease stress on the heart.

32. After having written many books, <u>the author was made popular</u>.

    (A) the author was made popular.

    (B) the author became popular.

(C) the man became a popular author.

(D) the author will become popular.

(E) the author is popular.

Revising Work in Progress

(1) I have recently found a new hobby and it gives me much pleasure. (2) I have had hobbies that took more time. (3) Even these hobbies were not as satisfying. (4) My new hobby of training dogs takes time, but its rewards are many.

(5) First, I tried gourmet cooking. (6) Since I live in a small Southern town, many of the ingredients were unobtainable. (7) Once the pheasants I had special ordered spoiled before the fresh mushrooms arrived four days later. (8) I found I had added 10 pounds in order not to waste the food. (9) For weeks my family did not eat the new dishes. (10) When I grew tired of the kitchen, I knew it was time to try something new.

(11) Secondly, I tried quilting. (12) The long hours of inactivity were unpleasant. (13) Again I had problems remaining indoors.

(14) When my dad took a business trip and left me in charge of his hunting dogs, I found a hobby I could love. (15) Training dogs gives me exercise and activity, does not consume much time, and allows me to enjoy the outdoors. (16) Sparkling, big, brown eyes and wagging tails at my approach are rewards no cooked goose or embroidered quilt can duplicate.

33. Which of the following is the best way to revise sentences 2 and 3 (reproduced below) so that the two sentences are combined?

    I have had hobbies *that took more time. Even these hobbies* were not as satisfying.

(A) that took more time, these hobbies

(B) that took more time; these hobbies in addition

(C) that were more time-consuming and in addition these hobbies

(D) that took more time but

(E) , more time-consuming and more satisfying.

34. Which of the following sentences, if added after sentence 4, would best link the first paragraph with the rest of the essay?

(A) A consideration of dog training is in order.

(B) I find dog training excels in comparison with my earlier hobbies.

(C) Let's look at my past hobbies.

(D) Other hobbies are also popular in America.

(E) The dictionary defines *hobby* as an activity that occupies one's spare time.

35. In the context of the second paragraph, which of the following is the best version of the portion of sentence 6 italicized below?

Since I live in a small southern town, *many of the ingredients were unobtainable.*

(A) many of the ingredients were unobtainable.

(B) many of the unobtainable ingredients.

(C) having ingredients is rare.

(D) I found it difficult to find the ingredients in local shops.

(E) the ingredients had been rare.

36. Which of the following is the best way to revise and combine sentences 9 and 10 (reproduced below)?

For weeks my family did not eat the new dishes. When I grew tired of the kitchen, I knew it was time to try something new.

(A) When my family did not eat the new dishes and when I grew tired of the kitchen, I knew it was time to try something new.

(B) As my family did not eat the new dishes, I grew tired of the kitchen and knew it was time to try something new.

(C) Due to the fact that my family did not eat the new dishes and when I grew tired of the kitchen, I knew it was time to try something new.

(D) Despite the fact that my family did not eat the new dishes for weeks and that I grew tired of the kitchen, I knew it was time to try something new.

(E) For weeks my family did not eat the new dishes, when I grew tired of the kitchen, I knew it was time to try something new.

37. All of the following strategies are used by the writer of the passage EXCEPT

(A) criticizing those whose opinions differ from the author's.

(B) making use of comparisons.

(C) making use of contrasts.

(D) selecting specific examples.

(E) telling a story to develop a point.

38. Which of the following words could best be placed at the beginning of the last sentence?

(A) Furthermore   (D) Excepting this

(B) Instead   (E) In contrast

(C) Nevertheless

39. Which of the following would best replace "Secondly" at the beginning of sentence 11?

(A) Furthermore,   (D) Later

(B) In addition,   (E) Nevertheless,

(C) Second,

40. Which is the best version of sentence 1?

(A) I have found a new hobby; giving me much pleasure.

(B) I have found a new hobby that gives me much pleasure.

(C) I have found a new hobby, it gives me much pleasure.

(D) I have found a new hobby; therefore it gives me much pleasure.

(E) I have found a new hobby; however it gives me much pleasure.

(1) The National Education Goals for the year 2000 were established by governors. (2) The first of these goals say that by the year 2000 all children should enter school ready to learn. (3) This goal may be accomplished by schools with difficulty.

(4) First, the schools were given the responsibility for correcting the social and economic conditions that hinder educational readiness by many children. (5) In many homes the purchase of pencils, papers, crayons, books, and other learning materials may be prohibited because of their cost. (6) A lack of learning materials may be a causative factor in some children's entering schools unready to learn.

(7) Second, social factors also prevent readiness. (8) The educational level of many parents prevents them from reading to and working with their children. (9) If all the adults in a family may work, their time to do these things is limited.

(10) The National Education Goals for 2000 are desirable, but they are not the responsibility of the schools alone. (11) Politics, parents, education, and society must all work to achieve these goals.

41. Which of the following is the best way to revise sentence 1 (reproduced below)?

The National Education Goals for the year 2000 were established by governors.

(A) The National Education Goals for the year 2000 were established by governors.

(B) The National Education Goals were established for the year 2000 by governors.

(C) Governors for the year 2000 established the National Education Goals.

(D) The National Education Goals were for the year 2000.

(E) Governors established the National Education Goals for the year 2000.

42. What treatment of sentence 6 (reproduced below) is most needed?

    A lack of learning materials may be a causative factor in some children's entering schools unready to learn.

    (A) A lack of learning materials may be a causative factor in some children's entering schools unready to learn.

    (B) Causing some children to enter school unready to learn, children may lack learning materials.

    (C) Causing some children to enter schools unready to learn is a lacking in learning materials.

    (D) It should be omitted since it does not logically follow the particular topic.

    (E) Learning materials may be a causative factor in some children's entering schools unready to learn.

43. Which is the best way to revise sentence 4 (reproduced below)?

    First, the schools were given the responsibility for correcting the social and economic conditions that hinder educational readiness by many children.

    (A) First, the schools were given the responsibility for correcting the social and economic conditions that hinder educational readiness by many children.

    (B) The schools first demanded the responsibility for correcting the social and economic conditions that hinder educational readiness by many children.

    (C) The governors gave the schools responsibility for correcting the social and economic conditions that hinder educational readiness by many children.

    (D) The correction of the social and economic conditions that hinder educational readiness by many children were given to the schools.

    (E) The correction of the social and economic conditions that hinder educational readiness by many children was given to the schools.

44. In sentence 9 *to do these things* refers to

    (A) reading to and working with their children.

(B) correcting the social and economic conditions that hinder educational readiness.

(C) entering school ready to learn.

(D) being a causative factor in some children's entering schools unready to learn.

(E) prohibiting the purchase of books and materials.

45. What is the best way to correct sentence 2 (reproduced below)?

The first of these goals say that by the year 2000 all children should enter school ready to learn.

(A) The first of these goals say that by the year 2000 all children should enter school ready to learn.

(B) The first of these goals says that by the year 2000 all children should enter school ready to learn.

(C) According to goals set by the governors, all 2000 children should enter school ready to learn.

(D) Because children are not entering schools ready to learn, goals have been set to ensure that they are ready to learn by the year 2000.

(E) Goals have been set to ensure that they are ready to learn by the year 2000.

46. Which is the best way to write sentence 8 (reproduced below)?

The educational level of many parents prevents them from reading to and working with their children.

(A) The educational level of many parents prevents them from reading to and working with their children.

(B) The educational level of many parents prevent them from reading to and working with their children.

(C) Many parents have been prevented from reading to and working with their children because of their educational level.

(D) Many children have been prevented from being read to and worked with by their parents because of their educational level.

(E) Reading to and working with children has been prevented by the educational level of parents.

47. Which is the best way to write sentence 5 (reproduced below)?

    In many homes the purchase of pencils, papers, crayons, books, and other learning materials may be prohibited because of their cost.

    (A) In many homes the purchase of pencils, papers, crayons, books, and other learning materials may be prohibited because of their cost.

    (B) The purchase of pencils, papers, crayons, books, and other learning materials may be prohibited because of their cost.

    (C) The purchase of pencils, papers, crayons, books, and other learning materials may be prohibited in many homes because of their cost.

    (D) The cost may prohibit the purchase of pencils, papers, crayons, books, and other learning materials.

    (E) Pencils, papers, crayons, books, and other learning materials may be unavailable in many homes due to their cost.

48. Which is the best word to place before sentence 9 (reproduced below)?

    If all the adults in a family may work, their time to do these things is limited.

    (A) However,   (D) In addition,

    (B) Nevertheless,   (E) Heretofore,

    (C) Therefore,

(1) Few people have a good word to say for the motorcyclist, generally considered a highway nuisance who makes the automobile and truck drivers nervous and he takes the joy out of driving. (2) It cannot be denied that some motorcyclists are showmen who believe the roadways were created for their exclusive use. (3) Yet, there are many motorcyclists who are responsible drivers. (4) Constantly tempting fate and fearlessly dodging in and out of the steady stream of traffic. (5) With increasing traffic and regulations more complicated, the motorcyclist would be wise to drive with care and caution. (6) Any driver which is really honest will admit that at times he has envied the freedom and the carefree maneuvers of the careful motorcyclist. (7) Nevertheless, the unpopularity of the motorcyclist on the crowded city street and on the superhighways survives for a number

of reasons.

(8) Motorcyclists usually enjoy the luxury of paying very low premiums on their vehicles. (9) Drivers of automobiles and trucks suffer bravely under a constant barrage of skyrocketing insurance billings. (10) Increasing accidents are the culprit. (11) They are often caused by the motorcyclists themselves. (12) Unhelmeted drivers, illegal in an increasing number of states, whiz by drivers who shake their heads disapprovingly at their risk taking. (13) Yet on balmy spring or crisp fall days, who could deny the thrill of weaving snakelike through a holiday stream of traffic or begrudge the beauty of casually touring an untraveled back road, leisurely on a motorcycle?

49. The writer developed the early draft primarily by

   (A) persuasion.

   (B) comparison and contrast.

   (C) narration.

   (D) description.

   (E) exposition.

50. Which is the best way to revise the section of sentence number 1 (reproduced below)?

   who makes the automobile and truck drivers nervous and he takes

   (A) who makes the automobile and truck drivers nervous and he takes

   (B) who make the automobile and truck drivers nervous and he takes

   (C) who makes the automobile and truck drivers nervous, he

   (D) making the automobile and truck drivers nervous, and he takes

   (E) , making the automobile and truck drivers nervous as he takes

51. Sentence number 4 is a classic example of

   (A) a dangling participle.

   (B) a sentence fragment.

   (C) onomatopoeia.

   (D) personification.

(E) a clause.

52. The most appropriate audience for this topic would be

(A) seat belt lobbyists.

(B) motorcycle enthusiasts.

(C) highway safety advocates.

(D) any general audience with interest in the pros and cons of motor-cycle driving.

(E) senior citizens.

53. Sentence number 3 should be placed most logically and strategically

(A) in the same spot (no change).

(B) at the beginning of paragraph two.

(C) before sentence 6.

(D) instead of sentence 11.

(E) as the concluding sentence.

54. Sentence number 6 contains an error in

(A) no part of the sentence.

(B) the relative clause.

(C) several parts of the sentence.

(D) verb tense.

(E) verb agreement.

55. Sentences 8 and 9 would be combined most effectively and correctly by which one of the following methods:

(A) cannot be combined.

(B) premiums on their vehicles, drivers of automobiles.

(C) premiums on their vehicles, and drivers of automobiles.

(D) premiums on their vehicles while drivers of automobiles.

(E) premiums on their vehicles, of drivers automobiles.

Section 2

TIME: 45 Minutes
1 Essay Question

DIRECTIONS: You will have 45 minutes to plan and write an essay on the topic specified. Read the topic carefully. Do not write on a topic other than the one specified. An essay on a topic of your own choice is not acceptable. Remember that how well you write is much more important than how much you write.

Essay Topic

The old saying, "experience is the best teacher," suggests to some people that they would benefit more from learning on the job or in the world than from continuing their formal education in the school or college classroom.

Assignment: Write an essay in which you discuss the relative values of experiential and academic learning. Support your view with specific examples from literature, history, current events, or personal experience.

CLEP ENGLISH COMPOSITION
WITH ESSAY QUESTION
TEST 3

ANSWER KEY

Section 1

1. (A)	12. (B)	23. (A)	34. (B)	45. (B)
2. (A)	13. (C)	24. (C)	35. (D)	46. (A)
3. (D)	14. (B)	25. (A)	36. (A)	47. (D)
4. (D)	15. (D)	26. (A)	37. (A)	48. (D)
5. (D)	16. (A)	27. (B)	38. (A)	49. (B)
6. (C)	17. (B)	28. (B)	39. (C)	50. (E)
7. (B)	18. (D)	29. (C)	40. (B)	51. (B)
8. (A)	19. (A)	30. (B)	41. (E)	52. (D)
9. (B)	20. (B)	31. (B)	42. (A)	53. (C)
10. (B)	21. (A)	32. (B)	43. (C)	54. (B)
11. (B)	22. (E)	33. (D)	44. (A)	55. (D)

DETAILED EXPLANATIONS
OF ANSWERS

TEST 3

Section 1

1.   **(A)** Two things are compared: 1) doing homework and watching television and 2) watching television and doing homework. Because only two things are compared, the writer should have chosen the comparative degree (*better*) rather than the superlative degree (*best*). Since the letter (A) is under the word *best*, (A) is the correct answer because it identifies the mistake in the sentence. The writer has used standard English for the rest of the sentence. *To do her homework* (B) is parallel with *to watch television* (C) and *to reverse the procedure* (D); (B), (C), and (D) are correctly written. Since there is an error, (E) – which indicates no error – is not an acceptable choice. Again, (A) is the best answer.

2.   **(A)** The writer has used *would of known* in place of the correct verb form *would have known*. Since the letter (A) is underneath the part of the sentence that should be changed, (A) is the correct choice. The rest of the sentence is standard English. (B) is correct English; there is nothing wrong with saying *it was going to rain*. There is nothing wrong with the subject-verb agreement in *the sisters* (C) and *would have taken* (D). The tense is appropriate in (D); the two choices (C) and (D) are in standard English. (E) cannot be chosen because it indicates that there is no error and an error is contained in the sentence; (E) is not a good choice.

3.   **(D)** The writer has used nonparallel structure by using a verb form ending with *-ing* (painting) *as* the third part of the compound verb. Rather than writing *paint,* which would fit with the other two verb forms (*sing* and *dance*), the writer has used the *-ing* form of the word *paint.* The letter (D) is the best answer since it is underneath the phrase *even painting a picture was easy.* The rest of the sentence is correct. There is nothing wrong with using *Mary* as the subject of the sentence; (A) is not the best choice since the test-taker is to choose the incorrect answer. (B) and (C)

are appropriate verbs. Both *sing* (B) and *dance* (C) are parallel in structure; therefore, neither (B) nor (C) are in error. Since there is a mistake in the sentence, (E) – which indicates that there is no error – is an incorrect choice.

4. **(D)** Since a principle (in this case Bernoulli's) holds true all the time, the writer should use the present tense. The writer used the past tense (*exerted*) rather than the present tense. The letter (D) is underneath the word *exerted.* (D) is the only incorrect part of the sentence. The verb *states* (A) is correct; the principle is still in use so the present tense is appropriate. Nothing is wrong with the adjective and noun *slow-moving air ;* (B) is correct as written. The verb *exerts* in the dependent clause is appropriate; (C) is correct. Since there is an error, (E) is false.

5. **(D)** To use parallel structure, the writer should have used the infinitive form of the word *add* (*to add*) rather than the *-ing* form. Since a (D) is underneath the *-ing* form, this is the mistake. The rest of the sentence is correct. The verb *has found* (A) is correct. There is no error in the dependent clause *it is* (B). The phrase *more difficult* (C) is correct; since there is no error in (C), the test-taker should not choose that answer. Since there is an error in the sentence, (E) – which states that there is no error – is not an appropriate choice.

6. **(C)** *Had regard* is a wordy, unclear term. One might correct the sentence by saying that one consulted books *related to* the subject, rather than books or resources that *had regard for* the subject. Since the letter (C) is underneath the words *had regard for,* (C) is the answer that should be chosen. The writer used standard English for the rest of the sentence. The introductory infinitive phrase, which serves as an adjective, is grammatically correct; (A) is correct as written. The noun *students,* which the infinitive phrase modifies, is certainly appropriate; (B) has no error. *The topic,* which serves as the subject of the sentence, is grammatically correct; (D) is not an appropriate choice. Since (E) indicates that there is no error, (E) is not a good selection.

7. **(B)** A plural noun requires a plural verb. In this case the plural noun (*shoppers*) is followed by a singular verb (*was*). Since (B) is underneath the word *was,* (B) should be selected; the word *was* (B) is incorrect. The rest of the sentence is correct. *Since two shoppers* is grammatically correct; *since* is an appropriate conjunction and *two shoppers* is an appropriate subject. (A) contains no error. The independent clause contains the

expletive *there* and the verb *was;* the verb agrees with the subject *hope.* (C) has no error. There is nothing grammatically incorrect about the object of the preposition *of; postponing the sale* (D) is an inappropriate choice for the answer sheet. (B) is an incorrect selection since there was a mistake in the sentence.

8.   **(A)** Sentence 8 contains a misplaced modifier. The phrase *knowing its importance to the entire family* does not modify the word *box.* The modifier should be near the word it modifies. Since the letter (A) is underneath the misplaced modifier, (A) should be marked on the answer sheet. The rest of the sentence is correct. The adjective *heavily-carved* (B) is correct; therefore, (B) is not an appropriate selection. The prepositional phrase *with the gold handles* (C) is an appropriate modifier for the word *box.* (C) is correct as it is. The prepositional phrase *to the boy* is correct; (D) is an inappropriate selection. The examinee should not mark (E) – no error – since there is an error in the sentence.

9.   **(B)** The subject of the sentence (*Either the animals or the zoo-keeper*) contains two subjects – *animals* and *zoo;* the author joined these two nouns by the conjunctions *either* and *or.* When these two conjunctions join two nouns and the number of the nouns is not the same, the verb must agree with the noun that is closer to it. In this case, *zookeeper* is singular and the verb *were making* (B) must also be singular. The examinee should change (B) to make the subject and verbs agree in number. (C) should not be changed since *was disturbing* is already singular. There is no need to change *circus performers* (D). Since there is an error in the sentence, (E) is an incorrect choice.

10.   **(B)** The subject of the sentence is *Everyone,* a singular pronoun; the other pronouns that refer to *everyone* must be singular to agree with the singular subject. In choice (B) the pronoun *their* is plural; (B) must be changed. The verb *should bring* is correct as written; (A) does not need modifying. (C) and (D) are also correct; they do not need to be changed. Since a change is necessary, (E) is an inappropriate answer.

11.   **(B)** When the writer joins a compound subject by *either-or,* the verb must agree with the number of the subject that is closest to the verb. In this case both subjects are singular; the examinee must change the verb *drive* (B) to the singular verb *drives.* The examinee should, therefore, select (B) as the answer. Since the subject (*her father or her mother*) is not

underlined, and since there is no line under the conjunction *either,* (A) is an incorrect choice. Choice C (*Mary is*) and choice (D) are correct; the examinee should not, therefore, change choices (C) or (D). (E) is not a viable option, since there is an error in the passage.

12. **(B)** The verb *is* must be changed to agree with the subject *years;* (B) contains the error. (A) cannot be changed because there are other references to *years* later in the sentence. The examinee should note that it is *years* (not *high school,* the object of the preposition *of*) that is the subject. There is no need to change *difficult* (C) or *adjusting to the new environment* (D); neither choice is correct. Since there is an error in the passage, (E) is not a correct choice.

13. **(C)** Since the dependent clause has a plural subject (*thoughts*), the verb in this clause must also be plural. The verb *was* (C) must be changed to *were* so that it will agree with *thoughts* (B). The verb in the independent clause (A) is correct as given, as is the prepositional phrase (D). Since there is an error, (E) is not a good choice.

14. **(B)** The verb (*go and cry*) is not in its best form; the examinee should change (B) to read merely *cry.* The contraction *It's* is correct as written in (A). The pronoun *its* (C) does not have an apostrophe. There are no errors in the two prepositional phrases in (D). Since there is an error, (E) is not a good alternative.

15. **(D)** The modifier *watching the train* is a misplaced modifier; since *Jane* is the word that the phrase modifies, the phrase should come closer to it. (D) is the phrase that the examinee should change. There is nothing wrong with the prepositional phrase (A), with the verb and the adverbial phrase *on a chair* (B), or with the phrase *near the window* (C). Since there is an error, (E) is not a good alternative.

16. **(A)** The double negative *wasn't nothing* is incorrect, so (A) is the correct choice. (B) The phrase *anyone could do* is correct. There are no errors in (C); the possessive pronoun *his* is correct before the *-ing* verb form. (D) is correct and does not need changing. Since there is an error, (E) is not a good alternative.

17. **(B)** *Laid,* the past tense of *lay* (to place), is needed in this context. (A) *Keenest* is appropriately used to mean acute or quick of mind. (C)

Principle is a correct choice of a word denoting a fundamental law. (D) The direct quotations signal that these are the speaker's exact words.

18. **(D)** The sentence parallels a noun and its appositive with an independent clause; the word *he* is unnecessary. (A) Contextually, *colorful* describes Byron as a compellingly interesting personage. (B) This is explanatory and is set off by commas. (C) The participial phrase correctly modifies the noun it follows.

19. **(A)** Commas designating the appositive, explanatory group of words, occur after *poltergeists* and after *night*. (B) In this context, *curious* means with a desire to investigate. (C) This adverb is a synonym for clearly. (D) The reference is to young children and teens.

20. **(B)** Correct standard English uses both words, *what is*. (A) and (C) both use the future perfect tense correctly since the proposed action has not yet occurred. (D) The use of *literally,* which dramatizes the factualness of the statistic, is correct in the sentence.

21. **(A)** This word is used incorrectly in the sentence, which states that it is past the time, *past time*. (B) The word is used effectively as a synonym for *realize*. (C) This relative pronoun refers back to *dictionaries*. (D) The phrase describes words that certain cultures would consider unflattering or offensive.

22. **(E)** The sentence contains no error. (A) and (B) correctly refer to archery's use through the years as survival in sustaining life. (C) This term refers to some people, while (D) refers to the unparalleled invention of the wheel.

23. **(A)** The simple subject, *method*, is singular and needs a singular verb, *is*, not *are*. (B) The parentheses indicate that the term is explanatory. (C) This is a commonly used phrase; whereas (D) is set off in quotation marks since it is used in a special sense.

24. **(C)** is the correct answer. *Due to the fact* is wordy; it should be replaced by the word *because* as in (C). (A) cannot be selected since it is as wordy as the original sentence. Choice (B) cannot be chosen; it does eliminate the wordiness of the original sentence, but it lacks the agreement between the subject *children* (plural) and the verb *was* (singular). (D) omits the noun *the children* and also does not include agreement between the subject *they* (plural) and the verb *was* (singular) in the dependent

clause. (E) is a poor choice because it includes the wordiness *Due to the fact* and also omits the noun *the children.*

25. **(A)** The sentence is correct; (A) is the best choice. Choice (B) does not have agreement between the subject *Keeping* (singular) and the verb *are* (plural). (C) is an incorrect choice because the word *its* has no antecedent. (D) is a poor choice because the subject *To keep* is singular but the verb is plural. If the examinee chooses choice (E), the result is an incomplete sentence; (E) is incorrect.

26. **(A)** The sentence is correct; (A) is the best choice. If the examinee chooses (B), the phrase *In writing A Tale of Two Cities* is a misplaced modifier. Since (C) contains passive voice, the examinee should not select (C). Since the Victorian Period did not actually produce the novel, (D) is a poor choice. (E) contains passive voice; the phrase *In writing A Tale of Two Cities* does not modify the word *Dickens,* which immediately follows it. (E) should not be selected because it has a misplaced modifier and passive voice.

27. **(B)** is the best answer since (B) is a complete sentence. (A) cannot be selected as the best answer since it is an incomplete sentence. (C) is also an incomplete sentence and cannot be selected as an appropriate choice. (D) is an incomplete sentence; it is not the correct choice. (E) is also an incomplete sentence.

28. **(B)** is the best choice. (A) and (C) cannot be chosen since *Seeing the three animated characters* does not modify the word *movie,* the word that comes directly after it. Neither (D) nor (E) can be correct choices since they do not give the complete sense of the sentence; each sentence either omits the excitement or the movie.

29. **(C)** is the best answer. Neither (A), (B), nor (E) can be chosen since they are wordy; in addition (B) contains incorrect punctuation since it contains a semicolon instead of a comma. (D) changes the meaning of the sentence and is a poor choice.

30. **(B)** is the best choice; the two complete clauses are correctly joined with a semicolon. (A) is a poor choice since the two complete clauses are joined by a comma. (C) is incorrect since the beginning of the second sentence would not have a capital letter. (D) changes the meaning of the

sentence and is not a good choice. (E) involves the passive voice; it also joins two complete clauses with a comma only.

31. **(B)** is the best answer. (C) is a poor choice because the result would be a sentence fragment. (A) is incorrect because the subject *Reducing* is singular and the verb *are* is plural; (A) is not a good choice. (C) would make the sentence a fragment – not a complete sentence – so it is incorrect. *Reducing one's weight* is a misplaced modifier; it does not modify *heart stress,* so (D) is an incorrect choice. (E) does not make sense in the sentence. The examinee should not choose (E).

32. **(B)** is the best answer. (A) is not a good choice because the sentence is in the passive voice. (C) is not a good choice because it changes the meaning; the author may or may not be a man. Since the tense changes in choices (D) and (E), neither is a good answer.

33. **(D)** is the best answer since it points out the contrasts between the earlier hobbies and the present hobby. (A) is not an appropriate answer since it is a run-on sentence; a comma should not connect two independent clauses. This sentence needs a contrasting connective; neither (B) nor (C) provide the contrasts. (E) is not a clear sentence; the examinee should remember that the part that is not italicized will remain as written.

34. **(B)** is the best answer since it provides a transition from dog training to earlier hobbies. Since the next sentences do not relate to dog training, (A) is not a good transition sentence. (C) is not the best answer; it is very informal in that it uses the word *Let's.* The paragraph does not discuss hobbies in America; (D) is not the best answer. Inserting a definition of *hobby* does not seem important to link the two paragraphs; (E) is not the best answer.

35. **(D)** Active voice – not passive voice – is preferable in writing. (D) allows the examinee to select active voice. (A) is passive and is not the best choice. Selecting (B) results in a sentence fragment; the examinee should not select this choice. (C) changes the meaning; it is not *all* ingredients that are rare but just *certain* ingredients. Since the tense of (E) is different from that of the rest of the passage, the examinee should not select (E).

36. **(A)** is the best answer; punctuation is correct. (B) changes the meaning of the sentence since the paragraph does not suggest that the

author grew tired of the kitchen just because the family did not eat the new dishes. (B) is also a poor choice since *as* is a weak connective; (B) is not a good choice. (C) uses the wordy expression *due to* instead of the word *because;* (C) is not the best choice. (D) is not a logical sentence; thus, it is not a good choice. (E) is a run-on sentence and is not a good choice.

37.   **(A)**   is the correct choice for this question, which asks which choice is NOT correct. The rest of the choices – (B), (C), (D), and (E) – are correct and should not be selected.

38.   **(A)**   is the best answer. The examinee is looking for a connective that would link two sentences with the same idea; *furthermore* is the correct choice. The other choices – (B), (C), (D), and (E) – are contrasting connectives and are not the best choices.

39.   **(C)**   is the best answer. The writer used the word *first* in the passage; the word *second* is parallel to the word *first.* Choices (A), (B), (D), and (E) are not parallel to the word *first.*

40.   **(B)**   is the best answer; the sentence expresses sentence 1 well. Choice (A) is supposedly two sentences joined by a semicolon; since the second part of the sentence is a fragment, however, (A) is not a good choice. (C) is a run-on sentence and so is not a good choice. (D) changes the meaning of the original sentence. (E) uses a contrasting connective and is therefore not a good choice.

41.   **(E)**   is the best answer; the original sentence was in passive voice and the best sentence uses active voice. (A) and (B) use passive voice and are not the best choices. (C) is in active voice, but it changes the original meaning for the sentence; this sentence is not acceptable. (D) leaves out some of the information and is not an acceptable choice.

42.   **(A)**   is the best answer; some examinees may not select this sentence because of the apostrophe, but the apostrophe is needed before the *-ing* form of the verbal. (B) changes the meaning of the sentence; it is not an appropriate choice. (C) is awkwardly constructed; it is not the best choice. Choice (D) suggests deleting the sentence. This is incorrect as the sentence adds information and is needed in the paragraph. (E) is not a good choice because, it is not the learning materials but rather the lack of learning materials that causes some children to enter school unprepared to learn.

43. **(C)** is the best answer since it eliminates the passive voice and makes clear who gave the schools the responsibility. (A) is not an acceptable answer since it retains the passive voice and the lack of clarity. (B) changes the meaning; the schools did not demand the responsibility. (D) retains the passive voice and contains a verb (*were*), which does not agree in number with the subject (*correction*).

44. **(A)** The antecedent of *to do these things* is (A), *reading to and working with their children.* The antecedent is not (B) *correcting the social and economic conditions that hinder educational readiness;* (C) *entering school ready to learn* (which is a changed meaning); (D) *being a causative factor in some children's entering schools unready to learn;* or (E) *prohibiting the purchase of books and materials.*

45. **(B)** is the best answer; with (B) the subject and verb agree in number. The subject *first* and the verb *say* do not agree in number in choice (A). (C) changes the meaning; there is no mention of 2,000 children named in the original passage. (D) uses passive voice and is not the best choice. (E) uses the pronoun *they* without a clear antecedent.

46. **(A)** is the best answer; the sentence is correct as written. (B) is incorrect because the subject and verb do not agree. (C), (D), and (E) use passive voice and are not the best choices.

47. **(D)** is in active voice and is the best choice. (A), (B), (C), and (E) are in passive voice; they are not the best answers.

48. **(D)** is the best answer; *in addition* shows that more information is available and forthcoming in the rest of the sentence. The contrasting connectives (A) and (B) are not appropriate. The next statement is not a cause-result statement, so the connective *therefore* (C) is not the best choice. The connective *heretofore* (E) is not a good choice.

49. **(B)** The writer compares and contrasts the advantages and the disadvantages of motorcycling. (A) The reader is not persuaded convincingly that all cyclists are a nuisance. (C) There is no story told and very little explanation given. (D) The description is limited to scenery and the highway.

50. **(E)** This modifying phrase is effectively placed next to the term *highway nuisance*. (A) contains errors of nonparallel structure, while (B) has a verb agreement error, and (C) is a run-on sentence.

51. **(B)** Sentence 4 is fragment that lacks a subject. (A) is not a verb form. (C) and (D) are poetic devices, not used here. (E) This is not a clause since it lacks a subject.

52. **(D)** Reasons for (pro) and against (con) motorcycling are presented. (A), (B), (C), and (E) represent special interest groups.

53. **(C)** Sentence 3 provides a logical transition to the context of sentence 6, which mentions the advantages of riding a motorcycle. No other choice provides a smooth transition.

54. **(B)** The subject of the relative clause should be *who*, the nominative case is indicated, rather than the objective.

55. **(D)** Combining the relative clause with the independent clause strengthens the sentence. (C) The coordinating conjunction cannot be used since it connects two unrelated clauses. (B) creates a run-on sentence error and (E) misplaces the prepositional phrase.

Section 2

ESSAY I

Try and remember some particular thing you learned in a school or college class from the past, say, how to factor an equation from algebra. Now try and remember the first time you learned to ride a bicycle or roller skating. Which one stands out in your mind? Which one could you do best right now: the algebra factoring or ridding a bicycle? You probably said you could still ride a bicycle but you can't factor an algebra equation without further study. This shows the relative value of learning by experience rather than academic learning.

Academic learning is something for school, not for real life. You hardly ever learn something in school you can use in real life. Most people get by school and don't remember much of what they learned. As kids, we want to play and have fun. School isn't much fun for most kids. What good does it do you to know how to spell a word you don't ever use? What good does it do for you to know the date of a particular historical event? Who cares when the Civil War began or ended. That was a long time ago. In other words academic learning is impractical compared with learning by experience.

Learning by experience does tend to stick with you. For instance, when I was a Boy Scout, I learned how to cook food over a campfire. Not just hot dogs or hamburgers but stews and biscuits and more complicated meals than grilled burgers or dogs. I've never forgotten how to do that even though I haven't gone camping in a long time. About the same time, I was taking algebra in junior high school, but I can't do most of the problems I learned how to do then. It's not very practical to me, so I don't remember it.

Learning from a book or a teacher's lecture is usually short-term learning. But if you try to learn something by doing it (trial and error), it sticks with you once you have done it. A friend of mine learned to sew before she took home economics classes in school. It was hard for her because her mother didn't want her to mess up her sewing machine, but she learned by experience, mostly on her own. Now she has a sewing job. She found it practical to keep up her sewing skills. Of course, she didn't do very well in French class. She hasn't had much opportunity to speak French since she left the class in high school.

So, what's better, school learning or learning by experience? I say learning by experience is like good solid food, it sticks with you. But school learning is sort of like fat free, tasteless diet food. It doesn't satisfy your hunger.

Analysis of Essay I

Essay I has a score range of 4-5. The essay states its main idea clearly and the introductory paragraph does its job reasonably well although the thesis is weak. The subordinate ideas in the following paragraphs are imprecise and lack supporting facts. The author weakens the essay by drawing on personal experience rather than citing facts or scholarly opinions to support his thesis. The conclusion lacks strength and the author's tone is too familiar for a scholarly essay. The essay

has several grammatical errors including nonparallel structure errors (<u>ridding</u> for <u>riding</u>), comma splice errors, sentence fragment errors, as well as apostrophe and question mark errors.

ESSAY II

Does anybody really not believe the old saying "experience is the best teacher"? It makes real good sense. Its true when you compare learning by experience to learning in school.

In school, you have to listen to boring teachers that don't know much about there subject. They just go on and on, but you don't learn much because its not interesting. I took a math class that was like that.

If the teacher isn't boring, then they've got some funny habit they do, like always calling on the same person for an answer to a question. That's not a good way for the whole class to learn.

Then, sometimes you get a teacher who wants to be doing something else. That's real aggravating. They always talk about whatever it is they want to do, instead of trying to make the class learn.

Of course, when you put your "hands-on" a job you learn it real fast. Somebody can talk for hours about pulling an engine out of a car, but until they do it with someone who knows what they are doing, they don't know hardly anything about pulling engines.

So, all in all, "experience is the best teacher."

Analysis of Essay II

Essay II has a score range of 2-3. The essay's introduction fails to develop a strong thesis and lacks details that would back up the author's claim. The body paragraphs are short, undeveloped, and do not naturally build upon one another or the thesis. The author relies heavily on personal experience rather than citing facts or scholarly sources, and the weak one-sentence conclusion evidences that the author did not think his topic through completely. Errors such as pronoun-antecedent disagreement, adjectives used instead of adverbs (*real* for *re-*

ally), **and double negatives (***don't hardly***) reveal a lack of college skill in writing.**

ESSAY III

Years ago, before formal education was available, everybody learned what they needed to know by experience. The prehistoric hunter-gatherers had assigned roles in the tribe or community, and each person learned their role by following an expert around and by practicing skills like hurling a spear or keeping a fire going. In a way, they were "learning on the job." Today, however, learning on the job no longer works for many of the technologically oriented jobs in the marketplace. People need some academic learning before or at the same time as experiential learning.

In the distant past of low technology, people learned how to do their work by practicing it under the direction of a parent or another experienced adult. Even the so-called primitive people had to learn how to hunt and what plants are edible in the process of becoming hunters and gatherers. There was no manuel and no school of hunting or gathering. They learned skills at the knee of their elders. As technology advanced, more knowledge became necessary. And when agricultural life began to dominate, skills such as knowing when and what to plant were learned by experience, often harsh experience at that. As technology advances farther into the use of complex machinery, more people will need more formal training. An IBM television commercial a few years ago showed how farmers can be more productive when they use an IBM personal computer to help manage their business. You don't have to go to college to learn how to use a computer, but you probably need some specialized formal training.

Today, job recruiters constantly say that they need workers who can learn by experience, who are prepared by academic training to learn work skills. If you want to work in accounting, for instance, you need to learn the rules and practices of accounting before you can start working. Then you learn even more in the practice of auditing other people's books. Some sales jobs also require a lot of formal education before you can work in that job. Real estate sales, for example, requires a state license that can only be acquired after a certain number of hours of formal training. Even relatively skilled jobs that do not requiring college degrees may require some prior academic training. If you have little or no knowledge of applied mathematics, you will have a hard time doing carpentry or machinery work.

On the other hand, classroom training is often out of touch with the "real world." Part of that is by design. Most people will not use directly a subject like algebra in their work. They won't write essays or interpret poetry. These academic skills often are used to do other academic work, but they can contribute to the ability to learn by experience. Algebra and poetry interpretation both train us in abstract thinking and creative problem solving, which should make us more valuable to an employer. Essay writing skills can be adapted fairly easily to business writing requirements. In other words, a large part of our academic learning prepares us to learn academically at a higher level or to apply the skills we learn in schools and college to real jobs.

Even college graduates are often assigned to a person on the job who is supposed to help the new employee learn by experience. Sometimes, though, there is no such help and the school of experience becomes the school of "hard knocks." Each time the new employee makes an error, they can either learn from that error and adapt or, ultimately, lose their job. By the same token, the new employee can learn through success as well. If they find out how to enter data into a microcomputer software program like a spreadsheet in accounting, they can build on that success and try to use or write a macro (a sort of mini-program) to help them become even more productive.

So, it seems that both academic learning and learning by experience are valuable in a technologically advanced culture. The best and most satisfying jobs aren't learned overnight or just in school or college. They require a mixture of academic or formal training and experience that helps them build on the academic learning.

Analysis of Essay III

Essay III has a score range of 5-6. The introduction is well thought-out and presents a strong thesis. The body paragraphs are detailed and support the thesis clearly and completely. Their sound structure steps through the author's argument clearly and there are few grammatical or punctuation errors. The conclusion could be stronger, but based on the length and considering the time constraints it is ad-

equate. The author uses language well except for a persistent pronoun-antecedent agreement problem, and a few grammatical errors.

PRACTICE
TEST 4
WITH ESSAY QUESTION

CLEP ENGLISH COMPOSITION
With Essay Question

Test 4

(Answer sheets appear in the back of the book.)

Section 1

TIME: 45 Minutes
55 Questions

Identifying Sentence Errors

DIRECTIONS: The following sentences test your knowledge of grammar, usage, diction (choice of words), and idiom.

Some sentences are correct.

No sentence contains more than one error.

You will find that the error, if there is one, is underlined and lettered. Assume that elements of the sentence that are not underlined are correct and cannot be changed. In choosing answers, follow the requirements of standard written English.

If there is an error, select the <u>one underlined part</u> that must be changed to make the sentence correct and fill in the corresponding oval on your answer sheet. If there is no error, fill in answer oval E.

Example:

<u>The other</u> football players and <u>him immediately</u> accepted the
   A   B

<u>offered contract</u> from the <u>state university.</u> <u>No error.</u>
      C   D   E

1. Mayor Wheeler of Kansas City proclaimed <u>October 3, 1971,</u>
                                                    A
    Satchel Paige Day since <u>the black athlete</u> was not allowed
                                   B
    <u>to pitch</u> for years <u>due to</u> racial discrimination. <u>No error.</u>
        C   D   E

2. Educators have <u>established</u> that a dramatic improvement in attitude
                        A
    toward reading <u>could occur</u> if parents would read <u>out loud</u> to
                        B   C
    their children, not only for the children, <u>but also</u> for their parents.
                                                   D

    <u>No error.</u>
        E

3. In October 1959, <u>a Russian moon probe – Luna 3 – circled</u>
                                          A
    behind the moon and took photographs <u>later transmitted</u> back to earth
                                               B
    <u>revealing</u> mountains, valleys, and craters <u>but</u> no sign of life. <u>No error.</u>
        C   D   E

4. <u>Cascading from</u> the starry <u>firmament,</u> the skiers watched <u>enraptured</u>
            A   B   C
    as the moon released<u> her bridal veil.</u> <u>No error.</u>
                              D   E

5. Within the <u>sepulcher,</u> a casket of solid gold held the <u>mummified</u>
                    A   B
    body of Tutankhamen, while over his face <u>lay</u> a gold mask
                                                  C
    inlaid with quartz; and after 3,300 years, a garland of flowers

    <u>still</u> with color. <u>No error.</u>
        D   E

6. In Massachusetts, <u>the first American compulsory school law,</u>
                              A
   <u>which</u> required the families of the colony to educate <u>their</u> youth,
      B   C
   was passed in 1642, <u>taking</u> a significant step forward in
                           D
   elementary education. <u>No error.</u>
                            E

7. When you are introduced to <u>someone's</u> brothers or sisters
                                 A
   for the first time, have you ever wondered how <u>siblings,</u>
                                                     B
   <u>born to the same parents,</u> could be so entirely
              C
   <u>different than</u> one another? <u>No error.</u>
        D   E

8. If the selection of the <u>President of the United States</u> <u>was</u>
                              A   B
   <u>solely</u> the responsibility of a handful of people, we <u>would</u> have an
      C   D
   oligarchy, not a democratic republic. <u>No error.</u>
                                            E

9. Writer Tom Wolfe says that many Americans <u>flaunt</u> religion by
                                               A
   <u>worshipping</u> art, <u>contributing</u> their money not to their
        B   C
   church or synagogue but to the <u>arts.</u> <u>No error.</u>
                                     D   E

10. The reason <u>astronomers</u> study quasars, small <u>quasi-stellar</u>
                   A   B
    objects, is <u>because</u> they <u>might</u> provide clues to the origin of the
                   C   D
    universe. <u>No error.</u>
                  E

11. English essayist Francis Bacon <u>proposed</u> a system of reasoning
                                    A
    referred to as induction, <u>and</u> is a <u>quasi-scientific</u> method
                              B   C
    involving the collecting and <u>inventorying</u> of a great mass of
                                 D
    observations from nature. <u>No error</u>.
                              E

12. <u>Due to</u> her pride in African-American culture, Zora Neale
    A
    Hurston <u>wrote</u> in the <u>1920's</u> that she was "the only Negro in
            B   C
    the United States" without an <u>Indian</u> chief for a grandfather.
                                  D
    <u>No error</u>.
    E

13. People from the <u>Middle East</u> and Latin America stand
                    A
    <u>more closely</u> to each other <u>when</u> holding a conversation than
         B   C
    <u>in the United States</u>. <u>No error</u>.
            D   E

14. Distinguished psychiatrist Karen Horney <u>claiming</u> <u>that</u>
                                            A   B
    the distrust between the sexes <u>cannot be explained away</u>
                                            C
    as existing only in individuals <u>because of</u> psychological forces
                                    D
    that exist in men and women. <u>No error</u>.
                                 E

15. An ethnic American, for example, an <u>Asian-American</u>, who
                                        A
    becomes an academic exists by definition in a culture separate

    from <u>their</u> nonacademic roots <u>and, therefore</u>, has difficulty
         B   C
    <u>reestablishing</u> ties to the ethnic community. <u>No error</u>.
         D   E

16. Curiously, there <u>are</u> <u>more</u> teachers of the English language in
                     A   B
    the Soviet Union <u>than there are</u> students of the <u>Russian language</u>
                           C   D
    in the United States. <u>No error.</u>
                              E

17. <u>Although</u> philosopher George Santayana assumed that the
     A
    material world was the source of <u>thought,</u> he believed that all
                                         B
    <u>that</u> was worthwhile in human experience <u>has</u> developed from
     C   D
    the imagination. <u>No error.</u>
                         E

18. To find the time <u>during which</u> our view of the natural world
                         A
    <u>came to be</u> expressed as an orderly mathematical model, we
     B
    must <u>refer back</u> to the <u>1600's</u> when Rene Descartes proposed
              C   D
    a clockwork model of the universe. <u>No error.</u>
                                           E

19. Gregor Mendel, the famous <u>monk</u> and early <u>geneticist,</u> studied
                                  A   B
    not only the <u>color</u> of the peas, but also <u>observed</u> the shapes
                     C   D
    of the seed. <u>No error.</u>
                     E

20. Many government officials <u>distrust</u> the people <u>who</u> they <u>serve;</u>
                                  A   B   C
    therefore, these officials arrogate decision-making power

    <u>to themselves.</u> <u>No error.</u>
         D   E

21. <u>Lamenting</u> the demise of the familiar <u>essay</u>, Joseph Wood
     A   B
Krutch wrote that no modern "live-wire" magazine editor

   would <u>never</u> publish nonfiction articles unless <u>they</u> were
             C   D
   factual, polemical, or reportorial. <u>No error</u>.
                                  E

22. Judith Martin, <u>writing as "Miss Manners,"</u> thinks Americans
                             A
   have <u>etiquette</u> problems <u>because</u> <u>we</u> believe people should
           B   C   D
   behave "naturally." <u>No error</u>.
                   E

23. Spaniard Santiago Ramon y <u>Cajal's</u> 1904 book on the human
                             A
   nervous system, <u>still</u> recognized as the most important single
               B
   work in <u>neurobiology</u>, <u>infers</u> that neuron interconnections
              C   D
   are highly structured. <u>No error</u>.
                       E

Improving Sentences

DIRECTIONS: The following sentences test correctness and effectiveness of expression. In choosing answers, follow the requirements of standard written English; that is, pay attention to grammar, diction (choice of words), sentence construction, and punctuation.

In each of the following sentences, part of the sentence or the entire sentence is underlined. Beneath each sentence you will find five versions of the underlined part. Choice (A) repeats the original; the other four are different.

Choose the answer that best expresses the meaning of the original sentence. If you think the original is better than any of the alternatives, choose it; otherwise, choose one of the others. Your choice should produce the most effective sentence – one that is clear and precise, without awkwardness or ambiguity.

Example:

Charlotte Bronte wrote <u>books and she was</u> not the only person in her family to do so.

Sample Answer Choice:

(A)   books and she was

(B)   books; she was

(C)   ; therefore she was

(D)   books, she was

(E)   books being

24. Devising good lessons involves establishing objectives for the students, <u>the preparation of procedures and activities</u>, and evaluating the students.

   (A) the preparation of procedures and activities,

   (B) which includes the preparation of procedures and activities

   (C) which included the preparation of procedures and activities

   (D) (the preparation of procedures and activities)

   (E) preparing procedures and activities.

25. The Old Satan Deluder Act sought to help people to read the Bible, and escape Satan.

    (A) , and escape Satan.

    (B) , and to escape Satan.

    (C) and escape Satan.

    (D) , for escaping Satan.

    (E) , escaping Satan.

26. For the grade the professor considered both attending the class and grades on the examinations.

    (A) both attending the class and grades on the examinations.

    (B) attending both the class and grades on the examinations.

    (C) both class attendance and examination grades.

    (D) both their attending the class and grades on their examinations.

    (E) the attendance of the class and the grades on their examinations.

27. The anonymous poem was considered the best of those in the class.

    (A) The anonymous poem was considered the best of those in the class.

    (B) The anonymous poem, considered the best of those in the class.

    (C) The best poem in the class was considered anonymous.

    (D) Considered the best of those in the class, the poem was anonymous.

    (E) The teacher considered the anonymous poem the best in the class.

28. Finding the book on top of the desk, it was placed on the shelf with the others by the librarian.

    (A) , it was placed on the shelf with the others by the librarian.

    (B) , it was placed with the others on the shelf by the librarian.

    (C) , the librarian placed it on the shelf with the others.

    (D) and placing it on the shelf with the others by the librarian.

(E) , it was placed on the shelf with the others by the librarian.

29. Keeping to the high roads, running as fast as she could, as well as not stopping for rest, allowed her to make the trip in record time.

    (A) , as well as not stopping for rest,

    (B) as well as not stopping for rest

    (C) , and not stopping for rest

    (D) , not stopping for rest,

    (E) stopping not for rest

30. The musicians carried four instruments, which is needed for the musical program.

    (A) , which is needed for the musical program.

    (B) , which may be needed for the musical program.

    (C) , probably helpful for the musical program.

    (D) , they are needed for the musical program.

    (E) , which are needed for the musical program.

31. If a person needs to leave the testing area, they should obtain verbal permission as well as a pass from the proctor.

    (A) they should obtain verbal permission as well as

    (B) they could obtain verbal permission as well as

    (C) you should obtain verbal permission as well as

    (D) he or she should obtain verbal permission as well as

    (E) they would obtain verbal permission as well as,

32. Is it historically verifiable that Abraham Lincoln wrote the Gettysburg Address while riding to Gettysburg on a scrap of paper?

    (A) while riding to Gettysburg on a scrap of paper?

    (B) as he rode to Gettysburg on a scrap of paper?

    (C) on a scrap of paper while riding to Gettysburg?

    (D) on a scrap of paper and he rode to Gettysburg?

    (E) while riding to Gettysburg on a train?

Revising Work in Progress

(1) Santiago, in Ernest Hemingway's novel, *The Old Man and the Sea,* displays admirable courage and strength in his fight with the marlin, which is really symbolic.

(2) The old fisherman also suffers a painful loss when sharks devouring his fish render him powerless, and it left him a skeleton to lug laboriously home.

(3) The novel, however, rises itself above the suffering and loss inherent in the general plot and brings a positive message of hope and greatness of the human spirit.

(4) The unique nobility of Santiago's character is revealed in his remarkable battle with the fish.

(5) Santiago ventures out deeper, and pressuring himself to fish at greater depths and farther distances than he has ever ventured before, he is rewarded with the capture of the great fish.

(6) This was not without great price.

33. Which of the following is the best way to revise the underlined portions of sentence 1 (reproduced below)?

    (1) Santiago, in Ernest Hemingway's novel, *The Old Man and the Sea,* displays admirable courage and strength <u>in his fight with the marlin, which is really symbolic</u>.

(A) As it is now

(B) in his symbolic fight with the marlin

(C) when he has his fight with the marlin, which is symbolic

(D) in his fight with the symbolic marlin

(E) in his, fight with the sharks

34. Which of the following is the best way to revise the underlined portions of sentence 2 (reproduced below)?

(2) The old fisherman also suffers a painful loss when sharks devouring his fish render him powerless, <u>and it left him a skeleton to lug laboriously home</u>.

(A) As it is now

(B) leaving him a skeleton to lug laboriously home

(C) leaving him a marlin to lug laboriously home

(D) it left him a skeleton to lug laboriously home

(E) and it leaves him a skeleton to lug laboriously home

35. The writer of the passage could best improve sentence 3 by

(A) leaving it as it is now.

(B) deleting the word *itself.*

(C) placing a period after *loss* and capitalizing *inherent.*

(D) combining sentence 2 with sentence 3 by placing a semicolon after *home.*

(E) substituting the word *raises* for *rises.*

36. Which of the following would provide the best introductory sentence for paragraph 2?

(A) Santiago catches the biggest fish he has ever seen.

(B) Santiago's relationship with the boy, Manolin, reveals his true character.

(C) The reward of capturing the marlin does not go without its price.

(D) From the first page of the novel, Santiago is portrayed differently from the other fishermen.

(E) The old man has gone without catching a fish for 84 days.

37. Combine the underlined elements of sentences 5 and 6 (reproduced below) into one correct sentence.

(5) , he is rewarded with the capture of the great fish.

(6) This was not without great price.

(A) He is rewarded with the capture of the great fish. This was not without great sacrifice.

(B) . He is rewarded the capture of the great fish, this was not without great price.

(C) . He is rewarded the capture of the great fish; not without great price.

(D) . Rewarded with the capture of the great fish, this was not without great price.

(E) . He is rewarded with the capture of the great fish; this was not without great price.

(1) Edgar Allan Poe left a lasting mark not only upon mystery fiction but the whole realm of literature. (2) He is credited for originating the detective story, and he defined the short story as a distinct literary form. (3) He did not, however, invent the mystery story. (4) Mystery stories were already written before Poe's time.

(5) Poe's famous detective Dupin was actually the first literary detective. (6) Only three stories were written about Dupin, which Poe called stories about ratiocination. (7) *The Purloined Letter* was the last of these three stories, containing, as all the others, the significant and special characteristics that have come to be associated with detective fiction.

(8) What exactly was it about Detective Dupin that made him an instant success in the world of literature? (9) What intriguing characteristics did this sleuth possess that caused great minds like Abraham Lincoln to read him over and over again? (10) Dupin's primary interest while investigating his case was never simply in solving the mystery or piecing the puzzle together, but in the analysis of the antagonist's motives and the working of their mind.

38. Which of the following is the best way to revise the underlined portion of sentence 1 (reproduced below)?

Edgar Allan Poe left a lasting mark <u>not only upon mystery fiction but the whole realm of literature</u>.

(A) not upon mystery fiction but the whole realm of literature.

(B) not only upon mystery fiction but also the whole realm of literature.

(C) only upon mystery fiction not the whole realm of literature

(D) on the whole realm of literature

(E) not only upon mystery fiction and the whole realm of literature

39. In the context of the first paragraph, which of the following is the best way to edit and revise the underlined portion of sentence 2 (reproduced below)?

He is credited <u>for originating the detective story, and he defined the short story</u> as a distinct literary form.

(A) because he originated the detective story, defining the short story

(B) for the originator of the detective story and the definition of the short story

(C) for originating the detective story and defining the short story

(D) originally for the detective story and the short story

(E) and he originated the detective story and defined the short story

40. Which of the following is the best way to revise the underlined portion of sentences 3 and 4 (reproduced below) so that the two are combined into one?

<u>He did not, however, invent the mystery story. Mystery stories</u> were already written before Poe's time.

(A) He did not, however, invent the mystery story and mystery stories

(B) He did not, however, invent the mystery story since mystery stories

(C) He did not, however, invent the mystery story since they

(D) Not inventing the mystery story since they were already written before Poe's time

(E) Since he did not invent the mystery story,

41. According to the context of this student draft, the word ratiocination in sentence 6 most closely means

(A) racial issues.

(B) defective thinking.

(C) the process of thinking and reasoning.

(D) a method of measuring.

(E) guesswork.

42. Sentence 7, reproduced below, contains:

The Purloined Letter was the last of these three stories, containing, as all the others, the significant and special characteristics that have come to be associated with detective fiction.

(A) no error.

(B) an error in comparison.

(C) an error in punctuation.

(D) an error in coordination.

(E) an appositive.

43. Sentence 8, reproduced below, is worded awkwardly.

What exactly was it about Detective Dupin that made him an instant success in the world of literature?

This could be corrected by:

(A) omitting the linking verb.

(B) beginning the sentence with the pronoun *it*.

(C) placing the adverb after the subject.

(D) placing the modifying adverb after the verb.

(E) deleting the entire clause.

44. The underlined section of sentence 9 (reproduced below) could best be improved for clarity by which one of the following revisions?

What intriguing characteristics did this sleuth possess <u>that cause great minds like Abraham Lincoln to read him over and over again</u>?

(A) that cause great minds like Abraham Lincoln

(B) for reading him over and over again

(C) that cause great men like Abraham Lincoln to read him over and over again

(D) that created great minds like Abraham Lincoln reading

(E) causing great men with minds like Abraham Lincoln to read

45. Sentence 10, reproduced below, can be corrected by:

Dupin's primary interest while investigating his case was never simply in solving the mystery or piecing the puzzle together, but in the analysis of the antagonist's motives and the working of their mind.

(A) omitting the apostrophe in the possessive noun.

(B) substituting a semicolon for the comma.

(C) omitting the word "but."

(D) changing "their" to "his."

(E) substituting "yet" for "but."

(1) Sandra Davis and her two children are finding out just how cold life can be when you're poor. (2) It's the beginning of Fall, and a chill wind briskly tosses red and gold leaves into a pile by the front door of the Davis home on Rand Street (3) But, the inside of the house is cold, too, because the gas has just been turned off for nonpayment of the bill. (4) Sandra is out of a job. (5) She suffers, but her children will suffer as much or more.

(6) In fact poor children across America are suffering. (7) According to the stereotype, we believe that poor children are born into large families in big cities, and these families are headed by minority, welfare mothers. (9) Nothing could be further from the truth. (9) More poor children live outside cities. (10) Nearly two-thirds of all poor families have only one or two children. (11) Most poor families' income comes from the wages of

one or more workers. (12) Most shocking of all is that even if every single-parent family was to disappear, the United States would still have one of the highest child poverty rates among industrialized nations. (13) This problem is a disgrace in a country as great as ours, but the government cannot legislate a solution. (14) The people of the United States must become concerned about child poverty and commit to a personal involvement before there can be an effective solution.

46. Which of the following is needed?

    (A) sentence 1: Delete the word "out."

    (B) sentence 3: Change the comma after "too" to a semicolon.

    (C) sentence 6: Place a comma after the phrase "In fact."

    (D) sentence 7: Place a colon after the word "stereotype."

    (E) None of the above.

47. Which of the following uses a nonstandard verb form?

    (A) sentence 11

    (B) sentence 12

    (C) sentence 13

    (D) sentence 14

    (E) None of the above.

(1) Although most new homes across the United States are finished in brick, stucco is an old finish that is becoming increasingly popular. (2) Stucco finishes, applied with a trowel, is composed of sand, water, and a cementing mixture. (3) The first coat or two is thicker, about 3/8 of an inch, with the final coat about 1/4 to 1/8 of an inch thick.

(4) Stucco has many advantages. (5) One of the most attractive selling features is that stucco is energy efficient. (6) In addition, a waterproof, low maintenance exterior is produced by coating the final application with a clear acrylic finish. (7) Since stucco finishes are mixed with color homeowners and designers can select from a wide range of shades. (8) Also, stucco is lightweight and quite inexpensive. (9) By substituting stucco for brick veneer, the typical home gains about 200 square feet of living space.

48. Which of the following, if added between sentences 2 and 3, is MOST consistent with the writer's purpose and audience.

    (A) Personally, I know people who think stucco is an ugly finish for a home.

    (B) Sometimes, Spanish and Indian style homes in the Southwest are finished with stucco on the interior walls.

    (C) Indeed, stucco creates a California ambiance many wish to emulate.

    (D) The plasterlike stucco is applied in two or three thin coats.

    (E) None of the above.

49. Which of the following is needed in the second paragraph?

    (A) sentence 5: Delete the second "is."

    (B) sentence 6: Move "in addition" after "finish."

    (C) sentence 7: Place a comma after "color."

    (D) sentence 8: Move "quite" after is.

    (E) None of the above.

50. Which of the following should be used in place of the underlined verb in sentence 2?

    (A) are

    (B) will be

    (C) being

    (D) should be

    (E) None of the above.

    (1) Consultative teaching models have gained much popularity lately. (2) The Content Mastery program is one such model designed to assist students who have been identified as learning disabled to achieve their maximum potential in normal classroom environments. (3) Learning disabled students are intelligent but need extra skills in order to overcome their disabilities. (4) A learning disabled student who is mainstreamed may have difficulties in a class where the teacher may not have the train-

ing necessary to help students with different disabilities. (5) The student who needs extra help can go to the Content Mastery classroom and work on an individualized basis under the guidance of the special programs teacher with the materials available there. (6) Students needing the Content Mastery program exhibit the following characteristics consistently low grades, poor performance, and gaps in skills.

(7) _____, Content Mastery is not just "a little extra help." (8) It also is not designed to "give" students the answers to worksheets and tests. (9) What Content Mastery does is offer increased stimulus variation in the form of many different strategies. (10) _____, the Content Mastery materials include taped textbooks, hi-lighted books and worksheets, and supplementary materials (such as laminated charts to practice labeling), as well as small study groups, individual counseling, sessions on test-taking strategies, and other types of problem-solving skills.

51. Which of the following, if inserted between sentences 4 and 5, is MOST consistent with the writer's purpose and audience?

    (A) Also, since class sizes vary, some classes may be too large for the teacher to give individualized instruction necessary for the success of these students.

    (B) I think some students use the Content Mastery classroom as a cop-out for getting out of work.

    (C) It has been clearly demonstrated that students below grade level in their psychomotor development benefit most from practicing tactile kinesthetic skills activities in Content Mastery.

    (D) Even though it is a problem-solving model, Content Mastery is not successful with all students.

    (E) The Content Mastery program was developed by fully trained, informed professionals.

52. Which of the following is needed?

    (A) sentence 1: Change "much" to "a lot."

    (B) sentence 3: Change "their" to "his or her."

    (C) sentence 6: Add a colon after "characteristics."

    (D) sentence 7: Remove the quotation marks around "a little extra help."

    (E) sentence 2: Change "who" to "which."

53. Which of the following, if used in order in the blanks of the second paragraph, BEST help the transition of ideas?

   (A) On one hand; In contrast

   (B) However; For example

   (C) Later; In addition

   (D) Furthermore; As long as

   (E) Yet; First of all

(1) Born Domenikos Theotokopoulos in Crete in 1541, El Greco became one of the world's great painters. (2) He earned his name, *El Greco,* meaning "The Greek," when he moved to Spain around 1577 after several frustrating years in Venice and Rome. (3) Probably because El Greco was unable to obtain important commissions during his years in Italy, he left for Spain in his mid-30s. (4) However, he had no better luck in Spain. (5) At that time, paintings were supposed to inspire prayer and teach religious doctrine, but El Greco did not always adhere to scripture. (6) For example, he put three Marys in *The Disrobing of Christ,* set biblical scenes in Toledo, Spain, and painted Roman soldiers in sixteenth century armor. (7) As a result, he lost the patronage of the Toledo Cathedral. (8) Later, he was able to gain the respect and patronage of Toledo's intellectuals who admired and supported El Greco. (9) This wide audience probably left the artist more freedom in developing his own style.

(10) El Greco's painting style is based on his early Venetian training. (11) The Venetian style, called *mannerism,* characterized by elongated forms, graceful lines, and metallic colors with white highlights. (12) El Greco's works show humans and animals such as horses extremely elongated, and his landscapes distorted. (13) Although some critics attribute these characteristics to a peculiar brand of mysticism, probably they show more freedom of experimentation, a freedom not allowed those artists painting politically correct scenes. (14) With loose brushstrokes and sharp contrasts in light and shadow, he anticipated the Expressionist style and profoundly influenced those painters in the 1900s.

54. Which of the following, if placed between sentences 4 and 5, BEST supports the writer's purpose and audience?

    (A) He sought work under King Philip of Spain, the most powerful monarch in Europe at that time.

    (B) El Greco sought to show the difference between the mundane and the supernatural by making his figures seem to glow with an inner radiance.

    (C) In his masterpiece *The Burial of Count Orgaz,* El Greco created a realistic lower, earthly half to contrast with abstract forms and distorted proportions in the upper, heavenly half.

    (D) The painter from Crete failed to win King Philip's favor with the painting *Martyrdom of St. Maurice.*

    (E) The Prado, in Madrid, houses one of the world's greatest collections of Titians.

55. Which of the following is a nonstandard sentence?

    (A) sentence 3   (D) sentence 13

    (B) sentence 8   (E) sentence 14

    (C) sentence 11

Section 2

TIME: 45 Minutes
1 Essay Question

DIRECTIONS: You will have 45 minutes to plan and write an essay on the topic specified. Read the topic carefully. Do not write on a topic other than the one specified. An essay on a topic of your own choice is not acceptable. Remember that how well you write is much more important than how much you write.

Essay Topic

Young people seem very conscious of wearing "trendy" or "brand name" clothing, especially the kind endorsed by sports figures or associated with popular musicians.

Assignment: Does this behavior reinforce or argue against the idea that "clothes make the man [or woman]"? Support your answer with specific examples.

CLEP ENGLISH COMPOSITION WITH ESSAY QUESTION TEST 4

ANSWER KEY

Section 1

1. (D)	12. (A)	23. (D)	34. (B)	45. (D)
2. (C)	13. (D)	24. (E)	35. (B)	46. (C)
3. (E)	14. (A)	25. (C)	36. (D)	47. (B)
4. (A)	15. (B)	26. (C)	37. (E)	48. (D)
5. (D)	16. (E)	27. (E)	38. (B)	49. (C)
6. (E)	17. (D)	28. (C)	39. (C)	50. (A)
7. (D)	18. (C)	29. (C)	40. (C)	51. (A)
8. (B)	19. (D)	30. (E)	41. (C)	52. (C)
9. (A)	20. (B)	31. (D)	42. (B)	53. (B)
10. (C)	21. (C)	32. (C)	43. (C)	54. (D)
11. (B)	22. (D)	33. (B)	44. (C)	55. (C)

DETAILED EXPLANATIONS
OF ANSWERS

TEST 4

Section 1

1. **(D)** *Because of* is the correct choice of terms and is not used interchangeably with "due to." (A) The commas correctly set off the date from the sentence. (B) The reference is to avoid ambiguity. (C) The use of an infinitive is structurally sound.

2. **(C)** *Aloud* is the acceptable word. (A) In this context, the word means proven factually. (B) The future perfect is accurately used. (D) Since *not only/but also* are used in pairs, this choice is accurate.

3. **(E)** The sentence is correct as it is. (A) The dash is effectively used for emphasis. (B) and (C) contain verbals with correct placement. (D) The word *but* is an effective substitute for *however* in this context.

4. **(A)** The participial phrase is misplaced and cannot logically modify the subject after the comma. (B) The word *firmament* is used as a synonym for *heavens*. (C) *Enraptured* is placed effectively after the verb as an adverb indicating how. (D) Figuratively, the moon is personified as a bride.

5. **(D)** After 3,300 years the garland of flowers *has* color; there is color *still*. (A) This is effective imagery since it is a place of burial for kings. (B) *Mummified* means *embalmed* here. (C) This is the correct verb form.

6. **(E)** No errors occur in this sentence. (A) The introductory phrase is set off by a comma. In (B) and (C), the correct relative and possessive pronouns appear, respectively. (D) The participle is effectively used.

7.   **(D)**   Different *from* is correct standard English. (A) The singular, possessive form of the pronoun is indicated. (B) Siblings denote children born to the same parents, which is set off as explanatory information in (C).

8.   **(B)**   Choice (A) raises questions of appropriate capitalization, but it is proper to capitalize this particular title, even without a name attached. Choice (C) might appear suspicious, but it is the correct spelling. Choice (D) is correct because "would" indicates a condition as suggested by the "If" at the beginning of the sentence. That leaves choices (E) and (B). One could argue that the electoral college constitutes an oligarchy because of its small size (E), but the sharp student will recognize that the sentence poses a condition contrary to fact, requiring the subjunctive, "were," choice (B).

9.   **(A)**   Choices (B) and (C) could look incorrect, except that both are parallel and appropriately balance each other. Choice (D) does not even merit scrutiny; nothing is improper there. Again, either there is no error (E), or we must look to choice (A). Knowledgeable students will know that confusion exists between *flaunt* and *flout*. *Flout* (to defy contemptuously) is correct in the context of the sentence; *flaunt* (to display arrogantly) is clearly incorrect.

10.   **(C)**   Choices (A) and (D) do not really require more than a cursory glance to show that they are acceptable. Choice (B) might require a second look because of the hyphen, but it is correct. Choice (C) is a clear example of faulty predication *reason...is because,* and is incorrect.

11.   **(B)**   Reading the sentence, the student should be jarred by the inappropriate coordination of the verb phrases beginning *proposed* and *is.* Changing *and* to *which* makes a much more euphonious and balanced sentence. That change would properly subordinate the definition of *induction.* None of the other choices should raise concern, except, perhaps (C), but it is a correctly hyphenated word.

12.   **(A)**   Both (C) and (D) are possible choices, but (C) correctly uses the apostrophe to indicate plural. (Usage varies on this issue, but it is considered correct either with the apostrophe – 1920's – or without – 1920s. Choice (D) also correctly capitalizes *Indian,* meaning American Indian. Nothing is amiss with choice (B) given the time noted and the subordinate clause verb *was.* Choice (A), however, incorrectly uses *due to*

to show causation with an active verb (*wrote*). *Because of* is the correct phrase.

13.   **(D)**   We have an illogical comparison in this sentence: *People from...* and *in the United States.*" Logical comparison demands that we compare like things to each other. In this case, the sentence compares people with the name of a nation. A logical comparison might read *...than people in the United States [do]*. All other choices are correct: capitalized name of a geographical region (A), comparative adverb used with the active verb *stand* (B), and appropriate subordinating adverb *when* (C).

14.   **(A)**   This one looks more difficult than it is. The sentence is a fragment because there is no verb except in the dependent clauses. Furthermore, one cannot correct the problem by eliminating the relative pronoun *that,* choice (B), or by changing choices (C) or (D). *Because of* correctly modifies *cannot be explained away.* By changing choice (A) to "claims," one completes the sentence and corrects the error.

15.   **(B)**   The problem should be spotted right away as a disagreement between the plural pronoun *their* and its singular antecedent *American,* choice (B). *Asian-American*, choice (A), is correctly hyphenated and capitalized. The phrase *and, therefore,* choice (C), is correctly punctuated because it links the compound verbs (*exists* and *has*). It is also precise (not wordy). The last choice, (D), is correctly spelled without a hyphen. Choice (E) in this instance would be a wild guess.

16.   **(E)**   One could quarrel with the use of the word *Curiously,* but it is not a choice. Otherwise, the sentence is a perfectly balanced logical comparison between like things (*teachers of the English language* and *students of the Russian language*). Even though students and teachers are not precisely parallel, one can compare them in this context. There is no reason to suspect the other choices.

17.   **(D)**   The problem here is sequence of verb tenses. Every verb in the sentence except choice (D) is in the simple past tense, meaning occurrences in the finite past (not over a period of time). In the sentence context, *has* must be changed to *had.* The only other possibility is choice (C). One could question the elegance of the repetition of *that,* but it is both correct and necessary. The first two occurrences of *that* could be omitted, but they are not choices, and the sentence would not be any clearer than it is with them as stated.

18.   **(C)**   The phrase *refer back* is a textbook example of classic wordiness. One neither refers *back* nor *ahead* (*forward?*); one simply refers *to* something without reference to time. Choice (A) correctly subordinates the following clause (*when* would be less precise here). Choice (B) is grammatically correct, if not particularly elegant. Again, (D) the plural of *1600* formed by adding the apostrophe could be questioned, but it is acceptable.

19.   **(D)**   Nonparallel structure is the key to this and many other test items. Because of the overwhelming importance of understanding balance and euphony in sentence structure, tests like this one emphasize parallel sentence structures. A noun phrase follows *not only,* but a verb phrase follows *but also.* The easiest way to balance the structure would be to omit the word *observed,* choice (D). Choice (A) is correctly lower case, and choices (B) and (C) arouse no suspicion.

20.   **(B)**   *Who* should be *whom*; the objective case is needed. Choices (A) and (C) should not cause a second glance. Choice (D) is the correct prepositional phrase. *Who* versus *whom* is an important debate, well worth attention.

21.   **(C)**   You probably will pick the right answer fairly easily here, because the use of *never* clearly causes a double negative (with *no* in the same sentence). Choice (A) could make you think, but it correctly suggests that Krutch feels regret that the familiar essay is hard to find. Choices (B) and (D) should not attract your attention unduly.

22.   **(D)**   This is a case of needlessly shifting pronoun voice from third person (...*Americans have*...) to first person (...*we believe*...). Choice (A) is correct, including the comma at the end of the interrupting phrase inside the quotation marks. Choice (B) is both spelled and used correctly. Choice (C) correctly uses *because* to show causation. Choice (E) obviously should be ignored in this case.

23.   **(D)**   Whenever you see *imply* or *infer?* as a choice, examine it carefully. Most likely, the usage will be in error, as it is here. An easy way to approach this pair of commonly confused words is to remember that generally only people *infer,* but written material and people can *imply.* In this case, the book cannot *infer.* Choice (A) correctly shows *ownership* of the book. Choice (B) correctly suggests that over 80 years after the book's

publication, it is important. Choice (C) correctly omits the hyphen in this word. Again, choice (E) does not figure in here.

24.   **(E)** is the best choice. (A) is not a good choice since the structure is not parallel. Since *the preparation of procedures and activities* does not describe the previous direct object, the word *which* is not needed; neither (B) nor (C) are correct answers. The phrase *the preparation of procedures and activities* is not a description of the subject *devising,* so (D) is not a good choice.

25.   **(C)** is the best answer; no comma is needed between the compound infinitive *read* and *escape.* Since the rest of the answers include a comma, (A), (B), (D), and (E) are incorrect choices. Without the comma, both (A) and (B) could be correct choices. Neither (D) nor (E) could be used as the correct answers because of the comma and because of the nonparallel structure – the *-ing* endings do not parallel the infinitive *to read.*

26.   **(C)** is the best answer; the words are concise and to the point and they are parallel in structure. (A), (B), and (D) are not suitable answers since they are nonparallel in structure. (E) changes the meaning of the sentence; it is the grade of the individual students and not the grade of the class as a whole that is used for the grades. (E) is unclear and should not be chosen.

27.   **(E)** is the best answer. (A) is not an acceptable answer because the verb is in passive voice. (B) is a sentence fragment and is not an appropriate choice. (C) is in passive voice and is not a good choice. (D) is unclear; who considers the poem the best in the class?

28.   **(C)** is the best answer. Choices (A), (B), and (E) have a misplaced modifier since *Finding the book on the table* does not describe the pronoun *it.* Choice (D) is an unacceptable answer since it is a sentence fragment.

29.   **(C)** is the best answer. It is less wordy to use the word *and* than to use the words *as well as.* (D) has a comma after the word *rest;* this means that the sentence contains a comma separating the subject from the verb. (D) is not a good choice. (A) is wordy because it uses the words *as well as.* (B) is not a good choice since the commas are not used; commas are needed in the list. (E) is not a good choice since no commas appear.

30. **(E)** is the best answer; (E) does not change the sense of the sentence and allows the verb form in the dependent clause to agree with the plural noun *instruments* to which it refers. (A) is not a good choice since the verb in the dependent clause does not agree with the noun *instruments*. (B) and (C) change the sense of the sentence, and so they should not be chosen. (D) is a run-on sentence and is not an appropriate choice.

31. **(D)** Since the subject of the introductory clause, *person*, is singular in number, the correct choice must agree in number. (A), (B), and (E) contain plural pronouns. (C) The shift in subject to the second person, *you*, creates an error.

32. **(C)** This choice clarifies the intended meaning by placing the prepositional phrase next to the noun it modifies. (A) and (B) state ambiguously that the ride was on paper. (D) The compound predicate indicates that the ride precedes the written message. (E) Omitting the "scrap of paper" alters the sentence's meaning.

33. **(B)** The correct choice uses the modifier *symbolic* definitively since it tells the reader what kind of a fight. (A) The clause is misplaced and confusing. (C) is awkwardly constructed. (D) It is the *marlin* that is real; the fight is symbolic. (E) Sentence 1 states that he fights with the marlin— not the sharks that sentence 2 describes.

34. **(B)** The correct choice places the modifying verbal strategically and in agreement with the verb in time of action. (A) incorrectly shifts in verb from present tense to past tense. (C) presents the wrong message since the marlin was devoured by sharks. (D) contains a run-on sentence error without a coordinating conjunction. (E) The tense is incorrect in this choice.

35. **(B)** By deleting *itself*, the word *rises* becomes contextually correct. (A) *Rises itself* is grammatically incorrect. (C) This would create a fragment. (D) Combining the sentences would create a run-on. Also, the sentences are not closely related and therefore should *not* be combined by any method. (E) *Raise* is generally followed by a direct object.

36. **(D)** This is the best choice, for the character of Santiago, qualified as a *unique nobility* in sentence 4, is central to the theme of the essay. Although (B) mentions the fisherman's character, it prematurely introduces the boy, who is not mentioned again in the draft. Both (C) and (E)

as choices are not suitable since they also mention isolated details from the novel.

37.   **(E)**   This choice correctly replaces the period with a semicolon and correlates two related thoughts. (A) incorrectly creates two complete sentences. (B) lacks a coordinating conjunction and creates a run-on sentence error. (C) The semicolon inappropriately connects a sentence and a fragment. (D) This is a complex sentence.

38.   **(B)**   The correlative conjunctions, (not only/but also), are used correctly in pairs. Both choices (A) and (C) create obscurity in the intended meaning. (D) incorrectly excludes the particular genre and thus changes the meaning the sentence conveys. (E) creates an incomplete thought.

39.   **(C)**   This choice smoothly and efficiently combines two parallel forms of the verb. (B) is an incorrect word choice; use *origin* or *origination*. (D) The error states *not credited originally* (from the first) and should state *credited for originating* (for creating). (E) is a rambling sentence error.

40.   **(C)**   This skillful revision combines two related ideas by using a pronoun and its antecedent. (A) uses the coordinating conjunction, *and*, incorrectly. (A) and (B) are unnecessarily repetitious. (D) offers the incorrect use of a verbal as a subject. (E) as it stands is a dependent clause which cannot stand alone.

41.   **(C)**   The use of pure reasoning and thinking were Dupin's attributes. (A) improperly substitutes *racial* for *rational*. Defective thinking (B) would be the polar opposite of the intended meaning as would (E) guesswork. (D) confuses the mathematical term ration with the intended *rational*.

42.   **(B)**   There were three Dupin stories; therefore, the original sentence contains an error in comparison and needs *other two*, not *others*. Therefore, (A) is incorrect. (C) The commas set off the intervening phrase. No error in comparison (B) nor coordination (D) is contained in the sentence. (E) Appositives identify or explain another noun or pronoun.

43.   **(C)**   This question places the subject *it* in inverted order. (B) transforms the interrogative into a declarative sentence. (D) misplaces an adverb in place of the verb. (E) becomes a sentence fragment error.

44. **(C)** Clearly stated is the intended message that Lincoln, a great man, read Dupin's stories over again. (A) The man, not the mind, read. (B) Lincoln is omitted in this choice. (D) Dupin did not create Lincoln's great mind. (E) Not great men like Lincoln, but Lincoln.

45. **(D)** Corrects the error in number and agreement of the noun and its antecedent. (A) The possessive case is correct as it is. (B) Independent clauses are divided by semicolons. Both (C) and (E) are erroneous since *but* is needed, meaning instead.

46. **(C)** In choice (C) a comma is indicated for the introductory phrase "In fact." Choice (A) creates no difference. Choice (B) would create a fragment in the second half of the sentence by isolating the subordinate clause beginning with "because." Choice (D) is incorrect because no colon should be used after the introductory phrase.

47. **(B)** Choice (B) has an incorrect verb form. The subjunctive mood "were" is needed in conditions contrary to fact. Thus, the sentence should read, "even if every single-parent family were to disappear" because the clause beginning with "if" signals condition contrary to fact. Choices (A), (C), and (D) are all correct.

48. **(D)** Choice (D) is the logical transition between sentence 2 which describes the composition of stucco and sentence 3 which describes how the finish is applied. Choice (A) contradicts the thesis and breaks voice, "I." Choice (B) and choice (C), although true facts, introduce extraneous ideas.

49. **(C)** In choice (C) a comma is necessary to set off the introductory adverbial clause that begins with "Since." Choice (A) would create an incoherent sentence. Choice (B) is incorrect as the transition "In addition" needs to be placed close to the beginning of a sentence, or at least in the middle, but not at the end. Choice (D) changes the meaning of the sentence since the cheapness is the main emphasis, not the weight.

50. **(A)** Choice (A) is correct because the plural verb "are" agrees with the plural subject "finishes." An intervening phrase, "applied with a trowel," does not affect the choice of verb, even if the phrase ends with a singular word, "trowel." Choice (B) is incorrect because future tense is not needed. Choice (C) would create a fragment. Choice (D) is conditional tense and

inappropriate because the composition for a stucco finish is clearly defined, not subject to condition.

51.   **(A)**   Choice (A) contains the transition word *Also* and another reason why the pull-out program, Content Mastery, is necessary. Choice (B) contains slang, *cop-out,* as well as a negative attitude not displayed in the rest of the passage. Choice (C) is far too formal in tone. Choice (D) refutes the thesis of the passage and the reason for instituting a Content Mastery program. Choice (E) may be correct, but is logically out of place here.

52.   **(C)**   In choice (C) a colon is necessary before a list introduced by *the following.* Choice (A) creates a grammar usage error; *a lot* is a parcel of land, not a unit of measurement. Choice (B) would change a correct plural pronoun *their,* referring to a plural antecedent *students,* to an incorrect singular one. Choice (D) would incorrectly remove necessary quotation marks around a commonly repeated phrase that breaks the tone of the essay. Choice (E) is incorrect because the antecedent is students, requiring the pronoun *who.*

53.   **(B)**   Choice (B) makes the clearest transitions. The word *However* indicates the argument that is the detractors' main objection. *For example* connects with an idea in the previous sentence, *many different strategies,* and leads into examples of Content Mastery materials. In choice (A), the first transition may be viable, but the second, *In contrast,* is clearly inappropriate for examples unless they are negative examples. Choice (C) is incorrect because the first transition listed, *Later,* is used for chronological sequence. In choice (D) the second transition is incorrect. Choice (E) is incorrect because the second transition introduces a sequence, of which there is none.

54.   **(D)**   Choice (D) is logical because it gives a specific example of El Greco's failure to win the patronage of an influential person, the king. Choice (A) may appear logical at first, but it does not show the result of the attempt to become employed by the king; therefore, it does not continue the idea of "no better luck in Spain." Choices (B) and (C), although true, deal with El Greco's style, not his failure to seek employment in Spain. Choice (E) introduces extraneous information.

55.   **(C)**   Choice (C) is a fragment. The subject *Venetian style* needs to be completed by the verb phrase *is characterized by.* Choices (A), (B), (D), and (E) are complete sentences.

Section 2

ESSAY I

Young people seem to be wearing "trendy" clothing, especially the kind endorsed by sports figures or associated with popular musicians. This suggests that "clothes make the person" due to the fact that young people want to be like the people wearing the clothes they wear.

For instance, a friend of mine wears nothing but only their favorite NBA team clothing. The whole outfit, from the cap on down to the shoes his favorite player wears in television commercials.

Another person I know thinks he's in a Seattle rock band. All he wears is thermal underwear top, plaid flannel shirts, torn jeans, a knit cap, and black boots. Even in warm weather. He hadn't got any musical talent, he just likes to wear the same clothes they wear.

I know a girl who wears those lacey tops that looks like fancy slips, the kind Madona used to wear. She thinks if she looks like Madonna she'll be popular.

Then there's the guy that wears a big black Garth Brooks hat, a western shirt with pearl buttons, jeans and cowboy boots. Does he work on the ranch? No, at a fast food place for a job after college classes. Its like he wants to be like a country western star.

Do "clothes make the man [or woman]? Yes, I guess so based on people I know.

Analysis of Essay I

Essay I has a score range of 2-3. The writer uses specific detail, but does not seem to have asserted a strong thesis and equally strong subordinate ideas. The writer repeats the statement of the topic word for word instead of composing an original introductory paragraph. The paragraphs do not have topic sentences. As a result, the essay reads like a string of examples loosely connected to the topic, but without any real thought about the implications of the examples re-

lated to the topic. **The weak ending seems like a concession to the time limit rather than a true conclusion. In addition, sentence fragments, subject-verb and pronoun-antecedent disagreements, spelling (*plad*, *lacey*) and apostrophe errors, weak word choice overall, and vague pronoun references go beyond the usage error rate expected of college students, even in timed writing assignments.**

ESSAY II

On television the other day, I saw a story about teenagers gambling and piling up big debts with bookies. One of the male students interviewed had the typical clothing of a high-school student: baseball cap, tee-shirt, jeans, even an earring. The old saying, "clothes make the man," came to mind when I saw that report. In this and other cases of teenagers wearing conforming clothing, especially if it differs from that worn by adults, clothing behavior follows the crowd rather than "making" the individual. In other words, young people conform almost blindly to the latest clothing trend in a desperate attempt to show that they are not like their parents and in an equally shallow attempt to be accepted rather than rejected by their peers. Perhaps their state of transition and their probing into the notion of who they are leads to wearing conforming clothing.

Conforming behavior in clothing among young people usually has some basis of rebellion in it. If their school has a code about skirt length, you can be sure that students will try to test it by wearing short skirts, if they are "in" that year, that is. Likewise, wearing torn jeans, whether torn at the knee or in different places, seems to signify that students are rejecting the middle-class value of having a wardrobe of nice clothes. The irony of the torn jeans reached its height a few years ago when jeans makers started selling pre-torn clothing at very high prices. If manufacturers are selling products like that, no doubt they are trendy, and that trend finally represents the normal when large numbers of young people buy and wear these products.

Teenagers often rebel against their parents as much as they do against school rules. After all, teens are going through the period in their lives when they are maturing sexually, if not emotionally and mentally. Their identities may not yet be revealed to themselves or others. So they are searching, but they are searching for something that sets them apart from their parents, because they are trying to be their own person. Ironically, this searching usually leads to role playing in fashion rather than identity discovery. A young woman I know decided to cut a design into her wrist as an identifying mark like the members of her teen "tribe." Her parents pointed out to her that she already had a "tribe," her family, but she did not see it that way. She probably knew that the scarification would annoy her parents, just as her wearing Seattle "grunge" clothing to conform to her friends' tastes had already done so. Technically, piercings, scarifications, and tattoos are not clothing, but they serve some of the same purposes of "decoration" that clothes do. So I think they fit into my points about conforming clothing behaviors of young people.

Conforming clothing among teenagers also has the effect of gaining acceptance among their peers. Teenagers can be very cruel to each other at a time in their lives when their emotions are already in turmoil. Teens seem to need some sort of acceptance, not necessarily for sharing interests or for earning self-esteem. In fact, teenagers who stand out by making good grades or by not smoking marijuana or not drinking alcohol find themselves lacking in popularity. So they may make up for it by dressing the way other teens in a particular group dress in order to be perceived as a member of that group. If the "cool" group clothing of the moment in their school is khaki trousers and plaid shirts, some teens will wear those clothes to make others think they are in that group, even if that it is not true. Where does the individual "man" or "woman" reveal himself or herself in that kind of behavior?

Some conforming clothing can lead to the "un-making" of the person in a different and tragic way. Four years ago where I live, a fifteen-year-old was shot and killed because he would not give up his very expensive Boston Celtics team jacket to thieves. In other cities, similar stories involving expensive Nike or other brand athletic shoes have been in the news the last few years. Young people, even pre-adolescents, have been killed for their popular, but expensive, athletic clothing. These killings suggest the conforming power of those clothes (and shoes). Young people who can't afford them just kill someone who does have them if they can't steal them.

Young people, especially teenagers, are going through a very difficult time in their lives at the turn of the millenium. The pressures on them seem more weighty than in previous generations. Their bodies and feelings are telling them they are growing up, but their experiential knowledge, wisdom, and mental maturity still need developing. In a way, they are like boats thrown around in stormy seas. They see clothing and outer markings that identify them with celebrities in sports and music as a way of finding a calm port in that storm. They do not seem to recognize that reaching that port means compromising their developing individuality to an extent.

Analysis of Essay II

Essay II has a score in the high range, perhaps even 7, certainly 6. It has an assertive thesis that controls the direction (structure) of the development. The subordinate ideas develop the main idea quite well, even though there seems to be a slight digression from discussing clothing to discussing scarifications, piercings, and tattooing. However, the writer does attempt to show that this digression is part of the same idea of conforming clothing being against the forming of the person's identity. It has few errors of any kind, and it uses specific examples to develop each subordinate idea. Both the introduction and the conclusion do their jobs well. The word choice and general language use are also quite good.

ESSAY III

When teenagers or young people in general wear clothes that are in style, they are usually wearing clothes popularized by celebrities, especially the athletes and musicians they look up to. A quick look around any group of young people will portray their fashion consciousness in their imitation of celebrities. This wearing of stylish clothing indicates in a strange way that young people's clothing suggests an identifying with a particular individual or type giving it a sort of identity. In other words, for them, "clothes do make the man [or woman]."

In any group of young people, you will probably see males wearing baseball-style caps, tee-shirts, and jeans. Some of these caps have college or professional basketball or football team emblems sewn on them other than a baseball team's logo. Usually, when a team wins a championship, sales of their gear soars, especially with young people. So when Duke University's basketball team won the college tournament a couple of years ago, alot of folks bought their caps and wore them. About the same time, you could see alot of blacks wearing caps with a large X on them, relating to Malcolm X, in which a biographical movie was being publicized by the filmmakers.

In that same crowd, you would find a lot of students, male and female, wearing Seattle grunge style clothing. This consists of plaid flannel shirt, the standard torn jeans, and boots, preferably Doc Martins' brand. The probably also are wearing a knit cap and have various body piercings. Again, these young folks are identifying with a kind of rebelliousness they see as "cool," or successful. They might even have bought the clothes at a Goodwill or Salvation Army second-hand clothing store, giving them a farther kind of identity that says they are rebelling against the adult clothing of jackets and ties for men and dresses or skirts and blouses for women. The fact that they look alike from a distance probably doesn't phase them, they think they are different.

You may actually find some young people wearing clothing their parents would like, neat, clean clothing for both sexes. As a way of identifying with adulthood, since these folks have seen their parents and their parents' friend wearing this kind of clothing on the weekends or at home in the evenings.

All in all, young people may be trying to use clothes to "make the man [or woman]." They are trying to identify with celebrities in sports and music, or they are not yet rebelling against their parents.

Analysis of Essay III

Essay III has a score range of 4-5. It has satisfactory introductory and concluding paragraphs, even if they could be improved. The development seems to run out of steam by the time it reached the third of its three subordinate ideas, perhaps running out of time. Word choice varies from good to weak. A few errors such as a sentence fragment, subject-verb disagreement, comma splices, wrong word (*The* for *They*; *phase* for *faze*), and misspelling (*alot*) seem to derive from the time limit more than from a lack of ability.

CHAPTER 2
HUMANITIES

PRACTICE
TEST 1

CLEP HUMANITIES
Test 1

(Answer sheets appear in the back of the book.)

Section 1

TIME: 45 Minutes
75 Questions

DIRECTIONS: Each of the questions or incomplete statements below is followed by five possible answers or completions. Select the best choice in each case and fill in the corresponding oval on the answer sheet.

---

1. In ancient Egyptian architecture, the large, sloping walls which flank the entrance to a temple complex are called

    (A) pyramids.

    (B) mastabas.

    (C) tombs.

    (D) pylons.

    (E) obelisks.

2. An improvised performance, usually held in churchyards or city squares, that was performed in a circle and involved playing the role of redeemers, by the act of scourging and whipping themselves, which made them move and gesture, was performed by

    (A) fools.

    (B) flagellants.

    (C) minnesingers.

    (D) mimes.

    (E) joculators.

3. An *a priori* truth is one that is known to be true

   (A) independently of experience.

   (B) after careful experimentation or observation.

   (C) as a result of mathematical calculation.

   (D) only by God.

   (E) because its denial is a contradiction.

4. The fourth degree of a major scale is given what name?

   (A) Tonic   (D) Subdominant

   (B) Dominant   (E) Mediant

   (C) Leading tone

5. A natural minor scale contains five whole steps and two half steps. Between which scale degrees do the half steps occur?

   (A) 2-3, 5-6   (D) 2-3, 7-8

   (B) 3-4, 7-8   (E) 3-4

   (C) 1-2, 7-8

6. An example of the use of primitivism can be found in which musical selection?

   (A) "Prelude a l'apres-midi d'un faune"

   (B) "Le Sacre du Printemps"

   (C) "Salome"

   (D) "Wozzeck"

   (E) "The Liberty Bell"

7. Which of the following is the earliest and clearest demonstration of the principles of romanticism?

   (A) Pope's "The Rape of the Lock"

   (B) Rousseau's *The Social Contract*

   (C) Blake's *Songs of Innocence and Experience*

(D) Dreiser's *Daisy Miller*

(E) Shakespeare's *Romeo and Juliet*

8. Which of the following works are known for defining the parameters of existentialism?

(A) *L'Etranger*

(B) *Morte D'Arthur*

(C) *Candide*

(D) *Saint Joan*

(E) *Le Misanthrope*

9. Which American classic is known for its comprehensive description of frontier families' lives in the Midwest during the nineteenth century?

(A) *The Last of the Mohicans*

(B) *The History of the Dividing Line*

(C) *On Plymouth Plantation*

(D) *My Antonia*

(E) *Huckleberry Finn*

10. Which of the following is a "coming of age" novel that utilizes the concept of the anti-hero?

(A) *Tom Sawyer*

(B) *Martin Chuzzlewit*

(C) *Catcher in the Rye*

(D) *The Great Gatsby*

(E) *Sister Carrie*

11. Of the following poems, which is known as one of the most poignant elegies to President Abraham Lincoln?

(A) "Elegy Written in a Country Churchyard"

(B) "When Lilacs Last in the Dooryard Bloomed"

(C) "After Death"

(D) "Howl"

(E) "Elegiac Stanzas"

QUESTION 12 refers to the following.

12. Which of the following is an important feature of the building pictured above?

(A) A dependence on rectilinear lines and angles

(B) An emphasis on the structural framework of the building

(C) An interplay of large and small geometric shapes

(D) The use of curvilinear forms to suggest organic growth or motion

(E) An orderly, classically inspired floor plan

QUESTIONS 13–15 refer to the following illustrations (A) through (E).

(A)

(C)

(B)

(D)

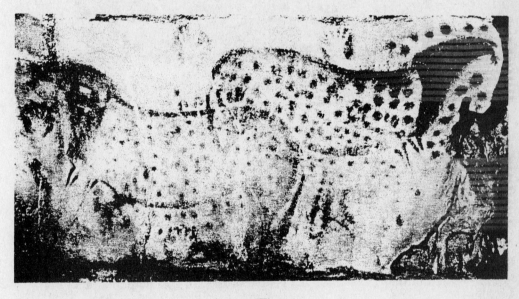

(E)

13. Which example is intent on a naturalistic rendering of an animal's anatomy?

14. Which example uses animals as a metaphor for human behavior?

15. In which example are animals seen in a magic or ritual context?

QUESTION 16 refers to the following.

16. The example pictured above most likely presents which of the following?

    (A) A passage from a classical epic

    (B) A scene from a Wagnerian opera

    (C) An eighteenth-century satire on human foibles

    (D) An episode from a Shakespearean drama

    (E) An incident from the French Revolution

17. Which of the following lines is an example of iambic pentameter?

    ◡ / ◡ / ◡ / ◡ /
    (A) Her deck / once red / with he/roes' blood /

    / ◡ / ◡ / ◡ / ◡
    (B) Here goes / the try / I've al/ways know /

    / ◡ / ◡◡ / ◡ ◡
    (C) She loves the / way I hold / her hand/

    / / ◡ / / ◡ / /
    (D) Although I/ knew the road / led home/

    ◡ / ◡ / / ◡ / /
    (E) As I lay / wait ing / for the / morn

QUESTIONS 18 and 19 refer to the following verses.

O God, do you hear it, this persecution,
These my sufferings from this hateful
Woman, this monster, murderess of children?
Still what I can do that I will do:
I will lament and cry upon heaven,
Calling the gods to bear me witness
How you have killed my boys to prevent me from
Touching their bodies or giving them burial.
I wish I never begot them to see them
Afterward slaughtered by you.

18. These lines are spoken by

   (A) the murderer.

   (B) the father of the dead children.

   (C) one of the gods.

   (D) a bystander.

   (E) a judge.

19. It can be inferred from this passage that

   (A) the woman had a right to kill her children.

   (B) the man deserved to lose his children.

   (C) the rites and ceremonies of burial are extremely important.

   (D) the gods decreed the death of the children.

   (E) the woman will get away with the murders.

QUESTIONS 20–22 refer to the following verses (A) through (E).

   (A) For shade to shade will come too drowsily,
        And drown the wakeful anguish of the soul.

   (B) Rocks, caves, lakes, fens, bogs, dens, and shades of death.

   (C) 'Twas brillig, and the slithy toves
        Did gyre and gimble in the wabe

(D) Because I could not stop for Death—
He kindly stopped for me—

(E) … yet from these flames
No light, but rather darkness visible

20. Which passage contains an oxymoron?

21. Which passage uses assonance?

22. Which passage is written in iambic pentameter?

23. Which of the following are African-American playwrights who won awards and critical recognition for their plays in the 1920s?

(A) August Wilson and Lorraine Hansberry

(B) Charles Gordone and Imamu Amiri Baraka

(C) Ed Bullins and Sonia Sanchez

(D) Zora Neale Hurston and Marita Bonner

(E) Eugene O'Neill and Clifford Odets

24. A well-made play may have all of the following EXCEPT

(A) a tight and logical construction.

(B) a plot based on a withheld secret.

(C) a misplaced letter and documents.

(D) an obligatory scene.

(E) an episodic structure.

25. Frank Lloyd Wright was the original architect/designer of which of the following twentieth-century museums?

(A) Solomon R. Guggenheim Museum, New York

(B) East Wing, National Gallery of Art, Washington, D.C.

(C) Museum of Architecture, Frankfurt-am-Main

(D) The High Museum of Art, Atlanta

(E) None of the above.

QUESTIONS 26–28 refer to the following ballet definitions.

(A) Quick springing movement that resembles a cat walk by alternating feet.

(B) Placing and applying body weight to one foot that is against the floor while sliding the other foot into fifth position.

(C) Positioning one foot in front of the other while the feet remain one step apart.

(D) Weight proportioned incorrectly, creating the body to shift and lean in that direction.

(E) One left leg lifted at a 45 degree angle rotating from front to outer side, from back to inner side.

26. Which description describes glissade?

27. Which description describes improper balance?

28. Which description is fourth position crossed?

29. The predecessor of the modern-day piano is the _____

   (A) lute.   (D) harp.

   (B) harpsichord.   (E) xylophone.

   (C) synthesizer.

30. A poem set to music is a(n) _____

   (A) madrigal.   (D) aria.

   (B) art song.   (E) symphony.

   (C) opera.

31. A high male voice is classified as a(n)

   (A) soprano.   (D) baritone.

   (B) tenor.   (E) alto.

   (C) bass.

32. Which of the following well-known writers is famous for his verses about the struggle for Irish independence?

(A) James Joyce   (D) G. B. Shaw

(B) J. P. Donleavy   (E) John O'Hara

(C) W. B. Yeats

33. The idea of evolution is propounded by which of the following English writers?

(A) Alfred Lord Tennyson

(B) Dr. Samuel Johnson

(C) Charles Darwin

(D) Robert Browning

(E) Thomas Henry Huxley

34. Which of the following early American novels deals with the author's personal attempt to exorcise many of the negative aspects of his Puritan heritage?

(A) Irving's *The History of New York*

(B) Melville's *Moby Dick*

(C) Brown's *Wieland*

(D) Cooper's *The Pathfinder*

(E) Hawthorne's *The Scarlet Letter*

35. Though condemned as indecent and controversial, this modern English autobiographical novel is now acclaimed for its originality.

(A) *The Metamorphosis*   (D) *The Heart of Darkness*

(B) *Sons and Lovers*   (E) *Ethan Frome*

(C) *Time and Again*

36. Known for its transcendentalist underpinnings, this early American work also emphasizes the importance of self-reliance.

    (A) *The Scarlet Letter*

    (B) *The Open Boat*

    (C) *Walden*

    (D) *The Last of the Mohicans*

    (E) *The Red Badge of Courage*

QUESTIONS 37–39 refer to illustrations (A) through (E).

(A)

(B)

(C)

(D)

(E)

37. Which example characterizes a culture which values logic and order?

38. In which example are architectural forms and materials used for a whimsical effect?

39. Which example best characterizes a culture which values technological precision and efficiency?

QUESTION 40 refers to the following.

40. In the building pictured above, the cantilevered horizontal forms do all of the following EXCEPT

    (A) echo the natural waterfall's rock ledge.

    (B) emphasize the structural framework of the building.

    (C) deny the mass and weight of the materials.

    (D) integrate the building with the natural setting.

    (E) rely on industrial construction materials.

QUESTION 41 refers to the following.

41. The architect of the building pictured above probably relied primarily on which of the following?

(A) Internal steel cables

(D) Stone masonry and mortar

(B) Prestressed concrete

(E) Sheet glass

(C) Oak timber framing

QUESTIONS 42 and 43 refer to the following poem.

The Sick Rose

O Rose, thou art sick.
 The invisible worm
 That flies in the night
 In the howling storm

Has found out thy bed
 Of crimson joy,

And his dárk sécret love
Does thy life destroy.

— *William Blake*

42. The imagery in this poem is mainly

(A) religious.   (D) light.

(B) sexual.   (E) darkness.

(C) animal.

43. The word "life" in line 8 means

(A) passion.   (D) beauty.

(B) spirit.   (E) memory.

(C) love.

QUESTIONS 44–46 refer to the following poem.

Apparently with no surprise
To any happy flower
The Frost beheads it at its play
In accidental power.
The blonde Assassin passes on,
The Sun proceeds unmoved
To measure off another Day
For an Approving God.

44. Line 3 demonstrates

(A) alliteration.   (D) assonance.

(B) personification.   (E) conceit.

(C) onomatopoeia.

45. "The blonde Assassin" line 5 refers to

(A) fate.   (D) the sun.

(B) disease.   (E) an approving god.

(C) the frost.

46. Which of the following best describes the meaning of the poem?

    (A) The cruelty of God

    (B) The inevitability of death

    (C) The indifference of God

    (D) The happiness of flowers

    (E) The inevitability of winter

47. Poetic drama is best described as

    (A) poetry in dialogue.

    (B) a poem in dialogue written for performance.

    (C) ancillary to action.

    (D) a one-act play.

    (E) a play with no well-defined scenes.

48. *The Three Penny Opera* is best described as

    (A) an adaptation of John Gay's *The Beggar's Opera*.

    (B) a melodrama.

    (C) a comedy.

    (D) an epic drama.

    (E) historification.

49. The belief that a human being has an absolute power to choose his or her own destiny is a hallmark of

    (A) existentialism.

    (B) essentialism.

    (C) pragmatism.

    (D) marxism.

    (E) platonism.

50. "Cyclopean" is a term which is often used to refer to the masonry building of which of the following civilizations?

    (A) Ancient Egyptian

    (B) Mesopotamian

    (C) Aztec

    (D) Roman

    (E) Mycenean

51. Descartes used his *cogito* argument ("I think; therefore, I am") to establish

    (A) an indubitable foundation for knowledge

    (B) the basis of personal identity.

    (C) metaphysics on a firm footing.

    (D) the existence of God.

    (E) the foundation of mathematics.

52. Which analysis represents a through-composed form?

    (A) AB

    (B) ABA

    (C) ABCDE

    (D) ABACA

    (E) A

53. Which of the following can be a synonym for Gregorian chant?

    (A) Plainchant

    (B) Motet

    (C) Canon

    (D) Aria

    (E) Fugue

54. Which composer is best know for his technique of weaving favorite melodies, often patriotic, into his compositions?

    (A) Sousa

    (B) Ives

    (C) Bernstein

    (D) Stravinsky

    (E) Haydn

55. Which of the following is perhaps the most curious – even hilarious – novel written in the eighteenth century?

   (A) *Tristram Shandy*

   (B) *Don Quixote*

   (C) *Candy*

   (D) *Catch-22*

   (E) *Where the Bee Sucks There Suck I*

56. Which Shakespeare play is considered by many critics to be the Bard's finest study of guilt and conscience following a crime?

   (A) *Julius Caesar*

   (B) *Macbeth*

   (C) *Hamlet*

   (D) *A Midsummer Night's Dream*

   (E) *Love's Labor Lost*

57. In which of the following tales is a house presented as a personification of a family?

   (A) *Anne of Green Gables*

   (B) *The House of Morgan*

   (C) *The Young Housewife*

   (D) *The House of the Seven Gables*

   (E) *An Angel on the Porch*

58. Which of the following is a twentieth-century novel about the Wild West written in the tradition of realistic movement?

   (A) *Huckleberry Finn*

   (B) *The Bird Comes to Yellow Sky*

   (C) *The Oxbow Incident*

   (D) *The Occurrence at Owl Creek Bridge*

   (E) *The Red Badge of Courage*

59. Which of the following poets is known as an American original who experimented with extensive works of detailed images and free verse?

(A) Alexander Pope

(B) Samuel Langhorne Clemens

(C) Walt Whitman

(D) Emily Dickinson

(E) Anne Bradstreet

QUESTION 60 refers to the following.

60. The pose of the horse in the sculpture pictured above serves to express

(A) physical aging and decay. (D) military prowess.

(B) massiveness and stability. (E) moral fortitude.

(C) lightness and motion.

QUESTION 61 refers to the following.

61. Which of the following best describes the example pictured above?

    (A) Monumental architecture dominates the scene.

    (B) The scene is viewed from the window of a passing train.

    (C) Human drama is the artist's main concern.

    (D) The composition has a dramatic central focus.

    (E) The scene is viewed as though from a second-story window.

QUESTION 62 refers to the following.

62. Which of the following is probably true of the sculpture pictured above?

(A) The artist modelled it with his hands.

(B) The artist poured it into a mold.

(C) The artist shaped his materials with a blowtorch and welding tools.

(D) The artist shaped natural materials with a chisel.

(E) The artist used industrial forms as he found them.

QUESTION 63 refers to the following.

63. Which of the following is the most important artistic device in the example shown above?

   (A) Line   (D) Volume

   (B) Tone   (E) Hue

   (C) Perspective

QUESTION 64 refers to the following.

64. Which of the following does NOT contribute to order and regularity in the example pictured on the previous page?

    (A) The repeated second-story window design

    (B) A facade which lacks deep recesses and voids

    (C) The use of columns at the center and corners of the building

    (D) A subtle use of the arch

    (E) The balustrade running across the roof line

QUESTIONS 65 and 66 refer to the following stanza.

> When my mother died I was very young
> And my father sold me while yet my tongue
> Could scarcely cry "'weep! 'weep! 'weep! 'weep!"
> So your chimneys I sweep, and in soot I sleep.

65. The above stanza was taken from a longer poem written by

    (A) Shakespeare.   (D) Blake.

    (B) Milton.   (E) Hardy.

    (C) Chaucer.

66. Which of the following best explains the use of the word "'weep!" in line 3 of the stanza?

    (A) The child is so young he cannot yet pronounce the word.

    (B) The child has a speech impediment because of neglect.

    (C) The child is weeping because he was sold as a chimney sweep.

    (D) The child wants to make you feel guilty about sweeping your chimneys.

    (E) The child is so young he is upset at having to sweep chimneys.

QUESTIONS 67–71 refer to the following epic poem.

> A whole day's journey high but wide remote
> From this Assyrian garden, where the Fiend
> Saw undelighted all delight, all kind
> Of living creatures new to sight and strange:
> Two of far nobler shape erect and tall,

God-like erect, with native honor clad
In naked majesty seemed lords of all,
And worthy seemed, for in their looks divine
The image of their Maker shone,
...
For contemplation he and valor formed,
For softness she and sweet attractive grace,
He for God only, she for God in him:

67. The term "epic" refers to

    (A) a long poem written in rhyming couplets about a hero.

    (B) a long poem translated from Latin.

    (C) a long poem written about heroic actions.

    (D) a long poem written by Virgil.

    (E) a long poem about death.

68. The above lines are from

    (A) Dante's *Inferno.*   (D) *Arabian Nights.*

    (B) Virgil's *Aeneid.*   (E) *Paradise Lost.*

    (C) *The Iliad.*

69. The view point of the lines is

    (A) Faust's.   (D) Satan's.

    (B) God's.   (E) Dante's.

    (C) Scheherazade's.

70. Which best describes the couple in lines 4-6?

    (A) Beowulf and Grendel's mother before the crucial fight.

    (B) Grendel and Grendel's mother after the crucial fight.

    (C) Adam and Eve before "The Fall."

    (D) Hector and his wife before the crucial battle.

    (E) Adam and Eve after "The Fall."

71. Which best describes the poet's views on the roles of men and women?

    (A) Men and women are equal.

    (B) Men are made for thoughtful action and women for beauty.

    (C) Women must be submissive to the god in men.

    (D) Men must be powerful and women soft.

    (E) Men are reasonable and strong and women soft and graceful.

72. Which of the following plays focuses on a marriage built on a lie and problems with eyesight?

    (A) *The Wild Duck*   (D) *Antigone*

    (B) *Oedipus*   (E) *Andromache*

    (C) *Electra*

73. *Tartuffe* is best described as a play about

    (A) the downfall of a noble king.

    (B) the problems of a marriage.

    (C) a man of considerable stature duped by a hypocrite.

    (D) individuals who wait and do not act.

    (E) children who are ingrates.

74. An *insula* refers to a(n)

    (A) Greek public meeting square.

    (B) multi-storied Roman apartment block.

    (C) western portion of a Carolingian church.

    (D) Greek cross plan.

    (E) vertical groove on the surface of a column.

75. Berkeley's famous dictum, "Esse est percipi," ("to be is to be perceived") is associated most strongly with the outlook known as

(A) idealism.

(B) pragmatism.

(C) empiricism.

(D) rationalism.

(E) phenomenology.

Section 2

TIME: 45 Minutes
75 Questions

DIRECTIONS: Each of the questions or incomplete statements below is followed by five possible answers or completions. Select the best choice in each case and fill in the corresponding oval on the answer sheet.

---

76. Which jazz saxophonist was named "Bird"?

    (A) Charlie Parker

    (B) John Coltrane

    (C) Dizzy Gillespie

    (D) Paul Desmond

    (E) Stan Getz

77. Which jazz tenor saxophonist is famous for his "Giant Steps"?

    (A) Charlie Parker

    (B) Stan Getz

    (C) John Coltrane

    (D) Coleman Hawkins

    (E) Ornette Coleman

78. A collaboration between Aaron Copland and the dance-choreographer Agnes de Mille resulted in the creation of which ballet suite?

    (A) "West Side Story"

    (B) "Rodeo"

    (C) "Porgy and Bess"

    (D) "Phantom of the Opera"

    (E) "Salome"

79. Which of the following novels of adventure presents the most detailed picture of eighteenth-century English manorial and city life?

    (A) *Great Expectations*

    (B) *Moby Dick*

    (C) *Jane Eyre*

    (D) *Tom Jones*

    (E) *Silas Marner*

80. Which of the following is among the most famous of English works by the group of writers called the "Decadents"?

(A) Coleridge's "Rime of the Ancient Mariner"

(B) Lawrence's *Sons and Lovers*

(C) Fielding's *Joseph Andrews*

(D) Wilde's *The Picture of Dorian Gray*

(E) Joyce's *The Dubliners*

81. The important literary concept of the "pathetic fallacy" was first set forth in

(A) Ruskin's *Modern Painters*.

(B) Emerson's *Nature*.

(C) Shakespeare's *As You Like It*.

(D) Thomas Lodge's *Rosalynde*.

(E) Samuel Johnson's *Dictionary*.

82. A reaction against utilitarianism – the theory of ethics formulated in England in the eighteenth century – can be seen in nineteenth-century literature, such as

(A) Eliot's *Middlemarch*.

(B) Dreiser's *Sister Carrie*.

(C) Melville's *Billy Budd*.

(D) James' *Washington Square*.

(E) Dickens' *David Copperfield*.

83. Which of the following writers participated energetically in the Celtic Revival of the eighteenth century?

(A) James Joyce

(B) John O'Hara

(C) J. P. Donleavy

(D) James Macpherson

(E) W. B. Yeats

QUESTION 84 refers to the following.

84. In the painting illustrated above, all of the following are important compositional devices EXCEPT

(A) the perspective grid of the checkerboard floor.

(B) the strong highlighting of the foreground figures.

(C) the arcade of arches in the background.

(D) the vigorous movement of the main figure group.

(E) the intersecting lines of the arms and the swords.

QUESTION 85 refers to the following.

85. The building pictured on the previous page was produced in which of the following countries?

(A) Japan   (D) Greece

(B) Indonesia   (E) Nigeria

(C) Easter Island

QUESTIONS 86–88 refer to the following illustrations (A) through (E) below.

(A)

(B)

(C)

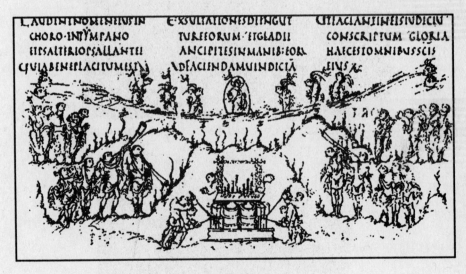

(D)

(E)

86. Which example seeks to give a schematic representation of a ceremonial event?

87. In which example is the human figure most stylized and repeated in order to fit its container?

88. In which example do the figures show the greatest tendency toward rhythmic calligraphy?

QUESTIONS 89–91 refer to the following lines.

As when in the sky the stars about the moon's shining
are seen in all their glory, when the air has fallen to stillness.
and all the high places of the hills are clear, and the shoulders out-
jutting,
and the deep ravines, as endless bright air spills from the heavens
and all the stars are seen, to make glad the heart of the shepherd:
such in their numbers blazed the watchfires the Trojans were burning
between the waters of Xanthos and the ships, before Ilion.

89. The lines above are an example of

    (A) a Homeric simile.

    (B) an extended metaphor.

    (C) Augustan couplets.

    (D) English heroic verse.

    (E) Miltonic free verse.

90. What is being described as what?

    (A) The stars are like hills.

    (B) The stars are like shepherds.

    (C) The stars are like rivers.

    (D) The Trojan fires are like the stars.

    (E) The Trojan ships are like the stars.

91. The shepherd is introduced in line 5 in order to

    (A) humanize the description.

    (B) give some humor to the description.

    (C) give some depth to the description.

    (D) give some gladness to the description.

    (E) glamorize the description.

QUESTIONS 92–95 refer to lines (A) through (E) below.

    (A) As soon as April pierces to the root
        The drought of March, and bathes each bud and shoot
        …

    (B) Of man's first disobedience, and the fruit
        Of that forbidden fruit whose mortal taste
        …

    (C) My heart leaps up when I behold
        A rainbow in the sky;
        …

    (D) I placed a jar in Tennessee,
         And round it was, upon a hill.

    (E) Because I could not stop for Death—
         He kindly stopped for me—

92. Which is written by a woman?

93. Which is by Chaucer?

94. Which represents the Romantic period?

95. Which represents the epic?

96. As Gregor Samsa awoke one morning from an uneasy dream he found himself transformed into a gigantic insect.

    This opening line is

    (A) Genet's   (D) Kafka's

    (B) Sartre's   (E) Tolstoy's

    (C) Ionesco's

97. The best definition for the original use of scapegoat is

    (A) a table ornament used when royalty was unable to appear.

    (B) a fur-bearing animal that was used to provide milk.

    (C) an animal tethered to lure animals terrorizing the village.

    (D) a victim sacrificed for the redemption of the tribe being driven into the wilderness.

    (E) a royal personage like Oedipus who went into exile.

98. Which of the following types of ancient Roman architecture most directly influenced the development of early Christian church planning?

    (A) Temple   (D) Forum

    (B) Basilica   (E) Villa

    (C) Bath

99. Dance was originated by

    (A) religious groups.   (D) Romans.

    (B) Egyptians.   (E) savage hunters.

    (C) Greeks.

100. The logical fallacy involved in concluding that the universe itself must have a cause because every event in the universe has cause is

    (A) the fallacy of composition.

    (B) the fallacy of division.

    (C) the slippery slope fallacy.

    (D) the *ad hominem* fallacy.

    (E) the fallacy of ignorance.

101. The themes of many musical compositions are often that of folk music. Which composer is most famous for his folk music settings for wind ensemble?

    (A) Sousa   (D) Strauss

    (B) Grainger   (E) Haydn

    (C) Beethoven

QUESTIONS 102-105 refer to the following musical notation.

102. What is the key of this excerpt?

    (A) B flat   (D) D

    (B) F   (E) A

    (C) C

103. The time signature for the above excerpt is not noted. What should it be?

(A) $\frac{4}{4}$ (D) $\frac{3}{4}$

(B) $\frac{2}{4}$ (E) $\frac{12}{8}$

(C) $\frac{6}{8}$

104. How many measures are present?

(A) 1   (D) 0

(B) 2   (E) 5

(C) 3

105. What is the arrow pointing towards?

(A) Key signature   (D) Repeat sign

(B) Clef sign   (E) Time signature

(C) Double bar

106. Which of the following is considered among the body of literature currently termed "American Ethnic"?

(A) James' *Daisy Miller*

(B) Poe's *Cask of Amontillado*

(C) Roth's *Goodbye Columbus*

(D) Updike's *Rabbit Redux*

(E) Hawthorne's *Scarlet Letter*

107. One of the most famous and prophetic descriptions of settlements in the young American nation was

(A) *The Journals of Lewis and Clark.*

(B) *Main Street.*

(C) *Letters From an American Farmer.*

(D) *The Last of the Mohicans.*

(E) *The Diary of Captain John Smith.*

108. Which of the following modern novels describes the difficulties faced by African-Americans in twentieth-century America?

    (A) *As I Lay Dying*

    (B) *Ethan Frome*

    (C) *Heart of Darkness*

    (D) *The Metamorphosis*

    (E) *The Invisible Man*

109. Which of the following nineteenth-century novels was used as an accurate travel guide well into this century?

    (A) *Journey to the Center of the Earth*

    (B) *The Mysterious Island*

    (C) *Robinson Crusoe*

    (D) *20,000 Leagues Under the Sea*

    (E) *Gulliver's Travels*

110. Which of the following novels recalls a time of medieval chivalry?

    (A) Eliot's *Middlemarch*

    (B) Scott's *Ivanhoe*

    (C) Poe's *The Fall of the House of Usher*

    (D) King's *The Shining*

    (E) Perelman's *The Dreamlife of Balso Shell*

111. It has been said that Victorian poetry is essentially a continuation of the poetry of the romantic movement. This can be seen in

    (A) Hemingway's veneration for Eliot.

    (B) Tennyson's veneration of Browning.

    (C) Arnold's veneration for Wordsworth.

    (D) Rossetti's veneration of Browning.

    (E) Wordsworth's veneration of Scott.

112. Which of the following is one of the most hilarious stories in *Huckleberry Finn* – one which demonstrates both the accepting nature and eventual canniness of the heartland Americans?

(A) *The Duke and the Dauphin*

(B) Tom Sawyer and his painted fence

(C) Huck's escape from Pap

(D) Jim's escape to freedom

(E) Huck "lighting out for the territories"

QUESTION 113 refers to the following.

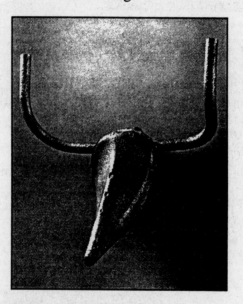

113. In combining found objects to make the sculpture shown above, the artist sought to create

(A) a contrast of line and tone.

(B) a religious symbol.

(C) a visual analogy to a living creature.

(D) a metaphor for human experience.

(E) a functional device.

QUESTIONS 114–116 refer to the following illustrations (A) through (E)

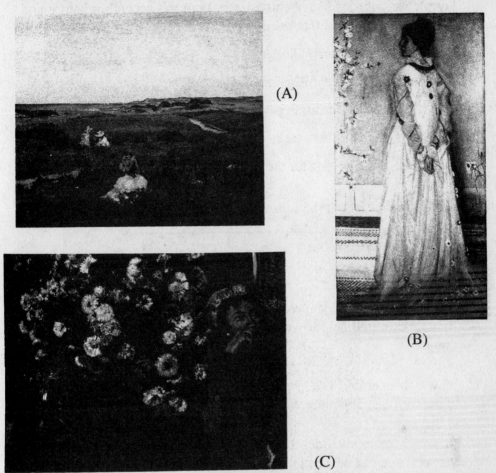

(A)

(B)

(C)

(D)

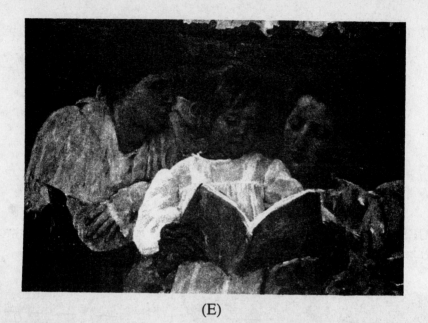

(E)

114. In which example do carefully rendered decorative details on the figure's costume help to visually relate the main subject to the background?

115. In which example is an off-center subject cropped to produce the effect of a casual photograph?

116. In which example does the subject's off-center position lead the viewer's eye out of the picture?

QUESTION 117 refers to the following.

117. The staircase in the Hotel van Eetvelde, designed by Victor Horta in 1895, illustrates which one of the following art historical styles?

    (A) Surrealism

    (B) Post-Modernism

    (C) Neo-Classicism

    (D) Post-Impressionsim

    (E) Art Nouveau

QUESTIONS 118 and 119 refer to the following illustrations (A) through (D) below.

(A)

(B)

(C)

(D)

118. Which is Gothic?

    (A) Building (A)   (D) Building (D)

    (B) Building (B)   (E) None of the above.

    (C) Building (C)

119. Which was NOT constructed as a place of religious worship?

    (A) Building (A)   (D) Building (D)

    (B) Building (B)   (E) None of the above.

    (C) Building (C)

QUESTIONS 120 and 121 refer to the following verse.

On the one-ton temple bell
a moonmoth, folded into sleep,
sits still.

120. The above is an example of

    (A) hyperbole.   (D) an epigram.

    (B) an ode.   (E) doggerel.

    (C) haiku.

121. The original of the above was written in

    (A) French.   (D) British English.

    (B) Japanese.   (E) Persian.

    (C) Chinese.

122. Which of the following best defines the term *bathos*?

    (A) A gross exaggeration

    (B) A build to a climax

    (C) An abrupt fall from climax

    (D) An abrupt fall from the beautiful to the funny

    (E) An abrupt build to a climax

123. Which poet gave us the term "negative capability"?

    (A) William Carlos Williams

    (B) T. S. Eliot

    (C) William Wordsworth

    (D) e. e. cummings

    (E) John Keats

124. If all tragedies are finished by death, and all comedies by a marriage, then which of the following is the best example of tragedy?

    (A) *A Death of a Salesman*

    (B) *A Midsummer's Night's Dream*

    (C) *Oedipus*

    (D) *The Tempest*

    (E) *The Bad-Tempered Man*

QUESTIONS 125–127 refer to what happens when:

    (A) misunderstandings are cleared up.

    (B) action not intended by the main character takes place.

    (C) the public is aided in its discovery of the villain.

    (D) the main character whispers an "aside" to the audience.

    (E) the hero's understanding of the true nature of the situation and the self changes.

125. Which of the choices best defines Anagnorisis, the Greek word for "recognition" or "discovery"?

126. Which choice best describes Mark Antony's intent in the public oration that he makes regarding Julius Caesar's death?

127. Which choice is best used to characterize Othello's description of himself as "one that loved not wisely, but too well"?

128.   "So the whole ear of Denmark
    Is by a forged process of my death
    Rankly abused."

    The speaker is

    (A) the Royal Dane.   (D) Falstaff.

    (B) King Lear.   (E) Caliban.

    (C) Puck.

129. The unglazed opening in the center of the dome of the Pantheon in Rome is called a(n)

    (A) window.   (D) stained-glass window.

    (B) oculus.   (E) clerestory.

    (C) splayed window.

130. Parallel feet, flat-footed steps, undulating torso, body isolation, and syncopated rhythms refer to

    (A) belidi dance (abdominal dance).

    (B) jazz dance.

(C) danse mora (Flamenco dance).

(D) tap dance.

(E) country dance.

131. Suppose two theories are equally powerful in explaining certain phenomena, but one of them (**X**) postulates a larger number of unobservable entities than the other (**Y**). Which is preferable and why?

(A) **Y**, because of Occam's Razor

(B) **Y**, because of the Principle of Plenitude

(C) **X**, because of the Open Question Argument

(D) **X**, because of Underdetermination

(E) **Y**, because of Scientific Realism

132. The hero of what nineteenth century novel states that "...vanity is a weakness indeed. But pride– where there is a real superiority of mind, pride will be always under good regulation."

(A) Silas Marner

(B) Emma

(C) Gone with the Wind

(D) Pride and Prejudice

(E) Gulliver's Travels

133. A trumpet can play different notes by adjusting the lip or by doing what?

(A) Pressing down a valve

(B) Striking a string

(C) Covering a hole

(D) Using an octave key

(E) Using a slide

QUESTIONS 134 and 135 refer to the following musical notation.

134. The diagram is an example of

(A) hemiola.   (D) crescendo.

(B) paradiddle.   (E) glissando.

(C) fermata.

135. The C in measure 1 is a C sharp. Therefore, the C in measure 2 is a

(A) C natural.   (D) B.

(B) C sharp.   (E) D.

(C) C flat.

136. What is another name for the bass clef?

(A) F clef   (D) Treble clef

(B) G clef   (E) Alto clef

(C) Tenor clef

137. One of the greatest modern chronicles of a famous incident during the Civil War is

(A) Hoover's *None Dare Call It Treason.*

(B) Wouk's *Caine Mutiny.*

(C) Mailer's *Naked and the Dead.*

(D) Catton's *A Stillness at Appomatox.*

(E) Crane's *Red Badge of Courage.*

138. Which of the following is Edward Albee's memorable drama of the trials and tribulations of a university professor and his wife?

(A) *Troilus and Cressida*

(B) *Who's Afraid of Virginia Woolf*

(C) *The American Dream*

(D) *Brighton Beach Memoirs*

(E) *A View From the Bridge*

139. One of the greatest diarists of the Restoration was

(A) Sir Laurence Olivier.   (D) Samuel Pepys.

(B) Laurence Sterne.   (E) Jonathan Swift.

(C) O. E. Rolvaag.

140. In the early 1800s, which American minister and writer promoted the philosophical and literary movement called transcendentalism?

(A) Jonathan Edwards   (D) Henry David Thoreau

(B) Sir William Pitt   (E) Dr. Samuel Fuller

(C) Ralph Waldo Emerson

141. Mystery plays were common during which of the following historical periods?

(A) The Middle Ages   (D) The Age of Innocence

(B) The Modern Age   (E) The Iron Age

(C) The Classical Age

142. During Dr. Samuel Johnson's time, the London stage was dominated by the

(A) Comedy of Manners.

(B) Comedy of Error.

(C) Situation Comedy.

(D) The Graveyard School of Comedy.

(E) Comedy of Practical Criticism.

143. Typically, in the medieval pastourelle poem,

(A) a princess is wooed by a man of higher standing.

(B) a king retreats to the country to reaffirm his wedding vows with his queen.

   (C) a scholar woos a woman of noble ranking.

   (D) a shepherdess is wooed by a man of higher social standing.

   (E) a queen woos the court jester when on a jaunt to the country.

144. According to Ruskin, the phrase "They rowed her in across the rolling foam / The cruel, crawling foam," is a

   (A) truism.

   (B) quatrain.

   (C) pathetic fallacy.

   (D) quip.

   (E) mythopoetic frame.

QUESTIONS 145 and 146 refer to the following.

145. The creator of this painting is

   (A) Van Gogh.   (D) Pollock.

   (B) Picasso.   (E) None of the above.

   (C) Dali.

146. The event that inspired it was

   (A) the Spanish-American War.

   (B) Homer's *Odyssey*.

(C) the bubonic plague.

(D) the first use of saturation bombing against civilians in modern warfare, during the Spanish Civil War.

(E) the yearly running of the bulls in Pamplona, Spain.

147. *To achieve a transcendent experience through faith in a spontaneous act of creation and by avoiding any representational subject matter which would relate to the physical, everyday world.*

The above statement best describes the goals of which twentieth century art movement?

(A) Surrealism
(D) Abstract expressionism

(B) Futurism
(E) Minimalism

(C) Cubism

QUESTIONS 148-150 refer to illustrations (A) and (B) below.

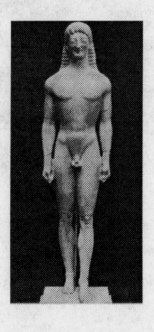

(A)   (B)

148. Which statue came first, chronologically?

    (A) Statue A

    (B) Statue B

    (C) Neither, they both date from roughly the same time period.

    (D) It is not possible to tell because each was made before dates were recorded for works of art.

    (E) It is not possible to tell simply from looking at them.

149. Statue (A) is

    (A) Egyptian.   (D) Roman.

    (B) Aegean.   (E) Byzantine.

    (C) Greek.

150. Statue (B) is

    (A) Egyptian.   (D) Roman.

    (B) Aegean.   (E) Byzantine.

    (C) Greek.

CLEP HUMANITIES
TEST 1

ANSWER KEY

Section 1

1. (D)	16. (C)	31. (B)	46. (B)	61. (E)
2. (B)	17. (A)	32. (C)	47. (B)	62. (C)
3. (A)	18. (B)	33. (C)	48. (D)	63. (A)
4. (D)	19. (C)	34. (E)	49. (A)	64. (D)
5. (A)	20. (E)	35. (B)	50. (E)	65. (D)
6. (B)	21. (B)	36. (C)	51. (A)	66. (A)
7. (C)	22. (A)	37. (A)	52. (C)	67. (C)
8. (A)	23. (D)	38. (D)	53. (A)	68. (E)
9. (D)	24. (E)	39. (B)	54. (B)	69. (D)
10. (C)	25. (A)	40. (B)	55. (A)	70. (C)
11. (B)	26. (B)	41. (D)	56. (B)	71. (E)
12. (D)	27. (D)	42. (B)	57. (D)	72. (A)
13. (D)	28. (C)	43. (D)	58. (C)	73. (C)
14. (A)	29. (B)	44. (B)	59. (C)	74. (B)
15. (E)	30. (B)	45. (C)	60. (C)	75. (A)

Section 2

76. (A)	91. (A)	106. (C)	121. (B)	136. (A)
77. (C)	92. (E)	107. (C)	122. (D)	137. (D)
78. (B)	93. (A)	108. (E)	123. (E)	138. (B)
79. (D)	94. (C)	109. (A)	124. (A)	139. (D)
80. (D)	95. (B)	110. (B)	125. (E)	140. (C)
81. (A)	96. (D)	111. (C)	126. (C)	141. (A)
82. (E)	97. (D)	112. (A)	127. (E)	142. (A)
83. (D)	98. (B)	113. (C)	128. (A)	143. (D)
84. (D)	99. (E)	114. (B)	129. (B)	144. (C)
85. (A)	100. (A)	115. (C)	130. (B)	145. (B)
86. (A)	101. (B)	116. (D)	131. (A)	146. (D)
87. (C)	102. (B)	117. (E)	132. (D)	147. (D)
88. (D)	103. (D)	118. (C)	133. (A)	148. (B)
89. (A)	104. (C)	119. (A)	134. (A)	149. (C)
90. (D)	105. (D)	120. (C)	135. (A)	150. (A)

DETAILED EXPLANATIONS
OF ANSWERS
TEST 1

Section 1

1.   **(D)** Pylons serve as large "gates" to ancient Egyptian temple complexes. Pyramids (A), mastabas (B), and tombs (C) were burial sites and were not as a rule located near the entrances of temples. (E) Obelisks, while positioned near the entrance to many Egyptian temple complexes, are tall, narrow, vertical shafts, which are physically quite unlike wide, massive pylon walls.

2.   **(B)** The group of performers who used such techniques for the purpose of displaying power were called flagellants. Fools used crude jokes and quick wit in their technique (A). Minnesingers were a group of entertainers who sang about war, political issues, and love (C). The mimes mimicked and acted out a situation without speech (D). Joculators were seen as actors and jesters, dancing mimes, acrobats, poets, and musicians (E).

3.   **(A)** Although the definition of an *a priori* truth is not altogether clear, it is usually said that such truths are known independently of experience or "from the first." Thus, (B) cannot be correct. Mathematical calculation can count as a kind of experience, so (C) is incorrect. Human beings are believed to know truth "from the first" by many philosophers; thus, (D) is incorrect. A truth whose denial is a contradiction (E) is called an "analytic" truth.

4.   **(D)** The fourth degree of a major scale is called the subdominant. Each degree is given a name to show its relation within the scale. Choice (D) is correct. The tonic is the first step of a scale; choice (A) is incorrect. The dominant is the fifth degree of the scale; choice (B) is incorrect. The leading tone is the seventh degree of the scale; choice (C) is incorrect. The mediant is the third degree of a scale; choice (E) is incorrect.

5. **(A)** A minor scale ascends from the tonic in the following pattern: $w \, 2 \, w \, w \, \frac{1}{2} \, w \, w$. Therefore, the half steps occur between the 2-3 and 5-6 scale degree, so choice (A) is correct. Half steps between steps 3-4 and 7-8 are found in a major scale, $w \, w \, 2 \, w \, w \, w \, 2$. Choice (B) is incorrect. Half steps between steps 1-2 and 7-8 and 2-3 and 7-8 are not defined scales; choices (C) and (D) are incorrect. A half step between the third and fourth degrees of a scale is found in the blues scale; choice (E) is incorrect.

6. **(B)** Stravinsky's "Le Sacre du Printemps" is an example of the use of primitivism – employing rhythms that are explosive and powerful; choice (B) is correct. Debussy employs impressionism for "Prelude a l'apres-midi d'un faune"; choice (A) is incorrect. "Salome" is a tone poem by Richard Strauss which experiments with atonality. Choice (C) is incorrect. "Wozzeck" is a 12-tone opera by Alban Berg; choice (D) is incorrect. "The Liberty Bell" is a march composed by John Phillip Sousa; choice (E) is incorrect.

7. **(C)** William Blake (1757-1827) has been described as "the first clear voice of romanticism" and perhaps his greatest work was *Songs of Innocence and Experience* (C), in which many of the characteristics of romantic poetry can be seen: the poetry expresses the poet's personal feelings, not the actions of other men; spontaneity and freedom; natural scenes and pictures of flora and fauna. Pope's (A) "hero-comical" poem from the seventeenth century demonstrates none of the above. *The Social Contract* (B) is a sociological and philosophical essay. *Romeo and Juliet* (E), while commonly understood to be a romance between two teenagers, is not "romantic," and predates romanticism by 200 years. Dreiser's novel (D) belongs to the American realist period.

8. **(A)** The titles presented here, of course, are mostly in French (except for (D) which is about a French historical figure) – the language of Albert Camus, the father of existentialism. Camus' *L'Etranger (The Stranger)* – the story of an expatriate Frenchman in Algeria – presents many of the precepts of existentialism: an emphasis on existence rather than essence, and the inadequacy of human reason to explain the enigma of the universe. *Morte D'Arthur* (B) was written in English by Tennyson; *Candide* (C) and *Le Misanthrope* (E) – a comedy of the 1700s, by Moliere. While the latter title might indicate existential estrangement, the work appears 200 years before the literary movement. *Saint Joan* (D), a dramatic tragedy by G. B. Shaw, is biographical.

9.   **(D)**   All of the writings listed here describe life on an American frontier – but only *My Antonia* deals with frontier life in the Midwest during the nineteenth century – the rough weather, the difficulties of farm life, and the blossoming of romance in harsh conditions. Cooper's famous work (A), while written during that century, refers to upstate New York during the eighteenth century. William Byrd's work (B) deals with defining the border between Virginia and North Carolina during the late eighteenth century. Bradford's diary (C) is a Pilgrim document written in colonial Massachusetts, and Twain's classic (E), while it tangentially involves Illinois and the shores of Iowa on the Mississippi River, does not deal with the Midwest per se.

10.   **(C)**   Salinger's work is recognized as a coming of age novel in which his main character, Holden Caulfield, is an "antihero" – a character whose appeal is that his flaws are dominant. *Tom Sawyer* (A) has always been viewed by critics as a children's novel, because Tom can be seen as the "All-American Boy," unlike Huck Finn, Twain's later, more complicated creation. Dickens' work (B) does not deal with coming of age. Dreiser's *Sister Carrie* (E), on the other hand, does concern itself with changes in the protagonist through time, but Carrie is more a classic heroine in her rigid self-reliance and conquest over adversity. Fitzgerald (D) creates a number of interesting figures – some, like Gatsby, who have antiheroic qualities – but all have basically "come of age" before the summer in which the story takes place.

11.   **(B)**   Whitman's poem is one of four elegies, entitled "memories of President Lincoln," which were made part of drum taps after Lincoln's death in 1864. Whitman, who volunteered as a male nurse in Washington during the Civil War – like so many Americans – mourned greatly for the president. The Englishman Gray's "Elegy" (A) is of a much earlier vintage (late 1700s). Christina Rossetti's "After Death" (C) is not an elegy, nor is Allen Ginsburg's "Howl" (D). Wordsworth's work (E) deals with the death of Sir George Beaumont, the poet's patron.

12.   **(D)**   The architect of the building illustrated was intent on avoiding traditional building forms in the search for a new, expressive use of space. The design pictured, therefore, carefully avoids all reminders of the symmetrical, balanced floor plans of classical and Renaissance architecture. It also dispenses with a conventional structural framework and with the geometric forms and angles of traditional buildings. Instead, it exploits fully the potential of a new material – in this case, poured concrete – to create

dynamic, curving forms whose arcs and spirals echo both the shape of growing organisms and the motion of wind and water.

13.   **(D)**   Answer choices (A), (B), and (E) each contain images of animals which are based to some degree on naturalistic observation. In each case, however, the animals are presented either as black-and-white line drawings or as schematic, two-dimensional renderings, with no attempt to model the forms of the animals; and in each case, the imagery functions in either a narrative or magical context and does not intend to explore anatomy. Answer choice (C) presents a basically realistic, well-modelled animal, based on naturalistic observation and with close attention to detail, but the addition of the wings adds a fantastic touch and the animal as a whole is elegantly designed and positioned to act as the functional handle of a jar. Only answer choice (D) explores the expressive forms of the animal's musculature, here conveying a sense of untamed emotion and animal energy through the tensed, swelling muscles of the crouched jaguar.

14.   **(A)**   Answer choices (B) and (E) each present somewhat schematic representations of animals, the first in order to document the character and activities of an Egyptian noble, and the second to fulfill a magical, ritual function. The animal in answer choice (C) exists solely as a decorative detail on a purely functional object. Answer choice (D) shows animal behavior which might be called analogous to human behavior – i.e., the violence of the strong over the weak – but the image itself does not intend to comment directly on human life. Only answer choice (A) uses animal imagery to directly caricature human behavior. In this case, the Japanese scroll employs monkeys, frogs, hares, and foxes to mimic Buddhist religious practices.

15.   **(E)**   Answer choice (E) presents animal images with a high degree of naturalism in a sophisticated, abstract, almost "modern" style. The artist, however, despite his naturalism, was not concerned with perspective or with conventional pictorial space, and concentrated solely on the overlapping images of the animals, which have no narrative function. He has included a print of his own hands, possibly to indicate his magical control over the animals through these images of them. These paintings were executed on the walls of a cave in what appears to be a sacred precinct, and seem to function as magical images to ensure success in the hunt.

16.   **(C)**   The example pictured, by the English painter William Hogarth, satirizes eighteenth-century English life in a comic way. In telling the

story of the human characters illustrated in the work, the picture uses a wealth of carefully chosen detail which the viewer is to "read" in a novelistic manner. The period details, therefore (as of dress, architecture, furnishings, etc.), and the attitudes and actions of the figures (the exasperated look, for instance, of the servant on the left) tell us that this is a human comedy set in the eighteenth century. Of the other answer choices, (A), (B), and (D), would be both historically anachronistic and weightier in subject matter. Answer choice (E) would fall roughly within the correct period, but it, too, would likely present a more dramatic content.

17.   **(A)**   Choice (A) is the only correct scanned line. It contains five iambic feet and is an example of iambic pentameter. The other examples have incorrectly marked accents and feet.

18.   **(B)**   This passage comes from the Greek play *Medea* by Euripides. Medea, a woman who is being cast aside so her husband, Jason, can marry a princess, kills their two sons in retaliation. This passage shows Jason lamenting over the boys' deaths and invoking the gods to punish his ex-wife.

19.   **(C)**   In the passage Jason mourns that Medea killed the boys "to prevent me from/Touching their bodies or giving them burial." In Greek society, the dead were honored by elaborate burial rites and ceremonies. To be buried without ceremony was considered to be dishonorable to the dead, especially when they were related to great warriors, such as Jason.

20.   **(E)**   An oxymoron is an apparent contradiction in terms, such as "jumbo shrimp," "cruel kindness," or (as some would say) "military intelligence." Passage (E) contains an oxymoron because it mentions flames which give "No light, but rather darkness." Choice (E) is the correct answer.

21.   **(B)**   Assonance is the repetition of vowel sounds in a single line of poetry. Passage (B) contains three examples of assonance: the words "Rocks" and "bogs," the words "caves," "lakes," and "shades," and the words "fens" and "dens." Thus, passage (B) is the correct answer.

22.   **(A)**   Iambic pentameter refers to the meter, or rhythm, of a line of poetry composed of five feet, each of which is an iamb, having one unstressed syllable followed by a stressed syllable. A line of poetry written in iambic pentameter is ten syllables long. Passage (A) contains two lines

of poetry written in iambic pentameter. When read aloud, the unstressed-stressed pattern emerges: "For SHADE to SHADE will COME too DROWsiLY, / And DROWN the WAKEful ANGuish OF the SOUL." Thus, choice (A) is the correct answer.

23. **(D)** is the correct answer. Zora Neale Hurston and Marita Bonner won awards and recognition for their plays in the 1920s. (A) Wilson and Hansberry are of different generations; Wilson is a contemporary playwright and Hansberry wrote her plays between 1961 and 1964. (B) Gordone and Baraka were best known in the 1970s. Ed Bullins was a novelist/poet who came to prominence in the late 1960s, too late for this question. Sonia Sanchez is a contemporary poet and is also too late to be considered as a correct answer for this question. O'Neill and Odets (E) are not African-American playwrights.

24. **(E)** is the correct answer. A well-made play is characterized by (A) tight and logical construction, (B) a plot based on a withheld secret, (C) misplaced letters or documents, and (D) obligatory scene. (E) Episodic structure is antithetical and characterized by little more than a series of incidents and has little logical arrangement; therefore, (E) is the exception to the well-made play and is the best answer.

25. **(A)** Solomon R. Guggenheim Museum, New York. The (B) East Wing of the National Gallery of Art in Washington, D.C. was designed by I. M. Pei. O. M. Ungers designed the (C) Museum of Architecture in Frankfurt-am-Main. Richard Meier was the architect of the (D) High Museum of Art in Atlanta.

26. **(B)** To brush one foot against the floor is glissade. Pas de chat is a quick "cat-like" step (A), feet positioned in front of one another with a step separating them and legs turned out is fourth position crossed (C), body weight shifted incorrectly is improper balance (D), and a pointed foot and extended leg moving in a circular motion is a demi-rond de jambe (E).

27. **(D)** Weight and body shifted incorrectly is improper balance. Choices pas de chat (A), glissade (B), fourth position crossed (C), and demi-rond de jambe (E) are specific ballet movements.

28. **(C)** One foot in front of the other with a step separating them describes fourth position crossed. Pas de chat (A) and glissade (B) are

steps in motion, improper balance is incorrect body alignment caused by uneven weight distribution (D), and demi-rond de jambe is a circular foot motion (E).

29.   **(B)** The harpsichord is the predecessor of the piano, also called a spinet. The strings of the harpsichord were plucked with quills; this limited dynamics and tone colors. The piano was called the piano forte because it could play dynamics based on the performer's force. The harpsichord was widely used during the baroque period; choice (B) is correct. The lute is similar to the guitar; choice (A) is incorrect. The synthesizer is an electronic keyboard using analog and/or digital technology to produce sound; choice (C) is incorrect. The harp is a stringed instrument that is plucked with the fingers; choice (D) is incorrect. The xylophone is a percussion instrument which is struck with a mallet; choice (E) is incorrect.

30.   **(B)** An art song, or "lieder," is a poem set to music, for solo voice and piano; choice (B) is correct. A madrigal is verse set to music for two or more voices, which often follows a prescribed form; choice (A) is incorrect. An opera is a theatrical drama which is sung, often with instrumental accompaniment; choice (C) is incorrect. An aria is a solo for voice with accompaniment, occurring during a longer form such as an opera; choice (D) is incorrect. A symphony is a three or four movement work for orchestra; choice (E) is incorrect.

31.   **(B)** A tenor is a high male voice; choice (B) is correct. The range of voices is classified from high to low; that is, soprano, alto, tenor, baritone, bass. A soprano is a high female voice; choice (A) is incorrect. A bass is the lowest male voice; choice (C) is incorrect. A baritone has a range between the tenor and the bass; choice (D) is incorrect. An alto is a medium female voice; choice (E) is incorrect.

32.   **(C)** W. B. Yeats is the correct answer. The famous Irish poet and essayist of the early twentieth century is always remembered for his devotion to Irish nationalism – most specifically in his volumes of collected poems such as "In the Seven Woods" and "The Green Helmet and Other Poems." James Joyce (A) is known for his depiction of Irish life, and dramatist G. B. Shaw (D) is generally regarded more in a strictly literary and not political tradition. The other two choices – Donleavy (B) and O'Hara (E) – are modern American writers, whose literary interests tend more to romance and mystery than Irish nationalism and unification.

33. **(C)** Charles Darwin's *Origin of Species* helped shape Victorian English thought as well as considerations of natural history throughout the world. Tracing the origin of man from mammals, and species before them, was a monumental scientific effort and a shock so great to the religious community that many still attempt to deny Darwin's Theory of Evolution. Tennyson (A) referred to Darwin's theory of evolution in some of his major poems. English scientist and essayist Huxley (E) was a proponent of Darwin's theories. Dr. Johnson's (B) degree was not in science; his work as an essayist, commentator, and lexicographer remains an enormous contribution to arts and letters. Browning's (D) wonderful poetic monologues, while written during the Victorian Age, in no way represent a suitable answer to the question.

34. **(E)** *The Scarlet Letter.* While much writing is autobiographical, some works are known more than others for serving particular personal purposes. Hawthorne's work is among them. Hathorne, a descendant of Judge Hathorne of Salem Witch Trial fame, believed that a curse on male members of his family was still a matter of personal concern during his life in the early 1800s. He changed the spelling of his name and wrote *The Scarlet Letter,* in which Puritan justice is seen as harsh, overreactive, and heartless. In this and other ways, he hoped to atone for the cruelty of his ancestors. Irving (A) was an entertaining historian with no such worries. Melville (B) and Cooper (D) were great tale tellers, and Charles Brockden Brown's (C) main claim to fame is as the first American novelist.

35. **(B)** Lawrence's *Sons and Lovers* shocked an entire generation of critics when it was published in the early 1900s. Its passionate prose and erotic evocations will still shock the more innocent contemporary reader. Kafka's novel (A) about a man who changes into a moth is dense with philosophy. Conrad's great work (D) is vivid in its natural descriptions, but hardly a novel to be "banned in Boston." Jack Finney's (C) modern novel of dimensional travel is also tame by any comparison, as most certainly is Edith Wharton's (E).

36. **(C)** Thoreau's *Walden* most clearly engages his friend Emerson's precepts of rugged individualism which the minister set down in his essay "Self Reliance." Thoreau writes about his month-long sojourn living off the land in a cabin near Walden Pond in Massachusetts. Hawthorne's work (A), while written at about the same time, demonstrates few of these concerns. Crane's works (B) and (E) are brilliant descriptions of an accident and warfare, and great stories – as is Cooper's (D) – but none are

based in transcendentalist theory – a reliance on individual and conscience – and expressed powerfully through prose.

37.   **(A)**   Answer choices (C), (D), and (E) illustrate buildings which employ arching, curving, cylindrical, and circular forms, often in elaborate, complex combinations, and suggest the play of emotion, fantasy, or romance, but do not seem founded on any general cultural need for logic and order. Choice (B) shows a modern building whose design certainly proceeds from logical precepts, but, of the principles offered in the answer choices, technological precision seems to best characterize this example. Example (A), however, the famous fifth century B. C. Parthenon in Athens, presents a building whose design reflects perfectly the logical philosophies which defined Classical Greek culture. The Parthenon's architects were careful to construct a building of simple, refined forms, methodically repeated according to calculated ratios of size and space. The result is an effect of perfect balance and order which would be undermined by altering any one of the building's essential components.

38.   **(D)**   Choices (A) and (B) illustrate structures whose severe, regularized forms seem to deny the possibility of humor and whimsy. Choice (C), a Gothic cathedral interior, uses soaring arches and strong vertical thrust to express spirituality and religious fervor, while choice (E), an Italian baroque church exterior, conveys a sense of intellectual, nervous agitation through a contrast of convex and concave curves and the use of an overabundance of ornamental detail. Only choice (D), a nineteenth-century English pleasure pavilion, combines a fanciful assortment of playful, whimsical shapes – as in the "Islamic" domes and minarets – to create an effect of exotic fantasy and underscore its function as a place of recreation.

39.   **(B)**   Alone among the five answer choices, example (B) pares its structural forms to an absolute minimum, stressing the industrial materials – the steel of its framework and its extensive window glass – to achieve an effect of absolute structural logic and clarity. This "international style" architecture typifies the skyscraper buildings in large cities throughout the industrial world and reflects the high cultural value placed on industrial and commercial efficiency in the modern urbanized society.

40.   **(B)**   In the example, the 1939 "Falling Water" house by the American architect Frank Lloyd Wright, the horizontal forms which project dramatically over the small waterfall do not emphasize the building's struc-

tural framework but, rather, deny the presence of a structural support altogether and seem almost to defy gravity. All of the other observations offered in the answer choices are valid. Consistent with Wright's conception of an "organic" architecture, the cantilevered forms echo the horizontal axis of the waterfall's rock shelf, and, even though they are rigidly cubic in form, help to merge the house with its setting. This bold construction was only possible to the architect through the use of such modern, industrial-strength building materials as poured, pre-stressed concrete, whose great strength and flexibility made possible the long projecting forms supported at one end only.

41.   **(D)**   The building pictured in the example, an eleventh-century Norman church in the north of France, shows the typically massive masonry construction of these early Romanesque churches. These buildings, which did not yet have the advantage of Gothic arches and flying buttresses, relied for strength and stability on thick, blank walls which were pierced only by small window openings. Stone masonry bonded by mortar was, therefore, the architects' fundamental material. Oak timbers were probably used here also, although they were likely restricted to roof and ceiling framing and to construction scaffolds. All of the other materials listed in the answer choices are industrial-age materials which were unavailable to the medieval architect.

42.   **(B)**   The rose has, for centuries, been a symbol of virginal love and beauty. By calling the rose "sick," the poet is implying that somehow this virginal beauty has been lost. This is due to, as the poet states, an "invisible worm," that has found the rose's "bed/Of crimson joy." The loss of virginity has been equated with "sickness," and the sex act causing the loss is alluded to in terms of "worms" and "beds of crimson joy."

43.   **(D)**   Because of the "worm," the "rose" is "sick"; choice (D) is the best answer because it addresses the archetypical symbol of the rose as virginal love and beauty. Since the rose is "sick," this beauty is gone. Some of the other choices may adequately answer the question, but not as well as (D).

44.   **(B)**   Personification means an object or emotion has been made into a person with human attributes – here the frost is seen beheading as if in battle as a show of power. Easily detected, the personified word is frequently capitalized. Alliteration (A) is a device that repeats the initial consonants (or vowels) as in "crowing cocks" or "weeping widows." Ono-

matopoeia (C) uses verbs that sound like the action, as in ooze or hiss or swish. Assonance repeats the vowel sounds in a line or sentence. In fact, lines 6-8 demonstrate assonance in the words "unmoved," "another," and "approving," but for the technique in line 3 (D) is incorrect. Conceit (E) is a term connected with the metaphysical poets like John Donne where outrageous comparisons are made between unlike objects – the most famous is Donne's use of a drawing compass to link two people saying good-bye. Here frost is referred to as a killer of flowers, not compared to a weed-whacker. Study hint: find a glossary in the back of a poetry anthology and learn these figures of speech.

45. **(C)** The frost has already been described as a killer beheading the flowers in line 3; it is a clear connection to see frost as blonde or icy white and the whole point of the poem is the killing power as of an assassin. Go through each of the possible suggestions and analyze the closest meaning of the line: fate (A) is part of the poem's *interpretation* but not the meaning of this particular line; disease (B) is not mentioned, rather, random acts of violence; the sun (D) follows the act of frost and is not involved in the killing; it is "unmoved." An approving god (E) watches but is not the assassin here. (C) is the best possible answer.

46. **(B)** Although the other choices have something to do with the meaning of the poem, the "best," meaning the central or core description of what the poem is about, is that death comes to everyone; it cannot be planned for nor avoided. Certainly a cruelty is indicated in the frost's action but that is not (A) God's cruelty. God is shown not to be indifferent, but in fact approving, so (C) is incorrect. The flowers being happy (D) suggests that we put human experience into plants, but this is not the poem's central theme, nor is the fact that we know winter comes each year, so (E) is likewise an idea that is in the poem but is not the central point.

47. **(B)** Note that what is required here is both a knowledge of drama as well as an awareness of qualifying terms in both the question stem and answer. You are asked what poetic drama is "best" described as, while (A) asks for a value judgment; (B) is a full description incorporating both the fact that poetic drama is comprised of poetry and performance. (C) demonstrates value judgment; (D) is too limiting; so, too, is (E).

48. **(D)** Bertolt Brecht described his work as (D) epic drama, not (B) melodrama. It was based on (A) John Gay's *The Beggar's Opera*, but this

is not the most important fact. The major characteristic of the *Three Penny Opera* is that Brecht's adaptation of it corresponds with his view of what drama should be. Brecht was concerned about defamiliarizing his audience with what they felt they knew. He thought that theaters should make things strange through (E) historification, the use of material drawn from other times and places, which allowed the audience to view the performance in a detached manner. This method of alienating the audience was the most important criterion for the development of an "epic" (meaning narrative, or non-dramatic) work. Since drama is antithetical to comedy, (C) should be eliminated immediately.

49.   **(A)**   Existentialism is a philosophy that arose in France and Germany in the late nineteenth century, which claims that "existence precedes essence" or that what one becomes is a matter of choice and not something usually called "human nature" or "essence." Essentialism (B) is thus incorrect because it is the opposite of existentialism. Pragmatism (C) is a distinctively American philosophy that the worth of an idea is its "cash value" or power to solve a problem. Marxism (D) depends on the supposition that humans have an essence or nature, as does Platonism (E). Platonists are clear examples of essentialist.

50.   **(E)**   The ancient Greeks, upon viewing the massive masonry blocks used in much Mycenean construction, believed that they could only have been placed by giants; thus they are referred to as "cyclopean" after the giant Cyclopes of Greek mythology. Although (A) ancient Egyptian, (B) Mesopotamian, (C) Aztec, and (D) Roman methods of construction often included the use of very large, heavy stone blocks, the term "cyclopean" is never used to identify them.

51.   **(A)**   The *cogito* resolves Descartes' methodological doubt and establishes a firm foundation for knowledge. He does not question the basis of personal identity (B) in the way that, say, Locke does. Descartes uses a separate argument to establish the existence of God (D). He then uses his proof of God's existence to put metaphysics (C) and mathematics (E) on firm foundations. The *cogito* is the foundation for his epistemology.

52.   **(C)**   Through-composed form is represented by ABCDE. This is because new music is created for each verse; choice (C) is correct. AB is binary form that starts in the tonic key and may modulate before the end. This is considered an open structure; choice (A) is incorrect. ABA is ternary form in which both A sections are in the tonic and the B section modulates and contains new material; choice (B) is incorrect. ABACA is a

rondo form that contains multisections. These utilize modulations with new material and return to the tonic; choice (D) is incorrect. A form of A would only contain one musical idea; choice (E) is incorrect.

53. **(A)** Gregorian chant is often referred to as plainchant. Plainchant is monophonic vocal music, which was primarily used in church; choice (A) is correct. A motet is a polyphonic vocal composition used in church music for two or more voices; choice (B) is incorrect. A canon is imitated polyphonic vocal composition consisting of two or more voices; choice (C) is incorrect. An aria is a vocal solo with accompaniment found in a larger composition; choice (D) is incorrect. A fugue is imitative polyphony with variations; choice (E) is incorrect.

54. **(B)** Charles Ives mastered the technique of weaving bits of patriotic melodies within his compositions; choice (B) is correct. Sousa popularized patriotic marches; choice (A) is incorrect. Bernstein worked in many genres using classical and jazz elements; choice (C) is incorrect. Stravinsky explored primitivism and tonalities; choice (D) is incorrect. Franz Joseph Haydn was a composer of the classical period; choice (E) is incorrect.

55. **(A)** *Tristram Shandy* was written by Laurence Sterne, a parish clergyman and small landowner. His sometimes bawdy, often hilarious novel demonstrated an extraordinary playfulness with the language, and with concepts of space and time in storytelling. Cervantes' (B) work was amusing, but the gentleman author was Spanish. *Candy* (C) is an American bawdy novel of the 1960s not to be confused with the French novel *Candide*. *Catch-22* (D) is at least as funny as the others, but is of the same vintage as the previous novel; and (E), though possessed an amusing title, is a Shakespearean song.

56. **(B)** Shakespeare's *Macbeth* deals with the powerful influence of guilt and conscience after the fact of an illicit deed. Lady Macbeth sleepwalks and tries to wash the imagined blood of King Duncan off of her hands, and Macbeth himself sees the ghost of the bloodied Banquo during a public celebration, thereby providing one more clue to the populace that he and his wife were responsible of the death of the rightful king. *Julius Caesar* (A) deals with many political themes including ambition – but conscience does not seem prominent. *Hamlet* (C) demonstrates the restraining power of conscience – even in the face of seeking revenge for a

vile act. The fantasy (D) and the comedy (E) are artful treatments of happier themes.

57. **(D)** Hawthorne's famous work is well known for its personification of the fading fortunes of the Pyncheon family in the famous seven gabled structure still to be visited in Salem, Massachusetts. The imploding and collapse of the structure at the end of the novel represents the end of the family that had been cursed during the witchcraft trials 150 years before. (A) of course, is a delightful children's book. (B), by Dos Passos, is a twentieth century description of the banking family. William Carlos Williams wrote the brief poem (C); and (E) was the first piece of fiction published by Thomas Wolfe, but does not deal with the subject in question.

58. **(C)** The 1940 book deals with a hanging in the fictional Western town of Bridger's Wells. While Realism was a nineteenth-century movement, Clark employs Realistic techniques – accurate usage of concrete details to raise interest or create an effect – in relating his compelling story. Twain's famous story (A) had realistic elements in it, but was written during the nineteenth century – though only in one section can he be said to deal with the Wild West. Crane's work (B) was realistic and was about the Wild West, but was a short story also written in the nineteenth century. Bierce's tale (D) – though again in a similar tradition, and while it also deals with a hanging – also takes place during the Civil War.

59. **(C)** Walt Whitman's poetry, including "Song of Myself" and "The Sleepers," presented American critics with a new American voice: one not bounded by the constraints of rhyme schemes and meter. His long listing of examples of American characters and prototypes are so detailed that they provide us with an accurate picture of the mid-nineteenth century nation of Whitman's day. The Englishman Pope (A) does not qualify for reason of nationality alone. Clemens (B) is the novelist Mark Twain's real name. Emily Dickinson (D) is known for short, rhyming verse, and Anne Bradstreet (E) – perhaps our first American poet – wrote in traditional rhyme schemes and meter.

60. **(C)** The second century Chinese bronze horse shown in the example effectively exploits the unexpected contrast between the huge massive animal and its graceful, almost delicate pose and action. The horse is elegantly poised on one rear hoof and seems to be flying or swimming through the air, rather than merely trotting. It therefore expresses lightness

and motion, not massiveness and stability, and completely denies any suggestion of physical decay. Additionally, although the horse in Chinese art was a symbol of majestic power, this sculpture does not allude in any specific way to either military prowess or moral fortitude.

61.   **(E)**   This city view by the French Impressionist Camille Pissarro is one of many in which the artist painted the scenes he saw beneath his second- or third-story Paris hotel windows; the correct answer is (E). The tilted perspective, with diagonal street axes and no horizon line, may owe a debt to photography, to Japanese prints, or to the example of his Impressionist peers. The resulting composition lacks not only a central focal point, but any single focal point at all; likewise, the only architecture visible does not dominate the scene, but, rather, acts as incidental local detail. The anonymous figures in the crowds below the artist's window share this lack of focus: they are busy in normal daily activity, without the least suggestion of drama. Finally, the idea that this scene was recorded from the window of a train lacks evidence: the scene is distinctly urban, not rural, and it is unlikely that a train would either pass through the crowded centers of a city or that it would be elevated to this height.

62.   **(C)**   In the work pictured, the American sculptor David Smith used power tools to cut, weld, and polish industrial-strength steel to create an ensemble in which the heavy, cubic forms balance in arrested motion. The sculptor obviously neither modelled the materials with his hands nor poured them into a mold: these forms have a rigid, machinelike, technological perfection to them and lack any such irregularities as those resulting from the molding action of human fingers. This same cubic perfection, and the gleaming, reflective surfaces, refute the idea of chisel work as well. And, finally, the erroneous suggestion that the artist merely joined ready-made industrial forms as he found them stems from this same sense of rigid, cubic perfection in the work's individual components.

63.   **(A)**   The seventeenth century Japanese ink-on-paper scroll painting shown in the example relies almost exclusively on the qualities of line to convey the graceful forms of two leaping deer. In this painting, called *Deer and Calligraphy,* both the animals and the scripted characters share the same quality of fluid, rhythmic, spontaneous "writing." Gradations of tone are unimportant here, since the images are defined by black line on white, and volume, too, is absent, since these forms show no shading or modulation of tone. Perspective is not an issue here since this drawing does not attempt to reproduce a third dimension.

64. **(D)** The arch, whether rounded or pointed, is completely absent from the building pictured in the example, even though the alternating use of windows with rounded pediments in the lower story seems to suggest the presence of arches. Otherwise, all of the other features listed in the answer choices do help regularize the design of this seventeenth-century English Renaissance structure. The uniform second-story windows assert a regularity over the alternating window designs below them; they also emphasize a strong horizontal thrust across the building's facade, which is repeated in the balustrade at roof-level. The nearly flush front surface of the building is broken only by the window openings and by the engaged columns at the building's center and the pilasters at the outer corners. Both of these features project just enough to establish a vertical contrast to the horizontal facade, but not enough to create a system of alternating solids and voids.

65. **(D)** You may not have come across this poem by William Blake so you need to look at the language and the topic. Blake often writes about the ugliness and horror of the Industrial Revolution – you may know "Tiger Tiger" – the topic of child labor gives you an immediate clue. Shakespeare (A), Milton (B), and Chaucer (C) may be familiar, so you can see the difference in their rhyme schemes and language. This rhyme and meter suggest a more modern style than the older writers. Hardy (E) often uses a similar simple rhyme and rhythm but his topics were more of fate and destiny, war and lost loves. By such a process of elimination, you will come to (D) as the correct answer.

66. **(A)** The word is cleverly used because it does suggest the child's weeping but the meaning of the line carries on from the opening line when he was sold before he could clearly say the chimney sweeper's cry for business: "Sweep! Sweep!" – not because of neglect (B), but because he is so young he still lisps on the "s" sound. The other suggestions all deal with emotions conjured up by the child's plight – of course he is upset at being sold (C); "the your" pronoun does make for guilt (D) but you are looking for the reason the poet chose this word, not the "message" of the poem. Of course he hates cleaning chimneys (E), but analyze the word's usage in the line itself and the best answer is (A).

67. **(C)** The epic is long and tells of heroes engaged in battles and actions involving valor. Look at the rhyme scheme and analyze. There are no rhyming couplets (A), epics are not all written in Latin (B), nor by Virgil (D), and although death (E) is usually featured, epics are not just about death.

68.   **(E)** If you do not know *Paradise Lost* look at the context – the garden idea, the noble couple made in God's image. Dante would be describing Hell so (A) is incorrect. Virgil (B) deals with family and honor in Latinate verse; *The Iliad* (C) deals with battles and the Greek gods; and *The Arabian Nights* (D) tells fantastic stories, so none of these apply.

69.   **(D)** The keyword here is viewpoint – not the one writing the poem or telling the main story. Even if you do not know *Paradise Lost,* you will no doubt have heard of the fiend – place that fiend in a garden and the answer is Satan; not Faust (A) which is another story; not God (B) – the fiend is watching God's creation; not Scheherazade (C) who tells of magical things not people in a garden; and not Dante (E) who watches fiends in hell – he is not a fiend himself.

70.   **(C)** The situation in the Garden is idyllic; the couple is naked – all such signs point to before the Fall. The references to God and "the image of their maker" eliminate both (A) and (B); the fiend is not a Homeric character, so (D) is incorrect; as stated, the idyllic setting indicates that this is before the Fall, so (E) is also incorrect.

71.   **(E)** The last three lines need to be carefully equated with each of the options: equality is not possible if she sees God in the man (A); women are not just made for beauty but softness and grace (B); and (C) and (D) tell only half the meaning of the lines.

72.   **(A)** is the correct answer. (B) *Oedipus* is also a play about a man who kills his father and blinds himself. In *The Wild Duck* Gregers returns home to find that Gina, who was once a maid in his family, is now married to Hjalmar. Gregers believe that Gina was impregnated by his father, Old Werle, who is slowly losing his eyesight. Gregers believes that Gina and Hjalmar's marriage is based on a lie. Old Werle's diminished eyesight may be read symbolically, but it does not hold the same significance as Oedipus' blinding. The eyesight motif joins *The Wild Duck* and *Oedipus* and makes it easier to eliminate the other three answer choices. Both Sophocles and Euripides wrote plays they titled *Electra;* Sophocles also wrote *Antigone* and Euripides' *Andromache.* Basically, these questions are meant to confuse; therefore, (C), (D), and (E) should be eliminated immediately.

73.   **(C)** is the correct answer. It is much more specific. Orgon is rich, middle class, and middle-aged. He is duped by Tartuffe, who assumes a

mask of religious piety. This question is testing your ability to recognize the situation of each play. For example, (A) is too vague, as the downfall of a king is a frequent theme in plays. (B) is also vague, as are (D) and (E).

74. **(B)** A multi-storied Roman apartment block, the type which existed in large numbers in urban areas of the Roman Empire. A Greek public meeting square (A) is called an *agora;* the western portion of a Carolingian church (C) is referred to as a *westwerk.* A Greek cross-plan (D) is that of a centrally planned church whose four arms are all of equal length. A vertical groove on the surface of a column (E) is called a *flute.*

75. **(A)** Berkeley held, in his famous dictum, that to be is to be perceived, or that only ideas are real. Hence, the view expressed is known as (A) idealism. Pragmatism (B) is the view that ideas which work should be believed true. Empiricism (C) and rationalism (D) are broad tendencies to answer a question about the source of knowledge either as in experience or in the mind itself. Phenomenology (E) is a position in metaphysics that takes a special view of experience. Berkeley is perhaps the clearest advocate of idealism in the history of philosophy.

Section 2

76. **(A)** Charlie Parker was nicknamed "Bird" due to his rapid alto saxophone Bebop figures. Choice (A) is correct. John Coltrane was a master of the tenor and soprano saxophone; choice (B) is incorrect. Dizzy Gillespie was a master of the trumpet; choice (C) is incorrect. Paul Desmond was the alto saxophonist in the Dave Brubeck Quartet, which played classical jazz styles; choice (D) is incorrect. Stan Getz was a tenor saxophonist of the "cool" jazz style; choice (E) is incorrect.

77. **(C)** John Coltrane made a lasting impact on the jazz scene with his album "Giant Steps." Choice (C) is correct. Charlie Parker played alto, not tenor saxophone, and performed such works as "Ko-ko" and "YardBird Suite"; choice (A) is incorrect. Stan Getz is the tenor saxophone player famous for his work on "The Girl from Ipanema"; choice (B) is incorrect. Coleman Hawkins is considered the father of jazz tenor saxophone; choice (D) is incorrect. Ornette Coleman experimented with "free jazz" on the alto saxophone; choice (E) is incorrect.

78.   **(B)** "Rodeo" is the result of a collaboration between Aaron Copland and Agnes de Mille. It incorporated music with dance; choice (B) is correct. "West Side Story" is a musical by Leonard Bernstein. It is a modern-day version of "Romeo and Juliet"; choice (A) is incorrect. "Porgy and Bess" is an opera with music by George Gershwin, portraying the struggles of black Americans in the South; choice (C) is incorrect. "The Phantom of the Opera" is a novel by Gaston LeRoux that has been adapted for film, stage, and most recently, a Broadway musical. Choice (D) is incorrect. "Salome" was a composition of Strauss; choice (E) is incorrect.

79.   **(D)** *Tom Jones,* Henry Fielding's (1707-1754) wonderful and raucous novel, is the only one here both written in and about the eighteenth century. Tom's travels take him from the seat of manorial propriety to the very bawdiest of tumbletown inns. Known for its wanton characterization and surprising turns of plot, it is considered by many to be one of the most picturesque of the picaresque novels (defined as the "life story of a rascal of low degree... consisting of a series of thrilling incidents"). Dickens' work (A) is about England in the following century, as are Bronte's *Jane Eyre* (C) and George Eliot's *Silas Marner* (E). *Moby Dick* (B) is an American work by Melville.

80.   **(D)** Oscar Wilde's famous work is in the well-known tradition of the Decadents – a group of writers in the late nineteenth and early twentieth century in France, England, and America. One of their major precepts was that the finest beauty was that of dying or deteriorating things. Thus, Dorian – a character of low virtues – ages grotesquely and supernaturally on a canvas, while the actual person seems to be forever young. The Mariner (A) may be aging, but the lengthy romantic poem is not in the Decadent tradition, nor written at that time. Fielding's work (C) may be about decadence, but was written 100 years earlier than the movement. The same might be said about Lawrence's mid-twentieth century work (B), and Joyce's *Dubliners* (E), which is even less a possibility.

81.   **(A)** Ruskin in *Modern Painters* actually introduced the phrase "pathetic fallacy" to denote a tendency of some poets and writers to credit nature with the emotions of human beings – as in the phrase, "the cruel, crawling foam." Nowadays it has come to mean writing that is false in its emotionalism – even if the topic considered is not nature. Emerson's work (B) is about the importance and reality of the natural world. Shakespeare's comedy (C) has nothing whatsoever to do with the topic, except that its plot does involve deception and falseness. Lodge's 1590 work (D) is considered a pastoral romance – in that it sets forth a romance in a beautiful

natural setting. Johnson's *Dictionary* (E) could not have listed the term, as it was published over 50 years before Ruskin invented it.

82.   **(E)** Dickens' *David Copperfield* is one of his many works that resent an opposing argument to utilitarianism – the powerful argument from the former century that defined utility in government and society as "the greatest happiness for the greatest number." The theory was proposed in the eighteenth century by Jeremy Bentham, and was modified and promoted in the nineteenth by James Mill and his son John Stuart Mill. Dickens' England is a place where misery counts – even for a statistical minority of orphans, waifs, and honest, if impoverished, men and women of the working class. Elliot's *Middlemarch* world (A) is the antithesis – as is James' *Washington Square* (D). Dreiser (B) does write about the seedier side of nineteenth century American life, but does not seem to "take sides" as far as the economic system itself is concerned. *Billy Budd* (C), of course, is an adventure novel by Melville.

83.   **(D)** While all of the writers suggested might claim Celtic origins, James Macpherson, the eighteenth-century composer of the poems "Fingal" (1762) and "Temora" (1763) is the most likely candidate. Macpherson invented, recorded, and reinterpreted Gaelic pieces preserved in the Scottish Highlands and published translations of the great early Celtic poet Ossian. His works, along with those of Thomas Gray, influenced many minor poets of the late eighteenth century. Joyce (A) and Yeats (E) were Irishmen of the twentieth century. O'Hara (B) and Donleavy (C) are contemporary American writers.

84.   **(D)** The late eighteenth-century neoclassical painting shown in the example illustrates an episode from ancient Roman legend and attempts to simulate the static, balanced, monumental character of much classical relief sculpture. The men in the main figure group, therefore, are represented in statuesque, absolutely motionless poses, and the correct answer choice here is (D). The compositional devices listed in all of the other answer choices are important to the painting. The figures stand within a shallow pictorial space, which is marked off by the arches in the background; these arches also serve to focus the man in the center. This shallow space, however, is modified somewhat by the checkerboard floor, which creates a slight perspective recession into the background and makes the figures' space seem logical and convincing. The strong highlighting on the foreground figures accentuates their static, sculptural quality, even as it pulls them to the absolute front of the picture. The intersecting lines of arms and swords establish the central focal point of the composition.

85.   **(A)** This question asks you to consider both geographical proximity and some general characteristics of Eastern architecture in order to logically determine who would have the most direct influence on Japanese style. Of the answer choices, Greece and Nigeria fall well outside the Asian sphere both in distance and in building styles, while Easter Island, a Pacific site, is not known for a distinctive native architecture. Indonesian temple buildings may share something of the exotic, heavily ornamented character of the structure pictured but the most representative Indonesian buildings are both much larger and are constructed of stone. The seventh century building pictured, in fact illustrates the strong dependence of Japan on the arts of China. The Chinese character of the structure is visible in the distinctive silhouette of the roof, with its long sweeping pitch and upturned corners in the heavy tiled roof, and in the wealth of elaborate brackets which support the dramatically projecting eaves.

86.   **(A)** Three of the answer choices – (A), (C), and (D) – show groups of figures engaged in activities which might be interpreted as ceremonial. Choice (C) illustrated a column of soldiers marching across the midsection of a ceramic vessel; while they may be marching in a ceremonial function such as a parade or assembly, they are most likely intended to be shown advancing into battle, and, in any case, their primary function on this vase is decorative. Choice (D) shows figures engaged in music-making activities in formally arranged groups, but here, too, the illustrations serve the secondary purpose of amplifying the accompanying text. Only answer choice (A), an ancient Persian relief sculpture, uses a rigidly schematized, formal composition and style to record an actual ceremonial event. Here, the clear-cut, well-defined figures are strictly arranged in three horizontal tiers, and each carries an accessory or attribute which identifies his role within this state occasion.

87.   **(C)** Only answer choices (A) and (C) repeat the simplified forms of the human figure within a sculptural or ceramic context. Choice (A) appears to continually repeat a series of nearly identical figures arranged on three horizontal levels, but close inspection reveals several types of figures here, each marked by a variety of detail in posture, costume, accessories, etc. Further, the figures are sculpted in a softly rounded, convincing style. The figures in choice (C), in contrast, are grouped in a horizontal sequence which appears to show variety and movement; close examination, however, shows that the artist here has simply repeated figures whose clothing, weapons, postures, positions, and facial features are identical. While this serves to illustrate an anonymous mass of marching soldiers, it is even more important in helping the group of figures fit neatly, conve-

niently, and decoratively into its allotted space on the round "belly" of the vase.

88. **(D)** Calligraphy, or "fine writing," implies a two-dimensional or graphic format. Three of the possible answer choices, (A), (B) and (E), are forms of sculpture or sculptural relief, and therefore contain no drawn, calligraphic elements. Choice (C) presents a flat, two-dimensional illustration painted in black and white and minimal color. However, the images here are rigidly formalized and static, and display none of the rhythmic curves or flourishes of artistic penmanship. Only choice (D), a ninth century manuscript illustration, links calligraphy with figure drawing in the same rhythmic, linear style. In this illustration of the Bible's Psalm 150, the text written in ink above accompanies the figures below. Each is drawn in the same bold, agitated black-and-white line, with a sketchy spontaneity that creates an animated, nervous tension.

89. **(A)** If you familiarize yourself with *The Iliad* and *Odysseus*, you will see how Homer uses the simile with the long-extended idea clinched at the end – look out for the words "such" or "so" which signal the last clause of the simile. An extended metaphor (B) is close except that the metaphor never has the signal words *as when, as if, like* (B); (C) is not an option as the verse is "free form" rather than rhymed couplets; the other options mix terms. Be on the lookout for terms that sound reasonable but, upon analysis, are gibberish.

90. **(D)** This is a case of working your way through the simile until you come to the signal word "such" which gives the image of the watchfires. The stars are not compared to hills (A), shepherds (B), rivers (C), or ships (E), so these are all incorrect choices.

91. **(A)** Again, the more familiar you become with Homer, the more you will see touches like this to humanize the lofty, godlike themes and characters, so the answer is (A). If this had been a medieval English piece, humor of a coarse, ribald kind, especially in the drama, might have been the answer, but there is no humor here (B). Depth in Homer comes from the poetry itself rather than the people who feature in the poetry (C). Gladness (D) takes a back seat to the power of the simile and in any poetry shepherds never glamorize (E)!

92. **(E)** Questions such as these rely on identification of famous lines; read through anthologies and see the often repeated poems. If you do not

recognize Emily Dickinson (the use of the long dash often gives her away – it is one of her "trademarks"), work your way through and eliminate. Obviously this is not Chaucerian, the language is stark and modern (A); nor is the passage epic in its voice or theme: think of lofty topics and rhythm and rhyme – this is conversational and choppy in its rhythm (B). However, (B) does fit all the criteria of epic so save that for the last answer. Wordsworth is taught in most high-school poetry classes and this opening line is much quoted – even if you do not recall the poem itself, you might recall that Wordsworth was not a woman (the Romantic males dominated the field of poetry), so the answer cannot be (C). The jar and Tennessee is unique and should immediately make you think of one of the most famous modern male American poets, Wallace Stevens, so (D) is incorrect.

93. **(A)** This is the famous opening line of *The Canterbury Tales*; it would be worth looking over the poem (this is in translation from the middle English language), as Chaucer is said to be the "father of English poetry." If you do not recognize the lines, look again at each of the answers and, as for the previous explanation, eliminate: (B) sounds too modern and conversational, as does (C) and (E), so eliminate both those on voice alone. (D) Tennessee did not exist in Chaucer's time and is definitely not the answer.

94. **(C)** Even if you do not recognize Wordsworth, the idea of a love of nature would clue you to the Romantics who looked upon nature as a rejuvenating force for the human spirit. You are working your way through elimination, narrowing down your field through language and topic, so none of the other possibilities apply.

95. **(B)** If you recognize the opening of *Paradise Lost*, this is straightforward; if not, think of epics that you have read with the lofty, heroic subjects – none of the others fit this category.

96. **(D)** is the correct answer. In your reading, be very aware of opening and closing lines in whatever genre. Kafka's famous opener from *Metamophosis* sets symbol and theme for the entire work. All the other possibilities involve striking writers, but Genet and Ionesco are primarily playwrights, and Sartre and Tolstoy have less dramatic starting points. Even if you don't remember the first line of the *Metamorphosis*, recall that the story was about a man who awoke one morning as a bug.

97. **(D)** is the correct answer. (A) refers to the coat of arms representing royal presence; (B) should be eliminated immediately because it is too

vague; the same is true of (C). While (E) Oedipus did go into exile, he was not sacrificed for the redemption of the tribe.

98.   **(B)**   The basilica, a large, hall-like building with a minimum of internal supporting members, served a variety of public functions in the Roman era and was designed to accommodate large crowds. The basilican plan was thus an appropriate building type to contain large numbers of Christian worshippers. Roman temples (A) were not designed to regulate crowds, and, with their overt pagan associations, were unacceptable for use within a Christian context. Roman baths (C) consisted of several bathing rooms and facilities, and did not adhere to a specific type of plan. A Roman forum (D) is an open air, public city square, not a building type. A Roman villa (E) is a private domestic dwelling, composed of multiple rooms and courtyards, the design of which is inappropriate for the containment and regulation of communal worship.

99.   **(E)**   Dance began with the savage hunters. Religious groups (A), Egyptians (B), Greeks (C), and Romans (D) succeeded the savage hunters and created their own style of dance for self-expression, religious and political rituals, and entertainment.

100.   **(A)**   The fallacy of composition (A), as the name suggests, consists in thinking that what is true of the parts of something must be true of the whole composed by those parts. For instance, it would be fallacious to think that because every member of a team is outstanding, the team must be outstanding, since teamwork is involved in the performance of the team in a way that it isn't with respect to its members. The fallacy of division (B) is just the opposite: what is true of the whole is incorrectly reasoned to be true of the parts. The slippery slope fallacy (C) is committed when one thinks small differences never add up to a significant difference, while the *ad hominem* fallacy (D) involves personal attacks. The fallacy of ignorance (E) is committed when one reasons that because something has not been proven false, it is true.

101.   **(B)**   Percy Grainger wrote extensively for wind ensemble. Most of his compositions were based on folk songs such as "Country Gardens" and "Ye Banks and Braes o' Bonnie Doon"; choice (B) is correct. Sousa composed primarily for military band; choice (A) is incorrect. Beethoven composed many works, including symphonies for orchestra and piano concertos. Choice (C) is incorrect. Strauss is famous for his tone poems; choice (D) is incorrect. Franz Joseph Haydn composed for the orchestra; choice (E) is incorrect.

102. **(B)** The key signature of this excerpt is F major. The key signature of F major contains a B flat, which can be determined by using the Circle of Fifths and proceeding counterclockwise from C to the scale with one flat, F. Choice (B) is correct. The B flat scale contains B flat and E flat; choice (A) is incorrect. The key of C contains no flats or sharps; choice (C) is incorrect. The key of D contains an F sharp and a C sharp; choice (D) is incorrect. The key signature of A major contains an F#, C#, and G#. Choice (E) is incorrect.

103. **(D)** The time signature of this excerpt should be $\frac{3}{4}$. The total number of beats in each measure is three, and a quarter note would equal one beat. Choice (D) is correct. A time signature of $\frac{4}{4}$ would require four beats in each measure; choice (A) is incorrect. A time signature of $\frac{2}{4}$ would require two beats in each measure; choice (B) is incorrect. A time signature of $\frac{6}{8}$ would have six beats in each measure; choice (C) is not correct. A time signature of $\frac{12}{8}$ would have 12 beats in each measure. Choice (E) is incorrect.

104. **(C)** The excerpt is divided into three measures. The measures are divided by the number of beats found in each and marked by a vertical line through the staff; choice (C) is correct. The following choices, one measure, two measures, and zero measures (choices (A), (B), and (D)) are incorrect. Five measures cannot be calculated from the material presented; choice (E) is incorrect.

105. **(D)** The arrow is pointing at the repeat sign. This directs the musician to repeat the selection; choice (D) is correct. The key signature is the B flat symbol; choice (A) is incorrect. The clef sign is the G clef; choice (B) is incorrect. The double bar is a symbol which denotes the end of the music; choice (C) is incorrect. The time signature is not in the figure. The time signature would be $\frac{4}{4}$. Choice (E) is incorrect.

106. **(C)** Philip Roth's *Goodbye Columbus* was a big literary hit in the late 1950s and was both part of and ushered in the age of the American Ethnic novelist. Roth's novel deals with the rocky road of young romance within a suburban New York Jewish-American context. It is both an American success story, and a recollection of transformation for generations between immigrant and native born. James' (A) novel concerns a pre-"recent" immigrant America of 100 years ago. Hawthorne's work (E) concerns the earliest Pilgrim immigrants, but ethnic Pilgrim has long been recognized as "ruling class standard." Updike's novels (D) of midwest

suburbia do not involve "ethnics" so much as the descendants of Hawthorne's folk – and Poe's famous short story (B) takes place in Italy, not America.

107. **(C)** Alexis de Toqueville's *Letters From an American Farmer* is considered one of the most perceptive and accurate portraits of the newly independent American nation. The Frenchman, who later became a citizen of the U.S. and a property owner, traveled widely and recorded his observations and perceptions. Lewis and Clark (A), the famed adventurers, explored the uninhabited West under orders from President Thomas Jefferson. Sinclair Lewis' novel (B) deals with the early decades of this century. Cooper's *Mohicans* (D) describes the frontier of New York State 200 years ago. Smith's *Diary* (E) predates the establishment of the United States by almost 200 years.

108. **(E)** Ralph Ellison's powerful novel defined for America of the 1950s the second class status of African-Americans and is still referred to as a great work of literature that galvanized a nation at the height of the battle for civil rights. Faulkner's work (A), while it may have a seemingly appropriate title, does not deal with this subject – neither does Wharton's (B), about a white man in New England. Conrad's (C) powerful novel deals with Africa, and Kafka's (D) strange novel superficially deals with a man's transformation into a bug.

109. **(A)** *Journey to the Center of the Earth* by Jules Verne has a remarkable history. Though its subject deals with a phenomenon – a hollow earth – that apparently does not exist, the description it gives of Iceland is so accurate that travelers there were urged to take the book with them well into the 1950s. Ironically, Verne rarely left Paris, never traveled to Iceland, and did all his research for the book in the libraries of the French capital. Stevenson's island (B) is invented, as is Defoe's (C). Verne's other work here (D) is not focused in its description of a single spot. Swift's "travel" novel (E) is not one at all, but rather a well-known political satire.

110. **(B)** Sir Walter Scott's famous nineteenth century romance *Ivanhoe* deals with the thirteenth century – now recognized by many scholars such as Barbara Tuchman as a dreadful period in history – but until recently it was thought of as the flower of the Middle Ages, replete with knights in shining armor and damsels in distress. Eliot's work (A) is a picture of manorial England in the nineteenth century and Poe's (C) of a formerly wealthy family in America at approximately the same time. King's terrify-

ing book (D) is modern and also American, as is Perelman's hilarious short novel (E).

111. **(C)** Like many Victorian poets, Matthew Arnold venerated the works of Wordsworth. In Arnold's preface to the "Poems" of 1853, he pleads for poets to turn to the epic or drama – as epitomized, perhaps, by Wordsworth in lyrical ballads such as "The Ruined Cottage." The major problems with the other possible answers here is one of time sequence. Hemingway and Eliot (A) are modern, not Victorian. Tennyson and Browning (B) are Victorian contemporaries, as are Rossetti and Browning (D). Wordsworth and Scott (E) are Romantic contemporaries.

112. **(A)** In the *Duke and the Dauphin,* Twain relates the story of a bogus pretender to the French throne and his accompli who perform what they hope will pass as Shakespeare to frontier audiences. Initially taken by the idea, the settlers get wise to their scam and chase them out of town. The famous fence painting scene (B) took place in *Tom Sawyer.* Huck's escape from Pap (C) does not prove the quote; neither does Jim seeking freedom (D). At the end of the famous novel, Huck "lights out for the territories" (E). The West certainly represented a future of promise to Huck and Twain, but again, clearly does not prove the point.

113. **(C)** In the example shown, the *Bull's Head* of 1943, the Spanish artist Pablo Picasso joined a bicycle seat and a set of handlebars in a clever, unexpected combination to produce a sculptural analogy to an actual bull. Thus, the artist was concerned here with form and substance, not with a contrast of line and tone and, even though the resulting artwork resembles a hat- or coat-rack the sculptor's first purpose was not to produce a functional device. Likewise, even though the bull has mythological connotations and figures prominently in many ancient religions, the artist was intent not on creating a religious symbol, but in exploring the visual unity of common objects brought together in new ways. The result is a strictly visual, sculptural effect, and in no way provides a metaphor for human experience.

114. **(B)** Three of the answer choices, (A), (C) and (E), illustrate Impressionist paintings, which tend to suppress or eliminate secondary or decorative detail in the search for a quick, spontaneous, and optically "true" impression of the subject. None can be said to concentrate on details in the figure's dress. Choice (D) shows a work of exhaustive detail, in which each tree branch, leaf, and grass stem, and the details and textures of clothing, stand out with stark realism. The main figure subject, how-

ever, far from merging into the background detail, is dramatically set off against it, especially in the face, neck, and arms. Only choice (B), by the American James MacNeill Whistler, accentuates decorative detail at the expense of the subject. In this case, the details of tiny flowers running up the back of the woman's dress connect visually to the delicate floral details in the wallpaper to the left, while the pale form of the woman's figure shades and merges into the background and almost reduces her to a flat pattern.

115. **(C)** Two of the answer choices crop, or cut off, the main subject, much as the arbitrary framing of a photograph might do. Choice (E), a study of two women and a child by the American Impressionist Mary Cassatt, pulls the figures to the very front of the picture plane, and cuts them off abruptly at the bottom edge and right side of the picture. The result seems to be an unposed, accidental image produced by a moment's glance. These figures, however, are firmly centered within the picture's borders, with a definite focal point in the image of the child with the book at center. Choice (C), by contrast, presents an extremely random composition in which the human subject is so far off-center and so dramatically cropped that she barely retains pictorial "presence" in the composition. This picture by the French Impressionist Edgar Degas produces an effect of seemingly unplanned, immediate realism which resembles a casually aimed photographic snapshot.

116. **(D)** Only two of the answer choices, (C) and (D), create their desired effect by positioning the primary subject noticeably off-center, thereby undermining the pictures formal visual balance. Choice (C), by the French painter Degas, shows a woman seated at a table on which rests an enormous bouquet of flowers. Even though the woman, apparently the main subject or sitter, glances out of the picture to the right and invites the viewer's gaze to follow, the huge bunch of flowers dominates the picture and calls the viewer's eye continually back to the painting's focal center. Answer choice (D), however, by the French Realist Bastien-Lepage clearly positions the primary subject off-center, as she stares and steps to the right with her arm outstretched. The figure seems to have just left the empty center of the picture and is about to exit the painting at the right. Her glance, her pose, and her position create a strongly directional thrust which draws the viewer's eye out of the picture as the figure moves.

117. **(E)** Art Nouveau is the correct answer. Art Nouveau is distinguished by the extensive use of such curvilinear, decorative details of interior design. Post-Modernism (B) is a later period in the history of architecture, and is not defined by such decorative elements. Neo-Classicism (C), a nineteenth-century era of architecture, is chracterized by the use of classical Greek and Roman architectural details, which are more austere in nature. Post-Impressionism (D) and surrealism (A) are movements in painting that have no equivalents in the history of architectural design.

118. **(C)** Reims Cathedral (ca. 1211-60) is an example of the High Gothic style. The sheer verticality of the twin towers, the overall upward movement, and the multitude of pinnacles are identifying characteristics of the Gothic style and would most clearly set Reims apart from the most closely related structure in this group, St. Peter's (D), a work of the late Renaissance in Rome. (A) The Taj Mahal, Agra, India, (1630-48) is incorrect because it is the most famous mausoleum of Islamic architecture. (B) The Parthenon, Acropolis, Athens (448-432 B.C.) is incorrect because it represents the classical phase of Greek architecture. (D) St. Peter's, Rome (1546-64), by Michelangelo is incorrect because it is an example of the colossal order in Renaissance architecture. It has a symmetrical plan crowned by a central dome, very different from the longitudinal emphasis of the Gothic cathedral. St. Peter's basilica lacks the exterior ornamentation of Reims, but its monumental dome creates a dramatic exterior profile.

119. **(A)** The Taj Mahal was built by Shah Jahan, one of the Moslem rulers of India, as a home for his wife. She died before it was finished and so in its completion the Taj Mahal became a memorial to her. (B) is incorrect because the Parthenon has served as a place of worship for four different faiths. It was originally built by the Greeks to honor the Goddess Athena. In Christian times it became the first Byzantine church, then a Catholic cathedral, and, finally, under Turkish rule, a mosque. (C) is incorrect because the Reims Cathedral is a Catholic church. (D) is incorrect because St. Peter's is a Roman Catholic church. (E) is incorrect because (A) was not constructed as a place of worship.

120. **(C)** Become aware of different types of poems: this is the short 17 syllable form that is highly evocative. Hyperbole (A) is characterized by

exaggeration, which is not present. Odes (B) honor or exalt a specific person or subject, also not present. An epigram (D) is usually a witty expression of a particular idea. A doggerel (E) describes loose, inferior verse.

121. **(B)** If you are not aware of the original language of the form, start discounting the others – French and Chinese would be more symbolic; British would not be so succinct and evocative; Persian would be on topics of love or religion.

122. **(D)** If you are not aware of the term, it is a useful one to learn – Pope uses it frequently to attain humor. Eliminate the other terms by what you know: (A) is hyperbole; (B) is crescendo; (C) is anticlimax; and (E) is not related to the question. Analyze that a climax suggests a building toward or upward.

123. **(E)** As well as learning meter, rhyme, and rhythm, look into what poets themselves say about poetry. Keats had a lot to say especially about the ways to read and the use of the imagination, as did Wordsworth and Coleridge, but they frequently tied their comments into poetry being of and for the common man: this phrase often bemuses the "average" man so (C) is incorrect. T. S. Eliot wrote copiously on the art of writing poetry but his comments are not so easily captured in a phrase, except perhaps "objective correlative," but this phrase can only be fit into a long explanation – definitely not (B). If you are not aware of the term, think of the sorts of poetry the others write: Keats is the only one here who wants the mystery (of something like the "Grecian Urn" for example); neither William Carlos Williams nor e.e. cummings wanted mystery, preferring to have cryptic to-the-point statements about their art, so clearly neither (A) nor (D) are correct.

124. **(A)** is the correct answer. Though you may disagree with the quotation, you must make your selection based on the quotation. (B) *A Midsummer Night's Dream* is a comedy. *Oedipus* (C) is indeed, a tragedy, but it does not fit the requirements for tragedy as established in the quotation. *Oedipus the King* is not completed by a death. Jocasta commits suicide, but Oedipus, the central character, remains within the walls of the city for many years before he is exiled. *Oedipus the King* is thus eliminated on the basis of this argument. (D) Shakespeare's *The Tempest* and (E) Menander's *The Bad-Tempered Man* should also be eliminated because both are comedies.

125. **(E)** is the correct answer. Anagnorisis means recognition or discovery. Therefore, when the hero's understanding of the true nature of the situation and the self is evident in drama or fiction, then this is an example of Anagnorisis. As a complete definition, this differs from (A), which is vague.

126. **(C)** is the correct answer. After the idealistic Brutus tells the people that he participated in Caesar's murder because he loved Rome more, he and the other conspirators make the mistake of allowing the wily Mark Antony to speak. Antony must aid the public or rabble in understanding the villainy of the murder of Caesar, no matter the motivation. Thus, the statement he makes is ironic as what he wishes to do is arouse the people to act against Caesar's murderers.

127. **(E)** is the correct answer. Othello's great weakness is his inability to recognize Iago's villainy and Desdemona's innocence. Iago is able to convince Othello that Desdemona is not the "chaste and heavenly true" wife she appears to be. Not until after he kills Desdemona does Othello understand the true nature of the situation and his own weakness.

128. **(A)** is the correct answer. Though all of the characters listed are from plays by Shakespeare, Dane and Denmark are the contextual clues here. One who comes from or resides in Denmark is called a Dane.

129. **(B)** Oculus, meaning "eye," refers to the round opening in the dome, which is without glass and thus open to the sky. The terms (A) window, (C) splayed window, and (D) stained-glass window are all defined as wall openings that are glazed in some form, which is not applicable here. A clerestory (E) refers to the upper portion of a building whose walls are pierced with windows and which emits light to the remainder of the building below; this type of construction refers to fenestrated walls only.

130. **(B)** The basic rules to jazz dance are parallel feet, flat-foot steps, undulating torso, body isolation, and syncopated rhythms. Belidi dance (abdominal dance) (A), danse mora (Flamenco dance) (C), tap dance (D), and country dance (E) each have their own different specific rules.

131. **(A)** Occam's Razor contends that one should not multiply entities beyond necessity: since both theories are equally powerful, choose the simpler one. The Plenitude Principle (B) says that the universe contains as

many types of things as possible. The Open Question Argument (C) applies to claims about the nature of goodness, not theories in general. The Underdetermination Principle (D) involves the notion that a given set of facts is compatible with many theories. Scientific Realism (E) is the view that the entities postulated by science actually exist.

132. **(D)** Jane Austen's *Pride and Prejudice* is the source of this quote. The word *pride*, found in both the quote and the title, should give you a clue to the correct answer, even if you have not read these books. (B) Austen's *Emma* and (C) Margaret Mitchell's *Gone with the Wind* also deal with the issues of pride and vanity, although to a lesser extent than does *Pride and Prejudice*. However, neither of these is the source of the quote. In addition, Mitchell's novel, although set in the nineteenth century, was written in 1936. (A) George Eliot's *Silas Marner*, written in 1861, is a story of an old linen-weaver and his adopted daughter. (E) Jonathan Swift's *Gulliver's Travels* describes the four voyages of Lemuel Gulliver; it was written in the 1720's.

133. **(A)** A trumpet can play different notes by pressing a valve down. A trumpet has three valves that, when combined in different prescribed combinations, help produce various notes; choice (A) is correct. Violins and pianos use strings to produce sound; choice (B) is incorrect. By covering and uncovering holes, the clarinet can change notes; choice (C) is incorrect. Saxophones use octave keys to change octaves; choice (D) is incorrect. Trombones use a slide to change pitches; choice (E) is incorrect.

134. **(A)** The diagram is an example of a hemiola. The hemiola is a rhythmic term that is used to define three notes of a given value occupying the space of two notes of the same value. It is also referred to as three against two; choice (A) is correct. A paradiddle is a percussion roll that follows a pattern such as RLRR LRLL; choice (B) is incorrect. A fermata, ꙮ, directs a musician to hold the note until the conductor cuts it off; choice (C) is incorrect. A crescendo, < , indicates to increase in volume; choice (D) is incorrect. A glissando is sliding through the pitches quickly; choice (E) is incorrect.

135. **(A)** The C in measure one is sharp because the accidental makes it sharp. This accidental affects all C's in the given measure. As a result the C in measure two is C natural because there are no accidentals before the note; choice (A) is correct. Consequently, the C is not sharp, flat, or a B. Choices (B), (C), and (D) are incorrect. A D would be located on the fourth line, choice (E) is incorrect.

136. **(A)** The bass clef is also referred to as the F clef. The symbol locates F below middle C, which is the fourth line; choice (A) is correct. The G clef and treble clef locate the G above middle C; choice (B) and (D) are incorrect. The tenor clef is used for cello, bassoon, and trombone to locate middle C; choice (C) is incorrect. The alto clef is used primarily by the viola; choice (E) is incorrect.

137. **(D)** Catton's work about the surrender of Lee at Appomatox stands as one of the great Civil War accounts, though it was written almost 100 years after the incident. The temptation here is to respond with (E) Crane's work, but *Red Badge* was written during the last century. Mailer's war novel (C) concerned WW II in the Pacific, as did Wouk's novel (B). That leaves Hoover's anti-Communist screed (A) written during the 1950s.

138. **(B)** Albee's 1960 popular play was made into a movie, starring Richard Burton and Elizabeth Taylor as the university professor and his wife, who display their troubled marriage to a young faculty couple who they had invited to their home for a visit. Albee's *American Dream* (C) does not concern itself with this subject matter. Miller's work (E) concerns longshoremen and immigrants in Red Hook, Brooklyn. Neil Simon's reflective comedy (D) also relates the experience of growing up in a distinctly blue collar, immigrant world. (A) is a medieval play.

139. **(D)** Pepys' diary, written during the restoration of the Stuarts and Charles II in 1660, is still compelling material, especially his account of the Great Fire of London. Many critics consider that Pepys pioneered the form as literature, though he was not the first by any means to keep a diary. The time factor alone eliminates from consideration the satirists Swift (E) and Sterne (B), who wrote in the late 1770s. O. E. Rolvaag (C) is a twentieth century Swedish novelist. Sir Laurence (A), of course, is the recent star of stage, screen, and Shakespeare.

140. **(C)** Ralph Waldo Emerson, Unitarian Minister, writer, and philosopher, is generally considered the chief promoter of transcendentalism. His influence was widely felt – on no less a personage than Henry David Thoreau (D) – with whom, eventually, Emerson had a falling out due to the inappropriate attentions Thoreau was said to have paid to Emerson's wife. Jonathan Edwards (A) was a New England minister of the early 1700s. Pitt (B) was a British parliamentarian of the American Revolutionary period. Dr. Samuel Fuller (E) was the only doctor to accompany the pilgrims to Massachusetts in 1620.

141. **(A)** Medieval religious plays based upon biblical history were called mystery plays. They were typically performed outdoors and were among the first "road shows" which traveled from town to town. While there are mystery plays (B) in the twentieth century (Ira Levin's "Deathtrap," for example), they are not known in the history of literature specifically as such. Edith Wharton wrote *The Age of Innocence* (D). The Iron Age (E) occurred before the invention of writing. The classical age of Greece or Rome (C) was of somewhat later vintage, but still 2,000 years ago.

142. **(A)** The term "Comedy of Manners" is used to designate the satirical comedy of the Restoration period in England – which occupies the last quarter of the seventeenth century. The form survives in the works of Wilde, Maugham, and Noel Coward, and is concerned with the conventions of highly sophisticated society. *The Comedy of Errors* (B) is a title of a Shakespeare play. (C) is, of course, of recent TV vintage. "Graveyard" (D) refers mostly to a school of poetry of the early 1700s. Practical Criticism (E) may often be humorous, but so far has not found a genre to be identified with.

143. **(D)** A pastourelle is a medieval type of dialogue poem in which a shepherdess is wooed by a man of higher social rank – usually a scholar or a poet. The method of explication is usually an argument. The wooing is not always successful. (C) is close in its participants, but the dynamics are opposite. (B) is not what happens at all. Neither, of course, is (E), in which it is proposed that the queen runs off with her court jester. (A), in which a princess is wooed by a gentleman of high standing, may be the subject of many romances, but does not concern the pastourelle.

144. **(C)** The lines by Ruskin quoted here contain an example of a pathetic fallacy – impassioned prose in which nature is credited with the emotions of human beings. When such a tendency is overdone, it is referred to as a "conceit." A truism (A) is a general truth; a quatrain (B) is four poetic lines; a quip is a brief joke (D); and a mythopoetic frame (E) is a term applied to writers who consciously create a mythical background in their stories.

145. **(B)** This is *Guernica* (1937), one of Picasso's most famous pieces and one of the most famous paintings of the twentieth century. It should be known to students and if not, Picasso's singular style should be. (A) is incorrect because Van Gogh was a post-impressionist painter who used thick paint and noticeable, dynamic brushstrokes. (C) is incorrect because

Dali was a surrealist who painted in an almost literal, realistic manner, not like the simplified, cartoonish figures here. (D) is incorrect because Pollock was an abstract expressionist painter who had no recognizable, figurative imagery in his paintings. (E) is incorrect because this piece is by (B) Picasso.

146. **(D)** Though this painting does not literally depict this event, it was inspired by the German bombing of the Spanish town of Guernica. Picasso uses a series of powerful images culled from mythology to evoke the horror of war. (A), (B), (C), and (E) are incorrect because Picasso himself explained that the German air attack on the Spanish town of Guernica was the inspiration for this piece, although it is meant to condemn all war.

147. **(D)** The abstract expressionists sought to charge form and color with a purely spiritual meaning by working from the unconscious with no preconceived idea for a painting and by avoiding any representational subject matter. (A) is incorrect because the surrealists, active in Europe from the 1920s through the 1940s, also aimed to work from the unconscious but their method was to transpose specific, illustrational dream imagery directly on to the canvas, the shock coming from the unreal, fantastic images being depicted in such a "realistic" manner. (B) is incorrect because the futurists were a group of Italian artists who in 1910 issued a manifesto rejecting the past and declaring a love for machines and new technology such as the locomotive and automated factories. They sought to emulate the dynamic movement of the industrial age in their paintings. They tried to achieve this by superimposing the successive phases of movement of their subjects on top of each other. (C) is incorrect because cubism, invented by Picasso and Georges Braque during the first decade of this century, fractured the picture plane into facets, thereby showing the same subject from many different angles simultaneously. This momentous development introduced the fourth dimension – time – into painting. (E) is incorrect because the minimalists were a group of painters and sculptors who sought extreme simplicity of shape and an increase of scale which would allow their work to enter the realm of architecture and envelop the viewer.

148. **(B)** *Mentemhet the Governor* is Egyptian from the 25th Dynasty (650 B.C.). Statue (A), *Kouros from Anavysos,* is Greek and dates from 540-515 B.C. The student should be able to see the obvious similarities in pose in both statues, so one has obviously influenced the other. More attempt has been made in statue (A) to depict the muscles and limbs of human anatomy. Students should recognize this as a step forward in the

development of human figurative sculpture, making (B) older. Also, the pose is slightly more lifelike and dynamic, traits which became more developed in later Greek and Roman figurative sculpture. (C) is incorrect because they don't both date from the same time period. (D) is incorrect because it is not true. (E) is also not true.

149.   **(C)**   The idealization and glorification of the human figure and the godlike scale and presence are some of the traits of Greek sculpture. Even though the pose is rigid, there is an obvious interest in depicting the human anatomy and how the pieces all fit together, which would differentiate the statue from an Egyptian piece (A), where the sculpted human figure was thought of as a smooth envelope of stone and where nudity would not be seen. (B) is incorrect because the art of the Aegeans dates from a much earlier time period (3000 B.C. – 950 B.C.), and the human figure in sculpture appears more as an idol than as a proportioned, detailed figure. (D) is incorrect because the Romans were interested in the figure in motion; in dynamic or dramatic poses with emotive facial expressions. (E) is incorrect because in Byzantine art, the figure usually appears in religious (Christian) mosaics.

150.   **(A)**   The correct answer is (A) for the above reasons. The student might also recognize the hieroglyphs at the base.

▼
PRACTICE
TEST 2

CLEP HUMANITIES
Test 2

(Answer sheets appear in the back of the book.)

Section 1

TIME: 45 Minutes
75 Questions

DIRECTIONS: Each of the questions or incomplete statements below is followed by five possible answers or completions. Select the best choice in each case and fill in the corresponding oval on the answer sheet.

QUESTION 1 refers to the following.

1. The "bridges" (labeled X and Y) on the exterior of the church above function as

    (A) arches.   (D) flying buttresses.

    (B) cantilevers.   (E) windows.

    (C) ribbed vaults.

2. Which of the following dance techniques has no established steps or patterns, and requires the dancer to create his or her own, emanating from movements of the body?

    (A) ballet

    (B) jazz

    (C) modern dance

    (D) danse mora (Flamenco dancing)

    (E) tap dancing

3. Who believed that a life of virtue or excellence is a matter of knowledge?

    (A) Socrates   (D) John Stuart Mill

    (B) Aristotle   (E) Rousseau

    (C) Kant

4. The following instruments are all members of the brass family EXCEPT the

    (A) trumpet.   (D) French horn.

    (B) tuba.   (E) trombone.

    (C) alto saxophone.

5. When a piece of music has a time signature of $\frac{4}{4}$, a quarter note receives ____ beats.

    (A) 4   (D) 3

    (B) 2   (E) $1\frac{1}{2}$

    (C) 1

6. Which musical style is characterized by a swing feel, a strong rhythmic beat, and improvisation?

    (A) Fugues   (D) Symphonies

    (B) Jazz   (E) Opera

    (C) Rock

QUESTION 7 refers to the following passage.

> 'Twas on a lofty vase's side,
> Where China's gayest art had dyed
> The azure flowers, that blow;
> Demurest of the tabby kind,
> The pensive Selima reclined,
> Gazed on the lake below.
>
> Her conscious tail her joy declared;
> The fair round face, the snowy beard,
> The velvet of her paws,
> Her coat that with the tortoise vies,
> Her eyes of jet, and emerald eyes,
> She saw; and purred applause.

7. What is the subject of the stanzas?

    (A) A snake

    (B) A turtle swimming in a lake

    (C) A vase

    (D) A dog watching a cat

    (E) A cat

QUESTION 8 refers to the following passage.

> The shore was fledged with palm trees. These stood or leaned or reclined against the light and their green feathers were a hundred feet up in the air. The ground beneath them was a bank covered with coarse grass, torn everywhere by the upheavals of fallen trees, scattered with decaying coconuts and palm saplings. Behind this was the darkness of the forest proper...

8. The above passage can best be described as

    (A) surrealistic.   (D) romantic.

    (B) expressionistic.   (E) Gothic.

    (C) realistic.

QUESTIONS 9 and 10 refer to the following passage.

Can we expect to glean information about places and times from a novel? Can anybody be so naive as to think he or she can learn anything about the past from those buxom best-sellers that are hawked around by book clubs under the heading of historical novels? But what about the masterpieces? Can we rely on Jane Austen's picture of landowning England with baronets and landscaped grounds when all she knew was a clergyman's parlor? And *Bleak House,* that **fantastic** romance within a **fantastic** London, can we call it a study of London a hundred years ago? Certainly not. And the same holds for other such novels in this series. The truth is that great novels are great fairy tales – and the novels in this series are supreme fairy tales.

9. The word "fantastic" in bold means

    (A) loaded with adventure.   (D) historical.

    (B) unreal.   (E) nonsensical.

    (C) ridiculous.

10. The author's attitude toward such writers as Jane Austen and Charles Dickens is one of

    (A) respect.   (D) disdain.

    (B) defiance.   (E) condescension.

    (C) mockery.

11. The Director of Companies was our captain and our host. We four affectionately watched his back as he stood in the bows looking to seaward. On the whole river there was nothing that looked half so nautical. He resembled a pilot, which to a seaman is trustworthiness personified.

    The above is an example of

(A) prose.

(B) unrhymed iambic pentameter.

(C) an elegy.

(D) a non sequitur.

(E) free verse.

12. A group of townspeople stood on the station siding of a little Kansas town, awaiting the coming of the night train, which was already 20 minutes overdue. The snow had fallen thick over everything; in the pale starlight the line of bluffs across the wide, white meadows south of the town made soft, smoke-colored curves against the sky.

   This passage is most likely taken from which of the following?

   (A) The conclusion of a short story

   (B) The beginning of a short story

   (C) The climax of a short story

   (D) The dénouement of a short story

   (E) None of the above.

QUESTION 13 refers to the following diagram.

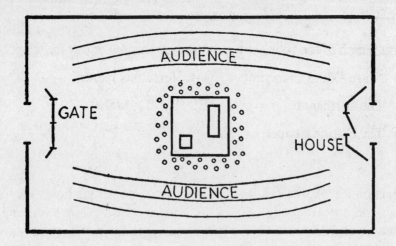

13. The picture shown on the previous page is an example of which of the following types of staging?

(A) Thrust   (D) Central

(B) Proscenium   (E) Open

(C) Theatre-in-the-Round

QUESTION 14 refers to the following.

14. From which of the following structures is the above picture taken?

(A) Notre Dame Cathedral   (D) Versailles Palace

(B) The Parthenon   (E) The Taj Mahal

(C) The Sistine Chapel

QUESTION 15 refers to the following.

15. The figure pictured above was most likely which of the following?

(A) A slave or menial servant (D) A farmer

(B) A knight's page   (E) A carpenter's apprentice

(C) A religious novice

QUESTION 16 refers to the following.

16. All of the following can be construed from the print above EXCEPT

   (A) the three figures portrayed are musicians.

   (B) the artwork conveys a strong sense of depth.

   (C) the drawing is representative of Egyptian tomb paintings.

   (D) the artist was not concerned with modeling the figures in three dimensions.

   (E) the artist employed a standardized figure type.

QUESTION 17 refers to the following.

17. Which of the following best describes the statue pictured above?

(A) Comic

(D) Imposing

(B) Tragic

(E) Introspective

(C) Ornate

QUESTION 18 refers to the following.

18. From this picture, one can assume that the music being played and sung is

    (A) an opera.   (D) a light, boisterous tune.

    (B) a sad, serious melody.   (E) a hymn.

    (C) a dirge.

QUESTIONS 19-21 refer to the following poem.

> My mistress' eyes are nothing like the sun;
> Coral is far more red than her lips' red;
> If snow be white, why then her breasts are dun;
> If hairs be wires, black wires grow on her head.
> I have seen roses damasked, red and white,
> But no such roses see I in her cheeks;
> And in some perfumes is there more delight
> Than in the breath that from my mistress reeks.
> I love to hear her speak, yet well I know
> That music hath a far more pleasing sound;
> I grant I never saw a goddess go;
> My mistress, when she walks treads on the ground.
> And yet, by heaven, I think my love as rare
> As any she belied with false compare.

19. This poem is different from other sonnets in that

    (A) it is Shakespearean.

    (B) it is Italian.

    (C) it describes the appearance of a beloved woman.

    (D) it does not describe the woman as beautiful.

    (E) it does not follow the proper sonnet conventions.

20. The last two lines of the poem

    (A) reaffirm the argument held throughout the poem.

    (B) start a new topic.

    (C) refute the argument held throughout the poem.

    (D) are a continuation of the ideas introduced in the poem.

    (E) use extensive metaphors.

21. The poem can best be described as

    (A) witty and satirical.   (D) brooding.

    (B) intense.   (E) sentimental.

    (C) sarcastic.

22. King: Take thy fair hour, Laertes; time be thine,
    And thy best graces spend it at thy will!
    But now, my cousin Hamlet, and my son, –

    Hamlet: *(Aside)* A little more than kin, and less than kind.

    In the above lines, what does the stage direction "*(Aside)*" mean?

    (A) The actor steps aside to make room for other action on stage.

    (B) The actor directly addresses only one particular actor on stage.

    (C) The actor directly addresses the audience, while out of hearing
    of the other actors.

    (D) The previous speaker steps aside to make room for this actor.

    (E) The actor speaks to someone off stage.

QUESTION 23 refers to the following.

23. The mask above represents which of the following cultural traditions?

(A) African

(B) Greek

(C) Roman

(D) Dutch

(E) Persian

QUESTION 24 refers to the following.

24. Hagia Sophia, shown above, in Constantinople (present-day Istanbul) was originally built as a

(A) Turkish mosque.

(B) Gothic cathedral.

(C) Byzantine palace church.

(D) Roman temple.

(E) monastic church.

25. The art of using movement instead of words to create a story refers to

    (A) pantomime.

    (B) mimetic imitation.

    (C) mime.

    (D) improvisation.

    (E) commedia dell'arte.

26. Every event has a cause, and so either there is some uncaused, primary cause or else the chain of causes goes backwards infinitely.

    This sentence expresses part of an argument. What is the argument called and what is it meant to prove?

    (A) The Cosmological Argument for the existence of God

    (B) A Slippery Slope argument for a first cause

    (C) The Ontological argument for the existence of God

    (D) A Physical Argument for the "Big Bang" theory

    (E) The Argument from Design for God

27. John Phillip Sousa, an American composer and band leader, popularized which style of music?

    (A) Opera

    (B) Marches

    (C) Symphonies

    (D) Fugues

    (E) Nocturnes

28. Which of the following composers was to music as Claude Monet was to art?

    (A) Stravinsky

    (B) Debussy

    (C) Gillespie

    (D) Bach

    (E) Mozart

29. All of the following educators/musicians/composers developed teaching methods. Of the group, whose method emphasizes the use of rote learning?

   (A) Gordon

   (B) Orff

   (C) Suzuki

   (D) Jaques-Dalcroze

   (E) Carabo-Cone

30. It pleased God that I was still spared, and very hearty and sound in health, but very impatient of being pent up within doors without air, as I had been for 14 days or thereabouts, and I could not restrain myself, but I would go to carry a letter for my brother to the post-house.

   The above is most likely an excerpt from which of the following?

   (A) Poem

   (B) Play

   (C) Journal

   (D) Myth

   (E) Song

31. In his "Speech in the Virginia Convention," Patrick Henry says, "Suffer not yourselves to be betrayed with a kiss." Which of the following best describes this quote?

   (A) An example of personification

   (B) A mixed metaphor

   (C) A Shakespearean illusion

   (D) Hyperbole

   (E) A biblical allusion

QUESTION 32 refers to the following passage.

From the mountains on every side rivulets descended that filled all the valley with verdure and fertility and formed a lake in the middle, inhabited by fish of every species and frequented by every fowl whom nature has taught to dip the wing in water. This lake discharged its superfluities by a stream, which entered a dark cleft of the mountain on the northern side, and fell with dreadful noise from precipice to precipice till it was heard no more.

32. The narrative technique in this passage can be described as

    (A) painstakingly descriptive.

    (B) full of comparisons and contrasts.

    (C) vague in its descriptions of landscape.

    (D) negative in connotation.

    (E) surrealistic.

QUESTION 33 refers to the following passage.

There was a time when I went every day into a church, since a girl I was in love with knelt there in prayer for half an hour in the evening and I was able to look at her in peace.

Once when she had not come and I was reluctantly eyeing the other supplicants I noticed a young fellow who had thrown his whole lean length along the floor. Every now and then he clutched his head as hard as he could and sighing loudly beat it in his upturned palms on the stone flags.

33. By using the term "supplicants," the author implies that

    (A) everyone in the church is there to celebrate a mass.

    (B) everyone in the church is devout.

    (C) everyone in the church is guilty of something.

    (D) everyone in the church is a hypocrite.

    (E) everyone in the church is damned.

QUESTIONS 34–36 refer to the following passage.

It was the best of times, it was the worst of times, it was the age of wisdom, it was the age of foolishness, it was the epoch of belief, it was the epoch of incredulity, it was the season of Light, it was the season of Darkness, it was the spring of hope, it was the winter of despair, we had everything before us, we had nothing before us, we were all going direct to Heaven, we were all going direct the other way – in short, the period was so far like the present period, that some of its noisiest authorities insisted on its being received, for good or for evil, in the superlative degree of comparison only.

There were a king with a large jaw, and a queen with a plain face, on the throne of England; there were a king with a large jaw, and a queen with a fair face, on the throne of France. In both countries it was clearer than crystal to the lords of the State preserves of loaves and fishes, that things in general were settled for ever.

34. The vast comparisons in the above passage indicate that the speaker is describing

(A) a placid historical time period.

(B) a time of extreme political upheaval.

(C) a public event.

(D) a time when anything was possible.

(E) the attitudes of people at war.

35. The last sentence of the passage

(A) mocks the self-assuredness of the governments of England and France.

(B) comments on the horrible poverty of the two nations.

(C) most likely foreshadows an upcoming famine or drought.

(D) attacks the two governments for neglecting the poor, hungry masses.

(E) alludes to the Bible to hint at the magnitude of the upcoming events.

36. The phrase, "some of its noisiest authorities insisted on its being received, for good or for evil, in the superlative degree of comparison only"

(A) mocks the arrogance of the governments.

(B) mocks the arrogance of the people.

(C) compares the attitude of the people to the attitude of the governments.

(D) Both (A) and (B).

(E) Both (B) and (C).

QUESTION 37 refers to the following.

Unité d'Habitation, Marseilles.

37. The designer of the building pictured above seems to have been concerned with which of the following?

(A) The amount of light available to the building's inhabitants

(B) Building a modern skyscraper

(C) Cylindrical shapes

(D) Hidden staircases

(E) Blending the building into its setting

QUESTION 38 refers to the following.

38. The building pictured above suggests which of the following?

    (A) Undulating waves of water

    (B) A congested city street

    (C) A chambered nautilus

    (D) A massive mountain

    (E) A tree with spreading branches

QUESTIONS 39–41 refer to the illustrations (A) through (E).

(A)

(B)

(C)

(D)

(E)

39. Which of the examples pictured does not share cultural heritage with the others?

40. In which example does the composition set up a circular motion within the picture's borders?

41. Which example tends most strongly to represent human features as a composite of stylized, abstracted forms?

QUESTION 42 refers to the following poem.

> Whilom ther was dwellynge at Oxenford
> A riche gnof, that gestes heeld to bord,
> And of his craft he was a carpenter.
> With hym ther was dwellynge a povre scoler.

42. What can we assume about this passage?

    (A) It is probably a translation of some other language into English.

    (B) It is written in Middle English.

    (C) It is romantic in style.

    (D) It is written in Elizabethan English.

    (E) The speaker is a foreigner.

QUESTIONS 43-45 refer to the following passages.

(A) That's my last duchess painted on the wall,
    Looking as if she were alive. I call
    That piece a wonder, now: Fra Pandolf's hands
    Worked busily a day, and there she stands.

(B) <u>Nov. 24.</u> A rainy morning. We were all well except that my head
    ached a little and I took my breakfast in bed. I read a little of
    Chaucer, prepared the goose for dinner, and then we all walked
    out. I was obliged to return for my fur tippet and Spenser it was
    so cold.

(C) There were times in early autumn – in September – when the
    greater circuses would come to town – the Ringling Brothers,
    Robinson's, and Barnum & Baily shows, and when I was a
    route-boy on the morning paper, on those mornings when the
    circus would be coming in, I would rush madly through my
    route in the cool and thrilling darkness that comes before the
    break of day, and then I would go back home and get my brother
    out of bed.

(D) This American government – what is it but a tradition, though a
    recent one, endeavoring to transmit itself unimpaired to poster-
    ity, but each instant losing some of its integrity? It has not the
    vitality and force of a single living man; for a single man can
    bend it to his will. It is a sort of wooden gun to the people
    themselves; and, if ever they should use it in earnest as a real
    one against each other, it will surely split.

(E) Miniver Cheevy, born too late,
        Scratched his head and kept on thinking;
    Miniver coughed, and called it fate,
        And kept on drinking.

43. Which of the above passages creates a mood of strange excitement?

44. Which of the passages is most likely taken from a dramatic mono-
    logue?

45. Which of the passages uses a metaphor to make a point?

QUESTION 46 refers to the following.

46. Which of the figures pictured above would be most appropriate for a medieval cycle play?

(A) 1   (D) 4

(B) 2   (E) 5

(C) 3

QUESTION 47 refers to the following passage.

(The veranda of the Voynitzevs' country house. It looks out onto a sunlit garden, with the tall trees of the forest beyond, bisected by a grassy walk.

The whoosh of a rocket taking off. The lights come up to reveal YAKOV in the garden with a large box of assorted fireworks in his arms. Beside him stands DR. TRILETZKY, a match in his hand. They are gazing up into the sky – DR. TRILETZKY with delight, YAKOV with apprehension. There is a smell of sulfur in the air. The rocket bursts, off.)

47. The above passage is most likely taken from

(A) a Victorian novel.

(B) the stage directions of a play.

(C) the critical notes to a literary work.

(D) the rough draft of a literary work.

(E) an epistolary novel.

48. The "skyscraper," as first pioneered by architects such as Henry Hobson Richardson and Louis Sullivan, saw its earliest development in which of the following cities?

    (A) Paris

    (B) London

    (C) New York

    (D) St. Louis

    (E) Chicago

49. The term "carole" or Reigen is a choral dance involving skipping and/or leaping to ring-shaped form, and probably falling. Which group in the early Middle Ages took joy in practicing this type of dance?

    (A) Royalty

    (B) Mime

    (C) Franciscan monks

    (D) Fools

    (E) Pantalone

50. The question whether knowledge is justified true belief is a question in what branch of philosophy; and is most closely associated with what famous philosopher?

    (A) Epistemology / Plato

    (B) Metaphysics / Aristotle

    (C) Epistemology / Descartes

    (D) Metaphysics / Plato

    (E) Epistemology / Spinoza

51. The following musicians/educators/composers developed teaching methods. Of these selected, who also researched and employed folk songs with his method?

    (A) Kodaly

    (B) Orff

    (C) Gordon

    (D) Carabo-Cone

    (E) Dalcroze

52. Edwin E. Gordon used the music learning theory to develop an appreciation for music. Which musical concept is essential in the music learning theory process?

    (A) Rhythm

    (B) Folk music

    (C) Eurythmics

    (D) Audiation

    (E) Rote learning

53. When a conductor reads a score with a time signature of $\frac{4}{4}$, which of the following conducting patterns should be executed?

(A)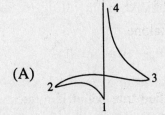

(D)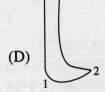

(B)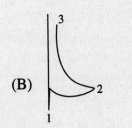

(E)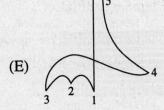

(C)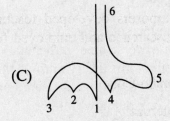

QUESTION 54 refers to the following passage.

Merry days were these at Thornfield Hall; and busy days too: how different from the first three months of stillness, monotony and solitude I had passed beneath its roof! All sad feelings seemed now driven from the house... there was life everywhere, movement all day long.

54. In the above passage, what is the significance of the three consecutive periods?

(A) They indicate a lapse in thought on the author's part.

(B) They indicate that the speaker is unable or unwilling to finish his/her sentence.

(C) They indicate that part of the quote has been omitted.

(D) They indicate that part of the original manuscript has been lost.

(E) They eliminate the need for further punctuation in the sentence.

QUESTIONS 55–57 refer to the following passages:

(A) Once upon a time and a very good time it was there was a moocow coming down along the road and this moocow that was coming down along the met a nicens little boy named baby tuckoo...

(B) And thus have these naked Nantucketers, these sea hermits, issuing from their ant-hill in the sea, overrun and conquered the watery world like so many Alexanders...

(C) A large rose tree stood near the entrance of the garden: the roses growing on it were white, but there were three gardeners at it, busily painting them red. Alice thought this a very curious thing, and she went nearer to watch them, and, just as she came up to them, she heard one of them say "Look out now, Five!"

(D) Emma was not required, by any subsequent discovery to retract her ill opinion of Mrs. Elton. Her observation had been pretty correct. Such as Mrs. Elton appeared to her on the second interview, such she appeared whenever they met again – self-important, presuming, familiar, ignorant, and ill-bred. She had a little beauty and a little accomplishment, but so little judgment that she thought herself coming with superior knowledge of the world, to enliven and improve a country neighborhood...

(E) TRUE! – nervous – very, very dreadfully nervous had I been and am; but why *will* you say that I am mad? The disease had sharpened my senses – not destroyed – not dulled them. Above all was in the sense of hearing acute. I heard all things in heaven and in the earth. I heard many things in hell.

55. Which passage makes use of allusion?

56. Which passage employs a discreet voice to imitate the speech of a character?

57. Which passage is most likely taken from a nineteenth-century novel of manners?

58. As he walked through the office, Raskolnikov noticed that many people were looking at him. Among them he saw the two porters from *the* house whom he has invited that night to the police-station. They stood there waiting. But he was no sooner on the stairs than he heard the voice of Porfiry Petrovitch behind him. Turning round, he saw the latter running after him, out of breath.

The preceding paragraph is most probably an excerpt from which of the following?

(A) British spy novel

(B) Nineteenth-century Russian novel

(C) A modern romance

(D) An existentialist short story

(E) A nineteenth-century Victorian novel

QUESTION 59 refers to the following.

59. Which of the following best identifies the medium of the work above?

(A) Oil painting on canvas

(B) Stained-glass window

(C) Marble sculpture

(D) Mosaic tile inlay

(E) Woven wool tapestry

QUESTIONS 60–62 refer to the illustrations (A) through (E).

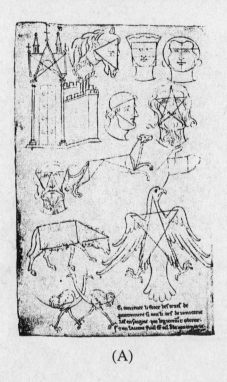

(A)

(B)

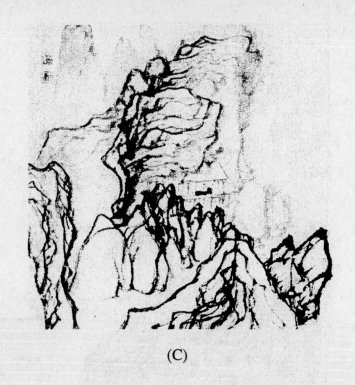

(C)

(D)

(E)

60. Which example depends most heavily on the decorative contrasts of black and white?

61. Which example seems to use coarse texture to emphasize an expressive effect?

62. In which example do the contents seem most like unrelated, documentary notations?

QUESTIONS 63–65 refer to the following passages.

    (A) Fair is foul and foul is fair.
          Hover through the fog and filthy air.

    (B) Weary of myself, and sick of asking
          What I am, and what I ought to be,
          At this vessel's prow I stand, which bears me
          Forward, forward o'er the starlit sea

And a look of passionate desire
O'er the sea and to the stars I send:
"Ye who from my childhood up have calmed me,
Calm me, ah, compose me to the end!

(C) There were a king with a large jaw and a queen with a plain face, on the throne of England; there were a king with a large jaw and a queen with a fair face on the throne of France. In both countries it was clearer than crystal to the lords of the state preserves of loaves and fishes, that things were in general settled for ever.

(D) no thats no way for him he has no manners nor no refinement nor no nothing in his nature slapping us behind like that on my bottom because I didnt call him Hugh the ignoramus doesnt know poetry from a cabbage thats what you get for not keeping them in their proper place

(E) The worthy woman bustled off, and I crouched nearer the fire; my head felt hot, and the rest of me chill; moreover I was excited, almost to a pitch of foolishness, through my nerves and brain. This caused me to feel, not uncomfortable, but rather fearful (as I am still) of serious effects from the incidents of today and yesterday.

63. Which passage describes a person seeking personal insight and solace?

64. Which passage uses the "stream of consciousness" technique to mimic the workings of the human mind?

65. Which passage contains examples of alliteration?

QUESTION 66 refers to the following verse.

The curfew tolls the knell of parting day,
The lowing herd wind slowly o'er the lea,
The plowman homeward plods his weary way,
And leaves the world to darkness and to me.

66. Which of the following sounds is NOT referred to in the above lines?

    (A) Bells

    (D) Cows

    (B) Wind through the trees

    (E) A man walking

    (C) Footsteps

QUESTION 67 refers to the following verse.

We think our fathers fools, so wise we grow;
Our wiser sons, no doubt, will think us so.

67. Which is the best paraphrase of the above lines?

    (A) As we grow older, we think our fathers wiser.

    (B) As we grow older, we think our fathers are fools, and our sons will probably think the same of us.

    (C) Sons always believe their fathers are fools, but fathers always think their sons are wise.

    (D) Fathers always think they are smarter than their sons.

    (E) Fathers and sons are always trying to prove that they are wiser than each other.

QUESTION 68 refers to the following.

68. The costumes pictured above would be most appropriate for which of the following?

(A) Ancient Greek drama

(B) A medieval cycle play

(C) A mid-nineteenth century play

(D) A passion play

(E) A Shakespearean play

QUESTION 69 refers to the following.

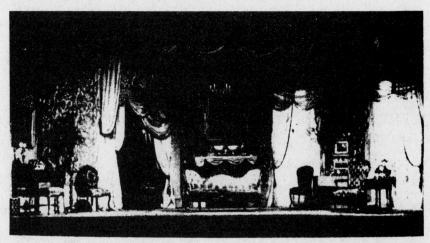

69. The setting pictured above is an example of which of the following?

    (A) Expressionism   (D) Realism

    (B) Symbolism   (E) None of the above.

    (C) Impressionism

QUESTION 70 refers to the following.

70. The church of St. Peter in the Vatican, Rome, was built according to which of the following architect's designs?

    (A) Michelangelo   (D) Bernini

    (B) Bramante   (E) Leonardo da Vinci

    (C) Borromini

QUESTIONS 71 and 72 refer to the following description of stage formats in theaters.

    (A) Typical in American theaters, this is a "picture frame" stage with a large space separating the audience from the stage.

    (B) A stage completely surrounded by the audience. This can also be described as "theater-in-the-round."

(C) An intimate theater space in which the audience typically is seated around three-quarters of the stage.

(D) A space without a specific format that can be adjusted to any desired arrangement.

(E) An area designed to accommodate 500-600 dancers and several thousand spectators. This dance area is circular in shape, resembling a large doughnut. The middle of the donut is the area where the dancer performs; the outer rim provides protection for the audience.

71. Which best describes a thrust stage?

72. Which is a proscenium stage?

73. A philosopher who speaks of true ideas as those which "work" or lead to satisfaction or success is best described as

(A) a pragmatist.

(B) an empiricist.

(C) a rationalist.

(D) a Correspondence theorist.

(E) a Coherentist.

74. Many directions are given on a music score. When a dot (♩) is over a note, this indicates to play the note

(A) tenuto.   (D) piano.

(B) staccato.   (E) loud.

(C) fortissimo.

75. Count Basie, a jazz pianist/band leader, employed which style of playing in his accompaniment?

(A) Comping   (D) Figured bass

(B) Scat singing   (E) Ghost note

(C) Riffs

Section 2

TIME: 45 Minutes
75 Questions

DIRECTIONS: Each of the questions or incomplete statements below is followed by five possible answers or completions. Select the best choice in each case and fill in the corresponding oval on the answer sheet.

---

76. Which one of the following scales contains three flats in the key signature?

    (A) B flat major

    (B) E flat major

    (C) F major

    (D) G major

    (E) D major

QUESTIONS 77-79 refer to the following passage.

It is very seldom that mere ordinary people like John and myself secure ancestral halls for the summer.

A colonial mansion, a hereditary estate, I would say a haunted house and reach the height of romantic felicity – but that would be asking too much of fate!

Still I will proudly declare that there is something queer about it.

Else, why should it be let so cheaply? And why have stood so long untenanted?

John laughs at me, of course, but one expects that.

John is practical in the extreme. He has no patience with faith, an intense horror of superstition, and he scoffs openly at any talk of things not to be felt and seen and put down in figures.

John is a physician, and *perhaps* (I would not say it to a living soul, of course, but this is dead paper and a great relief to my mind) – *perhaps* that is one reason I do not get well faster.

You see, he does not believe I am sick! And what can one do?

If a physician of high standing, and one's own husband, assures friends and relatives that there is really nothing the matter with one but temporary nervous depression – a slight hysterical tendency – what is one to do?

My brother is also a physician, and also of high standing, and he says the same thing.

So I take phosphates or phosphites – whichever it is – and tonics, and air and exercise, and journeys, and am absolutely forbidden to "work" until I am well again.

Personally, I disagree with their ideas.

77. John is characterized by the speaker as

(A) arrogant.

(D) realistic.

(B) trustworthy.

(E) possessive.

(C) cunning.

78. The speaker views writing as

(A) annoying.

(D) painful.

(B) therapeutic.

(E) whimsical.

(C) laborious.

79. We can infer from the passage that the speaker

(A) is insane.

(B) is of solid mental health.

(C) has no real occupation.

(D) strongly dislikes her husband.

(E) is planning to murder her husband.

QUESTIONS 80 and 81 refer to the following passage.

Come, now, there may as well be an end of this! Every time I meet your eyes squarely I detect the question just slipping out of them. If you had spoken it, or even boldly looked it; if you had shown in your motions the least sign of a fussy or fidgety concern on my account; if this were not the evening of my birthday and you the only friend who remembered it; if confession were not good for the soul, though harder than sin to some people, of whom I am one, – well, if all reasons were not at this instant converged into a focus, and burning me rather violently in that region where the seat of emotion is supposed to lie, I should keep my trouble to myself.

Bayaro Taylor, *Beauty and the Beast, Tales from Home* (1872)

80. The speaker of the above passage feels

(A) guilty.   (D) sorrowful.

(B) anxious.   (E) relieved.

(C) ashamed.

81. The speaker feels that confession is

(A) unnecessary.   (D) impossible.

(B) nonsensical.   (E) comical.

(C) healthy.

QUESTION 82 refers to the following verse.

<blockquote>
Gallants, attend, and hear a friend
Trill forth harmonious ditty:
Strange things I'll tell, which late befell
In Philadelphia city.
</blockquote>

82. Judging from the first stanza of this poem, which of the following is true?

(A) The poem has a serious tone.

(B) The poem has no predictable rhyme scheme.

(C) The poem may be satirical or humorous.

(D) The rhyme scheme will be a-b-a-b.

(E) The rhyme scheme will be a-a-b-b.

QUESTION 83 refers to the following.

83. Which of the following seems most true of the building pictured above?

    (A) It relies on broad areas of unbroken surfaces.

    (B) It uses industrial forms and materials to suggest a living organism.

    (C) It is conceived and designed on a human scale.

    (D) It owes a debt to the Classical past.

    (E) It achieves an effect of poetic calm, balance, and remove.

QUESTION 84 refers to the following.

84. Which of the following best describes the sculpture on the building pictured above?

    (A) It tells a detailed story with a definite sequence.

    (B) It dominates the facade of the building.

    (C) It draws heavily on classical mythology.

    (D) it is contained by the architectural forms of the doorways.

    (E) It was probably applied as an afterthought.

QUESTION 85 refers to the following.

85. The sculpture pictured above suggests which of the following?

   (A) The rolling motion of a wheel

   (B) The balanced action of a lever

   (C) The twisting spiral of a screw

   (D) The flowing motion of liquid

   (E) The interlocking action of gears

QUESTION 86 refers to the following.

86. In the example shown above, which of the following contributes most to the effect of a photographic snapshot?

(A) The inclusion of the horse and the dog

(B) The middle-class character of the subjects

(C) The perspective grid behind the figures

(D) The off-center composition and the random cropping of the figures

(E) The strong dependence on outline

QUESTION 87 refers to the following.

87. The building pictured on the previous page depends for its effect on

    (A) the interplay of diagonal and vertical lines.

    (B) the broad expanse of window glass.

    (C) a subtle arrangement of curving, rhythmic forms.

    (D) the viewer's point of view from ground level.

    (E) the bold massing of simple cubic forms.

QUESTIONS 88 and 89 refer to the following verse.

Now thou art dead no eye shall ever see,
For shape and service, spaniel like to thee.
This shall my love do, give thy sad death one
Tear, that deserves of me a million.

88. The above poem is an example of a(n)

    (A) allegory.   (D) kenning.

    (B) elegy.   (E) refrain.

    (C) ballad.

89. Lines 3-4 contain an example of

    (A) enjambment.   (D) Homeric simile.

    (B) personification.   (E) epigram.

    (C) onomatopoeia.

QUESTIONS 90–93 refer to the following verse.

Study is like the heaven's glorious sun,
That will not be deep-searched with saucy looks.
Small have continual plodders won
Save base authority from others' books.
These earthly godfathers of heaven's lights,
That give a name to every fixed star
Have no more profit of their shining nights
Than those who walk and wot* not what they are.
(*know)

90. The speaker of these lines is most likely a

    (A) student.   (D) thief.

    (B) professor.   (E) villain.

    (C) clergyman.

91. The lines "Small have continual plodders won / Save base authority from others' books" mean

    (A) books are key in the acquisition of knowledge.

    (B) only one's opinions are important – not facts found in books.

    (C) study is long and tedious, but ultimately rewarding.

    (D) knowledge and authority are eventually given to those who pursue them.

    (E) all that is gained by study are the simple and worthless opinions of others.

92. The last four lines of the passage suggest that

    (A) study is a pursuit for the old and tired.

    (B) anyone, whether he be a genius or simpleton, can name things and recite facts.

    (C) many geniuses are simpletons, and vice versa.

    (D) study ruins intuitive wonder, such as that caused by the stars.

    (E) All of the above.

93. "These earthly godfathers" are most likely

    (A) professors.   (D) lovers.

    (B) astronomers.   (E) poets.

    (C) artists.

94. This ruler has decided to retire and distribute his wealth and his responsibilities among his children, but he requires loyalty oaths from them. The action described above takes place in which of the following plays?

(A) *Tartuffe*

(D) *Hamlet*

(B) *Measure for Measure*

(E) *Waiting for Godot*

(C) *King Lear*

95. *Everyman* is one among a number of **morality** plays. Abstractions such as beauty, strength, discretion, and five wits are personified as Everyman's companions. Within the context of the preceding passage, which is the most precise meaning of morality?

(A) Ethics

(D) Diffidence

(B) Pride

(E) Sloth

(C) Mischief

96. The use of concrete as a construction material was first widely exploited during which of the following periods?

(A) Ancient Greek

(B) Ancient Rome

(C) The Middle Ages

(D) The eighteenth century

(E) The twentieth century

97. Which of the following choreographers was the first contributor to modern dance?

(A) Agnes de Mille

(D) Isadora Duncan

(B) Martha Graham

(E) Ted Shawn

(C) Ruth St. Denis

98. If a philosopher believes in reincarnation, that philosopher's general view in the philosophy of mind will be known as

(A) dualism.

(B) eliminative materialism.

(C) epiphenomenalism.

(D) functionalism.

(E) behaviorism.

99. What scale contains B flat, E flat, A flat, and D flat?

(A) C major

(D) A flat major

(B) F major

(E) C minor

(C) A minor

100. A scale composed of half steps is a _____ scale.

(A) major

(D) whole tone scale

(B) chromatic

(E) blues scale

(C) minor

101. How many sixteenth notes are equal to one quarter note?

(A) 1

(D) 4

(B) 3

(E) 6

(C) 2

QUESTION 102 refers to the following passage.

Nothing else was said; a new danger was being carried towards them by the river. Some wooden machinery had just given way on one of the wharves, and huge fragments were being floated along. The sun was rising now, and the wide area of watery desolation was spread out in dreadful clearness around them – in dreadful clearness floated onwards the hurry-ing, threatening masses. A large company in a boat that was working its way along under the Tofton houses, observed their danger, and shouted, "Get out of the current!"

But that could not be done at once, and Tom, looking before him, saw Death rushing on them. Huge fragments, clinging together in fatal fellow-ship, made one wide mass across the stream.

"It is coming, Maggie!" Tom said, in a deep hoarse voice, loosing the oars, and clasping her.

102. The above passage contains which of the following conflicts?

I.   Man vs. Man

IV. Man vs. Nature

II. Man vs. Society

V.   Man vs. Self

III. Man vs. God

(A) III only.

(D) I, II, and III only.

(B) IV only.

(E) I, II, IV, and V only.

(C) I and II only.

QUESTIONS 103 and 104 refer to the following passage.

Morning clatters with the first L train down Allen Street. Daylight rattles through the windows, shaking the old brick houses, splatters the girders of the L structure with bright confetti.

The cats are leaving the garbage cans, the chinches are going back into the walls, leaving sweaty limbs, leaving the grimetender necks of little children asleep. Men and women stir under blankets and bedquilts on mattresses in the corners of rooms, clots of kids begin to untangle to scream and kick.

At the corner of Riverton the old man with the hempen beard who sleeps where nobody knows is putting out his picklestand. Tubs of gherkins, pimentos, melonrind, piccalilli give out twining vines and cold tendrils of dank peppery fragrance that grow like a marsh garden out of the musky bedsmells and the rancid clangor of the cobbled awakening street.

The old man with the hempen beard who sleeps where nobody knows sits in the midst of it like Jonah under his gourd.

103. The language of this passage is reminiscent of

(A) the Bible.

(D) a literature textbook.

(B) Shakespeare.

(E) a rough draft.

(C) stage directions.

104. The man's namelessness lends him an air of

(A) anxiety.

(D) heroism.

(B) insignificance.

(E) humor.

(C) fear.

105. Often recalled as a medieval horror story of giants and demons, this magnificent epic was intended to outline the importance of leading a spiritual life.

The passage above discusses

(A) "The Pilgrim's Progress."

(B) "The Canterbury Tales."

(C) "The Song of Roland."

(D) "Beowulf."

(E) "The Divine Comedy."

106. Which of the following deals with a 20-year search for home?

(A) *Rip Van Winkle*   (D) "The Odyssey"

(B) *The Wizard of Oz*   (E) *Don Quixote*

(C) *Exodus*

QUESTION 107 refers to the following.

107. Which of the following is fundamental to the design of the building pictured above?

(A) A combination of intersecting diagonal lines

(B) A simple repetition of vertical and horizontal forms

(C) A continuous expanse of unbroken wall surface

(D) A combination of columns and arches

(E) A complex interplay of many varied shapes

QUESTIONS 108-110 refer to the following illustrations (A) through (E).

(A)

(B)

(C)

(D)   (E)

108. Which of the examples pictured above makes the most direct contact with the viewer?

109. In which example does the pose and expression of the sitter convey aristocratic disdain?

110. Which example breaks down the forms of the subject and merges them with the background?

QUESTION 111 refers to the following.

111. Which of the following seems most true of the example pictured above?

(A) The artist attempted a realistic depiction of three-dimensional space.

(B) The picture probably illustrates an episode in a narrative.

(C) The execution was slow, painstaking, and deliberate.

(D) Both the script and the leaves share a quality of quick, fluid calligraphy.

(E) The painting depends on a wide range of contrasting tones.

QUESTIONS 112–114 refer to the following passages.

(A) There was a knight who was a lusty liver.
One day as he came riding from the river
He saw a maiden walking all forlorn
Ahead of him, alone as she was born.
And of that maiden, spite of all she said,
By very force he took her maidenhead.

(B) That time of year thou mayst in me behold
When yellow leaves, or none, or few, do hang
Upon those boughs which shake against the cold,
Bare, ruined choirs where late the sweet bird sang.

(C) My love is like to ice, and I to fire.

(D) With how sad steps, O moon, thou climb'st the skies!
How silently, and with how wan a face.

(E) Hail to thee, blithe Spirit!
Bird thou never wert –
That from Heaven, or near it,
Pourest thy full heart
In profuse strains of unpremeditated art.

112. Which passage uses the literary device of simile?

113. Which passage employs personification?

114. Which passage uses the device of apostrophe?

QUESTIONS 115–117 refer to the following passages.

(A) Of man's first disobedience, and the fruit
Of that forbidden tree whose mortal taste
Brought death into the world, and all our woe,
With loss of Eden, till one great Man
Restore us, and regain the blissful seat,
Sing, Heavenly Muse...

(B) My poem's epic, and is meant to be
Divided in twelve books; each book containing,
With love, and war, a heavy gale at sea,
A list of ships, and captains, and kings reigning,
New characters; the episodes are three;
A panoramic view of Hell's in training,
After the style of Virgil and of Homer,
So that my name of Epic's no misnomer.

(C) Yet once more, O ye Laurels, and once more
Ye Myrtles brown, with Ivy never-sear,
I come to pluck your Berries harsh and crude,
And with forc'd fingers rude,
Shatter your leaves before the mellowing year.
Bitter constraint, and sad occasion dear,
Compels me to disturb your season due:
For Lycidas is dead, dead ere his prime...

(D) But at my back I always hear
     Time's winged chariot hurrying near;
     And yonder all before us lie
     Deserts of vast eternity.
     Thy beauty shall no more be found,
     Nor, in thy marble vault, shall sound
     My echoing song; then worms shall try
     That long-preserved virginity,
     And your quaint honor turn to dust,
     And into ashes all my lust:
     The grave's a fine and private place,
     But none, I think, do there embrace.

(E) Lo! 'tis a gala night
     Within the lonesome latter years!
     An angel throng, bewinged, bedight
     In veils, and drowned in tears,
     Sit in a theater, to see
     A play of hopes and fears,
     While the orchestra breathes fitfully
     The music of the spheres.

115. Which passage comes from a mock epic?

116. Which passage employs the theme of *carpe diem?*

117. Which passage is from a pastoral elegy?

118. She depended for her well-being upon the kindness of strangers; he
     relied upon being well-liked for his security.

   This statement describes which pairing of characters and plays?

   (A) Jocasta in *Oedipus;* Ekdal in *The Wild Duck*

   (B) The Caretaker in *The New Tenant; Walter* in A *Raisin in the Sun*

   (C) Blanche Dubois in A *Streetcar Named Desire;* Willy Loman in
        Death of a Salesman

   (D) Nora in A *Doll's House; Euelpides* in *Aristophanes*

   (E) Hedda in *Hedda Gabler;* Algernon in *The Importance of Being
        Earnest*

119. Why, what should be the fear?
    I do not set my life at a pin's fee,
    And for my soul, what can it do to that,
    Being a thing immortal as itself?
    It waves me forth again: I'll follow it.

    The preceding lines are from Shakespeare's *Hamlet*. Which of the following terms are best used to describe the "it" referred to in the passage?

    (A) An animal

    (B) An opponent

    (C) A path

    (D) A rule

    (E) A ghost

QUESTION 120 refers to the following.

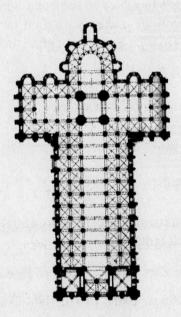

120. The plan illustrated above is an example of a type of medieval church that is commonly referred to as a(n)

    (A) early Christian monastic church.

    (B) Romanesque pilgrimage church.

    (C) subterranean crypt.

(D) Gothic cathedral.

(E) centrally planned church.

121. In ballet, the term *port de bras* refers to

(A) movement of the head, shoulders, and upper torso.

(B) all body parts in correct relative position with one another.

(C) exercises that help develop coordination, control, and balance. This is practiced by alternating feet.

(D) a pose standing on one leg while the other leg is raised up, turned out, and bent with the foot open in the opposite direction of the body.

(E) A group of exercises for the arms.

122. If a consequentialist in ethics is someone who believes that only the consequences of actions make them good or bad, then which of the following ethical theories is consequentialistic?

(A) Utilitarianism

(B) Kantianism

(C) Intuitionism

(D) Virtue ethics

(E) Aristotelian ethics

123. A chord (three or more pitches sounding simultaneously) in root position contains which order of notes?

(A) root, 3rd, 5th   (D) 5th, root, 3rd

(B) root, 2nd, 5th   (E) root, 2nd, 3rd

(C) 3rd, 5th, root

124. Which of the following scores tells the musician to play softly when the following dynamic marking is written below the staff?

(A) ff.   (D) decres.

(B) cres.   (E) rit.

(C) p.

125. How many beats are in each measure if the time signature is $\frac{6}{8}$?

    (A) 4   (D) 2

    (B) 6   (E) 8

    (C) 3

126. Which of the following seventeenth century works uses the satiric device of irony to superb effect?

    (A) "Paradise Lost"

    (B) *A Modest Proposal*

    (C) *Everyman*

    (D) *The Way of the World*

    (E) *The Lives of the Poets*

127. Which of the following is a great romantic epic considered by scholars to express the highest ideals of the Renaissance?

    (A) "The Faerie Queen"

    (B) "The Wife of Bath's Tale"

    (C) *Gulliver's Travels*

    (D) "The Rape of the Lock"

    (E) "Beowulf"

128. Which of the following deals with the dreadful working conditions in Chicago meat packing houses at the turn of the twentieth century?

    (A) *Martin Chuzzlewit*   (D) *My Antonia*

    (B) *The Jungle*   (E) *Main Street*

    (C) *Daisy Miller*

129. Often remembered as the play in which the main character killed his father and married his mother, which work is often cited as elucidating the Greek concept of "Hubris"?

(A) *Oedipus Rex*

(D) "The Aeneid"

(B) *Tiger at the Gates*

(E) "Il Purgatorio"

(C) *Zorba the Greek*

130. Which of the following Elizabethan works is often remembered as the play in which a son murders his uncle and stepfather for the murder of his father, and deals with the question: "Is justice delayed, justice denied?"

(A) *Twelve Angry Men*

(B) *Inherit the Wind*

(C) *Macbeth*

(D) *Hamlet*

(E) *Rosencrantz and Guildenstern Are Dead*

QUESTIONS 131-133 refer to illustrations (A) through (C) below.

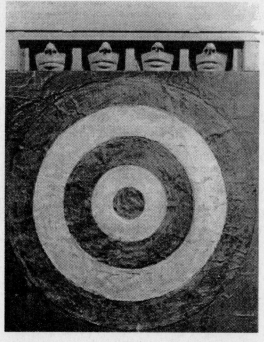

(A)

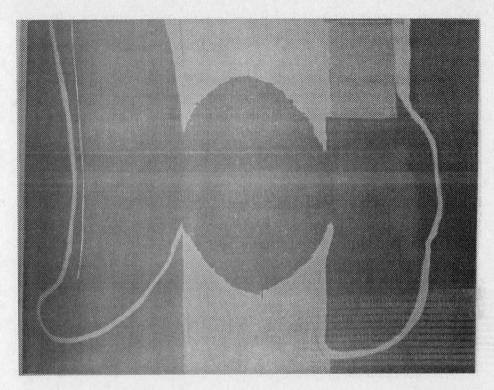

(B)

(C)

131. Which is NOT an abstract expressionist painting?

(A) Painting (A)

(D) All of the above.

(B) Painting (B)

(E) None of the above.

(C) Painting (C)

132. Which is a *mixed media* piece?

(A) Painting (A)

(D) All of the above.

(B) Painting (B)

(E) None of the above.

(C) Painting (C)

133. Which is by Jasper Johns?

(A) Painting (A)

(D) All of the above.

(B) Painting (B)

(E) None of the above.

(C) Painting (C)

QUESTION 134 refers to the following.

134. Who is the central focus in the picture above and why?

   (A) The two men at the lower right, because they are separate and thus draw attention

   (B) The guard at the top of the stairs, because he is the person at the highest elevation

   (C) The man to the left of the flag, because he rises above the crowd

   (D) The man on the middle of the stairs in the long, belted robe, because he is the focus of the other players

   (E) There is no central focus in the picture.

QUESTION 135 refers to the following.

135. In the example pictured above, which of the following contributes most to an effect of stability and changeless grandeur?

   (A) The strong horizontal thrust of the architecture

   (B) The wealth of elaborate ornamental detail

   (C) The vast open courtyard with its surrounding columns

(D) The simplified geometry of the massive forms and the sloping diagonal walls

(E) The enormous relief carvings of the pharaohs and the gods

QUESTIONS 136 and 137 refer to the following verse.

Careful observers may foretell the hour
(By sure prognostics) when to dread a shower:
While rain depends, the pensive cat gives o'er
Her frolics, and pursues her tail no more.
Returning home at night, you'll find the sink*
Strike your offended sense with double stink.
If you be wise, then go not far to dine;
You spend more in coach hire than save in wine.
A coming shower your shooting corns presage,
Old aches throb, your hollow tooth will rage.

(* sewer)

136. Which genre of poetry does this passage exemplify?

(A) Epic   (D) Ode

(B) Satiric   (E) Lyric

(C) Parodic

137. The phrase "(By sure prognostics)" is _____ in tone.

(A) sarcastic   (D) Both (A) and (B).

(B) playful   (E) Both (A) and (C).

(C) angry

QUESTIONS 138 and 139 refer to the following poem.

WHEN BRITAIN REALLY RULED THE WAVES

When Britain really ruled the waves
    (In good Queen Bess's time)—
The House of Peers made no pretense
To intellectual eminence,
    Or scholarship sublime;
Yet Britain won her proudest bays*
In good Queen Bess's glorious days!

When Wellington thrashed Bonaparte,
    As every child can tell,
The House of Peers, throughout the war,
Did nothing in particular,
    And did it very well:
Yet Britain set the world ablaze
In good King George's glorious days!

And while the House of Peers withholds
    Its legislative hand,
And noble statesman do not itch
To interfere with matters which
    They do not understand,
As bright will shine Great Britain's rays
As in good King George's glorious days!

(* honors)

138. In this poem, the ruling body of Britain is described as

    (A) a very successful legislative institution.

    (B) a body which makes wise decisions.

    (C) a body which is supported by the British.

    (D) a group of disinterested and unintelligent noblemen.

    (E) a group of highly talented diplomats and legislators.

139. The tone of this poem can be described as

    (A) lauding.   (D) satisfied.

    (B) parodic.   (E) patriotic.

    (C) satiric.

140. "Let Sleeping Dogs Lie" is a warning delivered in which of the following plays?

    (A) *The Cherry Orchard*   (D) *Aristophanes*

    (B) *Death of a Salesman*   (E) *Oedipus the King*

    (C) *Pygmalion*

141. Which play's conflict is divided between authorities and housewives who know the killer's identity because they recognize the "domestic" clues?

(A) *Ghosts*

(D) *Anna Christie*

(B) *Trifles*

(E) *Hamlet*

(C) *Pygmalion*

QUESTION 142 refers to the following.

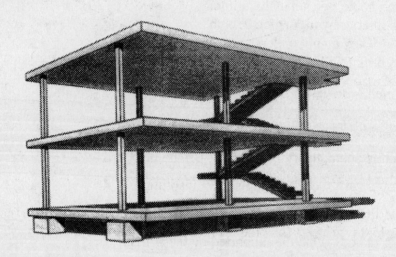

142. The primary function of *pilotis,* shown above, in Le Corbusier's Domino House, is to

(A) provide insulation.

(B) divide floors or stories.

(C) reinforce load-bearing walls.

(D) eliminate the need for load-bearing walls.

(E) elevate the structure above ground.

QUESTIONS 143–145 refer to the following diagram of a stage.

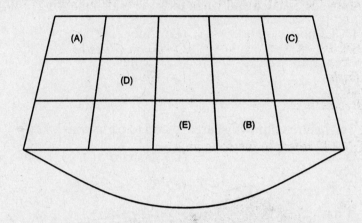

143. Which is downstage left center?

144. Which is upstage right?

145. Which is downstage center?

146. The theory of truth that regards a claim as true not when it fits the world, but when it fits other beliefs regarded as true is known

(A) the Coherence theory.

(B) the Correspondence theory.

(C) the Redundancy theory.

(D) the Pragmatic theory.

(E) the Performative theory.

147. A flat, sharp, or natural written in front of a note is called a(n)

(A) mistake.

(B) accidental.

(C) key signature.

(D) time signature.

(E) scale.

148. When reading music, the performers know to return to the sign and play to the designated end when they see which marking?

(A) DC al fine

(D) fine

(B) DS al fine

(E) decres.

(C) coda

149. A key signature with two sharps is said to be in which key?

(A) D

(D) F sharp

(B) A

(E) C

(C) B flat

150. Which of the following has as its central theme the spiritual decadence of the twentieth century?

(A) *Life on the Mississippi*

(B) *Portrait of a Lady*

(C) *The Outcasts of Poker Flat*

(D) "The Love Song of J. Alfred Prufrock"

(E) *The Man That Corrupted Hadleyburg*

CLEP HUMANITIES
TEST 2

ANSWER KEY

Section 1

1. (D)	16. (B)	31. (E)	46. (B)	61. (B)
2. (C)	17. (D)	32. (C)	47. (B)	62. (A)
3. (A)	18. (D)	33. (C)	48. (E)	63. (B)
4. (C)	19. (D)	34. (D)	49. (C)	64. (D)
5. (C)	20. (C)	35. (A)	50. (A)	65. (A)
6. (B)	21. (A)	36. (A)	51. (A)	66. (B)
7. (E)	22. (C)	37. (A)	52. (D)	67. (B)
8. (C)	23. (A)	38. (D)	53. (A)	68. (E)
9. (B)	24. (C)	39. (B)	54. (C)	69. (D)
10. (A)	25. (C)	40. (D)	55. (B)	70. (A)
11. (A)	26. (A)	41. (B)	56. (A)	71. (C)
12. (B)	27. (B)	42. (B)	57. (D)	72. (A)
13. (D)	28. (B)	43. (C)	58. (B)	73. (A)
14. (B)	29. (C)	44. (A)	59. (B)	74. (B)
15. (A)	30. (C)	45. (D)	60. (E)	75. (A)

Section 2

76. (B)	91. (E)	106. (D)	121. (E)	136. (B)
77. (D)	92. (D)	107. (B)	122. (A)	137. (D)
78. (B)	93. (B)	108. (C)	123. (A)	138. (D)
79. (C)	94. (C)	109. (B)	124. (C)	139. (C)
80. (B)	95. (A)	110. (A)	125. (B)	140. (E)
81. (C)	96. (B)	111. (D)	126. (B)	141. (B)
82. (C)	97. (D)	112. (C)	127. (A)	142. (D)
83. (B)	98. (A)	113. (D)	128. (B)	143. (B)
84. (D)	99. (D)	114. (E)	129. (A)	144. (A)
85. (B)	100. (B)	115. (B)	130. (D)	145. (E)
86. (D)	101. (D)	116. (D)	131. (A)	146. (A)
87. (E)	102. (B)	117. (C)	132. (A)	147. (B)
88. (B)	103. (C)	118. (C)	133. (A)	148. (B)
89. (A)	104. (B)	119. (E)	134. (D)	149. (A)
90. (A)	105. (E)	120. (B)	135. (D)	150. (D)

DETAILED EXPLANATIONS
OF ANSWERS
TEST 2

Section 1

1.   **(D)** These are flying buttresses, a feature of church construction used frequently during the Gothic period. They support, on the exterior of the building, key points of stress in the wall, where the lateral thrust of the roof vaults is greatest. While these members are in the approximate form of (A) arches, they do not *function,* in a supporting sense, as arches. (B) Cantilevers are supporting members which project independently from a wall or beam. This is a twentieth century invention, used in the context of modern building. (C) Ribbed vaults are also a feature of Gothic church construction, but are used *within* a church, not on the exterior. (E) Windows is not a correct choice because these structural members are obviously perpendicular to the wall, rather than parallel to it as windows are.

2.   **(C)** Of the choices given, a dance technique drawing its material from natural human movement allowing the artist to be free and create and build his or her own unique movements is modern dance. Ballet (A), jazz (B), danse mora (Flamenco dancing) (D), and tap dance (E) all require complete control of the body and are specific in the movements of each dance technique.

3.   **(A)** Although Socrates claimed not to know anything himself, he seems convinced that the unexamined life is not worth living because virtue and happiness come only with the search for knowledge. Aristotle (B) thought such a view placed too much emphasis on knowledge, for virtuous activity is largely a matter of habit and training. Kant (C) claimed that the only good thing is a good will, and that one can know what is right without willing it. Mill's utilitarianism (D), based on the idea that one should do what creates the most pleasure for the greatest number, is a radical departure from virtue ethics altogether. Rousseau (E) believed that

human beings are good by nature but are corrupted by their social environment.

4.   **(C)** Although it resembles a brass instrument, the alto saxophone is a member of the woodwind family. In order to produce a sound, air blown through the mouthpiece causes the reed to vibrate; choice (C) is correct. The trumpet, tuba, and French horn are all members of the brass family. These instruments are made of brass and produce sound by the vibration of the airstream from the lips through the mouthpiece. Choices (A), (B), and (D) are not correct. The trombone is a brass instrument. It changes notes by moving a slide. Choice (E) is incorrect.

5.   **(C)** The top number of a time signature is equal to the number of beats in a measure. The bottom number denotes which note is equal to one beat. For example, in $\frac{4}{4}$ there are four beats in each measure and a quarter note receives one beat. Therefore, choice (C) is correct. In $\frac{4}{4}$ a whole note would receive four beats, a half note would receive two beats, and a half quarter note would receive three beats. Therefore, choices (A), (B), and (D) are incorrect. A dotted quarter note receives one-and-a-half beats in $\frac{4}{4}$. Choice (E) is incorrect.

6.   **(B)** Jazz is a musical style that incorporates a swing feel, a strong rhythmic beat, and improvisation. Choice (B) is correct. Fugues employ one melodic fragment in variations; therefore, choice (A) is incorrect. Rock 'n' Roll combines elements of country, rhythm and blues, and other black idioms, such as gospel and the blues; therefore, choice (C) is not correct. A symphony is an orchestral work with three or four movements; therefore, choice (D) is incorrect. Opera is a vocal dramatic work; choice (E) is incorrect.

7.   **(E)** These two stanzas are taken from Robert Gray's "Ode on the Death of a Favorite Cat." There is no mention of a snake, so (A) is wrong. The passage does mention a "tortoise," but only because Gray is comparing the cat's coat with a tortoise's stripes; therefore, (B) is wrong. A vase is mentioned, but only because the cat "reclined" on it; (C) is also wrong. There is no mention at all of a dog, so (D) is wrong. The word "tabby" and such characteristics as "snowy beard" (whiskers) and "velvet paws" describe a cat, so (E) is correct.

8.   **(C)** This question asks you to read the excerpt from William Golding's *Lord of the Flies* and determine the literary movement to which

Golding ascribes. Surrealism (A) goes beyond the real into the realm of the "super-real" and often includes the world of the unconscious or dreams. Since there is nothing to suggest that this passage is anything but a true-to-life description, this choice is incorrect. Expressionistic writers (B) present life as they feel it to be, not as it appears. Again, this passage does not incorporate this style. Romantic writing (D) presents life as the writer wishes it could be and usually describes strange lands and adventures; this "normal" beach scene contains no romantic elements, so (D) is incorrect. Gothicism (E) is a style used by novelists of the eighteenth and nineteenth centuries which relies on greater-than-life heroes, villains, and a grandiose sense of the macabre. Since the passage features none of this, (E) is wrong. The correct answer is (C), because realistic writing concerns detailed descriptions of everyday life; "fledged with palm trees," "their green feathers were a hundred feet up in the air," "scattered with decaying coconuts," etc., are all realistic descriptions of the scene.

9. **(B)** The author's point here is that the so-called "historical novels" which exist in our canon of literature are, in fact, anything but "historical." "Fantastic" usually refers to something unreal, as it does here, making choice (B) the correct answer.

10. **(A)** If you selected anything but choice (A), you were too hasty in making your decision. The author is not mocking the famous *writers*, but those readers which read their works as historical treatises. The author refers to their novels as "fairy tales," but not in a condescending way; he is simply categorizing the novels as works of fiction ("supreme," in fact) which should be read as such.

11. **(A)** Prose is non-metrical language, the opposite of verse. Since this passage is not written in verse, (A) is the correct answer. Iambic pentameter is five units (or "feet") of an unstressed syllable followed by a stressed syllable, so (B) is incorrect. An elegy is a poem of lamentation for the dead, so (C) is wrong. A non sequitur is a type of reasoning pattern in which the conclusion does not follow the line of reasoning used to reach it, so (D) is incorrect.

12. **(B)** Since the selection seems to be creating a setting by describing the townspeople and weather in the "little Kansas town," choice (B) is correct. It seems highly unlikely that it is taken from the climax of a short story (C) (the point of highest tension where the elements of the plot are brought together), the dénouement (D) (the unwinding of the plot follow-

ing the climax), or the conclusion (A) (the final images or actions described by an author).

13.   **(D)**   The first four choices given are types of staging. Choice (E) is not; therefore, it is an invalid choice. Thrust staging has the stage projecting into the audience and the audience surrounding the stage on three sides. The audience in the picture is on only two sides of the stage, which is known as central staging (D). Proscenium (B) is traditional staging in a theatre with a proscenium arch. Theatre-in-the-round has the audience completely surrounding the playing area. Choice (D) is the correct answer.

14.   **(B)**   You are asked to determine which of the buildings named is pictured. Each edifice listed is built in a different style, which should be easily recognizable. Notre Dame Cathedral (A) is French, characterized by its flying buttresses. This is a picture of the frieze of the west cella of the Parthenon, which is characterized by Doric columns (as pictured) and the high-relief metopes of the Doric frieze. The Sistine Chapel (C), Michelangelo's masterpiece, is known for its frescoes and barrel-vaulted ceilings. Versailles (D) is the palace of Louis XIV, outside of Paris, and is an example of the ornate style of baroque grandeur. One distinguishing factor is that all the choices other than the Parthenon are structures which are in much better repair, since they are more recent than the pictured ruins of the Parthenon.

15.   **(A)**   The squatting position of the figure is indicative of a low position, like that of a slave (A). Since he is wearing only a cloak thrown back over one shoulder, this, too, indicates the clothing of a commoner or a person of low status. The action, that of sharpening a knife, is a job which would be designated to a slave. The muscle structure of the figure would not really indicate social level, making (B), (C), (D), and (E) unlikely choices.

16.   **(B)**   This question asks you to look at the print and come to some conclusions. Since each figure is holding or playing a musical instrument (double aulos, lute, and harp), it can be surmised that they are musicians (A). Choice (B) states that the artwork creates the illusion of depth. Since there is not a strong sense of depth, and you are looking for the exceptional choice, this is the correct answer. The lack of a three-dimensional aspect (D) and the absence of a background against which the figures are placed, all add to the conclusion that this is an Egyptian tomb painting (C).

17.   **(D)**   The pictured statue is a portrait of Augustus that was found near Rome. The effect of this figure, with the serious expression and gesture, is not comic (A). There is nothing in the stance, expression, or dress to suggest levity. Conversely, although the face is not smiling, it is also not a tragic figure (B). Although the breastplate or cuirass has scenes in low relief carved on it, the figure itself is not ornate or excessively decorated (C). Finally, the large gesture and stance of an imperator, or commander-in-chief, makes for an imposing figure (D). The carved armor, careful draping of the cloak and the rod the figure holds, all add to this impression. Thus, (D) is the correct answer.

18.   **(D)**   This question requires that you study the mood of the people in the picture and make a connection between the instruments pictured, the actions of those pictured, and the type of music being played. Since an opera (A) is usually a formal, upper-class form of music and the picture is of a coarse tavern scene, the music would not be operatic. The individuals appear festive and seem to be enjoying taking part in the merry-making, not singing a sad, serious melody (B), or a funeral hymn (C) dirge. Therefore, the correct answer is (D). The music is a light, boisterous tune.

19.   **(D)**   While the sonnet "My mistress' eyes are nothing like the sun" is Shakespearean, this does not make it different from other sonnets. A majority of sonnets are written in this form, so (A) is incorrect. The poem does describe the appearance of a beloved woman; this choice is incorrect, however, because many other sonnets do the same. Beautiful women were traditional subject matter for Elizabethan sonneteers. The sonnet does follow the proper conventions necessary to label it as one, so (E) is also wrong. (D) is the correct answer because Shakespeare undermines the traditional beauty of the women who are normally written about and states that his mistress is far more beautiful than the other "goddesses," even though she is realistically ordinary.

20.   **(C)**   The last two lines of a Shakespearean sonnet generally provide an ironic twist to the rest of the poem. In this sonnet, the lines refute the argument of the rest of the poem because the speaker states that even though his mistress is ordinary he still finds her beautiful. Thus, choice (C) is the correct answer.

21.   **(A)**   Choice (A) is correct because the poem is witty in the way it takes standard sonnet conventions (a woman's eyes, lips, hair, etc.) and twists them to make a point. By doing this, Shakespeare is also satirizing standard sonnet conventions of his time (which he himself never hesitated

to employ). The poem is not intense (B), sarcastic (C), brooding (D), or sentimental (E). "Sentimental" denotes "looking fondly back on," which the speaker is not doing; the woman is his mistress, not his past mistress.

22. **(C)** This question tests your knowledge of the use of the dramatic term "aside." An aside is a comment spoken directly to the audience that the other actors on stage are supposedly unable to hear. Thus, the correct answer is choice (C).

23. **(A)** You are asked to decide which culture this mask represents. The mask reproduced in the picture was designed to be worn by African tribesmen as they danced by firelight to the accompaniment of drums. The nonrealistic features are intended to conjure up the presence of an invisible spirit. The African tradition is noted due to the large features. The correct answer is (A). The mask is not representative of the Greek culture (B), whose sculpture is clean-lined and realistic, as is the Roman (C). The Dutch culture (D) is characterized by extremely domestic-related arts with a reality of simple truths. Thus, a mask showing elongated and distorted features would not characterize the Dutch culture. Persian art (E) also would not be distorted in the manner of this mask.

24. **(C)** The church of Hagia Sophia was built as part of the palace complex of the Byzantine Emperor Justinian in the first half of the sixth century. The building has the *appearance* of a (A) Turkish mosque; this is due to the four minarets which were added after the Moslem conquest of the Byzantine Empire, when the building was in fact converted (for a time) into a mosque. The building reveals no characteristics whatsoever that may be identified with (B) a Gothic cathedral, although the central-ized plan and large central dome are somewhat reminiscent of certain (D) Roman temples. Hagia Sophia was originally built as a *cathedral*, not as a (E) monastic church.

25. **(C)** Mime is the art of imaging the world together with an audi-ence. The best choice is mime. Pantomime is a composition of mime (A), mimetic imitation is the ability to adapt the body to the properties of things (B); improvisation is a technique in which a performer creates circumstances and applies it to games (D); and commedia dell'arte is a group of masked characters presenting plays in an improvisational form (E).

26.   **(A)** This sentence expresses part of the Cosmological Argument for God's existence, in which God is thought of as an Unmoved Mover. A Slippery Slope argument (B) is a logical fallacy that minimizes the differences between similar things or events and does not prove anything. The Ontological argument (C) is based not on causation but on the conception of God as the most perfect being. The "Big Bang" theory (D) does not answer the question, Why was there a Big Bang?, and so does not presuppose a first cause of all things. The Design Argument (E) takes God to be responsible not for the chain of causes but for the order of the universe: just as a watch presupposes a watchmaker, so an ordered universe presupposes a Cosmic Designer.

27.   **(B)** John Phillip Sousa composed and popularized marches. For example, "The Washington Post March" and "The Liberty Bell." He was known as the "March King"; so choice (B) is correct. Giuseppe Verdi is known for his operas, so choice (A) is incorrect. Symphonies were a specialty of Ludwig van Beethoven; therefore, choice (C) is not correct. Fugues are associated largely with Johann Sebastian Bach; therefore, choice (D) is incorrect. Frederic Chopin composed lyrical nocturnes for piano; choice (E) is incorrect.

28.   **(B)** Claude Debussy experimented with musical impressionism. His music painted a picture with sounds; choice (B) is correct. Stravinsky composed with a number of twentieth century styles, so choice (A) is not correct. Dizzy Gillespie was a composer and performer of jazz music; choice (C) is incorrect. Bach composed fugues, suites, concertos, and choral works during the Baroque period, so (D) is not correct. W.A. Mozart composed symphonies during the classical period. Choice (E) is incorrect.

29.   **(C)** Dr. Shin'ichi Suzuki developed a teaching philosophy called "Talent Education," which employed the "mother-tongue" method. Music is taught in a similar fashion to children learning their native language, by rote. The use of imitation, repetition, and observation are emphasized. Choice (C) is the correct answer. Edwin Gordon emphasized audiation, the use of inner hearing; choice (A) is incorrect. Carl Orff's approach employed the use of rhythm; choice (B) is not correct. Emile Jaques-Dalcroze is primarily recognized for the use of eurythmics and improvisation; choice (D) is incorrect. The Carabo-Cone method believed the students learn by using the body; choice (E) is incorrect.

30.   **(C)**   You are asked to decide the literary form of the quote. Since it seems to have no poetic form, the first choice is easily negated, as is choice (E), for songs are similar in form to poems. Although a long speech in a play could be similar to this, there is no dialogue, which would normally indicate a play (B). A journal, or diary, is written in first person, as the excerpt is. Also, it puts forth everyday events and feelings, the purpose we normally associate with a journal. A myth (D) is a traditional story, usually connected with the religion of people, and attempts to account for something in nature. This quote gives no indication of mythological allusions. The correct answer is (C).

31.   **(E)**   This quote from Patrick Henry's speech is a reference to Judas Iscariot who betrayed Jesus with a kiss, giving him up to the soldiers to be crucified. This is a biblical allusion from Luke 22: 47-48 (E). Since there is no personification in the line, nor is there a metaphorical comparison, (A) and (B) are incorrect. Choice (C) is incorrect because an "illusion" is a false idea or conception. Choice (D), hyperbole is also an incorrect choice, since there is no overstatement in the quote.

32.   **(C)**   is the correct response because the author of this passage does little to give the reader a sense of what the landscape looks like in detail. Phrases such as "filled all the valley with verdure and fertility" do nothing to describe the details of the scene, such as the flora and fauna "Fish of every species" and "every fowl whom nature has taught to dip the wing in water" are extremely vague, giving no description of what the fish and birds look like. The passage involves no comparisons or contrasts (B), and it does not have a negative connotation. Although the description is vague, it is still realistic, not surrealistic (E).

33.   **(C)**   A supplicant is one who seeks forgiveness in a religious sense. Therefore, by labeling the parishioners as such, the author is implying that they are all guilty of various crimes against their religion and have come to the church seeking forgiveness.

34.   **(D)**   The passage, which opens Charles Dickens's *A Tale of Two Cities,* contains numerous and vast comparisons. By making these comparisons and descriptions of the time period ("we had everything before us, we had nothing before us, we were all going direct to Heaven, we were all going direct the other way," etc.), Dickens is illustrating how during this period (just before the French Revolution) anything was possible: "wisdom," "foolishness," "Light," or "Darkness." This "anything is possible" tone also foreshadows the French Revolution, which the aristocracy

never expected. Dickens will, later in the novel, describe extreme political upheaval, but does not here, so (B) is wrong. (A) is wrong because "placid" implies settled and calm; if "anything is possible," then the times are the exact opposite. There is no mention of a public event or the attitudes of people at war, so (C) and (E) are also incorrect.

35.   **(A)** The Bible tells of how Christ was able to feed hundreds of hungry people with only seven loaves of bread and fish until all were satiated. By jokingly suggesting that the two governments contain the positions "lords of the state preserves of loaves and fishes," Dickens mocks their self-assuredness and unflinching certainty that the "preserves" will never be depleted and that "things in general [are] settled for ever." The phrase "clearer than crystal" helps, through its sarcasm, to give this attack more sting. All of the other choices are not alluded to or discussed in the passage, and are thus incorrect.

36.   **(A)** The "superlative degree" refers to the utmost degree of something being compared (the *hottest* day, the *fastest* runner, the *most beautiful* object, etc.). The phrase indicates that some of the time periods "noisiest authorities" (a sarcastic euphemism for members of the governments) wanted time to be remembered as the "most" or "best" of something – regardless of whether it was "the most evil" or "the most productive." All that mattered to these "authorities" was to be at the top of every comparison, regardless of its implications. Thus, (A) is correct. The people are not mentioned here, so (B) and (C) are both incorrect, as are (D) and (E).

37.   **(A)** Le Corbusier's Unité d'Habitation (Union for Living) is an apartment house in Marseilles. Corbusier set out to build apartments vibrating with light. This is obvious from the many windows almost covering the side of the building. Thus, choice (A) is correct. The building is obviously not a skyscraper (B), since there are no more than eight floors. The building is structured around rectangular and linear shapes, rather than cylindrical (C). And, the staircase at left is not hidden, but in full view (D).

38.   **(D)** You are asked to look at the structure of a building and relate to it in terms of natural forms. Since this contemporary building stacks and masses cubes or facets from a broad base to an increasingly narrow peak, much like a mountain, the correct answer is (D). It does not have wave-like lines which would connote undulating water, nor does it display any branch-like elements projecting from a trunk as on a tree. Likewise, it does

not reveal the concentric spirals of a snail or nautilus shell, while answer choice (B), a city street, offers an example of a man-made, not a natural object, and is therefore not relevant to the question.

39. **(B)** Answer choices (A), (C), (D), and (E) all share in some way the forms and ideals of the Western Classical tradition as it was established in the arts of Greece and Rome. This tradition emphasizes the value of the human individual and expresses its humanistic convictions, in part, through an idealized representation of the human figure. Answer choice (A), a Hellenistic marble relief of the second century B.C., shows this figure style in one of its earliest contexts. Examples (D) and (E), paintings from the Renaissance and Baroque periods in Europe, directly echo the ideal figure forms found in the Greek work. Choice (C), a modern work, abstracts and stylizes the human form somewhat more severely, but remains focused on the complete, nude human figure as a humanistic ideal. Only choice (B), a sixteenth-century African bronze head, falls outside of the long continuous stream of Western European culture.

40. **(D)** Answer choices (B) and (C) show static, isolated forms which display no motion at all. Choice (E) presents subjects arranged around a central focal point in a somewhat circular format, but the painting aspires to an effect of balanced calm and stillness and cannot be said to be at all animated. Choices (A) and (D) both exhibit vigorous movement, but the motion in (A), the Greek relief, depends on the counteracting thrust of intersecting diagonal lines and repeated V-forms. Only choice (D), the *Galatea* by the Renaissance painter Raphael, establishes a truly circular motion, in which the arched form of the cupid at the bottom of the picture leads the viewer's eye upwards to the right, through the cupids in the sky, all of whom circle around the main subject in the center of the picture.

41. **(B)** Answer choices (A), (D), and (E) all follow the Classical tradition of idealized figures presented in an illusionistic, well-modelled, three-dimensional mode. Only choices (B) and (C) begin to abstract the figure to any significant degree, although choice (C), a twentieth-century sculpted image of female nude, retains the sense of a rounded, softly-modelled, corporeal mass. Choice (B), however, an African bronze head, begins to facet the facial features into a series of angular planes and lines (evident in the sharp line from cheekbone to jaw) and overemphasizes the size and shape of the eyes.

42. **(B)** This question tests your knowledge of the development of the English language. This passage is taken from one of Chaucer's *Canter-*

bury Tales, written in the late fourteenth century. This is evident from the highly "irregular" spelling of words such as "dwellynge" ("dwelling") and "povre" ("poor"). (A) is incorrect because a translation would be translated into standard, modern English. Choice (C) is wrong, because while the poem may be romantic, it is impossible to tell from this passage. Elizabethan English is completely different from Middle English, so (D) is incorrect, and (E) is wrong because it is impossible to tell from the passage whether or not the speaker is a foreigner. (B) is the correct answer.

43. **(C)** This question asks you to read and determine the mood created by an author in a short selection. Passage (C), taken from Thomas Wolfe's "Circuses at Dawn," uses such words and phrases as "thrilling darkness" and "rush madly" to let the reader share the narrator's strange excitement as he anticipates the circus. Therefore, (C) is the correct answer.

44. **(A)** A dramatic monologue is a poem in the form of an extended speech by an identifiable character. Passage (A), the beginning of Robert Browning's "My Last Duchess," is unquestionably spoken by one character to another; therefore, (A) is the correct answer.

45. **(D)** A metaphor is a literary device whereby an author compares two seemingly unlike things to achieve an effect. Passage (D), taken from Henry David Thoreau's essay "Civil Disobedience," compares two seemingly unlike things – the American government and a wooden gun – to make a point; therefore, (D) is the correct answer.

46. **(B)** Figure 1 is an Elizabethan nobleman, appropriate for a play set in the 1600s. Figure 2 is a medieval old man and would be appropriate for a medieval cycle play. This is the style appropriate during the medieval period. Figure 3 is a Royalist trooper. Figure 4 is a Chinese Mandarin. Figure 5 is a late nineteenth-century "Dandy." Choice (B) is the correct answer.

47. **(B)** You can tell that this passage is taken from the stage directions of a play because of the visual and auditory descriptions you are given. Also, you are told that "lights come up" and a "rocket bursts, off," here meaning "offstage." (B) is the correct answer.

48. **(E)** These architects are known for their contributions to the development of urban architecture in Chicago, which, because of financial and land constraints, ultimately led to "skyscrapers." This is an American in-

vention in architecture, so (A) Paris and (B) London are incorrect. (C) New York is a seemingly logical answer due to the number of skyscrapers built there over the course of the past century and a half; however, while close behind Chicago in their development, key design features were first employed by architects working Chicago. (D) St. Louis did not play an important role in the early building of skyscrapers.

49.   **(C)** The Franciscan monks expressed their joy by singing, skipping, leaping, and falling. Royalty (A) would not be seen in public acting in an uncontrolled manner; mime (B) could mimic part of this dance solely through movement and no words; a fool (D) would cruelly mimic this type of expression; and (E) a commedia dell'arte character like Pantalone would improvise the movement and voice.

50.   **(A)** The question arises in the theory of knowledge, or epistemology (from the Greek word *episteme*), and Plato argues that knowledge is justified true belief: mere true belief is necessary but not sufficient for knowledge, because a true belief might be the product of a lucky guess. A person who knows has a good reason for the true belief. Metaphysics is the branch of philosophy that explores very general questions about what exists, so (B) and (D) are incorrect. (C) is incorrect because Descartes held that knowledge is a matter of clarity and distinctness, the resolution of doubt, and (E) is incorrect because Spinoza held that when we know, we know that we know and need no justification.

51.   **(A)** Zoltan Kodaly researched the folk music of Hungary. He believed using folk songs for study would strengthen a musical culture. Choice (A) is correct. Carl Orff used rhythm and participation; choice (B) is not correct. Gordon used audiation, inner hearing, as the foundation of his learning theory; choice (C) is incorrect. The Carabo-Cone method incorporated sensory-motor skills for students to use their bodies to learn music; choice (D) is incorrect. Emile Jaques-Dalcroze primarily used eurythmics and improvisation; choice (E) is incorrect.

52.   **(D)** Audiation, to hear music in the mind, is essential to Edwin E. Gordon Learning Theory. Musical context and technique are built upon the foundation of audiating skills. Choice (D) is the correct answer. Rhythm, the duration of tone or the pulse, is often incorporated in most learning methods; choice (A) is incorrect. Folk music is employed in the method of Zoltan Kodaly; choice (B) is incorrect. Eurythmics is a term used by Jaques-Dalcroze describing the physical response to music; choice (C) is

not correct. The core of Dr. Suzuki's method includes imitation, repetition; and rote learning; choice (E) is incorrect.

53.　**(A)**　In $\frac{4}{4}$ the top number of the time signature indicates four beats per measure. Therefore, a conductor would follow a four beat pattern because each point or movement represents one beat; choice (A) is correct. Choice (B) is incorrect because it contains a three beat pattern that would be utilized in $\frac{3}{4}$. Choice (C) contains a six beat pattern that would be used with six beats in a measure of $\frac{6}{8}$; choice (C) is incorrect. Choice (D) has a two beat pattern that would be used for two beats in each measure of $\frac{2}{4}$; choice (D) is incorrect. A pattern with five points would be used in a measure which contains five beats. Choice (E) is incorrect.

54.　**(C)**　This question asks you to demonstrate knowledge and awareness of a widely used symbol, the ellipsis. Within a sentence, three periods with a space after each period indicate that material has been purposefully omitted while quoting from the original. Thus, choice (C) is the correct answer.

55.　**(B)**　This passage from Melville's *Moby Dick* contains an allusion in the phrase, "like so many Alexanders." Melville is illustrating the strength and power of whalers ("naked Nantucketers") by alluding and comparing them to Alexander the Great, the famous conqueror who died in 323 B.C.

56.　**(A)**　This passage, which opens James Joyce's *A Portrait of the Artist as a Young Man,* is written in "baby talk" ("moocow," "nicens," "baby tukoo") to convey to readers the age, speech, and mental set of the narrator. While choice (E) does imitate the speech of a character, the voice used is not nearly as discreet as choice (A).

57.　**(D)**　Nineteenth-century novels of manners employed such themes as the importance (or unimportance) of "good breeding," the elation (and suffocation) caused by society, and the interaction of individuals within the confines of a closed country community (to name just a few). This passage, taken from Jane Austen's *Emma,* mentions "opinions" of other characters, the importance of "beauty" and "accomplishment" (note how Emma sees them as almost saving graces for Mrs. Elton), and the "improvement" of a "country neighborhood."

58.　**(B)**　This question asks you to judge, from the paragraph given, the type of literature from which the excerpt was taken. The only choice for which any support is given is choice (B), because the names given are Russian. The other choices can be ruled out, because there is nothing in the paragraph to support them as choices. We see no evidence of British terminology or dialect (A), nor are there specific elements of a modern romance (C). Likewise, there is not enough information to determine whether or not this is a short story with existentialist qualities (D). Therefore, you must choose the answer you *can* support, which is choice (B).

59. **(B)** This question asks that you view the picture and decide what type of artwork is pictured. This is a detail of a stained-glass window at Chartres Cathedral (B). The design is two-dimensional, a characteristic which artists of stained glass preferred. Stained glass is also characterized by the fine strips of lead that hold the small pieces of glass in place. These can be seen between the glass pieces in the picture. A mosaic design would have smaller pieces of tile making up the design (D). An oil painting (A) is characterized by dramatic use of high intensities to spotlight principal figures and deeper shadow for subordinate ones, subtle modeling of figures, and softness of contours. Even in a black-and-white photograph, it is easy to tell that there is little blending or softness in the figures and colors portrayed. Finally, a marble sculpture (C) would be three-dimensional and free standing. Thus, the correct answer is (B).

60. **(E)** Of the five possible answer choices, (A), (C), and (D) use predominantly a black outline on a white background, with (C) employing slight tonal (i.e., grey) qualities. Choices (B) and (E) share similar densities of pure black against a white ground. Answer choice (B), however, uses the pale white faces of the figures against the heavy black for an expressive effect; in this case, the technique serves the emotional content of the picture and avoids a purely decorative effect. Only choice (E) contrasts broad areas of pure black with a large field of pure white to establish a flowing linear rhythm and produce a sophisticated decorative result.

61. **(B)** Choices (A), (D), and (E) employ either pure black line on a white background or pure black line with broad areas of flat black. All avoid the use of contrasting textures almost completely, and only choices (B) and (C) develop textural effects to any noticeable degree. In choice (C), however, although a soft grey texture is used widely throughout the drawing, the predominant effect is that of black line against white, and there is no expressive human content in evidence. Choice (B), a woodblock print, uses the rough gouging to model and texture the grieving human faces, setting them off against the dense black and reinforcing the emotional content of the image.

62. **(A)** Choices (B), (C), and (E) all merge and join the forms on the page into integrated compositions, although in different ways and with differing effects. Only choices (A) and (D) present a number of unconnected images, drawn in fine black line on a white page. The images in choice (D), however, although they are separate and discrete, are arranged in a planned, composed manner which implies a motion to the left and suggests a narrative action of some sort. In contrast, choice (A), a page of sketches from a medieval architect's notebook, presents a random assortment of unrelated subjects and motifs which are composed in no special order and suggest no specific meaning.

63. **(B)** The first two lines tell us that the speaker has been doing some inner questioning and searching. The last two lines are almost a prayer to the sea, a prayer that asks the sea to calm the speaker and "compose (him) to the end." The line that reads, "Ye who from my childhood up have calmed me" suggests that the sea has been able to calm the speaker before; it is this same calming which the speaker now "passionately desire(s)."

64. **(D)** The "stream of consciousness" technique is a modern invention used by writers to mimic, and, if possible, duplicate, the quick workings of the human mind. This passage from James Joyce's *Ulysses* describes Molly Bloom's thoughts of the character Hugh as she thinks of him: how he slapped her "on my bottom," and how he is an "ignoramus" who "doesn't know poetry from a cabbage." The passage lacks punctuation because (as the technique ascribes) people do not think in properly punctuated sentences. The passage is meant to display how thoughts lead to other thoughts by association.

65. **(A)** Alliteration is a poetic device where writers repeat consonant sounds at the beginning of successive (or almost successive) words. "Fair is foul and foul is fair" is an example of alliteration because of the repeated "f" sound; the same is true for "fog and filthy."

66. **(B)** This question asks you to interpret the passage and look for specific sounds hinted at in the lines. Line 1 refers to the tolling of a bell (A). Line 2 refers to the "lowing herd" or sound of cows (D). Line 3 hints at the footsteps of the plowman as he "plods his weary way" (C); this is the same sound as a man walking (E). There is no mention of the wind, however, so (B) is the correct answer.

67. **(B)** This question asks you to choose the best paraphrase or re-statement of the quotation. The correct answer is (B). "We think our fathers fools, so wise we grow," means that as we grow older, we think our fathers are fools and *we* are wise. "Our wiser sons, no doubt, will think us so," means that our sons will do the same, and thus think of us in the same way. The other choices are misinterpretations of the lines.

68. **(E)** The costuming shown is Elizabethan dress and would be appropriate for most Shakespearean plays (E). The puffing and slashing sleeves, the farthingale skirt and the male's gartered hose are all indicative of this period. Choice (E) is correct.

69. **(D)** You are asked to view the setting of a play and determine which style of scene design has been used. Symbolism (B) is the visualization of a play's idea through special scenic treatment. Expressionism is exaggerated symbolism. It usually distorts the scenic elements (A). Impressionism (C) attempts to enable the audience to see through the character's eyes. It is usually expressed through exaggeration and contrasts. Since the setting pictured does not use distortion or exaggeration, but is a realistic presentation of a drawing room or living room, we realize it is a realistic setting. Choice (D) is correct.

70. **(A)** The design was by Michelangelo. Although (B) Bramante drew up plans for a new church of St. Peter prior to Michelangelo, his designs were never carried out. (C) Borromini is an architect of the Baroque period and therefore was working after the Renaissance church of St. Peter was constructed. (D) Bernini, also a Baroque-period architect, designed the large elliptical colonnade built in the piazza of St. Peter. (E) Leonardo da Vinci, although living at the time of the early planning of the church, was not involved in the design process.

71. **(C)** A thrust stage provides an intimate space for the audience, whereas a proscenium stage (A) is the "formal" stage most common in American theater. Choice (B) describes an arena stage, the type of stage where Greek dramas were first performed. In this arrangement, the audience encircles the stage. A black box theater (D) has no format and is commonly used for experimental theater performances. A dance arbor (E) is an outdoor theater space using the earth as the stage floor and the sky as the rooftop.

72. **(A)** A proscenium stage has a space separating the audience from the stage; whereas the arena stage (B), thrust stage (C), dance arbor (E),

and black box theater (D) all do not have an open space and are less "formal."

73. **(A)** A pragmatist, such as Dewey or James, thinks that truth is a matter of the utility of an idea, its "cash value," as it is sometimes metaphorically put. An Empiricist (B) would stress the origin of true ideas in sensory experience, while a rationalist (C) is someone who sees the origin of true ideas in the mind itself, independently of experience. Thus, (B) and (C) are incorrect. The Correspondence and Coherence theories of truth (D) and (E) are competitors of pragmatism, locating truth not in the success of an idea but in its correspondence with reality or coherence (its "fit") with other ideas.

74. **(B)** Staccato, to play the note detached or separated, is indicated by a dot over or under the note. Choice (B) is correct. Tenuto instructs to play the note for its full value; choice (A) is incorrect. Fortissimo is a dynamic marking to play very loud; choice (C) is not correct. Piano is a dynamic marking, which means to play soft; choice (D) is also incorrect. An "F" would be the dynamic marking for a loud volume; choice (E) is incorrect.

75. **(A)** Comping, which is short for accompaniment, is the style of playing that Count Basie mastered. Often used in jazz, comping had a bounce, syncopation, and flexibility that allowed soloists the freedom to improvise. Choice (A) is correct. Scat singing is also used in jazz. It is a vocal technique that does not use words. This was popularized by Louis Armstrong among others; choice (B) is incorrect. Riffs are short phrases often used as accompaniment; choice (C) is not correct. Figured bass is a notation below the bass line and tells the performer which chords to follow. This technique was incorporated into the composing of Johann Sebastian Bach; choice (D) is incorrect. A ghost note is a jazz technique often used by horn players in which a note is fingered but does not sound; choice (E) is incorrect.

Section 2

76. **(B)** E flat major has three flats. When building a scale upon E flat, the major pattern is w w $\frac{1}{2}$ w w w $\frac{1}{2}$. This pattern on E flat would result in B flat, E flat, and A flat. This can also be determined by using the Circle

of Fifths. Choice (B) is correct. A scale built upon B flat would result in a key signature of B flat and E flat; choice (A) is incorrect. A major scale on F would result in a B flat in the key signature; choice (C) in incorrect. A major scale upon G would result in an F sharp in the very signature; choice (D) is incorrect. The D major scale contains an F sharp and a C sharp; choice (E) is incorrect.

77.   **(D)**   John is described by the speaker as "practical in the extreme." We are also told that he has "no patience with faith, an intense horror of superstition, and scoffs openly at any talk of things not to be felt and seen and put down in figures." John is concerned with concrete reality, not "romantic felicity" as is the speaker. Choice (D) is the correct answer.

78.   **(B)**   The speaker says of her story that she "would not say it to a living soul, of course, but this is dead paper and a great relief to my mind." Writing is, for her, an outlet, a way for her to address her problems. Choice (B) is the correct answer.

79.   **(C)**   When not used to signal direct discourse, quotation marks indicate that the speaker or writer is being sarcastic and that the word being used has a different meaning than its dictionary definition. The fact that "work" (line 26) is in quotation marks tells us that the speaker is being sarcastic about her "occupation." Choice (C) is the correct answer.

80.   **(B)**   The passage serves to introduce an upcoming story to be told by the narrator. He begins by exclaiming, "there may as well be an end of this!" and then gives a list of reasons why he has finally decided not to "keep my trouble to myself." He is about to relate an event, or series of events, to his friend, because keeping silent has been "burning [him] rather violently." He is very excited about what he has to say; choice (B) is correct. There is no evidence that the speaker feels guilty, ashamed, sorrowful, or relieved, so (A), (C), (D), and (E) are all incorrect.

81.   **(C)**   The speaker gives, as one of the reasons for telling his story, "if confession were not good for the soul, though harder than sin to some people, of which I am one," showing that he regards confession as a healthy, although difficult activity. (C) is the correct answer. He never speaks of confession as being unnecessary, nonsensical, impossible, or comical, so (A), (B), (D), and (E) are all incorrect.

82.   **(C)**   This first stanza sets the tone for the rest of the poem. The poet tells us that this will be a "harmonious ditty," which clues us that the poem will not have a serious tone; therefore, (A) is wrong and (C) is correct. The rhyme scheme for this stanza is a-b-c-b, familiar, and will probably be repeated throughout the poem, so (B) is also incorrect. Choices (D) and (E) feature incorrect rhyme schemes for the stanza, and are, therefore, incorrect as well.

83.   **(B)**   The building pictured in the example – the contemporary "Beaubourg" art museum and cultural center in Paris – dispenses entirely with the ideas and philosophies of the classical past and with the styles and forms of traditional architecture. It is conceived instead on a huge industrial scale and, rather than projecting an atmosphere of quiet balance and poetic calm, it seeks to involve itself and its visitors in the dynamic life and culture of the modern city. Therefore, rather than concealing its structural and mechanical components behind a finished, exterior wall, the Beaubourg intentionally exposes its "anatomy," using pipes, ducts, tubes, and funnels of a modern industrial plant to reveal both its structure and its functions to the people in attendance. The visitor's ability to perceive the building's processes at work creates the sense that both building and people are part of a huge living organism.

84.   **(D)**   The jamb statues on the Early Gothic cathedral at Chartres, France (c. A.D. 1145-1170) draw their subject matter and thematic content not from classical mythology but from Christian ideology and belief. The figure groupings in the three main portals illustrate scenes from the Life and Passion of Christ, such as His birth, the Presentation in the Temple, and, in the center, the Second Coming. However, these scenes are not specifically arranged in a continuous narrative sequence and do not "tell a story." The sculpture itself, though it covers much of the building's facade, cannot be said to dominate, since it is strictly controlled and contained within the space allotted to it. The static, motionless figures conform closely to their architectural framework and are therefore subordinate to the structural forms of the doorways.

85.   **(B)**   The Renaissance sculptor who created the small figure group shown in the example was intent on conveying the physical stresses and strains of two wrestlers in violent conflict. To express the ferocity of the fight, he has exaggerated the tautness of the muscles and the rigid tension in the bodies; to illustrate the climatic moment at which one fighter lifts the other from the ground to break his back, he has shown the brief instant during which the raised figure is balanced against his opponent's stomach.

In the viewpoint shown, there is no suggestion of either the rolling motion of a wheel or the flowing of liquid, and there is apparently none of the spiral torsion of a screw. The figures do seem to interlock somewhat like a set of gears, but the simple machine they most resemble is the lever, with the fulcrum located at the balance point between the two men's abdomens.

86. **(D)** Edgar Degas (1834-1917), the French Impressionist artist who painted the picture shown in the example, was strongly influenced by the ability of the camera to capture a subject in a fleeting moment and in a spontaneous, seemingly unposed manner. In *Viscount Lepic and His Daughters,* 1873, the artist has constructed an off-center composition in which the main subject moves to the right and seems about to exit the picture. Both the viscount and his two young daughters are abruptly cut off at or near the waist, the dog is half-hidden behind one of the children, and the man standing to the left barely enters the picture. This random cropping of objects is reminiscent of a photographic snapshot. Further, the focal center of the picture is located in the empty plaza behind the figures. The painting therefore owes little either to Greek sculpture, which usually represented the full human figure in idealized form, or to Renaissance perspective, which carefully balanced its figures within an illusionistic space. It also shows no apparent debt to the numerous styles of children's book illustration or to the severe abstractions of much primitive art.

87. **(E)** The example shows the church of St. Michael's at Hildesheim, Germany (c. A.D. 1001-1031). It is typical of Early Romanesque architecture in its dependence on thick blank walls with little or no ornamental decoration, and in its massing of simple cubic and cylindrical forms. The effect of this building is less that of a structural framework supporting walls, roofs, and windows, than of a combination of building blocks which have been sectioned and then glued together. Except for the arched shape of the windows, with their tiny glassed areas, the building completely avoids curving forms, while the only diagonals are those of the roof lines, which are functionally necessary but not fundamental to the building's cubic character. Finally, a spectator's ground-level point of view might make this building seem larger and more dramatic, but it, too, is not essential to the architects' conception.

88. **(B)** An elegy is a serious poem lamenting the death of an individual or group of individuals. Passage (B) is Robert Herrick's "Upon His Spaniel Tracy," an elegy which mourns the death of his favorite dog. Thus, passage (B) is the correct answer.

89.   **(A)** Enjambment occurs when a line of poetry "runs on" to the next line, causing a slight pause in mid-sentence or thought. Line 3 reads, "This shall my love do, give thy sad death one." The reader is left wondering, "One what?" It is not until line 4 that the poet explains that he will give one "Tear." Thus, choice (A) is the correct answer.

90.   **(A)** The speaker of these lines is Berowne, a reluctant student in Shakespeare's *Love's Labor's Lost.* You can discern that the lines are spoken by a student because they are a reaction *against* study and those who pursue it ("Small have continual plodders won..."). It would be highly unusual for a professor to say such things, and the other three choices are, of course, possible, but not within the limited context of the passage.

91.   **(E)** Restated, the lines mean, "Little (small) have those who constantly (continually) plod through their studies gained (won), except (save) for some common, throwaway knowledge (base authority) from others' books." Choice (E) comes closest to this and is thus the correct answer.

92.   **(D)** These lines suggest that the astronomers who name "every fixed star" get no more out of their studies than simpletons "that walk and wot not what they are." Choice (D) comes closest to this meaning and is thus the correct answer.

93.   **(B)** The meaning of this phrase can be found in the words which follow it: "That give a name to every fixed star." Astronomers are usually responsible for the naming of stars, so choice (B) is correct.

94.   **(C)** *King Lear* is the correct answer. This question focuses on the main character in a drama as well as on the dramatic developments caused by his actions. Thus, the focus is on a single character of significant import. This should lead the reader to conclude that the answer focuses on a dramatic figure powerful enough to have a play named after him. Hamlet is a memorable character whose actions are central to the play of the same name. However, three plays in which the name of the play is the same as that of the main character requires a shift to the second level of reasoning: making distinctions among the three. (A) Tartuffe is unveiled as a hypocrite near the end of the play, while Lear's autocratic actions take place near the opening of the play. The same reasoning must be used to eliminate (E) *Waiting for Godot,* as this is a play in which the character of the same name is the person for whom the two characters are waiting. (B) *Measure for Measure* does not focus on a main character but on a group of characters.

95. **(A)** Ethics is the correct answer. Given the limitations of both possible answers and the parameters of the passage, this is the best possible answer. Though both evil and good exist within morality plays, the focus is on the choice one must make between the two. With the exception of (D) diffidence, which is an obvious variance from the other three choices, all other choices, (B) pride, (C) mischief, and (E) sloth, suggest characteristics that are either positive or negative. Only ethics encompasses both aspects; hence, morality concerns ethics.

96. **(B)** Concrete was one of the most significant contributions the ancient Romans made to the history of architecture. Mortar, but not concrete, was used by the (A) ancient Greeks; and the knowledge of concrete as a building material had somehow become lost by (C) the Middle Ages. Concrete was "rediscovered" and widely used once again by (D) the eighteenth century, and of course used almost exclusively in various forms in (E) the twentieth century.

97. **(D)** Isadora Duncan was the first choreographer to rebel against formality and to practice the expression of oneself through free bodily movement. Agnes de Mille (A), Martha Graham (B), Ruth St. Denis (C), and Ted Shawn (E) were choreographers who followed Isadora Duncan's ideas and concepts.

98. **(A)** Reincarnation, as the name implies, presupposes that a soul united with one body can become united with another. This belief in turn assumes that souls and bodies are not only distinct but separable. The view that a person consists of a body and a separable soul is dualism. An eliminative materialist (B) believes that the soul can be eliminated, that a person is nothing more than a complex material object. Since, on this view, souls do not exist, there can be no "incarnation" of the soul in a body and, hence, no reincarnation. An epiphenomenalist believes that the soul and body are distinct but inseparable, much as the bubbling of a brook is distinct but not separable from the brook. So (C) cannot be correct. Functionalism and behaviorism hold that the soul is really just a kind of state or condition of a body – a functional state or the condition of its behaving in a certain way. Hence, choices (D) and (E) cannot be correct.

99. **(D)** A flat major contains B flat, E flat, A flat, and D flat. This major scale has four flats. This is determined by following the major scale pattern, which is w w $\frac{1}{2}$ w w w $\frac{1}{2}$. Choice (D) is correct. C major contains no sharps or flats; choice (A) is incorrect. F major is found one scale

below C major on the Circle of Fifths counterclockwise from C, so as a result it contains one flat, B flat. Choice (B) is incorrect. A minor is parallel to C major, so it also contains no flats or sharps; choice (C) is incorrect. C minor is the relative minor of E flat major which contains three flats; choice (E) is incorrect.

100. **(B)** A chromatic scale is a scale of half steps. Within each octave a scale is divided into 12 notes. For example, between middle C and its octave, a chromatic scale would be all of the white and black keys. Choice (B) is correct. A major scale is a diatonic scale composed of two tetrachords. It follows the pattern w w $\frac{1}{2}$ w w w $\frac{1}{2}$. Choice (A) is not correct. A relative minor scale is composed of the pattern w $\frac{1}{2}$ w w $\frac{1}{2}$ w w. Choice (C) is incorrect. A whole tone scale is composed of all whole steps; choice (D) is incorrect. A blues scale is built on the tonic to a minor third, whole step, half step, minor third, and a whole step. Choice (E) is incorrect.

101. **(D)** Four sixteenth notes are equal to one quarter note. For example, $\frac{1}{4}=\frac{4}{16}$. The quarter note equals one beat: a down beat and an upbeat. This can be simplified into one eighth note on each part of the beat, therefore, two sixteenth notes need to be on the down beat and two on the upbeat in order to equal one full beat. Choice (D) is correct. One sixteenth note, three sixteenth notes, or two sixteenth notes would each only equal a fraction of the quarter note. Choices (A), (B), and (C) are incorrect. Six sixteenth notes would equal one-and-a-half beats; choice (E) is incorrect.

102. **(B)** The passage describes large pieces of machinery coming toward two characters in a boat. The pieces of machinery are propelled by the water, a force of nature, making (B) the correct answer. None of the other conflicts are present in this passage.

103. **(C)** The way in which the passage describes, in detail, the setting, as well as the way in which the focus narrows as the passage proceeds (it moves from an entire neighborhood to a single man) marks it similar in tone and style to the opening stage directions of a play. Choice (C) is correct.

104. **(B)** The fact that this character is known only as "the old man with the hempen beard who sleeps where nobody knows" lends him an air of insignificance – he is a type, not an individual, and is thus unworthy of a specific name. Choice (B) is correct.

105. **(E)** Dante Alighieri's (1265-1321) "The Divine Comedy" is the famous medieval epic of a journey through hell, purgatory, and paradise – replete with unforgettable references to frightening Satanic beasts (including Satan himself) and horrific landscapes. It is also viewed by scholars as Dante's spiritual autobiography – a story with a happy ending in which every person might attain redemption and the vision of God through Christianity. "The Pilgrim's Progress" (A), written 400 years after "The Divine Comedy," is perhaps the closest to Dante's famous epic, in that it also presents an allegory of the life of a Christian in this world. (B) and (C) are roughly of the same time period but of vastly different concerns, and (D), while it deals with giants, is an Anglo-Saxon work which predates Dante by at least five centuries.

106. **(D)** Homer's "Iliad" deals with events leading up to and including the Battle of Troy. His "Odyssey" concerns the hero Odysseus' attempt to return home after having helped win that battle. The voyage – which was delayed by storm, bad luck, and imprisonment – took 20 years. *Rip Van Winkle* (A) does deal with a return to home after approximately the same period of time, but Rip never left his hideaway in the Catskills and, in fact, never knew he was "gone" until he woke up two decades later. *The Wizard of Oz* (B) deals with an almost "instantaneous" departure and return, as Dorothy comes back to Kansas only a few moments after being knocked unconscious as a result of the tornado. *Exodus* (C) deals with the Hebrews coming out of Egypt and their 40 years of subsequent wandering, and (E) *Don Quixote* involves neither a return or a long period of absence.

107. **(B)** The Greek Doric temple pictured in the example illustrates a type of architecture known as post-and-lintel (or *trabeated*) construction, in which long horizontal beams rest atop a series of vertical supports. In the Greek temple, the cylindrical columns act as supports for the large marble "beam" (or the *architrave*), which, in turn, supports the roof. The Doric temple thus achieves an appearance of Classical balance and perfection through the calculated repetition of a minimum variety of forms. The temple avoids unbroken wall surfaces, instead playing off the solids and voids of the columns and the spaces between, while the only diagonals are those of the triangular front gable (the *pediment*). The building is completely devoid of arches, which were known to the Greeks but were rarely used and gained prominence only in Roman architecture.

108. **(C)** Two of the examples shown, choices (D) and (E) are profile portraits, in which the sitters do not turn their gazes out of the picture space, thus eliminating any possibility of eye contact with the viewer. Two

other examples, choices (A) and (B), show the subjects in nearly full face, but the sitter in choice (A) glances introspectively down to his left, while the subject in choice (B) looks toward us but, with aristocratic remove, keeps his own gaze just out of the line of our view. Only choice (C) presents a subject in full face who looks directly at the viewer with his large, warm eyes. This sarcophagus portrait from Roman Egypt, c. A.D. 160, intent on expressing the warmth and humanity of the deceased subject, not only effected full eye contact with the viewer, but also portrayed the subject's eyes as abnormally large and deep.

109. **(B)** Neither the clothing, the sitters, the expressions, nor the styles of choices (A) and (C) convey in any specific way that the subjects are aristocrats. Choice (E) appears to be a royal person and is therefore probably an aristocrat, but the painting is highly stylized and abstracted and projects little of the sitter's personality. Only choices (B) and (D) show subjects who are clearly wealthy, well-born, and well-bred. Choice (D), however, is a profile portrait which is so formalized as to be neutral and devoid of expression. Choice (B), by contrast, presents a subject whose rich clothing, haughty posture, elegantly cocked wrists, and, especially, distant expression mark him as a wealthy young man whose circumstances make him superior to most.

110. **(A)** The two Renaissance portraits, choices (B) and (D), show the forms and features of their subjects as clearly defined, well-modelled, and set within a basically naturalistic space. The portrait in choice (C), too, though painted in a sketchier style, models the forms of the face in a lucid, convincing, realistic manner in order to project the sitter's personality. Only choices (A) and (E) begin to abstract the figure and undermine the conventional sense of form in the search for new pictorial styles. Choice (E), however, stresses the flatness of the design and encloses all of its forms in a bold black outline. Only in choice (A), the *Boy in a Red Vest* by the French painter Paul Cézanne, is the specific subject less important than the way the artist treats it. Here, the painter breaks the outlines of the figure and disintegrates its forms, linking them with the background space in a new kind of picture construction.

111. **(D)** In the Chinese ink painting shown in the example, the artist exploited the fluid, calligraphic character of the ink-and-brush technique. In rendering the graceful bamboo leaves, he did not attempt to suggest illusionistic three-dimensional space, as a Western artist might, but let his forms lie firmly on the two-dimensional picture plane. Further, he restricted his range of tones to a dense black and one grey, and, even though

written script is included in the picture, this isolated image of the bamboo plant does not relate an episode in a story. Instead, the artist has drawn upon years of technical training and practice to create a picture in which both the script and the plant forms act as kind of spontaneous, rhythmic "writing."

112. **(C)** A simile is a literary device which uses the word "like" to compare two often unlike things. "My love is like to ice, and I to fire" suggests that the speaker's love interest is cold to him, while he or she is very much in love with the other.

113. **(D)** Personification is a literary device which gives human characteristics to inanimate objects or animals. In the phrase in choice (D), the moon is given a face which has a "wan" expression, and it is given legs, with which it "climb'st the skies." Thus, the moon has attained human aspects and is therefore personified.

114. **(E)** Apostrophe is the act of addressing someone or something directly in a poem. Choice (E) begins with "Hail to thee, blithe Spirit!" which is the first line of Percy Bysshe Shelley's "To a Skylark." The poet addresses the bird directly at the very start of the poem.

115. **(B)** This passage from Byron's "Don Juan" is an example of mock epic: a poem written in epic style designed to parody and satirize this literary tradition. The playful spirit of the passage ("So that my name of Epic's no misnomer") as well as its larger implications (epics are formulamatic and predictable) mark it, like Chaucer's *The Nun's Priest's Tale*, as a true mock epic.

116. **(D)** The theme of *carpe diem*, Latin for "seize the day," urges people to enjoy their present pleasures and lives, because the future is so uncertain. In Andrew Marvell's "To His Coy Mistress," the speaker is attempting to seduce his mistress by reasoning with her along these lines. He states that "time's winged chariot" is always near and that, once dead, she will no longer hear his "echoing song."

117. **(C)** A pastoral elegy is, by definition, a poem dealing with rural life which mourns the death of someone. Choice (C), taken from John Milton's "Lycidas," fits this description. It begins with the speaker plucking berries "harsh and crude" because "Lycidas is dead, dead ere his prime." The speaker is comparing the berry, whose leaves are "shattered

before the mellowing year," to Lycidas, who also died "ere his prime." (Actually, the poem is about a friend of Milton's, Edward King, who was drowned in the Irish Sea.) The combination of nature and death mark "Lycidas" as a pastoral elegy.

118. **(C)** Blanche DuBois in Tennessee Williams' A *Streetcar Named Desire* and Willy Loman in Arthur Miller's *Death of a Salesman*. Both these characters have become part of American folklore. Therefore, the reader who does not recognize both should be able to make a choice based on recognition of one of the pair.

119. **(E)** A ghost is the correct answer. Though based on a particular passage from a specific play, this question also depends upon the reader's ability to analyze prose. Hamlet, the speaker, is referring to the ghost of his father, the murdered King of Denmark. In these five lines, the speaker establishes clearly that the answer cannot be either (C) or (D), for these are inanimate objects. "Soul" and "it" are key words in line three; "immortal" and the verbs "being," "waves," and "follow" in lines four and five all combine to suggest that the "it" is a ghost. Because "it" is usually not used to refer to human, (B) an opponent, must also be eliminated.

120. **(B)** This is a Romanesque pilgrimage church, characterized most notably by the nave and side aisles, the transept, the ambulatory encircling the apse, and the chapels which radiate from the apse. Pilgrimage churches housed important relics and, in the Middle Ages in Western Europe, faithful Christians made pilgrimages to these churches to view the relics. Churches planned in this manner were designed to accommodate large crowds of people. (A) Early Christian monastic churches were often basilican in plan, but varied widely from one monastery to the next, and did not incorporate such elements as an ambulatory or radiating chapels. A (C) subterranean crypt is a burial chamber located *below* the main body of a church. (D) Gothic cathedrals were often similar in plan to pilgrimage churches, but the strict compartmentalization of the various elements of pilgrimage churches was abandoned in the Gothic period. (E) Centrally planned churches are those whose components radiate from a central point, unlike the church illustrated in this example, which is designed along a longitudinal axis.

121. **(E)** A group of arm exercises is *port de bras.* Epaulements is (A), alignment is (B), exercises au milieu is (C), and attitude is (D).

122. **(A)** Utilitarianism is the view that the goodness or badness of an action depends on whether it brings about the greatest amount of pleasure or happiness for the most people, compared to its alternatives. Hence, it is consequentialistic. Kant (B) argues that the only good thing is a good will, or that what makes an action right or wrong is the intention behind it, no matter what its consequences. Intuitionism (C) holds that an ethical principle is true if it appears to be true to a person with the necessary insight, independently of its consequences. Both virtue ethics (D) in general and Aristotelian ethics (E), a type of virtue ethics, assert that moral excellence is largely a matter of character and training, not the consequences of action.

123. **(A)** A chord in root position is built upon the root or tonic. From the root, the chord increases by thirds. Therefore, root, 3rd, 5th would be in root position. Choice (A) is correct. A chord built root, 2nd, 5th does not follow the pattern of increasing by thirds; choice (B) is incorrect. A chord built 3rd, 5th, root is considered to be in the first inversion; choice (C) is incorrect. A chord built 5th, root, 3rd is in second inversion; choice (D) is incorrect. A combination of a root, 2nd, 3rd would not produce a chord; choice (E) is incorrect.

124. **(C)** When a p is written below the staff, it directs the musician to play "piano" softly. Choice (C) is the correct answer. The dynamic marking ff directs the musician to play fortissimo or very loud; choice (A) is incorrect. Crescendo, notated as cres., directs the musician to gradually increase volume; choice (B) is incorrect. Decrescendo, notated as decres, indicates to gradually play softer; choice (D) is not correct. The abbreviation rit. denotes ritard or to slow down. Choice (E) is incorrect.

125. **(B)** When reading a time signature the top number indicates the number of beats in each measure and the bottom indicates which note receives each beat. So, in 16 there would be six beats in each measure. Choice (B) is correct. There would be four beats in each measure if the time signature were $\frac{4}{4}$; choice (A) is incorrect. There would be three beats in a measure of $\frac{3}{4}$; choice (C) is incorrect. A measure of $\frac{2}{4}$ would contain two beats per measure; choice (D) is incorrect. The eight in $\frac{6}{8}$ represents which note receives one beat, an eighth note; choice (E) is incorrect.

126. **(B)** *A Modest Proposal* is Jonathan Swift's famous tongue-in-cheek extended proposal that the Irish consider eating their young as a solution to poverty and starvation. From the use of the word "Modest" in his title,

to the last sentence (a profession of sincerity), Swift emphasizes the true horror of the state to which Ireland had been reduced by the absentee English landlords. Each of the other possibilities is serious in tone: *Everyman* (C) is a morality play; and "Paradise Lost" (A) is an epic of serious religious proportions. *The Way of the World* (D) is an example of a comedy of manners aiming at moral insight; and Cowley's *Lives of the Poets* (E) is a serious critical work.

127. **(A)** Spenser's (1552-1599) "The Faerie Queen" is strongly influenced by Renaissance Neoplatonism and in many ways expresses the spirit of experimentalism that characterized the Elizabethan age. Chaucer's "The Wife of Bath's Tale" (B) was written 200 years before, and, while the "Cantebury Tales" themselves might be considered an adventure, the Wife's tale is usually enjoyed as a bawdy revel. *Gulliver's Travels* (C) is a tale of adventure, but more certainly expresses the spirit of the Enlightenment. "The Rape of the Lock" (D) is based upon a trivial incident when Lord Petre cut off a lock of hair from the head of Arabella Fermor and has been called a "hero-comical poem." "Beowulf," the Anglo-Saxon adventure, was written in the first half of the eighth century (E).

128. **(B)** Upton Sinclair's powerful tract about conditions in Chicago led to Congressional passage of laws that were intended to ensure the health of industrial workers. Dreiser's *Daisy Miller* (C) was written about Chicago at the turn of the century, but did not concern itself with reform. *Main Street* (E) was written by Sinclair Lewis – he and Sinclair are sometimes confused – and is a classic in its own right, but deals with life in a small town in the Midwest. Cather's *My Antonia* (D) deals with frontier life in the Midwest; and Dickens' *Martin Chuzzlewit* (A), written 50 years beforehand, is based *on* his travels through England and America.

129. **(A)** *Oedipus Rex (Oedipus the King)* is the first in the famous trilogy *(Oedipus at Colonnus* and *Antigone* being the others) by Sophocles in which the Greek concept "pride going before a fall" (hubris), is presented through a plot that still shocks and surprises. Oedipus' hubris was not that he unknowingly sinned, but that he never considered that the King of Thebes could have been the "contagion" that was destroying his kingdom. *Tiger at the Gates* (B) and *Zorba the Greek* (C) are minor works with Greek themes. The "Aeneid" (D) was written by the Roman Virgil, and Dante's work "Il Purgatorio" (E) is of medieval origin.

130. **(D)** Shakespeare's *Hamlet* is both of Elizabethan origin and deals with the plot as described. Hamlet is famous for this speech that ends: "Thus, conscience doth make cowards of us all." The character Hamlet vacillates between inaction and plans to murder his uncle – so much so that the ghost of his father must appear to prod him on to revenge. The ghost's message is that, by delaying revenge, Hamlet is denying his father and Denmark proper justice for the heinous deeds that the king's brother has committed. *Macbeth* (C), while written in the same period, has a markedly different plot. *Twelve Angry Men* (A) and *Inherit the Wind* (B), while they deal with themes of justice, are of contemporary origin. *Rosencrantz* (E) is contemporary, though it purports to be an extension of the plot of Hamlet.

131. **(A)** *Target with Four Faces* (1955) is by Jasper Johns. This piece has none of the gestural mark-making crucial to an abstract expressionist painting. It also uses a recognizable image, a target and four plaster casts of faces. This piece has elements of surrealism and pop but is a post-expressionist painting historically and stylistically. (B) is incorrect because it is a famous abstract expressionist painting, *Irish Elegy* (1965) by Robert Motherwell. (C) is incorrect, it is a typical abstract expressionist painting by Franz Kline, *Painting* (1952). (D) is incorrect because only (A) is not an abstract expressionist painting. (E) is incorrect because (A) is not an abstract expressionist painting.

132. **(A)** Mixed media is a term that describes work that incorporates more materials than just the conventional paint and canvas. In this *piece,* Johns is mixing the media of wood, plaster, newspaper (underneath the target), and encaustic (oil paint mixed with beeswax). (B) is incorrect because Motherwell has only used oil paint on canvas in this piece. (C) is incorrect because Kline has used only oil paint on canvas in this piece. (D) is incorrect because only (A) is a mixed media piece. (E) is incorrect because (A) is a mixed media piece.

133. **(A)** *Target with Four Faces* (1955) is one of John's most famous works and one of the most famous works of the second half of the twentieth century and should be familiar to students. It has Johns' deadpan rendition of a common image but transformed in a way so that its meaning becomes mysterious. (B) is incorrect because it is by Robert Motherwell, one of the most famous of the abstract expressionists. (C) is incorrect because it is by Franz Kline, one of the most famous of the abstract expressionists. (D) is incorrect because only (A) is by Johns. (E) is incorrect because (A) is by Jasper Johns.

134. **(D)** This question tests your ability to determine the central focus in a staged dramatic production and to explain why there is such a focus. The central attraction in this picture is the man at the center of the stairs (D). Almost all eyes are turned to him, as well as the bodies of the other characters. The men in the right foreground (A) have their backs to the audience and are directing their attention to the central character. Since this character is in a full front position, he will draw more attention than those in profile or full back, which are weaker positions. Choice (D) is correct.

135. **(D)** The Egyptian Temple of Horus, c. 212 B.C., pictured in the example displays elements typical of the monumental architecture which developed during Egypt's Old Kingdom period (c. 2600-2100 B.C.) and continued until Egypt became a province of the Roman Empire (c. 31 B.C.). This architecture achieved an effect of imposing grandeur and durability through the use of simple, solid geometric forms, constructed on an overwhelming scale and laid out with exacting symmetry. The Temple of Horus avoids any emphasis on horizontal lines, and relies instead on the sloping outer walls to visually "pull" the massive building to the ground and make it seem immovable and eternal. Additionally, although the temple carries minor ornamental detail, displays huge reliefs of figures, and is set within a large open courtyard, all of these elements are secondary to the massive character of the building itself.

136. **(B)** The passage, taken from Jonathan Swift's "Description of a City Shower," is satiric in that it attacks, with humor, a subject or practice which the poet finds ridiculous; in this case, it is the practice of assigning meaning to seemingly "unrelated" occurrences to foretell the weather. Swift is mocking those who feel that such things as a cat which stops chasing its tail, the sewer letting out a "double stink," or even the raging of a "hollow tooth" could "foretell the hour... when to dread a shower."

137. **(D)** The phrase is certainly sarcastic because in this passage Swift is mocking those who feel that such things as sewers and "old aches" can foretell the weather; "By sure prognostics," then, comes to mean exactly the opposite, i.e., these "signs" foretell nothing! This phrase, like the rest of the passage, is also playful in tone, not angry as choice (C) states. Thus, choice (D), which covers both (A) and (B), is correct.

138. **(D)** This poem, written by William S. Gilbert in 1882, is a satiric look at the ineffectuality of the British Parliament and its inability (in the

poet's opinion) to do anything worthwhile. Phrases such as "The House of Peers made no pretense / To intellectual eminence" and "The House of Peers, throughout the war, / Did nothing in particular, / And did it very well" show the author's disdain for the noble men who inherited their Parliament seats and had no real interest in the political goings-on of England. The fact that, as the poet mentions, Britain becomes an empire in spite of the House of Peers adds to the satiric yet humorous tone of the poem.

139. **(C)** The satire in the poem is evident in the author's depiction of the success of Britain in spite of the ineffectual "House of Peers," and the satire is given a prophetic nature as the author wonders if the same success will continue, as if the Parliament will always be useless. The poem certainly does not laud (praise) the Parliament (A), and the poet is not satisfied (D) with the House's past performances. The poem is not a parody (B), and although the poet seems proud of England's successes, the poem is not patriotic in its tone (E).

140. **(E)** This often-used expression is from Sophocles' *Oedipus the King,* the Greek tragedy. Concerned that Oedipus is about to learn the terrible truth about his parentage, Jocasta urges him to stop making further inquiries – to "Let Sleeping Dogs Lie.

141. **(B)** *Trifles* is the correct answer. Trifles means something of slight importance. The opinions of the female characters are considered of little importance by male law officers investigating a murder. Yet, the females recognize the domestic clues. They know that Mrs. Wright has murdered the mentally abusive Mr. Wright before the authorities do. (A) *Ghosts,* too, is about a different kind of crime; however, this social crime is committed by Mr. Alving against his family as his son is born with the venereal disease Mr. Alving brought into the home. Mrs. Alving, like Mrs. Wright, is a long-suffering housewife. (C) *Pygmalion* should be eliminated immediately as it is the least logical answer choice. It is the story of a commoner who is tutored by a linguist and, hence, is able to pass herself off as a duchess. (D) *Anna Christie* shares the plight of Mrs. Wright as she, too, was a victim of abuse and understood cruelty. Moreover, the play's name is the main character's name. *Trifles* combines murder with abuse, and, of course, there is no transformation. (E) *Hamlet* is about murder and ghosts, but there are no noticeable housewives in the play.

142. **(D)** Pilotis eliminate the need for load-bearing walls. The pilotis in the Domino House are the slender vertical supports between the floor and roof slabs. Pilotis are constructed of thin steel or reinforced concrete and thus have greater load-bearing capability, thereby eliminating the necessity of heavy, supporting walls. While pilotis divide floors or stories (B), their *primary* function is that of support. Since pilotis eliminate the need for load-bearing walls, they do not (C) reinforce load-bearing walls. The structure is (E) slightly elevated above ground, but this is due to the small blocks located beneath the foundation level.

143. **(B)** The position closest to the audience on the extreme left of the stage is the left center; the correct answer is (B). Upstage right (A), upstage left (C), right center stage (D), and downstage center (E) are other locations on a stage.

144. **(A)** The area to the extreme right of the stage directly in front of the backdrop is upstage right. Downstage left center (B), upstage left (C), center stage right (D), and downstage center (E) are in other positions of the stage.

145. **(E)** The section on a stage nearest to the audience center stage is downstage center. Upstage right is to the right of the stage and in front of the backdrop (A), downstage left center is closest to the audience to the left of the stage center (B), upstage left is to the far left of the stage in front of the backdrop (C), and stage right center is in-between center and the extreme right of the stage (D).

146. **(A)** The Coherence Theory of Truth (A) holds that a claim is true just in case it coheres with or agrees with other beliefs one accepts as true. In this usage "coherence" amounts (at least) to the absence of contradiction. This theory arose in response to a rejection of the Correspondence theory (B), which was criticized on the grounds that no sense could be made of its central idea that a true claim "fits the facts." The Redundancy theory (C) holds that there is no difference between asserting a claim and asserting that it is true. The Pragmatic theory (D) asserts that a true claim is one that works or helps one to reach a goal. The Performative theory (E) rejects that notion that the predicate, "is true," describes a claim. Instead, "is true," performs the function of showing that a speaker agrees with a claim.

147. **(B)** A flat, sharp, or natural preceding a note is an accidental. The accidental alters the note for the measure it is located in, not for the entire piece. Choice (B) is correct. Choice (A), mistake, is not correct. A key signature is found at the beginning of a selection of music or when a change of key is needed. The key signature identifies the sharps and flats of the piece; choice (C) is incorrect. A time signature establishes the beats in each measure and which note will receive one beat; choice (D) is incorrect. A scale is a pattern of pitches from a tonic to an octave; choice (E) is incorrect.

148. **(B)** DS al fine, del segno a fine, translates as repeat to the sign and play till the end; choice (B) is correct. DC al fine, Da Capo al fine, means repeat to the beginning and play till the end; choice (A) is incorrect. Coda is a section found at the end used as a closing; choice (C) is incorrect. Fine is defined as "the end"; choice (D) is incorrect. Decres. is the abbreviation for decrescendo or to gradually get softer; choice (E) is incorrect.

149. **(A)** A key signature with two sharps is in the key of D major. When building a scale upon D and following the major pattern, w w 2 w w w 2, the F and C are sharp, so choice (A) is correct. When building a scale upon A major, there are three sharps, F, C, and G sharp. Choice (B) is not correct. A B flat scale does not contain sharps; choice (C) is incorrect. F sharp major contains six sharps, F, C, G, D, A, and E sharps; choice (D) is incorrect. A scale in the key of C major contains no sharps and no flats. Choice (E) is incorrect.

150. **(D)** "The Love Song of J. Alfred Prufrock," written in 1917, reflects T.S. Eliot's conviction that the debacle of World War I represented the failure of Western civilization and was a result of the moral decay of that civilization's citizens. Prufrock's chronic cowardice and hesitation ("Do I dare / Disturb the universe?") is representative of this; the world the poem describes (half-deserted streets... one night cheap hotels... sawdust restaurants) is as barren of outer life as Prufrock is of inner life. *Life on the Mississippi* (A) and *The Man That Corrupted Hadleyburg* (E) are two nineteenth century works by Twain – one a raucous chronicle of his times as a riverboat-man, the other a quaint short story of the American West. *Outcasts* (C), by O. Henry, is similar. Its theme, however, is quite the opposite of Prufrock – society – deemed decadent individuals can still have hearts of gold.

PRACTICE
TEST 3

CLEP HUMANITIES
Test 3

(Answer sheets appear in the back of the book.)

Section 1

TIME: 45 Minutes
75 Questions

DIRECTIONS: Each of the questions or incomplete statements below is followed by five possible answers or completions. Select the best choice in each case and fill in the corresponding oval on the answer sheet.

1.   The citadel of a Russian town or city is called a(n)

(A) palazzo pubblico.   (D) kremlin.

(B) atrium.   (E) forum.

(C) cathedral.

2.   The expression of rhythm through sound using footwork refers to

(A) ballroom dance.   (D) tap dance.

(B) jazz dance.   (E) country dance.

(C) dansa mora (Flamenco dance).

3.   The assumption that no two material things can occupy the same place at the same time plays a central role in which branch of philosophy?

(A) Metaphysics   (D) Ethics

(B) Philosophy of Mind   (E) Aesthetics

(C) Epistemology

4. What is another name for the treble clef?

   (A) G clef   (D) Bass clef

   (B) F clef   (E) C clef

   (C) B clef

5. The symbol, <, represents which dynamic?

   (A) Decrescendo   (D) Fermata

   (B) Crescendo   (E) Forte

   (C) Diminuendo

6. What direction does a fermata, ⌒, tell a musician?

   (A) Stop short

   (B) Crescendo

   (C) Hold until the conductor cuts off

   (D) Pause

   (E) Play soft

7. From the time of the ancient Greeks, the fortunes of the hero of a tragedy could be reversed by which of the following?

   (A) A harlequin   (D) Hellenism

   (B) Egocentricity   (E) Hamartia

   (C) Eccentricity

8. The Federalist period in American literature refers to

   (A) the period of the Confederacy.

   (B) the period of Reconstruction.

   (C) the period during which the Federalist party dominated.

   (D) the period during which the Federal Reserve was created.

   (E) the period during which the American army joined Mexican Federales in fighting Pancho Villa.

9. Milton's *Lycidas* is an example of

   (A) a pastourelle.

   (B) a pathetic fallacy.

   (C) a pastoral elegy.

   (D) a pastoral drama.

   (E) a pastoral narrative.

10. In poetry, a closed couplet refers to

   (A) the ending of a sonnet.

   (B) any two-line verse at the end of a stanza in which each line ends with the same sound and which expresses a complete, independent thought.

   (C) two lines in which the end rhyme rhymes with no other.

   (D) any two-line verse which expresses a complete, independent thought.

   (E) any poem by Alexander Pope.

11. In the typical Gothic novel

   (A) magic, mystery, ghost, and horrors abound.

   (B) churches are the main setting for the action.

   (C) barbarians invade more civilized societies.

   (D) emphasis is placed on the horrors of barbarism.

   (E) science fiction themes are predominant.

QUESTIONS 12–14 refer to the following illustrations (A-C).

(A)

(B)

(C)

12. Which painting is Early Renaissance?

    (A) Painting (A)   (D) Both (B) and (C).

    (B) Painting (B)   (E) None of the above.

    (C) Painting (C)

13. Which is Gothic?

    (A) Painting (A)   (D) Both (B) and (C).

    (B) Painting (B)   (E) None of the above.

    (C) Painting (C)

14. Which is by Raphael?

    (A) Painting (A)   (D) Both (B) and (C).

    (B) Painting (B)   (E) None of the above.

    (C) Painting (C)

QUESTIONS 15–17 refer to the following illustration.

15. What is the name of this structure?

    (A) Mount Vernon

    (B) Monticello

    (C) New Chiswick House

    (D) Charlottesville Manor

    (E) Valley Forge

16. It was home to which U.S. President?

    (A) Washington

    (D) Coolidge

    (B) Lincoln

    (E) Theodore Roosevelt

    (C) Jefferson

17. Its design

(A) was created by this president himself, combining features of many different styles of architecture.

(B) was taken from an identical structure in England, *Chiswick House.*

(C) was the first and only architectural project of John Singleton Copley, the colonial portrait painter.

(D) was the result of a session of Congress devoted to designing a house for the newly elected president which would show American advancements in architecture to the world.

(E) was taken from this president's childhood home.

QUESTIONS 18–21 refer to the following concluding lines from poems.

A) The blackbird sat
In the cedar limbs.

B) Such was their burial of Hektor, breaker of horses.

C) So long as men can breathe, or eyes can see,
So long lives this, and this gives life to thee.

D) And we are here as on a darkling plain
Swept with confused alarms of struggle and fight,
Where ignorant armies clash by night.

E) What immortal hand or eye
Dare frame thy fearful symmetry?

18. Which concludes an epic?

19. Which was written by Shakespeare?

20. Which was written by a twentieth-century poet?

21. Which was written by a Victorian?

QUESTIONS 22 and 23 refer to the following.

Does not the Heaven vault itself above us?
Is not the earth established fast below
And with their friendly glances do not
Eternal stars rise over us?

22. In this speech "vault" most likely means

    (A) wall safe.   (D) leap.

    (B) arch.   (E) discipline.

    (C) burial chamber.

23. "Established fast below" most likely means

    (A) firmly.   (D) cement.

    (B) verified.   (E) purge.

    (C) moving.

QUESTION 24 refers to the following.

24. The Chateau de Chambord, built in France in the sixteenth century, was originally constructed for use as a

    (A) hunting lodge.   (D) town hall.

    (B) fortress.   (E) church.

    (C) royal palace.

25. Which film was the most politically controversial?

    (A) Oliver Stone's *JFK*

    (B) Francis Ford Coppola's *The Godfather*

    (C) Jonathan Demme's *Silence of the Lambs*

    (D) Spike Lee's *Malcolm X*

    (E) Martin Scorsese's *The Last Temptation of Christ*

26. According to the Theory of Descriptions advanced by Bertrand Russell, a definite description like "the center of the universe"

    (A) has no meaning in its own right.

    (B) is really a name.

    (C) is always satisfied by some object.

    (D) is as meaningful as its component words.

    (E) is a logical constant.

27. Renaissance music predominantly contained which characteristics?

    (A) Religious, vocal, polyphony

    (B) Swing beat, improvisation

    (C) Homophonic, instrumental

    (D) Atonal, pagan

    (E) Monophonic

28. Composers of the Baroque period were predominantly employed through

    (A) the church.   (D) local arts guild.

    (B) the government.   (E) school.

    (C) self-employment.

29. Most of Bach's organ and vocal music was composed for

    (A) church.

    (B) government.

    (C) children.

    (D) theater.

    (E) taverns.

30. Which of the following is considered one of the best books about World War I by an American author?

    (A) *All Quiet on the Western Front*

    (B) *The Naked and the Dead*

    (C) *For Whom the Bell Tolls*

    (D) *The Sun Also Rises*

    (E) *The Caine Mutiny*

31. Which Shakespearean work is often subtitled: The Moor of Venice?

    (A) *King Lear*

    (B) *Hamlet*

    (C) *Othello*

    (D) *Richard III*

    (E) *Julius Caesar*

32. The works of Sir Walter Scott are generally considered part of which literary period?

    (A) Romantic

    (B) Realistic

    (C) Federal

    (D) Transcendental

    (E) Restoration

33. A Shakespearean sonnet is generally written in

    (A) iambic tetrameter.

    (B) dactylic hexameter.

    (C) trochaic pentameter.

(D) iambic pentameter.

(E) dactylic tetrameter.

34. James Boswell is best known for his

(A) biography of William Shakespeare.

(B) biography of William and Mary.

(C) biography of Ben Jonson.

(D) biography of Samuel Johnson.

(E) autobiography of Benjamin Franklin.

35. The term *chiaroscuro* refers to

(A) the underlying preliminary sketches done for murals during the Italian Renaissance, usually done with charcoal or thin sticks of charred wood.

(B) the practice of mixing pasta or wheat flour in with oil paint to add texture and to increase the opacity of the color.

(C) in painting, the contrast of light and shade to model form in three dimensions, as used dramatically by Caravaggio and Rembrandt.

(D) the Italian school of painters active during the High Renaissance period.

(E) in painting or sculpture, a representation of the free human stance in which the torso and pelvis tilt in opposition to each other around a central axis.

36. Which of the answer choices, (A) through (E), in question 35 defines the term contrapposto?

QUESTIONS 37-39 refer to illustrations (A) through (E) below.

(A)

(B)

(C)

(D)

(E)

37. Which is by Vermeer?

38. Which is by Caravaggio?

39. Which is an example of Dutch *genre painting?*

QUESTIONS 40–42 refer to the following stanza.

> After great pain a formal feeling comes
> The nerves sit ceremonious like tombs;
> The stiff Heart questions – was it He that bore?
> And yesterday – or centuries before?
>
> The feet mechanical
> Go round a wooden way
> Of ground or air or Ought, regardless grown,
> A quartz contentment like a stone.
>
> This is the hour of lead
> Remembered if outlived,
> As freezing persons recollect the snow –
> First chill, then stupor, then the letting go.

"After Great Pain," by Emily Dickinson

40. The "He" (line 3) is

    (A) the one who is instrumental in inflicting the pain.

    (B) the pain itself which has been personified.

    (C) the person who is inflicted with the pain.

    (D) a disinterested observer trying to understand the cause of the pain.

    (E) the poet herself.

41. The word "stiff" in line 3 is best described by the phrase

    (A) protected by a shield.

    (B) unwilling to bend.

    (C) poorly prepared.

(D) insensitive and unfeeling.

(E) haughty and proud.

42. Which of the following phrases is redundant and could be eliminated without altering the meaning of the poem?

(A) if outlived

(B) like tombs

(C) or centuries before

(D) a wooden way

(E) like a stone

43. *Woyzeck* has been called the first "proletarian" play. This means most likely that it focuses upon

(A) the hypocrisy of court life.

(B) life in the military.

(C) the world of court jester.

(D) mercenaries for hire.

(E) life among the working classes.

44. "Yes, I am. For once in my life I want to have the power to shape a man's destiny."

The speaker is

(A) Caliban.

(B) Mother Courage.

(C) Oenone.

(D) Hedda.

(E) Joan of Arc.

QUESTION 45 refers to the following.

45. The style of the Houses of Parliament in London can best be described as

    (A) classical.   (D) Gothic revival.

    (B) neo-Classical.   (E) Romanesque.

    (C) Gothic.

46. *Undulating arch* and *contraction walk* are terms in

    (A) ballet.   (D) country dance.

    (B) ballroom.   (E) tap dance.

    (C) beledi (abdominal dance).

47. If God knows everything, as some contend, then he knows what everyone will be doing tomorrow. If he knows what everyone will be doing tomorrow, he has always known this. Thus, there is a conflict between God's omniscience and

    (A) free will.

    (B) determinism.

    (C) God's omnibenevolence.

(D) the existence of time.

(E) God's love.

48. The oratorio made famous by G.F. Handel is

   (A) "St. Matthew's Passion."

   (B) "Mass in B minor."

   (C) "Also Sprach Zarathustra."

   (D) "Messiah."

   (E) "Wozzeck."

49. How many eighth notes are equal to one quarter note?

   (A) 2   (D) 4

   (B) 3   (E) 1

   (C) 8

50. If a clarinet sounds a G, what note is it in concert pitch?

   (A) F   (D) B flat

   (B) G   (E) A

   (C) C

51. In a Shakespearean tragedy,

   (A) only the hero or heroine dies.

   (B) both the hero and the heroine die.

   (C) the major characters survive, but the supporting characters die.

   (D) the supporting characters die, but the major characters live.

   (E) many of the major characters and many of the supporting characters die.

52. The famous words "Et tu, Brute" come from the play

   (A) *Measure for Measure.*

   (B) *Hamlet.*

   (C) *Loves Labors Lost.*

(D) *King Lear.*

(E) *Julius Caesar*

53. Often, in a Shakespearean history play, a murder of a famous person

(A) is a result of injustice and ushers in an era of stability and justice.

(B) is a result of ambition and leads to the destruction of the murderer.

(C) is a result of a widespread discontent or revolution.

(D) is a result of a previous leader being too just or too good.

(E) is a result of that person having been a tyrant.

54. Which of the following English works is often categorized as one of the earliest works of science fiction?

(A) Bradbury's *The Martian Chronicles*

(B) Wells' *The Time Machine*

(C) More's *Utopia*

(D) Shelley's *Frankenstein*

(E) Verne's *20,000 Leagues Under the Sea*

55. Which Classical work was one of the first to define the "epic hero"?

(A) *Mourning Become Electra*

(B) *The Old Testament*

(C) *Androcles and the Lion*

(D) *The Odyssey*

(E) *Gone With the Wind*

QUESTIONS 56-58 refer to illustrations (A) through (E) below.

(A)

(B)

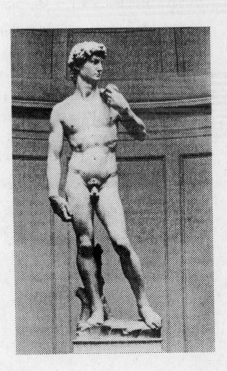

(C)

(D)

(E)

56. Which is baroque?

57. Which is Donatello's *David?*

58. Which of these sculptures was not chiseled from a block of material?

59. The term *Arte Povera* refers to

    (A) a school of Italian painting active during the seventeenth and eighteenth centuries which was devoted to depicting all aspects of the lives of the lower class.

    (B) art produced by untrained, "naive" artists, such as mental patients or those living in rural areas removed from popular culture.

    (C) graffiti and crude drawing.

    (D) minimal art produced with "humble" and commonly available materials such as sand, wood, stones, and newspaper.

    (E) Both (B) and (C).

60. Which of the answer choices from question 59 best defines the term *Art Brut?*

QUESTIONS 61–64 refer to the following lines taken from different poems.

    A) Some heart once pregnant with celestial fire;
       Hands that the rod of empire might have swayed,

    B) I am his Highness's dog at Kew;
       Pray tell me sir, whose dog are you?

    C) Oh young Lochinvar is come out of the west,
       Through all the wide Border his steed was the best;

    D)   ; and till action,
       Lust is perjured, murderous, bloody, full of blame
       Savage, extreme, rude, cruel, not to trust;

    E) The grave's a fine and private place,
       But none, I think do there embrace.

61. Which shows the figure of speech synecdoche?

62. Which shows irony?

63. Which shows cacophony?

64. Which shows the ballad form?

65. According to Aristotle, all of the following are important elements in the structure of a play EXCEPT

    (A) beginning.   (D) end.

    (B) plot.   (E) stage directions.

    (C) middle.

66. A "dumb show" appears in all of the following plays EXCEPT

    (A) *Hamlet.*   (D) *The Changeling.*

    (B) *The Tempest.*   (E) *Gorboduc.*

    (C) *Duchess of Malfi.*

67. In medieval churches, the portion of the building in which the main altar is placed is called the

    (A) ambulatory.   (D) nave.

    (B) apse.   (E) chapel.

    (C) transept.

QUESTIONS 68 and 69 refer to diagrams (A) through (E).

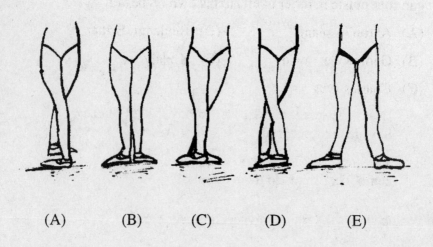

    (A)   (B)   (C)   (D)   (E)

68. Which is fifth position?

69. Which is third position?

70. In a recent book, the writer Camille Paglia argues that liberal feminists are "heirs to Rousseau." By this she means that feminists are people who think social relations can be improved by changing the social environment, given Rousseau's belief that

    (A) humans are by nature good.

    (B) humans are by nature bad.

    (C) humans are neither good nor bad by nature.

    (D) human nature has nothing to do with social relations.

    (E) the social environment is the only significant factor in human relations.

71. A cappella means

    (A) instrumental music.

    (B) vocal music without instruments.

    (C) sacred songs.

    (D) soft music.

    (E) piano.

72. Which American composer often combined jazz with hints of American folk music in order to create his own orchestral style?

    (A) Aaron Copland   (D) Benjamin Britten

    (B) George Gershwin   (E) Kodaly

    (C) Charles Ives

73. The preceding segment is from Beethoven's "Symphony No. 5." What musical term does this demonstrate?

    (A) Motif

    (B) Appoggiatura

    (C) Grace note

    (D) Trill

    (E) Slur

74. Greek tragedy is characterized by the

    (A) fall of a character from a person of high importance to one of low.

    (B) elimination of people of little importance by people of high importance.

    (C) trials and agony of any individual, no matter from what station in society.

    (D) loss by natural disaster or murder of any important group of individuals.

    (E) continuance of an unfortunate situation despite the best efforts of heroes and heroines to change it.

75. *Romeo and Juliet* adheres to many of the rules of tragedy as stated by Aristotle, among them

    (A) all main characters must die.

    (B) the hero will not triumph in the end.

    (C) no comedy is allowed.

    (D) use only dark stage lighting.

    (E) rule of five acts.

Section 2

TIME: 45 Minutes
75 Questions

DIRECTIONS: Each of the questions or incomplete statements below is followed by five possible answers or completions. Select the best choice in each case and fill in the corresponding oval on the answer sheet.

---

76. One of the longest running murder mysteries on the London stage was

    (A) A.C. Doyle's *Hound of the Baskervilles.*

    (B) Ira Levin's *Death Trap.*

    (C) Stephen King's *The Shining.*

    (D) Agatha Christie's *The Mousetrap.*

    (E) Larry McMurtry's *Texas.*

77. Colonial American writing consisted mostly of

    (A) adventure stories and religious poems.

    (B) diaries, sermons, and religious poetry.

    (C) short stories and diaries.

    (D) novels and short stories.

    (E) religious poetry, short stories, and travel guides.

78. Among the most popular early biographies of an early American was

    (A) Weem's biography of Washington.

    (B) Flexner's biography of Washington.

    (C) Sandberg's biography of Lincoln.

    (D) Franklin's autobiography.

    (E) Irving's *Rip Van Winkle.*

79. A style of painting, architecture, and interior decoration using soft colors and delicate curves to produce gay, elegant, and charming effects. The employment of common subject matter of pastoral scenes, courtship, and characters of comic opera was common with this style.

The above statement best describes which of the following styles?

(A) Rococo   (D) Art Deco

(B) Baroque   (E) Art Nouveau

(C) Romantic

QUESTIONS 80–82 refer to the following illustrations (A-D).

(A)

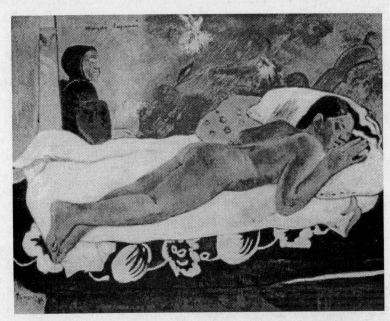

(B)

(C)

(D)

80. Which is impressionist?

   (A) Painting (A)   (D) Painting (D)

   (B) Painting (B)   (E) Paintings (B) and (D)

   (C) Painting (C)

81. Which is by Gauguin?

   (A) Painting (A)   (D) Painting (D)

   (B) Painting (B)   (E) All of the above.

   (C) Painting (C)

82. Which is post-impressionist?

   (A) Painting (A)   (D) Painting (D)

   (B) Painting (B)   (E) Paintings (B) and (D).

   (C) Painting (C)

QUESTIONS 83–86 refer to the following poem.

> A certain carelessness in dress
> Kindles in clothes a wantonness;
> A lawn* about the shoulders thrown   (*a linen stole)
> Into a fine distraction
> An erring lace which here and there
> Enthralls the crimson stomacher,*   (*a covering in the neckline)
> A cuff neglectful, and thereby
> Ribbands to flow confusedly
> A winning wave (deserving note)
> In the tempestuous petticoat,
> A careless shoe-string, in whose tie
> I see a wild civility;
> Do more bewitch me, than when any art
> Is too precise in every part.

83. The poem above is

    (A) a sonnet.   (D) a Petrarchan sonnet.

    (B) an ode.   (E) a villanelle.

    (C) an air

84. "Wild civility" in line 12 is

    (A) a paradox.

    (B) a metaphor.

    (C) an example of onomatopoeia.

    (D) an oxymoron.

    (E) hyperbole.

85. The word "erring" in line 5 could best be replaced by

    (A) straying.   (D) wandering.

    (B) untied.   (E) straight.

    (C) loose.

86. Which best describes the meaning of the poem?

    (A) The speaker does not like law and order.

    (B) The speaker likes to see untidy women.

    (C) The speaker likes to see a certain carelessness in a woman's dress.

    (D) The speaker is a voyeur and likes to see women undress.

    (E) The speaker prefers a little disorder to rigid order in a woman's dress.

87. Which of the following reacted after seeing a reflection of his guilt in a play-within-a-play, by calling for more light?

    (A) King Lear   (D) Richard II

    (B) Prospero   (E) Henry V

    (C) King Claudius

88. In which play is the fair a place of rogues and vendors who attempt to deceive the customers?

    (A) *Bartholomew Fair*

    (B) *Falstaff*

    (C) *Juliet*

    (D) *Merchant of Venice*

    (E) *The Duchess of Malfi*

QUESTION 89 refers to the following.

89. The building illustrated above, which was designed by Christopher Wren in 1675-1710, is

   (A) St. Paul's Cathedral, London.

   (B) Church of the Invalides, Paris.

   (C) The Pantheon (Ste. Genevieve), Paris.

   (D) Royal Pavilion, Brighton, England.

   (E) Baltimore Cathedral, Baltimore.

QUESTIONS 90–92 refer to the following groups of people.

   (A) Tim Rice, Andrew Lloyd Webber, Stephen Sondheim

   (B) Trevor Nunn, George C. Wolfe, Joseph Papp

   (C) Tommy Tune, Bob Fosse, Jerome Robbins

    (D) David Mamet, Edward Albee, Tony Kushner

    (E) Michael Crawford, Estelle Parsons, Betty Buckley

90. Which is a group of stage directors?

91. Which is a group of choreographers?

92. Which is a group of playwrights?

93. In Plato's utopian political philosophy, the relation between the human soul and the ideal republic is

    (A) microcosm to macrocosm.

    (B) part to whole.

    (C) cause to effect.

    (D) specimen to species.

    (E) particular to universal.

94. Beethoven's Symphony No. 3 in E flat major Op. 55, "Eroica" was originally composed for which historic figure?

    (A) Napoleon Bonaparte   (D) Jesus Christ

    (B) Joseph Stalin   (E) Mozart

    (C) George Washington

95. The duration or pulse of music is defined as

    (A) dynamics.   (D) clef.

    (B) rhythm.   (E) tone.

    (C) interval.

96. James Joyce (1882-1941) used "stream of consciousness" technique in his expressionistic writing. A composer who used similar techniques in music is

    (A) Igor Stravinsky.   (D) Arnold Schoenberg.

    (B) Claude Debussy.   (E) Handel.

    (C) Maurice Ravel.

97. One of the greatest New England poets of the twentieth century was

    (A) Henry Thoreau.   (D) Edward Taylor.

    (B) Walt Whitman.   (E) Robert Frost.

    (C) John Whittier.

98. The development of the modern English novel is deeply indebted to

    (A) the short stories of the Anglo-Saxons.

    (B) the long poetic epics of the ancient Greeks.

    (C) the oral tradition of rural America.

    (D) the picaresque novels of eighteenth-century England.

    (E) the Italian novella.

99. Some of the most popular medieval tales in England were carried to the American colonies and still survive in Appalachia. They are known as

    (A) Jack tales.

    (B) fairy tales.

    (C) Aesop's fables.

    (D) the stories of Hans Christian Anderson.

    (E) the Arthurian Cycle.

100. Oral and musical traditions from the Scottish and English border region that were transmitted to the American colonies are known as

    (A) chamber music.   (D) ballads.

    (B) folk tales.   (E) broadsides.

    (C) lullabies.

101. One of the greatest English poet laureates of the early nineteenth century was

    (A) William McGonigle.   (D) William Shakespeare.

    (B) T.S. Eliot.   (E) John Milton.

    (C) Alfred Tennyson.

102. Which of the following painters was not an impressionist?

(A) Pissarro   (D) Degas

(B) Monet   (E) Cassat

(C) Van Gogh

103. Which of the following painters is most famous for his pictures of ballerinas?

(A) Degas   (D) Renoir

(B) Manet   (E) Monet

(C) Toulouse-Lautrec

QUESTIONS 104–106 refer to the following.

(A)

(B)

(C)

104. Which of the above is most directly influenced by impressionism?

(A) Painting (A)

(B) Painting (B)

(C) Painting (C)

(D) Paintings (A) and (C) are equally influenced.

(E) Paintings (A), (B), and (C) are all equally influenced.

105. Which is by Matisse?

(A) Painting (A)   (D) Paintings (A) and (C)

(B) Painting (B)   (E) Paintings (A), (B), and (C)

(C) Painting (C)

106. Which of the above is an example of the Fauve style?

(A) Painting (A)   (D) Paintings (A) and (C)

(B) Painting (B)   (E) Paintings (A), (B), and (C)

(C) Painting (C)

QUESTIONS 107–109 refer to the following short poem.

With his venom

Irresistible
and bittersweet

that loosener of limbs, Love

reptile-like
strikes me down.

107. Which word best describes the tone of the speaker?

(A) Despondent   (D) Poignant

(B) Sarcastic   (E) Ecstatic

(C) Distraught

108. Line 4 shows the use of

    (A) alliteration.

    (B) assonance.

    (C) slant rhyme.

    (D) oxymoron.

    (E) paradox.

109. Which best describes the meaning of line 4?

    (A) The speaker is distressed by love.

    (B) The speaker is debilitated by love.

    (C) The speaker loves benign love.

    (D) The speaker hates being in love.

    (E) The speaker finds being in love irresistible.

110. Which of the following best defines an epigram?

    (A) A short poem with often a witty malicious "sting" at the end

    (B) A poem that laments the death of a particular person

    (C) A short poem related to a theme placed at the head of a work

    (D) A short poem placed on a tombstone

    (E) A short poem expressing the thought of one person

111. He is a man who allows his fool to speak the truth, but disinherits his daughter when she does so. Who is this man?

    (A) Lear

    (B) Creon

    (C) Macbeth

    (D) Polonius

    (E) Oedipus

112. The Captain confronts his willful wife with his decision to send their son to a boarding school. In her zeal to have her own way, Laura, the wife, reveals a secret. This describes a scene in which story?

    (A) *The Playboy of the Western World*

    (B) *The Cherry Orchard*

    (C) *The Father*

(D) *The Wild Duck*

(E) *The Misanthrope*

QUESTION 113 refers to the following.

113. The vertical "stacking" of different styles of columns, as shown here on the exterior of the Colosseum in Rome, is an example of

(A) piers.

(B) compound piers.

(C) colonnades.

(D) superimposed orders.

(E) blind arcades.

114. According to David Hume's widely accepted analysis of causal relations, if heating a metal bar to 1,000 degrees causes the bar simulta-

neously to glow, then heating the bar cannot be the cause of the bar's glowing. This is because, according to Hume,

(A) a cause always precedes its effect.

(B) there is no necessary connection between cause and effect.

(C) effects are regularly connected with their causes.

(D) not every event has a cause.

(E) there is no such thing as a cause.

115. Who is responsible for commissioning most of the compositions for use with the Russian Ballet?

(A) Igor Stravinsky   (D) Walt Disney

(B) Serge Diaghilev   (E) Mussorgsky

(C) Esterhazy

116. Which of the following is a folk opera set in the American south that portrays the struggles of black Americans?

(A) *The Barber of Seville*   (D) *Tristan and Isolde*

(B) *Porgy and Bess*   (E) *On the Town*

(C) *Carmen*

117. In Question 116, the correct answer was a composition of which composer?

(A) George Gershwin   (D) W.A. Mozart

(B) Giuseppe Verdi   (E) Salvador Dali

(C) Richard Wagner

118. In a *Modest Proposal,* Jonathan Swift satirically proposes

(A) cannibalism as a method of population control.

(B) germ warfare as a method of eliminating an enemy.

(C) forcing all people under English rule to speak French.

(D) encouraging the Scots and Irish to break off from England.

(E) calling out the king's forces to control scolding wives.

119. In which novel by Charles Dickens does a convict become the benefactor of an orphan boy?

(A) *David Copperfield*

(D) *Great Expectations*

(B) *Martin Chuzzlewit*

(E) *Bleak House*

(C) *Dombey and Sons*

120. Dickens often wrote about the poor and the criminal class because

(A) as a member of Parliament these were major concerns of the day.

(B) he often saw homeless orphans on his way to work in the Customs House.

(C) his father had been put in a debtor's prison.

(D) his mother had always encouraged him to help the poor.

(E) his own brother had been made homeless by the Industrial Revolution.

121. George Eliot was the pen name for

(A) Silas Marner.

(D) Mary Evans.

(B) Mary Shelley.

(E) Godfrey Cass.

(C) Molly Farren.

122. Joel Chandler Harris is known for writing

(A) the first accurate description of the foothills of the Rockies.

(B) the only known transcript of George Washington addressing his troops.

(C) the most accurate account of the sights and sounds during the Battle of Gettysburg.

(D) the first dependable representation of African-American slave dialects.

(E) the most extensive compendium of American Indian medicinal practices.

QUESTIONS 123–125 refer to the following illustrations (A-E).

(A)

(B)

(C)

(D)

(E)

123. In which example does the landscape act as a backdrop for a carefully composed figure group?

124. In which example does the location of the horizon line emphasize the figure's isolation?

125. Which example shows the greatest tendency to abstract and simplify the forms?

126. "I sleep very late. I commit suicide 65%. My life is very cheap, for me it is only 30% of life. My life contains 30% of life. It lacks arms, strings, and a few buttons. 5% is consecrated to a state of semi-lucid stupor accompanied by anemic rules... So you see that life is very cheap. Death is a little more expensive. But life is charming and death is charming too."

The statement on the previous page is an example of the writings of the members of which of the following twentieth century art movements?

(A) Surrealism

(D) Dada

(B) Impressionism

(E) Pop art

(C) Abstract expressionism

QUESTION 127 refers to the following.

127. In the example pictured on the previous page, the folds of the garment serve to

    (A) define the forms of the human figure.

    (B) counteract the vigorous motion of the figure.

    (C) establish a sense of three-dimensional space.

    (D) help tell the story behind the figure's movements.

    (E) create a dynamic surface pattern which dominates the composition.

QUESTIONS 128 and 129 refer to the following stanza.

    Gather ye rosebuds while ye may
    Old Time is still a flying
    And this same flower that smiles today,
    Tomorrow will be dying.

128. The above stanza demonstrates the concept of

    (A) epiphany   (D) euphony.

    (B) euphemism.   (E) cacophony.

    (C) carpe diem.

129. Which best defines the figure of speech *oxymoron?*

    (A) Variation from regular word order to make the rhyme

    (B) Repetition of a group of words

    (C) An object or action that carries more than the literal meaning

    (D) An abstract moral proposition

    (E) Contradictory ideas in close juxtaposition

130. The hero of a tragedy must be an essentially good individual whose character is marred by a fatal shortcoming or weakness powerful enough to cause ruin to the individual. This characteristic is known as

    (A) a tragic flaw.   (D) self-delusion.

    (B) dramatic discontinuity.   (E) pragmatism.

    (C) the third wall.

131. Which play focuses on "star-crossed lovers" and feuds?

(A) *Romeo and Juliet*

(B) *Macbeth*

(C) *Hamlet*

(D) *The Wild Duck*

(E) *Antony and Cleopatra*

QUESTION 132 refers to the following.

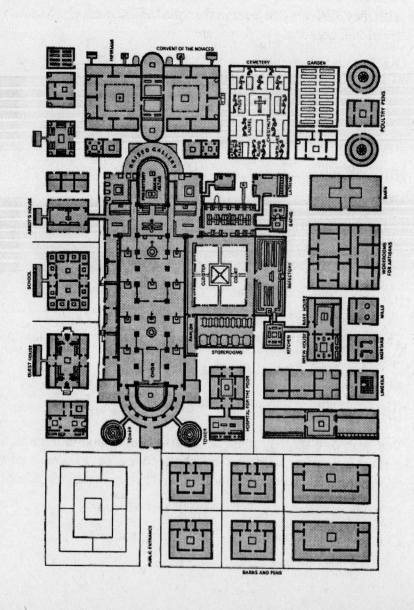

132. The "Plan of St. Gall," illustrated on the previous page, is a design for which of the following?

    (A) Carolingian monastery

    (B) Ottonian monastery

    (C) Islamic mosque

    (D) Byzantine palace complex

    (E) Anglo-Saxon fortress

133. Although both Aristotle and Plato are realists with respect to universals, they differ in one crucial respect: Plato, unlike Aristotle, believed that universals or forms are

    (A) separate from particulars.

    (B) distinct from but not separate from particulars.

    (C) immaterial.

    (D) eternal.

    (E) changeless.

134. Pitch is directly related to

    (A) shape.   (D) volume.

    (B) size.   (E) None of the above.

    (C) quantity.

135. The tempo marking "allegro" directs the musician to play at what speed?

    (A) Slow   (D) Very fast

    (B) Fast   (E) Detached

    (C) Moderately

136. Society is often revealed through the arts. Many artists, writers, and composers felt the stress of society and used these feelings for their themes. What style did they employ?

    (A) Expressionism

    (B) Impressionism

    (C) Classical

    (D) Baroque

    (E) Renaissance

137. Which of the following is an American naturalistic novel well known for its depiction of immorality and spiritual decay?

    (A) Twain's *Huckleberry Finn*

    (B) Melville's *Moby Dick*

    (C) Zola's *Nana*

    (D) Eliot's *Wasteland*

    (E) Dreiser's *Sister Carrie*

138. Known for its irreverent treatment of Victorian gentility which survived into the twentieth century, this Maryland journalist also wrote a famous work about American language and culture.

    (A) T.S. Eliot

    (B) k.d. lang

    (C) H.L. Mencken

    (D) ee cummings

    (E) A.E. Hotchner

139. Among the characters in Dickens' *Great Expectations* is

    (A) a young boy who believes in the American Dream.

    (B) an old man who spends most of his time at the spinning wheel.

    (C) a teenager who writes the novel from a sanitarium.

    (D) an old lady who was abandoned at the altar.

    (E) a priest who broke his vow of celibacy for the woman he loved.

140. The famous line: "Hail to thee, blithe Spirit!" appears at the beginning of

    (A) Shelley's "To a Skylark."

    (B) Coleridge's "Rime of the Ancient Mariner."

(C) Blake's "Songs of Innocence."

(D) Grey's "Elegy in a Country Churchyard."

(E) Wordsworth's "Michael."

141. Which famous poem begins with the lines: "Sunset and evening star,/ And one clear call for me!"?

(A) Blake's "Songs of Innocence"

(B) Browning's "Child Rolande"

(C) Joyce's "Ulysses"

(D) Tennyson's "Crossing the Bar"

(E) Shelley's "Ozymandias"

142. The term *readymade* was coined by

(A) Andy Warhol.

(B) Jackson Pollock.

(C) Marcel Duchamp.

(D) This term cannot be traced back to any single artist.

(E) None of the above.

143. A *readymade* is

(A) any previously existing object (except for a work of art) which an artist chooses to call a work of art.

(B) any object that an artist hires someone else to construct, which is then considered a work of art.

(C) a type of minimalist "painting" which consists simply of raw canvas stretched onto a frame.

(D) Both (A) and (B).

(E) (A), (B), and (C).

144. The American art movement of the 1950s that put New York at the center of the international art world for the first time was

(A) color-field painting.

(B) minimalism.

(C) pop art.

(D) abstract expressionism.

(E) the Hudson River school.

145. The dominant and most influential American art movement during the 1960s was

(A) abstract expressionism.

(B) minimalism.

(C) feminist art.

(D) pop art.

(E) environmental art.

146. The dominant American art movement of the 1970s which many consider to be the inevitable, final phase of modernism was

(A) abstract expressionism.

(B) minimalism.

(C) feminist art.

(D) pop art.

(E) environmental art.

QUESTIONS 147–150 refer to the following first half of a poem.

I see them standing at the formal gates of their colleges,
I see my father strolling out
under the ochre sandstone arch, the
red tiles glinting like bent
plates of blood behind his head, I
see my mother with a few light books at her hip
standing at the pillar made of tiny bricks with the
wrought-iron gate still open behind her, its
sword tips black in the May air,
they are about to graduate, they are about to get married,
they are kids, they are dumb, all they know is they are
innocent, they would never hurt anybody.

147. Lines 4-5 demonstrate which of the following?

   (A) Assonance
   (D) Irony
   (B) Caesura
   (E) Simile
   (C) Abstract language

148. Which best describes the figurative meaning of lines 4-5?

   (A) The roof tiles are glinting in the sun like blood.

   (B) The roof is red brick and radiating light behind the man's head.

   (C) There is an aura of romance glinting off the red tiles.

   (D) There is a feeling of violence reflected from the red roof tiles.

   (E) The red tiles are wet with rain as if with blood.

149. The words "still open behind her" in line 8 suggest

   (A) the woman has her life ahead of her.

   (B) the woman must face life now.

   (C) the woman can change her mind and go back.

   (D) the woman must go forward.

   (E) the woman cannot change her mind now but go onward.

150. Which best describes the figurative meaning of line 9?

   (A) The woman will have death in her future.

   (B) The woman will face violent battles in her future.

   (C) The woman will face death and rebirth in her life.

   (D) The woman should not marry this man.

   (E) The woman will bring death to this man.

CLEP HUMANITIES
TEST 3

ANSWER KEY

Section 1

1. (D)	16. (C)	31. (C)	46. (C)	61. (A)
2. (D)	17. (A)	32. (A)	47. (A)	62. (E)
3. (A)	18. (B)	33. (D)	48. (D)	63. (D)
4. (A)	19. (C)	34. (D)	49. (A)	64. (C)
5. (B)	20. (A)	35. (C)	50. (A)	65. (E)
6. (C)	21. (D)	36. (E)	51. (E)	66. (B)
7. (E)	22. (B)	37. (B)	52. (E)	67. (B)
8. (C)	23. (A)	38. (A)	53. (B)	68. (D)
9. (C)	24. (A)	39. (B)	54. (C)	69. (C)
10. (B)	25. (E)	40. (C)	55. (D)	70. (A)
11. (A)	26. (A)	41. (A)	56. (B)	71. (B)
12. (B)	27. (A)	42. (E)	57. (E)	72. (B)
13. (A)	28. (A)	43. (E)	58. (E)	73. (A)
14. (C)	29. (A)	44. (D)	59. (D)	74. (A)
15. (B)	30. (C)	45. (D)	60. (E)	75. (E)

Section 2

76. (D)	91. (C)	106. (E)	121. (D)	136. (A)
77. (B)	92. (D)	107. (D)	122. (D)	137. (E)
78. (A)	93. (A)	108. (A)	123. (A)	138. (C)
79. (A)	94. (A)	109. (B)	124. (D)	139. (D)
80. (C)	95. (B)	110. (A)	125. (E)	140. (A)
81. (B)	96. (B)	111. (A)	126. (D)	141. (D)
82. (E)	97. (E)	112. (C)	127. (E)	142. (C)
83. (A)	98. (E)	113. (D)	128. (C)	143. (A)
84. (D)	99. (A)	114. (A)	129. (E)	144. (D)
85. (A)	100. (D)	115. (B)	130. (A)	145. (D)
86. (E)	101. (C)	116. (B)	131. (A)	146. (B)
87. (C)	102. (C)	117. (A)	132. (A)	147. (E)
88. (A)	103. (A)	118. (A)	133. (A)	148. (D)
89. (A)	104. (B)	119. (D)	134. (B)	149. (C)
90. (B)	105. (D)	120. (C)	135. (B)	150. (B)

DETAILED EXPLANATIONS
OF ANSWERS
TEST 3

Section 1

1.   **(D)**   Kremlin, perhaps the most well-known of which is the Kremlin in Moscow. A palazzo pubblico (A) is the Italian term for a city hall. An atrium (B) is an open courtyard located in front of a private Roman house or villa, or in front of a church. A cathedral (C) is a church that contains the seat (*cathedra*) of a bishop. A forum (E) is an open-air public square from the ancient Roman era.

2.   **(D)**   The expression of rhythm through sound using footwork is tap dance. Ballroom dance (A), jazz dance (B), dansa mora (Flamenco dance) (C), and country dance (E) are not dependent on the sound of the footwork.

3.   **(A)**   If two material objects are qualitatively identical, then since we say there are two of them, they must occupy different places at the same time. This is a basic principle of metaphysics. (C) can be eliminated because the principle concerns the existence of things in space and time, not our knowledge of them. (B), (D), and (E) can be eliminated because philosophy of mind, ethics, and aesthetics are not concerned exclusively with material existence.

4.   **(A)**   The G clef is also called the treble clef. It locates the G above middle C; choice (A) is correct. The F clef and bass clef locate the F below middle C; choices (B) and (D) are incorrect. The B clef does not exist. Choice (C) is incorrect. The C clef locates C on the staff; choice (E) is incorrect.

5.   **(B)**   This dynamic marking represents a crescendo, which is the direction to go from soft to loud. Choice (B) is correct. A decrescendo gives the opposite direction, to go from loud to soft; choice (A) is incor-

rect. A diminuendo is notated as dim. and means to gradually get softer; choice (C) is incorrect. A fermata, ⌢, tells the musician to hold the note until the conductor cuts off the note; in the case of a soloist, the performer chooses the duration of the note; choice (D) is incorrect. Forte is notated as an f to indicate a loud volume; choice (E) is incorrect.

6.   **(C)** A fermata directs a musician to hold the given note until the conductor gives the direction to stop. Choice (C) is correct. There is no marking that would give the direction to stop short, unless a conductor gestures for a quick stop; choice (A) is incorrect. A crescendo, <, gives the direction from a soft dynamic and increase to a loud dynamic level; choice (B) is incorrect. A pause would be marked as //; this is often called "railroad tracks." A conductor would follow this marking and the ensemble would continue on his gesture; choice (D) is incorrect. The indication to play soft would be notated as p. Choice (E) is incorrect.

7.   **(E)** Fortunes of the greatest heroes can be reversed by a "great error or frailty" according to the rules of tragedy as first set forth by Aristotle. More commonly called the "tragic flaw" today, it may be bad judgment or some inherited character weakness. A harlequin (A) is a clown or fool. Egocentricity or eccentricity – (B) and (C) – may be flaws, but they are only two kinds of hamartia. The flowering of Hellenism (D) may have given us both Aristotle and the term hamartia, but it is not relevant to the question.

8.   **(C)** The Federalist period is perhaps one of the least studied periods in American literature. Generally, it refers to that time period in the late 1700s when the Federalist period of Alexander Hamilton dominated politics. It also refers to that time period just before the adoption of the Constitution when America was defining itself in the Federalist papers – a series of written debates among many of our important thinkers. The Confederacy (A) was 60 years later. The naming of the Federal Reserve (D) at roughly the same time is mostly coincidental. The Mexican Federales (E) are unrelated to this topic.

9.   **(C)** Milton's *Lycidas* is an example of a pastoral elegy – a poem dealing with shepherds and the rustic life. It is a highly conventionalized form of poetry and is often a lament in the form of the keening of a lovesick shepherd for her lover or an elegy for a dead friend. (B) denotes a general tendency toward false emotionalism. (A) is a specific type of medieval dialogue poem that employs characters such as a shepherd. (D) is a self-descriptive, less prescriptive term, and (E) is an invention.

10. **(B)** While it is true that many sonnets end with a couplet (A), not all sonnets do. This explanation also eliminates (D) as the answer, because couplets must rhyme. Pope used couplets, but they are not full poems (E). A couplet should express a complete thought, so (C) is not appropriate. Heroic couplets are found at the ends of Shakespearean sonnets and do express complete thoughts, but that is not the proposition here.

11. **(A)** The gothic novel has a long and continuing tradition – from the works of Edgar Allan Poe and Bulwer-Lytton to the shocking narratives of Stephen King. Typically, magic, mystery, horrors, and ghosts abound. While there are many Gothic-style churches (B), they are not a prerequisite for the genre. Similarly, while the Goths were barbarians – (C) and (D) – they do not seem to take any required part in Gothic fiction. Some science fictions may have Gothic elements, but the reverse is generally not true (E).

12. **(B)** *Annunciation* (1440-50) by Fra Angelico is an example of Italian Early Renaissance painting. Note the shallow, simple architectural space, the simplified, symbolic figures, and the sparse, peaceful composition. (A) *Lamentation* (1305-06) by Giotto is an example of late Gothic painting. Although there is a limited depth of space here as well, and large simple forms, the figures are treated more three-dimensionally and the grouping of figures is more dramatic. *School of Athens* (1510-11) by Raphael is a masterpiece of the High Renaissance with its deep, architectural perspective and complex composition. It is a tribute to the Athenian school of thought and shows a group of famous Greek philosophers gathered around Plato and Aristotle. Each figure represents a real individual and the placement of each one and their poses all have significance. (D) is incorrect because (C) is High, not Early, Renaissance. (E) is incorrect because (B) is Early Renaissance.

13. **(A)** The correct answer is (A). (B) is incorrect because it is Early Renaissance. (C) is incorrect because it is High Renaissance. (D) is incorrect because (B) is Early Renaissance. (E) is incorrect because (A) is Gothic.

14. **(C)** The correct answer is (C). (A) is incorrect because it is by Giotto. (B) is incorrect because it is by Fra Angelico. (D) is incorrect because neither is by Raphael. (E) is incorrect because (C) is by Raphael.

15. **(B)** *Monticello*, in Charlottesville, Virginia, was built between 1770-84 and 1796-1806. (A) is incorrect because this is not Mount Vernon. (C) is incorrect because there is no such thing as New Chiswick House. (D) is incorrect because there is no such thing as Charlottesville Manor. (E) is incorrect because this is not Valley Forge.

16. **(C)** Thomas Jefferson. (A) is incorrect because Washington lived at Mount Vernon. (B) is incorrect because Lincoln did not live here. (D) is incorrect because Coolidge did not live here. (E) is incorrect because Theodore Roosevelt did not live here.

17. **(A)** Jefferson designed *Monticello* in the Georgian style of colonial architecture which came from the English style Palladianism. Also popular in this colonial style of hybrid architecture were Greek or Roman columns. Usually Greek columns were used during this revival phase of neoclassicism, but Jefferson preferred the Roman Doric style. He was greatly influenced by *Chiswick House* (1725) but altered its design considerably for Monticello, so (B) is incorrect. (C) is incorrect because Copley was not involved in its design. (D) is incorrect because no session of Congress ever had anything to do with the design of *Monticello*. (E) is incorrect because the design for *Monticello* had nothing to do with the home where Jefferson grew up.

18. **(B)** This answer relies on recognition of the works, but if you are not aware of the work through your knowledge: epics deal with battles, heroes, death, lofty subjects – you may well have heard of Hektor, even if you are not sure of the context. (A) does not appear to come from an epic, nor do (C), (D), or (E).

19. **(C)** Remember that Shakespeare also wrote sonnets, so include these in your review. Even if you do not know this sonnet, you could separate out this answer by knowing that the Shakespearean or English sonnet always has a final rhyming couplet, and is written in iambic pentameter. (A), (B), (D), and (E) are not Shakespearean in language or metrical scheme.

20. **(A)** The simple, modern style reveals this poem to be relatively recent. Rarely are people referred to in modern works by an appellation such as "breaker of horses" (B). (C), (D), and (E) are clearly not in modern language.

21.   **(D)**   This is perhaps the most famous of Victorian poets, Matthew Arnold, and the poem, "Dover Beach," expresses the fear and darkness of an age threatened by Darwinism and technology – the language expresses this. (E) The famous "Tiger" poem of William Blake falls into the Romantic period. (A), (B), and (C) are similarly non-Victorian in their language.

22.   **(B)**   is the correct answer. The word "arch" is used as a metaphor for an architectural term of a structure arching over an expanse. (A) Though used to store valuables, a wall safe differs in size from a bank "vault" and in purpose from a (C) burial chamber. (D) Though "vault" is used as a verb in the speech, it does not mean "leap." (E) should be eliminated, immediately, as it is unrelated.

23.   **(A)**   is the correct answer. (B) is tenuously related to "established" but does not take into consideration the entire phrase. (C) suggests a relationship to fast, as in moving fast, but is not logically related. While the idea of the earth beneath our feet may be suggested in cement or terra firma, this too, does not capture the meaning of the phrase. (E) purge is not related. The best meaning for "established fast" within this context is "firmly."

24.   **(A)**   A hunting lodge is designed for use by the owner and his personal acquaintances. Although loosely based on designs of medieval donjons, giving the building a fortress-like appearance (B), the Chateau was not built for military or defensive purposes. (C) The Chateau influenced later architects of French palatial architecture, but was not itself constructed as such. The Chateau was built as a private domestic dwelling, not intended for use by the public, including as (D) a town hall or (E) a church.

25.   **(E)**   Martin Scorsese's *The Last Temptation of Christ* was the most politically controversial film (E). Oliver Stone's *JFK* (A), Francis Ford Coppola's *The Godfather* (B), Jonathan Demme's *Silence of the Lambs* (C), and Spike Lee's *Malcolm X* were also controversial.

26.   **(A)**   Russell's famous theory claims that definite descriptions have no meaning in their own right. Hence, definite descriptions are (B) not names, which do have meaning in their own right. Definite descriptions are often not satisfied (C) by any object ("The present King of France"). Hence, definite descriptions cannot be logical constants (E). Since they have no meaning in their own right, they cannot be as meaningful as their components (D).

27. **(A)** Renaissance music is predominantly vocal works composed for use in the church. The music is mainly polyphonic, which means two or more pitches or melodies occurring simultaneously. Choice (A) is correct. Music that contains a swing beat and improvisation is defined as jazz; choice (B) is incorrect. Homophonic, instrumental style consists of block chords or a melody with accompaniment chords, similar to a guitar with a soloist. Choice (C) is incorrect. Expressionism often experimented with the use of atonality and pagan themes. Choice (D) is incorrect. Monophonic music contains a single line of melody; choice (E) is incorrect.

28. **(A)** Although musicians may have been employed by all choices, musicians were predominantly composing for the church. Choice (A) is correct. The governments of the baroque period were often princes or noblemen who on occasion employed musicians to perform or compose. Choice (B) is incorrect. Musicians who were self-employed often were not as successful and needed to find other methods to support their musical endeavors; choice (C) is incorrect. The local arts guild was not the dominant employer of the baroque period; choice (D) is incorrect. Schools were not the primary employer of composers; choice (E) is incorrect.

29. **(A)** Bach composed extensively for the church, and his vocal works and instrumentals were used during the service. Bach was employed as director of music, organist, and teacher at several churches during his lifetime; choice (A) is correct. Though Bach may have composed compositions for the government, children, or theater, the mass of his compositions were for the church service. Choices (B), (C), and (D) are incorrect. Bach's compositions may have been played in taverns, but the compositions were not intended for the tavern. Choice (E) is incorrect.

30. **(C)** Hemingway's novel is based on his experience as an ambulance driver during World War I. The title is taken from the poem by Alexander Pope, as well as the lines: "Never ask for whom the bell tolls. It tolls for thee." Another of his novels (D) is set in post-WWI Europe. Remarque's novel (A) is probably the best French novel about WWI. Both Mailer's work (B) and Wouk's (E) take place in the Pacific during WWII.

31. **(C)** Othello – one of the few "multicultural" characters in Shakespeare's works, was a Moor: technically, a person whose origins are either in North Africa or on the Iberian peninsula. References in the play and tradition has it that Othello is black – or at least much darker than the average Englishman of the time – even though Moors, like Arabic people in general, vary widely in complexion.

32. **(A)** The author of *The Waverly Novels,* Scott also wrote such exciting classics as *Rob Roy* (1817), *Ivanhoe* (1819), *Kenilworth* (1821), and *Quentin Durward* (1823), and is generally considered to epitomize novels written during the English Romantic Age. These works often recall previous times – real or imagined – when men were more daring and their women more saintly. The public loved them.

33. **(D)** A Shakespearean sonnet is generally written in iambic pentameter: that is, with five unstressed and stressed syllables per line. An example of this is the opening line: "Shall I compare thee to a summer's day?" There are other characteristics: 14 lines with a heroic couplet as the last two, and a rhyme scheme throughout: ababcdcdefefgg. The sonnet is always a love poem, and is generally divided into three themes or questions, and the final two line resolution. There are many other types of sonnets with other rules, among which is the Petrarchian sonnet, first written by the Roman poet, Petrarch.

34. **(D)** James Boswell established the now familiar pattern of acolyte turned famed biographer when he wrote his magnificent work *The Life of Samuel Johnson* at the end of the eighteenth century. Familiar with the great man's ways, and mindful of his reputation, Boswell had regularly taken notes on Dr. Johnson's comings and goings in anticipation of writing his monumental work. Today, Boswell is almost as famous a writer as Johnson – though Boswell would be most shocked, as he respectfully stood in the great man's shadow for many years.

35. **(C)** The correct answer is (C). (A) is incorrect; there is no such thing. (B) is incorrect; there is no such thing. (D) is incorrect; there was no one school of painters active during this period. (E) is incorrect because it is the definition of *contrapposto.*

36. **(E)** The correct answer is (E). (A) is incorrect because there is no such thing. (B) is incorrect because there is no such thing. (C) is incorrect because it is the definition of *chiaroscuro.* (D) is incorrect because there was no one school of painters active during this period.

37. **(B)** *Young Woman with a Water Jug* (1665) is one of Vermeer's most famous works and students should recognize this as Vermeer – because of the solitary female figure going about an everyday task – a favorite subject of Vermeer. (D) is *Supper at Emmaus* (1648) by Rembrandt. This painting contains the key Rembrandt trademark of a large dark area

illuminated dramatically by an interior light source. The somber mood of the piece is also characteristic of Rembrandt's work. (A) is *Bacchus* (1597) by Caravaggio. It is his most famous painting and should be familiar to any student of art history. (C) is *Aurora* (1613) by Guido Reni, the Italian Baroque painter. (E) is Sir Joshua Reynolds' *Mrs. Siddons as the Tragic Muse* (1784).

38.　**(A)**　The correct answer is (A). (B) is incorrect because it is by Vermeer. (C) is incorrect because it is by Reni. (D) is incorrect because it is by Rembrandt. (E) is incorrect because it is by Reynolds.

39.　**(B)**　*Young Woman with a Water Jug* by Vermeer is correct. The woman's native Dutch attire should be a clue and it depicts an everyday domestic scene which is the definition of a *genre painting,* a category of subject matter first defined by Flemish and Dutch artists. Rembrandt, of course, is also Dutch, but his painting depicts a biblical scene. (A) is incorrect because it is an Italian baroque painting with a mythological subject. (C) is incorrect because it is an Italian baroque painting of a religious theme. (D) is incorrect because it is a religious scene, not a picture of daily life. (E) is incorrect because it is an English romantic painting.

40.　**(C)**　One might say also that the heart itself is a bearer of the pain for it is the heart that questions the pain's reality. The reference of the poem is general, and it describes a feeling experienced by anyone who goes through great pain.

41.　**(A)**　The point of the poem is that the formal feeling insulates or protects the emotions after the pain, much as we don a wetsuit when swimming in icy waters. Formal stiffness at such times is a defense against emotional disintegration.

42.　**(E)**　The phrase "like a stone" repeats the meaning of the word "quartz" and therefore adds nothing to the poem's message. Because it is the essence of poetry to avoid unnecessary words, this phrase might be pointed out as a weakness. All of the other phrases are essential to what the poet is telling us.

43.　**(E)**　is the correct answer. Georg Buchner's *Woyzeck* was called the first proletarian play because it did not focus on (A) the hypocrisy of court life, (B) life in the military, (C) the world of court jesters, (D) mercenaries for hire, or any other exotic or exciting fare; rather, the play focuses on (E) life among the working classes. Thus, proletarian is a key word in the question stem.

44. **(D)** is the correct answer. The best approach to answering this question is to recognize immediately that you are looking for an individual and not the title of a play. Therefore, all titles of plays should be eliminated. (B) *Mother Courage* and (E) *Joan of Arc* should be eliminated immediately. (A) Caliban is an individual character, but he is clearly as much a slave in *The Tempest* as Oenone is a servant in *Phaedre*. Only one possible choice is left, and that is Hedda of *Hedda Gabler*.

45. **(D)** Gothic Revival, a style common in the nineteenth-century Romantic period of architecture, in which earlier architectural styles, such as classical Greek and Roman, as well as medieval, were imitated. The spires and towers on the roof of the Houses of Parliament are derived from those of Gothic churches; the low, horizontal profile of the building itself is typical of English Gothic churches. Classical (A) architectural elements are absent; thus, the building is also not an example of (B) neo-classical architecture (another romantic style of architecture). Romanesque (E) architecture, an earlier medieval style, did not incorporate details such as tall spires and tracery comparable to those which appear on the Houses of Parliament.

46. **(C)** *Undulating arch* and *contraction walk* are terms in beledi (abdominal dance). In ballet (A), ballroom (B), country dance (D), and tap dance (E), one would not elevate the rib cage while the spine was arched carrying stretched arms.

47. **(A)** God's foreknowledge is often thought to be compatible with free will, because if God knows what someone will be in the future, that person cannot do otherwise. Human freedom seems to depend on the possibility that one might do otherwise than one did, choosing one action rather than another. (B) is incorrect because, according to this argument, God's foreknowledge entails determinism. (C) and (E) are implausible because God's love and universal benevolence are not obviously incompatible with determinism. (D) is incorrect because the problem presupposes that there is (future) time.

48. **(D)** G.F. Handel's famous oratorio is "Messiah." An oratorio is a dramatic work, religious in nature, for voices and orchestra. "Messiah"

describes the life of Christ. Choice (D) is correct. "St. Matthew's Passion" is an oratorio by Bach; choice (A) is incorrect. "Mass in B minor" is also a composition of Bach, a massive work on religious themes; choice (B) is incorrect. "Also Sprach Zarathustra" is a tone poem composed by Richard Strauss; choice (C) is incorrect. "Wozzeck" is an opera by Alban Berg; choice (E) is incorrect.

49. **(A)** Two eighth notes are equal to one quarter note, for example 4/8. A quarter note equals one beat, a down beat, and an upbeat. One eighth note is equal to half of one beat. Therefore, one eighth note is the down beat and the other is the upbeat. Choice (A) is correct. Three eight notes would equal a dotted quarter note because a dot adds half of the value of the note to the total value. Choice (B) is incorrect. Eight eighth notes equal four beats or a whole note; choice (C) is incorrect. Four eighth notes would equal a half note or two beats; choice (D) is incorrect. One eighth note is half of a quarter note; choice (E) is incorrect.

50. **(A)** If a clarinet sounds a G, it is the concert pitch of an F. This is because the clarinet is generally a B flat clarinet, so it needs to transpose up a major second to read concert pitch. Choice (A) is correct. A concert pitch of a G would be an A on the clarinet; choice (B) is incorrect. A concert pitch of a C would be a D on the clarinet; choice (C) is incorrect. A concert pitch of a B flat would be a C on the clarinet; choice (D) is incorrect. The pitch of A would be a B flat on the clarinet; choice (E) is incorrect.

51. **(E)** In Shakespearean tragedy it is common that the last scene is a heap of bodies – both high born and not so high – both major and supporting. Some have satirized this tradition – as well as the equally recognized tendency of a dying Shakespearean character such as Hamlet to announce "I am dead, Horatio," and then to continue speaking. At the end of *Hamlet,* in the same example, the Prince is dead on the floor, his old friend-turned-murderer Laertes is also, so is his mother and his step father – his father, Hamlet senior – having been assassinated in an orchard previously.

52. **(E)** In Shakespeare's *Julius Caesar,* the famous question and accusation, "Et tu, Brute," is uttered by the dying emperor. Finally, Brutus, his closest friend, has brutally and literally "stabbed him in the back," and at the realization of this, Caesar sees that the last of his world has turned against him. His last words are: "Then fall Caesar." The phrase has become generalized to mean a response to any formerly trusted friend.

53. **(B)** Ambition leads many of Shakespeare's characters to upset the balance of nature by assassination and/or conspiracy. This inevitably results in the eventual destruction of the assassin as the forces of the natural order strive to correct the imbalance caused by the unnatural act. Thus, Macbeth is destroyed and order is restored and Hamlet the elder's murder is avenged. Murder never results in stability (A); the people's discontent does not seem to enter into great affairs of state (C); evil and not benevolent weakness is always the problem (D); and most rulers have their bad points, but not so much that they should be destroyed (E). Shakespeare has, in fact, been accused by his critics of being overly sympathetic with the powers that have been because his company was funded by the Lord Chamberlain. The concept of the Great Chain of Being was also a widely held Elizabethan belief.

54. **(C)** In the 1500s Sir Thomas More wrote a curious work entitled *Utopia* – obviously about a perfect society as he imagined it. Many scholars of the genre consider this the first recognizable science fiction – although there were some ancient Greek fancies about traveling to the moon on a sailboat. At any rate, each of the other choices postdate More's work: Shelley and Verne wrote in the nineteenth century; Bradbury and Wells in the twentieth.

55. **(D)** Odysseus is the model for the classical hero – almost superhuman in his capabilities, charismatic and egocentric – he challenges giants and makes alliances with gods and goddesses. O'Neil's (A) work may have the name of a Greek goddess in its title, but was written during this century. The same is true of (C). The Old Testament (B) predates the Greek era. Michell's novel (E) – while full of interesting heroes – was written a little more than 50 years ago.

56. **(B)** *David* by Bernini is a quintessential baroque sculpture. The dynamic pose, the dramatic action, the windswept hair, and flowing robes amazingly captured in marble, and the mythological subject matter are all characteristics of baroque sculpture. (A) is *Pauline Borghese as Venus* (1808). It is a portrait of Napoleon's sister as a reclining Venus. It is a neoclassical sculpture, depicting, as was the custom, members of the social and political elite in mythological guise. (C) Michelangelo's *David* (1501-04) is a Renaissance masterpiece and his most famous work, one that should be familiar to all students. (D) is a *Pieta* by an unknown artist from the early fourteenth century. It is a Gothic devotional image, intended to arouse intense emotion through the stark depiction of suffering. (E) is Donatello's *David* (1430-32) from the Early Renaissance.

57. **(E)** Students should know which one is Michelangelo's *David* (C), and Bernini's *David* (B) is not consistent with Donatello's style. (A) is incorrect because it is neither a David nor is it by Donatello. (D) is incorrect for the same reason as (A).

58. **(E)** Donatello's *David* is bronze and thus was cast from a mold rather than chiseled from a block of marble (A, B, and C) or wood (D). It should be obvious from its color and shiny texture that Donatello's sculpture is bronze and could therefore not have been chiseled.

59. **(D)** *Arte Povera* is a twentieth century term coined by Italian critic Germano Celant. (A) is incorrect because no school exists. (B) is incorrect because it is the definition of *Art Brut.* (C) is incorrect because it is also a definition of *Art Brut.* (E) is incorrect because (B) and (C) both define *Art Brut.*

60. **(E)** Both (B) and (C) describe *Art Brut* as defined by twentieth century artist Jean Dubuffet who coined the term. (A) is incorrect because no such school exists. (B) alone is incorrect because (C) also defines *Art Brut.* (C) alone is incorrect because (B) also defines *Art Brut.* (D) is incorrect because it defines *Arte Povera.*

61. **(A)** A figure of speech where one part represents the whole: the heart and hands stand for the whole person. (B) illustrates personification; and (C) is from a ballad and does not contain a specific type of figure of speech. (D) contains elements of personification and cacophony, and (E) contains irony. This answer calls for recognizing techniques, forms, or figures of speech – again worth studying from the glossaries in anthologies.

62. **(E)** The irony is implied by the idea that people *could* embrace in a grave. (A), (B), (C), and (D) illustrate synecdoche, personification, ballad, and cacophony, respectively, not irony. Work your way through the examples to sift out the meanings.

63. **(D)** Cacophony is usually associated with discordant music; the term can also apply to words that break the rhyme or rhythm in a rough-sounding way, usually for the purpose of stressing a point. In this Shakespearean sonnet, the sound is discordant and the meter overturned to reflect the poet's unease with the subject of lust. (A), (B), (C), and (E) illustrate synecdoche, personification, ballad, and irony, respectively, not cacophony.

64. **(C)** The ballad form is one of the earliest forms of poetry and this is perhaps the best known example from Sir Walter Scott. In your review learn the rhyme and rhythm patterns so the ballad becomes easily recognized. (A), (B), (D), and (E) illustrate synecdoche, personification, cacophony, and irony, respectively, not a ballad.

65. **(E)** is the correct answer. According to Aristotle, (A) plot, (B) beginning, (C) middle, and (D) end are important structural elements in a play. (E) is not related to this question as it is not technically a part of structure.

66. **(B)** is the correct answer. Pantomimed performances, or dumb shows, were often a part of Elizabethan plays. The dumb show in (A) *Hamlet* was especially important because it served a particular purpose for Hamlet. Dumb shows appeared in (C) *Duchess of Malfi,* (D) *The Changeling,* and (E) *Gorboduc.* (B) *The Tempest* is the exception here, and is, therefore, the correct answer.

67. **(B)** The apse, a semicircular projection at the east end of a church, is considered the most sacred area of a church, and thus is the appropriate area for the performance of the most sacred Christian rite, the Eucharist. An (A) ambulatory is a passageway which encircles the apse, designed to direct worshippers around the altar. A (C) transept refers to the arms of a church which project from the (D) nave, the main body of a church. Many churches are constructed with (E) chapels, each of which contains a smaller altar, but the *main* altar of a church is never placed in such smaller chapels.

68. **(D)** In fifth position, the legs are turned out from the hips and one foot is directly in front of the other. The heel of the front foot should also be placed at the joint of the toe of the rear foot. Choice (A) is fourth position crossed, (B) is first position, (C) is third position, and (E) is second position.

69. **(C)** Third position is the heel of each foot touching the middle of the other foot while one foot is directly in front of the other. The legs must be turned out from the hips. Like third position, fourth position crossed (A), first position (B), fifth position (D), and second position (E) all must keep the legs turned out from the hips.

70. **(A)** Rousseau argues that humans are by nature good, and that bad behavior is a product of the social environment. Paglia believes that femi-

nists want to change the social environment because they think doing so will result in a happier situation for women, given that people are ultimately good. If humans were by nature bad (B), changing the social environment would not be sufficient for happier relations between the sexes. If (C) or (E) were correct, she would not say feminists are "heirs to Rousseau." Rousseau is not neutral about human nature, thinking that it might be neither good nor bad. So choice (D) is incorrect.

71.   **(B)**   A capella is vocal music without instrumental accompaniment. Choice (B) is correct. Instrumental music would not be a capella; choice (A) is incorrect. Sacred songs can be sung a capella, but they can have accompaniment; choice (C) is incorrect. Soft music merely describes a dynamic level and does not relate to style; choice (D) is incorrect. Piano is a dynamic level which instructs to play soft; choice (E) is incorrect.

72.   **(B)**   George Gershwin combined classical forms with folk music and jazz to create an original orchestral style: for example, "Rhapsody in Blue" and "American in Paris." Choice (B) is correct. Aaron Copland used folk themes in works such as "Appalachian Spring;" choice (A) is incorrect. Charles Ives composed music with hints of other compositions, such as "The Unanswered Question"; choice (C) is incorrect. Benjamin Britten is a British composer who employed neoclassical form as in "Peter Grimes"; choice (D) is not correct. Kodaly was a Hungarian composer/educator who researched folk music; choice (E) is incorrect.

73.   **(A)**   The diagram demonstrates the use of a motif, a phrase, or series of notes that is found throughout a composition, often in variations. Choice (A) is correct. A appoggiatura is a dissonant ornamental note that resolves by a step up or down. Choice (B) is incorrect. A grace note is an ornamental note played immediately before a counted beat; choice (C) is incorrect. A trill means to shake, to quickly play the notes above or below the given note; choice (D) is incorrect. A slur is a form of articulation which connects the pitches; choice (E) is incorrect.

74.   **(A)**   Greek tragedy is characterized by the fall of one person from a position of high esteem to one of little or none. There would be no tragedy – according to the Greeks – if the fall involved people of little importance (B). Their ordeals are ordinary (C). Similarly, the focus is on one important person rather than many (E). Simply coping with a bad situation from beginning to end is – to the Greeks, unlike ourselves – not heroic in the Classical sense. All of these precepts can be seen at work in Sophocles' play *Oedipus the King,* in which the King of Thebes is reduced to a blind

beggar and endures his own brand of agony – far different from the common kind.

75.   **(E)**   The tragedy of *Romeo and Juliet* not only adheres to the Aristotelian rule of five acts, but it also uses a chorus – at least in its introduction. In Shakespeare's use, this chorus has been reduced to one character; and in modern versions it has been changed into a voice-over or has been entirely eliminated. *Romeo and Juliet*'s chorus, however, is famous for its direct communication with the audience as well as the famous lines which mention the "two hour traffic upon our stage" during which time the "star crossed lovers take their lives." All of the other answers choices, (A) to (D), are not rules of tragedy by Aristotle. While some may apply to Shakespeare's tragedies, these answer choices are not rules for tragedy at all.

Section 2

76.   **(D)**   Christie's *Mousetrap* was seen on the London stage for almost 50 years. In this play she perfects her formula of the classic "Whodunnit" – a dwindling number of suspects in an increasing number of murders – all isolated in one place. Doyle's work (A) in general is only occasionally adapted for the stage; Levin's (B) is a wonderfully suspenseful play written in the 1970s. King's work (C) and Larry McMurtry's (E) are novels.

77.   **(B)**   From the diaries of William Byrd and John Smith to the sermons of Jonathan Edwards to the poetry of Edward Taylor, most early American writing was practical or instructive in nature. Entertaining works – short stories, plays, etc., either were imported from England, or were not permitted in strict settlements such as those in New England. Basically, however, the settlers – if they could read – had little time for literary diversion of any sort. American short stories and novels came later – beginning at the end of the eighteenth century, and finally being produced in impressive number by the middle of the nineteenth – 300 years or more after the initial settlement.

78.   **(A)**   Weems wrote one of the most popular and widely read biographies at the beginning of the nineteenth century – his biography of George Washington. Indeed, it was Weems who evidently "invented" the "I will not tell a lie" myth that apparently has no basis in fact. Flexner (B) wrote

his biography of the first president 150 years later; and Sandberg's of Lincoln (C) at approximately the same period in this century. Irving's work (E) was a short story; and Franklin's (D) is put here simply to trick the too casual reader and responder.

79.   **(A)** Rococo grew out of the Baroque style and is considered by many to be the final phase of that movement. However, the given statement for this question definitely best describes Rococo. (B) Baroque, the dominant style of European architecture, painting, and sculpture from about 1600-1750 is an ornate style marked by dramatic and complex compositions and subject matter. It led into the playful, more decorative style of Rococo which inherited its penchant for elaborate decoration and ornament but not its drama. (C) Romantic style is marked by a feeling for nature and an emphasis on emotion and a subjective sensibility as opposed to reason and scientific fact. This movement was at its height in Europe between the years of 1790-1840. (D) Art Deco is a modern style of architecture and interior decoration which was popular in Europe and the U.S. between the 1920s-40s. (E) Art Nouveau is a style of decoration and architecture which was popular in Europe from the 1890s through the early 1900s. A lot of wrought iron work was done in this style, with an emphasis on plant forms, such as to the entrances to the Paris Metro stations. There was also much furniture and glassware produced with similar motifs. Also, much magazine illustration was done in this graphic style, as typified by the work of Aubrey Beardsley.

80.   **(C)** *Le Moulin de la Galette* (1873) by Auguste Renoir. The impressionists (started in France; at its height 1870s-1886) sought to capture the movement of light and shade by avoiding outlines and instead covering their canvases with short, sketchy brush marks jutting up against each other, in contrasting colors. Up close the paintings seem to be a cacophony of random spots, but when the viewer steps back, the scene comes into focus. The thousands of individual brushstrokes unify, and illusory depth and light are created. Outdoor scenes were the focus of the impressionists because of the play of the natural light. (A) is *Autumn on the Hudson River* (1860) by Jasper Cropsey. This is an academic landscape painting, an example of the work of the Hudson River School, and American movement to glorify the domestic landscape, so named because the artists started in the Hudson River Valley of New York state and this was their subject matter. The paint is handled much too rigidly and the forms too outlined and individually illustrated for this piece to be an Impressionist work. (B) is *Spirit of the Dead Watching* (1892) by Paul Gauguin. The faux-primitive style in which this work is painted prevents it from being an impres-

sionist work. Its looseness of form and paint handling, and its departure from realistic representation both grew out of the innovations begun by the impressionist, but this is an example of one of the offshoot styles of impressionism, Fauvism, which followed impressionism and is thus a post-impressionist style. (D) is *Mont Sainte-Victoire Seen from Bibemus Quarry* (1898-1900) by Paul Cezanne. Cezanne takes the fractured pictured surface of individual, identifiable brushstrokes, a practice started by the impressionists, one step further. Cezanne bridges the gap between impressionism and cubism by starting to experiment with movement and the concept of time in his paintings, features more prominent in cubism. Cezanne is also an example of a post-Impressionist. (E) is incorrect because both are post-Impressionist work.

81. **(B)** *Spirit of the Dead Watching* (1892) by Gauguin. Gauguin is famous for having left his native France for Tahiti where he adapted that island's native style of painting to create a new and modern false-primitive style. Not only his technique was influenced by the natives; their ideas concerning spirituality and religion are also present in the work. In this painting, the moon and the earth are personified as a man and a woman. (A) is incorrect because it is by Cropsey, an American member of the Hudson River School. (C) is incorrect because it is by the impressionist Renoir. (D) is incorrect because it is by Cezanne, a post-impressionist of an entirely different style. (E) is incorrect because only (B) is by Gauguin.

82. **(E)** Both Gauguin's *Spirit of the Dead Watching* and Cezanne's *Mont Sainte-Victoire Seen from Bibemus Quarry* are historically (post-1886 and pre-1910s) and stylistically (influenced by aspects of Impressionism) post-Impressionist works. (A) is incorrect because it predates even Impressionism. (B) is incorrect because painting (D) is also post-Impressionist. Choice (C) is incorrect because it is impressionist. Choice (D) is incorrect because painting (B) is also post-Impressionist.

83. **(A)** The sonnet is easily recognized by counting the lines: 14. However, this sonnet is made up of rhyming couplets so it is not Petrarchan (D), sometimes known as Italian after the Italian poet Petrarch; nor is it Shakespearean, sometimes known as English. Learn the different rhyme patterns so you can recognize the types. An ode (B) addresses someone or something; an air (C) is a song; and a villanelle (E) is a complicated verse form: five tercets with a concluding quatrain.

84. **(D)** A figure of speech which juxtaposes two very dissimilar ideas or feelings is an oxymoron: civility is not usually associated with wildness

– the two terms contradict one another. A paradox (A) is a statement that contradicts itself but may still be true, i.e., "While I was at the library, I had some pizza." A metaphor (B) is when one object is said to be another, as in "necessity is the mother of invention." Necessity cannot literally be a mother, as it is said to, so it must be a metaphor. (C), an example of an onomatopoeia, is when a word sounds itself like the sound that it illustrates, i.e., "ding-dong" or "thud." Hyperbole (E) means great exaggeration, for example, "I'm so tired I could sleep for a year."

85. **(A)** Most of the words are close, but erring suggests a mistake which straying rather than wandering (D) captures; untied and loose, (B) and (C), suggest a deliberateness to the mistake, and straight (E), of course, contradicts the idea of carelessness in the dress – think of the term straight-laced person to see the difference.

86. **(E)** There is a spirit of fun behind the poem that (D) does not capture; the poet is not against law and order nor does he say he likes to see untidy women, (A) and (B). He does like a certain carelessness in a woman's dress (C), but the end of that thought is in preference to a rigid or precise artfulness, so (E) is the best answer.

87. **(C)** is the correct answer. When he sees a character in the dumb show staged by Hamlet pour a solution into the ear of the character playing the sleeping king, Claudius cries out: "Give me some light, Away!" and Polonius repeats this call: "Lights. Lights. Lights."

88. **(A)** is the correct answer. Note that the answer requires a play title and not a character name such as (B) Falstaff, the fool and Jester in *Henry IV: Part II* or (C) Juliet, from *Romeo and Juliet;* therefore, these can be eliminated immediately. You are left with (D) the *Merchant of Venice, a* play in which the issues of money-lending are raised; however, the characters are less "cut-throat" than those in Johnson's play.

89. **(A)** St. Paul's Cathedral, London, has as its distinguishing characteristics the two-storied facade, the dome, and the flanking towers. The Church of the Invalides, Paris (B), which was designed by Jules Hardouin-Mansart and built 1680-91, influenced Wren's design; however, the Church of the Invalides lacks flanking towers. The (C) Pantheon, Paris, designed by Jacques-Germain Soufflot; the (D) Royal Pavilion, Brighton, England, designed by John Nash; and the (E) Baltimore Cathedral, Baltimore, de-

signed by Benjamin Latrobe, all post-date St. Paul's Cathedral (1755-92; 1815-18; 1805-, respectively).

90. **(B)** Trevor Nunn, George C. Wolfe, and Joseph Papp are theatrical stage directors (B). Tim Rice, Andrew Lloyd Webber, and Stephen Sondheim are musical composers (A); Tommy Tune, Bob Fosse, and Jerome Robbins are choreographers (C); David Mamet, Edward Albee, and Tony Kushner are playwrights (D); and Michael Crawford, Estelle Parsons, and Betty Buckley are thespians (E).

91. **(C)** A group of choreographers is (C). A group of musical composers is (A), stage directors is (B), playwrights is (D), and thespians is (E).

92. **(D)** A group of playwrights is David Mamet, Edward Albee, and Tony Kushner. Musical composers (A), stage directors (B), choreographers (C), and thespians (E) are also working artists.

93. **(A)** Plato thought his ideal republic should mirror the human soul in its structure, and so the state is a macrocosm of the microcosmic soul. Since none of the others has this central feature of an isomorphic structure, only (A) can be regarded as correct. In any event, the soul is not part of the state (B), nor is it the cause (C) of the state. Certainly, the soul is not a specimen state (D), and no Platonists would have said that the soul is a particular instance of the state as a universal (E).

94. **(A)** Beethoven's Symphony No. 3 was originally composed for Napoleon Bonaparte. It depicted the battles of the young soldier. Choice (A) is correct. The composition was not composed for Joseph Stalin, George Washington, or Jesus Christ. Choices (B), (C), and (D) are incorrect. Although Mozart composed during the classical period, Beethoven did not dedicate "Eroica" to him; choice (E) is incorrect.

95. **(B)** Rhythm is the pulse or the duration of the notes. Choice (B) is correct. Dynamics are defined as the degrees of loudness in music; choice (A) is incorrect. An interval is the distance between notes; choice (C) is incorrect. A clef sign identifies the location of a certain pitch; choice (D) is incorrect. Tone is the pitch or the color of the note. Choice (E) is incorrect.

96. **(B)** Claude Debussy was an expressionistic composer attempting to paint pictures with music; choice (B) is correct. Stravinsky's work contained primitivism among other elements; choice (A) is incorrect. Maurice Ravel was an impressionistic composer who explored chromaticism; choice (C) is incorrect. Schoenberg developed serialism, the use of the 12 tones in order; choice (D) is incorrect. G.F. Handel was a composer of the Baroque period; choice (E) is incorrect.

97. **(E)** Robert Frost is truly one of the greatest American poets of the twentieth century and was the first poet ever to participate in a presidential inaugural (John Kennedy's in 1961). His poetry – from "Mending Wall" to "The Death of the Hired Hand" – is evocative of New England's people and places. All of the other choices – with the exception of Whitman – are known as New England poets, though all are from previous centuries. Whitman – some say the greatest American poet – wrote in the nineteenth century and was from Brooklyn.

98. **(E)** The Italian novella of the 1300s is generally recognized as the direct predecessor in form and intent of the modern novel. Typified by Boccaccio's *Decameron* (ca. 1348), they were stories of scandal in love, dishonest priests, fashionable nobles, and tough peasantry. By the sixteenth century, similar narratives were being written in England (e.g., Arcadia, ca. 1570). Picaresque novels (D) are also descendant of the Italian. Far back, Greek epics are vague ancestors (B), but are not direct, causal creative forces. The Anglo-Saxons (A) were not well known for their literacy, let alone for their short stories – a genre that did not exist then. The oral tradition of rural America (C) has not had that great of an effect on literature outside of the United States, making it impossible for these stories to have been a predecessor to the English novel.

99. **(A)** Every time parents tell their children the story "Jack and the Beanstalk" they are relating a "Jack tale" which had been told in its many variations in England since the Middle Ages. There are scores of Jack tales, and they are mainly told now in the Southern Appalachians where oral tradition remains strong and where most of the population are descended from English, Scottish, and Irish settlers. A Jack tale may be a fairy tale (B) but it is a more specific identification. Aesop's fables (C) are Greek in origin. (E) is English but relates to the mythical King Arthur. (D) is modern and passed down through written formats.

100. **(D)** Known today as "border ballads," songs such as "Barbara Allen," "Mary Hamilton," and "Lord Lovett" still are sung in the Southern

Appalachians of the United States. Originally from the border region of Scotland, these ballads were first catalogued by Child in the early years of this century, and sometimes go by the name of "Childe ballads." They may involve folk tales (B), but these are put to music. Again, they may be lullabies (C), but that would be only a subclass. Most were passed down orally, but in the eighteenth century other ballads were printed as "broadsides" (E) and distributed – again a subclass. Chamber music (A) is instrumental and of more "highborn" origins.

101. **(C)** Without specific knowledge of the question, it might still be answered correctly as long as the reader knows that Tennyson is the only poet listed who was famous during the early nineteenth century. William McGonigle (A) seriously called himself the "Poet Laureate of Scotland" later on in the century, but he was actually a national joke. The professor's extant poetry still leaves readers howling in laughing disbelief. Eliot (B) is of this century, and Shakespeare (D) and Milton (E) were of the seventeenth century.

102. **(C)** Though influenced by impressionism, Van Gogh was far more expressionistic with his thick application of paint and more violent brushwork. Van Gogh made no attempt at naturalistic color representation. (A), (B), (D), and (E) are all incorrect because all of these painters (Camille Pissarro, Claude Monet, Edgar Degas, and Mary Cassat, respectively) were impressionist.

103. **(A)** Edgar Degas is most well known for the hundreds of paintings, pastels, and sketches that he did depicting ballerinas warming up and in performance. (B) is incorrect because Manet is most well known for his landscapes. (C) is incorrect because Toulouse-Lautrec is most well known for his depiction's of the Paris nightlife of bars and dance halls. (D) is incorrect because Renoir is most famous for his paintings of voluptuous nude women. (E) is incorrect because Monet is most famous for his paintings of landscapes with subjects such as haystacks and waterlillies.

104. **(B)** *London* (1906) is by Andre Derain. In this piece Derain takes from the tradition of the impressionist landscape, focusing on the movement of light on a body of water. The brush strokes here, however, are bigger and spaced farther apart than in an impressionist painting. This piece is also more dynamic and abstract, making it a post-impressionist or Fauve painting, but the influence of impressionism is obvious when compared to any painting by Manet or Pissarro featuring a river view spanned

by a bridge. *The Open Window* (1905) by Henri Matisse is incorrect because, while the influence of impressionism is obvious in the water scene and the broken-up brush strokes, this piece departs more from the tradition than does (B). First of all, this is an interior and an exterior, not a pure landscape. Also, much of this painting is drawn in thick lines; only in certain areas do we see the fragmented brush strokes of the impressionists and here they are even less connected and more abstract than in Derain's piece. (C) *The Joy of Life* (1905-06) by Matisse is also incorrect because it is a wholly Fauve piece. It has figures drawn in bold outline with large, flat areas of solid color, not related directly at all to impressionism. (D) is incorrect because both (A) and (C) are less directly influenced by Impressionism than (B). (E) is incorrect because only (B) is clearly the most directly influenced by impressionism.

105. **(D)** Both (A) *The Window* and (C) *The Joy of Life* are by Henri Matisse. These are two off his most famous works and even in black-and-white reproduction, his singular style should be recognizable. (A) alone is incorrect because (C) is also by Matisse. (B) is incorrect because it is by Andre Derain. (C) alone is incorrect because (A) is also by Matisse. (E) is incorrect because (A) and (C) are by Matisse, but (B) is by Derain.

106. **(E)** All of these works are done in the post-impressionist style of fauvism. The paint handling is looser and the compositions more dynamic than impressionism, but all come out of the tradition. The fauves were known for their expressionistic landscapes and figures and for their wild use of color (fauve in French means beast or wild animal). Even though the color cannot be seen here, these pieces should still be recognizable as fauve paintings. (A), (B), (C), and (D) are all incorrect because all of these are fauve paintings not just any one or combination of two.

107. **(D)** The words irresistible and bittersweet provide a clue. The speaker is moved and yet not despondent (A), nor sarcastic (B), and certainly not distraught (C), because he can still write of his love with a sense of sweetness; above all he is not ecstatic (E)!

108. **(A)** Alliteration is perhaps the most easily recognized of figures of speech: the repetition of consonants, usually the initial consonant. Assonance (B) sounds similar but means the repetition of vowel sounds. (C) slant rhyme refers to imperfect rhymes. A slant rhyme is not present in this passage. An oxymoron (D) is a figure of speech which juxtaposes two very dissimilar ideas or feelings. A paradox (E) is a statement that contra-

dicts itself but may still be true, i.e., "While I was at the library, I had some pizza."

109. **(B)** Another way of saying this might be that love makes one "weak at the knees." Answer choices (A), (C), (D), and (E) all involve the emotions rather than the physical which this line clearly shows.

110. **(A)** Option (B) is a clear example of the sting in the tail of an epigram; here (B) is an elegy; (C) is an epigraph; (D) an epitaph; and (E) could be a monologue or soliloquy. All such terms are worth learning with examples so they are easily recognizable.

111. **(A)** is the correct answer. Both (A) Lear and (B) Creon are noted for their "stiff-necks" and (C) Macbeth for his weakness as a murderer and opportunist. (D) Polonius should be eliminated immediately; though he chides Ophelia for her love of Hamlet, he does not have power over a fool. So, too, should (E) Oedipus be eliminated immediately as it is the title of a play.

112. **(C)** is the correct answer. All other answer choices are plays which do not have characters named the Captain or Laura, so choices (A), (B), (D), and (E) are incorrect.

113. **(D)** The Pantheon contains columns of the Doric order on the lowest level, columns of the Ionic order on the second level, Corinthian columns on the third level, and pilasters on the uppermost level. Piers (A) are large supporting pillars, while (B) compound piers are such supports with attached half-columns or pilasters. A colonnade (C) refers to a row of freestanding columns. Blind arcades (E) are rows of columns attached to a wall which are connected by arches.

114. **(A)** Hume held that effects follow causes in time and so could not account for cases in which an effect and its cause occur simultaneously. (B) is true, since Hume believed that there is no necessary connection between a cause and its effect, but this point is irrelevant here, as are (C) and (D). Although Hume's analysis of causation is startling, choice (E) cannot be correct. Hume did not claim there are no causes but only that causation was not properly understood.

115. **(B)** Serge Diaghilev commissioned works of composers for use with the Russian Ballet; choice (B) is correct. Stravinsky often composed

for Diaghilev; choice (A) is incorrect. Esterhazy was the estate that employed Haydn; choice (C) is incorrect. Walt Disney, though he made the film "Fantasia," which used many famous classical pieces, he was not responsible for works for the Russian Ballet; choice (D) is incorrect. Modest Mussorgsky was a Russian composer of nationalistic music; choice (E) is incorrect.

116. **(B)** *Porgy and Bess* is a folk opera composed by George Gershwin, which portrays the lives and struggles of black Americans in the South. Choice (B) is correct. *The Barber of Seville* is an opera by Rossini; choice (A) is incorrect. *Carmen* is the famous opera by Bizet; choice (C) is incorrect. *Tristan and Isolde* is an opera by Wagner; choice (D) is incorrect. *On the Town* is a musical by Leonard Bernstein; choice (E) is incorrect.

117. **(A)** George Gershwin is the composer of "Porgy and Bess." Choice (A) is correct. Giuseppe Verdi was an Italian composer of operas such as "Rigoletto"; choice (B) is incorrect. Richard Wagner composed operas such as "Tristan and Isolde," a story of fate and passion; choice (C) is incorrect. W.A. Mozart composed many operas, including "Don Giovanni," the story of the famous Spanish nobleman who lived to seek pleasure; choice (D) is incorrect. Salvador Dali was a surrealist artist; choice (E) is incorrect.

118. **(A)** The Irish churchman Swift was appalled at the treatment of the Irish by the English and their ruling surrogates. Famine had spread throughout the island, and Swift and other critics blamed this mostly on England's cruel policies and on the incompetence and lack of concern on the part of the responsible government officials. In his *Modest Proposal,* Swift uses biting satire to suggest that, in order to "cure" the Irish problem of starvation, overpopulation, and dissuade, Irish babies might be boiled and eaten. Only (D) here is a feasible answer, but that wasn't Swift's purpose. Ironically, the correct answer sounds preposterous – though it is accurate.

119. **(D)** In *Great Expectations,* the hero, Pip, has been orphaned. In fact, the story begins before his parents' stones in the graveyard. Ironically, Magwitch, the escaped convict who attacks Pip in the graveyard, eventually becomes his mysterious benefactor. Each of the other works by Dickens cited here possess similar elements such as orphans (A), poverty (E), businesses that go awry (C), and young lads seeking fortunes (B), but none possess the exact characteristics asked for here.

120. **(C)** Though Dickens' father, John, had been a moderately successful businessman, he fell into debt and bankruptcy, the punishment for which was debtor's prison. John's circumstances later improved due to the surprise receipt of a legacy. Dickens was forced to go to work in a bootblacking factory at the age of nine to help support his family. This left a lasting mark on Dickens the man and on his literature. Thus, in *Great Expectations,* Pip receives support from a mysterious source, and honest, hard working people like Pip's Uncle Joe Gargery remain poor throughout their lives.

121. **(D)** Mary Anne Evans wrote *Silas Marner* (A) under the pen name George Eliot because, in Victorian England, it was generally considered improper for a woman to become an author, and because a man stood a greater chance of getting published. Mary Shelley (B) had earlier found success in her publication of *Frankenstein.* Godfrey Cass (E) and Molly Farren (C) are characters in Eliot's story of Silas, the sad old miser.

122. **(D)** Editor and writer Joel Chandler Harris is famous for his tales of Uncle Remus and for being the first writer to record a dependable representation of the African-American slave dialect. Harris, who was white, was fascinated by African-American and Native American folk tales – particularly those about animals and nature, and between the 1880s and 1908, he wrote and published many works. The other possibilities here are out of the scope of interest and lifetime of the Georgia writer.

123. **(A)** Of the five answer choices, only (A) and (B) can be said to show groups of figures in a landscape; choices (D) and (E) show one or two isolated figures in a landscape setting, and choice (C) contains no landscape elements at all. Choice (B), however, though it presents a number of figures within a topographic view, carefully avoids formally composed and arranged groups and seeks instead to achieve an effect of direct, unposed observation. Only choice (A) uses a composed group as its focal point: the line of schoolboys, seemingly engaged in a moment of spontaneous play, has been painstakingly arranged to lead the viewer's eye from the darker forms at the right to the white-shirted boy at the center. The entire group is set in a broad meadow against a distant, level horizon line which lends balance and stability to the whole composition.

124. **(D)** Only choices (A), (B), and (D) include visible horizon lines: in choice (A) the horizon is integrated with the figure group, and in choice (B) the figures, though small and insignificant within the broad landscape

space, are busy in normal workday activities and do not seem especially isolated. Choice (D), however, Andrew Wyeth's *Christina's World,* 1948, places a solitary figure in a broad, empty landscape space bounded by a high, distant horizon. The helpless isolation of the stricken woman in the field is emphasized by the distance which separates her from her home high on the horizon.

125. **(E)** Only choices (D) and (E) appear to simplify their contents in any significant way. Choice (D) simplifies by eliminating unnecessary subject matter and concentrating on a few essential images, such as the figure, the field and sky, and the buildings. Its style, however, is not abstract but realistic, and is based on close observation of actual details. Choice (E), in contrast, presents actual, observed forms, but distills and refines them into basic, almost abstract shapes: the trees to the right appear as a simple dark mass, while the houses are reduced to a combination of basic planes which reflect light and color. All secondary detail and texture, as of the wood siding of the houses, is carefully, rigorously suppressed.

126. **(D)** Dada is a movement that sprang up in Europe around the time of the First World War. In response to what they saw as an absurd, unspeakable event (the war), dadaists sought to ridicule the values of bourgeois society, the same society which supported the war. The pseudo-scientific, comic rantings of poet and artist Tristan Tzara exemplify the satire of the seriousness and self-important "rationality" of middle-class life in Europe. The dadaists believed that the only way to combat absurdity was with absurdity. (A) is incorrect because although dadaism led into surrealism, the surrealists did not include humor in their dramatic statements, although they also used absurdity to shock. (B) is incorrect because the impressionists were breaking down the formal barriers imposed by academic painting and wrote about such issues as light and color, etc. (C) is incorrect. The abstract expressionists wrote serious philosophical statements about the transcendence and holiness of paintings. (E) is incorrect because the pop artists, especially Warhol, did use absurdity in their statements, but drew their imagery from American popular culture.

127. **(E)** In the eighteenth century Japanese woodblock print pictured in the example, the artist used the folds of the garment and its bold design to create an animated surface pattern of diagonal lines and shapes. These diagonals, far from minimizing the motion of the dancer, emphasize his athletic leaps and turns, although they give no specific information about the story behind his dance. Further, the drapery folds do not cling to the dancer's body and define the three-dimensional forms of his anatomy, as

they would in a Western tradition, but, rather, obscure his body almost completely, reassert the picture surface, and deny any sense of actual, three-dimensional space.

128. **(C)** This term, meaning "Seize the Day," became popular after the film *Dead Poet's Society*. A number of older poems have this sense of making the most of one's time before it is too late. (A) Epiphany is a James Joyce term for a sudden enlightenment; (B) euphemism is a grandiose term for a simple idea; (D) euphony means sounds pleasant to the ear; and (E) cacaphony is an unpleasant sound.

129. **(E)** Working your way through this test you will have come across this word; now is the opportunity to work with definitions. (A) refers to recording, (B) to repetition, (C) to symbolism, and (D) to the theme of the poem.

130. **(A)** is the correct answer. (B) refers to a play's plot and (C) to the auditor-players relationship. While most tragic heroes suffer from (D) self-delusion, tragic flaw is a better choice. (E) pragmatism is not logically related.

131. **(A)** is the correct answer. (B) *Macbeth* focuses on a married couple who aid each other in murder (C) *Hamlet* on a couple whose marriage is plagued by problems such as secrets, disgruntled children, and murder. (D) *The Wild Duck* shares with *Hamlet* the device of a troubled marriage plagued by secrets that at least one disgruntled member of the family is determined to uncover. All of these are easily eliminated. However, it is less easy to eliminate *Antony and Cleopatra* since the lovers also die, differing only in the order of their death. One way of resolving this dilemma is to look again at the question stem where "star-crossed lovers" is emphasized. The phrase comes from *Romeo and Juliet*.

132. **(A)** The Plan of St. Gall was originally intended as an "ideal" monastic plan; it was designed to contain all buildings and facilities necessary to a monastic community. It was drafted in the Carolingian period (in about 800 C.E.), but was never built. The Ottonian period (B) succeeded the Carolingian (c. 00-1050 C.E.) and is of a later date than the Plan of St. Gall. The plan indicates that it is not a layout for (C) an Islamic mosque, for the church (a place of Christian worship) dominates the center of the complex. While various domestic quarters are indicated on the plan, they are quite simple, not at all similar to sumptuous (D) Byzantine palace

complexes. The presence of a church and domestic quarters, with no indication off any military facilities, indicate that this plan is not one for an Anglo-Saxon fortress (E).

133. **(A)** Plato's forms, unlike Aristotle's, are separate and "otherworldly." This difference was the principal metaphysical split between Plato and his pupil, Aristotle. Aristotle, not Plato, held that forms are immanent in things. Hence, (B) is incorrect. Both Plato and Aristotle agreed that forms or universals are (C) immaterial, (D) eternal, and (E) changeless. So these features do not differentiate Plato's view from Aristotle's.

134. **(B)** Pitch is related to size. The smaller the instrument, the higher the pitch range; consequently, the larger the instrument the lower the pitch range. Also, when tuning, a musician would push the tuning slide in, making the string smaller in order to raise the pitch, or pull the tuning slide out to lower the pitch. Choice (B) is correct. The shape of an instrument will affect the timbre and tone color; choice (A) is incorrect. The quantity does not directly affect pitch; choice (C) is incorrect. Volume may cause a change in pitch if the musician neglects to adjust it while playing; choice (D) is incorrect. Choice (E) is incorrect because pitch can be adjusted by lengthening or shortening the size of an instrument.

135. **(B)** Allegro directs a musician to play fast. Choice (B) is correct. A musician would play slowly if the word largo were provided; choice (A) is incorrect. Moderately would indicate tempo, or a dynamic such as mezzo forte, moderately loud; choice (C) is incorrect. Very fast would be related to vivace; choice (D) is incorrect. To play detached would be an articulation of stacatto; choice (E) is incorrect.

136. **(A)** Artists and musicians would express their feeling in their work. As a result they were called expressionists; choice (A) is correct. Impressionists used words or tone colors to portray events or scenes; choice (B) is incorrect. The classical musicians believed in form and style; choice (C) is incorrect. The baroque style was of the late sixteenth to eighteenth centuries and dealt with vocal church music and the use of melody; choice (D) is incorrect. Renaissance explored the techniques of imitative polyphony; choice (E) is incorrect.

137. **(E)** Dreiser's famous work fits well into the pattern of American Naturalism in it stark depiction of human suffering and moral decline. Set in Chicago and New York at the beginning of the century, the novel traces

the decline of the erstwhile salesman Hurstwood and his ill treatment of Carrie over many years. Eliot's work (D) is a poem of the modern age, though it also explores moral decline. Emile Zola (C) was a French author. Melville's famous work (B) explores the controlling nature of passion and obsession, and Twain's work (A), while naturalistic, is more entertaining and uplifting than Dreiser's work.

138. **(C)** H.L. Mencken was a distinguished Baltimore-based journalist who commented on American language and manners throughout his career, but particularly in his massive work "The American Language" first published in 1923. Each of the possibilities here are names which use the British/Southern America two initials in place of first names, but lang (B) is a Country Western singer; (D) is a famous American poet; (E) is a contemporary science fiction writer; and (A) is the famous American expatriate poet.

139. **(D)** One of Dickens' most memorable characters is Miss Havisham, who, decades after having been jilted at the altar, remains in her wedding dress, living mostly in a room with the original, now very moldy, wedding cake, warning anyone who will listen (especially her ward Estella) of the evils of men. (A) cannot be a possibility, because *Great Expectations* takes place in England. (B) is more likely to fit Eliot's *Silas Marner*. Salinger's Holden Caulfield writes *Catcher in the Rye* from a sanitarium (C), and (E) is a reference to the modern novel *The Thornbirds,* by McCullough.

140. **(A)** The line continues... "Bird thou never wert," and is taken from Shelley's "To a Skylark," one of the greatest of Romantic poems in which the bird is meant to symbolize the overvaulting potential of the human spirit. Coleridge (B), Blake (C), and Wordsworth (E) are also considered Romantics, but did not pen the famous line. Grey's "Elegy," a truly majestic poem, somewhat predates those offered here.

141. **(D)** Tennyson's most quoted work begins with these lines which continue with "And may there be no moaning of the bar/ When I put out to sea." The poem, about the poet facing death, is both brave in its sentiment (he hopes to see the "Pilot face to face") and rich in its imagery. Joyce's "Ulysses" (C) is not a poem. Though choices (A), (B), and (E) are poems, they do not begin with these lines.

142. **(C)** Marcel Duchamp coined the term in 1914. (A) is incorrect; Andy Warhol, the pop artist, did not coin this term. He was not even born when the term was first used. (B) is incorrect, Jackson Pollock, the abstract expressionist, did not coin this term. (D) is incorrect because the term can be traced back to Marcel Duchamp. (E) is incorrect because (C), Marcel Duchamp, did coin the term.

143. **(A)** A readymade, as defined by Marcel Duchamp, must be an object existing outside of the context of art which is transformed into a work of art simply by being chosen by an artist to be seen as such. (B) is incorrect because a readymade must be an object that was already finished and out in the world before any intervention by the artist. (C) is incorrect. Even if such a "painting" exists it still would not qualify as a readymade. (D) is incorrect because only (A) defines a readymade and (B) does not. (E) is incorrect because both (B) and (C) do not define readymade, only (A) does.

144. **(D)** Abstract expressionism was the first movement started in America to become internationally influential. The New York School of painters who started this movement includes, among others, Robert Motherwell, Jackson Pollock, and Mark Rothko. (A) is incorrect. Color-field painting grew out of abstract expressionism but the gesture was removed and the focus was on non-representational fields of pure color. (B) is incorrect. While minimalism was also an American movement, it did not become one until the 1960s-early 1970s. (C) is incorrect because although pop art was also an American movement, it did not gain coherence and critical support until the 1960s. (E) is incorrect. While the Hudson River School was an American movement as well, it was a late nineteenth century movement of landscape painters.

145. **(D)** Pop art is a reaction to the "purity" of abstract expressionism. The pop artists wanted to reflect contemporary American culture by using recognizable mass-media images as their subject matter. (A) is incorrect, Abstract expressionism was a movement of the 1950s. (B) is incorrect, Minimalism was a late 1960s–early 1970s movement. (C) is incorrect. While some feminist art was being made in the 1960s, it was a fringe movement, not a dominant, popular one. (E) is incorrect. Environmental art was a movement happening concurrently with minimalism during the late 1960s-early 1970s.

146. **(B)** Minimalism is believed by some to be the final phase of modernism because the image has been reduced down to its simplest, purest,

most elemental form – there is nowhere else to go from here. This can also be seen as inevitable because styles of art had been getting more and more abstract ever since impressionism and this seemed to be the final phase, total and utter abstraction, no image at all except the actual, physical body of the piece. (A) is incorrect, abstract expressionism was a movement of the 1950s. (C) is incorrect. Though feminist art continued and gained momentum through the 1970s, it was not dominant. (D) is incorrect; pop art was a movement of the 1960s. (E) is incorrect. Though environmental art was produced concurrently with minimalism, it was neither as popular nor as influential.

147. **(E)** Perhaps the simplest of forms, the simile gives a description of one thing in terms of another, introduced with the word "like" for a phrase or "as if" for a clause. Assonance (A) refers to the repetition of vowel sounds, as in "he may see the free bee." Caesura (B) means a clear break in a line. Abstract language (C) refers to language that gives no concrete image, but conveys a mood or idea. Irony (D) indicates a humorous contrast.

148. **(D)** Here you are asked to go with a deeper meaning than the surface or literal – what is the poet evoking (drawing out) with this image? (A), (B), and (E) are still working with the surface meaning; blood rarely conjures romance (C) but it does evoke violence. (D) gives the figurative meaning.

149. **(C)** The poet suggests it is not too late for the woman to go back and change her mind: the gate has not irrevocably closed behind her. (A), (B), (D), and (E) all indicate a meaning that would be conveyed by a closed gate. Reading this half of the poem carefully shows the idea that life involves choices, and how blindly we sometimes make those choices.

150. **(B)** Sword tips immediately evoke strife and battle; silver might have suggested angelic warfare (C), but black suggests hardship and violence. Death (A) is not indicated, and nothing specific points to (D) or (E).

CHAPTER 3

COLLEGE

MATHEMATICS

PRACTICE
TEST 1

CLEP COLLEGE MATHEMATICS
Test 1

(Answer sheets appear in the back of the book.)

Section 1

TIME: 45 Minutes
33 Questions

DIRECTIONS: Each of the questions below is followed by five suggested answers. Complete the question and select the answer that is best.

1. The solution set to the system $\begin{cases} 2x+3y=6 \\ y-2=\dfrac{-2x}{3} \end{cases}$ is

(A) $\{0, 2\}$.

(D) $\{8, 3\}$.

(B) $\{0, 0\}$.

(E) an infinite number of solutions.

(C) $\{\dfrac{1}{3}, 5\}$.

2. The number 120 is separated into two parts. The larger part exceeds three times the smaller by 12. The smaller part is

(A) 27.

(D) 39.

(B) 33.

(E) 29.

(C) 15.

3. For the following sequence of numbers, $\frac{1}{2}, \frac{1}{12}, \frac{1}{30}, \ldots$, the next number will be

(A) $\frac{1}{36}$.

(D) $\frac{1}{56}$.

(B) $\frac{1}{27}$.

(E) $\frac{1}{72}$.

(C) $\frac{1}{48}$.

4. Given the possibility of two events:

Event I: g is true

or

Event II: g and h are true

Which of the following always applies?

(A) g is true.

(D) g is true and h is false.

(B) g and h are true.

(E) h is false.

(C) h is true.

5. If a is an even integer and b is an odd integer, which of the following must be an even integer?

I. ab

II. $2(a + b)$

III. $\dfrac{ab - 2}{2}$

(A) I only

(D) II and III only

(B) II only

(E) I, II, and III

(C) I and II only

6. What is the solution set of the equation

$$\cos 2x + 3\sin^2 x - 6\sin x + 4 = 0?$$

(A) $\left\{2n\pi + \dfrac{\pi}{2}\right\}$ $n = 0, 1, 2, \ldots$

(B) $\{2n\pi\}$ $n = 0, 1, 2, 3, \ldots$

(C) $\{2(n-1)\pi\}$ $n = 0, 1, 2, 3, \ldots$

(D) $\{\ \}$

(E) $\left\{2n\pi + \dfrac{\pi}{2}\right\}$ $n = 0, 1, 2, 3, \ldots$

7. If $G = \{(4, 7), (8, 3), (x, 6), (10, y), (12, 15)\}$ is a function, then which of the following values can the pair (x, y) not take on?

(A) $\{9, 3\}$ (D) $\{5, 14\}$

(B) $\{2, 7\}$ (E) $\{8, 5\}$

(C) $\{2, 4\}$

8. If A is the set of odd integers, B is the set of multiples of 5, and C is the set of counting numbers, which of the following contains -7?

(A) $A \cap B$ (D) $B \cap C$

(B) $A \cup B$ (E) $A \cap C$

(C) A

9. In the system

$$ax + by = 20$$
$$bx + ay = 16$$

the solution is $x = 2$ and $y = 1$. What are the coefficients a and b?

(A) $a = 2$ (D) $a = 7$

     $b = 1$ $b = 14$

(B) $a = 8$ (E) $a = 9$

     $b = 7$ $b = 4$

(C) $a = 8$

     $b = 4$

10. In how many different ways can the letters *a, b, c,* and *d* be arranged, if they are selected three at a time?

(A) 8   (D) 4

(B) 12   (E) 48

(C) 24

11. Two statements, *p* and *q*, are defined as follows: $p : a + b < c + d$

$q : a < c, b < d$. Which of the following is true?

(A) *p* implies *q*.   (D) *q* is the contrapositive of *p*.

(B) *p* and *q* imply each other.   (E) Neither *q* nor *p* implies the other.

(C) *q* implies *p*.

12. The sum of the digits of a two-digit number is 9. The number is equal to 9 times the units digit. Find the number.

(A) 36   (D) 54

(B) 45   (E) 72

(C) 63

13. The first three terms of a progression are 3, 6, 12, …. What is the value of the tenth term?

(A) 1,200   (D) 1,536

(B) 2,468   (E) 3,272

(C) 188

14. What is the solution set of $|3x - 9| < 5$?

(A) $\dfrac{4}{3} < x < \dfrac{8}{3}$ (D) $\dfrac{4}{3} < x < \dfrac{13}{3}$

(B) $-\dfrac{4}{3} < x < \dfrac{7}{3}$ (E) $\dfrac{4}{3} < x < \dfrac{14}{3}$

(C) $-\dfrac{4}{3} < x < \dfrac{8}{3}$

15. "*p* or *q*" is logically equivalent to which of the following?

    (A) *p* is true.

    (B) *q* is true.

    (C) Both *p* and *q* are true.

    (D) Either *p* or *q* is true, but not both.

    (E) Either *p* or *q* is true, or both.

16. If $A \subset C$ and $B \subset C$, which of the following statements is true?

    (A) The set $A \cup C$ is also a subset of C.

    (B) The complement of A is also a subset of C.

    (C) The complement of B is also a subset of C.

    (D) The union of $\overline{A}$ and $\overline{B}$ contains C.

    (E) C is the universal set.

17. Find the solution set of the following equation:

    $$|3x - 2| = 7$$

    (A) $\left\{-\dfrac{5}{3}\right\}$ (D) $\left\{-\dfrac{7}{3}, 3\right\}$

    (B) $\left\{-\dfrac{5}{3}, -\dfrac{7}{3}\right\}$ (E) $\left\{3, -\dfrac{5}{3}\right\}$

    (C) $\{3\}$

18. Find the solution set of the following pair of equations

    $$\begin{cases} 3x + 4y = -6 \\ 5x + 6y = -8 \end{cases}$$

    (A) $\{(1, 2)\}$ (D) $\{(2, -3)\}$

    (B) $\{(1, 3)\}$ (E) $\{(3, -3)\}$

    (C) $\{(2, 3)\}$

19. Find the solution set of the inequality $2x + 5 > 11$.

    (A) $x < 6$ (D) $x < -3$

    (B) $x > 3$ (E) $x > 6$

    (C) $x = 3$

20. The sum of four consecutive even integers is 68. What is the value of the smallest one?

    (A) 12   (D) 18

    (B) 14   (E) None of the above

    (C) 7

21. If $x^2 - 3x - 4 < 0$, then the solution set is

    (A) $-4 < x < 1$.   (D) $-1 < x < 0$.

    (B) $-4 < x < -3$.   (E) $-1 < x < 4$.

    (C) $-3 < x < 0$.

22. Which of the following inequalities has a solution set on the real axis?

    (A) $x^2 < -1$ (D) $x^2 < -4$

    (B) $x^2 + 2x + 2 > 0$ (E) None of the above

    (C) $-3x^2 + x - 1 > 0$

23. The coordinates of the point of intersection of the lines having equations $3x + 2y = 5$ and $x - 4y = 1$ are

    (A) $\left(-\dfrac{11}{7}, \dfrac{-1}{7}\right)$.   (D) $\left(\dfrac{11}{7}, \dfrac{2}{7}\right)$.

    (B) $\left(-\dfrac{11}{7}, \dfrac{-2}{7}\right)$.   (E) $\left(\dfrac{11}{7}, \dfrac{16}{7}\right)$.

    (C) $\left(\dfrac{11}{7}, \dfrac{1}{7}\right)$.

24. The following instructions are executed by a computer:

    1. LET SUM = 0

    2. LET N = 1

    3. If N < = 5 GO TO INSTRUCTION 4 OTHERWISE GO TO INSTRUCTION 7

    4. LET SUM = SUM + N

    5. LET N = N + 1

    6. GO TO INSTRUCTION 3

    7. WRITE THE FINAL VALUE OF SUM

    What is the final value of SUM?

    (A) 5   (D) 21

    (B) 10   (E) 25

    (C) 15

25. If x is an odd integer and y is even, then which of the following must be an even integer?

    I. $2x + 3y$

    II. xy

    III. $x + y - 1$

    (A) I only   (D) II and III only

    (B) II only   (E) I, II, and III

    (C) I and II only

26. How many integers are in the solution set of $|\, 3x - 7 \,| < 2$?

    (A) None   (D) Three

    (B) One   (E) Six

    (C) Two

27. In how many ways can we arrange four letters (*a*, *b*, *c*, and *d*) in different orders?

    (A) 4

    (B) 8

    (C) 16

    (D) 24

    (E) 48

28. What is the biggest positive integer *k* for which $7 - k$ and $18 - k$ will be non-zero and have opposite signs?

    (A) 8

    (B) 0

    (C) 7

    (D) 17

    (E) 18

29. If the sum of three consecutive odd numbers is 51, then the first odd number of the sequence is

    (A) 11.

    (B) 13.

    (C) 15.

    (D) 17.

    (E) 19.

30. If $f(x) = 2x + 4$ and $g(x) = x^2 - 2$, then $(f \circ g)(x)$, where $(f \circ g)(x)$ is a composition of functions, is

    (A) $2x^2 - 8$.

    (B) $2x^2 + 8$.

    (C) $2x^2$.

    (D) $2x^3 + 4x^2 - 4x - 8$.

    (E) $4x^2 + 16x + 14$.

31. Consider the function $f(x) = x^3 + 3x - k$. If $f(2) = 10$, then $k =$

    (A) 4

    (B) –4

    (C) 0

    (D) 18

    (E) 14

32. If the functions f and g are defined by $f(x, y) = x^2 + 2y^2 - y$ and $g(h) = h + 7$, what is $f(3, g(-2))$?

(A) 24

(D) 64

(B) 54

(E) 19

(C) 59

33. Given the function $f(x) = x^2 - 2x + 7$, for what values of a does $f(a) = f(-a)$?

(A) {all positive integers}

(D) {1, 2, 3}

(B) {the empty set}

(E) {0}

(C) {3}

QUESTION 34 refers to the following graph:

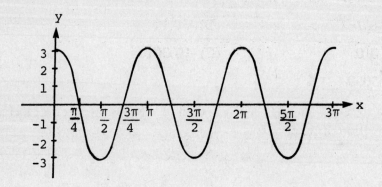

34. The graph represents the function

(A) $2 \sin 3x$.

(D) $2 \cos 3x$.

(B) $3 \sin 2x$.

(E) $\cos 2x$.

(C) $3 \cos 2x$.

35. If $f(x) = \{(2, 5), (6, 9), (11, 2), (x, 4)\}$ is a function, then x may not have which of the following values?

    (A) 7

    (B) 3

    (C) 9

    (D) 2

    (E) 4

36. Let n be an integer greater than or equal to 1. Which of the following is greater than 1?

    (A) $-(n)^3$

    (B) $(n)^{-\frac{1}{3}}$

    (C) $-(-n)^3$

    (D) $-(n + 1)^3$

    (E) $-(n + 1)^5$

37. Given $\log_{10} 2 = 0.3010$, find $\log_{10} 32$.

    (A) 0.6020

    (B) 3.010

    (C) 1.5050

    (D) 30.10

    (E) 0.03010

38. Express $\log_b 2 + \log_b \beta + \frac{1}{2}\log_b \gamma - \frac{1}{2}\log_b \omega$ as a single logarithm.

    (A) $\frac{1}{2}\log_b\left(2\beta\frac{\gamma}{\omega}\right)$

    (B) $2\log_b(2\beta\omega\gamma)$

    (C) $\log_b\left(2\beta\sqrt{\frac{\gamma}{\omega}}\right)$

    (D) $\frac{1}{2}\log_b\left(\beta\frac{\omega^2}{\gamma^2}\right)$

    (E) $2\log_b\left(\beta\sqrt{\frac{\omega}{\gamma}}\right)$

39. What is the value of $(0.0081)^{-\frac{3}{4}}$?

(A) $\dfrac{81}{27}$

(D) $\dfrac{8.10 \times 10^{-2}}{4}$

(B) $\dfrac{1,000}{27}$

(E) $\dfrac{8.10 \times 10^{-2}}{0.27}$

(C) $\dfrac{27}{81}$

40. The mathematical value of 0! is

(A) 0.

(D) e.

(B) indeterminate.

(E) $\dfrac{e}{\pi}$.

(C) 1.

41. If f is defined by $f(x) = \dfrac{5x - 8}{2}$ for each real number x, find the solution set for $f(x) > 2x$.

(A) $\{x \mid x > 6\}$

(D) $\{x \mid 6 < x < 8\}$

(B) $\{x \mid x > 8\}$

(E) None of the above

(C) $\{x \mid x < 8\}$

42. Find the range, R, of the function $f(x) = \dfrac{x}{|x|}$. The domain, D, consists of the set of non-zero real numbers.

(A) $R = \{1, 0\}$

(D) All positive integers

(B) $R = \{-1, 1\}$

(E) All non-zero real numbers

(C) $(1, -1, 0)$

43. Let $f : R \to R$ and $g : R \to R$ be two functions given by $f(x) = 2x + 5$ and $g(x) = 4x^2$, respectively, for all x in R, where R is the set of real numbers. Find expressions for the composition $(f \circ g)(x)$.

(A) $8x^3 + 20x^2$

(D) $8x^3 + 5$

(B) $4(2x + 5)^2$

(E) None of the above

(C) $8x^2 + 5$

44. Consider the function $P(x) = \sqrt{1-x^2}$ shown below and indicate which graph represents $P^{-1}\{-1 \le x \le 0\}$.

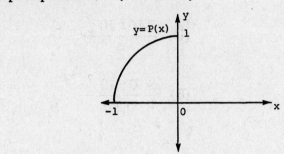

(A)

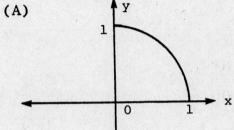

(B)

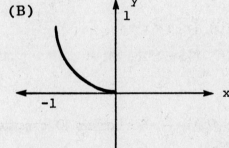

(C)

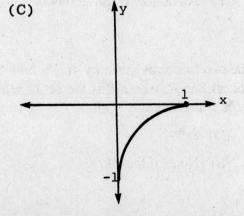

(D)

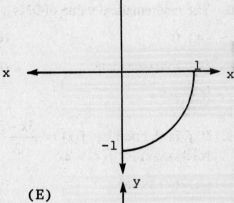

(E)

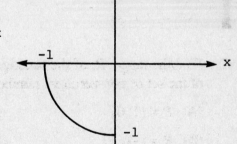

45. A single fair die is tossed. Find the probability of obtaining either a 3 or a 5.

(A) $\dfrac{1}{3}$ (D) $\dfrac{2}{5}$

(B) $\dfrac{2}{3}$ (E) $\dfrac{1}{6}$

(C) $\dfrac{1}{36}$

Section 2

TIME: 45 Minutes
33 Questions

DIRECTIONS: Each of the questions below is followed by five suggested answers. Complete the question and select the answer that is best.

46. Ten white balls and 19 red balls are in a box. If a man draws a ball from the box at random, what are the odds in favor of him drawing a red ball?

(A) 10 : 29

(B) 19 : 29

(C) 19 : 10

(D) $\dfrac{10}{19} : \dfrac{19}{29}$

(E) $\dfrac{19}{10} : \dfrac{29}{19}$

47. There are six knights of the round table. Given that Sir Lancelot must sit in a specific chair and that Sir Gawain must be directly on either side of him, in how many ways may the knights be seated?

(A) 24

(B) 120

(C) 48

(D) 25

(E) 720

48. What is the value of b in the relation $\log_b \dfrac{1}{25} = -2$?

(A) 2

(B) $\pm\sqrt{2}$

(C) 2^{25}

(D) 25^2

(E) ± 5

49. Solve for x: $\log(40x - 1) - \log(x - 1) = 3$.

(A) $\dfrac{333}{320}$

(D) $\dfrac{1,001}{960}$

(B) $\dfrac{333}{960}$

(E) Cannot be determined.

(C) 999

50. Given $\log_{10}33! = 37$, $\log_{10}37! = 43$, and $\log_{10}51! = 66$, evaluate N if $N = \dfrac{33!\,37!}{51!}$.

(A) 10^{14}

(D) $33 + 37 - 51$

(B) e^{14}

(E) Indeterminate

(C) e^{-14}

51. For $x \geq 0$, what is the minimum value of $(3i)^2 - (5 - x)$?

(A) -28

(D) $-\infty$

(B) $3i$

(E) -14

(C) 0

52. Let $[x]$ be the largest integer less than or equal to x. Determine $[2.1] + [-0.9] + [1.9]$.

(A) 0

(D) 3

(B) 1

(E) 4

(C) 2

53. After the following instructions are executed, what number is printed?

Step 1: Let $x = 1$.

Step 2: Let $A = x + 2$.

Step 3: Increase x by 2.

Step 4: If A is a prime number, then go back to Step 2.

Step 5: Print the value of x.

(A) 4   (D) 9

(B) 5   (E) 11

(C) 7

54. If the functions f and g are defined for all x by $f(x) = 2x^2 - 3x + 2$ and $g(x) = 2$, then $g(f(1)) =$

(A) 0.   (D) 3.

(B) 1.   (E) 4.

(C) 2.

55. The graph of the function, given in polar coordinates, $r(\theta) = c$, where c is a constant, is a

(A) circle.   (D) straight line.

(B) ellipse.   (E) None of the above.

(C) spiral.

56. If the functions f, g, and h are defined by $f(x) = x^3$, $g(x) = x - 2$, and $h(x) = \dfrac{x}{2}$, then $f(g(h(8))) =$

(A) 0.   (D) 27.

(B) 4.   (E) 62.

(C) 8.

57. If $f(x) = x^3$ and $g(x) = x^2 + 1$, which of the following are odd functions?

   I. $f(x) \bullet g(x)$

   II. $f(g(x))$

   III. $2g(f(x)) - 1$

(A) I only   (D) I and III only

(B) II only   (E) II and III only

(C) III only

58. If two fair dice are thrown, what is the probability that the sum of the number of dots on the top faces will be 7?

(A) $\dfrac{1}{2}$

(D) $\dfrac{1}{12}$

(B) $\dfrac{1}{6}$

(E) $\dfrac{1}{16}$

(C) $\dfrac{1}{9}$

59. Four officers must be chosen from a high school committee of eight freshmen and five sophomores, with exactly two officers to be chosen from each class. In how many ways can these officers be chosen?

(A) 1,600

(D) 980

(B) 1,120

(E) 1,260

(C) 1,680

60. A fair coin is tossed five times. What is the probability of two heads occurring?

(A) $\dfrac{1}{16}$

(D) $\dfrac{1}{4}$

(B) $\dfrac{5}{16}$

(E) $\dfrac{5}{8}$

(C) $\dfrac{5}{32}$

61. A table tennis tournament is to be round–robin; that is, each player plays one match against every other player. The winner of the tournament is determined by the best scores in the matches. How many matches will be played if five people enter the tournament?

(A) 10

(D) 105

(B) 15

(E) 120

(C) 20

62. If $f(x, y) = \dfrac{\log x}{\log y}$, then $f(4, 2)$ equals

   (A) 0.

   (B) $\dfrac{1}{2}$.

   (C) 1.

   (D) 2.

   (E) log 2.

63. $\log 3\left(\dfrac{1}{81}\right) =$

   (A) -4

   (B) $\dfrac{1}{4}$

   (C) 4

   (D) $-\dfrac{1}{4}$

   (E) 3

64. $\log(a^2 - b^2) =$

   (A) $\log a^2 - \log b^2$

   (B) $\log \dfrac{a^2}{b^2}$

   (C) $\log \dfrac{a+b}{a-b}$

   (D) $2 \cdot \log a - 2 \cdot \log b$

   (E) $\log(a + b) + \log(a - b)$

65. If $\log_8 3 = x\log_2 3$, then x equals

   (A) 4.

   (B) $\log_4 3$.

   (C) 3.

   (D) $\log_8 9$.

   (E) $\dfrac{1}{3}$.

66. If $b^2 - 4c = 0$, where b and c are real numbers, then the roots of the equation $x^2 + bx + c = 0$ are

(A) real and equal.

(D) complex and unequal.

(B) real and unequal.

(E) No solution.

(C) complex and equal.

67. Let $f(x) = x^2 - x - 6$. Where does the graph of the function cross the x-axis?

(A) $\{(0, -6)\}$

(D) $\{(3, 0), (-2, 0)\}$

(B) $\{(0, -3), (0, 2)\}$

(E) Does not cross the x-axis

(C) $\{(-3, 0), (2, 0)\}$

68. If the functions f, g, and h are defined by $f(x) = x^2$, $g(x) = \sin x$, and $h(x) = \dfrac{x}{2}$, then $f(g(h(\pi))) =$

(A) 0.

(D) $\dfrac{1}{4}$.

(B) 1.

(E) $\dfrac{\sqrt{2}}{2}$.

(C) $\dfrac{1}{2}$.

69. Find the minimum value of the function $f(x) = (x - 1)^2 + 3$.

(A) 0

(D) 3

(B) 1

(E) -2

(C) 2

70. Which of the following relations has an inverse which is not a function?

I. $y = \sqrt{x}$

II. $|y| = x$

III. $y = \sin x$

(A) I only   (D) I and II only

(B) II only   (E) I and III only

(C) III only

71. Which of the following are odd functions?

    I. $f(x) = 2x + 1$

    II. $g(x) = \tan x$

    III. $h(x) = x^3 + x^2$

(A) I only   (D) I, II, and III

(B) II only   (E) None of these

(C) I and II only

72. In a school of 300 students, 260 students take physics and 185 students take calculus. How many students take both physics and calculus if we know that any of the students at least takes one of the courses?

(A) 125   (D) 145

(B) 130   (E) 150

(C) 135

73. A bag contains six white balls, three red balls, and one blue ball. If one ball is drawn from the bag, what is the probability it will be white?

(A) 0.1   (D) 0.6

(B) 0.3   (E) $0.6\overline{6}$

(C) $0.3\overline{3}$

74. One card is drawn from a standard deck of cards. What is the probability of an ace being drawn?

    (A) $\dfrac{1}{10}$

    (D) $\dfrac{4}{13}$

    (B) $\dfrac{12}{13}$

    (E) $\dfrac{1}{52}$

    (C) $\dfrac{1}{13}$

75. A telephone number consists of seven digits. How many different telephone numbers exist if each digit appears only one time in the number?

    (A) 7!

    (D) 7^7

    (B) 10^7

    (E) $\dfrac{10!}{3!}$

    (C) 70

76. $\log_3\left(\dfrac{1}{27}\right) =$

    (A) –3

    (D) 3

    (B) $-\dfrac{1}{3}$

    (E) 9

    (C) $\dfrac{1}{3}$

77. Find all values of x for which $x^{\log_{10} x} = 100x$.

    (A) $\left\{1, \dfrac{1}{10}\right\}$

    (B) $\left\{\dfrac{1}{10}, 10\right\}$

(C) {100, 1,000}

(E) $\left\{\dfrac{1}{10}, 100\right\}$

(D) {10, 100}

78. Simplify the expression $\dfrac{4! + 3!}{5!}$.

(A) $\dfrac{3}{10}$

(D) $\dfrac{3}{20}$

(B) $\dfrac{1}{5}$

(E) $\dfrac{12}{5}$

(C) $\dfrac{1}{4}$

79. When a certain integer is divided by 6, the remainder is 2. What is the remainder when this integer is divided by 3?

(A) 0

(D) 3

(B) 1

(E) 4

(C) 2

80. If $x - 2$ is a factor of $x^3 - 7x^2 + kx - 12$, then k is

(A) 32.

(D) –32.

(B) 16.

(E) –16.

(C) 2.

81. How many four-digit numbers are there such that the first digit is odd, the second is even, and there is no repetition of digits?

(A) 1,200

(D) 1,400

(B) 1,625

(E) 1,600

(C) 200

82. Find the intersection of the parabola $y = 2x^2$ and its inverse.

(A) $(0, 0)$

(B) $(0, 0), \left(-\dfrac{1}{2}, \dfrac{1}{2}\right), \left(-\dfrac{1}{2}, -\dfrac{1}{2}\right)$

(C) $(0, 0), \left(\dfrac{1}{2}, \dfrac{1}{2}\right), \left(-\dfrac{1}{2}, \dfrac{1}{2}\right)$

(D) $(0, 0), \left(-\dfrac{1}{2}, \dfrac{1}{2}\right)$

(E) $(0, 0), \left(\dfrac{1}{2}, \dfrac{1}{2}\right)$

83. Which of the graphs below represents the function $y = 2 + \sin(x - \pi)$?

(A)

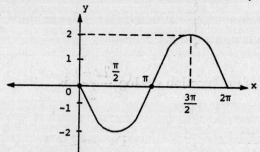

(B)

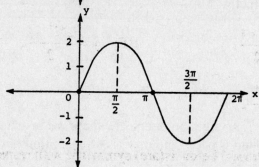

(C)

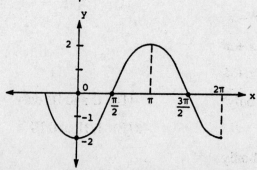

(D)

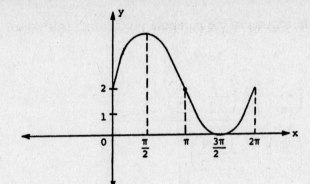

(E)

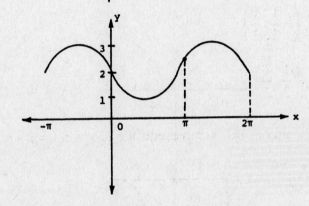

84. The inverse of the function $y = \log_2 \dfrac{2x-1}{2}$ is

(A) $y = \dfrac{4^x + 1}{2}.$

(D) $y = 2^x.$

(B) $y = \dfrac{2^x + 1}{2}.$

(E) $y = \dfrac{2^{x+1} + 1}{2}.$

(C) $y = \dfrac{2^{x+1}}{2}.$

85. Which function(s) below is(are) symmetric with respect to the origin?

I. $f(x) = x^3 - x$

II. $f(x) = 2x + x^5$

III. $f(x) = 2x + 4$

(A) I and II only

(D) II and III only

(B) I only

(E) I, II, and III

(C) I and III only

86. Which graph does not represent a function ($y = f(x)$)?

(A)

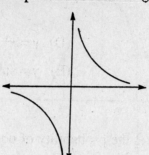

(B)

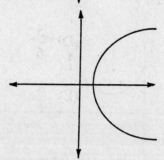

(C)

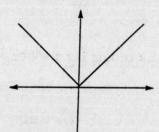

(D)

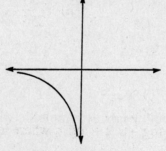

(E)

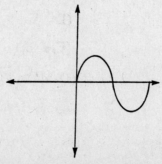

87. Which of the graphs of the functions below has symmetry with respect to the y-axis?

   (A) $y = x + 2$ (D) $y = x^2$

   (B) $y = 2^x$ (E) $y = \sin x$

   (C) $y = x^2 + x$

88. If a die is fair, what is the probability of obtaining an even number or a number greater than 3?

   (A) $\dfrac{2}{3}$ (D) $\dfrac{5}{6}$

   (B) 1 (E) $\dfrac{1}{6}$

   (C) $\dfrac{1}{3}$

89. If the probability of a certain team winning is $\dfrac{3}{4}$, what is the probability that this team will win its first three games and lose the fourth?

   (A) $\dfrac{3}{256}$ (D) $\dfrac{81}{256}$

   (B) $\dfrac{9}{256}$ (E) $\dfrac{27}{256}$

   (C) $\dfrac{1}{256}$

90. Find x if $\log 100 - \log \dfrac{1}{5} = 2 + \log x$, where $\log x$ means $\log_{10} x$.

   (A) 3   (D) 6

   (B) -1 (E) -3

   (C) 5

CLEP COLLEGE MATHEMATICS
TEST 1

ANSWER KEY

Section 1

1. (E)	10. (C)	19. (B)	28. (D)	37. (C)
2. (A)	11. (C)	20. (B)	29. (C)	38. (C)
3. (D)	12. (B)	21. (E)	30. (C)	39. (B)
4. (A)	13. (D)	22. (E)	31. (A)	40. (C)
5. (C)	14. (E)	23. (C)	32. (B)	41. (B)
6. (A)	15. (D)	24. (C)	33. (E)	42. (B)
7. (E)	16. (A)	25. (E)	34. (C)	43. (C)
8. (C)	17. (E)	26. (B)	35. (D)	44. (D)
9. (C)	18. (D)	27. (D)	36. (C)	45. (A)

Section 2

46. (C)	55. (A)	64. (E)	73. (D)	82. (E)
47. (C)	56. (C)	65. (E)	74. (C)	83. (E)
48. (E)	57. (A)	66. (A)	75. (E)	84. (E)
49. (A)	58. (B)	67. (D)	76. (A)	85. (A)
50. (A)	59. (B)	68. (B)	77. (E)	86. (B)
51. (E)	60. (B)	69. (D)	78. (C)	87. (D)
52. (C)	61. (A)	70. (C)	79. (C)	88. (A)
53. (D)	62. (D)	71. (B)	80. (B)	89. (E)
54. (C)	63. (A)	72. (D)	81. (D)	90. (C)

DETAILED EXPLANATIONS
OF ANSWERS

TEST 1

Section 1

1. **(E)** $2x + 3y = 6$

$$y - 2 = \frac{-2x}{3}$$

Multiplying the second equation by 3, we obtain:

$$3y - 6 = -2x.$$

Transposing, we obtain:

$$2x + 3y = 6.$$

Thus, both equations are equivalent and define one straight line. Since they intersect at every point, there are an infinite number of solutions.

2. **(A)** Let x = larger number

y = smaller number

$x + y = 120$

$x = 3y + 12$

This system is solved for y.

Substituting: $3y + 12 + y = 120$

$$4y = 108$$

Dividing by 4: $y = 27$.

3.   **(D)** To determine the next number, we look for a pattern among the previous terms. Only the denominators differ. We note by inspection that each denominator is equal to the product of two successive integers. For example

$$\text{the first term: } \frac{1}{2} = \frac{1}{1 \times 2}$$

$$\text{the second term: } \frac{1}{12} = \frac{1}{3 \times 4}$$

$$\text{the third term: } \frac{1}{30} = \frac{1}{5 \times 6}$$

Thus, the next term in the sequence can be expected to be

$$\frac{1}{7 \times 8} \text{ or } \frac{1}{56}.$$

4.   **(A)** The only condition that prevails in both events is the condition where g is true.

This can be proven by the logical theorem:

$$g + gh = g,$$

where addition is the logical "or" operation and multiplication represents the logical "and" operation.

5.   **(C)** When an even integer is multiplied by another integer, the result will be even, i.e., it will be divisible by 2.

Statement I satisfies this. (a is even.)

Statement II satisfies this. (The sum $a + b$ is multipled by 2, which is even.)

Statement III does not satisfy the criterion. (When we divide an even number by 2, the result can be either odd or even, e.g., $\frac{6}{2} = 3$.)

Thus, I and II is the answer.

6. **(A)** The equation given is

$$\cos 2x + 3\sin^2 x - 6\sin x + 4 = 0.$$

The identity for $\cos 2x$ is implemented:

$$\cos 2x = 1 - 2\sin^2 x. \qquad \text{Equation (1)}$$

Substituting in Equation (1) for $\cos 2x$:

$$1 - 2\sin^2 x + 3\sin^2 x - 6\sin x + 4 = 0.$$

Simplifying: $\sin^2 x - 6\sin x + 5 = 0.$

Factoring: $(\sin x - 5)(\sin x - 1) = 0.$

The two equations that are set up are:

$$\sin x - 5 = 0 \Rightarrow \sin x = 5. \qquad \text{Equation (2)}$$

$$\sin x - 1 = 0 \Rightarrow \sin x = 1. \qquad \text{Equation (3)}$$

Equation (2) has no solution because the function $\sin x$ takes on a maximum value of 1. That leaves Equation (3). Solving:

$$\sin x = 1$$

$$\sin^{-1}(\sin x) = \sin^{-1} 1$$

$$x = \sin^{-1} 1.$$

The angles which have sin 1 are

$$\frac{\pi}{2}, \frac{5\pi}{2}, \frac{9\pi}{2}, \dots$$

In other words, $2n\pi + \dfrac{\pi}{2}$ where $n = 0, 1, 2, 3....$ Thus, the solution set is

$$\left\{ x = 2n\pi + \frac{\pi}{2} \right\}.$$

7. **(E)** If G is to be a function, then no first component of its ordered pairs may have more than one second component. One second component can correspond to more than one first component. The pairs $(9, 3)$, $(2, 7)$, $(2, 4)$, and $(5, 14)$ are all valid because only one second component corresponds to each first. The pair $(8, 5)$ is not valid because the number 8 is a first component already paired with another number (3).

8. **(C)** To solve this problem we must know the meanings of the rules for the sets that have been stated.

The set of odd integers is:

$$\{ \ldots, -5, -3, -1, 1, 3, 5, \ldots \} = A.$$

The set of multiples of 5 is:

$$\{ \ldots, -10, -5, 0, 5, 10, \ldots \} = B.$$

The set of counting numbers is:

$$\{ 1, 2, 3, 4, 5, \ldots \} = C.$$

9. **(C)** Since the solutions of the system, x and y, are given, these values can be substituted into the two equations and the unknown coefficients are solved for.

Substituting $x = 2$ and $y = 1$:

$$2a + b = 20 \hspace{4cm} \text{Equation (1)}$$

$$2b + a = 16 \hspace{4cm} \text{Equation (2)}$$

We can solve for b by using Equation (1),

$$b = 20 - 2a.$$

Substituting this into Equation (2) yields:

$$2(20 - 2a) + a = 16.$$

Simplifying:

$$40 - 4a + a = 16$$

$$40 - 3a = 16$$

$$-3a = -4$$

$$3a = 24$$

$$a = 8$$

Substituting 8 for a in Equation (1) we obtain:

$$2(8) + b = 20$$

$$16 + b = 20$$

$$b = 4$$

10. **(C)** When we arrange a certain number of objects, taken a certain number of times, in every possible way, we are dealing with permutations. One permutation is an arrangement of r objects selected from n objects.

The applicable formula is:

$$P(n, r) = \frac{n!}{(n-r)!}$$

where $n!$ stands for n factorial and is defined as $n(n-1)(n-2) \times \ldots \times 1$. The letters $a, b, c,$ and d are four "objects." We are arranging them while taking them three at a time, e.g., $abc, cda,$ etc. Therefore, we solve

$$P(4, 3) = \frac{4!}{(4-3)!} = \frac{4!}{1!} = \frac{4 \times 3 \times 2 \times 1}{1} = 24 \text{ arrangements.}$$

11.   **(C)**   If $a < c$ and $b < d$, then $a + b$ must be less than $c + d$, thus q implies p. Note if we allow $a = 3$, $b = 2$, $c = 1$, and $d = 8$, then indeed $3 + 2 < 1 + 8$ or $5 < 9$ but 3 is not less than 1.

12.   **(B)**   The problem may best be solved by setting up a system of simultaneous equations. Since there are two unknowns, namely the units digit and the tens digit, two equations are needed to solve for these variables, u and t, respectively.

One equation can be obtained from the fact that the sum of the digits is 9. Thus,

$$t + u = 9.$$ Equation (1)

The other condition states that the number itself (which can be expressed as $10t + 1u$ since the number has t 10's and u units) is equal to 9 times the units digit. Therefore, we obtain:

$$10t + u = 9u.$$ Equation (2)

Solving Equation (1) for t, we have $t = 9 - u$. Now substituting this value of t into Equation (2), we obtain:

$$9u = 10(9 - u) + u.$$

Simplifying we obtain:

$$9u = 90 - 10u + u$$

$$9u = 90 - 9u$$

$$18u = 90$$

$$u = 90/18$$

$$u = 5$$

Substituting this value of u into Equation (1), we obtain 4 as the value of t; therefore, the required number is 45.

13.   **(D)** The progression given is a geometric progression. The expression for the nth term of a geometric progression is:

$$1_n = a_1 r^{n-1}$$

where a_1 is the first term and r is the common ratio between terms.

In the given sequence, the first term is 3. The common ratio is found to be $\dfrac{6}{3} = \dfrac{12}{6} = 2.$

Therefore, letting $n = 10$ (for the tenth term), we have:

$$1_{10} = 3(2)^{10-1} = 3(2)^9 .$$

Since $2^9 = 512$:

$$1_{10} = 3(512) = 1,536.$$

14.   **(E)** $|3x - 9| < 5$

$$-5 < (3x - 9) < 5$$

$$\frac{-5}{3} < x - 3 < \frac{5}{3}$$

$$\frac{4}{3} < x < \frac{14}{3}$$

15.   **(D)** All of the other choices do not logically come to the conclusion "p or q."

16.   **(A)** The set $A \cup B$ contains all elements which belong to either set A or set B. Since all elements, which belong to set A or set B, also belong to C, the set $A \cup B$ is a subset of C.

17.　**(E)**　$|3x-2|=7$

$$3x-2=7 \quad \text{or} \quad 3x-2=-7$$

$$3x=9 \qquad\qquad 3x=-5$$

$$x=3 \qquad\qquad x=-\frac{5}{3}$$

Therefore, the solution set is $\{\,3,-\dfrac{5}{3}\,\}$.

18.　**(D)**　$\begin{cases} 3x+4y=-6 \\ 5x+6y=-8 \end{cases}$　　　　Equation (1)
　　　　　　　　　　　　　　　Equation (2)

Multiply Equation (1) by 3 and Equation (2) by 2. Subtract Equation (2) from Equation (1):

$$9x+12y=-18$$

$$\underline{-(10x+12y=-16)}$$

$$-x=-2$$

$$x=2$$

Substitute $x=2$ into Equation (1):

$$3(2)+4y=-6$$

$$4y=-12$$

$$y=-3$$

Therefore, the solution set is $\{(2,-3)\}$.

19.　**(B)**　$2x+5>11$

$$2x>6$$

$$x>3$$

20.　**(B)**　Four consecutive integers can be represented by $2n$, $2n + 2$, $2n + 4$, and $2n + 6$.

$$(2n) + (2n + 2) + (2n + 4) + (2n + 6) = 68$$

$$8n + 12 = 68$$

$$8n = 56$$

$$2n = 14$$

Therefore, the value of the smallest one is 14.

21.　**(E)**　$x^2 - 3x - 4 < 0$

$$(x + 1)(x - 4) < 0$$

$$-1 < x < 4$$

22.　**(E)**　Since the square of a real number is non-negative, $x^2 < -1$ and $x^2 < -4$ do not have solution sets on the real axis.

Consider a quadratic inequality of the form $ax^2 + bx + c > 0$:

If the discriminant, $b^2 - 4ac$ is greater than or equal to zero, the inequality will have real roots; otherwise, the roots are complex.

Note　$2^2 - 4(1)(2) = -4$

and　$1^2 - 4(-3)(-1) = -11$.

Therefore, none of the choices are correct.

23.　**(C)**　$\begin{cases} 3x + 2y = 5 \\ x - 4y = 1 \end{cases}$　　　Equation (1)
　　　　　　　　　　　　　　　　　　　Equation (2)

Multiply Equation (1) by 2 and add to Equation (2):

$$6x + 4y = 10$$
$$\underline{+\ x - 4y =\ \ 1}$$
$$7x\qquad = 11$$

$$x = \frac{11}{7}$$

Substitute $x = \frac{11}{7}$ into (2):

$$\frac{11}{7} - 4y = 1$$

$$4y = \frac{4}{7}$$

$$y = \frac{1}{7}$$

Therefore, the solution set is $\left(\frac{11}{7}, \frac{1}{7} \right)$.

24. **(C)** This is a program which computes the summation of the first five integers starting from 1.

Therefore, SUM $= 1 + 2 + 3 + 4 + 5 = 15$.

25. **(E)** I. An odd integer times two will become an even integer. An even integer times any number will remain even. The sum of two even numbers is also an even number.

Therefore, $2x + 3y$ must be even.

II. An even integer times any number will remain even. Therefore, xy must be even.

III. The sum of an odd integer and an even integer is odd. An odd integer minus one will become even. Therefore, $x + y - 1$ must be even.

26. **(B)** $|3x - 7| < 2$

$$-2 < 3x - 7 < 2$$

$$5 < 3x < 9$$

$$\frac{5}{3} < x < 3$$

Therefore, the solution set is { 2 } and contains only one element.

27. **(D)** Choose a to be the first letter:

abcd, abdc, acbd, acdb, adbc, adcb.

Since each letter can be the first letter, there will be $4 \times 6 = 24$ different arrangements. $n!$ is the number of ways we can arrange n different objects.

$$n! = n(n-1)\,(n-2) \dots (1) \therefore 4! = 4\,(3)\,(2)\,(1) = 24$$

28. **(D)** $(7-k)\,(18-k) < 0$

$7 < k < 18$ (as both terms are non–zero and have opposite signs)

Therefore, the solution set is $\{8, 9, 10, 11, 12, 13, 14, 15, 16, 17\}$ and 17 is the biggest number from the solution set.

29. **(C)** Let x be the first odd number. Then,

$$x + (x+2) + (x+4) = 51$$

$$3x + 6 = 51$$

$$3x = 45$$

$$x = 15$$

30. **(C)** $(f \circ g)(x) = f(x) \circ g(x) = f(g(x))$.

This is the definition of the composition of functions. For the functions given in this problem we have

$$2(g(x)) + 4 = 2(x^2 - 2) + 4$$

$$= 2x^2 - 4 + 4 = 2x^2$$

31. **(A)** $f(x) = x^3 + 3x - k$

Since $f(2) = 10$, we have

$$10 = (2)^3 + 3(2) - k, \text{ or}$$

$$10 = 8 + 6 - 8 \Rightarrow k = 4$$

32. **(B)** $f(x, y) = x^2 + 2y^2 - y$ and $g(h) = h + 7$.

$$g(-2) = -2 + 7 = 5$$

$$f(3, g(-2)) = 3^2 + 2(g(-2))^2 - g(-2)$$

$$= 3^2 + 2(5)^2 - (5) = 9 + 50 - 5 = 54$$

33. **(E)** $f(a) = a^2 - 2a + 7$

$$f(-a) = (-a)^2 - 2(-a) + 7$$

$$= a^2 + 2a + 7$$

For $f(a) = f(-a)$ we must have:

$$a^2 - 2a + 7 = a^2 + 2a + 7$$

$$-2a = 2a$$

$$4a = 0$$

$$a = 0$$

Hence, $a = 0$ is the only solution.

34. **(C)** The coefficient of the function is 3, which means that the maximum and minimum values are 3 and –3, respectively. The period of the cosine function is the coefficient of x multiplied by $\dfrac{\pi}{2}$ radians. Therefore, the period of the cosine function given in this problem is

$$2\left(\frac{\pi}{2} \text{ radians}\right) = \pi \text{ radians}$$

35.   **(D)**   If x is a function, then each member of the domain is mapped into one and only one member of the range. Hence, x may not be 2, 6, or 11; these numbers are already first components of ordered pairs in x.

36.   **(C)**   A negative integer raised to any odd power is negative; the negative sign before the parentheses in $-(-n)^3$ makes the negative value of $(-n)^3$ always positive.

37.   **(C)**   Note that

$$32 = 2 \times 2 \times 2 \times 2 \times 2 = 2^5.$$

Thus,

$$\log_{10} 32 = \log_{10} 2^5.$$

Recall the logarithmic property,

$$\log_b x^y = y \log_b x.$$

Hence,

$$\log_{10} 32 = \log_{10} 2^5 = 5 \log_{10} 2$$

$$= 5 (0.3010)$$

$$= 1.5050$$

38.   **(C)**

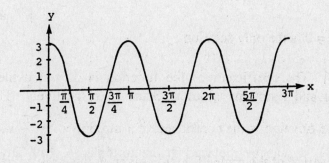

$$\log_b 2 + \log_b \beta + \frac{1}{2} \log_b \gamma - \frac{1}{2} \log_b \omega$$

$$= (\log_b 2 + \log_b \beta) + \frac{1}{2} (\log_b \gamma - \log_b \omega)$$

$$= \log_b(2\beta) + \frac{1}{2}\log_b\left(\frac{\gamma}{\omega}\right)$$

$$= \log_b\left(2\beta\left(\frac{\gamma}{\omega}\right)^{\frac{1}{2}}\right)$$

$$= \log_b\left(2\beta\sqrt{\frac{\gamma}{\omega}}\right)$$

39. **(B)** $(0.0081) = (0.3)^4$

Hence,

$$(0.0081)^{-\frac{3}{4}} = (0.3^4)^{-\frac{3}{4}} = (0.3)^{-3}$$

$$= \frac{1}{0.3^3} = \frac{1}{0.027} = \frac{1}{27/1,000} = \frac{1,000}{27}$$

40. **(C)** 0! (zero factorial) is defined as 1.

41. **(B)** To find the solution set of $f(x) > 2x$, we procede as follows:

$$\frac{5x-8}{2} > 2x$$

$$5x - 8 > 4x$$

which implies $x > 8$.

42. **(B)** x can be replaced in the formula $\frac{x}{|x|}$ with any real number

except 0, so if x is negative, $\frac{x}{|x|} = -1$, and if x is positive, $x = 1$. Thus, there are only the two numbers -1 and 1 in the range of our function; $R = \{-1, 1\}$.

43.　**(C)**　Consider functions $f : A \to B$ and $g : B \to C$, that is, where the codomain of f is the domain of g. Then the function $g \circ f$ is defined as $g \circ f : A \to C$ where $(g \circ f)(x) = g(f(x))$ for all x in A, and it is called the composition of f and g.

In another notation,

$$g \circ f = \{(x, z) \in A \times C \} \text{ for all } y \in B \text{ such that}$$

$$(x, y) \in f \text{ and } (y, z) \in g\}.$$

So　　　$(f \circ g)(x) = f(g(x))$

$$= f(4x^2)$$

$$= 2[4x^2] + 5$$

$$= 8x^2 + 5$$

44.　**(D)**　By reflecting $P(x)$ about the line $y = x$, we obtain $P^{-1}(x)$. Graph (D) is the result of such an operation and is therefore the correct choice.

45.　**(A)**　The die may land in any of six ways for a single toss. The probability of obtaining a 3 is:

$$P(3) = \frac{\text{Number of ways of obtaining a 3}}{\text{Number of ways the die may land}}$$

$$\therefore P(3) = \frac{1}{6}, \text{ similarly } P(5) = \frac{1}{6}$$

The probability therefore of obtaining either a 3 or a 5 is $P(3) + P(5)$, which equals

$$\frac{1}{6} + \frac{1}{6} = \frac{2}{6} = \frac{1}{3} \, .$$

Section 2

46.   **(C)** If an event can happen in p ways and fail to happen in q ways, then, if $p > q$, the odds are p to q in favor of the event happening.

If $p < q$, then the odds are q to p against the event happening. In this case, $p = 19$ and $q = 10$, $p > q$. Thus, the odds in favor of the event of drawing a red ball are 19:10.

47.   **(C)** Since Sir Lancelot must sit in an assigned chair, and Sir Gawain on either side of him, there are 4! or 24 ways of seating the other four. For each of these combinations, Sir Gawain can be in either of two seats, so the total number of ways of seating the knights is 24×2 or 48.

48.   **(E)** Since the statement

$$\log_b \frac{1}{25} = -2$$

is equivalent to

$$b^{-2} = \frac{1}{25}$$

and

$$b^{-2} = \frac{1}{b^2}$$

therefore,

$$\frac{1}{b^2} = \frac{1}{25}$$

Cross multiply to obtain the equivalent equation,

$$b^2 = 25.$$

Take the square root of both sides to find

$b = \pm 5.$

49. **(A)** By the law of the logarithm of a quotient of two numbers which states that $\log \dfrac{a}{b} = \log a - \log b$, $\log(40x - 1) - \log(x - 1) = \log \dfrac{40x - 1}{x - 1}$

$= 3.$ Hence, $\log_{10} \dfrac{40x - 1}{x - 1}$ $= 3.$ By the definition of a logarithm, if $\log_b N = x$, then $b^x = N$.

Therefore, $\log_{10} \dfrac{40x - 1}{x - 1} = 3$ means $10^3 = \dfrac{40x - 1}{x - 1}$. Thus $1{,}000 = \dfrac{40x - 1}{x - 1}$. Multiply both sides by $(x - 1)$:

$$(x - 1)\, 1{,}000 = (x - 1)\left(\dfrac{40x - 1}{x - 1}\right)$$

$$(x - 1)\, 1{,}000 = 40x - 1$$

Distributing, $1{,}000x - 1{,}000 = 40x - 1$. Subtract $40x$ from both sides to obtain:

$$960x - 1{,}000 = -1.$$

Add $1{,}000$ to both sides to obtain:

$$960x = 999.$$

Divide both sides by 960:

$$x = \dfrac{999}{960} = \dfrac{333}{320}.$$

50. **(A)** $N = \dfrac{33!\, 37!}{51!}$

$$\log_{10} N = \log_{10} 33! + \log_{10} 37! - \log_{10} 51!$$

$$= 37 + 43 - 66 = 14$$

Since $\qquad$ $\log_{10} N = 14$

then $\qquad$ $N = 10^{14}$

51. **(E)** $(3i)^2 - (5 - x)$

$\qquad$ $9i^2 - 5 + x$

$\qquad$ $-9 - 5 + x$

$\qquad$ $-14 + x$

$(-14 + x)$ has a minimum of -14 under the condition $x \geq 0$ when $x = 0$.

52. **(C)** $[2.1] = 2, [-0.9] = -1, [1.9] = 1, 2 - 1 + 1 = 2.$

53. **(D)** We may execute the instructions in a systematic way.

x	A
1	3
3	A is prime $\rightarrow$ continue
	5
5	A is prime $\rightarrow$ continue
	7
7	A is prime $\rightarrow$ continue
	9
9	A is not prime $\rightarrow$ write the value of x.

$x = 9.$

54. **(C)** Since $g(x) = 2$ for all x, $g(f(1)) = 2.$

55. **(A)**

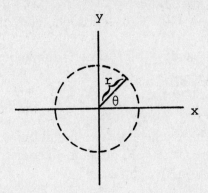

r is constant for all values of θ so the line segment in the diagram has constant length as it revolves through the $x - y$ plane.

56. **(C)** $f(g(h(8))) = f(g(4))$

$$= f(2) = 2^3 = 8$$

57. **(A)** $f(x)\, g(x) = x^3(x^2 + 1) = x^5 + x^3$

This is an odd function since $f(-x) = -f(x)$.

$$f(g(x)) = f(x^2 + 1) = (x^2 + 1)^3$$

This is not odd because x is squared first, then cubed. Positive and negative values of x yield the same result when raised to an even power.

$$2g(f(x)) - 1 = 2g(x^3) - 1 = 2(x^3)^2 + 2 - 1 = 2x^6 + 1$$

Again, x is raised to an even power so the function is not odd.

58. **(B)** There are 36 possible outcomes. Six of these produce the number 7:

$$(1, 6), (2, 5), (3, 4), (4, 3), (5, 2), \text{ and } (6, 1).$$

Hence, the probability is $\dfrac{6}{36} = \dfrac{1}{6}$

59. **(B)** There are: 8 choices for first freshman officer,

7 choices for second freshman officer,

5 for first sophomore officer,

and 4 for second sophomore officer.

Thus, $8 \times 7 \times 5 \times 4 = 1{,}120$.

60. **(B)** With each toss there are two possibilities, heads or tails. There are five tosses so there are $2^5 = 32$ possible outcomes. The number of ways to choose two heads from five tosses is

$$\binom{5}{2} = \frac{5!}{2!\,5!} = 10.$$

So the probability is

$$\frac{10}{32} = \frac{5}{16}.$$

61. **(A)** Label the players 1 through 5. Player 1 will have one match with each of the remaining four players. Player 2 (who has already played Player 1) will have matches with the remaining three players and so on. The total number of matches will be $4 + 3 + 2 + 1 = 10$.

62. **(D)** $f(4, 2) = \dfrac{\log 4}{\log 2} = \dfrac{\log 2^2}{\log 2} = \dfrac{2\log 2}{\log 2} = 2$

63. **(A)** $\log_3\left(\dfrac{1}{81}\right) = \log_3\left(\dfrac{1}{3^4}\right) = \log_3(3^{-4}) = -4$

64. **(E)** $\log(a^2 - b^2) = \log(a + b)(a - b)$ (difference of squares)

$$= \log(a + b) + \log(a - b). \quad \text{(law of logs)}$$

65. **(E)** Let $y = \log_8 3 = x\log_2 3$. Then

$$8^y = 3 \Rightarrow 2^{3y} = 3 \tag{1}$$

and $y = x\log_2 3 \Rightarrow 2^y = 3^x \tag{2}$

Substituting the expression for 2^y in (2) into (1), we obtain

$$3 = (2^y)^3 = (3^x)^3 = 3^{3x}.$$

Hence, $3x = 1 \Rightarrow x = \dfrac{1}{3}$.

66.   **(A)** If $x^2 + bx + c = 0$, then by the quadratic formula $x = \dfrac{-b \pm \sqrt{b^2 - 4c}}{2}$. We are given $b^2 - 4c = 0$, so the two roots $x_1 = \dfrac{-b + 0}{2}$ and $x_2 = \dfrac{-b - 0}{2}$. So x_1 and x_2 are real numbers and $x_1 = x_2$.

67.   **(D)** Any point which is located on the x-axis has a y-coordinate of zero. Therefore, to determine where the function crosses the x-axis, we must find these values of x for which $y = f(x) = 0$; i.e., we must solve $x^2 - x - 6 = 0$.

We obtain $(x - 3)(x + 2) = 0$ which has solutions $x = 3$ and $x = -2$. The points of intersection are thus $(3, 0)$ and $(-2, 0)$.

68.   **(B)** $f(g(h(\pi))) = f\left(g\left(\dfrac{\pi}{2} \right) \right) = f\left(\sin \dfrac{\pi}{2} \right) = f(1) = 1^2 = 1,$

since we have $h(\pi) = \dfrac{\pi}{2}$ and $g\left(\dfrac{\pi}{2} \right) = \sin \dfrac{\pi}{2} = 1.$

69.   **(D)** Since $(x - 1)^2 > 0$ for all x, the minimum value occurs when $(x - 1)^2 = 0$. Hence, $f(x) = 0 + 3 = 3$ is the minimum value. This conclusion can also be made by considering the graph of the function which is a parabola.

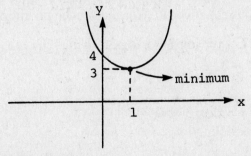

70.   **(C)** The domain of $y = \sqrt{x}$ is $\{x \in R \mid x \geq 0\}$; the range is also the same. The inverse is $x = \sqrt{y}$ or $y = x^2$, $x \geq 0$. This, of course, is a function. The relation $\mid y \mid = x$ is not a function; each x value, for example $x = 1$, has two corresponding y values, $y = \pm 1$. However, the inverse $y = \mid x \mid$, $x \in R$, is a function. The function $y = \sin x$ is periodic; the value assigned at x is the same as that assigned at $x + 2n\pi$, $n = 0, \pm 1, \pm 2, \ldots$. So the inverse will assign the same x values to y and $y + 2n\pi$. The y value must be unique to define a function, so the inverse is not a function. The curves below show each of the relations and their inverses.

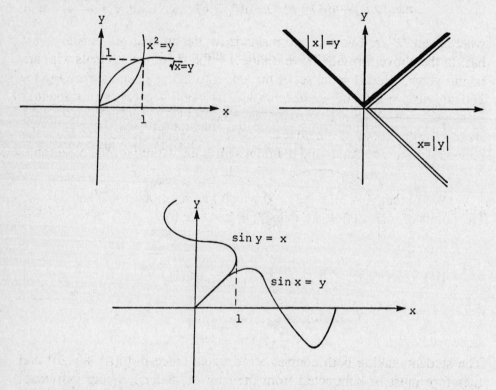

71.   **(B)** An odd function $f(x)$ has the property that whenever $x \in$ domain of f, then we have $(-x) \in$ domain and also: $F(-x) = -F(x)$. All of the functions below have the real number system as their domain, i.e., they are defined for any real number. Therefore, the first condition for being an odd function is satisfied. But for the second condition:

I. $f(-x) = -2x + 1$, $-f(x) = -2x - 1$. These are not equal.

II. $\tan(-x) = \dfrac{\sin(-x)}{\cos(-x)} = \dfrac{-\sin x}{\cos x} = -\tan x$. Thus, $g(x) = \tan x$ is an odd function.

III. $h(-x) = -x^3 + x^2$, $-h(x) = -x^3 - x^2$. These are not equal.

Hence, the only odd function is $g(x) = \tan x$.

72.   **(D)**   [all students] = [students taking physics] +

[students taking calculus] – [those taking both] .

This formula is a direct conclusion of the following relation:

$$n(A \cup B) = n(A) + n(B) - n(A \cap B)$$

where A and B are two sets and n stands for the number of elements a set has. In the above formula, if we define A = the set of the students who are taking physics and B = the set of the students taking calculus, then $n(A) = 260$ and $n(B) = 185$ and we have: $n(A \cup B) = 300$ because each student at least takes one of the two courses. Therefore, $(A \cap B)$ will be the set of the students taking both of the courses and $n(A \cap B)$ can be derived from the above relation. The following diagram shows the validity of the equation.

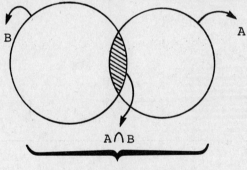

The students taking both courses are counted twice in $[n(A) + n(B)]$ and therefore must be subtracted from the sum of students taking individual courses.

We obtain $300 = 260 + 185 - x$

$= 445 - x$

Hence, $x = 145$.

73.   **(D)**   There are ten balls in all and six of them are white. Hence, the probability of drawing a white ball is $\dfrac{6}{10} = 0.6$

74. **(C)** There are four aces in a deck of 52 cards. Hence, the probability of drawing an ace is $\dfrac{4}{52} = \dfrac{1}{13}$.

75. **(E)** There are ten integers from 0 to 9; hence, there are ten choices for the first digit of the phone number. Since no digit can be repeated, we have only nine choices for the second digit. Similarly, there are eight choices for the third digit and so on. Since there are seven digits in a phone number, we have

$$10 \times 9 \times 8 \times 7 \times 6 \times 5 \times 4 = \frac{10!}{3!}$$

possible phone numbers.

76. **(A)** $\log_3\left(\dfrac{1}{27}\right) = \log_3\left(\dfrac{1}{3^3}\right) = \log_3(3^{-3}) = -3$

We could also use the identity:

$$\log_a b^c = c \log_a b$$

and write:

$$\log_3 \frac{1}{27} = \log_3 3^{-3} = -3 \log_3 3 = -3$$

77. **(E)** Take the log of both sides:

$$\log_{10}(x^{\log_{10}x}) = \log_{10}(100x)$$

$$(\log_{10}x)(\log_{10}x) = \log_{10}(100x)$$

because

$$\log_{10}x^a = a \log_{10}x,$$

setting $a = \log_{10}x$, we will arrive at the above conclusion.

$$(\log_{10}x)^2 = \log_{10}100 + \log_{10}x = 2 + \log_{10}x$$

or $\qquad (\log_{10}x)^2 - \log_{10}x - 2 = 0$

This is a quadratic equation and can be factored:

$$(\log_{10}x + 1)(\log_{10}x - 2) = 0$$

$$\log_{10}x = -1 \text{ and } \log_{10}x = 2$$

$$\Rightarrow x = 10^{-1} = \frac{1}{10} \text{ and } x = 10^2 = 100$$

78. **(C)** $\dfrac{4!+3!}{5!} = \dfrac{(4)\,3!+3!}{(5)\,(4)\,3!} = \dfrac{(4+1)\,3!}{(5)\,(4)\,3!}$

$$= \frac{4+1}{(5)\,4} = \frac{5}{20} = \frac{1}{4}$$

79. **(C)** If a certain integer y has a remainder 2 after division by 6, it can be written as:

$$\frac{y}{6} = q + \frac{2}{6}$$

It can be rewritten as:

$$y = 6q + 2$$

If we divide by 3, the result is:

$$\frac{y}{3} = \frac{6q+2}{3} = 2q + \frac{2}{3}$$

Therefore, the remainder is 2.

80. **(B)** If $(x - 2)$ is a factor, then 2 is a root so $f(2) = 0$. To obtain $f(2)$ we substitute 2 into the expression $x^3 - 7x^2 + kx - 12$, which results:

$$2^3 - 7(2)^2 + k(2) - 12 = 8 - 28 + 2k - 12$$

Since $f(2) = 0$, we obtain:

$$8 - 28 + 2k - 12 = 0$$

$$2k - 32 = 0$$

$$2k = 32$$

$$k = 16$$

81.   **(D)** There are five possibilities for the first (1, 3, 5, 7, 9), five for the second (0, 2, 4, 6, 8), eight possibilities for the third (10 − 2), and seven for the fourth (8 − 1) = 7. We subtracted 2 possibilities on the third and 3 on the fourth because there is no repetition, as shown below:

$$5 \times 5 \times (10 - 2)\,(8 - 1) = 5 \times 5 \times 8 \times 7 = 1{,}400$$

82.   **(E)** The equation of the parabola is $y = 2x^2$ and its inverse is given by $x = 2y^2$. The ordered pairs that satisfy both at the same time correspond to their intersection:

$$\begin{cases} y = 2x^2 \\ x = 2y^2 \end{cases}$$
$$\text{Equation (I)}$$
$$\text{Equation (II)}$$

If we substitute Equation (II) into Equation (I), we will obtain:

$$y = 2(2y^2)^2$$

$$y = 8y^4$$

$$y - 8y^4 = 0$$

$$y(1 - 8y^3) = 0 \Rightarrow y = 0 \text{ or } y = \frac{1}{2}$$

If $y = 0$ then $x = 0$. If $y = \frac{1}{2}$, from (I) $x = \pm\frac{1}{2}$.

Note that the ordered pair $(-\frac{1}{2}, \frac{1}{2})$ has to be eliminated, since it does not satisfy Equation (II). The solution consists of the pairs $(0, 0)$ and $(\frac{1}{2}, \frac{1}{2})$.

83.   **(E)** There are three steps to build this graph:

1st step: Draw the graph $y = \sin x$

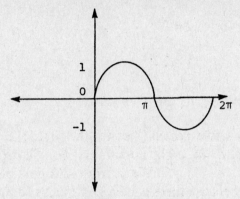

2nd step: Move the graph two units up, because it is $y = \sin(x - \pi) + 2$.

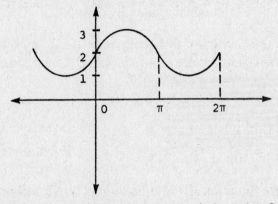

3rd step: Move the graph π units because it is $y = \sin(x - \pi) + 2$.

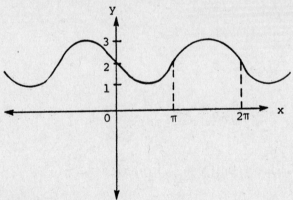

84. **(E)** To determine the inverse of a function, it is necessary to re-place the variable y by x and x by y.

The function $y = \log_2 \dfrac{2x - 1}{2}$ becomes:

$$x = \log_2 \frac{2y - 1}{2}$$

$$2^x = \frac{2y - 1}{2}$$

$$\frac{2^{x+1} + 1}{2} = y$$

85.　**(A)**　A function is symmetric with respect to the origin if replacing x by $-x$ and y by $-y$ produces an equivalent function.

(I)　　$y = f(x) = x^3 - x$

$(-y) = (-x)^3 - (-x)$

$-y = -x^3 + x$

$y = x^3 - x$

(I) is symmetric.

(II)　$y = f(x) = 2x + x^5$

$-y = 2(-x) + (-x)^5$

$-y = -2x - x^5$

$y = 2x + x^5$

(II) is symmetric.

(III)　$y = f(x) = 2x + 4$

$-y = 2(-x) + 4$

$-y = -2x + 4$

$y = 2x - 4$

(III) is not symmetric.

86.　**(B)**　To determine whether or not a graph represents a function it is possible to apply the "vertical line test." If any vertical line to the graph intersects it in more than one point, the graph is not a function. The only graph for which a vertical line passes through more than one point is (B). A relation is a function if for any x there is one and only one y.

87.　**(D)**　If we sketch the graphs of the functions, we will obtain:

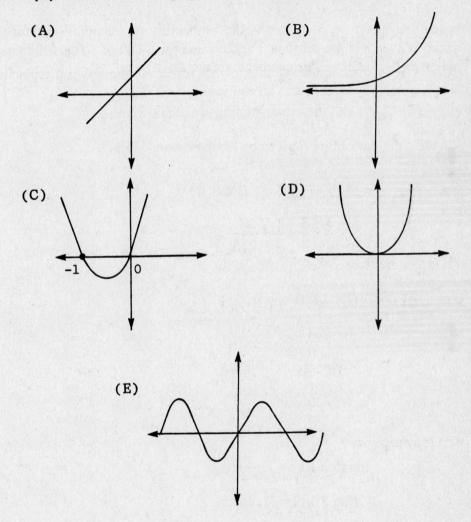

(A)

(B)

(C)

(D)

(E)

The only graph with symmetry with respect to the y-axis is choice (D).

Note: For a function to be symmetric with respect to the y-axis, $f(x)$ must equal $f(x)$ for all x. The answer to this problem can be determined that way.

88. **(A)** The probability of obtaining "even" or "greater than 3" is expressed below:

$$P(\text{even or} > 3) = P(\text{even}) + P(> 3) - P(\text{even} \cap > 3)$$

$$= \frac{3}{6} + \frac{3}{6} - \frac{2}{6} = \frac{4}{6} = \frac{2}{3}$$

Note that $P(\text{even} \cap > 3)$ means the probability of obtaining a number which is even and greater than 3 at the same time. Out of six possibilities, only two, "4," and "6," are even and greater than 3.

89. **(E)** Let's call the event winning A and not winning $\overline{A}$:

We want the probability P given by the expression below:

$$P = P(A) \times P(A) \times P(A) \times P(\overline{A})$$

$$= \frac{3}{4} \times \frac{3}{4} \times \frac{3}{4} \times \frac{1}{4} = \frac{27}{256}$$

90. **(C)** $\log 100 - \log \dfrac{1}{5} = 2 + \log x$

$$\log \frac{100}{\dfrac{1}{5}} = 2 + \log x$$

$$\log 500 = 2 + \log x$$

$$\log (5 \times 10^2) = 2 + \log x$$

$$(\log 5) + 2 = 2 + \log x$$

$$x = 5$$

PRACTICE
TEST 2

CLEP COLLEGE MATHEMATICS
Test 2

(Answer sheets appear in the back of the book.)

Section 1

TIME: 45 Minutes
33 Questions

DIRECTIONS: Each of the questions below is followed by five suggested answers. Complete the question and select the answer that is best.

---

1. $\log_2 \dfrac{\sqrt{2}}{8} =$

   (A) $\dfrac{5}{2}$ (D) $\dfrac{-5}{2}$

   (B) $\dfrac{1}{2}$ (E) $\dfrac{-1}{2}$

   (C) $\dfrac{3}{2}$

2. Determine a, b, and c, such that, for any real value of x, the ratio of $ax^2 - bx + 5$ to $3x^2 + 7x + c$ will be equal to 3.

   (A) $a = 3, b = 7, c = \dfrac{2}{3}$ (D) $a = 9, b = -21, c = \dfrac{5}{3}$

   (B) $a = 9, b = 21, c = \dfrac{3}{4}$ (E) $a = 9, b = -21, c = \dfrac{-5}{3}$

   (C) $a = 1, b = 1, c = -1$

3. Which one of the graphs below represents the inverse of the function $y = 3x + 4$?

(A)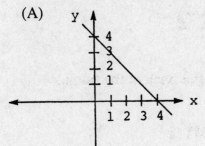

(D)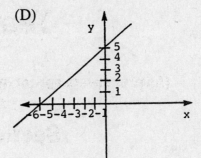

(B)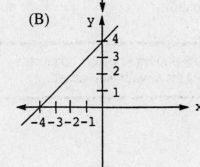

(E)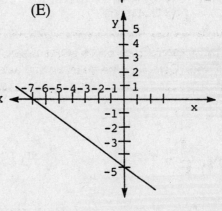

(C)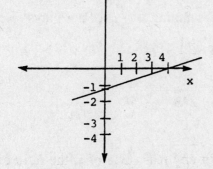

4. For what value of c will the graph of the function $y = 2x^2 + 5x + c$ NOT intersect the x-axis?

(A) 4

(D) 1

(B) –1

(E) 2

(C) 0

5. Suppose x is a prime number less than 12. What is the probability that $2 \leq x \leq 6$?

(A) $\dfrac{1}{2}$

(D) $\dfrac{1}{8}$

(B) $\dfrac{5}{6}$

(E) $\dfrac{5}{7}$

(C) $\dfrac{3}{5}$

6. If we toss a coin five times, the probability of obtaining exactly one head is

(A) $\dfrac{1}{32}$.

(D) $\dfrac{4}{32}$.

(B) $\dfrac{2}{32}$.

(E) $\dfrac{5}{32}$.

(C) $\dfrac{3}{32}$.

7. In a certain game the probability of winning is $\dfrac{1}{3}$. If Paul plays five times, what is the probability that he will win exactly once?

(A) $\dfrac{16}{243}$

(D) $\dfrac{80}{243}$

(B) $\dfrac{8}{243}$

(E) $\dfrac{2}{243}$

(C) $\dfrac{227}{243}$

8. By definition, the conjugate of a complex number $z = x + yi$ is represented by $\bar{z}$ and corresponds to $\bar{z} = x - yi$. Using this definition, find z such that $\bar{z} = -2zi$. Assume $i = \sqrt{-1}$ and $i^2 = -1$.

   (A) $0 + 0i$ (D) $-1 - i$

   (B) $1 + i$ (E) $2 + i$

   (C) $1 - i$

9. If k is an integer greater than zero, which of the following is always greater than zero?

   (A) $-k$ (D) e^k

   (B) $k - 1$ (E) None of the above

   (C) $\ln k$

10. If a and b are both positive, odd integers, and $a > b$, then for which of the following functions will $f(a)$ be greater than $f(b)$?

   I. $f(x) = e^x$

   II. $f(x) = x^{-3}$

   III. $f(x) = (-5)^x$

   (A) I only   (D) I and III only

   (B) II only   (E) I, II, and III

   (C) III only

11. For all non-negative real-numbers, $a \neq b$, $a * b$ is defined by the equation $a * b = \dfrac{a^2 - b}{a - b}$. If $5 * x = 11 * 0$, then $x =$

   (A) 0.   (D) 3.

   (B) 1.   (E) 4.

   (C) 2.

12. If $f(x) = (x - 1)^2 + (x + 1)^2$ for all real numbers x, which of the following are true?

   I. $f(x) = f(-x)$

   II. $f(x) = f(x + 1)$

   III. $f(x) = |f(x)|$

   (A) None of the above   (C) I and III only

   (B) III only   (D) II and III only

   (E) I, II, and III

13. What is the domain of the function defined by $y = f(x) = \sqrt{-x+1} + 5$?

   (A) $\{x|x \geq 0\}$ (D) $\{x|x \geq -1\}$

   (B) $\{x|x \leq 1\}$ (E) $\{x|x \leq -1\}$

   (C) $\{x|x \leq x \leq 1\}$

14. What is the range of the function given in Problem 13?

   (A) $\{y|y \geq 5\}$ (D) $\{y|0 < y \leq 5\}$

   (B) $\{y|y > 5\}$ (E) $\{$all real numbers$\}$

   (C) $\{y|y > 0\}$

15. If $f(x) = 2x - 4$, which of the following could be the graph of $y = f^{-1}(x)$, the inverse of f?

   (A)

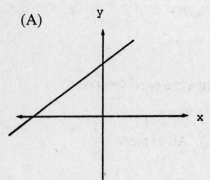

   (B)

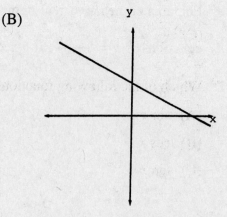

(C)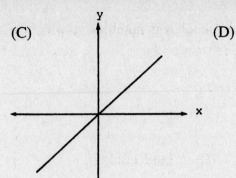

(D)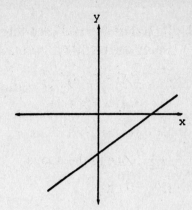

(E)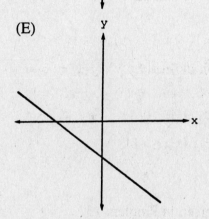

16. If $f(x) = \sin x + \cos x + 1$, $0 \le x \le \dfrac{\pi}{2}$, what is the minimum value of the function f?

(A) 0

(D) 2

(B) 1

(E) $\dfrac{\pi}{2}$

(C) $\dfrac{\pi}{4}$

17. Which of the following functions of x are even functions?

(A) $\sin x$

(D) $\cot x$

(B) $\cos x$

(E) All of these

(C) $\tan x$

18. If a fair coin is tossed three times, what is the probability of getting a head on the first toss, a tail on the second toss, and a head on the third toss?

(A) $\dfrac{1}{64}$ (D) $\dfrac{1}{4}$

(B) $\dfrac{1}{16}$ (E) $\dfrac{1}{2}$

(C) $\dfrac{1}{8}$

19. If $\Pr(A) = 0.2$ (the probability of event A is $\dfrac{1}{5}$), $\Pr(B) = 0.6$, and $\Pr(A \cap B) = 0.1$, what is $\Pr(A \cup B)$?

(A) 0.08   (D) 0.9

(B) 0.7   (E) 1.0

(C) 0.8

20. Using an ordinary deck of 52 playing cards, what is the probability of drawing three black cards in a row, without replacement?

(A) $\dfrac{1}{8}$ (D) $\dfrac{4}{33}$

(B) $\dfrac{2}{17}$ (E) $\dfrac{5}{41}$

(C) $\dfrac{3}{25}$

21. A counting number with exactly two different factors is called a prime number. Which of the following pairs of numbers are consecutive prime numbers?

(A) 27 and 29   (D) 37 and 39

(B) 31 and 33   (E) 41 and 43

(C) 35 and 37

22. If n is an integer, which of the following represents an odd number?

    (A) $2n + 3$ (D) $3n$

    (B) $2n$ (E) $n + 1$

    (C) $2n + 2$

23. Twelve more than twice a number is 31 less than three times the number. Find the number.

    (A) −43   (D) 19

    (B) −19   (E) 43

    (C) −9

24. What is the smallest positive number that leaves a remainder of 2 when the number is divided by 3, 4, or 5?

    (A) 22   (D) 122

    (B) 42   (E) 182

    (C) 62

25. Three times the first of three consecutive odd integers is three more than twice the third. What is the second of the three consecutive odd integers?

    (A) 7   (D) 13

    (B) 9   (E) 15

    (C) 11

26. If a and b are odd integers, which of the following must be an even integer?

    I. $\dfrac{a + b}{2}$

    II. $ab - 1$

    III. $\dfrac{ab + 1}{2}$

(A) I only   (D) II and III only

(B) II only   (E) I, II, and III

(C) I and II only

27. If m is an integer and the sum of m and the next integer larger than m is greater than 10, what is the smallest possible value of m?

(A) 4   (D) 7

(B) 3   (E) 6

(C) 5

28. What is the smallest positive integer that is divisible by each of the following numbers: 3, 4, 5, and 6?

(A) 18   (D) 60

(B) 42   (E) 72

(C) 54

29. If the sum of the digits of a two-digit positive whole number is 8 and the tens' digit is three times the units' digit, then what is the two-digit number?

(A) 93   (D) 71

(B) 31   (E) 62

(C) 26

30. Two consecutive even integers have a sum of 26. What is the result when they are multiplied?

(A) 168   (D) 182

(B) 120   (E) 121

(C) 169

31. The letters below represent consecutive integers on a number line.

```
  •   •   •   •   •   •   •   •   •   •
  a   b   c   d   e   f   g   h   i   j
```

If $2b + f = 13$, what is the value of b?

(A) 6   (D) 2

(B) 8   (E) 3

(C) 1

32. If n is the first of three consecutive odd numbers, which of the following represents the sum of the three numbers?

(A) $n + 2$ (D) $3n + 6$

(B) $n + 4$ (E) $6(3n)$

(C) $n + 6$

33. If the sum of four consecutive integers is 226, then the smallest of these numbers is

(A) 55.   (D) 58.

(B) 56.   (E) 59.

(C) 57.

34. If p and q are prime numbers greater than two, which of the following must be true?

I. $pq + 1$ is also a prime number.

II. $pq - 1$ is also a prime number.

III. p and q do not have a common factor.

(A) I only   (D) I and II only

(B) II only   (E) I and III only

(C) III only

35. What is the least prime number which is a divisor of $7^9 + 11^{25}$?

(A) 1

(D) 5

(B) 2

(E) $7^9 + 11^{25}$

(C) 3

36. What is the largest integer for which $(a + 3)(a - 7)$ is negative?

(A) 5

(D) 8

(B) 6

(E) 9

(C) 7

37. Find the smallest positive integer which is divisible by both 12 and 15.

(A) 36

(D) 80

(B) 48

(E) 90

(C) 60

38. Find the smallest of three consecutive positive integers such that when five times the largest is subtracted from the square of the middle one, the result exceeds three times the smallest by 7.

(A) 9

(D) 2

(B) 10

(E) 6

(C) 8

39. If m and n are consecutive integers, and $m < n$, which one of the following statements is always true?

(A) $n - m$ is even.

(D) $n^2 - m^2$ is odd.

(B) m must be odd.

(E) n must be even.

(C) $m^2 + n^2$ is even.

40. If x is an odd integer and y is even, then which of the following must be an even integer?

I. $2x + 3y$

II. xy

III. $x + y - 1$

(A) I only   (D) II and III only

(B) II only   (E) I, II, and III

(C) I and II only

41. The sum of four consecutive even integers is 68. What is the value of the smallest one?

(A) 12   (D) 18

(B) 14   (E) None of the above.

(C) 7

42. For any integer n, which of the following must be an even integer?

I. $2n + 1$

II. $2n + 2$

III. $2n - 1$

(A) I only   (D) I and II only

(B) II only   (E) II and III only

(C) III only

43. The mean IQ score for 1,500 students is 100, with a standard deviation of 15. Assuming normal curve distribution, how many students have an IQ between 85 and 115? Refer to the figure shown below.

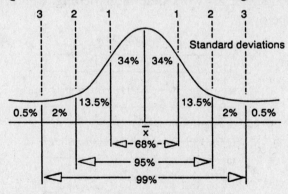

(A) 510   (D) 1,275

(B) 750   (E) 1,425

(C) 1,020

44. Two college roommates spent $2,000 for their total monthly expenses. A pie chart below indicates a record of their expenses.

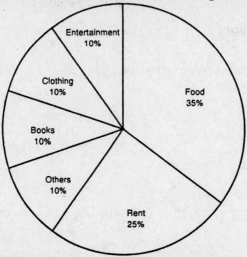

Based on the above information, which of the following statements is accurate?

(A) The roommates spent $700 on food alone.

(B) The roommates spent $550 on rent alone.

(C) The roommates spent $300 on entertainment alone.

(D) The roommates spent $300 on clothing alone.

(E) The roommates spent $300 on books alone.

45. Ralph kept track of his work time in gardening. Refer to the broken-line graph below:

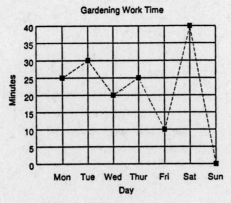

How many minutes did he average per day?

(A) 10 min.
(B) 20 min.
(C) 21.43 min.

(D) 23.05 min.
(E) 25 min.

Section 2

TIME: 45 Minutes
33 Questions

DIRECTIONS: Each of the questions below is followed by five suggested answers. Complete the question and select the answer that is best.

46. Mary had been selling printed shirts in her neighborhood. She made this pictograph to show how much money she made each week.

WEEKLY SALES

Each $ stands for $12.

How many weeks were sales more than $55?

(A) 1 week   (D) 4 weeks

(B) 2 weeks   (E) 5 weeks

(C) 3 weeks

47. The result of Mary's spring semester grades follow. Find her grade point average for the term ($A = 4$, $B = 3$, $C = 2$, $D = 1$, $F = 0$).

Course	Credits	Grades
Biology	5	A
English	3	C
Math	3	A
French	3	D
P.E.	2	B

(A) 3.80   (D) 2.00

(B) 3.50   (E) 1.86

(C) 2.94

48. The wear-out mileage of a certain tire is normally distributed with a mean of 30,000 miles and a standard deviation of 2,500 miles, as shown below.

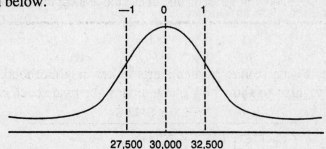

27,500 30,000 32,500

What will be the percentage of tires that will last at least 30,000 miles?

(A) 40%   (D) 55%

(B) 45%   (E) 60%

(C) 50%

49. Which of the following is an example of a rational number?

(A) $\sqrt{17}$ (D) $7+\sqrt{9}$

(B) $6+3\sqrt{7}$ (E) $2-\sqrt{15}$

(C) $4\sqrt{11}$

50. Which of the following statements includes a cardinal number?

(A) There are 15 volumes in the set of periodicals.

(B) I received my 14th volume recently.

(C) The students meet at Room 304.

(D) My phone number is 213–617–8442.

(E) James lives on 3448 Lucky Avenue.

51. Twice the sum of 10 and a number is 28. Find the number.

(A) 4   (D) 14

(B) 8   (E) 24

(C) 12

52. In a biology class at International University, the grades on the final examination were as follows:

91	81	65	81
50	70	81	93
36	90	43	87
96	81	75	81

Find the mode.

(A) 36   (D) 87

(B) 70   (E) 96

(C) 81

53. One commonly used standard score is a z-score. A z-score gives the number of standard deviations by which the score differs from the mean, as shown in the following example.

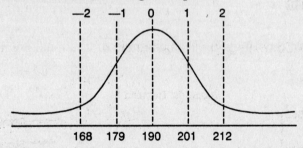

As shown above, the mean ($\bar{x}$) is 190 and the standard deviation(s) is 11. The score of 201 has a z-score of 1 and a score of 168 has a z-score of -2. Consider the mean height of a certain group of people as 190 cm with a standard deviation of 11 cm. Suppose Glenn's height has a z-score of 1.6, what is his height? (Note $z = \dfrac{x - \bar{x}}{\text{s.d.}}$)

(A) 20.760 cm   (D) 179 cm

(B) 190 cm   (E) 212 cm

(C) 201 cm

QUESTION 54 refers to the following chart.

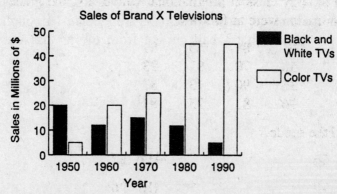

Sales of Brand X Televisions

54. According to the chart, in what year was the total sales of Brand X televisions the greatest?

(A) 1950   (D) 1980

(B) 1960   (E) 1990

(C) 1970

QUESTION 55 refers to the following chart.

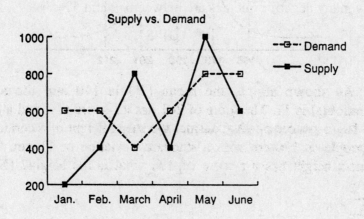

Supply vs. Demand

55. According to the graph, during how many months was supply greater than demand?

(A) 0   (D) 3

(B) 1   (E) 4

(C) 2

56. A jar contains 20 balls. These balls are labeled 1 through 20. What is the probability that a ball chosen from the jar has a number on it which is divisible by 4?

(A) $\dfrac{1}{20}$ (D) 4

(B) $\dfrac{1}{5}$ (E) 5

(C) $\dfrac{1}{4}$

57. How many odd prime numbers are there between 1 and 20?

(A) 7   (D) 10

(B) 8   (E) 11

(C) 9

58. How many negative integers are between −9 and 5?

(A) 13   (D) 8

(B) 10   (E) 6

(C) 9

59. On what interval is the below function positive?

(A) [0, 2]   (D) [1, 5]

(B) (0, 2)   (E) (1, 5)

(C) (0, 2]

60. Concerning the number π, which statement is the most accurate?

(A) $\pi = 3.14$.   (D) π cannot be calculated.

(B) $\pi = 3.1416$.   (E) π is an irrational number.

(C) $\pi = \dfrac{22}{7}$.

61. The smallest even integer n for which $(0.5)^n$ is less than 0.1 is

(A) 2.   (D) 8.

(B) 4.   (E) 10.

(C) 6.

62. What percent of 3.6 is 0.9?

(A) $\dfrac{1}{4}$ (D) 40

(B) 4   (E) 60

(C) 25

63. What is $\dfrac{1}{2}$ of $\dfrac{4}{5}$ divided into $\dfrac{2}{3}$ of 60%?

(A) $\dfrac{4}{5}$ (D) $\dfrac{4}{25}$

(B) $\dfrac{2}{5}$ (E) 1

(C) $1\dfrac{1}{2}$

64. How many twelfths are there in $33\frac{1}{3}\%$?

   (A) 1   (D) 100

   (B) 4   (E) 400

   (C) 33

65. Neal spent $\frac{3}{4}$ of his money for a shirt. If he was left with $20.00, how much did he have originally?

   (A) $15   (D) $80

   (B) $25   (E) $100

   (C) $60

66. A board 3 feet long is to be cut into three pieces such that the first piece is one-third the length of the second and the third piece is five times the length of the first. Find the length of the longest piece.

   (A) $\frac{1}{3}$ foot   (D) $1\frac{2}{3}$ foot

   (B) 1 foot   (E) $1\frac{3}{4}$ foot

   (C) $1\frac{1}{2}$ foot

67. Simplify the following:

$$\frac{\dfrac{1}{3}}{1+\dfrac{2}{4+5}}$$

(A) $\dfrac{7}{24}$

(D) 1

(B) $\dfrac{3}{11} \to \dfrac{3}{11}$

(E) $\dfrac{1}{3}$

(C) $\dfrac{8}{21}$

68. A restaurant buys cans of corn in bulk. If three cans of corn sell for $8.00, how much will one gross cost the restaurant?

(A) $24

(D) $384

(B) $80

(E) $1,152

(C) $246

69. Estimate to the nearest hundred:

$$\frac{(7{,}592)\,(4{,}892)}{(3{,}810)\,(70)}.$$

(A) 98

(D) 1,000

(B) 100

(E) 4,900

(C) 980

70. Sam has $1,000 to invest. He would like to invest $\dfrac{3}{5}$ of it at 6% simple interest. The remainder would be invested at 8% simple interest. How much interest would he have earned after one year?

(A) $32

(D) $70

(B) $36

(E) $140

(C) $68

71. What is the largest prime number factor of 156?

(A) 2

(D) 13

(B) 3

(E) 39

(C) 12

72. Rewrite the repeating decimal 0.252525... in fraction form.

    (A) $\dfrac{1}{4}$ (D) $\dfrac{4}{25}$

    (B) $\dfrac{1}{25}$ (E) $\dfrac{25}{99}$

    (C) $\dfrac{4}{17}$

73. The denominator of a fraction is four more than the numerator. If the numerator is doubled and the denominator is increased by five, the resulting fraction is equal to $\dfrac{1}{2}$. What is the original fraction?

    (A) $\dfrac{3}{7}$ (D) $\dfrac{7}{3}$

    (B) $\dfrac{5}{9}$ (E) $\dfrac{9}{5}$

    (C) $\dfrac{1}{5}$

74. Evaluate the following: $48 - 24 \div 3 + 5 \times 2$.

    (A) 6   (D) 26

    (B) 12   (E) 50

    (C) 18

75. Simplify $7.5 \times 1\dfrac{7}{9} - 1.333...$

    (A) $\dfrac{1}{18}$ (D) 12

    (B) $5\dfrac{5}{8}$ (E) $17\dfrac{7}{9}$

    (C) $6\dfrac{2}{3}$

76. Solve for x: $2x - 7 = 3x + 2$

    (A) −14   (D) $\dfrac{9}{5}$

    (B) −9   (E) $\dfrac{14}{5}$

    (C) 1

77. There are 25 students in a chemistry class and 23 students taking physics. Seven students are in both classes. How many individuals are enrolled in either of the classes or both?

    (A) 24   (D) 41

    (B) 34   (E) 48

    (C) 38

78. Scott can pot 100 plants in 30 minutes. Henri can do the same job in 60 minutes. If they worked together, how many minutes would it take them to pot 200 plants?

    (A) 20   (D) 60

    (B) 30   (E) 90

    (C) 40

79. Twenty-five students rented a bus to attend a play. At the last moment, five students decided not to go. The others were each assessed an additional $1.00 to their share of the fare to cover the total cost of the bus rental. How much was the bus rental?

    (A) $80   (D) $110

    (B) $100   (E) $125

    (C) $120

80. What is the least common multiple of $8x$ and $24xy$?

    (A) 2   (B) $2xy$

(C) $6x$

(E) $72xy$

(D) 48

81. A floor that measures 10 feet by 20 feet is to be tiled with square tiles that are 36 square inches in area. How many tiles are needed to cover the entire floor?

(A) 200

(D) 800

(B) 360

(E) 1,200

(C) 600

82. A recipe for chicken divan will serve eight people. Jann has invited 17 friends over for dinner. By how much does she need to increase the recipe in order to have enough servings?

(A) $1\dfrac{3}{4}$ times

(D) $3\dfrac{1}{2}$ times

(B) 2 times

(E) 9 times

(C) $2\dfrac{1}{4}$ times

83. Lance traveled 90 miles in 2 hours. How much faster does he need to go in order to return in 1.5 hours?

(A) 15 mph

(D) 45 mph

(B) 25 mph

(E) 60 mph

(C) 35 mph

84. Two cars 660 miles apart start traveling toward each other, agreeing to meet midway. One car averages 40 mph, the other 55 mph. How long will the faster car have to wait in order to meet the slower car at the halfway point?

(A) 2 hours

(D) 6 hours

(B) $2\dfrac{1}{4}$ hours

(E) $8\dfrac{1}{4}$ hours

(C) 4 hours

85. A group of children share a package of cookies, each having six. If two more children join the group, they can each have four cookies. How many cookies were in the package, assuming none are left over?

(A) 8   (D) 24

(B) 10   (E) 36

(C) 16

86. A bike wheel has a radius of 12 inches. How many revolutions will it take to cover one mile? (Use 1 mile = 5,280 feet, and $\pi = \dfrac{22}{7}$.)

(A) 70   (D) 840

(B) 84   (E) 1,020

(C) 120

87. Mike is $8\dfrac{1}{2}$ times older than his son, Derek. The sum of their ages is 38. How old is Mike?

(A) 32   (D) 38

(B) 34   (E) 40

(C) 36

88. Four less than three times x is greater than 6. Find all values of x.

(A) $x < \dfrac{10}{3}$ (D) $x > \dfrac{2}{3}$

(B) $x > \dfrac{10}{3}$ (E) $x > 8$

(C) $x < 5$

89. Sandy was x years old four years ago. What expression represents how old she will be four years from now?

(A) x (D) $x + 8$

(B) $x + 4$ (E) $16x$

(C) $4x + 4$

90. Simplify and express in factored form $6(x-2) - 4(x+4)$.

(A) $2(x+1)$ (D) $2(x-14)$

(B) $2(x+2)$ (E) $2(x-8)$

(C) $2(x+7)$

CLEP COLLEGE MATHEMATICS
TEST 2

ANSWER KEY

Section 1

1. (D)	10. (A)	19. (B)	28. (D)	37. (C)
2. (D)	11. (D)	20. (B)	29. (E)	38. (C)
3. (C)	12. (C)	21. (E)	30. (A)	39. (D)
4. (A)	13. (B)	22. (A)	31. (E)	40. (E)
5. (C)	14. (A)	23. (E)	32. (D)	41. (B)
6. (E)	15. (A)	24. (C)	33. (A)	42. (B)
7. (D)	16. (D)	25. (D)	34. (C)	43. (C)
8. (A)	17. (B)	26. (B)	35. (B)	44. (A)
9. (D)	18. (C)	27. (C)	36. (B)	45. (C)

Section 2

46. (B)	55. (C)	64. (B)	73. (A)	82. (C)
47. (C)	56. (C)	65. (D)	74. (E)	83. (A)
48. (C)	57. (A)	66. (D)	75. (D)	84. (B)
49. (D)	58. (D)	67. (B)	76. (B)	85. (D)
50. (A)	59. (E)	68. (D)	77. (D)	86. (D)
51. (A)	60. (E)	69. (B)	78. (C)	87. (B)
52. (C)	61. (D)	70. (C)	79. (B)	88. (B)
53. (A)	62. (C)	71. (D)	80. (E)	89. (D)
54. (D)	63. (E)	72. (E)	81. (D)	90. (D)

DETAILED EXPLANATIONS
OF ANSWERS

TEST 2

Section 1

1. **(D)** The expression $\log_2 \dfrac{\sqrt{2}}{8}$ can be rewritten as:

$\log_2 \dfrac{2^{\frac{1}{2}}}{2^3}$ and by subtracting the exponents:

$$\log_2 2^{\frac{1}{2}-3} = \log_2 2^{\frac{-5}{2}} = \frac{-5}{2}$$

2. **(D)** If $\dfrac{ax^2 - bx + 5}{3x^2 + 7x + c}$ is constant and equal to 3, then we conclude:

$ax^2 - bx + 5 = 3(3x^2 + 7x + c)$

$ax^2 - bx + 5 = 9x^2 + 21x + 3c$

$a = 9$

$b = -21$

$c = \dfrac{5}{3}$

3. **(C)** The inverse of the function $f(x) = 3x + 4$ is obtained by replacing y by x and x by y.

$$y = 3x + 4$$

$$x = 3y + 4 \Rightarrow 3y = x - 4 \Rightarrow y = \frac{x-4}{3}$$

The graph of $y = \dfrac{x-4}{3}$ is given below:

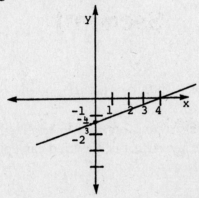

4.   **(A)**   The function $y = 2x^2 + 5x + c$ can be represented graphically as a parabola.

If its discriminant $D = b^2 - 4ac$ is negative, then the parabola will not intersect the x-axis. This occurs because the equation $0 = 2x^2 + 5x + c$ will have no real solutions when $D < 0$. Setting $D < 0$, we obtain:

$$D = b^2 - 4ac = 25 - 4(2)c < 0$$

$$25 - 8c < 0$$

$$25 < 8c$$

$$\frac{25}{8} < c$$

$$c > \frac{25}{8},$$

so the only choice among those given is $c = 4$.

5.   **(C)** There are five prime numbers less than 12: 2, 3, 5, 7, 11. There are three which fall between 2 and 6, namely 2, 3, and 5. So the probability is $\dfrac{3}{5}$.

6.   **(E)** The probability of obtaining a head the first time and tails the other four times is:

$$\left(\frac{1}{2}\right) \times \left(\frac{1}{2}\right) \times \left(\frac{1}{2}\right) \times \left(\frac{1}{2}\right) \times \left(\frac{1}{2}\right)$$

  p(head) p(tail) p(tail) p(tail) p(tail)

Since we could also have obtained a head on the second, third, fourth, or fifth time we played (that is, the head can come up in any one of five tosses), the probability is

$$5 \times \left(\frac{1}{2}\right) \times \left(\frac{1}{2}\right) \times \left(\frac{1}{2}\right) \times \left(\frac{1}{2}\right) \times \left(\frac{1}{2}\right) = \frac{5}{32}$$

7.   **(D)** The probability of winning the first time is:

$$\left(\frac{1}{3}\right) \times \left(\frac{2}{3}\right) \times \left(\frac{2}{3}\right) \times \left(\frac{2}{3}\right) \times \left(\frac{2}{3}\right) = \frac{16}{243}$$

But since he plays five times and he could win any of them (the second, third, fourth, or fifth), the probability of winning at least once is given by:

$$5 \times \frac{16}{243} = \frac{80}{243}$$

8.   **(A)** Considering $z = x + yi$ and $\bar{z} = x - yi$, if $z = -2zi$, we can substitute as follows:

$$(x - yi) = -2(x + yi)i$$

$$x - yi = 2y - 2xi$$

$$\begin{cases} x = 2y \\ y = 2x \end{cases} \Rightarrow x = 0 \text{ and } y = 0$$

9. **(D)** Choice (A): No, $-k < 0$ for all $k > 0$

Choice (B): No, $k - 1 = 0$ when $k = 1$

Choice (C): No, $\ln k = 0$ when $k = 1$

Choice (D): Yes, $e^k > 0$ for all integers $k > 0$.

10. **(A)** Let's take two arbitrary, positive, odd integers for our analysis. The use of these numbers will provide counter-examples for II and III.

I.   Since e^x is an increasing function (grows larger as x gets larger), we see that

$a > b \Rightarrow e^a > e^b$, so $f(a) > f(b)$

II. $f(3) = 3^{-3} = \dfrac{1}{27}$ and $f(1) = 1^{-3} = 1$, letting $a = 3, b = 1$

$\dfrac{1}{27} < 1 \Rightarrow$ No, $f(a) \not> f(b)$

III. $f(3) = (-5)^3 = -125$ and $f(1) = (-5)^1 = -5$, letting $a = 3$, $b = 1$

$-125 < -5 \Rightarrow$ No, $f(a) \not> f(b)$

11. **(D)** $5 * x = \dfrac{5^2 - x}{5 - x}$

$11 * 0 = \dfrac{11^2 - 0}{11 - 0} = 11$

$\dfrac{25 - x}{5 - x} = 11$

$25 - x = 11(5 - x)$

$$10x = 30$$

$$x = 3$$

12. **(C)** I. True: $f(-x) = (-x-1)^2 + (-x+1)^2$

$$= [-(x+1)]^2 + [-(x-1)]^2$$

$$= (x+1)^2 + (x-1)^2 = f(x)$$

II. False: $f(x+1) = (x+1-1)^2 + (x+1+1)^2$

$$= x^2 + (x+2)^2 \neq f(x)$$

III. True: $|f(x)| = |(x-1)^2 + (x+1)^2|$

$$= (x-1)^2 + (x+1)^2 = f(x)$$

13. **(B)** The only restriction for the domain is that $-x+1$ must be greater than or equal to zero.

$$-x+1 \geq 0$$

$$\Rightarrow 1 \geq x$$

14. **(A)**

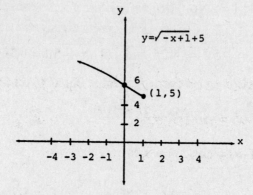

15. **(A)** To find the inverse of a function, exchange the variables x and y, and solve for y.

$$f(x) = 2x - 4 = y$$

$$2y - 4 = x$$

$$y = \frac{1}{2}x + 2 = f^{-1}(x)$$

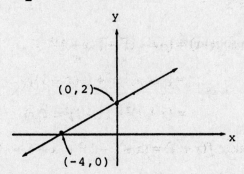

16. **(D)** The minimum of f, in the first quadrant, occurs when $\sin x = 0$ and $\cos x = 1$ or when $\sin x = 1$ and $\cos x = 0$.

17. **(B)**

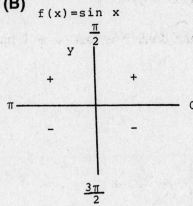

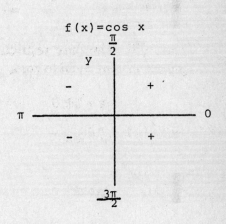

For a function to be even, $f(x)$ must equal $f(-x)$ for all x.

$$\sin(-x) = -\sin(x) \Rightarrow \text{No}$$

$$\cos(-x) = \cos(x) \Rightarrow \text{Yes}$$

$$\tan(-x) = \frac{\sin(-x)}{\cos(-x)} = \frac{-\sin x}{\cos x} = -\tan x \Rightarrow \text{No}$$

$$\cot(-x) = \frac{\cos(-x)}{\sin(-x)} = \frac{\cos x}{-\sin x} = -\cot x \Rightarrow \text{No}$$

18. **(C)** The probability of a head = Pr(head) = $\dfrac{1}{2}$

The probability of a tail = Pr(tail) = $\dfrac{1}{2}$

Pr(head, tail, head) = Pr(head on 1st) × Pr(tail on 2nd) × Pr(head on 3rd)

$$= \left(\frac{1}{2}\right) \times \left(\frac{1}{2}\right) \times \left(\frac{1}{2}\right) = \frac{1}{8}$$

19. **(B)** The probability of the union of two events equals the sum of the probabilities of each event separately minus the probability of the intersection.

$$Pr(A \cup B) = Pr(A) + Pr(B) - Pr(A \cap B)$$

$$= 0.2 + 0.6 - 0.1 = 0.7$$

20. **(B)** Pr(black card on first draw) = $\dfrac{26}{52}$

Pr(black card on second draw) = $\dfrac{25}{51}$

Pr(black card on third draw) = $\dfrac{24}{50}$

Pr(drawing three straight black cards) = $\dfrac{26}{52} \times \dfrac{25}{51} \times \dfrac{24}{50} = \dfrac{2}{17}$

21. **(E)** To test whether a number, N, is prime, we need to test if N is divisible by any of the prime numbers $\{2, 3, 5, 7, 11, 13, \ldots\}$ up to the largest natural number, k, whose square is less than or equal to the number we are testing, N. If N is divisible by any of the prime numbers $P \le k$, where $k^2 \le N$, then N is not a prime number. If N is not divisible by any of the prime numbers $P \le k$, where $k^2 \le N$, then N is a prime number. For example, to test whether 29 is a prime number, we need to test if 29 is divisible by any of the prime numbers starting with 2 and up to 5, that is,

we test if 29 is divisible by 2, 3, or 5, since $6^2 = 36$ is > 29. Since 29 is not divisible by any of these primes, 29 is a prime number.

Since all the prime numbers, except 2, are odd, it follows that the difference between any two consecutive prime numbers is 2. Thus, each of the pairs of numbers given in the answer choices as possible answers are two consecutive odd numbers.

Thus, to answer this question, we need to test if any of the pairs of numbers given in the answer choices is a pair of prime numbers. Testing these pairs of numbers yields,

(A)   27 and 29. Since $6^2 = 36$, and since $36 > 27$, and $36 > 29$, we need to test if 27 or 29 is divisible by any of the prime numbers less than or equal to 5. That is, if 27 or 29 is divisible by 2, 3, or 5. Since 27 is divisible by 3, then 27 and 29 is not a pair of consecutive prime numbers.

(B)   31 and 33. Again, $6^2 = 36$, $36 > 31$, and $36 > 33$. Hence, we need to test if 31 or 33 is divisible by any of the prime numbers less than or equal to 5. That is, if 31 or 33 is divisible by any of the primes 2, 3, and 5. Since 33 is divisible by 3, then 31 and 33 is not a pair of two consecutive prime numbers.

(C)   35 and 37. Since 35 is divisible by 5, then 35 and 37 is not a pair of prime numbers.

(D)   37 and 39. Since 39 is divisible by 3, then 37 and 39 is not a pair of prime numbers.

(E)   41 and 43. Since $7^2 = 49$, $49 > 41$, and $49 > 43$, it follows that we need to test if 41 or 49 is divisible by any of the prime numbers less than or equal to 6. That is, if 41 or 49 is divisible by any of the primes 2, 3, and 5. Since 41 is not divisible by any of these three primes and 43 is not divisible by any of these three primes either, it follows that 41 and 43 is a pair of consecutive prime numbers.

22.   **(A)** n is an integer means n can be an odd number or an even number. If n is odd, then $3n$ is odd (odd $\times$ odd $=$ odd). If n is even, then $3n$ is even (odd $\times$ even $=$ even). This simple discussion eliminates answer choice (D). Answer choice (E) is eliminated because if n is odd, then $(n + 1)$ is even, and if n is even, then $(n + 1)$ is odd.

If n is an integer (odd or even), then $2n$ is even (any integer $\times 2 =$ an even integer), and $(2n + 2)$ is even (since even + even = even). Thus, answer choices (B) and (C) are eliminated.

If n is an integer, then $2n$ is even and $2n + 3$ is odd (even + odd = odd).

23.   **(E)** Let $x =$ number. Write an equation from the question, "Twelve more than twice a number is 31 less than three times the number":

$$
\begin{array}{ll}
2x + 12 = 3x - 31 & \text{Solve the equation.} \\
\underline{-3x \qquad\quad -3x} & \text{Subtract } 3x \text{ from each side of the equation.} \\
-x + 12 = -31 & \\
\underline{\quad -12 \quad -12\quad} & \text{Subtract 12 from each side of the equation.} \\
\dfrac{-x}{-1} = \dfrac{-43}{-1} & \text{Divide both sides by} - 1. \\
x = 43 & \text{Correct answer is 43.}
\end{array}
$$

24.   **(C)** First find the least common multiple (LCM) of 3, 4, and 5 which is simply

$$3 \times 4 \times 5 = 60.$$

Since 3 divides 60, 4 divides 60, and 5 divides 60, then one needs only to add 2 to 60 in order to guarantee that the remainder in each case will be 2 when 3, 4, and 5, respectively, are divided into 62.

25.   **(D)** Let $x =$ the first odd integer, $x + 2 =$ the second consecutive odd integer, and $x + 4 =$ the third consecutive odd integer. Then, the following equation can be written based on what is given in the problem. Solve the equation.

$$3x = 2(x + 4) + 3$$

$$3x = 2x + 8 + 3$$

$$3x - 2x = 11$$

$$x = 11,$$

the first odd integer.

So, the second consecutive odd integer is

$$x + 2 = 11 + 2 = 13.$$

26. **(B)** We can express odd integers as

$$a = 2x + 1 \text{ and } b = 2y + 1$$

where x and y are integers.

I. $$\frac{a+b}{2} = \frac{(2x+1)+(2y+1)}{2}$$
$$= \frac{2x+2y+2}{2}$$
$$= x + y + 1$$

which is not necessarily even.

II. $$ab - 1 = (2x + 1)(2y + 1) - 1$$
$$= (4xy + 2x + 2y + 1) - 1$$
$$= 2(2xy + x + y)$$

which is always even (divisible by 2).

III. $$\frac{ab+1}{2} = \frac{(4xy+2x+2y+1)+1}{2}$$
$$= 2xy + x + y + 1$$

27. **(C)** The correct response is (C). The next integer larger than m would be represented by $m + 1$. As we are told, the sum of m and $m + 1$ must be greater than 10; therefore, we can set up the following inequality:

$$m + (m + 1) > 10$$

$2m + 1 > 10$ Combine like terms.

$2m + 1 - 1 > 10 - 1$ Place variables on one side and constants on the other.

$2m > 9$ Simplify.

$$\frac{2m}{2} > \frac{9}{2}$$ Divide both sides by the coefficient of the variable.

$m > 4.5$ Simplify.

The smallest integer greater than 4.5 is 5.

28. **(D)** The easiest way to do this problem is to consecutively consider each multiple of the largest number given (6) until we arrive at a number that is divisible by all the numbers.

6   not divisible by 5

12   not divisible by 5

18   not divisible by 5

24   not divisible by 5

30   not divisible by 4

36   not divisible by 5

42   not divisible by 5

48   not divisible by 5

54   not divisible by 5

60   divisible by 5, 4, and 3

$60 \div 6 = 10$

$60 \div 5 = 12$

$60 \div 4 = 15$

$60 \div 3 = 20$

A number is evenly divisible by another number when the second number divides into the first number without any remainder.

29. **(E)** Let U represent the units' digit and T represent the tens' digit. If the sum of the digits is 8, we can write the equation

$$U + T = 8$$

And, if the tens' digit is three times the units' digit, we can write the equation

$$3U = T$$

We now have two equations with two unknowns. Because we know that $T = 3U$, every place in the first equation where we see a T, we can substitute in $3U$. Thus,

$$U + T = 8 \quad \text{Original equation.}$$

$$U + 3U = 8 \quad \text{Substitute.}$$

$$4U = 8 \quad \text{Combine like terms.}$$

$$\frac{4U}{4} = \frac{8}{4} \quad \text{Divide both sides by the coefficient of the variable.}$$

$$U = 2 \quad \text{Thus the units' digit is 2.}$$

If the tens' digit is three times the units' digit, the tens' digit would be $3 \times 2 = 6$.

If the tens' digit is 6 and the units' digit is 2, the number is 62.

30. **(A)** Let $x = $ the smaller of the two integers. Then $x + 2 = $ the larger of the two integers. We are told their sum equals 26. Thus,

$$(x) + (x + 2) = 26$$

$$2x + 2 = 26 \quad \text{Combine like terms.}$$

$$2x + 2 - 2 = 26 - 2 \quad \text{Place variables on one side and constants on the other.}$$

$$2x = 24 \quad \text{Simplify.}$$

$$\frac{2x}{2} = \frac{24}{2}$$ Divide both sides by the coefficient of the variable.

$x = 12$ Simplify.

$x + 2 = 12 + 2 = 14$ Larger integer.

Thus, the numbers are 12 and 14 and their product is 168.

31. **(E)** We were told this is a number line, and on any number line numbers become greater as we move to the right. Thus, we know that $f > b$.

Additionally, because the letters represent consecutive integers and f is four spaces to the right of b, we know that $b + 4 = f$.

In the question, we were told that

$2b + f = 13$ Because we know that $b + 4 = f$, we can substitute.

$2b + (b + 4) = 13$ Substitute.

$3b + 4 = 13$ Combine like terms.

$3b + 4 - 4 = 13 - 4$ Place variables on one side and constants on the other.

$3b = 9$ Simplify.

$$\frac{3b}{3} = \frac{9}{3}$$ Divide both sides by the coefficient of the variable.

$b = 3$

32. **(D)** With n being the first odd number, it follows that $n + 2$ and $n + 4$ are the next two odd numbers. This eliminates answer choices (A) and (B) on the basis that each one of them represents only one of the two consecutive odd numbers that follow n. Since the sum of the three consecutive odd numbers is

$$n + (n + 2) + (n + 4) = 3n + 6,$$

it follows that neither of answer choices (C) nor (E) is correct, which leaves answer choice (D) as correct.

33. **(A)** If the smallest number is x, then

$$X + (X + 1) + (X + 2) + (X + 3) = 226,$$

giving $4X + 6 = 226.$

Therefore, $4X = 220$ or $X = 55$.

34. **(C)** If we want to prove a statement is false, we only have to give a counter example.

Let $p = 3$ and $q = 5$

$pq + 1 = 16$ (not prime)

$pq - 1 = 14$ (not prime)

Therefore, I and II are false. Since p and q are prime, they cannot possibly have a common factor. Thus, III is true.

35. **(B)** Since 7^9 and 11^{25} are both odd numbers, their sum is even. Thus, 2 is a divisor of $7^9 + 11^{25}$. Also, 2 is the smallest (least) prime.

36. **(B)** For the product of $(a + 3)$ $(a - 7)$ to be negative, one of the terms must be positive and the other must be negative. (Note: a negative multiplied by a negative is a positive, a positive multiplied by a positive is a positive, but a positive multiplied by a negative is a negative.)

In looking at the terms $(a + 3)$ and $(a - 7)$, we soon realize that $(a + 3)$ must always be greater than $(a - 7)$. (Regardless of what value we pick for a, adding 3 to it will also yield a greater number than subtracting 7 from it.)

Because $(a + 3)$ is a greater term, we want to find out the range of values for which $(a + 3)$ will be positive, which means $(a + 3)$ will be greater than 0. We can use an inequality.

$$a + 3 > 0$$

$a + 3 - 3 > 0 - 3$ Place constants on one side and variables on the other.

$a > -3$ Simplify.

Thus, if a is greater than -3, $a - 3$ will be positive.

Now we must find when $(a - 7)$ is negative, or less than 0.

$a - 7 < 0$

$a - 7 + 7 < 0 + 7$ Place constants on one side and variables on the other.

$a < 7$ Simplify.

Thus, if a is less than 7, $a - 7$ will be negative.

Thus, the product of $(a - 7)$ and $(a + 3)$ will be negative when $a < 7$ and $a > -3$. This can more clearly be expressed as $-3 < a < 7$.

The largest integer, therefore, that will yield a negative number for $(a - 7)$ and a positive number for $(a + 3)$ would be 6.

(If one tries to let $a = 7$, then $(a - 7) = 0$, which when multiplied by anything would yield a product of 0. If $a > 7$, then $(a - 7) > 0$ and $(a + 3) > 0$, which would yield a positive product.)

37. **(C)** $12 = 2 \times 2 \times 3$

$15 = 3 \times 5$

LCM $(12, 15) = 2 \times 2 \times 3 \times 5 = 60$

38. **(C)** Let x be the smallest number; this implies that the three consecutive numbers are x, $x + 1$, and $x + 2$. Therefore,

$(x + 1)^2 - 5(x + 2) = 3x + 7$

$x^2 + 2x + 1 - 5x - 10 = 3x + 7$

which leads to

$x^2 - 6x - 16 = 0$

or $\quad (x-8)(x+2)=0 \implies x=-2$ or 8.

But x cannot be a negative integer, so $x=8$ is the answer.

39. **(D)** If m and n are consecutive integers, and $m<n$, it follows that

$$n=m+1$$

Now, we can check each of the answer choices (A) through (E) as follows:

(A) $\quad n-m=(m+1)-m=m+1-m=1,$

which is odd. Thus, the statement in answer choice (A) is false.

(B) $\cdot$ Since no specific information is given about the integer m, m can be an odd integer or an even integer. So, the statement in answer choice (B) is false.

(C) $\quad m^2+n^2=m^2+(m+1)^2=m^2+m^2+2m+1$

$$=2m^2+2m+1$$

$$=2(m^2+m)+1$$

Since 2 times any integer (even or odd) yields an even integer, it follows that $2(m^2+m)$ is an even integer, and hence $2(m^2+m)+1$ is an odd integer. Hence, the statement in answer choice (C) is false.

(D) $\quad n^2-m^2-(m+1)^2-m^2=m^2+2m+1-m^2$

$$=2m+1$$

Again, since 2 times any integer (even or odd) yields an even integer, it follows that $2m$ is an even integer and $2m+1$ is always an odd integer. Hence, the statement in answer choice (D) is correct.

(E) Since m and n are any pair of two consecutive integers, it follows that m can be an even integer or an odd integer. Since $n=m+1$, it follows that if m is odd, then n is even and if m is even, then n is odd. Thus, the statement in answer choice (E) is false.

40. **(E)** I. An odd integer times two will become an even integer. An even integer times any number will remain even. The sum of two even numbers is also an even number.

Therefore, $2x + 3y$ must be even.

II.   An even integer times any number will remain even. Therefore, xy must be even.

III.   The sum of an odd integer and an even integer is odd. An odd integer minus one will become even. Therefore, $x + y - 1$ must be even.

41.   **(B)** Four consecutive integers can be represented by $2n$, $2n + 2$, $2n + 4$, and $2n + 6$.

$$(2n) + (2n + 2) + (2n + 4) + (2n + 6) = 68$$

$$8n + 12 = 68$$

$$8n = 56$$

$$2n = 14$$

Therefore, the value of the smallest one is 14.

42.   **(B)** For any integer n, $2n + 1$ as well as $2n - 1$ must always be odd integers and $2n + 2$ must always be even.

43.   **(C)** The mean IQ score of 100 is given. One standard deviation above the mean is 34% of the cases, with an IQ score up to 115. One standard deviation below the mean is another 34% of the cases, with an IQ score till 85. So, a total of 68% of the students have an IQ between 85 and 115. Therefore, $1,500 \times 0.68 = 1,020$.

44.   **(A)** $\$2,000 \times 0.35 = \$700$. The rest have wrong computations.

45.   **(C)** Find the sum of the seven days. Thus: M = 25; T = 30; W= 20; Th = 25; F = 10; Sat = 40; Sun = 0, or a total of 150 minutes. Find the average by dividing 150 by $7 = 21.43$ minutes.

Section 2

46.   **(B)** If each $\boxed{\$}$ stands for $12, only weeks 3 and 4 had a sale of $72 and $60, respectively. The rest are below $55.

47. **(C)** Total the number of credits earned (in this case, 16 credits). Multiply the credit and the weight for the earned grade per subject (e.g., biology = $5 \times 4 = 20$). Then add the total of the products of the credits and corresponding weights (in this case, 47). Then divide 47 by 16 to get the grade point average of 2.94. See table below.

$$\text{Biology} = 5 \times 4 = 20$$

$$\text{English} = 3 \times 2 = 6$$

$$\text{Math} = 3 \times 4 = 12$$

$$\text{French} = 3 \times 1 = 3$$

$$\text{P.E.} = \frac{2}{16} \text{ credit} \times 3 = \frac{6}{47} \text{ credit} \times \text{grade weight}$$

$$\text{GPA} = \frac{\text{total credit} \times \text{weight}}{\text{total credit}}$$

$$= \frac{47}{16} = 2.94$$

48. **(C)** In a normal distribution, half the data are always above the mean. Since 30,000 miles is the mean, half or 50% of the tires will last at least 30,000 miles.

49. **(D)** Nine is the square of an integer. 17, 11, and 15 are not squares of an integer; therefore, they are irrational numbers. 7 is not the cube of an integer; hence, it is an irrational number as well.

50. **(A)** 15 is used as a cardinal number. The rest are either ordinal (B) or nominal [(C), (D), (E)] numbers.

51. **(A)** $(10 + x)2 = 28$

$$20 + 2x = 28$$

$$2x = 28 - 20$$

$$2x = 8$$

$$x = \frac{8}{2}$$

$$x = 4$$

52. **(C)** Mode is the most frequent score. 81 appeared five times and is therefore the mode.

53. **(A)** Following the formula $z = \dfrac{x - \bar{x}}{\text{s.d.}}$, thus

$$1.6 = x - \frac{190}{11}$$

$$17.60 = x - 190$$

$$x = 190 + 17.60$$

$$x = 207.60 \text{ cm (Glenn's height)}$$

54. **(D)** First find the total sales for each year by reading the graph for the sales of (i) black and white televisions and (ii) color televisions. Then combine these numbers:

1950	$20,000,000 + $5,000,000 = $25,000,000
1960	$10,000,000 + $20,000,000 = $30,000,000
1970	$15,000,000 + $25,000,000 = $40,000,000
1980	$10,000,000 + $45,000,000 = $55,000,000
1990	$5,000,000 + $45,000,000 = $50,000,000

The greatest total sales occurred in 1980.

55. **(C)** According to the graph, the supply was greater than the demand in March and May only.

56. **(C)** Note that the numbers 4, 8, 12, 16, and 20 are the only numbers from 1 through 20 that are divisible by 4. The probability that a ball chosen from the jar has a number on it which is divisible by 4 is given by

$$\frac{\text{total number of balls with numbers that are divisible by 4}}{\text{total number of possible outcomes}} =$$

$$\frac{5}{20} = \frac{1}{4}.$$

57.   **(A)**   A prime number is an integer which is greater than one and which has no integer divisors other than 1 and itself. So, the prime numbers between 1 and 20 (not including 1 and 20) are 2, 3, 5, 7, 11, 13, 17, and 19. But 2 is not an odd number, so the odd primes between 1 and 20 are 3, 5, 7, 11, 13, 17, and 19. Hence, there are seven odd primes between 1 and 20.

58.   **(D)**   The list of all the negative integers between −9 and 5 is: −8, −7, −6, −5, −4, −3, −2, −1.

59.   **(E)**   A function is positive when the points on its graph lie above the x-axis. In our graph this occurs when x is between 1 and 5 or (1, 5).

60.   **(E)** π is an irrational number, while (A), (B), and (C) are all approximate rational values of π, and the statement (D) is vague.

61.   **(D)**   Since

$$(0.5)^2 = 0.25, (0.5)^4 = (0.25)^2 = 0.0625$$

$$(0.5)^6 = 0.015625 > 0.01$$

$$(0.5)^8 = (0.25)(0.015625) < 0.01$$

and n is an even integer, n must equal 8.

62.   **(C)**   Percents that are set up as proportions such as

$$\frac{\text{Percent}}{100} = \frac{\text{is}}{\text{of}}$$

or

$$\frac{\text{Percent}}{100} = \frac{\text{part}}{\text{whole}}$$

are the easiest to remember and solve. Identify the various parts of the proportion in the problem such as:

Percent = ?

"is" or "part" = 0.9

"of" or "whole" = 3.6

Now set up the proportion:

$$\frac{?}{100} = \frac{0.9}{3.6}$$

Simplify:

$$\frac{0.9}{3.6} = \frac{9}{36} = \frac{1}{4}$$

Therefore,

$$\frac{?}{100} = \frac{1}{4}$$

$$? = 25$$

63. **(E)** $\frac{1}{2}$ of $\frac{4}{5}$ is interpreted as:

$$\frac{1}{2} \times \frac{4}{5} = \frac{2}{5}$$

$\frac{2}{3}$ of 60% is translated into:

$$\frac{2}{3} \times \frac{60}{100} = \frac{2}{3} \times \frac{3}{5} = \frac{2}{5}$$

Following the problem then:

$$\frac{2}{5} \div \frac{2}{5} = 1$$

64. **(B)** Convert $33\frac{1}{3}\%$ into a fraction, remembering that the percent sign is equivalent to $\frac{1}{100}$.

Now, $\quad 33\frac{1}{3}\% = \frac{100}{3} \times \frac{1}{100} = \frac{1}{3}$

$$\frac{1}{3} = \frac{4}{12}$$

Therefore, there are 4 twelfths in $33\frac{1}{3}\%$.

65. **(D)** Since Neal was left with only $20.00 or $\frac{1}{4}$ of what he had originally, he must have spent 3($20.00) = $60.00 for his shirt. The cost of the shirt added to the $20.00 is $80.00 that he originally had.

66. **(D)** To make the problem easier to understand, first translate the phrase "the first piece is one-third the length of the second" into "the second piece is three times the first." Because the third piece is five times the first, the pieces are in a ratio of 1: 3 : 5. The board must be divided into nine equal parts of $\frac{1}{3}$ ft. which equals 4 inches. The longest piece takes five parts or 20 inches, which is:

$$\frac{20 \text{ inches}}{12 \text{ inches}} = 1\frac{2}{3} \text{ ft.}$$

67. **(B)** Complex fractions such as this one can be solved one of two ways. The first method would be to work on the numerator and denominator separately so they are each simplified to simple fractions, then treat them as a quotient of two fractions. Therefore,

$$\frac{\dfrac{1}{3}}{1+\dfrac{2}{4+5}} = \frac{\dfrac{1}{3}}{1+\dfrac{2}{9}}$$

$$= \frac{\dfrac{1}{3}}{\dfrac{11}{9}}$$

$$= \frac{1}{3} \times \frac{9}{11}$$

$$= \frac{3}{11}$$

In the second method, multiply every term by the common denominator (g) to cancel all of the denominators of the complex fraction, then work to simplify what is left:

$$\frac{\dfrac{1}{3}}{1+\dfrac{2}{4+5}} = \frac{\dfrac{1}{3}}{1+\dfrac{2}{9}}$$

$$= \frac{9 \times \dfrac{1}{3}}{(9 \times 1) + \left(9 \times \dfrac{2}{9}\right)}$$

$$= \frac{3}{9+2} = \frac{3}{11}$$

68. **(D)** One gross amounts to 144 cans. Since each set of three cans will cost \$8.00, and there are $\dfrac{144}{3} = 48$ sets, (48 sets) (\$8) = \$384.

69.   **(B)** In estimating an answer to the nearest hundred, round off to the nearest hundred all the numbers of the expression. This will create a much easier problem to simplify with less chance of a mistake.

$$\frac{(7,592)\ (4,892)}{(3,810)\ (70)}$$

is rounded off to:

$$\frac{(7,600)\ (4,900)}{(3,800)\ (100)} = (2)\ (49) = 98$$

98 rounded off to the nearest hundred is 100.

70.   **(C)** Because Sam is making two investments, first find $\frac{3}{5}$ of $1,000.

Divide $1,000 into five equal parts ($\frac{1,000}{5}$ = $200) and take three parts ($600).

$600 is invested at 6% simple interest, which yields:

$$\$600\ (6\%) = \$600\ (0.06) = \$36$$

The remaining $400 is invested at 8% simple interest, which yields:

$$\$400\ (8\%) = \$400\ (0.08) = \$32$$

The total interest earned is $36 + $32 = $68.

71.   **(D)** Prime factorize 156:

$$156 = 2 \times 78$$

$$= 2 \times 2 \times 39$$

$$= 2 \times 2 \times 3 \times 13$$

The largest prime factor of 156 is 13.

72.   **(E)** The most difficult part to deal with in a repeating decimal is the fact that it seemingly continues indefinitely. Eliminate this difficulty by eliminating the repeating portion of the decimal number using this algebraic method. Let:

$$x = 0.252525$$

and $$100x = 25.252525$$

By subtracting the first equation from the second, obtain:

$$100x = 25.252525...$$
$$- (x = 0.252525...)$$
$$\overline{99x = 25}$$

$$x = \frac{25}{99}$$

73.   **(A)** Let x = the numerator and $x + 4$ - the denominator. Therefore, the fraction is expressed as:

$$\frac{x}{x+4}$$

When the numerator is doubled and the denominator is increased by five, the expression for the new fraction is:

$$\frac{2x}{(x+4)+5}$$

Now set up the equation and solve for x:

$$\frac{2x}{x+9} = \frac{1}{2}$$

$$4x = x+9$$

$$3x = 9$$

$$x = 3$$

$$x+4 = 7$$

The original fraction is $\dfrac{3}{7}$.

74. **(E)** When evaluating an expression without grouping symbols to indicate what operation should be done first, always do all multiplication and division first as they appear from left to right, then do any addition or subtraction, again as they appear from left to right. Therefore,

$$48 - 24 \div 3 + 5 \times 2 = 48 - 8 + 10$$

$$= 40 + 10 = 50$$

75. **(D)** First, change all the numbers to the same form and simplify:

$$7.5 \times 1\frac{7}{9} - 1.3333... = 7\frac{1}{2} \times \frac{16}{9} - 1\frac{1}{3}$$

$$= \frac{15}{2} \times \frac{16}{9} - \frac{4}{3}$$

$$= \frac{240}{18} - \frac{4}{3}$$

$$= \frac{240}{18} - \frac{24}{18}$$

$$= \frac{216}{18}$$

$$= 12$$

76. **(B)** To solve any equation, use some simple rules of algebra. First, get the like terms on one side of the equation, then simplify to solve for the variable.

$$2x - 7 = 3x + 2$$

becomes

$$2x - 3x = 2 + 7$$

$$-x = 9 \text{ or } x = -9$$

77.　**(D)**　Of the 25 chemistry students, 7 are also in physics. There are 23 − 7 = 16 remaining students taking only physics. Therefore, 25 + 16 = 41 individual students are enrolled in the two science classes.

78.　**(C)**　Because this is a rate of work problem, consider what fraction of the job would get done in one minute. Scott would get 1/30th of the job done while Henri would get 1/60th of the job done in one minute. Together, they would get:

$$\frac{1}{30} + \frac{1}{60} = \frac{2}{60} + \frac{1}{60} = \frac{3}{60} = \frac{1}{20}$$

of the job done in one minute. Therefore, 20 minutes would be needed to pot 100 plants, and 40 minutes to pot all 200 plants.

79.　**(B)**　The 20 students that actually went to the play were assessed an additional $20.00 total to cover the remaining cost of the bus when the other five students decided not to go. Therefore, each of the five students were paying $4.00 for their share of the bus rental along with the other 20 students.

$$(\$4.00)\ (25\ students) = \$100.00$$

was the cost of the bus rental.

80.　**(E)**　The least common multiple or LCM of $18x$ and $24xy$ is the smallest number that both of these numbers can divide into evenly without a remainder. To find the LCM, prime factorize $18x$ and $24xy$ into:

$$18x = (2)\ (3)\ (3)\ (x)$$

$$24xy = (2)\ (2)\ (2)\ (3)\ (x)\ (y)$$

Now, take the largest group of each number and variable represented. Of the 2's, the larger group is the (2) (2) (2) from the $24xy$. Of the 3's, the larger group is the (3) (3) from the $18x$. There is also one x and one y to be represented. Therefore, the LCM of $18x$ and $24xy$ is (2) (2) (2) (3) (3) (xy) = $72xy$.

The LCM may also be calculated by a modified form of long division, as follows:

$$6x \mid 18x \quad 24xy$$

$$3x \mid 3 \quad 4y$$

$$4y \mid 1 \quad 4y$$

$$1$$

Then $(6x)(3)(4y) = 72xy$.

81. **(D)** The floor that measures 10 ft. by 20 ft. has an area of 10×20 = 200 sq. ft. The tiles with 36 sq. in. of area must measure 6 in. by 6 in. or $\frac{1}{2}$ ft. by $\frac{1}{2}$ ft. for $\frac{1}{4}$ sq. ft. of area. Because it would take four tiles to cover 1 sq. ft., $4 \times (200$ sq. ft.$) = 800$ tiles would be needed to cover the entire floor.

82. **(C)** There will be a total of 18 people for dinner, Jann and her 17 guests. Doubling her recipe will serve only 16 people, so another $\frac{1}{4}$ of the recipe must be included to feed the remaining two people. Jann needs to increase her recipe to $2\frac{1}{4}$ times the original.

83. **(A)** Ninety miles in two hours is equivalent to 45 miles in one hour (60 minutes) or 45 mph. If Lance has only 1.5 hours or 90 minutes to cover the same 90 miles when he returns, he needs to travel one mile a minute, which translates into 60 mph, 15 mph faster than his original speed.

84. **(B)** The car traveling 55 mph can get to the halfway point 330 miles away in $\frac{330}{55} = 6$ hours. The 40 mph car covers the same distance in $\frac{330}{40} = 8\frac{1}{4}$ hours. The faster car will have to wait:

$$8\frac{1}{4} - 6 = 2\frac{1}{4} \text{ hours}$$

85. **(D)** Using some algebraic expressions to represent the unknown should help here. Let:

x = the number of children in the original group

$6x$ = the number of cookies in the package.

When two more children join the group, the expressions are:

$x + 2$ = the number of children

$4(x + 2)$ = the number of cookies in the package.

Notice that there are two expressions for "the number of cookies in the package." These are equivalent expressions, so setup an equation and solve for x.

$$6x = 4(x + 2)$$

$$6x = 4x + 8$$

$$2x = 8$$

$$x = 4$$

86. **(D)** The circumference of the wheel is:

$$C = 2\pi \ (1 \text{ ft.})$$

$$C = 2\left(\frac{22}{7}\right) = \frac{44}{7} \text{ ft.}$$

To find the number of revolutions the wheel takes, calculate:

$$5{,}280 \div \frac{44}{7} = 5{,}280 \times \frac{7}{44}$$

$$= 120 \times 7 = 840 \text{ revolutions}$$

87. **(B)** Because the indicated operation in this problem is addition, find the two expressions that are to be added together. Let:

$$x = \text{Derek's age}$$

$$\frac{17}{2}x = \text{Mike's age}$$

Now add the expressions for a sum of 38.

$$\frac{17}{2}x + x = 38$$

$$17x + 2x = 76$$

$$19x = 78$$

$$x = 4$$

Derek is 4-years-old, and Mike is $38 - 4 = 34$-years-old.

88. **(B)** Set up the inequality in mathematical symbols and solve.

$$3x - 4 > 6$$

$$3x > 6 + 4$$

$$3x > 10$$

$$x > \frac{10}{3}$$

89. **(D)** x represents Sandy's age four years ago. Therefore, she is now $x + 4$ years old. Adding another four years to $x + 4$, in other words, $(x + 4) + 4$, will yield $x + 8$ as Sandy's age four years from now.

90. **(D)** Use the distributive property and collect like terms:

$$6(x - 2) - 4(x + 4) = 6x - 12 - 4x - 16$$

$$= 2x - 28$$

$$= 2(x - 14) \qquad \text{(in factored form)}$$

PRACTICE
TEST 3

CLEP COLLEGE MATHEMATICS
Test 3

(Answer sheets appear in the back of the book.)

Section 1

TIME: 45 Minutes
33 Questions

DIRECTIONS: Each of the questions below is followed by five suggested answers. Complete the question and select the answer that is best.

1. The angles of a triangle are in a ratio of 3 : 5 : 10. How many degrees is the largest angle?

    (A) 10   (D) 150

    (B) 18   (E) 180

    (C) 100

2. *ABCD* is a square. Given that $s = 2$, find its total area.

    (A) 8   (D) 12

    (B) 6   (E) 16

    (C) 4

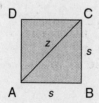

3. Find the area of the polygon.

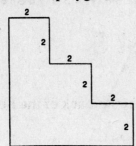

(A) 8   (D) 24

(B) 12   (E) 30

(C) 20

4. Triangles *ABC* and *A'B'C'* are similar right triangles. Find the length of side *AC*.

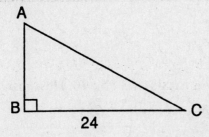   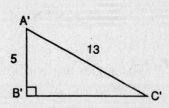

(A) 10   (D) 16

(B) 12   (E) 26

(C) 13

5. A cylindrical can measures 4.2 inches in height. Its circular bases of $1\frac{1}{2}$ inch radii are removed, and the cylinder is cut open from top to bottom. What is the surface area of the cylinder? (Use 3.14 for π.)

(A) $9\frac{3}{7}$ sq. in.   (D) $1\frac{4}{7}$ sq. in.

(B) 6.3 sq. in.   (E) 66 sq. in.

(C) 39.6 sq. in.

6. In the diagram, the triangle is isosceles, how many degrees is *x*?

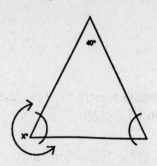

(A) 70   (D) 290

(B) 110   (E) 320

(C) 140

7. Line *AB* is a straight line. The measure of angle *CEB* is eight times the measure of angle *AED*. Find the degree measure of angle *DEB*.

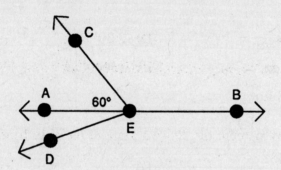

(A) 15   (D) 165

(B) 60   (E) 175

(C) 120

8. Find the area of the isosceles trapezoid.

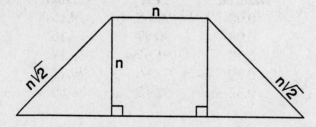

(A) n^2　　　　　　　　　　(D) $4n$

(B) $2n^2$　　　　　　　　　　(E) $4n + 2n \sqrt{2}$

(C) $4n^2$

9. How much more did Kristen's weight increase during the first 6 months as compared to her second 6 months?

QUESTIONS 9 and 10 refer to the following chart.

Kristen's Growth Chart

Age in months	Birth	6	12	18
Length in inches	20	$27\frac{1}{2}$	$30\frac{3}{4}$	33
Weight in lbs./oz.	$\frac{7}{4}$	$\frac{19}{15}$	$\frac{22}{6}$	$\frac{24}{8}$

(A) 10 lbs. 4 oz.　　　　　　(D) 7 lbs. 8 oz.

(B) 2 lbs. 5 oz.　　　　　　　(E) 4 lbs. 4 oz.

(C) 12 lbs. 11 oz.

10. By how many percent did Kristen's height increase from birth to 18 months of age?

(A) 13　　　　　　　　　　(D) 65

(B) 22　　　　　　　　　　(E) 75

(C) 42

QUESTIONS 11-12 refer to the following.

	Rainfall	Year	Normal
Monday	0.08	90.88	79.15
Tuesday	0.09	90.97	79.16
Wednesday	0.70	91.67	79.17
Thursday	0.19	91.86	79.17
Friday	0.32	92.18	79.50

11. Find the average rainfall for the week.

    (A) 1.38

    (B) 0.276

    (C) 0.32

    (D) 0.237

    (E) 0.138

12. Using Monday's reading and rounding off to the nearest one percent, the year-to-date record is what percent of the normal reading?

    (A) 13

    (B) 15

    (C) 87

    (D) 105

    (E) 115

13. Joan won at tennis four out of six matches. What percentage did she win?

    (A) $33\frac{1}{3}\%$

    (B) $66\frac{2}{3}\%$

    (C) 40%

    (D) 60%

    (E) 80%

14. Simplify $38 + (-17) + 91 + (-58)$.

    (A) 204

    (B) 58

    (C) -54

    (D) -58

    (E) 54

15. ABOUT how much is 75% of $9.89?

    (A) $75.00

    (B) $7.50

    (C) $5.00

    (D) $2.50

    (E) $6.00

16. Alex's grades in math class were 90, 75, 100, 60, and 75. Find the mean.

    (A) 400   (D) 100

    (B) 75   (E) 60

    (C) 80

17. What would Sammy's score on the next algebra test have to be to have an average of 95? His grades so far are 93, 100, 92, and 100.

    (A) 95   (D) 90

    (B) 93   (E) 100

    (C) 96

18. Laura spent $3.89 for milk, $1.29 for bread, and $4.99 for lunchmeat. Lana spent $3.45 for milk, $1.39 for bread, and $5.50 for lunchmeat. Who spent more and how much more?

    (A) Laura spent 27 cents more.

    (B) Lana spent 27 cents more.

    (C) Laura spent 17 cents more.

    (D) Lana spent 17 cents more.

    (E) They spent the same amount.

19. A sports car lease is $621 per month. This is 8% more than the lease for last year's model. How much was the monthly lease last year?

    (A) $670.68   (D) $575.00

    (B) $571.32   (E) $579.32

    (C) $613.00

20. Harry bought a sofa priced at $995 and a chair priced at $149. The sales tax is 8%. How much must he pay for the sofa and chair and tax?

    (A) $1,144   (D) $1,224.72

    (B) $91.52   (E) $1,235.52

    (C) $1,134

21. Juan found a portable TV that normally costs $225, but now it is on sale at 30% off. What is the sale price?

    (A) $157.50   (D) $195.00

    (B) $67.50   (E) Not enough information is given.

    (C) $199.95

22. A shirt sold at a 20% discount. The sale price was $36. What was the original price before the sale?

    (A) $43.20   (D) $39.95

    (B) $45.00   (E) $49.95

    (C) $56.00

23. Mountain High has 245 sophomores. Sixty percent have brown eyes. What percent of them do NOT have brown eyes?

    (A) 60%   (D) 98%

    (B) 40%   (E) 50%

    (C) 147%

24. John was looking for the smallest wrench in his tool box. If he has five wrenches, and the sizes are $\frac{1}{2}$ inch, $\frac{3}{8}$ inch, $\frac{7}{8}$ inch, $\frac{3}{4}$ inch, and $\frac{9}{16}$ inch, then which is smallest?

    (A) $\frac{1}{2}$ in.   (D) $\frac{3}{4}$ in.

    (B) $\frac{3}{8}$ in.   (E) $\frac{9}{16}$ in.

    (C) $\frac{7}{8}$ in.

25. There are 650 seniors at Warm Weather High School. What percentage of the seniors are girls if 351 of the seniors are boys?

   (A) 85.1%   (D) 54%

   (B) 2.17%   (E) 299%

   (C) 46%

26. Jerry wanted to buy a new pickup truck. In his hometown he found one he liked for $11,558, but the sales tax in his state is 6% on vehicles. He lived near another state with lower sales tax. He found a truck there for $11,599. How much would it cost him to buy it in the next state?

   (A) $12,251.48   (D) $12,062.95

   (B) $12,294.94   (E) Not enough information is given.

   (C) $12,178.95

27. Shawn bought a 10-foot board. He found it actually measured 9 feet $11\frac{5}{8}$ inches. He cut off a piece exactly $5\frac{1}{2}$ feet long. How much is left?

   (A) $4\frac{1}{2}$ ft.   (D) 5 ft. $5\frac{5}{8}$ in.

   (B) 4 ft. 6 in.   (E) 4 ft. $6\frac{5}{8}$ in.

   (C) 4 ft. $5\frac{5}{8}$ in.

28. Robert is doing a population study and needs to find 36.59% of 11,356. He should multiply 11,356 by

   (A) 36.59   (D) 0.03659

   (B) 3.659   (E) 365.9

   (C) 0.3659

29. Solve for the value of x: $4x + 7 = 27$

    (A) $\dfrac{27}{4}$ (D) 5

    (B) $\dfrac{17}{2}$ (E) –5

    (C) 4

30. $\dfrac{1}{4}x + 3 = 15$

    (A) $15\dfrac{1}{4}$ (D) 12

    (B) $12\dfrac{1}{4}$ (E) 48

    (C) 3

31. Evaluate the expression $x^2 + 2x - y + 3$ when $x = -2$ and $y = 3$.

    (A) –5   (D) –3

    (B) 3   (E) 5

    (C) 0

32. Simplify $15 - 4(x + 2) + (6x + 2)$.

    (A) $2x + 7$ (D) $10x + 9$

    (B) $2x + 9$ (E) $2x + 25$

    (C) $10x + 25$

33. Laura went cruising in her motor boat. She cruised for 2 hours and 20 minutes and found she had traveled 21 nautical miles. What was her speed to the nearest knot? (One knot = one nautical mile in one hour.)

    (A) 7 knots   (D) 9 knots

    (B) $2\dfrac{1}{3}$ knots   (E) 49 knots

    (C) 21 knots

34. Multiply $(x + 1)(4x + 3)$.

    (A) $4x^2 + 4$ (D) $4x^2 + 7x + 3$

    (B) $4x^2 + 3$ (E) $4x^2 - 7x - 4$

    (C) $4x^2 + 4x + 3$

35. Multiply $10(-3w + 2)$.

    (A) $30w + 2$ (D) $-30w - 20$

    (B) $-30w + 2$ (E) $-30w + 20$

    (C) $-30w - 2$

36. The sum of an even integer and twice the next consecutive even integer is 40. To find the integers, which equation represents the correct solution?

    (A) $x \times x = 40$ (D) $x(x + 2) = 40$

    (B) $x(x + 1) = 40$ (E) $x + 2(x + 2) = 40$

    (C) $x + 2(x + 1) = 40$

37. Factor completely $x^4 - 81$.

    (A) $(x^2 + 9)(x^2 + 9)$ (D) $(x^2 + 9)(x + 3)(x - 3)$

    (B) $(x^2 + 9)(x^2 - 9)$ (E) $(x^2 - 9)(x^2 - 9)$

    (C) $(x^2 + 9)(x - 3)(x - 3)$

38. The students were having a bake sale at Mountain Elementary School. Maria baked $5\frac{1}{2}$ dozen cookies. Her little brother ate $\frac{1}{3}$ of a dozen of them. How many cookies did Maria have left to take to the bake sale?

    (A) 62   (D) 63

    (B) 60   (E) 52

    (C) 66

39. Sam Sanchez got a new compact car. His car can go 100 miles on 3 gallons of gas. He drove 300 miles on a weekend trip. How many gallons of gas did he use?

    (A) 100 gal.   (D) 3 gal.

    (B) 33 gal.   (E) 10 gal.

    (C) 9 gal.

40. Factor $x^2 - 6x + 9$.

    (A) $x(x + 6)$ (D) $(x + 3)^2$

    (B) $(x + 3)(x + 3)$ (E) $(x + 3)(x - 3)$

    (C) $(x - 3)^2$

41. George took his dog for three long walks Saturday. First, they walked 1 mile, then they walked 720 yards, and for the last walk, they walked 3,500 feet. How many feet did they walk?

    (A) 4,221 ft.   (D) 11,340 ft.

    (B) 9,500 ft.   (E) 10,660 ft.

    (C) 3,780 ft.

42. $g(x) = x^2 + 4$, find $g(-3)$.

    (A) -3 (D) 3

    (B) 4   (E) 13

    (C) -5

43. Fresh pears are two pounds for $0.96. How much would three pounds cost?

    (A) $5.76   (D) $1.44

    (B) $4.80   (E) $1.50

    (C) $0.48

44. Bowling Balls Unlimited wants to know how much to sell their new shipment of bowling balls for if they bought them for $68.00 each?

$S = (p \times 1.6) + \$4.00$, where S = selling price and p = purchase price

(A) $73.60

(D) $112.80

(B) $108.80

(E) $272.00

(C) $278.40

45. What is the name of this figure?

(A) Rectangle

(D) Hexagon

(B) Trapezoid

(E) Heptagon

(C) Pentagon

Section 2

TIME: 45 Minutes
33 Questions

DIRECTIONS: Each of the questions below is followed by five suggested answers. Complete the question and select the answer that is best.

46. Classify this triangle.

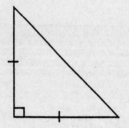

(A) Scalene   (D) Equilateral

(B) Isosceles   (E) Acute

(C) Obtuse

47. What is the measure of angle Q?

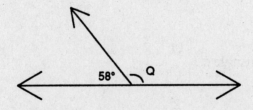

(A) 58°   (D) 32°

(B) 100°   (E) 180°

(C) 122°

48. What is the measure of angle *A*?

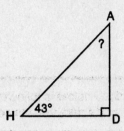

(A) 43°   (D) 137°

(B) 47°   (E) 57°

(C) 90°

49. Line *a* is parallel to line *b*. Angle *BFE* measures 80°. What is the measure of angle *CGF*?

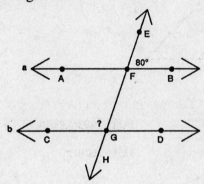

(A) 100°   (D) 20°

(B) 80°   (E) 120°

(C) 180°

50. How many degrees is angle *X*?

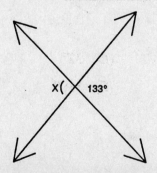

(A) 47°   (D) 223°

(B) 360°   (E) 133°

(C) 180°

51. $\overline{AB}$ is perpendicular to $\overline{BC}$. How many degrees is angle ABD?

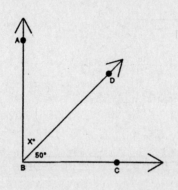

(A) 90°   (D) 40°

(B) 30°   (E) 130°

(C) 60°

52. In triangle ABC what is the measure of angle B?

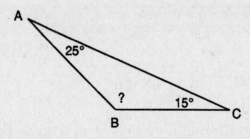

(A) 140°   (D) 40°

(B) 25°   (E) 100°

(C) 15°

53. What is the volume, in cubic centimeters, of this cylinder?

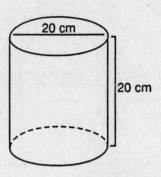

(A) 6,280 cu. cm.   (D) 200 cu. cm.

(B) 25,120 cu. cm.   (E) 628 cu. cm.

(C) 400 cu. cm.

54. Mary wants to cover a small chest with contact paper. The chest is 24" × 12" × 10". How much contact paper is needed?

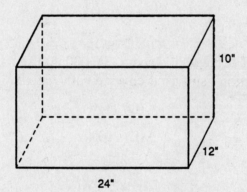

(A) 5 sq. ft.   (D) $1\frac{2}{3}$ sq. ft.

(B) 4 sq. ft.   (E) 720 sq. ft.

(C) 9 sq. ft.

QUESTIONS 55 and 56 refer to the following pie chart.

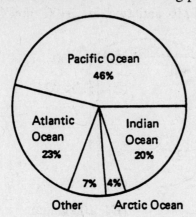

55. The total area of our world's oceans is about 140,000,000 square miles. What is the area of the Pacific Ocean?

    (A) 46,000,000 sq. mi.   (D) 86,000,000 sq. mi.

    (B) 64,400,000 sq. mi.   (E) 6,440,000 sq. mi.

    (C) 94,000,000 sq. mi.

56. The total area of our world is about 200,000,000 square miles. What percent of our world's surface is covered with water?

    (A) 7%   (D) 28%

    (B) 70%   (E) 60%

    (C) 14%

57. Simplify $4x^4 \times x^6$.

    (A) $4x^{10}$ (D) $24x^4$

    (B) $4x^{24}$ (E) x^{22}

    (C) $16x^{10}$

58. A travel agent earns 10% commission on each ticket sold. If the agent sold one ticket for $210 and two for $400, how much would his commission be?

(A) $18.60

(D) $80.00

(B) $21.00

(E) $101.00

(C) $40.00

59. What percent of 80 is 32?

(A) 40%

(D) 25%

(B) 0.4%

(E) 400%

(C) 2.5%

60. Medical insurance costs Maria $26.03 per week. What is the annual cost?

(A) $312.36

(D) $104.12

(B) $1,301.50

(E) $1,367.60

(C) $1,353.56

61. Sally entered a certain sweepstakes eight times. There were 1,600 entries. What are her chances of winning?

(A) 0.5%

(D) 12.8%

(B) 5%

(E) 128%

(C) 50%

62. Samantha works at a clothing store. Employees are given a 20% discount on clothes they buy there. Last year she spent $592.86 on clothes there. What was her annual benefit (employee discount)?

(A) $592.86

(D) $118.57

(B) $612.86

(E) $711.43

(C) $474.29

63. George and Mary open a savings account with $550 in it. They earn 8.2% annual interest if they leave the money in the account for one full year. How much will they have at the end of one year?

(A) $45.10

(D) $1,091.20

(B) $595.10

(E) $451.00

(C) $541.20

64. There are 90 students in the junior class at Mountain High School. Of these, 36 are girls. What percent are boys?

(A) 36%

(D) 60%

(B) 54%

(E) Not enough information is given.

(C) 40%

65. Solve $x + 35 = 70$ for x.

(A) 105

(D) −35

(B) 35

(E) 2

(C) −105

66. Johnny has 17 marbles. Mary has twice as many marbles as Johnny and half as many as Joe. How many marbles does Mary have?

(A) 9

(D) 17

(B) 43

(E) Not enough information is given.

(C) 34

67. Solve for x: $12x = 156$.

(A) 144

(D) 15

(B) −13

(E) −15

(C) 13

68. Taxi fare from a large hotel to the airport is $15. How much would a taxi driver earn if he made ten trips to the airport, but had to return to the hotel without a fare?

    (A) $1.50   (D) $150.00

    (B) $25.00   (E) $300.00

    (C) $15.00

69. Multiply $(x + 1)(3x + 4)$.

    (A) $3x^2 + 5$ (D) $3x^2 - 7x + 5$

    (B) $3x^2 + 4$ (E) $3x^2 + 7x + 4$

    (C) $3x^2 - 7x - 4$

70. Apples are two pounds for $0.98. How much would five pounds cost?

    (A) $9.80   (D) $2.45

    (B) $4.90   (E) $0.49

    (C) $1.96

71. Multiply $7(-4y + 2)$.

    (A) $28y + 2$ (D) $-42y$

    (B) $28y + 14$ (E) $-28y + 14$

    (C) $-14y$

72. An airplane made a six-hour trip with the wind blowing in the same direction as the airplane. The return flight against the wind took eight hours. What was the speed of the airplane in still air?

    (A) 420 km./hr.   (D) 400 km./hr.

    (B) 480 km./hr.   (E) 500 km./hr.

    (C) 360 km./hr.

73. $f(x) = -x + 4$, find $f(-3)$.

(A) -3 (D) 3

(B) 4   (E) 7

(C) 1

74. Simplify $\dfrac{x^{11}}{x^4}$.

(A) x^{44} (D) $\dfrac{1}{x^4}$

(B) x^7 (E) $\dfrac{1}{x^7}$

(C) x^6

75. Factor $x^4 - 1$.

(A) $(x^2 + 1)(x^2 + 1)$ (D) $(x^2 + 1)(x + 1)(x - 1)$

(B) $(x^2 + 1)(x^2 - 1)$ (E) $(x^2 - 1)(x^2 - 1)$

(C) $(x^2 + 1)(x - 1)(x - 1)$

76. Factor $x^2 + 6x + 9$.

(A) $x(x + 6)$ (D) $(x - 3)^2$

(B) $(x - 3)(x - 3)$ (E) $(x - 3)(x + 3)$

(C) $(x + 3)^2$

77. What is the measure of angle R?

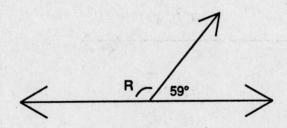

(A) 59°   (D) 31°

(B) 100°   (E) 180°

(C) 121°

78. What is the measure of angle *S* as shown in the figure below?

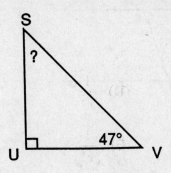

(A) 43°   (D) 54°

(B) 47°   (E) 133°

(C) 90°

79. What is the measure of exterior angle *ACD* as shown in the figure below?

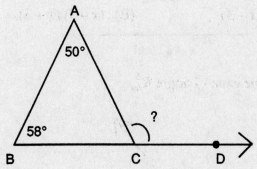

(A) 58°   (D) 108°

(B) 50°   (E) 130°

(C) 72°

80. The figure below shows two parallel lines *l* and *m*. Line *H* is intersecting both lines *l* and *m*. Angle *GEB* measures 40°. What is the measure of angle *CFE*?

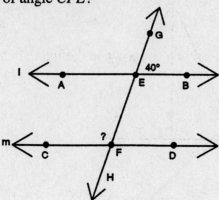

(A) 40°

(B) 180°

(C) 140°

(D) 120°

(E) Not enough information is given.

81. Ira has enough seed to plant a garden of 220 square feet. He has a place 20 feet long to put the garden. How wide must it be to have exactly 220 square feet?

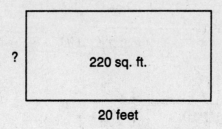

(A) 20 ft.

(B) 10 ft.

(C) 12 ft.

(D) 11 ft.

(E) 9.5 ft.

82. What is the height (altitude) of an equilateral triangle with the length of a side 6 centimeters?

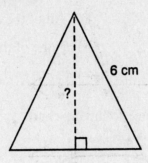

6 cm

?

(A) $3\sqrt{2}$ cm.

(D) 9 cm.

(B) $3\sqrt{3}$ cm.

(E) 3 cm.

(C) 6 cm.

QUESTIONS 83 and 85 refer to the following bar graph. The graph shows the amount of real estate sold by the XYZ Company.

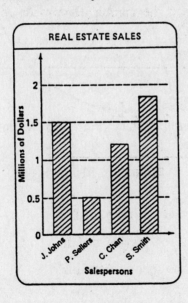

REAL ESTATE SALES

Millions of Dollars

Salespersons

83. Which salesperson sold $1,500,000 worth of real estate?

(A) J. Johns

(D) S. Smith

(B) P. Sellers

(E) None of the above.

(C) C. Chan

84. Which person sold about three times the amount of property as P. Sellers?

(A) J. Johns

(D) All of the above.

(B) C. Chan

(E) None of the above.

(C) S. Smith

QUESTIONS 85-87 refer to the following chart.

MYRNA'S MONTHLY BUDGET

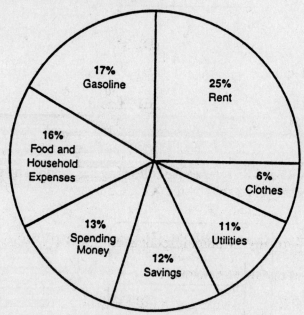

85. If Myrna makes a monthly salary of $2,500.00, how much will she spend on rent in one year?

(A) $7,500

(D) $156.25

(B) $625

(E) $2,500

(C) $32,500

86. What percentage does she spend for utilities?

(A) 275%

(D) 16%

(B) 11%

(E) 13%

(C) 132%

87. What amount does she save each month?

(A) $12

(D) $1,200

(B) $300

(E) $325

(C) $3,600

88. Simplify $\left(\dfrac{x^2}{y}\right)^5$.

(A) $\dfrac{x^2}{y^5}$

(D) x^8

(B) $\dfrac{x^7}{y}$

(E) $\dfrac{x^{10}}{y^5}$

(C) $\dfrac{x^7}{y^5}$

89. I filled $\dfrac{2}{3}$ of my swimming pool with 1,800 ft³. What is the total capacity of my swimming pool?

(A) 2,400 ft³

(D) 3,600 ft³

(B) 2,700 ft³

(E) 3,200 ft³

(C) 3,000 ft³

90. A jug will hold $\dfrac{2}{3}$ gallon of punch. How much punch is in the jug when it is $\dfrac{3}{4}$ full?

(A) $\dfrac{5}{7}$ gallon

(D) $\dfrac{2}{3}$ gallon

(B) $\dfrac{1}{2}$ gallon

(E) $\dfrac{1}{12}$ gallon

(C) $\dfrac{1}{4}$ gallon

CLEP COLLEGE MATHEMATICS
TEST 3

ANSWER KEY

Section 1

1. (C)	10. (D)	19. (D)	28. (C)	37. (D)
2. (C)	11. (B)	20. (E)	29. (D)	38. (A)
3. (D)	12. (E)	21. (A)	30. (E)	39. (C)
4. (E)	13. (B)	22. (B)	31. (C)	40. (C)
5. (C)	14. (E)	23. (B)	32. (B)	41. (D)
6. (D)	15. (B)	24. (B)	33. (D)	42. (E)
7. (D)	16. (C)	25. (C)	34. (D)	43. (D)
8. (B)	17. (D)	26. (E)	35. (E)	44. (D)
9. (A)	18. (D)	27. (C)	36. (E)	45. (D)

Section 2

46. (B)	55. (B)	64. (D)	73. (E)	82. (B)
47. (C)	56. (B)	65. (B)	74. (B)	83. (A)
48. (B)	57. (A)	66. (C)	75. (D)	84. (A)
49. (A)	58. (E)	67. (C)	76. (C)	85. (A)
50. (E)	59. (A)	68. (D)	77. (C)	86. (B)
51. (D)	60. (C)	69. (E)	78. (A)	87. (B)
52. (A)	61. (A)	70. (D)	79. (D)	88. (E)
53. (A)	62. (D)	71. (E)	80. (C)	89. (B)
54. (C)	63. (B)	72. (A)	81. (D)	90. (B)

DETAILED EXPLANATIONS
OF ANSWERS

TEST 3

Section 1

1.   **(C)** The ratio 3 : 5 : 10 indicates that the 180° of the triangle must be divided into 3 + 5 + 10 = 18 equal parts or 10° for each part. The largest angle is made up of ten 10° parts or 100°.

2.   **(C)** The area, A, of square ABCD, with side s, is given by the formula $A = s^2$. Since $s = 2$, the area of the square is 4. The corollary to this theorem is that the area of a square of diagonal z is equal to one-half the square of z.

3.   **(D)** The polygon can be divided into three rectangles whose areas are easy to calculate by using the formula: area = (length) (width).

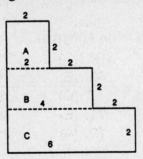

Rectangle A = 2(2) = 4

Rectangle B = 2(4) = 8

Rectangle C = 2(6) = 12

The sum $4 + 8 + 12 = 24$ is the area of the polygon.

4.   **(E)** The sides of similar triangles are in proportion. Using the Pythagorean Theorem the length of $B'C'$ is:

$$5^2 + (B'C')^2 = 13^2$$

$$25 + (B'C')^2 = 169$$

$$(B'C')^2 = 144$$

$$B'C' = 12$$

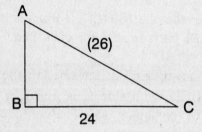

BC and B'C' are corresponding sides of similar triangles in a ratio of 24:12 or 2:1. Similarly, side AC and $A'C'$ have the same ratio; AC must be twice as long as $A'C'$. In other words, $AC = 2 (13) = 26$.

5.   **(C)** When the can is cut open and flattened out, its shape will be a rectangle.

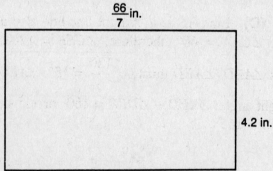

The length, which is the circumference of the circular base, is:

$$C = 2\pi \text{ (radius)}$$

$$C + 2\pi \left(\frac{3}{2} \text{ inches}\right)$$

$$C = 3\pi$$

$$C = 3\frac{22}{7} = \frac{66}{7}$$

The area of the rectangle is (length) (width):

$$A = \left(\frac{66}{7}\right)(4.2)$$

$$A = (66.6)(0.6) = 39.6 \text{ sq. in.}$$

6. **(D)** The diagram is of an isosceles triangle, as indicated by the two equal base angles.

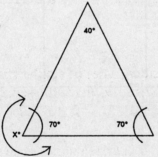

7. **(D)** Line *AB* is a straight line and also a straight angle measuring 180°. ∠*CEA* = 60°, therefore, ∠*CEB* = 120°. Because ∠*CEB* is eight times ∠*AED*, ∠*AED* must be $\frac{120}{5}$ = 15°. ∠*AED* and ∠*DEB* form another straight angle: ∠*AED* + ∠*DEB* = 180° or 15° + ∠*DEB* = 180°. Therefore, ∠*DEB* = 165°.

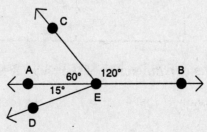

8.　　**(B)**　The formula for the area of a trapezoid is:

$$A = \frac{1}{2} \text{ (height) (first base + second base)}.$$

To find the length of the second base, use the Pythagorean Theorem to find the bases of the two congruent triangles on either side of the square.

$$(\text{base})^2 + n^2 = (n\sqrt{2})^2$$

$$(\text{base})^2 + n^2 = 2n^2$$

$$\text{base}^2 = n^2$$

$$\text{base} = n$$

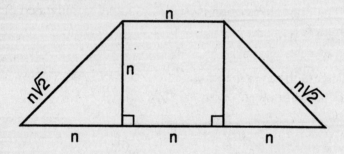

The base of the trapezoid is $3n$. Using the area formula:

$$A = \frac{1}{2}(n)(n + 3n)$$

$$A = \frac{1}{2}(n)(4n)$$

$$A = 2n^2$$

9.　　**(A)**　In the first six months, Kristen's weight gain is:

19 lbs. 15 oz. − 7 lbs. 4 oz. = 12 lbs. 11 oz.

During the following six months, her weight gain is:

22 lbs. 6 oz. − 19 lbs. 15 oz. = 21 lbs. 22 oz. − 19 lbs. 15 oz.

= 2 lbs. 7 oz.

Therefore, Kristen gained:

12 lbs. 11 oz. − 2 lbs. 7 oz. = 10 lbs. 4 oz. more.

10. **(D)** Kristen grew 13 inches in 18 months. Setting up a proportion yields the following:

$$\frac{percent}{100} = \frac{13}{20}$$

$$percent = \frac{13}{20}(100)$$

$$percent = 65$$

11. **(B)** To find the average rainfall for the week, add the five amounts in the "rainfall" column, then divide by five.

$$\frac{0.08 + 0.09 + 0.70 + 0.19 + 0.32}{5} = \frac{1.38}{5}$$

$$= 0.276 \text{ in.}$$

12. **(E)** The problem may be restated, "90.88 is what percent of 79.15?" Rounding off the numbers will simplify the calculations and not change the choice significantly. Therefore, set up the proportion and solve:

$$\frac{percent}{100} = \frac{91}{79}$$

$$percent = \frac{9,100}{79} = 115$$

13. **(B)** 4 divided by 6 is $\frac{4}{6}$ and reduces to $\frac{2}{3}$, or use long division to divide 6 into 4. Either way, this is $66\frac{2}{3}\%$. Choice (A) is the percent she lost.

14. **(E)** You may either combine each two terms as you get to them, $38 - 17 = 21$ and $21 + 91 = 112$ and $112 - 58 = 54$, or you may combine all of the positive numbers and then combine all of the negative numbers and then combine the two choices. This gives $38 + 91 = 129$ and $-17 + (-58) = -75$, and $129 - 75 = 54$.

15. **(B)** This is another estimation problem. $9.89 is about $10.00, and 75% of $10.00 is $7.50. Choice (A) has a misplaced decimal point.

16. **(C)** The mean is the average we usually find for grades. Add the scores and divide by the number of scores. The sum is 400, and 400 divided by 5 is 80. Choice (A) is the total points, choice (B) is both the median and the mode, choice (D) is the high score, choice (E) is the low score.

17. **(D)** All of his grades added together and divided by 5 must equal 95. Multiply both sides of that equation by 5 and $93 + 100 + 92 + 100 + x = 475$. Then $385 + x = 475$ and $x = 90$.

18. **(D)** Laura spent $10.17 and Lana spent $10.34, so Lana spent 17 cents more than Laura. Choice (B) represents a subtraction error.

19. **(D)** Let x equal the amount of the lease last year. This year is 8% more. $x + 0.08x = 621$ is the equation. Add 1 and 0.08 and get $1.08x = 621$, then $x = \$575$.

20. **(E)** $995 + 149 = 1{,}144$ and $1{,}144 \times 0.08 = 91.52$ tax. $1,144 + $91.52 = $1,235.52. Choice (A) is the cost of the sofa and chair without tax. Choice (B) is the tax. Choice (C) results from an addition error, and choice (D) results from adding tax to the incorrect choice (C).

21. **(A)** An easy way to work this is to think that if the TV set is 30% OFF, then it is 70% ON, and 70% of $225 is $157.50. The traditional way to work this is to take 30% of $225, which is $67.50, and subtract this from $225, giving $157.50. Choice (B) is the 30% discount. Choice (D) is obtained by simply subtracting $30.00 from $225.

22. **(B)** Let x equal the original price. Then $x - 0.20x = 36$ and $0.80x = 36$ and $x = 45$. Choice (A) adds 36 and 20% of 36, while choice (C) adds 20 and 36. Choices (D) and (E) are distractors for those who might want to guess.

23. **(B)** If 60% have brown eyes then 100% − 60% = 40% DO NOT have brown eyes. Forty percent of 245 is 98 and is written as a percent for choice (D); 60% of 245 is 147 and that is written as a percent for choice (C).

24. **(B)** Choices (C), (D), and (E) are each more than $\frac{1}{2}$. Choice (A) is $\frac{1}{2}$. Only choice (B) is less than $\frac{1}{2}$.

25. **(C)** You may either find the percent of boys (351 divided by 650) and then subtract from 100% to find the percent of girls, or you may subtract 351 from 650 and find that there are 299 girls and divide this by 650 to get 46% girls. Choice (A) is 650 divided by 351, and choice (B) is 650 divided by 299. Choice (D) is the percent of boys, and choice (E) is the number of girls written as a percent.

26. **(E)** There is not enough information given to find the cost in the next state. The tax rate in that state is needed. Choice (A) is the cost in his state, and the other choices are costs with tax rates of 6%, 5%, and 4%, respectively.

27. **(C)** Subtract:
$$9 \text{ ft. } 11\frac{5}{8} \text{ in.}$$
$$-5 \text{ ft. } \quad 6 \text{ in.}$$
$$\overline{\quad\quad\quad\quad\quad\quad}$$
$$4 \text{ ft. } 5\frac{5}{8} \text{ in.}$$

Choice (A) is obtained by subtracting $5\frac{1}{2}$ from 10. Choice (B) is the same, only written in feet and inches. Choice (D) represents a subtraction error. Choice (E) mistakenly subtracts 5.5 as 5 ft. 5 in.

28. **(C)** To change 36.59% to a decimal, divide by 100, or move the decimal point two places to the left.

29. **(D)** Subtracting 7 from each side of the equation gives $4x = 20$. Divide both sides of the equation by 4 and get $x = 5$. Choice (A) is not

correct because 7 was not subtracted before dividing by 4. Choice (B) is not correct because 7 was ADDED to 27. Choice (E) is not correct because of the incorrect sign.

30. **(E)** First subtract 3 from both sides of the equation, then multiply both sides by 4. This gives $x = 48$. Choice (C) is the result if 12 is mistakenly multiplied by $\frac{1}{4}$ rather than by 4.

31. **(C)** To evaluate an expression, simply replace the x or y with the equivalent number, $(-2)^2 + 2(-2) - 3 + 3 = 4 - 4 - 3 + 3 = 0$.

32. **(B)** To simplify, remove parentheses and collect like terms. $15 - 4x - 8 + 6x + 2 = 2x + 9$. The most common error is failure to distribute the minus sign with the 4.

33. **(D)** The formula $D = rt$ is the one to use for this problem. $21 = r \times 2\frac{1}{3}$ and $r = 9$ knots. Choice (B) is the time, choice (C) is the distance, and choice (E) is obtained by multiplying 21 by 2 rather than by dividing.

34. **(D)** Multiplying x and $4x$ gives $4x^2$. Multiplying x and 3 gives $3x$. Multiplying 1 and $4x$ gives $4x$. Multiplying 1 and 3 gives 3 and collecting like terms gives $4x^2 + 7x + 3$. Choice (A) is incorrect because 1 and 3 were ADDED, and the middle term is missing. Choice (B) is incorrect because the middle term is missing. Choice (C) is incorrect because the middle term is incorrect. Choice (E) is incorrect because the sign of the middle term is incorrect and the last term is incorrect.

35. **(E)** Distribute the 10 to both terms inside the parenthesis. Choice (E) is correct because 10 times $(-3w)$ is $(-30w)$ and 10 times 2 is 20. Choice (A) is incorrect because the negative sign was omitted from the first term, and the second term was not multiplied by 10. Choice (B) is incorrect because the second term was not multiplied by 10. In choice (C), the second term was not multiplied by 10, but the sign was changed. Choice (D) is incorrect because the sign of the second term was erroneously changed.

36. **(E)** If one integer is represented by x, then the next consecutive even integer is $(x + 2)$. The product of one even integer and twice the next

even integer is represented by $x + 2(x + 2)$. This is set equal to 40 to form the equation. Choice (A) is simply an integer times itself. Choice (B) represents the product of any two consecutive integers. Choice (C) represents the sum of one integer and twice the next consecutive integer. Finally, choice (D) represents the product of two even or odd integers.

37. **(D)** We want to find what binomials multiplied together would give $(x^4 - 81)$. $(x^2 + 9)$ and $(x^2 - 9)$ would give the results, but $(x^2 - 9)$ can also be factored into $(x + 3)$ and $(x - 3)$, so $(x^2 + 9) (x + 3) (x - 3)$ are the prime factors. Choice (B) is not the best choice because it is not the prime factors.

38. **(A)** There are 12 in a dozen, so Maria baked 66 cookies. Her little brother ate $\frac{1}{3}$ of 12 or 4 cookies. This left 62 $(66 - 4 = 62)$.

39. **(C)** His car can go 100 miles on 3 gallons, so it can go 300 miles on x gallons. Set up a proportion $\frac{100}{3} = \frac{300}{x}$. Then $x = 9$.

40. **(C)** This expression is of the form $A^2 - 2AB + B^2$, which is the square of a binomial $(A - B)^2$. So the choice is $(x - 3)^2$. Choice (A) ignores the third term. When choice (D) is squared, the middle term is positive. Choice (B) is the same as choice (D) only in a different form. When the factors of choice (E) are multiplied together, the last term of the trinomial formed is negative.

41. **(D)** First convert all measurements to feet, since the choices are in feet. One mile is 5,280 ft., 720 yds. is 2,160 ft. The sum is 11,340 ft. Choice (A) is obtained by adding all numbers without converting them to the same measure. Choice (B) is obtained by converting 1 mile to 5,280 ft. and then adding 720 and 3,500. Choice (E) mistakenly converts 1 mile to 5,000 ft.

42. **(E)** To find $g(-3)$ simply substitute (-3) for x. This gives $g(-3) = (-3)^2 + 4$. $(-3)^2$ is 9 and $9 + 4$ equals 13.

43. **(D)** 96 divided by 2 gives the cost of one pound, which is $0.48. Then $0.48 times 3 is $1.44. Choice (A) incorrectly multiplies 2 times 96 times 3. Choice (B) multiplies 96 times 3. Choice (C) is the cost for one pound, and choice (E) is a distractor.

44.   **(D)**   Substitute the values given into the formula: $s = (68 \times 1.6) + 4$, then $108.8 + 4 = \$112.80$.

45.   **(D)**   The figure has six sides; this is a hexagon. A rectangle has four sides, a pentagon has five sides, and a heptagon has seven sides.

Section 2

46.   **(B)**   This right triangle is isosceles. A scalene triangle has no sides the same length. An equilateral triangle has all sides the same length. An obtuse triangle has one obtuse angle, and an acute triangle has three acute angles.

47.   **(C)**   The two angles pictured form a linear pair, and together they form a straight angle. The sum of the measures of angle Q and 58 is 180°, the number of degrees in a straight angle. To obtain the correct choice, subtract 58 from 180.

48.   **(B)**   The sum of the measures of the angles of a triangle is 180°. Angle D is marked as a right angle, which is 90°. This leaves the other two angles to make up the other 90°. So the correct choice is obtained by subtracting 43 from 90. Also you could add 90 and 43 to get 133 and subtract 133 from 180. The choice is the same.

49.   **(A)**   Angle BFG and angle CGF are alternate interior angles and are therefore congruent, or equal in measure. If we can find the measure of either one, we will know the measure of angle CGF. We know that angle BFG and angle BFE form a linear pair, and are supplementary, and we know angle BFE measures 80°. Subtracting 80 from 180 we find that angle BFG is 100°. Since CGF is an alternate interior angle and congruent to angle BFG, the measure of angle CGF is 100°.

50.   **(E)**   Two lines intersect to form vertical angles. The angle marked 133° and the one marked X are vertical angles. Vertical angles are congruent. This means $X = 133°$.

51.   **(D)**   Since the two segments are perpendicular, they form a right angle. A right angle measures 90°, so the two marked angles must add up to 90°. $50 + X = 90$, therefore $X = 40$.

52. **(A)** The sum of the measures of the angles of a triangle equals 180°. $25 + 15 = 40$ and $180 - 40 = 140$.

53. **(A)** The volume of any solid is the area of the base multiplied by the height. The base of a cylinder is a circle. The formula for the area of a circle is $A = \pi r^2$. The diameter is marked 20 cm on the figure, so the radius is 10 cm. $10 \times 10 = 100$ and $100 \times 3.14 = 314$. This is the area of the base. Now multiply by the height, 20, and the answer is 6,280 cubic cm.

54. **(C)** The problem is really to find the surface area of the rectangular solid. This is done by finding the sum of the areas of every side, including the top and bottom. This problem is complicated by the fact that the measurements in the problem are given in inches, and the choices are given in square feet. We must convert to the same unit of measure. If we convert the inches to feet, the dimensions of the chest are $1' \times 2' \times \dfrac{5'}{6}$. A formula to find the lateral area (area of all the sides, but not the top and bottom) is $L = ph$, where p = perimeter of the base and h = the height. The perimeter of the base is $1 + 2 + 1 + 2$ or 6. Then $6 \times \dfrac{5}{6} = 5$ sq. ft. for the sides. Now find the area of the top and bottom and add it to the sides. The bottom is a rectangle and the area $= lw$, where l = length and w = width. So the area is 2×1 or 2 sq. ft. This is the bottom, but the top is the same. Finally add the area of the sides and the top and the bottom: $5 + 2 + 2 = 9$ sq. ft.

55. **(B)** The Pacific is 46% of the 140 million square miles, or $0.46 \times 140{,}000{,}000$. Choice (E) has a misplaced decimal point, choice (B) is the 46 written as 46 million, and choice (C) subtracts 46 million from 140 million.

56. **(B)** In problem 55 you were told that about 140 million square miles of our Earth's surface are covered with oceans. This problem adds the information that the total surface of our Earth is about 200 million square miles. The percentage is 140 divided by 200, or about 70%. Choice (A) has a misplaced decimal point, and choice (E) is $200 - 140$.

57. **(A)** The form $a^m a^n = a^{m+n}$ is the same form as $4\,(x^4 \times x^6)$, which equals $4x^{10}$. Choice (B) represents a common mistake of multiplying the exponents.

58.   **(E)**   Two tickets times $400 equals $800, plus $210 equals $1,010. Multiplying by 0.1 (for 10%) the choice is $101.

59.   **(A)**   This may be solved by "translating" the problem directly into algebraic symbols. "What" = x, percent = 0.01, "of" = multiply or times, and "in" = equals. Put this together and you have an equation, x (0.01) (80) = 32. Solve for x and $x = 40$. This is the percent. Another way to work this problem is to divide 32 by 80 and multiply by 100. A third way to work percent problems is by setting up a proportion, with the "parts" on top and the "wholes" on the bottom.

percent   quantity

$$\frac{x}{100} = \frac{32}{80}$$

By solving the proportion, you find the choice to the problem. You may use a proportion to solve any percent problem by letting X fill in the unknown place in the proportion.

60.   **(C)**   There are 52 weeks in a year, therefore, multiply the weekly cost of $26.03 by 52.

61.   **(A)**   Her chances are 8 out of 1,600 or $\frac{8}{1,600}$. This is one out of 200 or 0.5%.

62.   **(D)**   Her annual benefit is the amount she receives as her discount. It is 20% of the amount she spends at that store. It is found by multiplying $592.86 by 0.2.

63.   **(B)**   They will have the $550 plus the interest. The interest is 0.082 times the $550, or $45.10. So they will have $550 plus $45.10 or $595.10.

64.   **(D)**   There are two easy ways to solve this. First, if there are 36 girls, then there are 90 – 36 or 54 boys. 54 divided by 90 times 100 gives the percent of boys. Another way is to divide 36 by 90 then multiply by 100 to give 40% girls. If there are 40% girls, then 100% – 40% = 60% boys.

65.   **(B)**   Subtracting 35 from each side of the equation gives $x = 35$.

66. **(C)** 2 times 17 is 34. The number of marbles Joe has is not known and is not needed.

67. **(C)** Dividing both sides of the equation by 12 yields $x = 13$.

68. **(D)** $15 times 10 is $150. Choices (A) and (C) have the decimal point in the wrong place. Choice (E) would be correct if he received $10.00 going and another $10.00 returning from the airport, but he returned to the hotel without a fare.

69. **(E)** Multiplying x and $3x$ gives $3x^2$. Multiplying x and 4 gives $4x$. Multiplying 1 and $3x$ gives $3x$. Multiplying 1 and 4 gives 4, collecting like terms gives $3x^2 + 7x + 4$.

70. **(D)** 98 divided by 2 gives the cost of one pound, which is $0.49. Then $0.49 times 5 is $2.45. Choice (A) incorrectly multiplies 2 times 98 times 5.

71. **(E)** Choice (E) is correct because 7 times $(-4y)$ is $(-28y)$, and 7 times 2 is 14.

72. **(A)** The easiest way to solve this is with a chart. The chart below represents the trip going and the trip returning. The distance is the same for both trips. The trip going has the speed of the airplane plus the tail wind. The trip returning has the speed of the airplane minus the tail wind. The times are as stated.

D =		r	t
going ⟹	D	r + 60	6
returning ⟸	D	r − 60	8

Since the distance equals the rate times the time and the distances are equal, set up an equation of representations of the equal distances and solve: $6(r + 60) = 8(r - 60)$. $6r + 360 = 8r - 480$. Then $r = 420$.

73. **(E)** To find the $f(-3)$ simply substitute (-3) for x. This gives $f(-3)$ $= -(-3) + 4$, which is 7, because $-(-3) = +3$.

74. **(B)** The rule for dividing variables with exponents is a^N divided by $a^M = a^{N-M}$. So the exponents are just subtracted — the one in the denominator subtracted from the one in the numerator.

75. **(D)** We want to find what binomials multiplied together would give $(x^4 - 1)$. $(x^2 + 1)$ and $(x^2 - 1)$ would give the results, but $(x^2 - 1)$ can also be factored into $(x + 1)$ and $(x - 1)$.

76. **(C)** This problem is in the form of $A^2 + 2AB + B^2$, which is the square of a binomial $(A + B)^2$ So the choice is $(x + 3)^2$.

77. **(C)** The two angles pictured form a linear pair, and together they form a straight angle. The sum of the measure of angle R and 59 is 180, the number of degrees in a straight angle. To obtain the choice, subtract 59 from 180.

78. **(A)** The sum of the measures of the angles of a triangle is $180°$. Angle U is marked as a right angle, which is $90°$. This leaves the other two angles to make up the other $90°$. So the correct choice is obtained by subtracting 47 from 90. Also, you could add 90 and 47 to get 137 and subtract 137 from 180. The choice is the same.

79. **(D)** Angle ACD is called an exterior angle of the triangle, and it is equal to the sum of the two remote interior angles. This means you add the two opposite angles inside the triangle and the choice is the measure of angle ACD.

Another way to obtain the choice is to find the measure of the interior angle of the triangle at C, by adding the other two angles and then subtracting from 180. Angle C is $72°$. Then the two angles at point C form a linear pair whose sum is 180. So subtract 72 from 180 and you have the measure of angle ACD.

80. **(C)** Angle BEF and angle CFE are alternate interior angles and are therefore congruent, or equal in measure. If we can find the measure of either one, we will know the measure of angle CFE. We know that angle GEB and angle BEF form a linear pair, and we know angle GEB measures $40°$. Subtracting 40 from 180, we find that angle BEF is $140°$. Since CFE

is an alternate interior angle and congruent to angle *BEF*, the measure of angle *CFE* is 140°.

81.   **(D)**   The problem is asking, "20 times what equals 220." You must know at the length times the width of a rectangle is the area, and then use algebra to solve for the unknown. $20x = 220$. Divide both sides by 20 to find $x = 11$. Also, for a problem like this, you may try each choice to find the one which gives 220.

82.   **(B)**   All sides of an equilateral triangle are congruent, or have the same measure. The altitude is the perpendicular bisector of the base and the bisector of the vertex angle. So the altitude divides the triangle into two triangles that have angles of 30°–60°–90°. The sides of this kind of triangle have the special relationship $1 : \sqrt{3} : 2$. This makes the length of the altitude of our triangle $3\sqrt{3}$.

83.   **(A)**   To read the graph properly, notice that the columns represent millions of dollars, so locate 1.5 for the $1,500,000. Then look down to the bottom of the column to read the name of the salesperson. It is J. Johns.

84.   **(A)**   First find the amount sold by P. Sellers. Look to the top of the column above his name and read the amount to the left. It is 0.5 or one half of a million dollars. Three times that would be 1.5 million. The person selling 1.5 million is J. Johns. C. Chan did not sell that much, and S. Smith sold more.

85.   **(A)**   This is found by taking 25%, or $\dfrac{1}{4}$, of $2,500 and then multiplying by 12 months.

86.   **(B)**   The correct answer is clearly written on the graph under the section labeled "utilities."

87.   **(B)**   She saves 12% of $2,500, or $300.

88.   **(E)**   When a fraction is raised to a power, both the numerator and the denominator is raised to that power. So, x^2 taken as a factor 5 times is x^{10}, and y taken as a factor 5 times is y^5.

89. **(B)** Let x be the total capacity of the swimming pool, then $\frac{2}{3}x = 1,800$.

$$x = \frac{1,800 \times 3}{2} = 2,700 \text{ ft}^3$$

90. **(B)** Since the jug is $\frac{2}{3}$ full and the jug holds $\frac{3}{4}$ gallon of punch, the jug has $\frac{2}{3}$ of $\frac{3}{4}$ or $\frac{1}{2}$ gallon.

CHAPTER 4
NATURAL SCIENCES

PRACTICE
TEST 1

CLEP NATURAL SCIENCES
Test 1

(Answer sheets appear in the back of the book.)

Section 1

TIME: 45 Minutes
60 Questions

DIRECTIONS: Each of the questions or incomplete statements below is followed by five possible answers or completions. Select the best choice in each case and fill in the corresponding oval on the answer sheet.

---

1. Cell organelles containing enzymes necessary for aerobic respiration are called

    (A) mitochondria.

    (B) Golgi bodies.

    (C) vacuoles.

    (D) centrioles.

    (E) endoplasmic reticulum.

2. DNA is a polymer made up of repeating groups known as

    (A) phosphate units.

    (B) nucleotides.

    (C) nitrogenous bases.

    (D) deoxyribose units.

    (E) ribose units.

3. RNA nucleotides contain the nitrogenous bases

    (A) cytosine, thymine, uracil, and guanine.

    (B) adenine, thymine, guanine, and uracil.

    (C) thymine, adenine, cytosine, and guanine.

(D) uracil, adenine, cytosine, and guanine.

(E) thymine, cytosine, guanine, and uracil.

4. A cell organelle known to function in the transport of cell products from place to place within the cell is the

(A) endoplasmic reticulum.   (D) vacuole.

(B) mitochondria.   (E) ribosome.

(C) Golgi body.

5. The process by which chromatids exchange segments with each other is called

(A) crossing-over.   (D) replication.

(B) nondisjunction.   (E) polyploidy.

(C) gene linkage.

6. Which sequence shows decreasing complexity of levels of ecological organization?

(A) Biosphere, ecosphere, community, population

(B) Biosphere, community, ecosphere, population

(C) Ecosphere, biosphere, community, population

(D) Biosphere, ecosphere, population, community

(E) Population, community, ecosphere, biosphere

7. A small dense organelle that serves as a site for the manufacture of proteins within the cell is the

(A) Golgi complex.   (D) lysosome.

(B) chloroplast.   (E) vacuole.

(C) ribosome.

8. Photosynthesis occurs in which cellular structure?

(A) Cell wall   (D) Chloroplast

(B) Endoplasmic reticulum   (E) Lysosome

(C) Mitochondria

9. The cell wall surrounds the cell giving it rigidity. It is composed mainly of

   (A) cellulose.   (D) sugars.

   (B) lipids.   (E) amino acids.

   (C) proteins.

10. When a cell is in the prophase stage of mitosis,

    (A) the centromeres replicate and separate.

    (B) the nuclear membrane disintegrates and spindle fibers are formed.

    (C) the chromatids are pulled apart.

    (D) the separated chromatids become the chromosomes of the daughter cells that are to form.

    (E) two new nuclear membranes form.

11. A structure that is not found during animal cell mitosis but is present during plant cell mitosis is the

    (A) centriole.   (D) cell plate.

    (B) chromatid.   (E) mitochondria.

    (C) gamete.

12. A fertilized egg is also called a

    (A) gamete.   (D) zygote.

    (B) gland.   (E) chromatid.

    (C) xylem.

13. Which sequence correctly represents the process of mitosis?

    (A) Metaphase, prophase, anaphase, telophase

    (B) Prophase, anaphase, metaphase, telophase

    (C) Anaphase, metaphase, prophase, telophase

    (D) Prophase, metaphase, anaphase, telophase

    (E) Telophase, anaphase, prophase, metaphase

14. A physically expressed characteristic is referred to as

(A) a phenotype.

(D) a genotype.

(B) an allele.

(E) a linkage.

(C) a monohybrid cross.

15. What are the phenotype ratios of the offspring produced from a cross between a heterozygous tall pea plant and a homozygous short pea plant?

(A) 50% tall, 50% short

(D) 75% tall, 25% short

(B) 25% tall, 75% short

(E) 100% short

(C) 100% tall

16. What would be the ratios for the phenotypes of offspring from a cross between two heterozygous tall pea plants?

(A) 100% tall

(D) 25% tall, 75% short

(B) 75% tall, 25% short

(E) 100% short

(C) 50% tall, 50% short

17. Molecules which aid in the transport of amino acids to ribosomes are

(A) chromosomes.

(D) polysaccharides.

(B) lipases.

(E) chromatids.

(C) RNA molecules.

18. The region of the chromosome to which spindle fibers attach is called the

(A) centromere.

(D) gamete.

(B) spindle.

(E) equatorial plane.

(C) nucleus.

19. The cross between a homozygous tall pea plant and a homozygous short pea plant will result in offspring with the following genotype(s):

(A) TT and tt.   (D) Tt.

(B) TT and Tt.   (E) TT.

(C) Tt and tt.

QUESTIONS 20-22 are based on the following information and on your knowledge of biology.

In some cases of allele pairs, neither one exhibits dominance over the other. In heterozygous offspring, both alleles are expressed as a "blend." For example, when red petal four o'clocks are crossed with white petal four o'clocks, the F1 generation is pink in color. When F1 generation plants are crossed with each other, we obtain an F2 generation of red, white, and pink petal plants.

20. The blending of the phenotypes of both parents in the offspring is termed

(A) recombination.   (D) crossing-over.

(B) codominance.   (E) polyploidy.

(C) segregation.

21. When a pink petal four o'clock is crossed with another pink petal four o'clock, the offspring will show a phenotype ratio of

(A) 1 red: 1 pink: 2 white.

(B) 1 red: 3 pink: 1 white.

(C) 1 red: 2 pink: 1 white.

(D) 2 red: 1 pink: 1 white.

(E) 2 red: 1 pink: 2 white.

22. When a pink petal four o'clock is crossed with a white petal four o'clock, what percentage of the offspring will be white?

(A) 50%   (D) 75%

(B) 100%   (E) 33%

(C) 25%

23. Which is a genetic disorder in humans caused by the nondisjunction of chromosomes?

    (A) Color blindness   (D) Hemophilia

    (B) Tay-Sachs disease   (E) Down's Syndrome

    (C) Sickle-cell anemia

24. A man who is color-blind marries a woman who is carrying the gene for color-blindness. What is the chance that a son will be color-blind?

    (A) 1 out of 4   (D) 4 out of 4

    (B) 1 out of 2   (E) No chance

    (C) 1 out of 3

25. The presence of one or more extra sets of chromosomes is called

    (A) translocation.   (D) crossing-over.

    (B) deletion.   (E) transpiration.

    (C) polyploidy

26. Most mutations

    (A) result in hybrid vigor.

    (B) are reversible.

    (C) are recessive and detrimental to the organism.

    (D) are beneficial to the organism.

    (E) Both (A) and (B).

27. The number of chromosomes found in human gametes is

    (A) 46.   (D) 23.

    (B) 22.   (E) 21.

    (C) 47.

28. If two carriers for Tay-Sachs disease marry and have a child, what is the risk that this child will have the disease?

    (A) One in four   (D) Two in three

    (B) One in two   (E) One in five

    (C) One in three

29. Free ear lobe is a dominant trait, while attached ear lobe is a recessive trait. If two parents who are heterozygous for free ear lobes have children, the ear lobe phenotype of the children will be

    (A) 100% free.

    (B) 50% free, 50% attached.

    (C) 25% free, 75% attached.

    (D) 75% free, 25% attached.

    (E) 100% attached.

30. For a particular trait, a heterozygous individual has the same appearance as a homozygous dominant individual. A test cross is performed to determine whether an organism is homozygous dominant or heterozygous. This is best done by crossing the unknown individual with

    (A) a homozygous dominant organism.

    (B) a homozygous recessive organism.

    (C) a heterozygous organism.

    (D) None of the above

    (E) Choices (A), (B), and (C)

31. A certain strain of plant produces pink flowers when the temperature is above 65°. However, when the temperature is below 65°, the flowers are orange. Which statement best explains this phenomenon?

    (A) The environment influences gene action.

    (B) Polyploidy results in color change.

    (C) Chromosomal nondisjunction has occurred.

    (D) Crossing-over occurred.

    (E) A mutation has occurred.

32. In human beings, which of the following are examples of dominant traits?

    (A) Brown eyes   (D) Free earlobes

    (B) Attached earlobes   (E) Choices A and D

    (C) Straight hair

33. Animal breeders often mate members of the same litter with one another in order to maintain desirable traits. This procedure is known as

    (A) natural selection.   (D) crossing-over.

    (B) inbreeding.   (E) polyploidy.

    (C) hybridization.

34. When two snapdragon plants are crossed, 51% pink petal plants and 49% red petal plants are produced. The phenotypes of the parents are

    (A) red and white.   (D) red and red.

    (B) white and pink.   (E) pink and red.

    (C) pink and pink.

35. A person who is homozygous for blood type O has a genotype that may be represented by

    (A) ii.   (D) I^ai.

    (B) I^aI^a.   (E) I^bi.

    (C) I^aI^b.

36. A man with type O blood marries a woman with type AB blood. What are the possible blood types of their offspring?

    (A) AB only   (D) A, B, and AB

    (B) A and B only   (E) AB and O only

    (C) A, B, and O

37. A person with type AB blood has the following genotype

(A) I^aI^b.

(D) ii.

(B) I^ai.

(E) i.

(C) I^bi.

QUESTIONS 38-40 are based on the pedigree chart below and on your knowledge of biology. The chart depicts a family with a history of color blindness. The gene for normal vision (N) is dominant over the gene for color blindness (n).

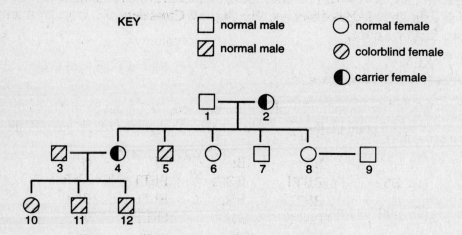

38. What is the genetic make up of person 4?

(A) X^NX^n

(D) X^nY

(B) X^NX^N

(E) X^NY

(C) X^nX^n

39. If female 6 marries a color-blind male and has four daughters, what percentage of their daughters will have normal vision?

(A) 0%

(D) 50%

(B) 20%

(E) 100%

(C) 25%

40. If female 10 marries a normal male, which will be true of their children?

    (A) Only the daughters will be color-blind.

    (B) Only the sons will be color-blind.

    (C) All the children will be color-blind.

    (D) All the children will have normal vision.

    (E) 50 percent of the sons will be color-blind.

QUESTIONS 41-44 are based on the information in the Punnett Cross below and your knowledge of biology. The Punnett Cross depicts a cross between two dihybrid mice.

KEY
B = mice with black fur
b = mice with tan fur
T = mice with long tails
t = mice with short tails

	BT	Bt	bT	bt
BT	BBTT	BBTt	BbTT	BbTt
Bt	BBTt	BBtt	BbTt	Bbtt
bT	BbTT	BbTt	bbTT	bbTt
bt	BbTt	Bbtt	bbTt	bbtt

41. The results of this dihybrid cross illustrates what principle?

    (A) Segregation

    (B) Incomplete dominance

    (C) Independent assortment

    (D) Gene linkage

    (E) Crossing-over

42. What is the ratio of black, short tail mice to tan, short tail mice?

    (A) 3:1   (D) 4:1

    (B) 16:1   (E) 2:1

    (C) 4:3

43. What is the ratio obtained of mice with black fur to those with tan fur?

    (A) 4:1   (D) 10:6

    (B) 12:4   (E) 8:1

    (C) 15:1

44. How many offspring out of a total of 16 can be expected to have the same genotype as the parent dihybrid?

    (A) 8   (D) 4

    (B) 12   (E) 1

    (C) 3

45. DNA coding for a particular amino acid contains a sequence of how many nucleotides?

    (A) 5   (D) 2

    (B) 4   (E) 1

    (C) 3

46. Which DNA strand represents the base sequence complementary to the portion of a DNA strand represented directly below?

    A-G-C-C-T

    (A) A-G-C-C-T   (D) U-C-G-G-A

    (B) T-C-G-G-U   (E) C-G-A-A-U

    (C) T-C-G-G-A

47. All of the following statements about RNA are true EXCEPT

    (A) RNA molecules are single stranded.

    (B) RNA molecules contain a 5-carbon sugar ribose.

    (C) RNA exists in three functional forms.

    (D) RNA contains thymine.

    (E) RNA contains uracil.

48. During replication, the strands of the DNA molecule separate from each other when bonds between which groups are broken?

    (A) 5-carbon deoxy sugars

    (B) Phosphate groups

    (C) Amino acids

    (D) Nitrogenous bases

    (E) Carbon-oxygen bonds

49. In the equation $p^2 + 2pq + q^2 = 1$, from the Hardy-Weinberg principle, q represents the frequency of the

    (A) dominant allele.

    (B) recessive allele.

    (C) hybrid individual.

    (D) homozygous individual.

    (E) heterozygous individual.

50. The establishment of a single species per niche in a climax community is most probably the result of

    (A) competition.   (D) mutation.

    (B) mutualism.   (E) overproduction.

    (C) overpopulation.

51. A lichen is composed of an alga and a fungus. Neither of these organisms can live alone on bare rock as the lichen does. This relationship is an example of

    (A) competition.   (D) selective breeding.

    (B) symbiosis.   (E) cross selection.

    (C) parasitism.

52. The interaction between biotic factors and abiotic factors in a pond is called

    (A) an ecosystem.   (D) a population.

    (B) a community.   (E) a biome.

    (C) a niche.

53. The occurrence of an antibiotic-resistant strain of bacteria is an example of an evolutionary process known as

    (A) use and disuse.

    (B) species preservation.

    (C) natural selection.

    (D) segregation.

    (E) polyploidy.

54. The term "gene pool" refers to

    (A) the proportion of each allele for a particular trait that is present.

    (B) a technique for the detection of genetic disorders in which bodily fluids are analyzed.

    (C) the total of all the inheritable genes for the traits in a population.

    (D) a gene mutation.

    (E) a gene linkage.

55. A heterotroph which benefits at the expense of its living host is called a

    (A) parasite.   (D) saprophyte.

    (B) scavenger.   (E) consumer.

    (C) decomposer.

56. The relationship between nitrogen-fixing bacteria and the roots of the legume plants on which they live can best be described as

    (A) parasitism.

    (B) autotrophism.

    (C) heterotropism.

    (D) mutualism.

    (E) commensalism.

57. After a major forest fire totally destroys a wooded area, the land is converted to barren soil. Which of the following best describes the sequence in which changes in vegetation occur in the area?

    (A) Grasses, shrubs, pine trees, maple trees

    (B) Lichen, grasses, maple trees, pine trees

    (C) Grasses, lichen, pine trees, maple trees

    (D) Shrubs, lichen, pine trees, maple trees

    (E) Shrubs, grasses, maple trees, pine trees

58. Abiotic factors include all of the following EXCEPT

    (A) the wastes produced by a member of the species.

    (B) temperature range.

    (C) availability of minerals.

    (D) acidity of the system.

    (E) amount of moisture available.

59. Organisms that eat both plant and animal matter as part of their regular diet are termed

    (A) autotrophs.

    (B) omnivores.

    (C) herbivores.

    (D) producers.

    (E) carnivores.

60. The relationship between athlete's foot fungus and human beings is best described as

    (A) mutualism.

    (B) commensalism.

    (C) parasitis

    (D) autotrophic behavior.

    (E) a food chain.

Section 2

TIME: 45 Minutes
60 Questions

DIRECTIONS: Each of the questions or incomplete statements below is followed by five possible answers or completions. Select the best choice in each case and fill in the corresponding oval on the answer sheet.

QUESTIONS 61 to 62 refer to the following passage.

In an ionic bond, the entities bonded together are ions of opposite charge. Electrons must be transferred to form an ionic bond. In a covalent bond, which is a strong bond, electrons are shared between two neutral atoms. Hard substances, such as diamonds, consist of covalently bonded atoms.

61. Sodium chloride is best described as a(n)

   (A) covalent compound consisting of Na^+ cations and Cl^- anions.

   (B) ionic compound consisting of Na^+ cations and Cl^- anions.

   (C) covalent compound consisting of Na^- anions and Cl^+ cations.

   (D) ionic compound consisting of Na^- anions and Cl^+ cations.

   (E) ionic compound consisting of Na^+ anions and Cl^- cations.

62. An example of a substance joined by one or several covalent bonds would be

   (A) H_2.   (D) a diamond.

   (B) Cl_2.   (E) Choices (A), (B), and (D)

   (C) NaCl.

QUESTIONS 63 to 65 refer to the following information.

Electrons are arranged in orbitals, each possessing various amounts of energy. A hydrogen atom has only one electron and its electron configuration is 1s. When two electrons reside in the same orbital, their spins must be paired as opposed to being parallel.

63. Rank the orbitals from highest energy to lowest energy as found in a multielectron atom.

   (A) 1s, 2s, 2p, 3s, 3p

   (B) 3p, 3s, 2p, 2s, 1s

   (C) 1s, 2p, 2s, 3p, 3s

   (D) 3s, 3p, 2s, 2p, 1s

   (E) 3d, 2p, 2s, 1p, 1s

64. An example of two electrons in the same orbital with paired spin quantum numbers (m_s) would be

   (A) $m_s = +1/2$, $m_s = -1/2$

   (B) $m_s = +1/2$, $m_s = +1/2$

   (C) $m_s = -1/2$, $m_s = -1/2$

   (D) $m_s = +1$, $m_s = +1$

   (E) Choices B and C

65. Fluorine has nine electrons. What is its ground state electronic configuration?

   (A) 1s nine

   (B) 1s2s2p

   (C) $1s^2 2s^2 2p^5$

   (D) $1s^2 2p^2 2s^5$

   (E) $2p^3$

QUESTIONS 66 to 68 refer to the following information.

Ernest Rutherford's (1871-1937) experiment provided the basis for the description of an atom's structure. In his experiment, alpha particles were directed toward a thin gold foil. Most particles went through the foil in a fairly straight line, but a few particles were deflected at sharp angles. A diagram of the experiment is shown below.

RUTHERFORD'S APPARATUS FOR OBSERVING THE SCATTERING OF ALPHA PARTICLES BY A METAL FOIL (within a vacuum chamber)

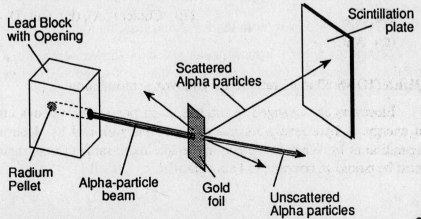

66. Why were some alpha particles deflected at sharp angles?

    (A) The particles did not have enough velocity to penetrate the gold foil, which may have been too thick in some areas.

    (B) The alpha particles were hitting electrons.

    (C) The alpha particles were colliding with atomic nuclei.

    (D) The alpha particles were being repelled from the gold since both alpha particles and gold possess the same charge.

    (E) The surrounding air pulled the alpha particles from the area where the gold foil was located.

67. Why do most alpha particles pass through the gold foil without being deflected?

    (A) Most of the atom is empty space which alpha particles can pass through unaffected.

    (B) The gold foil was mostly thin enough to allow alpha particles to pass through.

    (C) The electrons did not get in the way.

    (D) The atomic nuclei are semipermeable.

    (E) The alpha particles move so fast that they push the atomic nuclei out of the way.

68. The symbol for gold is

    (A) Ga.   (D) Na.

    (B) Hg.   (E) Au.

    (C) He.

QUESTIONS 69 to 72 refer to the following information.

A graph of a car's instantaneous speed is shown below for a time period of 30 seconds. Assume that when the car's speed is negative, it is backing up, and that it can only move in a straight line.

Instantaneous Speed vs. Time

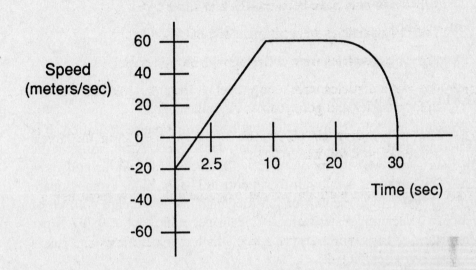

69. How long in seconds is the car moving forward?

(A) 30 seconds

(D) 10 seconds

(B) 27.5 seconds

(E) 2.5 seconds

(C) 15 seconds

70. During what time period is the car moving at a constant speed?

(A) Never

(D) 20–30 seconds

(B) 0–10 seconds

(E) 2.5–10 seconds

(C) 10–20 seconds

71. During the first 30 seconds, the maximum speed reached by the car is

(A) 20 meters/sec.

(D) 50 meters/sec.

(B) 30 meters/sec.

(E) 60 meters/sec.

(C) 40 meters/sec.

72. The car changes its speed the greatest (i.e., has the greatest acceleration or deceleration) during the period

(A) 0–2.5 seconds.   (D) 20–25 seconds.

(B) 2.5–10 seconds.   (E) 25–30 seconds.

(C) 15–20 seconds.

QUESTIONS 73 to 76 refer to the following information.

Pressure is a concept in physics that has a very precise definition. It is the force acting divided by the area upon which it acts. Air pressure at the Earth's surface is 14.7 lbs/in² or 1.013×105 N/m². (1.0 lb/in² is known as a PSI.) This pressure is enough to support a 34-foot high, 1-inch square column of water in a vacuum or 2.5-foot high, 1-inch square column of mercury in a vacuum. Water weighs 62.4 lbs per cubic foot or 9,797 N per cubic meter.

73. Comparing identical volumes of liquid, mercury weighs

(A) 157 times more than water.

(B) 68.1 times more than water.

(C) 13.6 times more than water.

(D) 2.3 times more than water.

(E) the same as water.

74. A 200 lb man standing on snow with boots each having a bottom area of 35 square inches will exert a downward pressure due to his weight equal to

(A) 200 PSI   (D) 2.86 PSI

(B) 100 PSI   (E) 1.93 PSI

(C) 5.71 PSI

75. A young girl wearing snow skis weighs 110 lbs. If the total area of the skis touching the snow is 330 square inches, then the air pressure on the snow is about

(A) 11 times that of the girl.   (D) 44 times that of the girl.

(B) 22 times that of the girl.   (E) 55 times that of the girl.

(C) 33 times that of the girl.

76. An air pressure of 14.7 PSI can support a one square foot column of water in a vacuum that is

(A) 34 feet high.

(D) 2.83 inches high.

(B) 17 feet high.

(E) less than an inch high.

(C) 2.83 feet high.

QUESTIONS 77 to 79 refer to the following information.

An electroscope is a device used to detect the presence of electric charge. One such device consists of a pair of gold foil leaves suspended from a metal rod that is electrically connected to the outside of a metal and glass enclosure as shown below. An insulator prevents charge from leaking from the leaves and metal rod to the enclosure.

ELECTROSCOPE

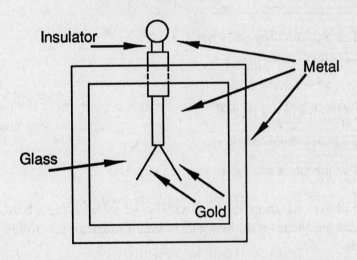

If a piece of vinyl is rubbed with a wool cloth and then brought near the top metal knob, then the gold leaves separate, indicating that the vinyl has acquired a certain amount of charge, either positive or negative. Only electrons (negatively charged particles) are allowed to move on the surface of the metal rod and gold leaves. The amount of spread in the gold leaves indicates the strength of the charge. Touching the top knob with your finger immediately makes the leaves come together, indicating that electrons are either added to or taken away from the electroscope to neutralize it.

77. An electroscope measures

   (A) only the presence of electrons.

   (B) only the absence of electrons.

   (C) the presence of nearby charge.

   (D) the amount of gold electrons.

   (E) the presence of protons in the knob.

78. Suppose a positively charged vinyl rod is brought near the top knob of a neutral electroscope.

   (A) The gold leaves will not spread.

   (B) The gold leaves spread because they become positively charged and they repel each other.

   (C) The gold leaves become negatively charged.

   (D) The top knob becomes positively charged.

   (E) The top knob remains neutral.

79. Suppose a negatively charged vinyl rod is brought near the top knob of an electroscope with its gold leaves separated because they both are negatively charged and repel each other.

   (A) The top knob will become more negative.

   (B) The gold leaves will tend to separate even more.

   (C) The gold leaf separation will remain the same.

   (D) The gold leaves will tend to come together.

   (E) Both (A) and (D).

QUESTIONS 80 and 81 refer to the following map.

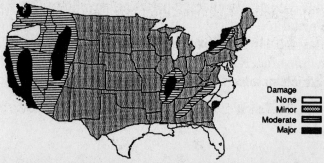

Seismic risk map for the U.S. issued January 1969, showing earthquake damage areas of reasonable expectancy in the next 100 years. Derived from U.S. Coast and Geodetic Survey, ESSA Rel. ES-1, January 14, 1969.

80. People living in which state have little need for earthquake insurance?

(A) Rhode Island   (D) California

(B) Wyoming   (E) Washington

(C) Illinois

81. Data from the map indicates that

(A) a major earthquake will definitely occur within 100 years.

(B) a major earthquake will definitely occur in California within 100 years.

(C) an earthquake can never occur in Texas.

(D) nothing can be concluded from this map concerning the location of earthquakes.

(E) few states are safe from earthquakes.

QUESTIONS 82 to 84 refer to the following passage.

The term "volcanic activity" can mean erupting volcanoes complete with lava and pyroclastic display, or it can mean a simple gaseous emission. It is believed that volcanic activity formed the early Earth's atmosphere. Volcanic gases typically include water vapor, carbon dioxide, hydrogen sulfide, sulfur dioxide, chlorine, and fluorine.

82. Which statement can be drawn in conclusion from the above information?

(A) Volcanic gases can be more dangerous than lava.

(B) Erupting volcanoes always emit both lava and gas.

(C) The term "volcanic activity" is always clear in its meaning.

(D) Erupting volcanoes emit lava only.

(E) Erupting volcanoes emit gases only.

83. Which statement is false?

(A) The early Earth's atmosphere contained no free oxygen.

(B) The early Earth's atmosphere was poisonous to present-day life forms.

(C) Current Earth's atmosphere must be formed by factors other than volcanic activity.

(D) Volcanic activity today emits oxygen to the atmosphere.

(E) None of the above.

84. "Pyroclastic display" is best defined as

(A) a fallout of ice and snow.

(B) trees that fall near the volcano.

(C) a mushroom-type cloud.

(D) a hot, green vapor.

(E) fire and rock particles.

QUESTIONS 85 to 87 refer to the following diagram.

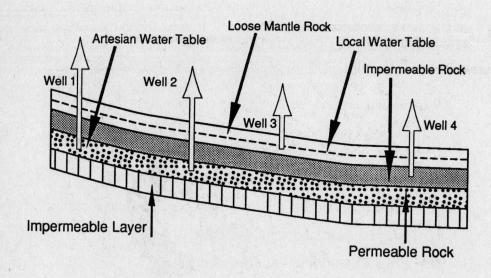

An artesian well system is based on the fact that a water-bearing rock layer (aquifer) is trapped between two impermeable rock layers.

85. Which well is an artesian well that will flow out under its own power?

    (A) Well 1   (D) Well 4

    (B) Well 2   (E) None of the above.

    (C) Well 3

86. Which well is an aquifer well that would require a pumping stem to bring water to the surface?

    (A) Well 1   (D) Well 4

    (B) Well 2   (E) None of the above.

    (C) Well 3

87. Which well is a common well subject to regional weather conditions?

    (A) Well 1   (D) Well 4

    (B) Well 2   (E) None of the above.

    (C) Well 3

QUESTIONS 88 to 90 refer to the following map.

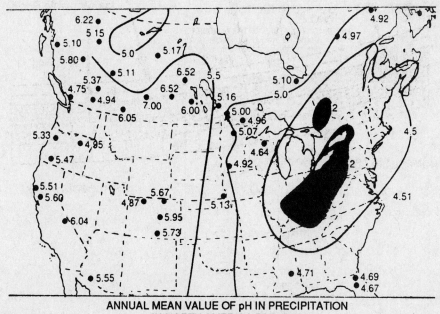

ANNUAL MEAN VALUE OF pH IN PRECIPITATION
IN NORTH AMERICA FOR 1980

88. Which part of the United States and Canada has the most serious acid rain problem?

(A) Northern

(D) Southwest

(B) Southern

(E) Northwest

(C) Northeast

89. The Great Lake(s) in most serious danger from acid rain are

I.   Superior.

IV. Erie.

II. Huron.

V.   Ontario.

III. Michigan.

(A) All the above.

(D) IV and V.

(B) I and II.

(E) None of the above.

(C) II and III.

90. Which factor could not account for variation in pH readings?

(A) Forest cover

(D) Population densities

(B) Industry

(E) Rainfall variations

(C) Prevailing westerly winds

QUESTIONS 91 to 93 refer to the following graph.

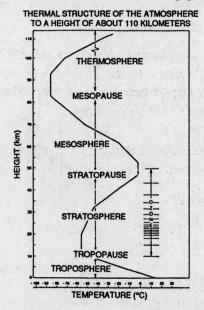

THERMAL STRUCTURE OF THE ATMOSPHERE
TO A HEIGHT OF ABOUT 110 KILOMETERS

91. The warmest place in the atmosphere is near the ground because

    (A) the ground is under the ozone layer.

    (B) the ground can store heat.

    (C) the ground is covered by ice in some regions.

    (D) the Earth is both land and water.

    (E) All of the above.

92. The coolest layer of the atmosphere is the

    (A) Mesopause.   (D) Stratopause.

    (B) Thermosphere.   (E) Stratosphere.

    (C) Mesosphere.

93. Which would be a reason for temperature changes as you travel up through the atmosphere?

    (A) Distance from the sun decreases

    (B) Weather disruptions cause mixing of the temperatures

    (C) Presence of ozone

    (D) Presence of man

    (E) Changes in composition

QUESTION 94 refers to the following passage.

Salinity is a measure of dissolved solids in water. On the average, 1,000 grams of typical sea water contains 35 grams of salts. The level of salinity is below average in areas where large amounts of fresh water enter the ocean, and above average in hot, arid climates.

94. The Mediterranean Sea and the Red Sea are adjacent to deserts. The water in these two seas would be expected to have

    (A) above-average salinity.

    (B) below-average salinity.

    (C) average salinity.

    (D) no salt content whatsoever.

    (E) cold temperatures.

QUESTIONS 95 to 97 refer to the following passage.

All matter can be divided into two categories: pure substances and mixtures. The pure substances can be further subdivided into elements and compounds, while mixtures can either be homogeneous or heterogeneous.

95. According to the paragraph, which one of the following statements is true?

   (A) A homogeneous mixture is a pure substance.

   (B) Pure substances and mixtures are equivalent terms for the same type of matter.

   (C) A compound can be a pure substance.

   (D) A heterogeneous mixture is only composed of one type of element.

   (E) All matter is one lump that cannot be categorized.

96. If a homogeneous mixture is combined with a heterogeneous mixture, what type of matter will result?

   (A) A homogeneous mixture

   (B) A heterogeneous mixture

   (C) A pure substance

   (D) The two mixtures will not combine because they are too different.

   (E) A new type of matter will result that has not yet been classified.

97. A substance that cannot be decomposed is called an element. Which one of the following is not an element?

   (A) Zinc   (D) Tin

   (B) Sodium   (E) Zinc sulfide

   (C) Iron

QUESTIONS 98 to 101 are based on the following passage.

Every living thing contains proteins. A protein molecule is composed of molecules called amino acids. These amino acids are chemically bonded together to form a chain (the protein molecule). Amino acids are generally composed of carbon, hydrogen, oxygen, and nitrogen. Every amino acid is basically alike except for one molecular component. That component, called the "R" factor, makes the amino acid unique. There are 20 different amino acids that make up hundreds of thousands of different kinds of proteins. Proteins are what make up our skin, our hair, our muscles, our cartilage, and many other components of our body. There is very little that is found in a living organism that is not composed, in part, of protein molecules. Protein molecules are specific to the organism of which they are a part. Therefore, cow muscle protein cannot be found in the muscles of humans, and neither can chicken muscle protein be found in the muscles of hawks.

98. If a chain of amino acids makes up a protein molecule, then one protein can be different from another protein by

(A) only the length of the protein molecule.

(B) the length of the protein molecule, and the order and type of amino acids in the protein molecule.

(C) only the type of amino acids found in the protein molecule.

(D) only the number of chemical bonds found in the protein molecule.

(E) only the order of amino acids in the protein.

99. How many different kinds of "R" factors are there?

(A) 20   (D) 1,000

(B) 50   (E) 100,000

(C) 100

100. Proteins are

(A) chains of sugar molecules.   (D) loops of cellulose molecules.

(B) chains of fat molecules.   (E) chains of amino acids.

(C) rings of carbon.

101. Which of the following is NOT made of protein?

(A) Hair   (D) Skin

(B) Fingernails   (E) Muscle tissue

(C) Rock

QUESTIONS 102 and 103 refer to the following information.

Substance	Length of Molecules
gasoline	short
tar	long
lubricating oil	medium

A liquid that flows with ease has molecules that do not tend to tangle. Tangles occur easily when long chains of atoms flow by one another. Viscosity is the resistance of liquids to flow.

102. According to the above information, which substance is most viscous?

(A) Tar

(B) Gasoline

(C) Lubricating oil

(D) Tar and lubricating oil are equally viscous.

(E) Gasoline and tar have equal viscosity.

103. Why does the viscosity of most substances decrease as the temperature rises?

(A) Chains join to form much longer chains.

(B) Thermal energy rises and chains vibrate more, which causes more tangling.

(C) The chains vaporize and less are present to tangle.

(D) Most chains circularize.

(E) Long chains break to form shorter chains.

QUESTIONS 104 to 107 refer to the following passage.

An easy method of experimentally determining the acceleration due to gravity "g" is by measuring the period of one complete vibration of a simple pendulum of known length. If all the mass of the pendulum can be considered to be concentrated in the bob at the bottom, and if the amplitude of the vibration is kept small (less than a 5° arc), then g will be proportional to the length of the pendulum and inversely proportional to the square of the period. For example, on the Earth's surface where g is about 9.8 meters/sec^2, a 1-meter long pendulum has a vibrational period of

2.0 seconds and a 2-meter long pendulum has a vibrational period of 2.84 seconds.

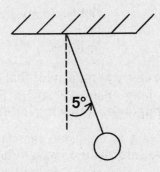

104. If the acceleration due to gravity "g" on the Earth is determined by using a pendulum with a period of four seconds, then its length must be about

    (A) One meter.   (D) Four meters.

    (B) Two meters.   (E) Five meters.

    (C) Three meters.

105. On the moon the acceleration due to gravity is about one-sixth of what is here on the Earth. If a simple pendulum is to have a two-second period on the moon, its length must be close to

    (A) 1/2 meter.   (D) 1/5 meter.

    (B) 1/3 meter.   (E) 1/6 meter.

    (C) 1/4 meter.

106. Which of the following does NOT seem to affect the period of a simple pendulum?

    (A) The acceleration due to gravity

    (B) The mass of the bob

    (C) The amplitude of the swing

    (D) The length of the pendulum

    (E) All of the above.

107. The units used to express the acceleration due to gravity express a measure of

    (A) velocity over time.   (D) velocity over distance.

    (B) distance over time.   (E) force over distance.

    (C) weight over time.

QUESTIONS 108 to 111 refer to the following information.

Issac Newton was the first to point out that every mass in the universe attracts every other mass. This statement is known as the Law of Universal Gravitation. This attraction between bodies is proportional to the mass of each and is inversely proportional to the square of the distance between their centers. Also, by Newton's Third Law of Motion, this attraction must be the same on each pair of masses but in an opposite direction. For example, it is known that Earth pulls on the moon with an average force of 2×10^{20} N and the moon pulls on Earth with an average force of 2×10^{20} N.

**Relative Masses and Average Separations
Moon, Earth and Sun**

108. Newton's Universal Law of Gravitation implies that

    (A) the attraction between the moon and the sun is the same as that between the moon and Earth.

    (B) the attraction between Earth and the sun is the same as that between the moon and Earth.

(C) the pull of the sun on Earth is the same as the pull of Earth on the sun.

(D) the pull of the sun on the moon must be 3×10^{19} N.

(E) the pull of Earth on the sun must be 8×10^{24} N.

109. The pull of the sun on Earth is

(A) about 82 times stronger than the pull of the sun on the moon.

(B) about 82 times weaker than the pull of the sun on the moon.

(C) about 393 times stronger than the pull of the sun on the moon.

(D) about 393 times weaker than the pull of the sun on the moon.

(E) about the same as the pull of the sun on the moon.

110. If the distance between the moon and Earth was doubled, then the gravitational pull of Earth on the moon would be

(A) 8×10^{20} N.   (D) 5×10^{19} N.

(B) 4×10^{20} N.   (E) 1×10^{19} N.

(C) 2×10^{20} N.

111. If Earth and the sun had the same mass, then the pull of the moon on Earth would be about

(A) the same as the pull of the moon on the sun.

(B) 393 times greater than the pull of the moon on the sun.

(C) 393 times weaker than the pull of the moon on the sun.

(D) 154,450 times greater than the pull of the moon on the sun.

(E) 154,450 times weaker than the pull of the moon on the sun.

QUESTIONS 112 and 113 refer to the following passage.

Matter is found in three states: solid, liquid, and gas. Gases are both compressible and expandable. The liquid state and the solid state are both condensed phases since molecules "stick" together by attractive forces.

112. Why do two Br_2 molecules "stick" together at low temperatures?

(A) Ice forms between the molecules and prevents their separation.

(B) An increase in thermal energy causes the molecules to approach each other.

(C) The attraction between the molecules is stronger than the thermal energy pushing them apart, causing them to "stick."

(D) The Br_2 molecules expand quickly and bump into one another.

(E) Br_2 molecules cannot "stick" together because Br_2 is a gas at all temperatures.

113. If the states of matter were organized in terms of randomness of the molecular arrangements, from most random to least random, the order would be

(A) solid, liquid, gas.

(D) gas, liquid, solid.

(B) liquid, solid, gas.

(E) liquid, gas, solid.

(C) gas, solid, liquid.

QUESTIONS 114 to 116 refer to the following passage.

The boiling point of a liquid in an open system is the temperature where atmospheric pressure is equivalent to the vapor pressure of the liquid. Additionally, the boiling point of a liquid is the highest temperature at which there can be liquid as a component of a system.

114. Bubbles form in a boiling liquid because

(A) air from the atmosphere is entering the liquid.

(B) the liquid is condensing to form a gas.

(C) helium gas, which is lighter than any liquid, is rising.

(D) the liquid is vaporizing.

(E) microorganisms in the liquid are carrying out respiration.

115. A kettle containing water is heated to a boil. If the water is allowed to boil for 15 minutes, what effect will this have on the volume of the water?

(A) The volume will increase as water molecules are created in the hot air over the kettle.

(B) The volume will remain constant.

(C) The volume will occasionally increase and decrease due to the effects of atmospheric pressure.

(D) The volume will decrease.

(E) The volume will remain constant only if the kettle is uncovered.

116. Which of the following statements about boiling liquids is FALSE?

(A) Boiling liquids contain both gas and liquid.

(B) All boiling liquids feel extremely hot to the human touch.

(C) It will take longer to boil two liters of water compared to one liter of water over the same flame.

(D) Below the boiling point for a liquid, the external pressure prevents the formation of gas bubbles.

(E) Vapor pressure equals atmospheric pressure at the boiling point.

QUESTIONS 117 to 120 refer to the following diagram.

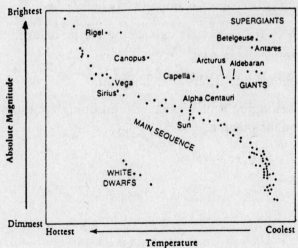

Diagram of the major constellations

117. Most stars represented belong to which group?

    (A) Giants   (D) White Dwarfs

    (B) Main Sequence   (E) Alpha Centauri

    (C) Supergiants

118. Compared to our sun, Sirius is

    (A) cooler and dimmer.   (D) warmer and brighter.

    (B) cooler and brighter.   (E) similar in all respects.

    (C) warmer and dimmer.

119. Which star is matched with an incorrect group?

    (A) Vega – Main Sequence   (D) Canopus – White Dwarf

    (B) Aldebaran – Giant   (E) Antares – Supergiant

    (C) Betelgeuse – Supergiant

120. Which statement is correct?

    (A) Our sun is similar to most other stars in the universe.

    (B) Our sun is very unique among stars.

    (C) Distances between stars can accurately be determined from this diagram.

    (D) Our night sky looks like this diagram.

    (E) Stars belonging to the supergiant grouping are by far the largest stars on the diagram.

CLEP NATURAL SCIENCES
TEST 1

ANSWER KEY

Section 1

1. (A)	13. (D)	25. (C)	37. (A)	49. (B)
2. (B)	14. (A)	26. (C)	38. (B)	50. (A)
3. (D)	15. (A)	27. (D)	39. (E)	51. (B)
4. (A)	16. (B)	28. (A)	40. (B)	52. (A)
5. (A)	17. (C)	29. (D)	41. (C)	53. (C)
6. (A)	18. (A)	30. (B)	42. (A)	54. (C)
7. (C)	19. (D)	31. (A)	43. (B)	55. (A)
8. (D)	20. (B)	32. (E)	44. (D)	56. (D)
9. (A)	21. (C)	33. (B)	45. (C)	57. (A)
10. (B)	22. (A)	34. (E)	46. (C)	58. (A)
11. (D)	23. (E)	35. (A)	47. (D)	59. (B)
12. (D)	24. (B)	36. (B)	48. (D)	60. (C)

Section 2

61. (B)	73. (C)	85. (B)	97. (E)	109. (A)
62. (E)	74. (D)	86. (A)	98. (B)	110. (D)
63. (B)	75. (D)	87. (C)	99. (A)	111. (D)
64. (A)	76. (A)	88. (C)	100. (E)	112. (C)
65. (C)	77. (C)	89. (D)	101. (C)	113. (D)
66. (C)	78. (B)	90. (E)	102. (A)	114. (D)
67. (A)	79. (B)	91. (B)	103. (E)	115. (D)
68. (E)	80. (B)	92. (B)	104. (D)	116. (B)
69. (B)	81. (E)	93. (E)	105. (E)	117. (B)
70. (C)	82. (A)	94. (A)	106. (B)	118. (D)
71. (E)	83. (D)	95. (C)	107. (A)	119. (D)
72. (E)	84. (E)	96. (B)	108. (C)	120. (A)

DETAILED EXPLANATIONS
OF ANSWERS
TEST 1

Section 1

1.　**(A)**　The mitochondria are cell organelles that contain enzymes necessary for aerobic respiration. Golgi bodies (B) are organelles that package and move cell products to the plasma membrane. Vacuoles (C) are cell organelles that may contain water or store nutrients and waste products inside the cell. Centrioles (D) are cell organelles that function in the process of cell division. The endoplasmic reticulum (E) is a series of intracellular membranes that function in the transportation of cellular products within the cell.

2.　**(B)**　DNA is a polymer made up of repeating units known as nucleotides. A nucleotide is composed of a phosphate group, a deoxyribose group, and a nitrogenous base. Choices (A), (C), and (D) are only parts of a nucleotide. Ribose units (E) are found in RNA. Deoxyribose is the 5-carbon sugar found in DNA nucleotides.

3.　**(D)**　Some RNA nucleotides contain the nitrogenous base uracil, while some DNA nucleotides contain thymine.

4.　**(A)**　The endoplasmic reticulum is a series of intracellular membranes that function in the transportation of cellular products within the cell. The mitochondria (B) are cell organelles that contain enzymes necessary for aerobic cellular respiration. Golgi bodies (C) are organelles that package and move cell products to the plasma membrane. Vacuoles (D) are cell organelles that contain water and store nutrients and waste products inside the cell. Ribosomes (E) are cell organelles that serve as a site of protein synthesis.

5.　**(A)**　Crossing-over is the breakage and exchange of corresponding segments of homologous chromosomes at one or more sites resulting in genetic recombination in the next generation. Nondisjunction (B) is the failure of a pair of chromosomes to separate during meiosis. Gene linkage (C) is a pattern of inheritance in which genes located in different places along the same chromosome tend to remain together. Replication (D) is the exact self-duplication of a chromosome during cell division. Polyploidy (E) is a type of chromosome mutation in which sets of homologous chromosomes fail to separate.

6.   **(A)**   The biosphere is the portion of the earth in which living things exist. An ecosystem is a self-sustaining dynamic community of plants and animals. A community consists of all organisms in a given environment. A population consists of all the members of a species inhabiting a given area.

7.   **(C)**   Ribosomes are organelles that are the site of protein synthesis. A Golgi complex (A) is a membrane-bound channel in which materials are synthesized or packaged. Lysosomes (D) are structures that contain digestive enzymes. Chloroplasts (B) are structures found in plant cells that contain chlorophyll and are the site of photosynthesis. Vacuoles (E) are cell organelles that contain water and store nutrients and waste products inside the cell.

8.   **(D)**   Photosynthesis occurs in the chloroplast. The cell wall (A) is a structure that surrounds the plant cell. The endoplasmic reticulum (B) is a channel network in the cytoplasm that aids in synthesizing, transporting, and storing substances made inside the cell. A lysosome (E) is a cell organelle that contains digestive enzymes. Mitochondria (C) are organelles responsible for the majority of the reactions of cellular respiration.

9.   **(A)**   Cellulose, a complex carbohydrate, is the main constituent of the cell wall. Lipids (B), proteins (C), sugars (D), and amino acids (E) are found within the cell.

10.   **(B)**   The nuclear membrane disintegrates and spindle fibers are formed. Prophase is the first stage of mitosis. Choices (A), (C), and (D) describe anaphase. Choice (E) describes telophase.

11.   **(D)**   The cell plate forms in plant cells and becomes a new cell wall dividing the cytoplasm into two parts. A centriole (A) is an organelle found in animal cells that is involved in cell division. Chromatid (B) is one of the strands of a double chromosome. A gamete (C) is a specialized

reproductive cell. Mitochondria (E) are cell organelles that contain enzymes necessary for cellular respiration.

12. **(D)** A zygote is a fertilized egg. A gamete (A) is a specialized reproductive cell. A gland (B) is an organ that produces certain chemicals that are released within the body. Xylem (C) is the tissue that conducts minerals and water from the roots upward through the plant. A chromatid (E) is one strand of a double-stranded chromosome.

13. **(D)** Prophase is the first stage of mitosis. The nuclear membrane disintegrates. Spindle fibers form. In the second stage, metaphase, the chromosomes become attached to the spindle fibers at the centromeres. During the third stage, anaphase, the centromeres replicate and separate. The separated chromatids become chromosomes of the new cells that are about to form. During the last stage, telophase, a new nuclear membrane forms around each new set of chromosomes, forming two new nuclei.

14. **(A)** A phenotype is the expression of a genotype in an observable trait. An allele (B) is one of a pair of genes that exist at the same location on a pair of homologous chromosomes. A monohybrid cross (C) is the genetic cross between organisms that are heterozygous for a trait. Linkage (E) refers to genes that are located on the same chromosomes. The genotype (D) is the genetic makeup of an organism.

15. **(A)** Using a Punnett Cross, this cross is easy to visualize. T represents tall, and t, short:

	t	t
T	Tt	Tt
t	tt	tt

When we cross Tt with tt, 50% of the offspring we obtain will be Tt, which will exhibit a tall appearance. The other 50% will be tt. The phenotype of these offspring will be short.

16. **(B)** When we cross two heterozygous tall pea plants, we obtain offspring that are 75% tall and 25% short in appearance. Using a Punnett Cross, this cross is easy to visualize.

	T	t
T	TT	Tt
t	Tt	tt

The offspring who are TT and Tt in genotype will exhibit a tall appearance, while the offspring with a tt genotype will exhibit a short phenotype.

17. **(C)** Transfer RNA molecules are responsible for transporting amino acids to ribosomes. Chromosomes (A) are structures found in the nucleus. Lipases (B) are enzymes that break down lipids. Polysaccharides (D) are long chains of repeating sugar units formed by joining simple sugars. A chromatid (E) is one of the two strands of a double chromosome.

18. **(A)** The centromere is the structure that holds chromatids together in double-stranded chromosomes. It is the region of the chromosome to which spindle fibers attach. The spindle (B) is the cell's fibrous network formed during mitosis. It mediates movement of the sister chromatids and the spindle poles. The nucleus (C) controls the activities of the cell. The gamete (D) is a specialized reproductive cell that unites with a cell of the opposite sex to form a zygote. The equatorial plane (E) is where the chromosomes align during the metaphase stage of mitosis. It lies in the center of the cell between spindle poles.

19. **(D)** TT is the genotype for a homozygous tall plant. tt is the genotype for a homozygous short plant. Tt is the genotype that results from a cross between a homozygous tall plant and a homozygous short plant.

	T	T
t	Tt	Tt
t	Tt	Tt

20. **(B)** Codominance results in the simultaneous expression of two dominant alleles. Recombination (A) is the process by which members of separated allele pairs are randomly recombined. Segregation (C) is the random separation of the members of allele pairs that occurs during meiosis. Polyploidy (E) is a condition in which cells have some multiple of the normal chromosome number.

21. **(C)** The phenotype ratios can be found using a Punnett Cross. RR is red; Rw is pink; and WW is white. We obtain 1 red plant, 2 pink plants, and 1 white plant.

	R	W
R	RR	RW
W	RW	WW

22.   **(A)** The best way to visualize this answer is to make a Punnett Cross.

$$
\begin{array}{ccc}
 & W & W \\
R & RW & RW \\
W & WW & WW
\end{array}
$$

We see that two out of the four offspring (50%) will have the genotype WW, which will result in white phenotype.

23.   **(E)** Down's Syndrome is a genetic disorder caused by the nondisjunction of chromosome 21 resulting in the presence of an extra chromosome. Color-blindness (A) and hemophilia (D) are examples of sex-linked traits. Tay-Sachs disease (B) is a genetic disease in which an enzyme necessary for the breakdown of lipids is missing. Sickle-cell anemia (C) is a genetic disease in which the red blood cells have an abnormal hemoglobin molecule.

24.   **(B)** Color-blindness is a sex-linked trait. The man has one Y chromosome and one X chromosome that carries the gene for color-blindness. Since his wife is a carrier, she has one X chromosome that carries the gene for color-blindness. Since his wife is a carrier, she has one X chromosome with the color-blind gene and one normal X chromosome. The chance of a "color-blind X" from the man joining with a "color-blind X" from the woman. "is 1 out of 2."

25.   **(C)** Polyploidy is a condition in which the cells have some multiple of the normal number of chromosomes. Translocation (A) is not the correct choice because it is a type of chromosome mutation in which a section of a chromosome is transferred to a nonhomologous chromosome. A deletion (B) refers to a chromosome mutation in which a piece of chromosome is lost. Crossing-over (D) refers to a pattern of inheritance where linked genes may be separated and then exchanged. Transpiration (E) is the evaporation of water from leaf stomates.

26.   **(C)** Mutations are recessive and detrimental to the organism. Hybrid vigor (A) results from the crossing of two homozygous parents to produce heterozygous offspring with more desirable traits. Most mutations are not reversible (B) or beneficial to the organism (D).

27.   **(D)** Human gametes contain 23 chromosomes. When an egg is fertilized, the number of chromosomes on the zygote formed is 46 (A).

There are 22 (B) non-sex chromosome pairs in the human species called autosomes. 47 (C) chromosomes are found in a person with Down's Syndrome.

28. **(A)** The female carrier produces two possible gametes T and t, where T is a normal gamete and t represents a gamete carrying the disease. The male carrier also produces two possible gametes Ta and t. The answer can be visualized using a Punnett Cross.

woman carrier		male carrier	
Tt		Tt	
T	t	T	t (possible gametes)

	T	t
T	TT	Tt
t	Tt	tt

The TT offspring will be normal. The two offspring that are Tt will be normal but will be carriers of the disease. The offspring who inherits both gametes that carry the disease will exhibit the disease. Choices (B) through (E) are not mathematical possibilities.

29. **(D)** The answer can be demonstrated using a Punnett Cross. The genotype of both parents can be represented by Ff, where F represents the dominant gene for free ear lobe and f represents the recessive gene for attached ear lobe.

Ff × Ff		
	F	f
F	FF	Ff
f	Ff	ff

The offspring with genotypes FF and Ff will demonstrate the free ear phenotype. The offspring with the genotype ff will exhibit the recessive phenotype attached ear lobes. Choice (A), (B), (C), and (E) are mathematically impossible.

30. **(B)** If any of the offspring produced show the recessive phenotype, then it indicates that the test organism was heterozygous. If all the offspring produced show the dominant phenotype, then the organism was homozygous for the dominant trait. A test cross always involves an indi-

vidual with a known genotype and an unknown. Choice (A) is incorrect because a cross between an unknown and a dominant organism will result in 100% expression of the dominant gene. Choice (C) will also result in the production of recessive offspring if the unknown is heterozygous, but this is not the best answer because of the increased possibility of inaccurate results.

31. **(A)** The environment influences gene action. Polyploidy (B) is an abnormality in which an entire set of homologous chromosomes fail to separate during the disjunction phase of meiosis, leading to multiple numbers of chromosomes. Chromosomal nondisjunction (C) occurs when members of a pair of homologous chromosomes fail to separate. Crossing-over (D) refers to a pattern of inheritance in which sections of homologous chromosomes may be exchanged. Choices (B) through (E) do not best explain the reason for the color change.

32. **(E)** Brown eyes and free earlobes are dominant traits in human being. Choices (B) and (C) are incorrect because attached earlobes and straight hair are examples of recessive human traits.

33. **(B)** Inbreeding occurs when breeders mate members of the same family with each other. Natural selection (A) states that individuals best adapted to their environment tend to survive. Hybridization (C) occurs when two varieties of the same species or members of different species are cross bred. Crossing-over (D) is a pattern of inheritance in which sections of homologous chromosomes are exchanged. Polyploidy (E) is a type of chromosome mutation in which sets of chromosomes fail to separate, resulting in multiple numbers of chromosomes.

34. **(E)** This is an example of incomplete dominance. Pink petals result from the cross between a homozygous red plant and a homozygous white plant. When a homozygous plant is crossed with a hybrid, both phenotypes are displayed in a 1:1 ratio. This can be visualized by setting up a Punnett Cross between RR and RW.

	R	R
R	RR	RR
W	RW	RW

The crossing of a red plant with a white plant would produce 100% pink plants. The crossing of a white plant with a pink plant would result in a 1:1

ratio of white to pink plants. The crossing of a pink plant with another pink plant would result in a 1:1:2 ratio of red to white to pink plants. The crossing of a red petal plant with another red petal plant would result in all red offspring.

35. **(A)** There are three alleles for blood type, I^a, I^b, and i. Blood type is determined by the combination of alleles. Blood type O is represented by ii. Choice (B) is incorrect because a person with type A blood would have a genotype of I^aI^a. Choice (C) is incorrect because when both I^a and I^b alleles occur in the same person, the person has type AB blood. Choice (D), I^ai represents a person with type A blood since the I^a allele is dominant over the i allele. Likewise, choice (E) is incorrect because it represents someone with type B blood.

36. **(B)**

	A	B
O	AO	BO
O	AO	BO

Type reflects the presence of both an A allele and a B allele. The offspring of a cross between a man with type O blood and a woman with type AB blood would produce offspring with blood types A and B. Blood type AB would not be produced. Type O blood would also not be produced.

37. **(A)** When both I^a and I^b alleles occur in the same person, the person has type AB blood. Choice (B) is incorrect because the genotype I^ai represents a person with type A blood since the I^a allele is dominant over the i allele. Choice (C) is incorrect because the I^bi genotype represents a person with type B blood since the I^b allele is dominant over the i allele. Choice (D) is incorrect because the genotype ii represents a person with type O blood. Choice (E) is incorrect because two alleles must be present.

38. **(B)** Person 4 is a female and a carrier for color-blindness. Choice (A) is incorrect because X^nX^n depicts a normal female. Choice (C) is wrong because X^nX^n represents a color-blind female. Choice (D) describes a color-blind male. Choice (E) is incorrect because X^NY represents a normal male.

39. **(E)** Female 6 has two genes for normal color vision. A male has only one X chromosome and has one gene for color-blindness. The daugh-

ters will all have normal vision, and they will all be carriers for color-blindness. Choices (A) through (D) are incorrect because they are not mathematically possible.

$$X^N X^N \quad \times \quad X^n Y$$

	X^N	X^N
X^n	$X^N X^n$	$X^N X^n$
Y	$X^N Y$	$X^N Y$

$X^N X^n$ represents a normal female who is a carrier for color-blindness.

40. **(B)** A male with normal vision has normal genes for the trait. Female 10 is color-blind. Setting up a Punnett Cross, we see that only the sons will be color-blind.

$$X^n X^n \quad \times \quad X^N Y$$

	X^n	X^n
X^N	$X^N X^n$	$X^N X^n$
Y	$X^n Y$	$X^n Y$

41. **(C)** The principle of independent assortment states that different traits are inherited independently of one another. Choice (A) is incorrect because the law of segregation states that during meiosis alleles separate randomly. Choice (B) is incorrect because incomplete dominance (also called codominance) is a type of inheritance in which two dominant alleles with contrasting characteristics are simultaneously expressed. Choice (D) is incorrect because gene linkage is a pattern of inheritance in which genes located along the same chromosome are prevented from assorting independently. Choice (E) is incorrect because crossing-over is the process in which pieces of homologous chromosomes are exchanged.

42. **(A)** Black mice with short tails would have BB or Bb and tt in the genotype expression. Tan mice with short tails would have bb and tt in their genotype expression. From the Punnett Cross we obtain 1 BBtt and 2 Bbtt which adds up to 3. The genotype expression for tan, short tail mice is bbtt. In the Punnett Cross we see only 1 bbtt. Therefore, the ratio is 3:1. Choices (B) through (E) are mathematically incorrect.

43. **(B)** Animals with black fur have a genotype expression of BB or Bb. Those with a tan fur phenotype must be bb, which is pure recessive.

From the Punnett Cross we see that there are 12 offspring with a BB or Bb genotype. These will express themselves in a black fur phenotype. There are only four offspring with a bb genotype which will result in four tan offspring. Therefore, the ratio obtained is 12:4. Choices (A), (C), (D), and (E) are not mathematically possible.

44. **(D)** From the Punnett Cross we can see that there are four off-spring with the BbTt genotype. These four are genetically identical to the parent dihybrid. Choices (A), (B), (C), and (E) are not possible.

45. **(C)** Each group of three nucleotides (called a triplet codon) provides the necessary information to code for a single amino acid. Choices (A), (B), (D), and (E) are incorrect.

46. **(C)** Nucleotides containing adenine are attracted by nucleotides containing thymine. Nucleotides containing cytosine are attracted to nucleotides containing guanine. Choice (A) is incorrect because it is an exact replica of the DNA strand shown. Choices (B) and (D) are incorrect because they contain uracil. Uracil is found in RNA. Choice (E) contains many errors in pairing.

47. **(D)** Thymine is found in DNA and is not a component of RNA. Choices (A), (B), (C), and (E) are true. RNA can exist as messenger RNA, transfer RNA, or ribosomal RNA.

48. **(D)** The two strands of DNA separate from each other by breaking the bonds between the pairs of nitrogenous bases. Choices (A), (B), and (C) are incorrect because they represent components of DNA whose bonds are not broken during replication. There are no carbon-oxygen bonds broken during DNA replication, thus (E) is an incorrect choice.

49. **(B)** Choice (A) is incorrect because the dominant allele in the gene pool is represented by the letter p. Homozygous individuals (D) in the population are represented by p and q. Heterozygous individuals (E) in the population are represented by $2pq$.

50. **(A)** If two species occupy the same niche they must have the same food requirement. The species best able to secure food will survive at the expense of the other species. Choice (B) is incorrect because mutualism occurs when two organisms live together for their mutual benefit. Choice (C) is incorrect because overpopulation is the production of more indi-

viduals than can be supported. Choice (D) is incorrect because a mutation is a change in genetic structure. Choice (E) is incorrect because overproduction would aid in the establishment of a niche.

51.   **(B)** When two organisms of different species live together and benefit each other, the relationship is called symbiosis. Choice (A) is incorrect because competition is a condition that occurs when different species in the same habitat attempt to use the same limited resources. Choice (C) is incorrect because parasitism occurs when one organism in the relationship benefits at the expense of the other. Choices (D) and (E) have no bearing on the problem.

52.   **(A)** An ecosystem consists of living species and the nonliving environment and the interaction between them. A community (B) is a collection of different species that live and interact in a given region. A niche (C) is the role that an organism plays in its environment. A population (D) consists of organisms of the same species that live in a particular location. A biome (E) is a major geographical grouping of similar ecosystems.

53.   **(C)** Natural selection states that individuals best adapted to their environments tend to survive. The antibiotic resistant strain of bacteria had probably mutated and was therefore able to survive treatment with the antibiotic. Choice (A) is incorrect because "use and disuse" is a term associated with the evolutionary theory of Lamarck. Choice (B) is incorrect because species preservation is the establishment of gamelands and wildlife refuges that have helped endangered species recover. Choice (D) is incorrect because segregation refers to random separation of members of allele pairs. Choice (E) is incorrect because polyploidy is a situation resulting from the failure of entire sets of chromosomes to separate.

54.   **(C)** A gene pool is the total of all the inheritable genes for the traits in a population. Choice (A) is incorrect because a gene frequency is the proportion of each allele that is present. Choice (B) is incorrect because it is a definition of genetic screening. Choice (D) is incorrect because a gene mutation is an alteration of the chemical nature of the gene. Choice (E) is incorrect because gene linkage is a pattern of inheritance in which genes located along the same chromosome are linked together in their inheritance.

55.   **(A)**   A parasite is a heterotroph which benefits at the expense of its living host. Choice (B) is incorrect because a scavenger is an organism that feeds on uneaten remains of dead animals and plants. Choice (C) is incorrect because a decomposer recycles materials by releasing minerals from dead plants and animals. Choice (D) is incorrect because saprophytes are organisms that feed on dead organic matter. Choice (E) is incorrect because a consumer is an organism that obtains nutrients from other organisms.

56.   **(D)**   Mutualism is a form of symbiosis in which both organism benefit. The nitrogen-fixing bacteria benefit by having a stable environment while the legume plant benefits from the nitrates produced by the bacteria. Choice (A) is incorrect because in parasitism one organism benefits at the expense of the other. Choice (C) is incorrect because a heterotroph is an organism that must depend on other organisms for its food. Choice (E) is incorrect because commensalism occurs when one organism benefits while the other organism is neither helped nor harmed.

57.   **(A)**   Choices (B) and (C) are examples of abiotic factors. Choices (B) through (E) are incorrect because one or more types of vegetation is out of sequence.

58.   **(A)**   Choices (B) and (C) are examples of abiotic factors. Abiotic factors are the chemical and physical factors in the environment upon which life depends.

59.   **(B)**   Omnivores are both plant and animal eaters. Choice (A) is incorrect because autotrophs are organisms capable of producing their own food. Choice (C) is incorrect because herbivores are animals that ingest only plants. Choice (D) is incorrect because producers are green plants and algae that use the sun's energy to manufacture organic compounds. Choice (E) is incorrect because carnivores consume the bodies of other animals for food.

60.   **(C)**   The fungus acts as a parasite which benefits at the expense of the human. The fungus obtains nutrients from the skin and causes it to become itchy and swell. Choice (A) is incorrect because in a mutalistic relationship both organisms benefit. Choice (B) is incorrect because in commensalism one organism benefits while the other organism is unaffected. Choice (D) is incorrect because autotropic behavior is exhibited when an organism synthesizes its own food. Choice (E) is incorrect be-

cause a food chain is a series of organisms through which food energy is passed on.

Section 2

61.   **(B)** For Na(s) and $Cl_2(g)$ to react, they must each first become ions. Na will form Na^+ ions by losing an electron, while a Cl atom forms Cl^- ions by gaining an electron. Thus, the electron is removed from the sodium and transferred to the chlorine atom. This transfer shows that NaCl is an ionic compound. Na^+ is a cation since it carries a positive electric charge, and Cl is an anion since it has a negative electric charge (since it gained an additional electron).

62.   **(E)** The bonds in H_2 (A) and Cl_2 (B) are covalent because the two identical atoms share the electrons equally. Additionally, diamonds (D) are covalently bonded. To be so hard, a diamond cannot have any weak bonds. NaCl (C) is ionic because Na^+ and Cl^- are ions of opposite charge.

63.   **(B)** Electrons will fill the 1s orbital first, then 2s, then 2p, then 3s, 3p, 4s, 3d, etc. Each electron is placed in the lowest-energy orbital available. Since hydrogen occupies 1s, the 1s orbital must be of lowest energy. Thus, (A) and (C) can be excluded from consideration. (E) is wrong because a 1p orbital does not exist. (D) is wrong because an s orbital has lower energy than a p orbital.

64.   **(A)** The spins of electrons are paired when they are spinning in opposite directions, or one has $m_s = +1/2$ and the other has $m_s = -1/2$. (B) and (C) are wrong because these electrons cannot occupy the same orbital if they have the same spin. Thus, (E) is also wrong. (D) is wrong because spin is designated by +1/2, not +1. Additionally, the spins shown here are the same (both positive) so the electrons could not both be present in the same orbital.

65.   **(C)** Two electrons fill the 1s orbital, two electrons fill the 2s orbital, which can hold six electrons. (B) shows the right energy levels but the superscripts are missing. (D) is wrong because 2s is not higher in energy than 2p. (A) is wrong because the 1s can only hold two electrons. (E) is wrong because the 1s orbital fills first, and all nine electrons cannot fit in the 2p orbital.

66. **(C)** Rutherford concluded that the particles were colliding with the nucleus of the gold atom which is where most of the mass of the atom is concentrated. (A) is incorrect because the particles do have enough velocity to pass through the empty space surrounding the nuclei. (B) is wrong because the electrons have a mass too small to repel alpha particles. (D) is wrong because although alpha rays and gold nuclei are both positively charged, this would not cause the large deflection. (E) is wrong because air cannot pull alpha particles in any way.

67. **(A)** It is true that most of the atom is empty space. (B) is wrong because the thickness of the gold foil does not affect the movement of the alpha particles. If a nucleus was in the path of the particle, the particle would then be deflected. (C) is wrong because the electrons are too small to influence the alpha particles. (D) is incorrect; atomic nuclei are not semipermeable. They are dense and cause the alpha particles to be deflected. (E) is wrong because the nuclei will not be moved by the alpha particles. Instead, the alpha particles collide with the nuclei and bounce off at an angle.

68. **(E)** Au is the correct choice. (D) Na is the chemical symbol for sodium. (C) He is the symbol for helium. (B) Hg, is mercury, and (A), Ga, is the symbol for gallium.

69. **(B)** If the car's speed is considered negative when backing up, then it must be going forward when it is positive. The graph shows positive speed for all times past approximately the 2.5 second mark. Since the total time is 30 seconds, the time it must be moving forward is 27.5 seconds. Note the car is backing up at 20 meters per second when the time starts and constantly slows down to a rest and increased in speed until it is going 60 meters per second, which is about 134 mph.

70. **(C)** The vertical axis represents the speed of the car. For it to be constant, the vertical movement on the graph must be zero. That is, the curve must remain horizontal. This happens between the 10 and 20 second marks. Before that, the car is accelerating in the forward direction, and after that, the car is slowing down to rest.

71. **(E)** The vertical axis represents the speed of the car. The maximum speed it has backing up is 20 meters per second and the maximum speed it has going forward is 60 meters per second. It is the highest value reached on the vertical axis. The average speed of the car during the first

10 seconds is 20 meters per second and the distance covered during the first 10 seconds is 200 meters or 656 feet.

72. **(E)** Acceleration is change in velocity over change in time. During the first 2.5 seconds, the acceleration is (20/2.5) 8 m/s². During the 2.5–10 second interval, the acceleration is (60/7.5) 8 m/s². During the 15–20 second interval, the acceleration is (0/5) 0 m/s². During the 20–25 second interval, the acceleration is (10/5) 2 m/s². During the 25–30 second interval the acceleration, or actually, deceleration, is greatest. It's the steepest part of the graph. The brakes are being applied!

73. **(C)** The water column is 34 feet high while the mercury column under the same conditions is only 2.5 feet high. Since the columns have the same cross-sectional area, the weight of the mercury must be 34/2.5 times that of water. This ratio is 13.6 to 1. Mercury is 13.6 times more dense than water. This is why air pressure was formerly measured with mercury barometers rather than water barometers. The latter would not fit in a normal classroom.

74. **(D)** The pressure is defined to be force per unit area. Weight is a force. The weight of the man divided by the area of the boots is 200 lb/70 square inches. This is a pressure of about 2.86 PSI. Notice that this is only about one-fifth of what the air applies to snow.

75. **(D)** The pressure is defined to be force per unit area. Weight is a force. The weight of the girl is 110 pounds and the area of the skis is 330 square inches. This is a pressure of (110/330) 0.333 PSI. Since air applies a pressure of 14.7 PSI, it is greater by a factor of about 44. This explains why sleds and snowshoes are so useful in traveling great distances over snow-covered terrain.

76. **(A)** Since air exerts the same pressure whether it is viewed over one square inch or over one square mile, the one square foot column of water will be forced to the same 34-foot height. It is the total force that is greater on the larger area, but it is the ratio of force divided by area that is the same. The larger diameter column of fluid needs more force to reach the same height but the area is larger so that the pressure stays the same.

77. **(C)** An electroscope can measure whether electrons are added to it or taken away. It can also measure whether a charged object is brought near by either attracting electrons to its top knob or driving electrons down

the rod and into the gold leaves. Choice (D) makes no sense. The source of the electrons is either from without by direct contact or from the knob above or from the gold itself. However, the electroscope does not indicate how many electrons the gold contains. Choice (E) is meaningless. The electroscope responds to the surplus or deficiency of electrons, not to the surplus or deficiency of protons.

78. **(B)** When a positively charged rod is brought near the top, elec-trons will be drawn from the gold up the internal rod to the knob. This leaves the gold leaves positively charged. If they are close to the same mass, they both will give up the same number of electrons and will result in the same positive charge. They then repel each other and separate. The knob has become negative, but the entire electroscope is still neutral since no charge has been added to it or taken away. All that has happened is that charge has been rearranged upon it due to the presence of an outside electrical field provided by the positively charged rod.

79. **(B)** If the gold leaves of an electroscope are separated before the vinyl is brought near, it must mean that some charge has been added to or taken from the electroscope. In this case electrons have been added to the electroscope so that it is charged negatively. When a negative vinyl is now brought near, electrons in the knob will be repelled down the internal rod to the gold leaves. They will now acquire a greater negative charge and tend to spread even further apart.

80. **(B)** Wyoming is located in an area of predicted minor damage. (A), (C), (D), and (E) are all states that are predicted to have more serious earthquakes.

81. **(E)** The map indicates that earthquakes of varying degrees can occur in almost every state. (A) and (B) are incorrect because the map is making predictions about where earthquakes might occur, rather than where earthquakes will definitely occur. (C) is wrong because according to the map, Texas might suffer minor damage in the next 100 years. (D) is incorrect, because many theories and conclusions can be drawn from the information given.

82. **(A)** is correct, because all of the gases listed are dangerous to life. (B) is wrong because volcanoes, according to the passage, do not always emit both lava and gas. (C) is incorrect, because "volcanic activity" is a

term that relates to different types of events. (D) and (E) are wrong, and the first sentence of this passage confirms this.

83. **(D)** In the passage a list of gases emitted from volcanoes is given and oxygen is not listed. (A) and (B) are incorrect choices as stated in the paragraph. (C) is an incorrect choice since the volcanoes formed the early atmosphere, and the earth now has oxygen, the oxygen must have come from some other activity.

84. **(E)** "Pyroclastic" comes from the term pyro," meaning fire. A "pyroclastic display" is a shower of fire and debris from a volcano.

85. **(B)** Only Well 2 breaks through the surface at a point below the artesian water table, causing water pressure to force water to the surface. (A) is incorrect because Well 1 would require a pump to bring water to the surface. (C) is incorrect; Well 3 does not extend into the aquifer. (D) is incorrect because Well 4 is in impermeable rock which does not contain water.

86. **(A)** Well 1 reaches into the aquifer, yet it is above the water table and would need a pump. (B) is incorrect as this well would gush water due to the pressure of an artesian system. (C) and (D) are incorrect as neither reaches the aquifer.

87. **(C)** Well 1 is incorrect because it is the only well to be in the local water table. (A) and (B) are incorrect as they are aquifer wells. (D) is incorrect as this well is dry, being in the impermeable rock layer.

88. **(C)** In reading the graph, the lowest numbers are located in the Northeast, and these numbers indicate the more concentrated acid. (A), (B), (D), and (E) are all incorrect as these areas all have higher readings, which indicate lower pH.

89. **(D)** Both Lakes Erie and Ontario are located in the area of lowest pH reading. (A) is incorrect; not all lakes are located in areas of low pH. (B) Lake Superior is in the least danger from acid rain. (C) is incorrect as Lakes Huron and Michigan are not in areas of low pH.

90. **(E)** The amount of rainfall does not affect the pH of the rain. (A), (B), (C), and (D) are all factors that concentrate pH or direct the pattern of rainfall.

91. **(B)** The physical properties of the ground allow it to absorb heat. (A) is incorrect, because the troposphere is under the ozone layer. (C) is incorrect, because ice cover affects only the place it is covering, not the entire planet. (D) is incorrect, because land and water have different rates of heating and cooling.

92. **(B)** According to the chart, the lowest temperatures are in the thermosphere, reaching –80°C. (A) and (D) are incorrect; they are boundaries, not layers. (C) and (E) are incorrect; they are layers, yet their temperatures are well above that of the thermosphere.

93. **(E)** Changes in composition would cause different rates of heating. (A) is incorrect, because change in distance is insignificant. (B) is incorrect, because weather is only found in the lowest atmospheric layer. (C) is incorrect, because ozone is only found in one layer. (D) is incorrect, because man does not affect the atmosphere.

94. **(A)** Desert areas increase evaporation of the water that is present, causing a concentration of salts. Therefore, the remaining choices are incorrect.

95. **(C)** A compound can be a pure substance. The passage states that pure substances are either elements or compounds. It is easier to see the relationships posed in the choices by this simple chart:

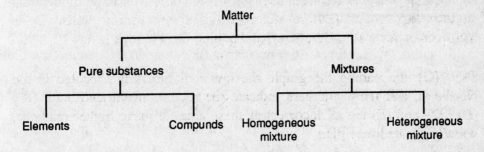

By studying this chart, which shows the relationships described in the passage, it becomes possible to eliminate the incorrect answer choices. (A) is wrong because a homogeneous mixture is a mixture, not a pure substance. (B) is incorrect since pure substances and mixtures are two distinctly different types of matter. (D) is wrong because the term "heterogeneous" implies being composed of parts with visibly different properties.

Since one type of element, such as a lump of lead, has consistency with respect to its physical properties, then this one element cannot simultaneously possess visibly different properties. (E) is wrong because matter can be categorized, as shown in the above diagram.

96. **(B)** This can be proven by visualizing a homogeneous mixture to be water (which has the same properties throughout) and a heterogeneous mixture to be water with rocks in it (since this combination would be composed of parts with visibly different properties). If the water is combined with water plus rocks, the resulting mixture will be water plus rocks, which is a heterogeneous mixture. (A) is wrong because the mixture will not be homogeneous; rocks have very different properties in comparison to water. (C) is wrong since a pure substance is entirely a different branch of matter from mixtures. (D) is wrong because these two mixtures will indeed be miscible, and (E) is incorrect because the resulting solution can be classified as a heterogeneous mixture.

97. **(E)** Only (E), zinc sulfide, is not an element, because it can undergo a chemical change when it is heated to form two substances, zinc and sulfur. Zinc (A), sodium (B), iron (C), and tin (D) are all elements. They can each be found in a periodic table of the elements. None can be broken down further to any other type of matter.

98. **(B)** Answer choice (B) is the correct answer since proteins can be of different lengths; they can contain different types of amino acids; the amino acids can be in different orders in the protein. (A) cannot be the correct choice since proteins can also differ by the order of their amino acids and/or by the types of amino acids they contain. (C) cannot be the correct choice since proteins can also differ in length and/or by the order of their amino acids. (D) cannot be the correct choice since it is not mentioned as being one of the factors by which proteins can be different. (E) cannot be the correct choice since proteins can differ by the length of the protein and/or the type of amino acids found in the protein.

99. **(A)** Answer choice (A), 20, is the correct choice since there are 20 different types of "R" factor which produce 20 different types of amino acids. 50 (B) cannot be the correct choice since there are only 20 different types of "R" factor which produce 20 different types of amino acids. 100 (C) cannot be the correct choice since there are only 20 different types of "R" factor which produce 20 different types of amino acids. 1,000 (D) cannot be the correct choice since there are only 20 different types of "R" factor which produce 20 different types of amino acids. 100,000 (E) can-

not be the correct choice since there are only 20 different types of "R" factor which produce 20 different types of amino acids.

100. **(E)** Answer choice (E) chains of amino acids is the correct choice since amino acids are bonded together to form a chain. Chains of sugar molecules (A) cannot be the correct choice since only amino acid chains make protein. Chains of fat molecules (B) cannot be the correct choice since fat molecules are not part of a protein chain, and they are not mentioned in the paragraph. Rings of carbon (C) cannot be the correct choice since carbon rings form structures other than protein, and proteins which are composed of amino acids have no carbon rings. Loops of cellulose molecules (D) cannot be the correct choice since proteins are composed of amino acid chains.

101. **(C)** Answer choice (C) is the correct choice since rock is not composed of amino acids. Hair (A) cannot be the correct choice since hair is composed of protein. Fingernails (B) cannot be the correct choice since they are composed of protein. Skin (D) cannot be the correct choice since its major components are protein. Muscle tissue (E) cannot be the correct choice since its bulk is derived from protein.

102. **(A)** Tar is the most viscous because the molecules composing tar are long and thus tangle easily. Lubricating oil (C) and gasoline (B) are composed of shorter molecules and thus flow easier, or are less viscous. (D) is wrong because tar and lubricating oil, or gasoline and tar (E) have molecules of different lengths and thus different viscosities.

103. **(E)** Long chains breaking to form shorter chains will help the substance to flow better, and viscosity will be reduced. (A) is wrong because the formation of long chains will result in increased viscosity. (B) is wrong because although thermal energy does increase, it will cause chain breakage, not increased tangling. (C) is wrong because chain vaporization has never been observed. (D) is wrong for the same reason.

104. **(D)** The longer the pendulum, the greater the time for one complete vibrational period. Since the acceleration due to gravity is constant, the length of the pendulum must be directly proportional to the square of the period. Here on Earth a two-second pendulum is one meter long. Doubling the period to four seconds implies a quadrupling of the length to four meters. Tripling the period to six seconds implies increasing the pendulum's length nine times.

105. **(E)** If the period of a pendulum is to remain constant while it is moved to a different position in space, then the length is directly proportional to the acceleration due to gravity "g." On the moon the acceleration due to gravity is one-sixth what it is on Earth, so that to have the same-period pendulum on the moon means its length must also be one-sixth of what it is on Earth. Similarly, on Jupiter the acceleration due to gravity at its cloud tops is over 2.3 times what it is on Earth, so that there the same pendulum would have to be over 2.3 times longer.

106. **(B)** From the information given, it is apparent that the period depends on "g" (A), on the fact that the amplitude must be less than 5° (C), and on the length (D). No mention of the mass (B) was made. Hence, we can assume it makes no difference for what we need here. The only difference a greater mass could make is increasing the effective length of the pendulum by taking up more space. The length of the pendulum is defined to be from the pivot point at the top to the bob's center of mass.

107. **(A)** The units of "g" were given as meters/sec^2. This is distance divided by (time × time). This can be rearranged to read distance (divided by time) divided by time. This is speed divided by time. And that is exactly what acceleration means: how fast is the speed changing in time. Weight (C) and force (E) are concepts that require mass. Distance over time (B) is speed. Velocity over distance (D) is the inverse of time.

108. **(C)** By Newton's Third Law of Motion, the gravitational pull of a first body on a second must be equal and opposite to the pull of the second back on the first, no matter what the mass of each body is or what the motion of each body is. Therefore, I pull back on the Earth with the same force Earth pulls on me, but in the opposite direction. But, because my mass is so small, I accelerate downward a great deal (9.8 m/s^2) while the mass of Earth is so large that it accelerates minutely.

109. **(A)** The gravitational pull between two masses is proportional to the product of their masses. Hence, doubling the two masses would increase the pull by four times. Since Earth is 82 times more massive than the moon, the pull between the sun and Earth must be 82 times greater than the pull between Earth and moon if their separations were the same. Actually, the smaller distance between Earth and moon makes the pull between the sun and Earth only 175 times the pull between Earth and moon.

110. **(D)** The gravitational pull between any two masses is inversely proportional to the square of the distance between them. The pull between the moon and Earth was given as 2×10^{20} N. If their separation was increased by two, then the force between them would have to decrease by four. A force of 2×10^{20} N divided by four is 5×10^{19} N.

111. **(D)** Since each choice given involves the pull between the moon and sun, the key factor is the relative distances between the bodies. The distance between the sun and moon is on the average 393 times greater than the distance between the moon and Earth. Remembering that the pull is inversely proportional to the square of the distance, the pull between the moon and Earth must be 393^2 or 154,449 times the pull between the sun and moon.

112. **(C)** The Br_2 molecules "stick" together at low temperatures because attractive forces between the molecules become stronger than the thermal energy, which tends to cause separation of molecules. Thus, choice (C) is correct. Choice (A) does not apply because the electrostatic forces of attraction are what cause the molecules to "stick." Ice is not involved. (B) is incorrect because molecules at low temperatures have decreased thermal energy, not increased thermal energy. (D) is wrong because gases tend to condense at low temperatures, not expand. (E) is wrong because Br_2 molecules, and most elements in general, will compress at low temperatures and go into a liquid phase.

113. **(D)** Gases contain molecules that move freely in space. Gases are thus the most random. Liquids still move but attractive forces between molecules prevent totally random motion. The solid state contains molecules that are ordered and close together. Thus, the rigid state of a solid renders it least random. The correct order is gas, liquid, solid.

114. **(D)** The liquid is vaporizing to form a gas at the boiling point. Air does not enter from the atmosphere (A) because the atmospheric pressure is equivalent to the vapor pressure; there is not a higher external pressure forcing air into the liquid. (B) is wrong because although liquid does form a gas at the boiling point, it does so by expanding, not by condensing. (C) is incorrect because the passage does not mention helium gas in the liquid as the cause of the bubbles. Helium gas is rare on Earth. (E) is wrong because microorganisms do not cause bubbles in boiling liquid. In fact, most microorganisms would not thrive at the boiling points of most naturally occurring liquids, such as water.

115. **(D)** As water boils, the liquid water evaporates. Water loss occurs in the form of steam, and the volume of water decreases. Choice (A) is incorrect because water molecules are not created over the hot steam. Choice (B) is wrong because the volume decreases rather than remains constant. Atmospheric pressure will not cause the volume to increase and decrease as choice (C) describes, and choice (E) is also incorrect.

116. **(B)** Choice (B) is the false statement. Many liquids boil below 100°C (when water boils) and thus would not be considered extremely hot. Liquid nitrogen boils at room temperature, for instance. (A) and (E) are true statements that are discussed briefly in the passage. (C) is true because more heat will be needed to heat more water. (D) is also true in that the external pressure is relatively higher in comparison to the lower vapor pressure below the boiling point and thus prevents gas bubble formation.

117. **(B)** The dots representing the most number of stars are clustered in the area called Main Sequence; therefore, (B) is the correct choice. (A), (C), and (D) are incorrect because the number of stars in these areas is less than those of the Main Sequence area, and (E) is incorrect because Alpha Centauri is the name of a star, not of a group.

118. **(D)** Sirius is located to the upper left of the sun in this diagram, which shows it is in a warmer and brighter position than the sun. (A), (B), (C), and (E) are all locations that Sirius is not in.

119. **(D)** Canopus is a Main Sequence star.

120. **(A)** Answer choice (A) is correct because our sun is located in the middle of the diagram, making it average in many respects. (B) is incorrect. The sun is a Main Sequence star, making it similar to many other stars. (C) is incorrect because distances are not included on this diagram. (D) is incorrect because many of these stars are invisible to the unaided eye. (E) is incorrect because no data regarding star size is provided.

PRACTICE
TEST 2

CLEP NATURAL SCIENCES
Test 2

(Answer sheets appear in the back of the book.)

Section 1

TIME: 45 Minutes
          60 Questions

DIRECTIONS: Each of the questions or incomplete statements below is followed by five possible answers or completions. Select the best choice in each case and fill in the corresponding oval on the answer sheet.

---

1. Australia is a continent where many species of marsupials are found. These marsupials are not found anywhere else on Earth. The existence of these unique species is most likely the result of

    (A) mutation.   (D) variations.

    (B) geographic isolation.   (E) overpopulation.

    (C) random mating.

2. The age of fossils has often been determined using the radioactive isotope

    (A) carbon-14.   (D) hydrogen-2.

    (B) carbon-12.   (E) oxygen-18.

    (C) nitrogen-15.

3. A mule is in many ways superior to either of its parents. This is an example of

   (A) dominance.   (D) inbreeding.

   (B) selection.   (E) mutation.

   (C) hybrid vigor.

4. According to the Hardy-Weinberg Principle, which of the following conditions will occur within a given population from generation to generation if there is random mating, no mutation, and no migration?

   (A) The gene frequency will remain stable.

   (B) The frequency of dominant genes will increase.

   (C) The frequency of recessive genes will increase.

   (D) The frequency of dominant genes will decrease.

   (E) The frequency of recessive genes will decrease.

5. Certain insecticides have been found to accumulate in the fat tissues of humans. Which statement best explains the accumulation?

   (A) Insecticides can be absorbed directly into fat cells from the air.

   (B) Insecticides are absorbed through skin cuts directly into the blood stream.

   (C) Insecticides are passed along the food chain.

   (D) Insecticides are transported through the air.

   (E) Insecticides can act as by-products of cellular respiration.

6. Plants that produce covered seeds which develop within the ovary of a flower are classified as

   (A) gymnosperms.   (D) angiosperms.

   (B) perennials.   (E) biennuals.

   (C) Filicineae.

7. Why does the densest population of most marine organisms occur close to the surface of the ocean?

   (A) There is less pollution on the ocean surface.

(B) Water contains a higher salt concentration at the surface.

(C) The intensity of light that reaches ocean organisms decreases with depth.

(D) There are less minerals available as depth increases.

(E) All of the above.

8. A tropical rain forest is best characterized by which of the following descriptions?

(A) Abundant rainfall throughout the year

(B) A diversity of species

(C) The temperature is always above freezing.

(D) Lacy, open trees

(E) Both (A) and (C).

9. The Use and Disuse Theory of Evolution was first presented by

(A) Darwin.

(D) Muller.

(B) Lamarck.

(E) Watson and Crick.

(C) DeVries.

10. Most of Earth's photosynthesis takes place in which one of the following biomes?

(A) Oceans

(D) Deserts

(B) Tundra

(E) Tropical forests

(C) Deciduous forests

11. An example of a vestigial structure is the

(A) elephant's trunk.

(D) appendix of man.

(B) claw of a crab.

(E) man's thumb.

(C) ear muscles of a cat.

12. A blue-eyed child may be born to two parents who both have brown eyes. An explanation for this would be that

    (A) a mutation has occurred.

    (B) one parent is homozygous for brown eyes.

    (C) crossing-over has occurred.

    (D) one parent is recessive for blue eyes.

    (E) both parents are heterozygous.

13. Sickle-cell anemia is a disease resulting from

    (A) a substitution in an amino acid in the hemoglobin molecule.

    (B) a gene-induced inability to produce a hormone.

    (C) an inability to produce a certain enzyme.

    (D) a vitamin deficiency.

    (E) None of the above.

14. During DNA replication, a nucleotide base that would bond with guanine is

    (A) adenine.   (D) guanine.

    (B) cytosine.   (E) thymine.

    (C) uracil.

15. In a DNA molecule, the number of nucleotides containing adenine must equal the number of nucleotides containing

    (A) cytosine.   (D) uracil.

    (B) thymine.   (E) m-RNA.

    (C) guanine.

16. Because whales are classified as mammals, you would expect them to have all of the following characteristics EXCEPT

    (A) a vertebral column.

    (B) a dorsal hollow nerve cord.

(C) scales.

(D) warm-bloodedness.

(E) ability to nurse their young.

17. The term primary productivity refers to which part of the food chain?

(A) Herbivores

(B) Carnivores

(C) Omnivores

(D) Plants

(E) Decomposers

18. An ecological community with permafrost is the

(A) tropical rain forest.

(B) taiga.

(C) tundra.

(D) temperate forest.

(E) grassland.

19. Assuming the environmental factors remain constant, which of the following successional stages represents the most stable community?

(A) A lake

(B) Freshwater marsh

(C) Meadow

(D) Low shrubs

(E) Forest

20. A community of organisms interacting with abiotic environmental factors composes a(n)

(A) biogeochemical cycle.

(B) food chain.

(C) ecosystem.

(D) niche.

(E) population.

21. Which statement about cells, the basic building blocks of everything that is living, is true?

(A) Animals, unlike plants, have cells.

(B) Plant cells, unlike animal cells, have a nonliving cell wall.

(C) Chlorophyll is found only in the cells of plants.

(D) Animal cells, unlike plant cells, contain the DNA molecule used to carry genetic information.

(E) The cells of fungi are rich in chlorophyll, which aid in their manufacture of food.

22. Which of the following situations might cause harm to an embryo?

(A) The father is RH-positive; the mother, RH-negative.

(B) The mother had German measles during the first trimester of pregnancy.

(C) The father is RH-negative; the mother, RH-positive.

(D) Both (A) and (B).

(E) Both (B) and (C).

23. Which of the following lists contains an organ which is NOT a part of the digestive system?

(A) Pancreas, small intestine, large intestine

(B) Gall bladder, stomach, rectum

(C) Esophagus, stomach, small intestine

(D) Spleen, stomach, small intestine

(E) Mouth, liver, salivary glands

24. Which of the following contains an item that is NOT a function of all living things?

I. Food getting, transporting

II. Assimilating, respirating

III. Responding to environmental stimuli, reproducing

IV. Communicating, digesting

V. Producing food, excreting

(A) I and IV.   (D) IV and V.

(B) II and III.   (E) I and V.

(C) III and IV.

25. Heavy infections of *Trichinella* in people may cause a disease called trichinosis; such a situation may best be described as which of the following?

    (A) Parasitism   (D) Benevolent

    (B) Mutualism   (E) Benign

    (C) Commercialism

26. Most scientists would agree with all the following statements about the routine use of pesticides EXCEPT

    (A) as a result of the widespread use of DDT, a new type of housefly emerged.

    (B) pesticides tend to become progressively less effective as the organisms become immune.

    (C) chemical control of pests should be used routinely, since it may result in the evolution of exciting new types of organisms.

    (D) application of chemical substances endanger both foes and friends (like honeybees) so routine use of chemicals seems inadvisable.

    (E) a pesticide may kill not only the intended insects but also the birds which feed on them.

27. Enzymes in the digestive tract serve which function(s)?

    (A) To enable molecules to pass into the bloodstream by passing through the membranes of the small intestine

    (B) To transform complex molecules into a form in which the cells of the body can use them for energy or for building new structures

    (C) To cause the fusion of food molecules so that they can be absorbed by the parts of the body

    (D) All the above.

    (E) Both (A) and (B).

28. All of the following are parts of the circulatory system EXCEPT

    (A) arteries.   (D) the heart.

    (B) capillaries.   (E) seminal vesicles.

    (C) veins.

29. All of the following are true of food webs and chains EXCEPT

    (A) implicit in a food chain and a food web is a natural system of checks and balances.

    (B) the shorter the food chain the greater the efficiency from the standpoint of energy flow.

    (C) an example of the shortest food chain is the people in India and China who feed primarily on plant foods.

    (D) the introduction of cattle between people and plants in a food chain reduces the efficiency.

    (E) the food chain is non-continuous; it does not require a flow of energy or a recycling of materials from consumer back to producer.

30. Listed below are five animals. Identify the phylum in which each belongs by choosing from the phylums below the sequence which matches the sequence of the animals.

    earthworm   oysters   bees   starfish   fish

    (A) Annelida, Molluska, Arthropoda, Echinodermata, Vertebrata

    (B) Mulluska, Annelida, Arthropoda, Vertebrata, Echinodermata

    (C) Arthropoda, Molluska, Annelida, Echinodermata, Vertebrata

    (D) Echinodermata, Annelida, Molluska, Echinodermata, Vertebrata

    (E) Annelida, Molluska, Echinodermata, Vertebrata, Arthropoda

31. Which of the following is NOT a characteristic of reptiles?

    (A) Their young are developed from land eggs.

    (B) Their bodies are covered by scales or bony plates.

    (C) They are air-breathing throughout life.

(D) Reptiles have a variable body temperature.

(E) Their young are gill-breathing throughout life.

32. Which of the following is NOT true about changes in plants and animals?

(A) Changes (modifications) in plants and animals may occur very rapidly.

(B) Physical changes in the earth have brought about changes in plant and animal forms.

(C) Many plants and animals once living on Earth have disappeared.

(D) Intelligence is a factor in changes.

(E) Natural selection plays a part in changes in plants and animals.

33. Which of the following are usual functions of the digestive system?

I. Transportation

II. Assimilation

III. Excretion

IV. Reproduction

V. Response to environmental stimuli

(A) All of the above.   (D) IV and V only.

(B) None of the above.   (E) I, II, and III only.

(C) I, IV, and V only.

34. Which of the following is NOT a reproductive part of a flower?

(A) Stigma   (D) Antler

(B) Stamen   (E) Sperm

(C) Pistil

35. All of the following are parts of the respiratory system of humans EXCEPT

   (A) the trachea.   (D) bronchial tubes.

   (B) the spleen.   (E) the lungs.

   (C) the diaphragm.

36. Enzymes in the digestive tract serve

   (A) to enable molecules to enter into the bloodstream by helping them pass through the membranes of the small intestine.

   (B) to transform complex molecules into a form in which the cells of the body can use them.

   (C) Enzymes are essential since they cause molecules to fuse and to be utilized effectively by all parts of the body.

   (D) Both (A) and (B).

   (E) None of the above.

37. Listed below are four parts of a plant. Their functions are listed below.

   leaf   stem   root   flower

   I.   Transporter and supporter

   II.   Anchor and absorber

   III. Seed producer

   IV.   Food producer

   V.   Seed disperser and communication

   Match the function with the part by selecting the choice below which gives the function in the same order as the part with which it corresponds.

   (A) V, IV, III, II   (D) III, II, I, IV

   (B) IV, I, II, III   (E) I, II, III, IV

   (C) IV, II, I, II

38. All of the following statements about plants are true EXCEPT

    (A) the plant kingdom is divided into two major phyla called the tracheophytes and the bryophytes.

    (B) the plant kingdom is divided into two broad groups: plants that produce seeds and plants that do not produce seeds.

    (C) plants are living things that can make their own food.

    (D) chlorosynthesis is the process by which plants utilize light energy to create their own food.

    (E) gymnosperms are a class of woody plants which bear their seeds in a cone.

39. Which of the following is NOT a mammal?

    (A) A bat   (D) An elephant

    (B) A whale   (E) A shark

    (C) A gibbon

40. Which of the following best describes people in general?

    (A) Herbivorous   (D) Migratory

    (B) Carnivorous   (E) Hibernating

    (C) Omnivorous

41. Which of the following statements about protozoans is FALSE?

    (A) Protozoans are tiny, simple, one-celled animals.

    (B) They are made up of single cells.

    (C) The amoeba is the simplest protozoan.

    (D) A slipper-shaped protozoan is the euglena.

    (E) Protozoans are very tiny, simple, one-celled protists.

42. All of the following are true of plants EXCEPT

    (A) seed plants may be divided into angiosperms and gymnosperms.

    (B) the seeds of angiosperms are enclosed in a protective coat called a fruit.

(C) gymnosperms are also called conifers because they produce woody cones.

(D) the cone is the "fruit" of the conifers and is made up of scales.

(E) most conifers have leaves which drop off during the fall season; they are said to be deciduous.

43. Which of the following is true of the roots of plants?

(A) Roots generally can do little to hold plants in the ground since most soils are so shallow.

(B) In a diffuse root system, there is a primary root that grows until it is the largest root in the root system.

(C) In a taproot system the primary taproot grows until it is the major root in the system.

(D) Only plants with a diffuse root system store food in the roots since the taproots live for such a short time.

(E) Roots help with absorption of water and minerals, support of the plant, and storage of food, but they cannot help with reproduction.

44. The two long, pointed teeth near the front of the human mouth are properly called

(A) central incisors.   (D) molars.

(B) canines.   (E) lateral incisors.

(C) premolars.

45. Which of the following is the number of permanent teeth normally in the mouth of an adult human?

(A) 24   (D) 20

(B) 28   (E) 32

(C) 36

46. Which of the following statements about stems is NOT true?

(A) Herbaceous stems are usually soft and green and have no woody tissue in them.

(B) Woody stems are stiff and grow longer and thicker than herbaceous stems.

(C) Removal of bark in a circular section all the way around a tree is called girdling and will result in a thicker bark and a healthier plant or tree.

(D) The cambium is the thin tissue between the bark and wood which forms new wood and a growth ring.

(E) The formation of layers in a woody stem makes it possible to estimate the age of a tree if one counts the number of annual rings.

47. Which of the following is NOT a means used for controlling harmful insects?

(A) Destroy the environment in which the insects live.

(B) Establish quarantine laws to prevent the importing of insects into a country.

(C) Use chemicals to control harmful insects.

(D) Import or make use of local natural enemies.

(E) Use nuclear fusion to destroy colonies.

QUESTIONS 48 to 50 refer to the following table.

ERA	PERIOD	EVENTS	BEGAN MILLIONS OF YEARS AGO
	Quaternary	Age of humans. Four major glacial advances.	2
CENOZOIC	Tertiary	Increase in mammals. Appearance of primates. Mountain building in Europe and Asia.	65
	Cretaceous	Extinction of dinosaurs. Increase in flowering plants and reptiles.	140
MESOZOIC	Jurassic	Birds. Mammals. Dominance of dinosaurs. Mountain building in western North America.	195
	Triassic	Beginning of dinosaurs and primitive mammals.	230
	Permian	Reptiles spread and develop. Evaporate deposits. Glaciation in Southern Hemisphere.	280
	Carboniferous	Abundant amphibians. Reptiles appear.	345

PALEOZOIC	Devonian	Age of fishes. First amphibians. First abundant forests on land.	395
	Silurian	First land plants. Mountain building in Europe.	435
	Ordovician	First fishes and vertebrates.	500
	Cambrian	Age of marine invertebrates.	600
PRECAMBRIAN TIME		Beginning of life. At least five times longer than all geologic time following.	

48. Which of the following statements is true?

   (A) Earth's history is divided into time blocks, determined by geo-logic events only.

   (B) Earth's history is divided into equal divisions of time.

   (C) Earth's history is divided into time blocks of differing amounts of time.

   (D) Each period of Earth's history is divided into time blocks called eras.

   (E) Three major events are grouped under each period.

49. Which sequence of life is correct?

   (A) Invertebrates, fish, reptiles, mammals

   (B) Fish, invertebrates, mammals, birds

   (C) Plants, invertebrates, forests, fish

   (D) Invertebrates, mammals, birds, plants

   (E) Mammals, plants, birds, reptiles

50. According to the table, what period would have marked the appear-ance of the first relatives of the common alligator?

   (A) Silurian (D) Carboniferous

   (B) Triassic (E) Cambrian

   (C) Tertiary

QUESTIONS 51 to 53 refer to the following passage.

Over 300 years ago, a British scientist named Robert Hooke was looking through a microscope at thin sections of cork. He noticed that there were many cavities in the cork. He coined the term "cells" to refer to these cavities. In 1835, Felix Dujardin was able to view living cells through a microscope. In 1838, Matthias Schleiden proposed that all plants are composed of cells, and in 1840, Theodor Schwann stated that all animals are made of cells. Approximately 20 years later, Rudolf Virchow published his observations that disease affected only living things. Today, we know that the information gained by these men is summed up in what is known as "The Cell Theory." The Cell Theory states that: 1) all living things are composed of cells; 2) cells carry on the life processes such as using energy, taking in nutrients, organizing protoplasm, having a life span, reproduction, adapting, and having irritability; and 3) all cells are produced from pre-existing cells.

51. Which of the following would NOT be considered a living thing?

    (A) A rose   (D) An amoeba

    (B) A fungus   (E) A sponge

    (C) A virus

52. According to the Cell Theory, an icicle is

    (A) alive because it grows by the addition of more water.

    (B) alive because it has a life span which involves a beginning, growth, a period of maturity, a period of decline, and finally, death.

    (C) alive because it can reproduce.

    (D) not alive because it is composed of cells.

    (E) not alive because it is not composed of cells, it cannot reproduce, and it does not carry out any of the life functions.

53. The basic or common unit of life is

    (A) a cell.   (D) an organ system.

    (B) an organ.   (E) an organism.

    (C) a chemical compound.

QUESTIONS 54 to 59 refer to the following paragraph.

Cells contain chromosomes. The number of chromosomes that are in a cell varies. In sexually reproducing organisms, the cells usually have two sets of chromosomes. Cells like these are said to be "diploid." In organisms that reproduce asexually, the cells are usually "haploid," or having one set of chromosomes. Cells reproduce themselves by means of a process called mitosis. Some organisms can reproduce themselves by budding, or breaking, when there is no sexual reproduction. Sexually reproducing organisms undergo a process whereby they produce haploid cells from diploid cells. These haploid cells are called sperms or eggs. When a sperm and an egg are united, they fuse to form a single cell called a zygote. The zygote of a human has 46 chromosomes. A zygote is a diploid cell and will undergo mitosis to produce a mature organism.

54. There are 46 chromosomes found in the cheek cell of a human male. If this cell were to undergo mitosis, how many chromosomes would be found in each resulting daughter cell?

    (A) 2   (D) 46

    (B) 10   (E) 92

    (C) 24

55. Humans have 46 chromosomes in their body cells. How many chromosomes are found in the zygote?

    (A) 2   (D) 46

    (B) 10   (E) 92

    (C) 23

56. If mitosis were not to occur in both a male and a female human and their sperm and egg were to unite to form a zygote, how many chromosomes would the zygote have?

    (A) 2   (D) 92

    (B) 23   (E) 184

    (C) 46

57. Which of the following relates to a zygote?

    (A) A single organism composed of two cells

    (B) Haploid

    (C) Undergoes meiosis to produce four sperm

    (D) Diploid

    (E) Undergoes meiosis to produce four eggs

58. Which of the following relates to a sperm?

    (A) A single organism composed of two cells

    (B) Haploid

    (C) Undergoes meiosis to produce four zygotes

    (D) Diploid

    (E) Undergoes meiosis to produce four eggs

59. Which of the following relates to an egg?

    (A) A single organism composed of two cells

    (B) Haploid

    (C) Undergoes meiosis to produce four sperm

    (D) Diploid

    (E) Undergoes meiosis to produce four zygotes

60. The relationship between human eyelashes and the human eye is similar to the relationship between comblike hooks found on antennae and antennae themselves. What is this relationship?

    (A) The comblike hooks blink periodically to moisten the antennae.

    (B) The comblike hooks keep the antennae free from dust and dirt.

    (C) The comblike hooks are attractive to male ants when female ants move their antennae in a blinking manner.

    (D) The length of the comblike hooks and the antennae determine the age of the ants.

    (E) The comblike hooks help an ant find its way, similar to the function of eyelashes.

Section 2

TIME: 45 Minutes
60 Questions

DIRECTIONS: Each of the questions or incomplete statements below is followed by five possible answers or completions. Select the best choice in each case and fill in the corresponding oval on the answer sheet.

QUESTIONS 61 to 64 refer to the following passage.

When an earthquake occurs, some of the energy released travels through the ground as waves. Two general types of waves are generated. One type, called the P wave, is a compression wave that alternately compresses and stretches the rock layers as it travels. A second type is a shear wave, called the S wave, which moves the rocks in an up and down manner.

A graph can be made of the travel times of these waves.

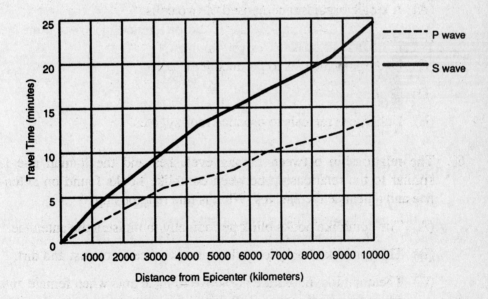

61. The main reason that a Time-Travel graph can be used to determine distance to an earthquake's point of occurrence is that

(A) S waves move up and down.

(B) P waves are compressional.

(C) P waves travel faster than S waves.

(D) S waves travel faster than P waves.

(E) P and S waves travel together.

62. Approximately how many minutes does it take a P wave to travel 8,000 km?

(A) 6 minutes   (D) 15 minutes

(B) 12 minutes   (E) 18 minutes

(C) 3 minutes

63. An earthquake occurs at noon, and the recording station receives the S wave at 12:05 p.m. How far away is the earthquake?

(A) 1,000 km   (D) 4,000 km

(B) 2,000 km   (E) 5,000 km

(C) 3,000 km

64. How far away is an earthquake if the difference in arrival time between the P and S waves is seven minutes?

(A) 1,000 km   (D) 7,000 km

(B) 3,000 km   (E) 9,000 km

(C) 4,000 km

QUESTIONS 65 to 67 refer to the following information.

The solubility of a substance is the maximum amount of that substance that can dissolve in a given quantity of solvent. A like substance can dissolve a like substance. A solution containing the maximum amount of solute is saturated.

65. If a solid substance is added to a solution but will not dissolve, one can hypothesize that

(A) the solution is unsaturated.

(B) the substance is insoluble in that solvent.

(C) the solution is saturated.

(D) one solution may never contain more than one type of solute.

(E) Either (B) or (C).

66. A solute dissolves in a solvent because

    (A) like substances dissolve in like substances, such as oil dissolving in water.

    (B) like substances do not dissolve in like substances.

    (C) like substances dissolve in unlike substances.

    (D) like substances do not dissolve in unlike substances, such as NaCl not dissolving in water.

    (E) like substances dissolve in like substances.

67. If a liquid-liquid solution is made, then

    (A) the liquid in greater quantity is the solute.

    (B) the appearance of two separate layers means that the liquids are miscible.

    (C) no solutes can be dissolved in this solution.

    (D) the liquid in greater quantity is always the solvent.

    (E) Either (A) or (C)

QUESTIONS 68 to 70 refer to the passage below.

Most substances are denser during the solid phase than during the liquid phase. Water is an exception to this rule. Additionally, water has a very high boiling point compared to other hydrides of nonmetals. Water has several other unusual properties that are related to the structure and composition of the water molecules.

68. Which of the following statements is NOT true about water?

    (A) Ice cubes float because solid water is less dense than liquid water.

    (B) Water exists as both a liquid and a solid at normal Earth temperatures.

    (C) Hydrogen bonding is especially weak in water.

    (D) The bonds between the oxygen and the hydrogens of water are covalent.

(E) A water molecule can be both an electron donor and an electron acceptor.

69. The unusually high boiling and melting points of water result from

(A) a great amount of intermolecular attraction in water.

(B) low surface tension.

(C) a low amount of hydrogen bonding between water molecules.

(D) the low heat capacity of water.

(E) strong covalent bonds between water molecules.

70. On the centigrade temperature scale, water freezes at _____ °C and boils at _____ °C.

(A) 32; 100   (D) 32; 212

(B) 0; 212   (E) 0; 100

(C) 32; 98.6

QUESTIONS 71 to 74 refer to the following information.

When assigning oxidation numbers, simple rules can be followed: 1) The sum of all oxidation numbers of the atoms in an electrically neutral chemical substance is zero. 2) The sum of the oxidation numbers must equal the charge on the ion for polyatomic ions. 3) The oxidation number of an atom in a monatomic ion is its charge. 4) Hydrogen always has the oxidation number +1 when combined with nonmetals and −1 when combined with metals.

71. Which rule(s) must be applied to find the oxidation number of H_2S?

(A) 1   (D) 1, 4

(B) 4   (E) 2, 4

(C) 1, 2

72. What is the oxidation number of the Mn in the neutral compound $KMnO_4$ if the oxidation number of K is +1 and the oxidation number for one oxygen atom (O) is −2?

(A) +1   (D) +3

(B) +7   (E) –3

(C) 0

73. Calculate the oxidation number of the P atom in HPO_4^{2-} if the oxidation number of one oxygen atom is –2?

(A) +1   (D) 0

(B) +7   (E) +2

(C) +5

74. Which rule(s) is/are used to find the oxidation numbers of HPO_4^{2-} and the oxidation numbers of the atoms comprising this compound?

(A) 2   (D) 2, 4

(B) 3, 4   (E) 1, 2, 4

(C) 4

QUESTIONS 75 and 76 refer to the following diagram.

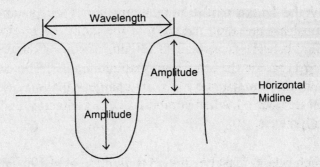

75. The wavelength is

(A) the distance between any two peaks.

(B) the distance between two adjacent peaks.

(C) the distance between the height of a wave and the low point of a wave.

(D) the rate of motion of the peak.

(E) the length of the horizontal midline.

76. A wave does not carry along the medium through which it travels. Thus, it follows that

   (A) molecules of water in the ocean are pushed to shore by waves.

   (B) the ocean's water molecules are thoroughly mixed each day by waves.

   (C) debris in the ocean is washed ashore by waves.

   (D) individual water molecules do not travel toward shore, but wave peaks do.

   (E) waves move water, not swimmers.

QUESTIONS 77 and 78 refer to the following information.

It has been suggested (R. McNeill Alexander, *Dynamics of Dinosaurs and Other Extinct Giants,* New York: Columbia University Press, 1989) that one can figure out what a dinosaur sounded like by measuring the length of its nasal cavity. One dinosaur has a cavity about 150 cm long that runs from the nose to the back of its throat. It was a plant eater that ground its food much like cows and horses do. The cavity is assumed to function much like an open-tube instrument such as the flute. The frequency in cycles per second played by the tube is approximately 170 divided by the length of the tube in meters. The frequencies of some standard musical notes are given below.

Note	Frequency*	Note	Frequency*
F_2	87	D_3	147
G_2	98	E_3	165
A_2	110	F_3	175
B_2	123	G_3	196
C_3	131	A_3	220

*Notice that the same note one octave higher is doubled in frequency.

77. The note sounded by this dinosaur when grinding its food is closest to

   (A) F_2.

   (B) A_2.

   (C) C_3.

   (D) G_3.

   (E) A_3.

78. A baby dinosaur which has a skull one-third the size of an adult would sound

   (A) a note six times higher in frequency than the adult.

   (B) a note six times lower in frequency than the adult.

   (C) the same note as the adult.

   (D) a note three times higher in frequency than the adult.

   (E) a note three times lower in frequency than the adult.

QUESTIONS 79 and 80 refer to the following information.

The average home use of electricity in the United States as compared to a developing country like Brazil is shown in the table below. The amount of electrical energy used is given in kilowatt-hours (KWH) per household per year. (October 1990, *Scientific American*, p. 113)

Use	United States	Brazil
Lighting	1,000	350
Cooking	635	15
Water Heating	1,540	380
Air-Conditioning	1,180	45
Refrigeration	1,810	470
Other	1,180	200

79. Which of the statements below is the best conclusion based on the data provided?

   (A) The total electrical consumption by the average U.S. household is about twice that of the typical Brazilian home wired for electricity.

   (B) Because it is warmer in Brazil, the percentage of electricity used in air-conditioning is greater than that used in the United States.

   (C) The greatest amount of electricity use in both countries is for lighting.

(D) United States households use more electricity for water heating than lighting, while Brazilian households use more electricity for lighting than water heating.

(E) Both countries have a somewhat similar pattern of electricity consumption.

80. How much more electrical energy per household does the United States consume than developing Brazil?

(A) 3 times   (D) 6 times

(B) 4 times   (E) 7 times

(C) 5 times

QUESTION 81 refers to the following information.

The graph below shows how the relative light energy given off by a tungsten lamp (3,000 K) and a fluorescent lamp compared with that of average sunlight at the earth's surface. The wavelength of 4,000 A is at the blue end of the spectrum, and 7,000 A is at the red end.

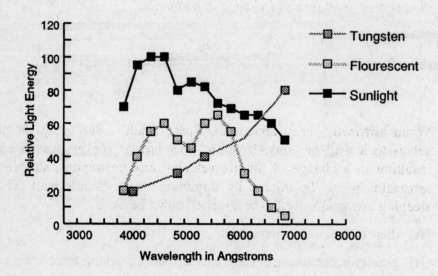

81. Which source tends to be the reddest?

(A) Tungsten filament lamp

(B) Fluorescent lamp

(C) Sunlight

(D) Sunlight and fluorescent lamp

(E) Each lamp has the same amount of red

QUESTIONS 82 to 84 refer to the following information.

The discoveries of Galileo Galilei (1564-1642) and Isaac Newton (1642-1727) precipitated the scientific revolution of the seventeenth century. Stressing the use of detailed measurements during experimentation enabled them to frame several universal laws of nature and to overthrow many of Aristotle's (384-322 B.C.) erroneous ideas about motion which were based on sheer reasoning alone. One of these universal laws is now known as the "Law of Inertia" or Newton's First Law of Motion. According to this law, objects in motion tend to stay in motion and objects at rest tend to stay at rest unless acted upon by external force. The more mass (inertia) an object has, the more resistance it offers to changes in its state of motion.

82. According to the Law of Inertia, which of the following would offer the greatest resistance to a change in its motion?

(A) A pellet of lead shot   (D) A feather

(B) A golf ball   (E) A sheet of notepaper

(C) A large watermelon

83. When astronauts sleep aboard the Space Shuttle, they strap themselves to a wall or bunk. If one of the thruster rockets was fired, resulting in a change of Shuttle velocity, any unstrapped, sleeping astronauts would be injured by slamming into a Shuttle wall. The sleeping astronauts need to be strapped down because

(A) their bodies have inertia.

(B) gravity is not strong enough to keep them touching their beds.

(C) their body functions need to be constantly monitored.

(D) astronauts cannot sleep while floating free in space.

(E) their bodies need a reaction force.

84. In Einstein's famous equation, $E = mc^2$, which of the following is most closely associated with a body's inertia?

   (A) The energy = E

   (B) The mass = m

   (C) The speed of light = c

   (D) The speed of light squared = c^2

   (E) The momentum = mc

QUESTIONS 85 to 87 refer to the following map.

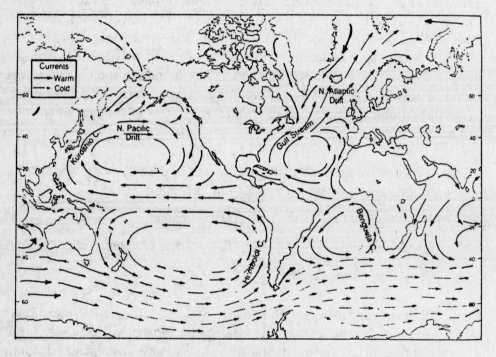

85. Which statement is true?

   (A) The east coasts of the continents are usually washed by warm currents.

   (B) The west coasts of the continents are usually washed by warm currents.

   (C) The east coasts of continents are washed by cold currents.

   (D) No pattern exists.

   (E) The pattern is hard to distinguish.

86. Both London, England, and Hudson Bay, Canada, are on the same North Latitude, yet London's winters average 35°F warmer. What could account for this difference?

(A) England is an island.

(B) The waters of the Gulf Stream wash the English coast.

(C) Latitude is not a factor in determining temperature.

(D) Warm winds from France moderate the weather in England.

(E) The waters of the Gulf Stream wash the Canadian coast.

87. A bottle with a message is tossed into the ocean on the east side of Japan. Where can it be expected to wash ashore?

(A) Australia

(B) Western North America

(C) Siberian Peninsula, U.S.S.R.

(D) Eastern Mexico

(E) Western South America

QUESTIONS 88 to 90 refer to the following diagram.

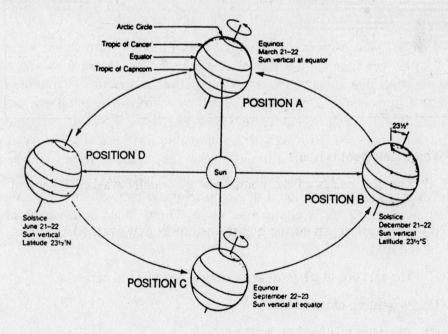

88. Which position(s) in the above diagram result(s) in the North Polar regions being referred to as the Land of the Midnight Sun?

(A) Position A   (D) Position D

(B) Position B   (E) Positions B and D

(C) Position C

89. Which position results in equal day and night?

(A) Position A   (D) Position D

(B) Position B   (E) Positions A and C

(C) Position C

90. Earth's seasons are caused by the

(A) tilt of Earth's axis.

(B) distance from the sun to the planet.

(C) rotation of the sun.

(D) rotation of Earth.

(E) effects of the moon's position.

QUESTIONS 91 to 93 refer to the following information.

Surface water waves are fundamentally different from sound waves in that the vibration of the former is perpendicular to the direction of motion, while that of sound is always parallel to the direction of motion. If a large disturbance in a material is created by a strong external blow, then it is possible for shear or transverse waves (like water waves) to propagate through the material. However, it is impossible for these shear waves to travel through the inside of a liquid or gas; the attractive forces between the molecules are so weak that there is little restoring force to cause displaced sections of the liquid or gas to return to their original positions which is required for a continuous wave. These shear or S-waves are known to travel through the earth at about 4.25 kilometers/sec.

91. Shear (transverse) waves, set up by a strong blow to the material, are able to travel through which of the following at room temperature?

    (A) Water

    (B) Carbon dioxide

    (C) Mercury

    (D) Air

    (E) Granite

92. Shear (or S-waves) created by an earthquake are known to stop at a depth of about 2,900 kilometers below Earth's surface. This is evidence that the Earth has

    (A) a diameter of 2,900 kilometers.

    (B) a liquid portion that starts 2,900 kilometers below Earth's surface.

    (C) a solid core that starts 2,900 kilometers below Earth's surface.

    (D) a radius of 2,900 kilometers.

    (E) mostly a liquid surface to reflect the waves down to 2,900 kilometers.

93. Earthquakes cause pressure-type waves (P-waves), which travel about twice as fast as the associated S-waves. If a seismographic station records an earthquake's P-waves arriving four minutes after the earthquake occurs, its distance away from the station must be about

    (A) 500 kilometers.

    (B) 1,000 kilometers.

    (C) 2,000 kilometers.

    (D) 3,000 kilometers.

    (E) 4,000 kilometers.

QUESTIONS 94 and 95 refer to the following map.

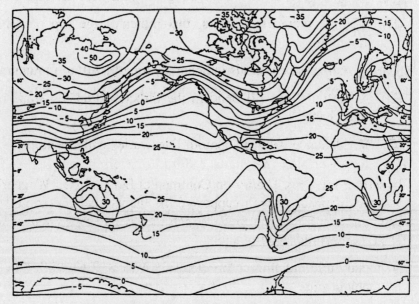

WORLD MEAN SEA-LEVEL TEMPERATURES IN JANUARY IN °C

94. Latitude is the distance in degrees north or south of the equator. The latitude of the equator is 0°, and the poles are at 90°. Longitude is the distance in degrees east or west of the prime meridian. The meridians are semicircles drawn around the globe from pole to pole. Which statement is true?

(A) The distance between latitude lines increases as you move toward the poles.

(B) The distance between longitude lines increases as you move toward the poles.

(C) The distance between latitude lines decreases as you move toward the poles.

(D) The distance between longitude lines decreases as you move toward the poles.

(E) The distance between latitude and longitude is never changing.

95. Contour lines are used in mapmaking. Contour lines give exact elevation above sea level and show the shape of the land at the same time. Which statement is FALSE?

    (A) When contour lines are close together, the land is steep.

    (B) When contour lines cross, this indicates the top of a hill or mountain.

    (C) Closed circles or ovals indicate the top of a hill or mountain.

    (D) A contour line will bend in the direction that the slope of the land changes.

    (E) The distance between contour lines varies with the slope.

96. In setting forth his Theory on Continental Drift, Alfred Wegner gave a series of proofs which supported his theory that the continents at one time were all connected. Which of the statements below would NOT support his idea?

    (A) The coasts of South America and Africa fit together like a jigsaw puzzle.

    (B) When continents are placed together, their mountain ranges connect.

    (C) The weather conditions on matching continents are similar.

    (D) Fossils of the same age and type are found on connecting continents.

    (E) Rocks of the same age and type are found on connecting continents.

97. Two main factors of climate are temperature and rainfall, and these factors depend on a whole set of conditions called climatic controls. Which of the following would not be a climatic control?

    (A) Latitude

    (B) Prevailing winds

    (C) Population density

    (D) Topography

    (E) Distance from large bodies of water

98. Which of the following is the main difference between an organic and an inorganic compound?

    (A) The former is a living compound, while the latter is a nonliving compound.

    (B) There are many more of the latter than of the former.

    (C) The latter can be synthesized only by living organisms.

    (D) The latter can be synthesized only by nonliving organisms.

    (E) The former are those that contain carbon.

99. Which of the following is NOT a part of the molecular theory of matter?

    (A) Matter is composed of exceedingly small particles called molecules.

    (B) Each different kind of matter is made up of its own particular kind of molecules.

    (C) Molecules are in rapid and ceaseless motion.

    (D) Molecules attract each other.

    (E) When molecules of water are split (perhaps with the aid of an electric current), the result is even smaller particles of the water.

100. On the periodic table, the symbol Pb represents which of the following?

    (A) Iron   (D) Plutonium

    (B) Phosphorus   (E) Potassium

    (C) Lead

101. A litmus test conducted on HCl would have which of the following results?

    (A) There is no effect on the color of the litmus paper.

    (B) The litmus paper disintegrates.

    (C) The litmus paper turns blue.

    (D) The litmus paper turns red.

    (E) The carbonation causes oxygen bubbles to rise to the top.

102. Water is which of the following?

    (A) A base   (D) All of the above.

    (B) An acid   (E) None of the above.

    (C) A compound

103. Which of the following statements about elements is true?

    (A) Elements are found in nature; nonelements are made by scientists.

    (B) Elements are made by scientists; nonelements are found in nature.

    (C) Some elements are found in nature, but others are made by scientists.

    (D) There are 110 presently known atoms, so there are 220 identified elements.

    (E) Steel, brass, and water are common elements.

104. Which is NOT true of protein?

    (A) All proteins are identical in their chemical makeup.

    (B) Proteins are made up of smaller units called amino acids.

    (C) A variety of protein from different sources is required in a good diet to provide the essential amino acids.

    (D) Some amino acids cannot be synthesized by humans and are known as the essential amino acids.

    (E) Proteins of animal origin have the highest nutritious value for humans.

105. Which of the following is true?

    (A) Energy may be converted from one form to another.

    (B) Energy may not be converted from one form to another.

    (C) The energy that a moving object possesses because of its motion is correctly known as potential energy.

    (D) Objects which possess energy because of their position are said to have kinetic energy.

(E) Nuclear fission will be the chief source of energy for the world by the year 2050.

106. Almost all interactions of matter result from the operation of which of the forces listed below?

(A) Gravitational force   (D) All of the above.

(B) Electromagnetic force   (E) None of the above.

(C) Nuclear force

107. To determine the amount of heat energy needed to raise the temperature of 50 grams of water at 50°C to water at 90°C, one must use which of the following factors?

I. The heat needed to melt a gram of ice.

II. The heat needed to change a gram of water to gas.

III. The heat needed to raise by 1° the temperature of a gram of water.

IV. The heat needed to raise by 1° the temperature of a gram of ice.

(A) I and III only.   (D) III only.

(B) II and IV only.   (E) I only.

(C) I, II, and III only.

108. Which of the following is NOT true?

(A) Comets generally have elongated, elliptical orbits.

(B) Comets may circle the sun in any direction.

(C) Despite their size, comets are mostly "empty space."

(D) Comets glow by their own light.

(E) It is believed comets are the mosr primitive objects in the solar system.

109. Which of the following statements is/are TRUE?

I. A cupful of water and a potful of water at 100°C have molecules with the same degree of activity.

II. A potful of water has a greater number of active molecules than does a cupful of water.

III. It takes more burning of gas to produce a potful of boiling water than a cupful.

IV. The unit used in measuring the quantity of heat is the calorie.

V. A calorie is the amount of heat necessary to raise 1 gram of pure water one degree Celsius.

A) All the above.   (D) I, III, and IV only.

(B) None of the above.   (E) III, IV, and V only.

(C) I, II, and III only.

110. Which of the following is FALSE?

(A) The apparent motion of stars each night is due to the turning of Earth.

(B) The apparent brightness of a star depends on several factors: distance from Earth, size, temperature.

(C) The Milky Way is the galaxy of the universe.

(D) The sun is a star.

(E) Constellations are patterns of stars.

111. All of the following are fundamental ideas of Dalton's atomic theory EXCEPT

(A) all matter is composed of a limited number of basic particles called atoms.

(B) each atom of an element is identical to all others.

(C) atoms can be broken into simpler substances by chemical means in a laboratory.

(D) molecules consist of a definite combination of atoms; all molecules of one particular kind have an identical atomic construction.

(E) new combinations of atoms to produce new molecules and new substances may be brought about by chemical changes.

112. Which of the following is NOT true?

    I.   Atoms are composed of electrons, protons, and neutrons; other particles have been discovered but these are the most important.

    II.   Electrons are extremely light atomic particles possessing a quantity of electricity designated as a positive charge.

    III. The rapidly moving electron is held in its orbit by the proton in the nucleus, which has a negative charge.

    IV. The charges of the electron and the proton are equal and opposite.

    (A) All of the above.   (D) III and IV only.

    (B) I and II only.   (E) I and IV only.

    (C) II and III only.

113. Which of the following statements about the structure of matter is a true statement?

    (A) Elements cannot be broken down into simpler substances.

    (B) Molecules built of more than one kind of atom are known as elements.

    (C) There are more than four million known elements used to create the more than four million identified compounds.

    (D) All elements are equally abundant in nature.

    (E) Compounds might be compared to the 26 letters of the alphabet; elements to the hundreds of thousands of words constructed from the alphabet.

114. Which of the following statements are true of gravitational force?

    I.   The production of an electromagnet is an example of gravitational force.

    II.   The rhythm of tides is an example of the effect of gravitational force.

    III. The law of gravity states that all bodies in the universe attract each other.

    IV. The strength of gravitational force between two bodies depends on the mass (quantity of material) in them.

V. The strength of gravitational force between two bodies depends on the distance between them.

(A) All of the above.   (D) II, III, IV, and V only.

(B) None of the above.   (E) III, IV, and V only.

(C) I, II, and III only.

115. All of the following are means of heat transfer EXCEPT

I. condensation.

II. conduction.

III. radiation.

IV. convection.

V. transportation.

(A) III, IV, and V only.   (D) I and V only.

(B) I, II, and III only.   (E) III and V only.

(C) II, III, and IV only.

116. The magnetism of a substance is NOT due essentially to which of the following?

(A) The magnetic properties of its atoms

(B) The arrangement of its atoms

(C) The position of its poles

(D) All the above

(E) Both (A) and (B).

117. Moving a coil of wire near a magnet or moving a magnet near a coil of wire

(A) causes electrons to flow in the coil.

(B) causes a weak link in the electric circuit.

(C) results in atomic fusion.

(D) is the principle of the generator.

(E) both (A) and (D).

118. Which of the statements below are examples of observing, predicting, and generalizing in that order?

    I.   Magnetized needles point in a north-south direction when suspended freely.

    II.   The magnet will probably attract this nail since it is made of iron.

    III. The magnet attracted all our objects made of iron.

    IV. The students did not have time to compare large and small magnets.

(A) I, II, and III only.   (D) III, II, and I only.

(B) I, II, and IV only.   (E) III, I, and II only.

(C) II, III, and IV only.

119. By which means do we measure a calendar year?

(A) Tilt of Earth on its axis.

(B) Rotation of Earth about the sun.

(C) Revolution of Earth about the sun.

(D) All the above.

(E) Both (A) and (B).

120. The sun has been burning and radiating energy into space for billions of years, according to some scientists. Which of the following refute this theory?

(A) The sun could burn for a *total* of 80,000 years.

(B) A newer theory is gravitation as a source of energy; if particles fall closer together because of their mutual attraction, the energy is converted into heat.

(C) In the case of the sun serving like a nuclear reactor, hydrogen atoms join to form helium atoms.

(D) All the above.

(E) Both (A) and (B).

CLEP NATURAL SCIENCES
TEST 2

$$\boxed{\textbf{ANSWER KEY}}$$

Section 1

1. (B)	13. (A)	25. (A)	37. (B)	49. (A)
2. (A)	14. (B)	26. (C)	38. (D)	50. (D)
3. (C)	15. (B)	27. (E)	39. (E)	51. (C)
4. (A)	16. (C)	28. (E)	40. (C)	52. (E)
5. (C)	17. (D)	29. (E)	41. (D)	53. (A)
6. (D)	18. (C)	30. (A)	42. (E)	54. (D)
7. (C)	19. (E)	31. (E)	43. (C)	55. (D)
8. (E)	20. (C)	32. (A)	44. (B)	56. (D)
9. (B)	21. (B)	33. (E)	45. (E)	57. (D)
10. (A)	22. (D)	34. (D)	46. (C)	58. (B)
11. (D)	23. (D)	35. (B)	47. (E)	59. (B)
12. (E)	24. (D)	36. (D)	48. (C)	60. (B)

Section 2

61. (C)	73. (C)	85. (A)	97. (C)	109. (A)
62. (B)	74. (D)	86. (B)	98. (E)	110. (C)
63. (A)	75. (B)	87. (B)	99. (E)	111. (E)
64. (C)	76. (D)	88. (D)	100. (C)	112. (C)
65. (E)	77. (B)	89. (E)	101. (D)	113. (A)
66. (E)	78. (D)	90. (A)	102. (D)	114. (D)
67. (D)	79. (E)	91. (E)	103. (C)	115. (C)
68. (C)	80. (C)	92. (B)	104. (A)	116. (E)
69. (A)	81. (A)	93. (C)	105. (A)	117. (E)
70. (E)	82. (C)	94. (D)	106. (D)	118. (D)
71. (D)	83. (A)	95. (B)	107. (D)	119. (C)
72. (B)	84. (B)	96. (C)	108. (D)	120. (A)

DETAILED EXPLANATIONS
OF ANSWERS
TEST 2

Section 1

1.   **(B)** Marsupials evolved before placental animals. After the continent of Australia separated from the rest of the land mass, the placental animals did not have a chance to reach Australia. Choice (A) is incorrect because a mutation reflects the presence of a new allele on a chromosome. Choice (C) is incorrect because random mating would not explain the presence of marsupials. Choice (D) is incorrect because variations refer to the range of adaptation which can be observed in all species. Choice (E) is incorrect because overpopulation is the production of more of a species than can adequately be taken care of and would not explain the presence of marsupials.

2.   **(A)** Half of any given quantity of carbon-14 decomposes in about 5,700 years. The ratio of carbon-14 to ordinary carbon-12 in living things is constant. After an organism dies, no additional carbon is taken in. The carbon-14 disintegrates. As a result, the amount of carbon-14 in the dead organism decreases while the amount of carbon-12 remains the same. By determining the ratio of carbon-14 to carbon-12 in a fossil, scientists have been able to determine when the organism died. Carbon-12 is not radioactive. Nitrogen-15 (C), hydrogen-2 (D), and oxygen-18 (E) are radioactive but not found in fossils.

3.   **(C)** A mule is the offspring of a male donkey and a female horse. The mule is bigger than a donkey and tougher than either the donkey or horse. Mules are more manageable than donkeys and more sure-footed than horses. Choice (A) is incorrect because dominance is the genetic principle in which the dominant trait will appear in the phenotype of offspring and mask the recessive trait. Choice (B) is incorrect because selection is a technique where only those organisms with the most desirable traits are allowed to breed. Choice (D) is incorrect because inbreeding

refs to breeding between members of the same family in order to maintain a desired trait. Choice (E) is incorrect because a mutation is the appearance of a new allele on a chromosome.

4. **(A)** The gene frequency will remain the same. The Hardy-Weinberg Principle states that the gene frequency of a population from generation to generation will remain stable as long as mating is random, there is no mutation, and migration does not occur. Choices (B) through (E) are incorrect because a change in dominant or recessive genes does not occur.

5. **(C)** Insecticides are passed along the food chain. Insecticides kill insects and enter the food chain when the insects are eaten by birds and fish. The insecticide is carried from organism to organism, concentrating itself in fat tissue. Choice (A) is incorrect because insecticides cannot be absorbed directly into fat cells from the air. Choices (B) and (D) do not explain how insecticides are concentrated in fat tissue. Choice (E) is incorrect because insecticides are no by-products of cellular respiration.

6. **(D)** Angiosperms have covered seeds which develop in the ovary of the flower. Choice (A) is incorrect because gymnosperms form "naked seeds" that are usually produced on the scales of a cone. Pine and spruce trees fall into this category. Choice (B) is incorrect because perennials are plants that live year after year. Choice (C) is incorrect because Filicineae is the family of plants that includes ferns; plants that do not produce seeds. Choice (E) is incorrect because biennials are plants that complete their life cycle in two years.

7. **(C)** The intensity of light that reaches organisms decreases as ocean depth increases. Plants and other organisms such as algae need light for photosynthesis. Choices (A), (B), and (D) may or may not be correct.

8. **(E)** Tropical rain forests are characterized by abundant rainfall throughout the year. The temperature is always above freezing. Choice (B) is incorrect because there is not a diversity of species. Choice (D) is incorrect because lacy, open trees are not characteristic of rain forests.

9. **(B)** Lamarck formulated a theory of evolution, now disproved, that emphasized use and disuse. He proposed that acquired characteristics were inherited. Darwin (A) is responsible for proposing the theory of evolution that stresses natural selection or "survival of the fittest." DeVries (C) presented a theory of evolution based on mutation. Muller (D) discovered

that the rate of mutation could be increased in fruit flies by exposure to X-rays. Watson and Crick (E) are scientists responsible for working out the structure of DNA.

10.   **(A)** Over 70 percent of the Earth's surface is covered by water. The great majority of the Earth's photosynthesis takes place near the surface where light can penetrate. Choices (B) through (E) are examples of terrestrial biomes. Terrestrial biomes comprise less than 30 percent of the Earth's surface and are very sensitive to extremes in climatic conditions. These extremes in climate reduce photosynthetic activity. The smaller surface area of terrestrial biomes, as well as their sensitivity to climatic changes, make choice choices (B) through (E) incorrect.

11.   **(D)** A vestigial structure is a structure that serves no useful purpose. It most probably was functional in an ancestral relative. Choices (A), (B), (C), and (E) are structures that still serve a useful purpose.

12.   **(E)** Both parents are heterozygous. They must both carry the recessive gene for blue eyes. The choice can also be visually demonstrated using a Punnett Cross. The parents must both be Bb, where B represents the gene for brown eyes and b represents the gene for blue eyes.

	Bb × Bb	
	B	b
B	BB	Bb
b	Bb	bb

The child with blue eyes will have a genotype of bb. Choice (A) is incorrect because a mutation has not occurred. Choice (B) is incorrect because if one parent were pure dominant for brown eyes then all the offspring would have brown eyes. Choice (C) is incorrect because crossing-over is the process in which pieces of chromosomes are exchanged. Choice (D) is incorrect because we are told that both parents are brown-eyed, and brown is a dominant trait.

13.   **(A)**   a substitution in an amino acid in the hemoglobin molecule. A mutation of a gene that controls the synthesis of hemoglobin substitutes valine for glutamic acid at a single point on the molecule. Choices (B) through (E) are incorrect because they do not describe sickle-cell anemia.

14.   **(B)**   Guanine always bonds with cytosine. Choice (A) is incorrect because adenine bonds with thymine. Choice (C) is incorrect because uracil is found in RNA. Choice (D) is incorrect because guanine will not bond with another guanine. Choice (E) is incorrect because thymine will bond with adenine.

15.   **(B)**   The complementary base for adenine is thymine. Choice (A) is incorrect because cytosine is the complementary base of guanine. Choice (C) is incorrect because guanine is the complementary base for cytosine. Choice (D) is incorrect because uracil is found only in RNA. Choice (E) does not apply.

16.   **(C)**   To answer this question you must apply your knowledge of the classification of mammals to a specific situation – you must predict the characteristics that you would expect whales to have. Vertebrates, in general, have a vertebral column (A) and dorsal hollow nerve cord (B). Since mammals are vertebrates, they would also have these characteristics. Birds and mammals are warm-blooded (D), and mammals nurse their young (E). Scales (C) are a characteristic of fish and reptiles, and would not be expected on whales.

17.   **(D)**   This question relates to energy flow in a food chain. Primary productivity is the amount of energy from the sun that is converted to chemical bond energy during photosynthesis. Plants are the only members of the ecosystem that can accomplish this conversion. Energy can then move to other organisms (herbivores, carnivores, omnivores, decomposers) through the food chain.

18.   **(C)**   Knowledge of the different kinds of ecosystems on Earth is necessary for answering this question. Permafrost is a layer of frozen ground that never thaws. It has ecological implications in terms of the types of plants that will grow on this type of land. Permafrost is found in the areas closest to the poles – in the tundra.

19.   **(E)**   The most stable community is the climax community. This type of community is marked by a large biomass, complex organization, and the fact that it does not change its environment. A lake tends to fill in with the accumulation of organic material. It will first become a marsh and then a meadow. A meadow provides open areas for the growth of shrubs, and trees then replace the shrubs.

20.   **(C)**   This is a straight definition of an ecological system.

21.   **(B)**   Both plants and animals are made of cells; (A) is not the correct choice. Plant cells usually have a nonliving cell wall; (B) is true. The euglena (C) is a single-celled organism that swims freely like a typical animal; it can, however, manufacture food with its green chlorophyll like a plant. This is one instance of a "non-plant" with chlorophyll. (C) is incorrect. Both plant and animal cells contain DNA. (D) is, therefore, not the right choice. Fungi (E) do not manufacture their own food. They do not contain chlorophyll. (E) is a wrong choice and should not be chosen.

22.   **(D)**   The result of a father who is RH-positive and a mother who is RH-negative may be a child with *erythroblastosis fetalis* – a disease brought on by incompatibility of the mother's blood and the child's blood; the red cells of the child may be damaged to the extent that the child is unable to obtain sufficient oxygen. German measles during the first trimester of pregnancy may cause problems with the development of the unborn child. Since (D) allows you to choose both the RH-positive father and the onset of German measles during the first trimester, (D) is the correct choice. (A) is a correct choice but (B) is also correct; (D) is the only right answer since it allows the reader to choose both. (C) is an incorrect choice since there is no danger if the father is RH-negative and the mother is RH-positive. (E) should not be selected since it includes (C) a wrong choice – along with the correct (B).

23.   **(D)**   All three choices are parts of the digestive system. The pancreas secretes pancreatic juice for digestion; both the small and large intestines are readily identified as parts of the system. Since you are looking, however, for the list containing an organ that is not a part of the system, (A) should not be chosen. Bile, which comes from the gall bladder, aids digestion. All three organs in (B) aid digestion. (B) should not be chosen. All three parts named in (C) belong to the digestive system. The spleen (D) is not a part of the digestive system. Since (D) contains an organ which is not a part of the digestive system, it should be selected as the correct choice. All three parts in (E) belong to the digestive system. The liver, for instance, secretes bile into the gall bladder. Since all three parts belong to the digestive system, (E) is a wrong choice.

24.   **(D)**   All the choices listed EXCEPT communicating and producing food are functions of living things; many animals, for instance, do not produce food, and plants do not seem to communicate. Item IV (men-

tioned in (D)) contains "communicating" and item V (mentioned in (D)) contains "producing food." (D) is the correct choice.

25. **(A)** Trichinella (wormlike parasites often spread from improperly cooked pork) may enter the body of the person and live there at a disadvantage to the individual. Since mutualism (B) indicates two organisms which survive at a benefit to each, (B) is not correct. Trichinosis is not of benefit to the host, which might be people. Commercialism (C) is not an appropriate choice since it does not relate at all to the question about trichinosis. Commercialism refers to the commercial spirit or mercantilism. (C) should not be chosen. Benevolent (D) is not a term relating to a situation where the host organism develops a disease like trichinosis. Benevolent means kind, charitable, disposed to promote the prosperity of another. (D) is not the best choice. Since benign (E) means mild or favorable, it does not adequately describe a situation in which the organism causes danger to the host or person. (E) should not be chosen.

26. **(C)** A housefly resistant to DDT (A) did emerge as a result of the use of the pesticide. Since the directions instruct you to find the one with which scientists would not agree, (A) should not be chosen. (B) is not the right choice since it is true and, in this particular instance, you are searching for a false answer. (C) is the correct choice. Scientists would not advocate the regular use of chemicals to try to bring about "the evolution of exciting new types of organisms." Since the statement is not one that scientists would agree with, it is the choice for this question. Since (D) is a true statement, it is not the correct choice. (E) is a true statement, and not the best answer to a question asking for an incorrect choice.

27. **(E)** Both (A) and (B) are correct. Enzymes enable molecules to pass into the bloodstream after the transformation of complex molecules into a simpler form. (C) is totally incorrect since it discusses fusing the molecules, not breaking down the food molecules. Choice (D) cannot be selected since it includes the correct choices (A) and (B) and the incorrect (C).

28. **(E)** All parts listed are parts of the circulatory system except the seminal vesicles (E); the seminal vesicles are saclike structures in the male used to store sperm. The vesicles, then, are part of the reproductive system – not part of the circulatory system. Choices (A), (B), (C), and (D) are all correct and should not be chosen since an incorrect choice is needed.

29. **(E)** The food chain is continuous – not non-continuous. Since the directions ask for the choice which is not true, (E) is the correct choice. All the other choices (A), (B), (C), and (D) are true and cannot be selected as the correct choice since a false choice (E) is needed.

30. **(A)** The first sequence is the correct one. *Annelida* refers to segmented worms, like the earthworms. *Molluska* has hard-shelled animals, like the oysters. *Arthropoda* has six-legged insects, like the bees. *Echinodermata* has spiny-skinned animals, like the starfish. *Vertebrata* have backbones; fish fit into that category. The sequence of the other phyla prevent the other choices – (B), (C), (D), and (E) – from being correct.

31. **(E)** Since reptiles are not gill-breathing throughout life, (E) is NOT a characteristic of reptiles and, consequently, is the correct choice. The rest of the choices – (A), (B), (C), and (D) – are true and not to be selected.

32. **(A)** Changes (modifications) in plants and animals usually occur very slowly over a period of time. Choice (A) suggests that these changes occur rapidly, it is false. Choice (A) should be selected. The rest of the choices – (B), (C), (D), and (E) – are true and should not be selected.

33. **(E)** The digestive system carries food from the mouth to the esophagus, to the stomach, and to the intestines; the organs are set up to allow the absorption of food though their walls and to allow the food to be sent to all parts of the body. Transportation (I) is one duty of the digestive system. The digestive system assimilates (digests, absorbs) food so II is also a feature of the digestive system. The last function of the digestive system is excretion. Only one choice (E) enables the reader to select I, II, and III. All of the other choices are not appropriate. Reproduction (IV) is a function of the reproductive system, not the digestive system. Choices (A), (C), and (D), which include (IV), cannot be selected. The nervous system is primarily responsible for the individual's response to environmental stimuli. Choices (A), (C), and (D), which include (V), cannot be chosen. Since statements (I), (II), and (III) are correct, (B) cannot be chosen.

34. **(D)** If you considered antler to be the correct choice you may have read the word as *anther* (the pollen-bearing part of the flower) rather than *antler* (a branching horn). The other choices are reproductive parts of a flower. A stigma (A) is the top of the style which is equipped with hairs

and a sticky secretion to hold pollen grains. A stamen (B) is the part involved in pollen-making. A pistil (C) consists of three parts – ovary, style, and stigma. A sperm (E) is the male reproductive nucleus.

35.   **(B)** All the parts listed – except the spleen (B) – are part of the respiratory system. The trachea (A) is another name for the windpipe. The diaphragm (C) is a muscle below the lungs which allows the chest cavity to become larger or smaller. The bronchial tubes (D) are tubes leading into the lungs. The lungs (E), of course, are the saclike respiratory organs. The spleen, on the other hand, is the organ near the stomach or intestine of most vertebrates; it is concerned with the final destruction of blood cells, the storage of blood and the production of lymphocytes.

36.   **(D)** Enzymes serve two main functions – both of which are stated in (A) and (B). Choice (D) allows you to choose both the correct choices. Choices (A) only or (B) only would be incomplete. Choice (C) suggests fusion of food molecules rather than the breaking down of food molecules. Choice (C) should not be chosen. Choice (E) is clearly the wrong choice and it should not be chosen.

37.   **(B)** Leaves produce food (IV). Stems transport and support a plant (I). The roots anchor the plant in the soil and absorb water and minerals for the plant (II). The flower produces seeds (III). (B) gives the functions in that order so (B) should be selected as the correct choice.

38.   **(D)** Since the reader is looking for the one choice that is incorrect, (D) must be chosen. Photosynthesis is the process by which plants create their own food. The other choices – (A), (B), (C), and (E) – are correct statements and should not be chosen.

39.   **(E)** A shark (E) is not a mammal; rather it is classified as a fish. Since it is NOT a mammal, a shark (E) is the correct choice. All the other choices (a bat, a whale, a gibbon [ape], and an elephant) are mammals; (A), (B), (C), and (D) may not be chosen.

40.   **(C)** Most people are omnivorous (both plant and animal eating), so (C) is the correct choice. Herbivorous (A) or plant-eating (vegetarianism) does not describe most people. Carnivorous (B) or meat-eating does not describe most people. People do not generally migrate (D) or move from one area to another according to the season. Hibernating (E) or sleeping during the winter is not an activity typical of people. (A), (B), (D), or (E) should not be chosen.

41. **(D)** The question asks for the false statement about protozoans. (D) is false. A slipper-shaped protozoan is the paramecium, not the euglena. The other choices – (A), (B), (C), and (E) – are true statements and should not be selected.

42. **(E)** Conifers do not have leaves which drop off during the fall season usually; the conifers are often called evergreens and have needles, not leaves. (E) is a false statement and is, therefore, the one to be selected. All the other choices – (A), (B), (C), and (D) – are true and cannot be chosen.

43. **(C)** In a taproot system there is a primary taproot that grows until it is the major root in the system. An example of a plant that has a taproot system would be a carrot. (A) is a false statement; roots generally help to hold the plant in the ground. In a diffuse root system there is a network of roots. The primary root lives only for a short time, so (B) is false. Both diffuse and taproot systems may be used to store food in the roots; (D), therefore, is false. (E) is partially true; roots do help with absorption, support, and storage; roots, however, also help with reproduction. For instance, a gardener would plant dahlia bulbs (roots) to grow new dahlias.

44. **(B)** The two, long, pointed teeth near the front of the human mouth are properly called canines. The central incisors are the two front teeth; they are straight across the bottom. (A) is not a correct choice. The premolars (C) are located behind the canines; they are broad and flat for chewing. Molars, like premolars, are broad, flat teeth for chewing. Molars (D) are located to the back of the mouth. Lateral incisors (E) are located to each side of the central incisors. Lateral incisors are flat across the bottom. Choice (E) should not be chosen.

45. **(E)** There are normally 32 permanent teeth in the adult mouth. Without the wisdom teeth, there are 28 teeth (B). A child has about 28 teeth from the time the 12-year molar is cut until the cutting of the wisdom teeth at age 18; (B) is an incorrect choice. The other choices – (A), (C), and (D) – are inappropriate numbers of teeth to select.

46. **(C)** Girdling a tree or plant will kill it. Choice (C) should be chosen since a false response is needed. You should not choose (A), (B), (D), or (E) because they are true.

47.   **(E)**   Using nuclear fusion to destroy colonies of insects seems drastic at this time. It is doubtful that such means would be used in the near future just to control insects! The other statements – (A), (B), (C), and (D) – are all true methods being used to control insects. None of them should be chosen since the question is to pick a means not used for controlling insects. Choice (A) might be chosen by some respondents. In that case, the reader needs to remember that draining swamps was a means used in some countries to eliminate the mosquito, which was causing disease.

48.   **(C)**   Examination of the fourth column reveals that there is no pattern to the divisions of time; therefore, (C) is the correct choice. (A) is incorrect because the events listed are biological in nature rather than geological. (B) is incorrect, as the time blocks are of differing amounts. (D) is wrong because the eras are divided into periods and not the reverse.

49.   **(A)**   The sequence of life listed in (A) is correct, so answer choice (A) should be chosen. (B) is incorrect because invertebrates evolved before fish. (C) is incorrect because the first fish appeared much earlier than the first forests. Plants were present before birds, so (D) is wrong, and (E) is incorrect because reptiles had evolved before mammals.

50.   **(D)**   The common alligator is a reptile. Answer choice (D) is correct because the Carboniferous Period saw the emergence of the first reptiles. Answer choices (A), (B), (C), and (E) are incorrect, because they represent the emergence periods of organisms other than reptiles.

51.   **(C)**   Answer choice (C), a virus, is the correct choice since a virus is not composed of cells, nor does it organize protoplasm into cells, and it does not come from pre-existing cells. A rose (A) cannot be the correct choice since it is a living thing composed of cells; it came from a cell; and it carries on all of the life processes. A fungus (B) cannot be the correct choice since it is a living thing composed of cells; it came from a cell; and it carries on all of the life processes. An amoeba (D) cannot be the correct choice since it is a living thing composed of cells; it came from a cell; and it carries on all of the life processes. A sponge (E) cannot be the correct choice since it is a living thing composed of cells; it came from a cell; and it carries on all of the life processes.

52.   **(E)**   is correct since icicles are made of only water and not cells. Choice (A) cannot be the correct choice since icicle grow by accumulation of water freezing to the outside, and not by assimilation where food is chemically broken down, absorbed, and incorporated into the body of the

organism. Choice (B) is wrong because there is no proper beginning (from a preexisting cell); growth is not of the right kind; no "maturity" is exhibited; and no decline (breaking down of cells due to age) is exhibited; no death is exhibited. Choice (C) cannot be the correct choice since icicles cannot reproduce. Choice (D) cannot be the correct choice since icicles are composed of water, not cells.

53.   **(A)**   A cell is the correct choice since all living things are composed of cells. An organ (B) cannot be the correct choice since organs are composed of tissues, which are composed of cells. A chemical compound (C) cannot be the correct choice since living things must be composed of cells, and chemical compounds are not cells. An organ system (D) or an organism (E) cannot be correct choices since an organism is composed of organ systems, which are composed of organs, which are composed of tissues, which are composed of cells.

54.   **(D)**   46 is the correct choice since a cell undergoing mitosis will first double its chromosome number and then divide and during that division the chromosomes will be evenly and correctly divided between the two daughter cells. 2 (A) cannot be the correct choice since the information in the questions states that a cell starts out with 46 chromosomes. 10 (B) cannot be the correct choice since this number is still too small to make up even one set of chromosomes, much less two. 24 (C) cannot be the correct choice since humans are sexually reproducing organisms and in a body cell there are two sets of chromosomes; therefore, 24 would be more than a single set but less than two sets. 92 (E) cannot be the correct choice since this number would indicate a doubling of the chromosome number without a cell division taking place.

55.   **(D)**   46 is the correct choice since the zygote of a human is a cell derived from a sperm containing 23 chromosomes and an egg containing 23 chromosomes. 2 (A) cannot be the correct choice since it represents too few chromosomes for either a haploid sex cell or a diploid body cell. 10 (B) cannot be the correct choice since it also represents too few chromosomes for either a haploid sex cell or a diploid body cell. 23 (C) cannot be the correct choice since it represents the number of chromosomes in a sperm or an egg. 92 (E) cannot be the correct choice since it represents the number of chromosomes in a diploid cell that has doubled its chromosome number without dividing.

56. **(D)** 92 is the correct choice since the egg and the sperm, in this case, would have the diploid number of chromosomes (46), and if they were to unite, then the number of chromosomes would be doubled. 2 (A) cannot be the correct choice since this number represents too few chromosomes for even a human sex cell. 23 (B) cannot be the correct choice since this is the haploid chromosome number of a normal human sex cell. 46 (C) cannot be the correct choice since this is the diploid chromosome number of a normal zygote. 184 (E) cannot be the correct choice since this number is greater than a zygote with twice the normal number of chromosomes.

57. **(D)** Diploid is the correct choice since a zygote is a diploid cell formed from the union of two haploid sex cells. A single organism composed of two cells (A) cannot be the correct choice since a zygote is not composed of two cells, it is composed of one cell. Haploid (B) cannot be the correct choice since a zygote is formed from the union of two haploid sex cells and is a diploid cell. Undergoes meiosis to produce four sperm (C) cannot be the correct choice since zygotes do not undergo meiosis. Undergoes meiosis to produce four eggs (E) cannot be the correct choice since zygotes do not undergo meiosis.

58. **(B)** Haploid is the correct choice since a sperm is a product of meiosis and has only one set of chromosomes. A single organism composed of two cells (A) cannot be the correct choice since a sperm is a single cell that has only one set of chromosomes. Undergoes meiosis to produce four zygotes (C) cannot be the correct choice since sperm do not undergo meiosis, and zygotes are not produced by meiosis. Diploid (D) cannot be the correct choice since sperm contain only one set of chromosomes and are haploid. Undergoes meiosis to produce four eggs (E) cannot be the correct choice since sperm do not undergo meiosis and they do not produce eggs.

59. **(B)** Haploid is the correct choice since an egg is a product of meiosis and has only one set of chromosomes. A single organism composed of two cells (A) cannot be the correct choice since an egg is a single cell that has only one set of chromosomes. Undergoes meiosis to produce four sperm (C) cannot be the correct choice since eggs do not undergo meiosis, and they do not produce sperm. Diploid (D) cannot be the correct choice since sperm contain only one set of chromosomes and are haploid. Undergoes meiosis to produce four zygotes (E) cannot be the correct choice since eggs do not undergo meiosis and they do not produce zygotes.

60. **(B)** Human eyelashes help keep dust and dirt out of the eye. Similarly, the hooks have tiny comblike ridges on them and they keep the antennae free from dust and dirt. Thus, (B) is correct. (A) is wrong because hooks are structures on the antennae that do not blink. (C) is wrong because the hooks are not involved in attraction between male and female ants. (D) is incorrect because the length of these structures is not indicative of the age of the ant. (E) is wrong because eyelashes do not help people find their way.

Section 2

61. **(C)** The difference between the P and S waves is the P wave travels faster. It can be seen on the graph that the P wave covers a greater distance in less time. (A) and (B) are incorrect as they are descriptions of the waves rather than an explanation. (D) is incorrect as an examination of the graph reveals the S wave to be slower. (E) is incorrect; if the P and S wave traveled together they would both occupy the same line.

62. **(B)** Locate the position labeled 8,000 km and look up until you reach the P wave line and read across to the time. (A) is incorrect; it would be 3,000 km. (C) is incorrect; it would be 1,000 km. (D) is incorrect; it would be > 10,000 km. (E) is incorrect; it would be > 10,000.

63. **(A)** You must locate the place on the graph where the S wave has traveled 5 minutes and read down to find the distance. (B) is incorrect; it would be 7 minutes. (C) is incorrect; it would be 10 minutes. (D) is incorrect; it would be 13 minutes. (E) is incorrect; it would be 15 minutes.

64. **(C)** You must locate on the graph the place where the space between the P and S wave lines is 7 minutes; then look down and read the distance scale. (A) is incorrect; it would be 2 minutes. (B) is incorrect; it would be 4 minutes. (D) is incorrect; it would be 9 minutes. (E) is incorrect; it would be 10 minutes.

65. **(E)** Either the added substance may be insoluble in the solvent, or the solution may already be saturated, or both may be true. (A) is wrong because the substance would dissolve in an unsaturated solution. (D) is wrong because a solution often does contain more than one type of solute.

66. **(E)** The rule is that like substances dissolve in like substances. Here, "like" means that both substances are polar or both are nonpolar. (A) is wrong because oil will dissolve in water. (B) is incorrect because like does dissolve in like. (C) is wrong for the same reason. (D) is incorrect because, again, the example states incorrect information. NaCl does, in fact, dissolve in water.

67. **(D)** The major component of a solution is the solvent. (A) is thus wrong. (B) is wrong because two layers indicate the two liquids are immiscible. (C) is wrong because additional solutes can be dissolved in a solution until the saturation point. Since (A) and (C) are wrong, (E) is wrong.

68. **(C)** is the correct answer. Hydrogen bonding is especially strong in water, not weak. (A), (B), (D), and (E) are all true statements about water.

69. **(A)** Intermolecular attraction, namely, hydrogen bonding, leads to the high boiling and melting point. (B) is wrong because water has high surface tension. (C) is wrong because there is a great deal of hydrogen bonding between water molecules. (D) is wrong because water has a high heat capacity. (E) is wrong because hydrogen bonds, not covalent bonds, are present between the oxygen and hydrogen of one water molecule.

70. **(E)** Water, at standard atmospheric pressure, freezes at 0°C and boils at 100°C. Therefore, the correct choice is (E). Choice (D) is the freezing and boiling points of water on the Fahrenheit scale. The other choices are also incorrect.

71. **(D)** To find the oxidation number of H_2S, rule 1 says that the sum of the oxidation numbers of the atoms must be zero. Rule 1 is important here, so choices (B) and (E) can be disqualified from being correct. Also, rule 4 states that hydrogen has a charge of +1 when combined with non-metals (such as sulfur). Rule 2 concerns polyatomic ions. H_2S, however, is not an ion. It is not monatomic, but polyatomic, so rule 3 does not apply.

72. **(B)** The sum of all of the oxidation numbers must equal zero. O_4 must be $4 \times 2 = -8$. K is +1. $-8 + 1 = -7$. To equal zero, then, Mn must equal +7.

73. **(C)** Since H is combined with a nonmetal (P), H must have a charge of +1. The four oxygen atoms have a combined charge of −8 since

$4 \times -2 = -8$. The charge on the ion is -2. Thus, P must have a charge of $+5$ since $5 + 1 - 8 = -2$.

74. **(D)** Rules 2 and 4 are necessary to find the charges of H, P, O_4, and the combined ion. Specifically, rule 2 states that HPO_4^{2-} must have a net charge of -2. Rule 4 helps in determining the charge of the hydrogen. Rule 1 is not applicable since HPO_4^{2-} is not a neutral substance. Rule 3 does not apply because HPO_4^{2-} is polyatomic, not monatomic.

75. **(B)** The distance between the two adjacent peaks is labelled as the wavelength. If the peaks are not adjacent, more than one wavelength will be measured, as in (A). (C) is wrong because the distance described is twice the wave amplitude, not wavelength. (D) is describing velocity, not wavelength. (E) is incorrect because the horizontal midline is only an imaginary line to divide the height of a wave from a trough.

76. **(D)** The water molecules, which is the medium, is not carried, but the wave peaks do move toward shore. (A) states the opposite of what is mentioned in the question. (B) is wrong because although the ocean is somewhat mixed each day, this mixing is due to currents and turbulence, not by waves. (C) is wrong because debris washes ashore by currents and turbulence, not by waves. (E) is incorrect because waves move neither water nor swimmers. The waves travel through the water and the swimmer will bob up and down but will not be carried by the wave. Again, currents and turbulence are responsible for moving both water and swimmers.

77. **(B)** The formula given to find the note is: 170 divided by the length of the cavity in meters will equal the frequency. Here, 170 is divided by 1.5 m (150 cm) which gives 113 cycles per second. The closest note in the table is at 110 cycles per second, or A_2, more than 1 octave below middle C, which is at 262 cycles per second. All musical scales use A_4 or 440 cycles per second as a standard reference.

78. **(D)** The size of the skull will give the length of the nasal cavity. If the baby's skull is one-third the adult size, then the nasal cavity is also one-third in length. The frequency sounded by the baby grinding its teeth will be 170 divided by (1.5 meters $\div$ 3) which is 170 divided by 0.5, which is 340 cycles per second or about 3 times greater than the adult.

79. **(E)** is correct. Choice (A) is unacceptable because in each area of use, the U.S. household utilizes far more than twice the electrical energy

of the Brazilian household. Choice (B) is incorrect because the percent used in air-conditioning is greater in the U.S. than in Brazil. Choice (C) is invalid since the greatest use in both countries is for refrigeration. Choice (D) is incorrect since in Brazil more electrical energy is used for water heating than for lighting. By the process of elimination, choice (E) is left and supported by the observations that both countries use the least for cooking and the most for refrigeration.

80. **(C)** Both columns of electrical energy in KWH must be totaled. The U.S. household consumes 7,345 KWH while the Brazilian household consumes 1,460 KWH per year. This is a ratio of 5 to 1. It is interesting to note that the Third World developing countries mimic the United States in their usage of technology.

81. **(A)** Visible light consists of waves which have wavelengths from blue at 4,000 angstroms to red at 7,000 angstroms. For the three sources plotted in the displayed graph, the tungsten filament lamp has the greatest relative energy output at the red end, with a reading of slightly greater than 80. This compares with the lower red readings of about 57 for daylight and about 7 for the fluorescent lamp. Note average daylight is far brighter than the other two sources, explaining why camera exposures inside under artificial lights need to be longer than those for outside on a normal day.

82. **(C)** The property of an object which determines the object's resistance to motion is its mass. A large watermelon has a far greater mass than the pellet of lead shot, golf ball, feather, or notepaper. The mass of an object never changes. It is equal to an object's weight divided by the acceleration due to gravity "g" at its current position in space.

83. **(A)** The sleeping astronauts would continue their motion in a straight line if the Shuttle suddenly changed velocity due to the firing of its thrusters. If the Shuttle slowed down, the astronauts would move forward relative to the walls. This is all due to the fact that the astronauts have mass, or inertia. Gravity is so weak that it is negligible on the astronauts. They can be monitored by battery driven devices which allow them to move around, and they can certainly sleep without being strapped. Bodies do not need a reaction force to sleep.

84. **(B)** Inertia is measured by mass, m. Choices (A) and (E) do contain mass but also involve other complicating factors like the speed of light, c, which invalidate the choice. There are two ways to measure mass: gravitationally through an object's weight, and inertially through an object's

resistance to motion. Both measures, gravitational mass and inertial mass, have always been found to be the same for a given object.

85.   **(A)**   An examination of the ocean currents shows that the eastern seaboards of all the continents are washed by warm currents from the equator, and the western seaboards are washed by cold polar currents. (B) is incorrect as west coasts are washed by cold water from the poles. (C) is incorrect as it is the opposite of choice (A). (D) is incorrect because a pattern clearly exists.

86.   **(B)**   The Gulf Stream consists of warm equatorial currents that raise the temperature of the winds that pass over England, thus warming the land. (A) is incorrect. Being an island would not make it warmer. (C) is incorrect. Latitude does affect temperature, the higher the latitude the greater the sun's angle and the cooler the air. (D) is incorrect as the winds that affect England do not come from France.

87.   **(B)**   A bottle tossed from Japan will ride the Kuroshio current to the North Pacific Drift and wash ashore on the western side of North America. (A), (C), (D), and (E) are all incorrect as no currents travel from Japan to these locations.

88.   **(D)**   At this location, the North Pole is tilted toward the sun, resulting in continual daylight. (A) and (C) are incorrect, because in this position the pole is neither pointing toward nor from the sun, and equal hours of night and day would occur. (B) is not the right choice because the North Pole is pointing away from the sun and is in continual darkness. (E) is incorrect; these two positions are so very different.

89.   **(E)**   Both of these positions are parallel to the sun, and this results in equal day and night. (B) is not the right choice because the North Pole is pointing away from the sun and is in continual darkness. (D) is not the right choice as the North Pole is facing the sun and is in continual daylight. (A) and (C) are only partially correct.

90.   **(A)**   It is the varying angle of the sunrays in relationship to the poles that causes the change in seasons. (B) is incorrect, because the changes in distance as the Earth revolves around the sun are not great enough to account for the changes in the seasons. (C), (D), and (E) have no bearing on the seasons.

91. **(E)** Liquid substances and gases are unable to transmit transverse shear waves. Each of the choices provided are liquids or gases at standard conditions except the igneous rock, granite (E). Mountains of granite on the earth transmit the three types of waves generated by earthquakes: P-, S-, and L-waves.

92. **(B)** If the S-waves are stopped at 2,900 kilometers below the surface, there must be liquid present there. The radius of the Earth is about 6,400 kilometers, or 3,960 miles. This implies that this liquid outer core must have a radius of about 3,500 kilometers, or about 2,170 miles.

93. **(C)** For this problem, S-waves travel at 4.25 km/sec and the P-waves at about 8.5 km/sec. Using the equation that distance equals rate multiplied by time, we see that the distance must be equal to 8.5 km/sec times 4 minutes (240 seconds) to get 2,040 kilometers. This is closest to the 2,000 km of choice (C). The associated S-waves would arrive about 4 minutes after the P-waves.

94. **(D)** All longitude lines converge at the poles. (A) and (C) are incorrect; latitude lines never vary in distance. (B) is incorrect as it is opposite to the correct choice. (E) is incorrect; since longitude lines vary, the relationship between latitude and longitude must change.

95. **(B)** is the false statement; if two lines cross then that place would have two elevations, which is not possible. (A), (C), (D), and (E) are all correct statements.

96. **(C)** is the false statement; weather is a modern-day phenomenon and is not a reflection on past conditions. (A), (B), (D), and (E) are all true statements.

97. **(C)** The number of people in an area does not affect the weather at that location. (A) affects the weather by changing the amount of sunlight received; (B) winds bring weather from other locations; (D) the shape of the land influences rainfall. (E) distance from water influences rainfall.

98. **(E)** Since the word organic (A) means pertaining to or derived from living organisms, or (in chemistry) a compound containing carbon (and in some cases oxygen), choice (A) is inappropriate. Choice (B) is incorrect; there are more organic compounds than inorganic. Since inorganic compounds (C) can be synthesized in a laboratory, (C) is incorrect.

(D) does not seem logical; dead organisms cannot synthesize a compound. (D) should not be selected. (E) is the correct choice. All organic compounds contain carbon.

99. **(E)** is the correct answer. (A) should not be chosen because it is a true statement, and the question asks the reader to select the one which is not a part of the theory. (B) is not the right choice because the statement is a true one. (C) is an incorrect choice. Molecules are believed to be in rapid and ceaseless motion. (D) is not the best choice, since the statement is a true part of the molecular theory. When a molecule of water is split, it is separated into hydrogen and oxygen – not smaller molecules of water. Since (E) is not a part of the molecular theory, it should be chosen.

100. **(C)** The symbol for iron is Fe. (A) is incorrect. Despite the fact that both phosphorous and the symbol Pb begin with p, (B) is not the correct choice. The correct representation for this common element of lead is Pb; therefore, (C) is the correct choice. Even though plutonium and Pb both begin with p, (D) is not the correct choice. Both potassium and Pb begin with p, but (E) is not the right choice.

101. **(D)** You would first have to recognize that HCl is hydrochloric acid, which is an acid and not a base. Then you would have to know that litmus paper turns pink in an acid. After this reasoning, the reader is now ready to make the correct choice. (A) is false; there should be a reaction. The paper should turn red. (A) is not the correct choice. Since the litmus paper does not disintegrate but instead turns red, (B) is not the best choice. Litmus paper turns blue in a base. Since HCl is an acid, the paper turns red, not blue. (C) is an incorrect choice. The litmus paper does turn red with an acid; (D) is the correct choice. There are no oxygen bubbles rising to the top because of carbonation at the time the litmus paper is inserted. (E) is wrong, therefore, and should not be chosen.

102. **(D)** Water has properties of a base; it also has properties of an acid and is classified as a compound. For these reasons, (A), (B), and (C) alone may not be selected. Since (A), (B), and (C) are all correct, (D) allows you to choose all three choices. Since choices (A), (B), and (C) are correct, (E) (none of the above) cannot be chosen.

103. **(C)** Some elements are found in nature, but others may be made by scientists. (A) is not the correct choice. Elements may or may not be made by scientists; the nonelements are made by scientists. (B) should not be chosen. (C) is the correct choice; some elements are found in nature;

others may be made by scientists. There are 110 identified elements – hence 110 presently known atoms; (D) is incorrect. Steel (carbon and iron), brass (copper and zinc), and water (hydrogen and oxygen) are compounds; (E) is wrong and should not be chosen.

104. **(A)** is not true; all proteins are not identical in their chemical makeup. Since you must select the false statement, (A) is the right choice. (B) is true and may not be selected. Since (C) is a true statement, (C) should not be chosen. (D) is not the best choice, since it is true. (E) is a true statement; since a false one should be selected, (E) should not be chosen.

105. **(A)** is the correct choice. Energy may be converted from one form to another. For example, electrical energy may be converted to light energy in the case of an electric light bulb; (B) is not the correct choice. Since kinetic energy is energy that an object possesses because of its motion; (C) is not the right choice. Potential energy (D) is that which objects possess because of their position. (D) is not the right choice and should not be chosen. Nuclear fission (E), most scientists agree, will not be the chief source of energy for the world by the year 2050, because of the many problems involved. Some of the problems involved include how to properly dispose of the nuclear waste, as well as the safety of the process. (E) is incorrect.

106. **(D)** Gravitational force is one of the forces that operates to cause interactions of matter. Since it is not the only force, however, (A) cannot be selected. Since electromagnetic force (B) is only one of the forces from which interactions of matter result, (B) should not be chosen. Nuclear force (C) is an important force from which interactions of matter result, but it is not the only such force. (C) is an incorrect choice. All three of the forces listed in (D) – gravitational, electromagnetic, and nuclear – are correct. (D), therefore, is correct. (E) "None of the above" is an incorrect choice since all the forces listed may result in the interactions of matter.

107. **(D)** The amount of heat necessary to melt ice (A) is not a relevant fact since water of 50°C is not ice. (A) should not be chosen. Changing water to gas (B) does not involve raising the temperature from 50° to 90°C. (B) is not the right choice. Since I and II in (C) mention ice and gas (two forms of water not relevant to water of the temperature 50-90°C), (C) is not the best choice. (D) is the best choice. It alone contains information appropriate only to water of the temperature 50° to 90°C. (E) is wrong. It refers to a gram of ice; water of the temperature 50° to 90°C is not ice.

108. **(D)** Since comets glow from reflected light, not their own light. (D) is false and the answer sought. When comets are close to the sun, they shine by fluorescence. The sun's ultraviolet radiation sets the gases of the comet aglow. The rest of the choices – (A), (B), (C), and (E) – are true but are not to be selected since the directions ask for the answer which is NOT true. (D) is the only appropriate choice.

109. **(A)** Since all the statements are true, (A) is the best – and only – answer. The other items, (B), (C), (D), and (E), omit important true statements.

110. **(C)** is correct. Since (A) is a true statement, it cannot be selected. The question asks you to find the false statement. (B) is a true statement as well, and cannot be selected. Since there are many galaxies in the universe (C), stating that the Milky Way is *the* galaxy is false. (D) is not the best choice, since it is a true statement. (E) is not the best choice since it, too, is a true statement.

111. **(E)** All the choices except (E) are indeed part of the fundamental ideas of Dalton's atomic theory. Atoms cannot be broken into anything simpler by ordinary chemical means; (E) should be selected. The other choices, (A), (B), (C), and (D), are true as they are stated.

112. **(C)** is the correct choice since it includes the two false statements II and III; the question asks for the statements which are not true. Statement II is false since electrons have a negative – not a positive – charge. Statement III is false since the proton in the nucleus has a positive charge, not a negative charge as the statement reads. The rest of the choices are true. No other choices include both false statements only. Therefore, (C) is a satisfactory answer.

113. **(A)** Since elements cannot be broken down into simpler substances, (A) is a true statement and the right answer. (B) is incorrect since molecules which are built of more than one kind of atom are known as compounds – not elements. Choice (C) is not to be selected because there are only 107 identified elements. (D) should not be selected as the right choice since all elements are not equally abundant in nature; some are more plentiful than others. (E) is an incorrect choice because elements – not compounds – might be compared to the 26 letters of the alphabet; compounds – not elements – might be compared to the words.

114. **(D)** All the statements about gravitational force are true except for I. Since (D) enables the reader to select all the statements (II, III, IV, and V) except I, it is the best choice to the question. It is evident that the production of an electromagnet is the result of electricity and not the result of gravitational force; I is incorrect and is not included in (D) – the right choice.

115. **(C)** Conduction (a method of heat transfer in which energy is moved from molecule to molecule by collision or bombardment), convection (heat transfer when the heavier, colder air pushes the warmer, lighter air upward and a whole volume of heated material circulates), and radiation (heat transfer by waves) are the only three correct means of heat transfer listed; (C) contains all of these. Since transportation and condensation are not means of heat transfer, their inclusion in choices (A), (B), (D), and (E) precludes the selection of these choices as the correct ones; (conduction, radiation, and convection), no choice but (C) is suitable.

116. **(E)** Since the magnetism of a substance is due BOTH to the magnetic properties of its atoms AND the arrangement of its atoms. Both (A) and (B) are the correct choices. Although (A) and (B) are both true, the reader who selects only one or the other has omitted part of the correct choice. The position of the poles (C) does not determine the magnetism of a substance; therefore (C) alone should not be selected. (D), which includes the incorrect choice (C), should not be selected. The only totally correct and complete choice is (E).

117. **(E)** When a magnet moves near a coil of wire or when a coil of wire moves near a magnet, the electrons flow and electricity can be generated (the principle of the generator). Choice (E) incorporates both of these concepts and is the correct choice. Neither a weak link in the electric circuit nor atomic fusion result from such movement, so neither (B) nor (C) can be correctly chosen.

118. **(D)** Three types of choices were asked for in this question. First, the reader was asked to identify an observation; statement III ("The magnet attracted all our objects made of iron.") is an observation. Second, the question asked for a prediction; statement II ("The magnet will probably attract this nail since it is made of iron.") is an example of a such a prediction. Third, the question asked for a generalization; statement I ("Magnetized needles point in a north-south direction when suspended freely.") Only one choice (D) gives the choices in this order; (D) is, therefore, the

correct choice. The other choices – (A), (B), (C), and (E) – do not include all the correct responses or do not include them in the correct order; therefore, none of them should be selected.

119. **(C)** It takes approximately 365 days for the Earth to revolve around the sun; by this means we measure the calendar year. (C) is the correct choice. The tilt of the Earth on its axis causes the concentration/lack of concentration of the sun's rays on certain parts of the Earth; the result is the seasons of the year – not the calendar year. (A) should not, therefore, be chosen. As a result of the rotation of the Earth about the sun, the Earth has day and night – not a calendar year. (B) is an incorrect response. The phases of the moon do not necessarily coincide with the calendar year; (D) is incorrect. The sun does not revolve about the Earth; rather the Earth revolves about the sun. (E) is an incorrect choice.

120. **(A)** "The sun could burn for a *total* of 80,000 years" (A) refutes the theory of the sun's having burned for billions of years; (A) best refutes the theory. (B) Energy converted to heat because of gravitational attraction does not necessarily refute the theory and should not be selected. Hydrogen atoms could join to form helium atoms and result in the "burning" of the sun; since (C) does not refute the theory, it is not the choice to be selected. (D) encompasses all the above choices and should not be chosen. (E) includes both (A) – a correct choice – and (B) – an incorrect choice – and should not be selected.

PRACTICE
TEST 3

CLEP NATURAL SCIENCES
Test 3

(Answer sheets appear in the back of the book.)

Section 1

TIME: 45 Minutes
60 Questions

DIRECTIONS: Each of the questions or incomplete statements below is followed by five possible answers or completions. Select the best choice in each case and fill in the corresponding oval on the answer sheet.

QUESTIONS 1 to 4 refer to the following passage.

Ants are insects with two body parts, a thorax and abdomen, plus a head. Antennae protrude from the head. These antennae serve in communicating with other ants and examining food, and possess several other purposes. Ants have fixed compound eyes which are made of many small lenses. Ants leave a trail when they travel; they never seem to get lost. Ants which have been trapped in resin and preserved for millions of years seem to be very similar to the ants of today.

1. When an ant finds food, it leaves a trail behind it which has a different odor than the trail left by any other ant colony. This trail is most likely made of

    (A) food.

    (B) broken pieces of antennae.

    (C) drops of liquid from the abdomen.

    (D) lenses of compound eyes.

    (E) tiny pebbles.

2. How is a compound eye advantageous to an ant?

   (A) The ant sees multiple images of everything.

   (B) If one lens breaks, the ant still can see.

   (C) The eye can rotate and gives the ant better vision.

   (D) The ant can see moving objects more easily than objects which stand still.

   (E) Like a compound microscope, a compound eye magnifies objects a thousand times.

3. Ants are considered to be most related to

   (A) bees.   (D) fleas.

   (B) spiders.   (E) crabs.

   (C) fungus.

4. Ants did not change or evolve much from prehistoric ants because

   (A) ants could not adjust themselves to changing conditions.

   (B) ants could not protect themselves against enemies.

   (C) no Earth changes were severe enough to disturb ants.

   (D) ants were unable to find food for their young.

   (E) ants were unable to find shelter.

5. If a person has a lung infection, the germs probably entered via

   (A) the nose.   (D) a cut on the chest.

   (B) a cut on the finger.   (E) the underside of a fingernail.

   (C) a cut on the foot.

6. Germs on the body surface of a healthy individual

   (A) are infecting the body.

   (B) are causing disturbance to the body.

   (C) are never contagious.

   (D) are not infecting the body.

   (E) cannot enter the body in any manner.

7.   Which one of the following microbes are considered harmful?

   (A) Yeast used in making bread

   (B) Mold that gives blue cheese its flavor

   (C) Bacterial cultures in yogurt

   (D) Malaria germs carried by mosquitoes

   (E) Microorganisms used in fermentation for beer preparation

8.   If a person swallows a great number of microbes with food,

   (A) acidic stomach juice will destroy most microbes.

   (B) basic stomach juice will destroy most microbes.

   (C) the destruction of all of the microbes will cause food poisoning.

   (D) powerful microbes that were not destroyed cannot cause food poisoning.

   (E) a great proportion of the microbes swallowed are most likely very harmful.

QUESTIONS 9 to 15 refer to the following paragraph.

A flower is composed of several different modified leaves. The sepals are modified leaves that encircle the flower when it is in "bud." Sepals are green and protect the bud while it is developing into a flower. Just inside the sepals are the petals. The petals are usually large, showy, and brightly colored. They serve as a means of advertisement for animal pollinators that are attracted to bright patterns. Inside the petals are the stamens. The stamens are a two-part structure made up of the anther and the filament. The filament supports the anther. The anther is a structure which houses the developing pollen grains. In the very center of the flower is the pistil. The pistil is a series of modified leaves (the carpels) that contain the ovules. A pistil is composed of three basic parts: the stigma, the style, and the ovary/ovaries. The stigma is a sticky knob that receives the pollen. The pollen germinate and grow downward into the filamentous style and into the ovary and ultimately fertilize the egg that is contained within the ovary.

9. The modified leaves that produce the ovules are the

   (A) sepals.   (D) stigmas.

   (B) petals.   (E) styles.

   (C) carpels.

10. The flower part that supports the stigma is the

   (A) sepal.   (D) stigma.

   (B) petal.   (E) style.

   (C) anther.

11. _____ fertilizes the egg.

   (A) Stigmas   (D) Radicals

   (B) Styles   (E) Anthers

   (C) Pollen

12. Some children pass by a bunch of flowers. After this interaction, bees are no longer attracted to the flowers. What did the children do?

   (A) They separated the sepals from the rest of the bud.

   (B) They crushed the pollen.

   (C) They crushed the stigma, which receives the pollen.

   (D) They plucked off all of the petals.

   (E) They separated the anther from the filament.

13. If a bug invades a flower which has not yet budded and causes damage to the petals, the bug must also have the ability to damage the

   (A) sepals.   (D) style.

   (B) stamens.   (E) ovary.

   (C) pistil.

14. In what way does the stigma most likely receive the pollen?

   (A) Gale winds are necessary to blow the pollen to the stigma.

   (B) Pollen sticks to pollinators and then is transferred to the stigma as the pollinator moves.

   (C) Picking flowers causes the flowers to pollinate.

   (D) The pollen is negatively charged and the stigma is positively charged.

   (E) The pollen slides from the anther to the stigma by way of the style.

15. Flowers are similar to female animals in that

   (A) both are composed of modified leaves.

   (B) both have ovaries and eggs.

   (C) both have ovaries and stigmas.

   (D) both have male and female reproductive organs.

   (E) both have eggs and sperm.

QUESTIONS 16 to 20 refer to the following passage.

Scientific investigation involves two areas: pure science and applied science. Pure science is basic research, or the attempt to answer questions simply for the sake of knowledge itself. Applied science uses the knowledge gained from pure science to solve practical problems. Consider the following example: A biologist wants to know how insects attract mates. After much research, observation, and experimentation she discovers a substance called a pheromone is produced by the female insect and released into the air as an invisible gas, much like perfume. Pheromones are chemicals that are given off by organisms and affect or influence the behavior or the development of an individual organism. Pheromones are also known as "sex attractants" and are specific according to the type of organism. She found that pheromones produced by some organisms can be detected miles away by male organisms of the same species. This allows the male to find the female much faster than by looking or listening for the female insect. Pheromones are so powerful that the insect attracted pays no attention to anything other than trying to reach the female so that mating can begin.

16. The biologist that did the research on pheromones was engaged in

    (A) basic research.

    (B) applied research.

    (C) government research.

    (D) library research.

    (E) methods to produce great numbers of insects.

17. Pheromones

    (A) are used only in insects.   (D) can be seen.

    (B) are used by all animals.   (E) can be felt.

    (C) are found in many organisms.

18. If another biologist placed a cockroach pheromone on a cork and then placed the cork in a dish containing a solution poisonous to cockroaches, what would probably be the result?

    (A) No cockroaches would be affected.

    (B) Over a period of time, the dish would gradually be filled with dead cockroaches that crawled through the poison in an attempt to mate with the cork.

    (C) Moths would be attracted to the pheromone impregnated cork.

    (D) Cockroaches would surround the dish but not cross the poison.

    (E) Not enough data has been given.

19. If a biologist used pheromones to attract male cockroaches to a cork containing a contact poison in hopes of ridding his home of cockroaches, what would this be an example of?

    (A) Pure science   (D) Government research

    (B) Basic research   (E) The scientific method

    (C) Applied science

20. Pheromones are sexual attractants of insects. This has been a great discovery in itself. If scientists took this information and used it to make a trap where the insects would die, this would be an example of

(A) entomology.

(D) pure science.

(B) botany.

(E) scientific method.

(C) applied science.

QUESTIONS 21 to 23 refer to the following passage.

For five years Charles Darwin traveled around the world aboard the H.M.S. *Beagle*. During that time he observed many things, especially the plants and animals of South America and the Galapagos Islands. Later, he published his famous book, *On The Origin of Species,* which made sense of what he saw. His theory may be summarized by the following four observations: (1) individuals vary genetically; (2) generally, organisms will produce more offspring than the environment can support; (3) even though there are large numbers of offspring, the population remains fairly constant; and (4) the environment all over the planet is in a constant state of change. From these four observations Darwin concluded that: (a) in every population there is competition for available resources; (b) those organisms that have favorable genetic variation will be able to live and reproduce; and (c) those genetic variations that allowed the parents to survive will be handed down to offspring through generations and will accumulate in the population until the whole population will have these favorable genes. In this way, Darwin could see how things change or evolve.

21. It is a well-known fact that clams release millions of eggs and sperm. If 50 percent of all eggs were fertilized, would this be consistent with Darwin's conclusions?

(A) Yes, because favorable variations occur.

(B) Yes, because there are more offspring produced than the environment could support, and only some of the clams would survive.

(C) Yes, because the environment is constantly changing.

(D) No, because individual sperm and egg are different genetically.

(E) No, because genetic variation does not allow for natural selection.

22. It is estimated that a single fern can produce upwards of 50 million spores in a single year. It is easy to realize that all of the spores do not grow into a mature adult fern, because if they did, whole continents would be covered with ferns. What did Darwin observe that would explain this?

    (A) Organisms produce more offspring than the environment can support, so a population will remain constant because there are not enough resources for all offspring.

    (B) The environment is slowly changing all over the world, which prevents all of the offspring from maturing.

    (C) Genetic variation is allowing the ferns to keep the same level of population.

    (D) Genetic variation, which allows for survival, will accumulate.

    (E) Individuals vary genetically.

23. Which person would be helped by having a better understanding of Darwin's observations and conclusions in order to have a more productive business?

    (A) Cattle rancher   (D) Refinery chemist

    (B) Oilman   (E) Hairstylist

    (C) Engineer

QUESTIONS 24 to 26 refer to the following paragraphs.

Carolus Linnaeus introduced a scientific system of naming organisms. He developed this because there were so many names for the same organism. For example, a mountain lion could be called a puma, mountain lion, panther, cougar, red lion, etc. In order to avoid this confusion, he set up what is known as the binomial system of nomenclature. This means that for the name of the animal, one would use two names. Carolus used Latin names because Latin is a dead language that is not spoken by anyone; therefore, it is not subject to change. In a two-word name, the first name refers to the animals' genus and the second name to its species.

Carolus Linnaeus also set up a system of grouping organisms. He began by dividing up all living things into two groups. These he named kingdoms. Today there are five kingdoms: Animalia, Plantae, Monera, Protista, and Fungi. The classification (grouping) hierarchy of today is: kingdom, phylum, class, order, family, genus, species. Note that members of a genus group can have a special name like *Felis* (cat) or *Canis* (dog). Every type of animal has a unique species name, which also places them in a single grouping. For example, *Canis lupis* (wolf) and *Canis latrans* (coyote) are two different species of the dog family. *Canis* is the genus name; *latrans* and *lupis* are species names. *Felis domesticus* and *Canis familiaris* are not the same and their genus names tell us so.

24. The panda bear, *Aleropoda melanoleuca,* is not a bear like the black bear, *Ursus americanus,* or the grizzly bear, *Ursus horribilis.* How can this distinction be shown?

    (A) Panda bears live only in China.

    (B) Pandas are not bears, and their genus name, *Aleropoda,* indicates this.

    (C) Pandas are not bears, and their species name, *melanoleuca,* indicates this.

    (D) Pandas are on the endangered list and have black and white fur.

    (E) Pandas are not bears because they are really called "pandas."

25. Given: 2 animals. Animal #1 is called *Linius alba,* and animal #2 is called *Canis alba.* Which of the following is true?

    (A) The species name indicates that there is a close genetic relationship.

    (B) The species name indicates a filial relationship.

    (C) The genus names indicate that there is no relationship.

    (D) The genus names indicate there is a filial relationship.

    (E) Both animals are totally black.

26. Some members of the kingdom Animalia include the

    (A) insects, amphibians, reptiles, fish, birds, and mammals.

    (B) insects, fungi, amphibians, reptiles, fish, birds, and mammals.

    (C) mushrooms, amphibians, reptiles, fish, birds, and mammals.

    (D) slime molds, autotrophic algae, rusts, trees, and blue-green algae.

    (E) insects, crabs, sponges, trees, fish, birds, and reptiles.

27. The first name of a scientific name, such as *Happlopappus gracilis,* is the

    (A) kingdom name.   (D) order name.

    (B) phylum name.   (E) genus name.

    (C) class name.

QUESTIONS 28 to 31 refer to the following paragraph.

Protein synthesis is very important in living things. All cells contain protein and the making of protein is controlled by DNA (deoxyribonucleic acid), which is a major constituent of the chromosomes. DNA molecules contain information in the form of 64 chemical "code words." This information is also known as the "genetic code." Since DNA is only found in the nucleus of cells, the information that is needed for protein synthesis must be carried to the portion of the cell involved with protein synthesis, the endoplasmic reticulum (ER) and the ribosomes. This is done by a molecule called messenger ribonucleic acid (mRNA), which is made by DNA. Once the mRNA is in the ER, the ribosomes begin to "read" the instructions on the mRNA. As the instructions are read, transfer ribonucleic acid (tRNA) brings to the ribosomes, from the cytoplasm, the proper amino acids. The ribosomes then bond these amino acids together in the proper order until a long chain of amino acids (the protein) is formed.

28. Imagine that a cosmic ray obliterates a "code word" in a single DNA molecule. What happens when the DNA molecule is read so that mRNA can be built?

    (A) Nothing happens.

    (B) The message of the mRNA is different from the DNA before the event.

    (C) mRNA cannot be made.

    (D) Triplets can no longer be produced, so doublets are used.

    (E) DNA repairs itself perfectly.

29. DNA nucleotides are found in what part of the cell?

    (A) The lysosomes

    (B) The endoplasmic reticulum

(C) The cytoplasmic matrix

(D) The nucleus

(E) The Golgi bodies

30. DNA strands that are coiled around and interwoven with protein molecules form

(A) RNA.   (D) genes.

(B) chromosomes.   (E) ribosomes.

(C) nucleotides.

31. If the "code words" for a DNA molecule were changed around, or reversed, what would happen to the resulting protein?

(A) The resulting protein would remain the same.

(B) The resulting protein would definitely be smaller.

(C) The resulting protein would definitely be larger.

(D) The resulting protein would be wrapped around the DNA.

(E) The resulting protein would be changed in some way, either in length, number, or type or arrangement of amino acids.

QUESTIONS 32 to 35 refer to the following paragraph.

Skin is the flexible outer covering on the bodies of vertebrate animals. The thickness varies on different body areas. Human skin is composed of an outer layer called the epidermis and an inner layer called the dermis. The epidermis has several layers. Near the outside is the stratum corneum. Under it is the layer of Malpighi which quickly grows to replace the cells of the stratum corneum which wear away. Human skin protects the body from injury, helps get rid of waste products, regulates water, and regulates temperature.

32. What area of the skin is most likely the thinnest?

(A) The soles of the feet   (D) The back

(B) The palms of the hand   (E) The heel

(C) Skin covering the eyeballs

33. What is the order of the layers of skin from the outside of the body proceeding inward?

    (A) Layer of Malpighi, stratum corneum, epidermis

    (B) Stratum corneum, layer of Malpighi, epidermis

    (C) Dermis, layer of Malpighi, stratum corneum

    (D) Dermis, stratum corneum, layer of Malpighi

    (E) Stratum corneum, layer of Malpighi, dermis

34. How does the body regulate temperature or water through the skin?

    (A) Respiration   (D) Sensation

    (B) Transpiration   (E) Coagulation

    (C) Perspiration

35. Since the stratum corneum is constantly wearing away, structures such as blood vessels, nerve endings, and sweat glands must be found in

    (A) the layer of Malpighi.   (D) the dermis.

    (B) the stratum corneum.   (E) the muscle tissue.

    (C) the epidermis.

QUESTIONS 36 to 38 refer to the following paragraph.

Chameleons are lizards found mainly in Africa. The popular belief that chameleons change color to match their environment is largely false. Temperature, sunlight, and emotion affect the chameleon more than the color of its surroundings. A chameleon can swiftly shoot out its sticky tongue to a distance longer than the length of its body. In this way, it can catch its food.

36. If chameleons are mainly found in Africa, it follows that

    (A) no chameleons can be found on any other continent.

    (B) the greater proportion of chameleons are found on the other continents.

    (C) a lizard found on another continent cannot be a chameleon.

(D) chameleons tend to migrate to all parts of the world in great numbers.

(E) some species may possibly live in India, but in small number.

37. A chameleon sitting on a black rock turns black in color. This color change is most likely because

(A) the chameleon is hiding from a predator.

(B) the chameleon is attempting to blend into its surroundings.

(C) the chameleon is most likely dying.

(D) the chameleon is cold, causing the animal to darken.

(E) the animal is preparing to extend its long tongue.

38. The chameleon's tongue catches prey because

(A) prey will stick to the sticky substance covering the tongue.

(B) the fork on the end of the tongue spears the prey.

(C) the tongue wraps around the prey in the same way that a snake will squeeze its prey to death.

(D) the tongue contains poisonous glands that kill their prey.

(E) the prey is stunned to see the chameleon change color.

QUESTIONS 39 to 44 refer to the following information.

One way of describing animals is to describe how their body parts are arranged. The arrangement of body parts is called symmetry. If an organism has no definite shape, then it is said to be asymmetrical. No matter which way the organism is sliced, no two halves will look similar. If an organism is shaped like a ball, then it is said to have spherical symmetry. No matter how you slice it, both halves will look similar. If an organism is bilaterally symmetrical, then it will have a right and a left side. If an organism has radial symmetry, then it will have the general shape of a cylinder, with its body parts extending outward from the middle of the cylinder (radiating). However, one must be careful when considering radial symmetry. Sometimes the cylindrical shape will be flattened.

39. What type of symmetry is exhibited by the animal shown to the right?

(A) Asymmetry

(B) Radial symmetry

(C) Spherical symmetry

(D) Bilateral symmetry

(E) Longitudinal symmetry

40. The organism to the right exhibits what type of symmetry?

(A) Asymmetry

(B) Radial symmetry

(C) Bilateral symmetry

(D) Spherical symmetry

(E) Triradial symmetry

41. What type of symmetry is exhibited by the figure on the right?

(A) Asymmetry

(B) Radial symmetry

(C) Spherical symmetry

(D) Bilateral symmetry

(E) Longitudinal symmetry

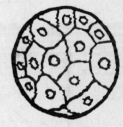

42. What type of symmetry is exhibited by the organism shown at the right?

(A) Asymmetry

(B) Radial symmetry

(C) Bilateral symmetry

(D) Spherical symmetry

(E) Longitudinal symmetry

43. If an organism has a right side and a left side, it is said to be

   (A) asymmetrical.   (D) cylindrically symmetrical.

   (B) bilaterally symmetrical.   (E) radially symmetrical.

   (C) spherically symmetrical.

44. A starfish, since it has rays radiating out from a central point, would be

   (A) asymmetrical.   (D) cylindrically symmetrical.

   (B) bilaterally symmetrical.   (E) radially symmetrical.

   (C) spherically symmetrical.

QUESTIONS 45 to 48 refer to the following graph.

   In the graph below, the dark black line represents the growth in a ranch's population of mule deer. The shaded line represents the growth of a population of whitetail deer in the same area. In both cases, sufficient food is supplied, and no other outside influences or diseases affect either population.

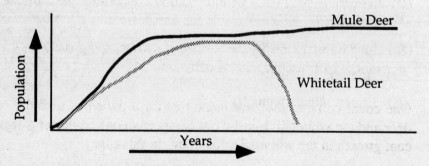

45. According to the graph, two species with the same living requirements cannot live long together in the same environment. Competition will eliminate one of the two.

   (A) This conclusion is supported by the data.

   (B) This conclusion is not supported by the data.

   (C) This conclusion includes the effect of hunting and is supported by the data.

   (D) This conclusion includes the effect caused by a drought and is supported by the data.

(E) This conclusion takes into consideration that a fire ruined half of the ranch and is supported by the data.

46. If one comes to the conclusion that the idea of survival of the fittest is supported by this graph, then

   (A) the conclusion is supported by the data.

   (B) the conclusion is refuted by the data.

   (C) the conclusion is refuted because only one kind of deer survived.

   (D) the conclusion is refuted because the two kinds of deer do not compete with each other, and the data supports this.

   (E) the conclusion is right, but the data is wrong.

47. If one comes to the conclusion that the mule deer are better adapted to the environment than are the whitetail deer, then

   (A) the conclusion is supported by the data.

   (B) the conclusion is refuted by the data.

   (C) the conclusion is neither supported nor refuted by the data.

   (D) the data gives plenty of information concerning the mule deer's adaptability, which supports the conclusion.

   (E) the data gives plenty of information concerning the type of terrain, which supports the conclusion.

48. One could come to the conclusion that for a period of time the mule deer and the whitetail deer did not compete so one could see a significant growth in the whitetail population. In this case,

   (A) the conclusion is supported by the data.

   (B) the conclusion is refuted by the data.

   (C) the conclusion is neither supported nor refuted by the data.

   (D) the data gives plenty of information concerning the mule deer's adaptability, which supports the conclusion.

   (E) the data gives plenty of information concerning the type of terrain, which supports the conclusion.

QUESTIONS 49 and 50 refer to the following paragraph.

Sharks are vertebrate animals and their skeleton is composed of carti-lage. Sharks are not in the class Osteichthyes because sharks do not have bony skeletons. The shark is a member of the class Chondrichthyes. Other members of this class included the rays, skates, and dogfishes. Sharks have a very rough skin which is covered with little toothlike appendages called denticles. Their teeth are enlarged versions of the denticles. Even though most sharks are ferocious predators, the two largest sharks are filter feeders. Sharks have internal fertilization with the female retaining the eggs within her body. Some of these sharks are ovoviparous, which means that the embryo gets all of its nourishment or food from the yolk of the egg. Other sharks are viviparous, which means that the embryo gets its nourishment from close contact of the blood vessels of the mother's ovi-duct with the blood vessels of the yolk.

49. Sharks have what type of fertilization?

    (A) Denticle   (D) External

    (B) Viviparous   (E) Internal

    (C) Ovoviparous

50. Sharks are members of the

    (A) phylum Reptilia.   (D) class Osteichthyes.

    (B) class Aves.   (E) class Chondrichthyes.

    (C) class Vertebrata.

QUESTIONS 51 to 54 refer to the following paragraph.

An animal cell is composed of many parts. The outside of the cell is surrounded by a membrane. The cell membrane is selective, which means that it only allows certain things in or out of the cell. The inside of the cell is composed of various cell organelles (little organs) and the matrix in which they are suspended. The matrix is called the cytoplasm. One of the most conspicuous objects in the cytoplasm is the nucleus. The nucleus is a large spherical structure. It is composed of a nuclear membrane which, like the cell membrane, is selective. Inside the nucleus is a viscous matrix, the nucleoplasm. Suspended in the nucleoplasm are the chromosomes and the nucleoli. The nucleoli are dark staining spherical structures that are thought to function in the production of ribosomes, which are involved in protein synthesis. The chromosomes, the number of which may vary from organism to organism, are elongated threadlike structures that cannot be seen with a normal microscope. However, during cell division, the chromosomes coil up and become visible. Some other cell organelles include the mitochondria and the vacuoles. The mitochondria produce energy for the cell. The vacuoles are used as storage centers. They may store food, water, or waste products.

51. Which of the following is the first barrier of defense that a foreign molecule must face upon entering an animal cell?

    (A) Nucleoplasm   (D) Chromosomes

    (B) Cytoplasm   (E) Cell membrane

    (C) Nuclear membrane

52. The number of elongated threadlike chromosomes that can be visualized during cell division

    (A) depends on the random manner in which the chromosomes reassemble during coiling.

    (B) varies among the different types of somatic cells within one organism.

    (C) depends on the strength of the microscope.

    (D) is the same for somatic cells within one individual.

    (E) is influenced by the presence of the nucleoli, which are also suspended in the nucleoplasm.

53. Since nucleoli are involved in the formation of ribosomes, it follows that

    (A) ribosomes must be located in the nucleus so as not to be far from their origin.

    (B) ribosomes must be transferred from the nucleus to the cytoplasm in order to function in protein synthesis.

    (C) ribosomes must be transferred to the area where they can produce energy for the cell.

    (D) the coiling of the chromosomes always hinders the formation of the ribosomes.

    (E) ribosomes must also be dark staining.

54. Since the cell membrane and nuclear membrane are selective in nature, they can be considered

(A) totally permeable.   (D) opaque.

(B) nonpermeable.   (E) translucent.

(C) semipermeable.

QUESTIONS 55 refers to the following paragraph.

Most of the land plants that one observes have vascular tissue. This tissue transports substances between various regions of the plant. There are two types of vascular tissue: phloem and xylem. The phloem transports or conducts organic materials, mainly food, from where they are made to various storage sites or regions of use. Xylem transports water and minerals from the roots to the stems and leaves and flowers. Another function of the xylem is that of support. To prevent drying out, the surface of a plant is covered with a waxy cuticle. The cuticle is impermeable to gases, such as carbon dioxide and oxygen, and to water. Since the plant needs carbon dioxide and oxygen to carry on photosynthesis, these gases are exchanged through tiny pores in the leaf called stomata. Each stomata is surrounded by two guard cells which regulate the size of the opening of the pore.

55. The tissue that is able to conduct food to specialized areas in the plant is the

(A) xylem.   (D) stomata.

(B) phloem.   (E) cuticle.

(C) precambrium.

QUESTIONS 56 to 60 refer to the following paragraph.

Life in the sea has its advantages and its disadvantages. Most of the food is found near the surface. The fish, which are vertebrates, have the advantage of being able to maintain position while cruising through the sea looking for food. Few invertebrates are powerful enough swimmers to do this. However, invertebrates have become adapted to remain small enough to float. These zooplankton are subject to the whims of the currents. An alternate adaptation that is exhibited by some invertebrates is to remain firmly anchored (sessile) to the sea floor or some solid object in the sea. Some of these animals, such as oysters and clams, are filter feeders, and filter the water for microscopic animals and plants which are their food. Since they are sessile, they must also have a means of protection from the mobile predators of the sea. That is why many of these animals have either a passive protection, such as a thick, hard, outer shell, or an active protection, such as stinging cells or an unappetizing, toxic mucus covering their body.

56. Fish are

    (A) filter feeders.   (D) zooplankton.

    (B) invertebrates.   (E) phytoplankton.

    (C) vertebrates.

57. Zooplankton are

    (A) invertebrates.   (D) toxic mucus.

    (B) vertebrates.   (E) mobile predators.

    (C) fish.

58. Those organisms that strain their food from the water could be called

    (A) fish.   (D) filter feeders.

    (B) vertebrates.   (E) toxic mobile predators.

    (C) phytoplankton.

59. Sessile means to

    (A) move around.   (D) float on the surface.

    (B) swim freely.   (E) be firmly attached.

    (C) crawl along the sea floor.

60. Invertebrates such as zooplankton are

    (A) voracious predators.

    (B) powerful swimmers.

    (C) fish.

    (D) voluntarily able to move from one ocean current to another.

    (E) tiny enough to float near the surface.

Section 2

TIME: 45 Minutes
60 Questions

DIRECTIONS: Each of the questions or incomplete statements below is followed by five possible answers or completions. Select the best choice in each case and fill in the corresponding oval on the answer sheet.

61. Which of the following statements about matter is false?

    (A) Matter exhibits three states: atoms, molecules, cells.

    (B) Atoms contain nuclei and are composed of smaller particles.

    (C) A wide variety of substances results from atoms which combine in various ways.

    (D) All matter is composed of atoms.

    (E) Atoms are divisible and they may also be combined.

62. Sulfur contains 16 electrons; this means that it contains _____ protons and that its atomic number is _____ .

    (A) 16, 16

    (B) 16, 32

    (C) 8, 24

    (D) 32, 48

    (E) an indefinite number, undetermined from information given

63. Which of the following statements is/are true?

    I.   A cupful of water and a potful of water at 100°C have molecules with the same degree of activity.

    II. A potful of water has a greater number of active molecules than does a cupful of water.

    III. It takes more burning of gas to produce a potful of boiling water than a cupful.

IV. The unit used in measuring the quantity of heat is the calorie.

V. A calorie is the amount of heat necessary to raise one gram of pure water one degree Celsius.

(A) All of the above.

(D) I, III, and IV only.

(B) None of the above.

(E) III, IV, and V only.

(C) I, II, and III only.

64. All of the following are true EXCEPT

(A) solids usually expand when they are heated and contract when they are cooled.

(B) water is a unique liquid in that at certain temperatures it reverses the rule that liquids contract when cooled; from 39°F to 32°F (its usual freezing point) water expands slightly instead of contracting.

(C) when water freezes into solid crystals of ice, the spaces between the molecules become large.

(D) gases contract when heated and expand when cooled.

(E) a liquid may be described as a substance which takes the shape of its container but has a size of its own.

65. Which of the following is/are NOT true of an electromagnet?

(A) When electricity flows through a wire, the wire becomes a magnet.

(B) An electromagnet is a permanent magnet.

(C) The strength of an electromagnet is limited and cannot be increased easily.

(D) Both (B) and (C).

(E) (A), (B), and (C).

66. What causes the phases of the moon?

(A) A shadow is thrown on the moon by the Earth.

(B) A shadow is thrown on the moon by the sun.

(C) At times the Earth is not in a position to see the moon which is always lit by the sun.

(D) The rays of the moon do not always have time to reach the Earth; therefore, at times the Earth sees only part of the moon.

(E) The moon is turning and shows a different part of its surface to the Earth at each phase.

67. Which of the following is NOT true?

(A) Comets generally have elongated, elliptical orbits.

(B) Comets may circle the sun in any direction.

(C) Despite their size, comets are mostly "empty space."

(D) Comets glow by their own light.

(E) It is believed comets are the most primitive objects in the solar system.

68. Which of the following is the symbol on the periodic table for hydrogen?

(A) H   (D) Hi

(B) Hy   (E) Hn

(C) He

69. Which of the following is true of chemical energy?

I.   Chemical energy is really a form of potential energy.

II. Chemical energy is really a form of kinetic energy.

III. Chemical energy is released when a chemical reaction takes place and new substances are formed.

IV. New substances are formed from the action between the electrons in the outermost shells or the energy levels in atoms of the different substances.

V.   Chemical energy comes from the nucleus of the atom when the atom splits in two.

(A) I, II, and III only.   (D) I, III, and IV only.

(B) II, III, and IV only.   (E) I, II, and V only.

(C) III, IV, and V only.

70. Which of the following is true of heat energy?

    I.   Heat energy is the energy produced by moving molecules.

    II.   The faster the molecules move, the more kinetic energy the substance has.

    III. The faster the molecules move, the hotter a substance becomes.

    IV. To produce the faster speed, molecules use heat so the substance is cooler.

    V.   The slower the molecules move, the more heat is produced in a substance since molecules are not using heat.

    (A) I, II, and III only.   (D) IV and V only.

    (B) I and II only.   (E) V only.

    (C) II and III only.

71. Sound energy is a type of

    (A) mechanical energy.   (D) nuclear energy.

    (B) electrical energy.   (E) heat energy.

    (C) wave energy.

72. What kind of energy includes light and radio waves?

    (A) Mechanical energy   (D) Radiant energy

    (B) Heat energy   (E) Nuclear energy

    (C) Electrical energy

73. Which of the following statements about magnets is FALSE?

    (A) Magnets are materials that will attract items made of iron, steel, cobalt, and nickel.

    (B) Natural magnets found in the ground are called lodestones.

    (C) Magnetized atoms group together in domains, or large clusters, which line up with north-seeking poles at one end and south-seeking poles at the other.

    (D) The older theory which said that magnetism was due to molecules behaving as tiny magnets with all the north-seeking poles facing in one direction and the south-seeking poles facing in the other is not currently held as true by most scientists.

(E) The earth does not behave as a huge magnet because it is not a magnet.

74. How many neutrons are there in the nucleus of an element of molecular weight 197?

(A) 43

(D) 100

(B) 79

(E) 118

(C) 83

75. The radioactive decay of plutonium-238 ($_{96}Pu^{238}$) produces an alpha particle and a new atom. That new atom is:

(A) Pu

(D) $_{96}Pu^{242}$

(B) $_{92}U^{234}$

(E) $_{92}Cm^{234}$

(C) 234

76. The element with atomic number 32 describes

(A) a metal.

(D) a halogen.

(B) a nonmetal.

(E) a noble gas.

(C) a metalloid.

77. Which of the following has the smallest mass?

(A) A hydrogen nucleus

(D) A helium nucleus

(B) An alpha particle

(E) A beta particle

(C) A neutron

78. Which of the following best represents the geometry and atomic radii in a carbon dioxide molecule?

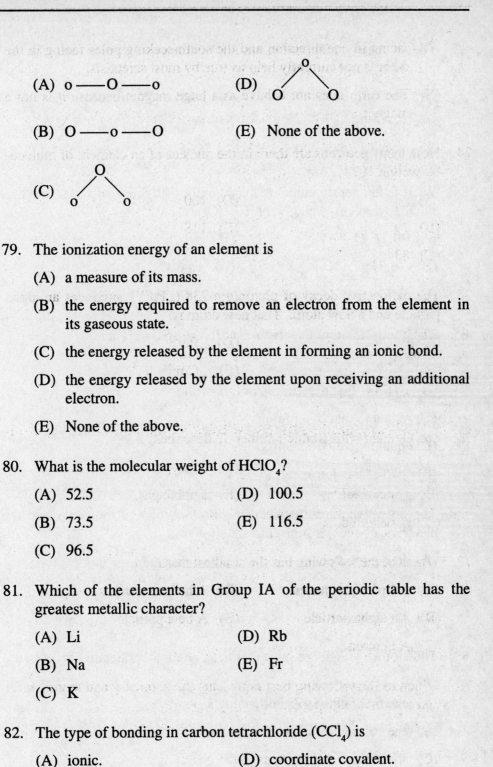

(A) o —— O —— o

(D)

(B) O —— o —— O

(E) None of the above.

(C)

79. The ionization energy of an element is

(A) a measure of its mass.

(B) the energy required to remove an electron from the element in its gaseous state.

(C) the energy released by the element in forming an ionic bond.

(D) the energy released by the element upon receiving an additional electron.

(E) None of the above.

80. What is the molecular weight of $HClO_4$?

(A) 52.5

(D) 100.5

(B) 73.5

(E) 116.5

(C) 96.5

81. Which of the elements in Group IA of the periodic table has the greatest metallic character?

(A) Li

(D) Rb

(B) Na

(E) Fr

(C) K

82. The type of bonding in carbon tetrachloride (CCl_4) is

(A) ionic.

(D) coordinate covalent.

(B) covalent.

(E) hydrogen.

(C) polar covalent.

83. The extremely high melting point of diamond (carbon) may be explained by large numbers of

    (A) covalent bonds.   (D) van der Waals forces.

    (B) ionic bonds.   (E) None of the above.

    (C) hydrogen bonds.

84. What is the approximate melting point of 0.2 liters of water containing 6.20 g of ethylene glycol ($C_2H_6O_2$)?

    (A) −1.86°C   (D) 0.93°C

    (B) −0.93°C   (E) 1.86°C

    (C) 0°C

85. The contribution of the electron to the atomic weight is

    (A) zero.

    (B) 1/1,837 that of a proton or a neutron.

    (C) equal to that of a proton.

    (D) equal to that of a neutron.

    (E) two of the above.

86. The attractive force between the protons of one molecule and the electrons of another molecule are strongest

    (A) in the solid phase.   (D) during sublimation.

    (B) in the liquid phase.   (E) during fusion.

    (C) in the gas phase.

87. The atomic weights of most elements are not whole numbers because of

    (A) the first law of thermodynamics.

    (B) the second law of thermodynamics.

    (C) the presence of isotopes.

    (D) the mass of the electrons.

    (E) the mass defect.

88. According to the following equation,

$$_{13}Al^{27} + {}_2He^4 \rightarrow {}_{15}P^{30} + X + \text{energy}$$

particle X is which atomic particle?

(A) Neutrons   (D) Protons

(B) Positrons   (E) Helium atoms

(C) Alpha particles

89. The time it takes for a plane to change its speed from 100 m/s to 500 m/s with a uniform acceleration in a distance of 1,200 m is

(A) 1 s.   (D) 4 s.

(B) 2 s.   (E) 5 s.

(C) 3 s.

90. The graph shows the speed of an object as a function of time. The average speed of the object during the time interval shown is

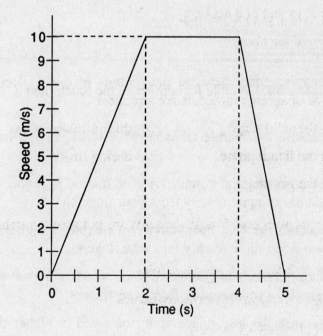

(A) 3 m/s.   (D) 8 m/s.

(B) 5 m/s.   (E) 10 m/s.

(C) 7 m/s.

91. A graph of displacement vs. time for an object moving in a straight line is shown below. The acceleration of the object must be

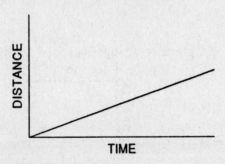

(A) zero.

(B) increasing.

(C) decreasing.

(D) constant and greater than zero.

(E) equal to g.

92. Why does a marble table feel cooler to the touch than a wooden table top?

(A) Because the marble table never absorbs enough heat to reach room temperature.

(B) Because the heat conductivity of marble is higher than wood, heat flows more readily from your fingers.

(C) Because the heat conductivity of marble is higher than wood, heat flows more readily into your fingers.

(D) Because the heat conductivity of wood is higher than marble, heat flows more readily from your fingers.

(E) Because the heat conductivity of wood is higher than marble, heat flows more readily into your fingers.

QUESTIONS 93 and 94 refer to the following graphs.

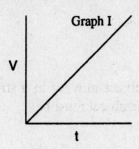

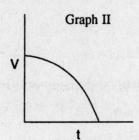

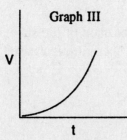

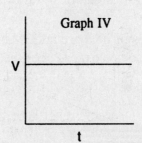

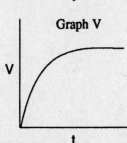

93. A graph that best describes the motion of a mass at rest and pulled by a constant force is

(A) Graph I.   (D) Graph IV.

(B) Graph II.   (E) Graph V.

(C) Graph III.

94. The graph that best describes the motion of a mass pulled by a force that is equal to the frictional force acting on it is

(A) Graph I.   (D) Graph IV.

(B) Graph II.   (E) Graph V.

(C) Graph III.

QUESTION 95 refers to the following specific heats of some common substances.

I. Lead – 0.03 calories/gram C

II. Silver – 0.06 calories/gram C

III. Iron – 0.11 calories/gram C

IV. Aluminum – 0.21 calories/gram C

V. Water – 1.0 calories/gram C

95. Ten calories of heat are added to one gram of each of the substances. Which substance experiences the greatest temperature increase?

(A) I   (D) IV

(B) II   (E) V

(C) III

QUESTION 96 refers to the following diagram.

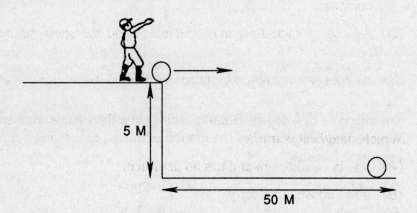

96. Given that the ball lands in one second, how fast did the child throw the ball horizontally?

(A) 5 meters/sec   (D) 500 meters/sec

(B) 50 meters/sec   (E) 1,000 meters/sec

(C) 100 meters/sec

97. When the sun is low on the horizon in the evening, it appears "redder." The best explanation for this is that

    (A) the sun is further away from the earth.

    (B) the sun is cooler in the evening.

    (C) the earth's atmosphere scatters the shorter wavelength, blue light.

    (D) the earth's atmosphere absorbs blue and green wavelengths.

    (E) the earth's atmosphere diffracts the light from the sun.

98. Which of the following statements is true under Einstein's Theory of Relativity?

    (A) As energy increases, the speed of light increases and mass is constant.

    (B) As energy increases, mass increases and the speed of light is constant.

    (C) As energy increases, the speed of light decreases and mass is constant.

    (D) As energy increases, mass decreases and the speed of light is constant.

    (E) As energy increases, the speed of light and mass will increase.

99. The moon is in a nearly circular orbit above the earth's atmosphere. Which statement is true?

    (A) It is in equilibrium and has no net force.

    (B) It has constant velocity.

    (C) It continues to use up its energy rapidly like a spaceship and is falling back to earth.

    (D) It is accelerating toward the earth.

    (E) Its acceleration is in the same direction as its velocity.

100. Which of the following is the dominant source of all or nearly all of the Earth's energy?

    (A) Plants

    (B) Animals

    (C) Natural gas

    (D) Oil

    (E) The sun

101. Which of the following resources are renewable?

   (A) Coal, oil, gas

   (B) Metals, minerals, coal

   (C) Soil, vegetation, animals

   (D) Freshwater, coal, vegetation

   (E) Oil, soil, vegetation

102. The rhythm of the tides on the Earth are the result of which of the following?

   I.   The gravitational pull of the moon

   II.   The rotation of the Earth

   III.   The pull of the planets

   IV.   Nuclear fission

   V.   Condensation and evaporation

   (A) All of the above.

   (B) None of the above.

   (C) I and II only.

   (D) V only.

   (E) II and V only.

103. All these statements illustrate recycling in nature EXCEPT

   (A) carbon dioxide (a waste from respiration) is recycled by plants as a raw material for food production.

   (B) nitrogen found in plant and animal waste may be reclaimed by the soil and used by plants in manufacturing protein.

   (C) tin-coated steel cans rust away and disappear into the environment.

   (D) aluminum cans are nonbiodegradable.

   (E) some bacteria that live deep in marshes, mud, and soil can live and grow in the absence of oxygen; these microbes (anaerobic bacteria) decompose organic matter.

104. Which best describes the nature of the environmental crisis?

   (A) The advance of technology has reached a level where processes and products threaten the earth's environment.

   (B) The environmental crisis is limited to highly industrialized areas.

(C) The oceans and atmospheres purify pollutants.

(D) All the above.

(E) Both (B) and (C).

105. All of the following are true of the structure of the Earth EXCEPT

(A) the uttermost shell of the Earth which extends for about 25 miles is the crust.

(B) the hot liquid rock in pockets within the crust is called magma.

(C) beneath the crust is the mantle.

(D) at the center of the Earth is a metallic core.

(E) the thickest of the Earth's three parts (crust, mantle, core) is the core.

106. A nuclide with a half-life of 2 days is tested after 6 days. What fraction of the sample has decayed?

(A) 1/2   (D) 3/4

(B) 1/4   (E) 7/8

(C) 3/8

107. The weather instrument designed by scientists to measure moisture in the air is a(n)

(A) hygrometer.   (D) thermometer.

(B) anemometer.   (E) altimeter.

(C) barometer.

108. Which items are harmful to the environment?

I.   Acid rain   IV. Greenhouse effect

II. Pollutants   V.   Water table.

III. Ozone hole

(A) None of the above.   (D) II, III, IV, and V only.

(B) All of the above.   (E) I, II, III, and V only.

(C) I, II, III, and IV only.

109. Which of the following measures could help prevent and cure the problems of pollution?

(A) Heat from electrical power plants should be discharged into adjacent waters to rid the environment of the heat more quickly.

(B) Sewage should be dumped into the salty waters of the ocean for purification rather than dumped into freshwater.

(C) Waste tars and oils must be dumped into ocean waters rather than into freshwater or the soil to prevent pollution.

(D) Industrial waste must be treated to remove toxic chemicals, phosphates, and other pollutants.

(E) Recycling must be discontinued; the recyclable items should never be manufactured in the first place.

110. Scientists divide the history of the earth into eras. Which of the following arranges these eras into their proper sequence from oldest to most recent?

(A) Cenozoic, mesozoic, paleozoic, precambrian

(B) Precambrian, paleozoic, mesozoic, cenozoic

(C) Mesozoic, cenozoic, paleozoic, precambrian

(D) Paleozoic, precambrian, cenozoic, mesozoic

(E) Precambrian, cenozoic, paleozoic, mesozoic

111. Which of the following temperatures marks the boiling point of water?

(A) 98.6°F

(B) 212°C

(C) 100°C

(D) 100 K

(E) 0°C

112. Even the most complex machines of today contain some simple machines. Which of the following statements about simple machines is NOT true?

(A) Some machines produce a gain in force, a gain in speed, or a change in direction of force.

(B) A gain in force is at the expense of speed; a gain in speed is at the expense of force.

(C) Friction (the rubbing together of two substances) is not an asset to the work of machines.

(D) Wheels, rollers, and ball bearings may be used to substitute rolling for sliding to reduce friction.

(E) The work put into a machine equals the work put out if one disregards friction.

113. When two glass tumblers are stuck, one inside the other, they can be loosened best by

(A) allowing them both to cool in a cool, dry place.

(B) by pouring hot water on the outside tumbler after filling the inside tumbler with equally hot water.

(C) by pouring hot water on the outside tumbler after filling the inside tumbler with cold water.

(D) by pouring cold water on the outside tumbler after filling the inside tumbler with cold water.

(E) by pouring cold water on the outside tumbler after filling the inside tumbler with hot water.

114. All of the following statements about the refrigerator found in most American homes are true EXCEPT

(A) inside the pipe in the refrigerator is a gas called Freon.

(B) a compressor changes the gas into a liquid.

(C) the Freon travels under pressure to the freezer; here the pressure is taken away.

(D) when the pressure is taken away, the Freon becomes a gas again; as it evaporates it takes heat with it.

(E) the Freon is then in gas form and is discharged into the air surrounding the refrigerator.

115. What type of radiation is emitted when uranium decays by the nuclear reaction

$$_{92}U^{238} \rightarrow {}_{90}Th^{234} + \text{?radiation}$$

(A) No radiation is emitted.   (D) Cosmic

(B) Beta   (E) Gamma

(C) Alpha

116. How many times faster will hydrogen effuse from the same effusion apparatus than nitrogen at the same temperature?

(A) 14.0   (D) 3.8

(B) .3   (E) 2.7

(C) 5.3

117. What is the normality of a solution that contains 23.2 g of H_2SO_4 and enough water to make 400 ml of solution?

(A) 2.4   (D) 6.0

(B) 0.60   (E) 0.50

(C) 1.2

118. If a certain number of moles of a gas occupied a volume of 200 ml at 25°C, what volume would it occupy if it was heated to 40°C at a constant pressure?

(A) 210 ml   (D) 500 ml

(B) 320 ml   (E) 120 ml

(C) 230 ml

119. Using molecular orbital theory, predict the bond order of He_2^+.

(A) 1/2   (D) 3

(B) 1   (E) 1/4

(C) 0

120. Which one of the following accounts for the disappearance of the purple color of MnO_4^- ion when it reacts with Fe^{2+} in acid solution.

(A) MnO_4^- forms a complex with Fe^{2+}.

(B) The MnO_4^- is reduced to the colorless Mn^{2+} ion.

(C) The MnO_4^- is oxidized.

(D) MnO_4^- is colorless in acid solution.

(E) None of the above.

CLEP NATURAL SCIENCES
TEST 3

ANSWER KEY

Section 1

1. (C)	13. (A)	25. (C)	37. (D)	49. (E)
2. (D)	14. (B)	26. (A)	38. (A)	50. (E)
3. (A)	15. (B)	27. (E)	39. (D)	51. (E)
4. (C)	16. (A)	28. (B)	40. (A)	52. (D)
5. (A)	17. (C)	29. (D)	41. (C)	53. (B)
6. (D)	18. (B)	30. (B)	42. (B)	54. (C)
7. (D)	19. (C)	31. (E)	43. (B)	55. (B)
8. (A)	20. (C)	32. (C)	44. (E)	56. (C)
9. (C)	21. (B)	33. (E)	45. (A)	57. (A)
10. (E)	22. (A)	34. (C)	46. (A)	58. (D)
11. (C)	23. (A)	35. (D)	47. (C)	59. (E)
12. (D)	24. (B)	36. (E)	48. (A)	60. (E)

Section 2

61. (A)	73. (E)	85. (B)	97. (C)	109. (D)
62. (A)	74. (E)	86. (A)	98. (B)	110. (B)
63. (A)	75. (B)	87. (C)	99. (D)	111. (C)
64. (D)	76. (C)	88. (A)	100. (E)	112. (C)
65. (D)	77. (E)	89. (D)	101. (C)	113. (C)
66. (C)	78. (A)	90. (C)	102. (C)	114. (E)
67. (D)	79. (B)	91. (A)	103. (D)	115. (C)
68. (A)	80. (D)	92. (B)	104. (A)	116. (D)
69. (D)	81. (E)	93. (A)	105. (E)	117. (C)
70. (A)	82. (C)	94. (D)	106. (E)	118. (A)
71. (C)	83. (A)	95. (A)	107. (A)	119. (A)
72. (D)	84. (B)	96. (B)	108. (C)	120. (B)

DETAILED EXPLANATIONS
OF ANSWERS
TEST 3

Section 1

1.   **(C)**   For the trail to be different from any other trail of another ant colony, the trail must have a unique composition. The trail is drops of liquid from the abdomen. Each ant colony has its own odor. Thus, (C) is correct. Ants do not use food (A), broken pieces of antennae (B), lenses of compound eyes (D), or tiny pebbles (E) to mark their trail.

2.   **(D)**   The compound eye permits the ant to see moving objects more easily than objects which stand still. Thus, (D) is correct. If an ant saw multiple images (A), its perception would be distorted. The same is true if images were highly magnified (E). (C) is wrong because a compound eye is fixed and cannot rotate. (B) is wrong because the whole compound eye works together in vision; all parts of it are needed for good vision.

3.   **(A)**   Ants are most related to bees. Ants, bees, and wasps are all classified in the order called Hymenoptera. These insects are social and live in communities rather than living alone. The body is similar to that of a bee. (B) spiders are different from ants in body structure and number of legs. Fungus (C) is very different from ants since fungus is a simple plantlike organism. Fleas (D) have a different body structure and do not live in communities. Crabs (E) are ten-legged crustaceans and are very different from ants.

4.   **(C)**   Ants did not change much because ants were always able to fight enemies, find food, find shelter, protect their young, and stand up to any environmental changes. Thus, (C) is correct because no changes were severe enough to cause much change in ants through the years. Answer choices (A), (B), (D), and (E) would all have resulted in extinction of the ant population. Since ants are not extinct, these answer choices are all incorrect.

5.   **(A)** The nose provides a direct route to the lungs via the bronchi. Thus, choice (A) is correct. A cut on the finger (B), the foot (C), or the chest (D) may cause infectious organisms to enter the body but these are not direct routes to the lungs like the nose is. (E), the underside of the fingernail, is not an entrance because skin blocks organisms from entering this way in a healthy organism.

6.   **(D)** Germs on the body surface of a healthy individual are not infecting the body. They are simply living on the body surface without causing disturbance to the body. Thus, choices (A) and (B) are wrong. Only if germs grow and affect the body does infection take place. These germs on the surface can be contagious, so (C) is wrong. Also, these germs can indeed enter the body if the opportunity arises, so choice (E) is incorrect.

7.   **(D)** Of all of the types of microbes mentioned in choices (A) to (E), only the malaria microbe is harmful. Malaria is an infectious disease. Yeast (A), cheese mold (B), yogurt cultures (C), and fermenting microorganisms (E) are used in the preparation of food and drink. They are approved methods because these microbes are not harmful.

8.   **(A)** Acidic stomach juice can destroy many microbes which otherwise could cause food poisoning. Thus, choice (A) is correct. (B) is wrong because stomach juice is acidic, not basic. (C) is wrong because destroying the microbes will eliminate the cause of food poisoning. (D) is wrong because any microbes that do survive have the possibility of causing food poisoning. (E) is wrong because most microbes swallowed are not harmful; food poisoning is a relatively rare occurrence.

9.   **(C)** Answer choice (C) carpels, is the correct choice since these are the modified leaves that produced the ovules. Sepals (A) cannot be the correct choice since the sepals are the modified leaves that surround the flower while it is in the bud. Petals (B) cannot be the correct choice since these are the modified showy leaves used to attract insects to aid in pollination. Stigmas (D) cannot be the correct choice since they are the portions of the pistil that are sticky and receive the pollen. Styles (E) cannot be the correct choice since they are the portions of the pistil that are beneath the stigmas.

10.   **(E)** Answer choice (E) style is the correct choice since it is the portion of the pistil that is beneath the stigmas. Sepals (A) cannot be the

correct choice since the sepals are the modified leaves that surround the flower while it is in the bud. Petals (B) cannot be the correct choice since these are the modified showy leaves used to attract insects to aid in pollination. Anthers (C) cannot be the answer since these are the modified leaves that produced the ovules. Stigmas (D) cannot be the correct choice since they are the portions of the pistil that are sticky and receive the pollen.

11.   **(C)**   Answer choice (C) pollen is the correct choice since the pollen contain the nucleus that combines with the nucleus in the ovule to produce the embryonic plant. Stigmas (A) cannot be the correct choice since stigmas receive the pollen. Styles (B) cannot be the correct choice since styles are found beneath stigmas. Radicals (D) cannot be the correct choice since these are growing regions that produce the root system. Anthers (E) cannot be the correct choice since an anther is a container that produces the pollen.

12.   **(D)**   The reason why bees are attracted to flowers is because of the bright and showy petals. If these are removed, the bees will not notice the flowers. Thus, (D) is correct. In (A), separating the sepals from the bud will still put the petals in a prominent position to be viewed by the bees. (B) is wrong because the pollen does not affect the bees' attraction for the flowers. (C) is incorrect because crushing the stigma will affect pollination but not bee attraction. (E), separating the anther from the filament, will break structures within the flower but will not affect the ability of the petals to attract bees.

13.   **(A)**   Since the sepal is the protective covering over the petals, the sepal must have been invaded if the petals are to be reached. Stamens (B), the pistil (C), the style (D), and the ovary (E) are all reproductive portions of the flower and are not involved in protecting the petals from damage.

14.   **(B)**   The main way in which the pollen travels to the stigma is by way of pollinators that transfer the pollen to the stigma through their movements. Thus, choice (B) is correct. (A) is false because although wind may help in pollination, gale winds (very strong winds) are not necessary. (C) is incorrect because picking flowers simply does not stimulate pollination. (D) is an incorrect statement because the pollen and stigma do not possess opposite charges. (E) is wrong because the style is the structure through which an already germinated pollen structure is passed to the ovary.

15. **(B)** It is true that female animals, like female humans, possess both ovaries and eggs. Flowers also possess ovaries and eggs. (A) is wrong because animals are not composed of modified leaves. (C) is wrong because animals do not have stigmas. (D) is wrong because animals in general possess either male or female organs, but not both. (E) is wrong because only animals have sperm; flowers do not.

16. **(A)** Answer choice (A) basic research is the correct choice since the biologist wanted to gain the knowledge simply for the sake of curiosity or knowledge itself. Applied research (B) cannot be the correct choice since it involves using knowledge that has been gained from basic research or pure research and used to solve a problem. Government research (C) cannot be the correct choice since it may be either basic research or applied research, and in the paragraph there is no mention of who is funding the research. Library research (D) cannot be the correct choice even though in scientific research there is work done in the library; the paragraph deals with the major theme of a biologist doing "basic research." Methods to produce great amounts of insects (E) cannot be the correct choice since nothing is mentioned in the paragraph concerning a reason for producing large numbers of insects.

17. **(C)** Answer choice (C), are found in many organisms, is the correct choice since there are organisms other than insects that produce chemical sexual attractants. Are used only in insects (A) cannot be the correct choice since there are other animals that produce chemical sexual attractants. Are used by all animals (B) cannot be the correct choice since there are some animals, especially the "lower," such as sponges and coelenterates, that have not been found to produce sexual attractants. Can be seen (D) cannot be the correct choice since the pheromones are invisible. Can be felt (E) cannot be the correct choice since no mention of feeling is mentioned in the paragraph, and it would be like standing next to someone wearing a perfume and "feeling it."

18. **(B)** Answer choice (B) is the correct choice since they would attempt to crawl to the cork thinking that it is a female. (A) cannot be the correct choice since the pheromone would definitely affect the insect. (C) cannot be the correct choice since the biologist in the question was not using a moth pheromone and pheromones are specific. (D) cannot be the correct choice since the cockroach would not notice what it is crawling through. (E) cannot be the correct choice since it is mentioned that the pheromone is so powerful that the insect does not pay attention to its own safety.

19. **(C)** Answer choice (C) applied science is the correct choice since the biologist is solving a problem by applying the information gained from the basic research or pure science. Pure science (A) cannot be the correct choice since the biologist is not experimenting out of curiosity or for only the sake of knowledge. Basic research (B) cannot be the correct choice since it is the same thing as "pure science." Government research (D) cannot be the correct choice since "government" would imply who is sponsoring the research, and not whether it is pure science/basic research or applied science/research. The scientific method (E) cannot be the correct choice since there is no mention of the methodology of a controlled experiment.

20. **(C)** Answer choice (C) applied science would be the correct choice since the scientists are using information gained from basic research/pure science to solve a problem. Entomology (A) cannot be the correct choice since it is the study of insects. Botany (B) cannot be the correct choice since it is the study of plants. Pure science (D) cannot be the correct choice since the scientists are not trying to gain knowledge simply for the sake of knowledge itself. Scientific method (E) cannot be the correct choice since it does not address the question of why the information is being sought or how the information is being used.

21. **(B)** Answer choice (B) is the correct choice since it is consistent with the second of Darwin's observations and the first of his conclusions. (A) cannot be the correct choice since the question has nothing to do with the variation. (C) cannot be the correct choice since even though the environment is constantly changing, the change is not fast enough to affect the single release of clam's sex cells. (D) cannot be the correct choice since this is not consistent with any of Darwin's observations nor with any of his conclusions. (E) cannot be the correct choice since it is not consistent with any of Darwin's observations or conclusions.

22. **(A)** Answer choice (A) is the correct choice since it is consistent with Darwin's observations and conclusions. (B) cannot be the correct choice since the environment does not change that quickly. (C) cannot be the correct choice since genetic variation has nothing to do with the leveling of the population of ferns. (D) cannot be the correct choice since the survival characteristics, which can accumulate, do not do so quickly enough for this to occur in a single year. (E) cannot be the correct choice since this is not a source which would prevent all of the spores from maturing.

23.   **(A)**   Answer choice (A), cattle rancher, is the correct choice since cattle ranchers are always trying to have the best-bred cattle. Oilman (B) cannot be the correct choice since this person would be more interested in the finding and refining of oil. Engineer (C) cannot be the correct choice since engineers function in constructing things. Refinery chemist (D) cannot be the correct choice since a refinery chemist's main function is to develop new products or to maintain the quality control of the products produced at the refinery. Hairstylist (E) cannot be the correct choice since a hairstylist is mainly interested in hair fashions.

24.   **(B)**   Answer choice (B) is the correct choice. Since *Ursus* is the genus name of bears, *Aleropoda* would indicate that the panda is not a bear. (A) cannot be the correct choice since where a panda lives does not indicate that it is a bear. (C) cannot be the correct choice since species names are not used to designate the grouping. (D) cannot be the correct choice since being on the endangered list and the color of fur does not make the panda a bear. (E) cannot be the correct choice since the only way to tell what pandas are is to compare the genus name of the bear *Ursus* and the genus name of the panda, *Aleropoda,* and, if they are the same, then the panda is a bear. Simply calling it a "panda" is using its common name which tells one nothing about its classification.

25.   **(C)**   Answer choice (C) is the correct choice since the genus names of the two animals are different. (A) cannot be the correct choice since the species name does not show genetic relationships. (B) cannot be the correct choice since the species name is not used to show a genetic relationship. (D) cannot be the correct choice since the two names are different. (E) cannot be the correct choice since not enough information is given.

26.   **(A)**   Answer choice (A) is the correct choice since every organism listed is a member of the kingdom Animalia. (B) cannot be the correct choice since fungus is in the kingdom Fungi. (C) cannot be the correct choice since mushrooms are in the kingdom Fungi. (D) cannot be the correct choice since these are members of several kingdoms, none of which are animals. (E) cannot be the correct choice since trees are members of the kingdom Plantae.

27.   **(E)**   Answer choice (E), genus name, is the correct choice since all scientific names begin with the genus name. Kingdom name (A) cannot be the correct choice since a kingdom name is never used in an organism's scientific name. Phylum name (B) cannot be the correct choice since a

phylum name is never used in an organism's scientific name. Class name (C) cannot be the correct choice since a class name is never used in an organism's scientific name. Order name (D) cannot be the correct choice since an order name is never used in an organism's scientific name.

28.   **(B)**   Answer choice (B) is the correct choice. Since the DNA contains the information for the mRNA, the mRNA made after the event will be different because the DNA will be changed. Since DNA makes mRNA, the mRNA will be changed whenever the DNA is changed. (A) cannot be the correct choice since the removal of a "code word" is at least considered a point mutation, and the resulting mRNA will be changed. (C) cannot be the correct choice since many of the DNA "code words" would have to be destroyed before this would happen. (D) cannot be the correct choice since "code words" are always "read" by threes (triplets). (E) cannot be the correct choice since although DNA can repair itself, the mechanism for repair is often flawed.

29.   **(D)**   Answer choice (D), the nucleus, is the correct choice since the nucleus contains the chromosomes, which are composed of DNA nucleotides and some protein. The lysosomes (A) cannot be the correct choice since lysosomes contain digestive enzymes. The endoplasmic reticulum (B) cannot be the correct choice since it is a series of membranes found in the cytoplasm and it serves as a site of protein synthesis. "They are found floating in the cytoplasmic matrix" (C) cannot be the correct choice since DNA nucleotides are not found outside of the nucleus. Golgi bodies (E) cannot be the correct choice since ribosomes are found in the cytoplasm and are in the endoplasmic reticulum.

30.   **(B)**   Answer choice (B), chromosomes, is the correct choice since DNA and its associated proteins form these rodlike or threadlike structures. RNA (A) cannot be the correct choice since RNA does not interweave itself with proteins to form chromosomes. Nucleotides (C) cannot be the correct choice since DNA strands are composed of nucleotides; DNA and protein cannot make nucleotides. Genes (D) cannot be the correct choice since genes are composed of DNA and make up chromosomes. Golgi bodies (E) cannot be the correct choice since ribosomes are composed of RNA.

31.   **(E)**   Answer choice (E) is the correct choice since all proteins are made of amino acids, which are bonded together sequentially as dictated by the mRNA which was made by the DNA. (A) cannot be the correct

choice since any change in the DNA molecule would result in the change of the mRNA which would result in a changed protein. (B) cannot be the correct choice since only the order of the amino acids would be changed. (C) cannot be the correct choice since only the order of the amino acids would be changed. (D) cannot be the correct choice since DNA does not enter into the actual construction of the protein molecule.

32. **(C)** Skin covering the eyeballs is generally the thinnest skin on the body. The soles of the feet (A), the palms of the hand (B), and the heel (E) are often involved in laborious activities, and the skin is thick in these areas. The back (D) also has thick skin. Thus, (C) is the correct choice.

33. **(E)** The epidermis is made of two layers: the layer of Malpighi and the stratum corneum. The stratum corneum is the outer layer, and the layer of Malpighi is directly under it. Under these two layers of the epidermis is the dermis. Choice choices (A) through (D) do not have these layers arranged in the correct order. (A) and (B) are wrong because the two layers mentioned are both part of the epidermis. (C) is wrong because this is the order from the inside out. (D) is wrong because the dermis is not on the outside.

34. **(C)** The body regulates water and heat through perspiration. Transpiration describes a process not involving humans. Thus, (B) is not correct. Respiration (A) is breathing in humans and will cause some water loss. However, the question asks for how the body regulates substances through the skin. (D) sensation is the ability to process or perceive. The skin does have nerve endings that can sense, but this does not involve temperature or water regulation. Coagulation (E) is a term referring to a change from a liquid to a thickened mass. This term does not relate to the question.

35. **(D)** The nerve endings, blood vessels, and sweat glands are found in the dermis. They are not in the layer of Malpighi, since this layer's main function is to grow to replace the stratum corneum that quickly wears away. Thus, (A) is wrong. It would not be beneficial to have these important structures in a layer that wears away; thus, they are not found in the stratum corneum. (B) must be wrong. Since the layer of Malpighi and the stratum corneum are the two layers of the epidermis, (C) must be wrong. Since it is known that nerve endings and sweat glands are in skin, they could not be contained in the muscle tissue, or (E). (D) must be correct.

36. **(E)** It is true that chameleons are mostly found in Africa, but this does not prohibit the existence of some chameleons on other continents. In fact, some species do live in India. Thus, (E) is correct, and it follows that (A) is incorrect. (B) is incorrect because the majority of the chameleons are found in Africa, and this must be the greater proportion. (C) is wrong because a chameleon may be found on another continent. (D) is wrong because chameleons tend to be located in Africa; they are not evenly spread throughout the world.

37. **(D)** A chameleon changes color mostly due to temperature, sunlight, and emotion. Thus, a black chameleon is probably black because it is cold. Thus, (D) is correct. It is a false belief that chameleons change color to match their environment. Thus, (B) is wrong. (A) is wrong because hiding is a possibility for a color change but not a main reason why a color change occurs. (C) is wrong because color changes are normal occurrences for chameleons and do not signify that the animal is dying. (E) is incorrect because extending the tongue is not necessarily preceded by a color change.

38. **(A)** The sticky substance on the tongue aids in catching prey. Thus, (A) is correct. (B) is incorrect because the fork on the end of a tongue is too soft to spear prey. (C) is wrong because the tongue flicks the prey into the chameleon's mouth; the tongue does not squeeze the prey. In this case, the length of the tongue is helpful for catching prey at a distance. (D) is wrong because the chameleon does not have poisonous glands. (E) is wrong because the color change of a chameleon will not distract the prey.

39. **(D)** Answer choice (D), bilateral symmetry, is the correct choice Since the bird has a right and a left side. Asymmetry (A) cannot be the correct choice since asymmetry refers to something that has no definite shape. Radial symmetry (B) cannot be the correct choice since radial symmetry refers to organisms that have their parts radiating outward as in a cylindrical shape or a flattened cylindrical shape. Spherical symmetry (C) cannot be the correct choice since the bird is not shaped like a sphere. Longitudinal symmetry (E) cannot be the correct choice since there is no such terminology.

40. **(A)** Answer choice (A), asymmetry, is the correct choice since the amoeba is constantly changing shape. Radial symmetry (B) cannot be the correct choice since radial symmetry refers to organisms that have their parts radiating outward as in a cylindrical shape or a flattened cylindrical shape. Spherical symmetry (D) cannot be the correct choice since the

amoeba is not shaped like a sphere. Bilateral symmetry (C) cannot be the correct choice since the figure has no right or left side. Triradial symmetry (E) cannot be the correct choice since there is no such terminology.

41.   **(C)**   Answer choice (C), spherical symmetry, is the correct choice since the figure is ball-shaped. Asymmetry (A) cannot be the correct choice since asymmetry refers to something that has no definite shape. Radial symmetry (B) cannot be the correct choice since radial symmetry refers to organisms that have their parts radiating outward as in a cylindrical shape or flattened cylindrical shape. Bilateral symmetry (D) cannot be the correct choice since the figure has no right or left side. Longitudinal symmetry (E) cannot be the correct choice since there is no such terminology.

42.   **(B)**   Answer choice (B), radial symmetry, is the correct choice since the organism resembles a flattened cylinder with body parts radiating outward. Asymmetry (A) cannot be the correct choice since asymmetry refers to something that has no definite shape. Spherical symmetry (D) cannot be the correct choice since the organism is not shaped like a sphere. Bilateral symmetry (C) cannot be the correct choice since the figure has no right or left side. Longitudinal symmetry (E) cannot be the correct choice since there is no such terminology.

43.   **(B)**   Answer choice (B), bilaterally symmetrical, is the correct choice since bilateral organisms have a right and left side. Asymmetrical (A) cannot be the correct choice since asymmetrical organisms have no definite shape. Spherically symmetrical (C) cannot be the correct choice since balls have no right or left side. Cylindrically symmetrical (D) cannot be the correct choice since no definition was given for this term. Radially symmetrical (E) cannot be the correct choice since body parts do not necessarily radiate outward in an organism with a right and left side.

44.   **(E)**   Answer choice (E), radially symmetrical, is the correct choice since the "rays" of the starfish radiate outward from a central disk. Asymmetry (A) cannot be the correct choice since asymmetrical organisms have no definite shape. Bilaterally symmetrical (B) is not the correct choice since bilateral organisms have a right and a left side. Spherically symmetrical (C) cannot be the correct choice since a starfish is not shaped like a ball. Cylindrically symmetrical (D) cannot be the correct choice since no definition was given for this term.

45.   **(A)**   Answer choice (A) is the correct choice since the gray line representing the whitetail deer population drops over a period of time, and

the mule deer (black line) stays the same or shows an increase in population. (B) cannot be the correct choice since one can determine that there are fewer whitetail deer over a period of time. (C) cannot be the correct choice since it is stated in the paragraph that hunting was not allowed. (D) cannot be the correct choice since no drought was mentioned in the data. (E) cannot be the correct choice since a proper conclusion can only be based on the data, and if that data is incorrect, then the conclusion must also be incorrect.

46. **(A)** Answer choice (A) is the correct choice since the mule deer survived and the whitetail deer did not survive. (B) cannot be the correct choice since the fittest, in this case, were the mule deer. (C) cannot be the correct choice since there is no data indicating that any of the whitetail deer survived. (D) cannot be the correct choice since both animals had the same food and opportunities. (E) cannot be the correct choice since a conclusion is based on data and if the data is wrong, then the conclusion must also be wrong, and there is no evidence of that.

47. **(C)** Answer choice (C) is correct since there is no data concerning any special adaptations to the environment. (A) cannot be the correct choice since there is no data concerning any special adaptations to the environment. (B) cannot be the correct choice since environmental adaptations are not addressed by the graph. (D) cannot be the correct choice since there are no data about adaptability. (E) cannot be the correct choice since no information is given about the terrain.

48. **(A)** Answer choice (A), is the correct choice since the graph shows an early increase in both populations of deer. (B) cannot be the correct choice since the graph shows an early increase in both populations of deer. (C) cannot be the correct choice since the conclusion is supported by the early increase in both populations of deer. (D) cannot be the correct choice since adaptability is not a part of the graph. (E) cannot be the correct choice since no data is given concerning the terrain.

49. **(E)** Answer choice (E) internal is the correct choice since sharks do not lay their eggs to be externally fertilized by the male shark. Denticle (A) cannot be the correct choice since denticles are the little toothlike appendages found on the skin of a shark. Viviparous (B) cannot be the correct choice since this term refers to how the embryos of some kinds of shark get their nourishment. Ovoviparous (C) cannot be the correct choice since this term refers to how the embryos of some kinds of shark get their

nourishment. External (D) cannot be the correct choice since sharks do not lay eggs to be externally fertilized by the male shark.

50.   **(E)**   Answer choice (E) class Chondrichthyes is the correct choice since sharks, rays, skates, and dogfishes are members of this class. Phylum Reptilia (A) cannot be the correct choice since there is no phylum Reptilia, and it is not mentioned in the paragraph. Class Aves (B) cannot be the correct choice since this is a class/group of birds, and it is not mentioned in the paragraph. Class Vertebrata (C) cannot be the correct choice since there is no class Vertebrata, even though the shark is a vertebrate animal. Class Osteichthyes (D) cannot be the correct choice since this is the class of fish that have skeletons composed of bone.

51.   **(E)**   The cell membrane, which surrounds the outside of a cell, is the first barrier that a foreign molecule will meet. Nucleoplasm (A) is the substance inside the nucleus and is far from the outside of a cell. Cytoplasm (B) is immediately inside the cell membrane, so the foreign molecule must pass the cell membrane first before reaching the cytoplasm. Both the nuclear membrane (C) and the chromosomes (D) are inside the cell and will not be the first structure reached by an approaching foreign molecule.

52.   **(D)**   There is a constant number of chromosomes for any somatic cell within an organism. Thus, choice (D) is correct. (A) is incorrect because the chromosomes do not assemble randomly. (B) is incorrect because it is the opposite of the correct answer. (C) is incorrect because the strength of the microscope will not change or affect the number of chromosomes. Also, during cell division, all of the chromosomes should be easily visible. (E) is incorrect because there is no evidence for nucleoli interfering with chromosome coiling.

53.   **(B)**   It is true that ribosomes function in protein synthesis, which occurs in the cytoplasm. Thus, the ribosomes must move from the site of their synthesis in the nucleus to the cytoplasm. Choice (B) is correct. (A) is incorrect because the ribosomes are located in the cytoplasm. (C) is incorrect because mitochondria, not ribosomes, produce the energy for a cell. (D) is wrong since there is no evidence that chromosome coiling interferes with ribosome formation. (E) is incorrect because one cannot assume that the product (the ribosome) of a dark staining organelle (the nucleolus) will also stain dark.

54. **(C)** A selective membrane is considered semipermeable (C) because some things pass through while others do not. Thus, (A) and (B) are wrong. The terms opaque (D) and translucent (E) refer to the ability of light to pass through. These terms are unrelated to selective membranes.

55. **(B)** Answer choice (B) phloem is the correct choice since phloem conducts food to the storage areas of the plant. Xylem (A) cannot be the correct choice since xylem conducts water from the roots throughout the plant. Precambrium (C) cannot be the correct choice since this is a geologic age. Stomata (D) cannot be the correct choice since stomata are the openings on the underside of leaves. Cuticle (E) cannot be the correct choice since the cuticle is a thin, waxy covering that waterproofs the leaf.

56. **(C)** Answer choice (C) vertebrates is the correct choice since fish have a backbone (vertebrate). Filter feeders (A) cannot be the correct choice since these are animals like clams and oysters which have no backbones. Invertebrates (B) cannot be the correct choice since invertebrates do not have backbones. Zooplankton (D) are very small invertebrate animals that are carried by the currents and have no backbones. Phytoplankton (E) cannot be the correct choice since they are one- to few-celled plants and do not have backbones.

57. **(A)** Answer choice (A) invertebrates is the correct choice since zooplankton are very small animals without backbones. Vertebrates (B) cannot be the correct choice since vertebrates have backbones and zooplankton are not vertebrates. Phytoplankton (C) cannot be the correct choice since they are plantlike organisms. Toxic mucus (D) cannot be the correct choice since it is not mentioned in relation to being a type of organisms, but it is a protective device. Toxic mobile predators (E) cannot be the correct choice since zooplankton are carried by the currents, they are not extremely mobile, and they are not toxic.

58. **(D)** Answer choice (D) filter feeders is the correct choice since organisms like the clam, which filter their food by straining it from the water by passing it over their gills, would be called filter feeders. Fish (A) cannot be the correct choice since fish do not use any means of filtering the water for food. Vertebrates (B) cannot be the correct choice since no mention is made of vertebrates filtering the water. Phytoplankton (C) cannot be the correct choice since they are plantlike organisms and are not mentioned in the paragraph. Toxic mobile predators (E) cannot be the correct choice since no mention of these are made in the paragraph.

59. **(E)** Answer choice (E), be firmly attached, is the correct choice since being sessile is to be anchored or attached to something. Move around (A) cannot be the correct choice since sessile means to be attached or anchored to something. Swim freely (B) cannot be the correct choice since sessile means to be attached or anchored to something. Crawl along the sea floor (C) cannot be the correct choice since sessile means to be attached or anchored to something. Float on the surface (D), is also wrong because something which floats is not sessile.

60. **(E)** Answer choice (E) is the correct choice since zooplankton are very small and they are easily buoyed up by the water. Voracious predators (A) cannot be the correct choice since nothing of this nature is mentioned in the paragraph. Powerful swimmers (B) cannot be the correct choice since zooplankton are invertebrates and it is mentioned that invertebrates are not powerful swimmers. Fish (C) cannot be the correct choice since fish are not invertebrates. Voluntarily able to move (D) cannot be the correct choice since this implies being able to be a powerful swimmer, which zooplankton are not.

Section 2

61. **(A)** Matter exhibits the three states of solids, liquids, and gases. (A) says that matter exhibits the states of atoms, molecules, and cells; (A) is an incorrect statement and therefore the correct answer since the question asks for the false answer. The rest of the choices (B), (C), (D), and (E) are not appropriate since they are true statements and the question calls for the false statement.

62. **(A)** Since the number of electrons is the same as the number of protons in an atom and since the atomic number equals the number of electrons and also equals the number of protons, (A) is the correct choice. (A) states that the atomic number of sulphur is 16 and the number of protons and the atomic number is also 16; this is correct. Choices (B), (C), and (D) contain multiples of 8 but do not include the correct choices and should not be selected. Choice (E) which states that "an indefinite number, undetermined from information given" is incorrect and should not be chosen; the choice can be determined since the number of electrons is given.

63.   **(A)**   Since all the statements are true, (A) is the best – and only choice. The other items (B), (C), (D), and (E) omit important true statements.

64.   **(D)**   All the statements about liquids, expansion, and contraction are true – except for (D). Gases actually expand when heated and contract when cooled – the opposite of what the statement reads. Choice (D) should be selected since the incorrect answer is sought.

65.   **(D)**   An electromagnet is not a permanent magnet; it ceases to be a magnet when the electricity ceases to flow through the wire. The strength of an electromagnet can be increased when the number of coils in the wire are increased. Since (D) allows the choice of (B) which states that an electromagnet is permanent and (C) which states that the strength of a magnet is limited, (D) should be chosen; (D) includes both incorrect answers. (A) is a true statement and should not be chosen as the correct answer. (E) includes (A) and should not be selected.

66.   **(C)**   Since the moon is always lit by the sun, the reason the moon is not entirely seen by Earth is because of Earth's position while revolving around the sun. (C), therefore, is the correct answer. (A) describing a shadow thrown on the moon by Earth, is not the correct answer since it describes an eclipse. The sun does not cast a shadow on the moon; it lights the moon. (B) which describes the casting of a shadow by the Sun instead of the casting of light by the sun, is incorrect. (D), which states that the rays of the moon do not always reach Earth and gives that as the reason for phases of the moon is incorrect; the moon has no light of its own. Since the moon only shows Earth one of its sides, (E) is not an appropriate choice.

67.   **(D)**   Since comets glow from reflected light, not their own light, (D) is a false answer and the choice sought. When comets are close to the sun, they shine by fluorescence when the gases are set aglow by ultraviolet radiation from the sun. The rest of the choices – (A), (B), (C), and (E) – are true choices but are not to be selected since the question asks for the choice which is NOT true. (D) is the only appropriate choice.

68.   **(A)**   The symbol for hydrogen is H. The other items are not symbols for hydrogen. No element on the periodic table of the elements is represented by Hy (B). He (C) is the symbol for helium, not hydrogen. Hi is not a symbol on the periodic table; therefore, (D) should not be chosen.

Since Hn is not a symbol on the periodic table, (E) should not be selected as a symbol for hydrogen.

69. **(D)** Three statements about chemical energy in this question are true: I, III, and IV. Only choice (D) allows the reader to choose these three items. II [which is included in (A), (B), and (E)] is a false statement since chemical energy is really a form of potential – not kinetic – energy. V is a false statement; the defmition given is really the definition of nuclear fission – a form of energy. V is included in (E). Since both II and V are included in (E), (E) should not be chosen. It is apparent then that (A), (B), (C), and (E) are erroneous statements and should not be selected.

70. **(A)** Since heat energy is produced by moving molecules (I), and since the faster the movement the more heat energy the substance has (II) and the hotter the substance becomes (III), choice (A) is correct. Choice (B) omits (III) which is true and must be included; (B) should not be selected. Choice (C) omits (I) which is true and must be listed; (C) should not be chosen. A substance is not cooler as a result of the movement of its molecules. The movement results in a hotter substance. (IV) is false and should not be selected. Since (D) contains (IV) it is an inappropriate choice. (E) cannot be chosen because it not only omits (I), (II), and (III) but also includes (V), which is an erroneous statement. Slow moving molecules do not produce heat in a substance (V) and, therefore, (E) is false.

71. **(C)** Sound energy is a type of wave energy, so (C) is correct. Mechanical energy (A) is the most common form of energy about us. All moving bodies produce mechanical energy. The energy produced from machines is also mechanical energy. It is apparent that sound energy does not fit in this category. (A) is not the correct choice. Electrical energy (B) is the energy produced by the moving of electrons through a substance; electrical energy runs motors, lights homes, and makes telephones work. Sound energy is not a type of electrical energy. Choice (B) is incorrect. Nuclear energy (D) comes from the nucleus of an atom when it splits into two parts or when nuclei of atoms are fused together. Clearly sound waves do not fit into this classification. (D) is incorrect. Heat energy (E) is a form of radiant energy; sound energy does not fit under the category of heat energy. Sound energy would not fit under the category of radiant energy since radiant energy (another form of wave energy) includes light rays, infrared rays, radio waves, cosmic rays, radiant heat, X-rays, and ultraviolet rays. (E) should not be selected. (C) is the correct choice.

72.   **(D)**   is the correct answer because it allows you to choose radiant energy, of which light and radio waves are examples. Radiant energy is a form of wave energy. Mechanical energy (A) is the energy form seen most. All moving bodies produce mechanical energy; energy produced by machines of all kinds is mechanical energy. Radio waves do not fit this category. Heat energy (B) is produced by the movement of molecules; the faster their rate of movement, the hotter the substance becomes. Since radio waves do not fit under the heat energy category, (B) is not appropriate. Electrical energy is the energy produced when electrons move through a substance; radio waves do not fit this category so (C) should not be chosen. Nuclear energy is a result of the splitting of the nucleus of the atom or from the fusion of the nuclei of atoms; (E) is not an appropriate choice since radio waves are not the result of this fusion or fission.

73.   **(E)**   The earth behaves as a huge magnet; it has a north pole and a south pole. Choice (E), therefore, is false. It is the correct answer because it is a false statement. All the other choices – (A), (B), (C), and (D) – are true and cannot be chosen.

74.   **(E)**   The element of molecular weight 197 is gold (Au-atomic number 79). Since the molecular weight is equal to the number of protons and neutrons in the nucleus and the atomic number is equal to the number of protons in the nucleus, the number of neutrons in the nucleus is 197–79 or 118.

75.   **(B)**   Plutonium-238 has a mass of 238 and an atomic number of 94 ($_{94}Pu^{238}$). The atomic mass tells us the number of protons and neutrons in the nucleus while the atomic number tells us the number of protons. An alpha particle $_2\alpha^4$ is a helium nucleus composed of two neutrons and two protons (atomic mass of 4). Hence, upon emitting an alpha particle, the atomic number decreases by two and the atomic mass decreases by four. This gives us $_{92}X^{234}$. Examining the periodic table we find that element 92 is uranium. Thus our new atom is $_{92}U^{234}$. $_{92}Pu^{234}$ and $_{92}Cm^{234}$ are impossible since the atomic number of plutonium is 94 and that of curium is 96. $_{92}Pu^{242}$ and $_{96}Cm^{242}$ are impossible since these nuclei could only be produced by fusion of $_{96}Pu^{242}$ with an alpha particle. In addition, $_{96}Pu^{242}$ is incorrectly named.

$$\therefore \text{ The reaction (decay) is } _{94}Pu^{238} \rightarrow {}_{92}U^{234} + {}_2\alpha^4$$

76. **(C)** Referring to the periodic table, we see that element 32 is germanium. Germanium is a metalloid as are boron, silicon, arsenic, antimony, tellurium, polonium, and astatine. Chemically, metalloids exhibit both positive and negative oxidation states and combine with metals and nonmetals. They are characterized by approximately half-filled outer electron shells and electronegativity values between those of the metals and the nonmetals.

77. **(E)** A beta particle is a fast electron of mass 9.11×10^{-28} g, while a proton and a neutron both have a mass of 1.67×10^{-24} g. A hydrogen nucleus is a proton, and an alpha particle is a helium nucleus (two protons and two neutrons). Thus, the electron (beta particle) has the smallest mass of the choices given.

78. **(A)** Atomic radius decreases as one goes from left to right across a period, so the atomic radius of carbon is greater than that of oxygen. This eliminates choices (B) and (D). Now we must determine whether the CO_2 molecule is linear or bent. Linearity means the O–C–O bond angle is 180°. Recall that the nuclei of a molecule orient themselves so as to experience the smallest repulsions of the positive nuclei. Thus, a triatomic molecule is expected to be linear as is CO_2. However, this is not always true. The lone electron pairs on oxygen in a water molecule bend the molecule so that the hydrogen nuclei and the two electron pairs occupy the corners of a tetrahedron. Thus, the water molecule is bent. The same effect occurs in ammonia, NH_3, where a lone pair of electrons on nitrogen distorts the expected trigonal planar geometry. The shape of a CO_2 molecule is

$$:\ddot{O} = C = \ddot{O}:$$
$$\underset{180°}{\underbrace{\qquad\qquad}}$$

79. **(B)** The ionization energy is defined as the energy required to remove the most loosely bound electron from an element in the gaseous state. The energy released by an element in forming an ionic solid with another element is the lattice energy of that ionic compound. The electronegativity of an element gives the relative strength with which the atoms of that element attract valence electrons in a chemical bond.

80. **(D)** The molecular weight of a compound is the sum of its constituents atomic weights. Elements or groups followed by a subscript have their atomic weight multiplied by that subscript. Thus, the molecular weight of perchloric acid ($HClO_4$) is

atomic weight of H + atomic weight of Cl + 4 × atomic weight of O

or $1 + 35.5 + 4 \times 16 = 100.5$

81.   **(E)**   The metals are found on the left side of the periodic table, with metallic character increasing as one goes down a group. All the choices given are in Group IA, so the one farthest down in the group has the greatest metallic character. This is francium (Fr).

82.   **(C)**   The type of bonding in an element or a compound may be determined by the difference in electronegativities of the atoms engaged in the bond. The bonding is covalent if the electronegativity difference is less than 0.5, polar covalent if from 0.5 to 1.7, and ionic if greater than 1.7. Coordinate covalent bonding is characterized by one atom supplying two electrons to the bond while the other supplies none. Hydrogen bonding occurs between protons of one molecule and highly electronegative (especially oxygen) atoms of another molecule. The electronegativities of carbon and chlorine are 2.5 and 3.0, respectively. The electronegativity difference is 0.5 making the bonding polar covalent.

83.   **(A)**   Diamond, composed solely of carbon, cannot have ionic bonds or hydrogen bonds. Van der Waals attraction between the nucleus of one atom and the electrons of an adjacent atom are relatively weak compared to the covalent bonding network (sp^3 hybrid) between the carbon atoms in diamond. On the other hand, graphite (another allotropic form of carbon) is sp^2 hybrid and not strongly bonded as compared to diamond.

84.   **(B)**   First we determine the number of moles present in a solution taking the molecular weight of ethylene glycol to be 62 g. Thus,

$$6.20 \text{ g} \times \frac{1 \text{ mole}}{62 \text{ g}} = 0.1 \text{ mole of ethylene glycol}$$

We must also know the molality – the ratio of moles of solute to kilograms of solvent. The number of kilograms of solvent is

$$0.2 \, 1 \times \frac{1 \text{ kg}}{1 \, 1} = 0.2 \text{ kg}$$

since the density of water is 1g/ml. The molality of the solution is

$$\frac{0.1 \text{ mole}}{0.2 \text{ kg}} = 0.5 \text{ molal}$$

For H_2O, the molal freezing point depression constant is 1.86°C/molal. Thus, the freezing point depression is

$$0.5 \text{ molal} \times \frac{1.86°C}{\text{molal}} = 0.93°C$$

Thus, the melting point would be

$$0°C - 0.93°C = -0.93°C$$

85.   **(B)**   The mass of an electron is 1/1,837 that of a proton or that of a neutron.

86.   **(A)**   The attractive force between the protons of one atom and the electrons of another is inversely proportional to the distance between the atoms, i.e., ($F\alpha1/d$) where F = force and d = distance between two atoms. This shows that the attraction is strongest at small distances (as in solids) and weakest at large distances (as in gases).

87.   **(C)**   The atomic weights of the elements are usually not whole numbers since they are calculated as a weighted average of all naturally occurring isotopes (isotopes of the same element have the same number of protons and electrons, but different number of neutrons).

88.   **(A)**   In this question, the rules for the conservation of charge and mass in nuclear reactions must be utilized. On the left-hand side of the equation, there are represented a total of 15 protons (2 + 13), and there are also 15 represented on the right side. On the left side, a total mass number of 31 (neutrons and protons) is represented, while on the right only 30 are represented. Since protons are conserved from right to left, and the mass number of P is 30, X must be a neutron.

89.   **(D)**   Time equals distance divided by average velocity if the acceleration is uniform. The average velocity is

(100 m/s + 500 m/s) ÷ 2 or 300 m/s.

1,200 m ÷ 300 m/s = 4 s and the correct choice is (D).

90. **(C)** The average speed for each second during which the speed is either constant or changes uniformly may be calculated.

0 – 1 s, V_{av} = 2.5m/s;

1 – 2 s, V_{av} = 7.5 m/s;

2 – 3 s, V_{av} = 10 m/s;

3 – 4 s, V_{av} = 10 m/s;

4 – 5 s, V_{av} = 5m/s.

These average speeds may in turn be averaged:

(2.5 + 7.5 + 10 + 10 + 5) ÷ 5 = 35 ÷ 5 = 7 m/s.

Thus, the average speed is 7 m/s and the correct choice is (C).

91. **(A)** The slope of the line is constant, indicating that the distance covered per time is constant. An object traveling in a straight line must be traveling at a constant velocity to cover the same distance in the same time. Acceleration is a measure of the change in velocity per time. No change in velocity results in zero acceleration.

92. **(B)** Because marble is a good conductor of heat, it has a high conductivity and heat will be able to flow easily from your finger into the rock making it feel cool.

93. **(A)** A mass at rest being acted on by a constant force will accelerate constantly, or its change in velocity per unit time will be a constant (with a beginning velocity of zero). Thus, a plot of velocity versus time for this mass would be a straight diagonal line passing through the origin.

94. **(D)** If the force pulling on a mass equals the force of friction between the mass and the surface it is sitting on, then the net force on the mass is zero. According to Newton's First Law, if the net force is zero, an

object will move at a constant velocity, or remains motionless. Graph IV describes a mass moving with a constant velocity.

95. **(A)** A specific heat value, if read like a sentence, explains the number of calories required to raise one gram of a substance one degree centigrade. Therefore, the substance in the table with the lowest specific heat will experience the greatest temperature increase, when equal numbers of calories are added to an equal mass of each substance.

96. **(B)** The time it takes for the ball to travel 50 meters horizontally is exactly equal to the time it takes for the ball to travel 5 meters to the ground. For an object to travel 50 meters in one second, it must be traveling at a velocity of 50 meters per second.

97. **(C)** The dust, water particles, etc., in the Earth's atmosphere scatter the shorter wavelengths, blue and green light waves. When the sun is on the horizon, the light from the sun must travel a longer distance through the Earth's atmosphere, decreasing the amount of blue and green wavelengths reaching the Earth's surface.

98. **(B)** Einstein's energy equation,

$$E = mc^2,$$

is based on the premise that the speed of light for all observers is constant, and that energy is directly proportional to mass. As energy increases, so does the mass. (A), (C), and (E) are incorrect because the speed of light is considered constant. (D) is incorrect because the mass and energy values must increase or decrease simultaneously.

99. **(D)** The gravitational force between the Earth and the moon produces a centripetal acceleration. Since the moon is not moving in a straight line, there must be a net force, eliminating (A). Since it is changing direction, it does not have a constant velocity (though it has a near constant speed) eliminating (B). Though there may be insignificant energy losses, *Conservation of Angular Momentum and Energy* are dominant factors and do not allow the moon to slow down appreciably or fall back to the Earth, thus eliminating choice (C). Its velocity is always tangent to its path at any moment while its acceleration is always directed toward the Earth, nearly perpendicular to its path at any moment, thus choice (E) is incorrect.

100. **(E)** Contrary to choice (A), all of the Earth's energy does not come from plants. In fact, there would be no plants without the sun; the sun is necessary for the plants to make food. (A) is incorrect. Since animals (B), like plants, are dependent on the sun to provide energy, and since the sun provides all or nearly all of the Earth's energy, (B) could not be correct. Natural gas (C) is fossil fuel made from plants. All of the Earth's energy does not come from oil (D).

101. **(C)** (A) Neither coal, oil, nor gas are renewable. These fuels would take years to form even if all of the needed conditions and elements are present. (A) is not the correct choice. The items in (B) are nonrenewable; (B) should not be chosen. Soil, vegetation, and animals can be renewed in a relatively short period of time. (C) is the best choice. Although the other two items in item (D) are renewable, coal (a fossil fuel) is not; (D)is not the correct choice. Oil, a fossil fuel, is not renewable. Since it is nonrenewable (E) should also be avoided.

102. **(C)** Only the gravitational pull of the moon and the rotation of the Earth cause the rhythm of the tides. (C) is correct. The other choices, (A), (B), (D0, and (E), are therefore, incorrect.

103. **(D)** (A) is not the best choice, since it is an example of recycling. The reclaiming of nitrogen by the soil (B) is an example of recycling, and is not the correct choice. The rusting away of the cans (C) is an example of recycling, and not the correct choice. The non-biodegradable can (D) is NOT an example of recycling. (D) is the correct choice. Since (E) is an example of recycling, it is not the right choice.

104. **(A)** Since the advance of technology has reached a level where processes and products threaten the Earth's environment, (A) is correct. It is the only acceptable choice. (B) is false; the environmental crisis is not limited to highly industrialized areas but is global in nature. (B) cannot be chosen. The oceans and atmospheres do not purify pollutants as (C) suggests; rather the oceans and atmosphere distribute the life-destroying pollutants everywhere. Since choice (D) suggest that all the above are correct, it cannot be selected. Since both (B) and (C) are false, choice (E), which includes both those choices, should not be chosen.

105. **(E)** All the answers given are correct as they are written except (E) which is incorrect. Since the question asks for the choice which is not true, (E) is the correct choice. The thickest of the Earth's three parts is the

mantle, not the core; the mantle, of course, is the layer between the crust and the core, or center.

106. **(E)** After only two days, 1/2 the sample has decayed and 1/2 remains, so choice (A) is incorrect. After four days, 1/2 of the 1/2, or 1/4, remains, so 3/4 has decayed. Thus choices (B), (C), and (D) are not possible. After six days, 1/2 of the 1/4, or 1/8, remains, which means 7/8 of the original amount hass decayed.

107. **(A)** Since a hygrometer does indeed measure moisture in the air, (A) should be selected. An anemometer (B) measures wind speed and is not to be chosen. A barometer (C) measures air pressure; (C), therefore, cannot be chosen. A thermometer (D) measures temperature; it, too, is the incorrect choice. An altimeter (E) measures height; it cannot be selected as the correct choice.

108. **(C)** Acid rain, pollutants, ozone hole, and the greenhouse effect are harmful to the environment; choice (C) includes all these items and is, therefore, the correct answer. Choice (A) cannot be selected since it includes "None of the above." Choice (B) cannot be selected since (B) states "All of the above." The water table is necessary to our environment; choices (D) and (E) which include this item are incorrect. Choice (D) also omits (I), so it should be avoided. Choice (E), in addition to including (V), excludes (IV), and should not be chosen.

109. **(D)** The only way to prevent and/or cure the problems of pollution is to treat industrial waste before it is discharged into the environment; (D) is the correct choice. Discharging heat into adjacent waters (A) will kill the plant and animal life there; (A) is not acceptable for preventing and curing the problems of pollution. Dumping sewage, tars, and oils into salty water (B) or ocean waters (C) does not eliminate the problem of pollution. This process simply spreads the problem. Recycling (E) helps with the problem; it should not be discontinued as choice (E) suggests. The best choice is (D).

110. **(B)** Choice (B) gives the correct order of the eras. The rest of the choices – (A), (C), (D), and (E) – do not sequence the eras correctly and none of them should be selected.

111. **(C)** The boiling point of water is generally regarded as 100°C or 212°F. Only choice (C) gives this correct information. Choice (A) gives

the normal body temperature; (B) is followed by a C instead of an F. The other choices are incorrect

112. **(C)** All of the statements about machines are true except (C); (C) is, therefore, the correct choice. Friction can be an asset in certain cases-contrary to what (C) would have the reader to believe. For instance, friction (the rubbing together of two substances) can prevent slipping in the work of machines.

113. **(C)** Heat normally causes a solid to expand; cold normally causes a solid to contract. Hot water would cause the outside tumbler to expand; if the inside tumbler is cooled, it would contract. This procedure should cause the two tumblers to slip apart. Allowing the two tumblers to cool would probably not result in their slipping apart. (A) should not be chosen. Heating both tumblers would cause both to expand and the result would probably be a tighter fit. (B) is incorrect. Cooling both tumblers (D) would result in a contracting of the two and a probable tightening of the fit; (D) is inappropriate. Contracting the outside tumbler by the use of cold and expanding the inside tumbler by the use of heat would only result in a tighter fit. (E) is incorrect.

114. **(E)** If the refrigerator is working properly, the Freon never leaves the refrigerator since the system is sealed. Warm air is discharged into the air, not Freon. (E) is the false choice and is the choice to be selected. All the other choices – (A), (B), (C), and (D) – are true and cannot be selected since a false choice is needed.

115. **(C)** Radioactive elements will spontaneously emit radiation of three principal types, alpha (α), beta (β), and gamma (γ) rays. The properties of these three types are summarized below:

	mass	charge	corresponds to
alpha	4	+2	He^{2+}
beta		−1	electrons
gamma	0	0	electromagnetic radiation

In the decay of $_{92}U^{238}$ to $_{90}Th^{234}$, we recognize a change in both atomic number, 92 to 90, and mass number, 238 and 234. To account for this difference an alpha particle, $_2He^4$, which consists of two neutrons and two protons, must have been emitted.

116. **(D)** Graham's law of effusion states that the rates of effusion of gases are inversely proportional to the square roots of their molecular weights or densities.

$$\text{rate of effusion} \propto \frac{1}{\sqrt{MW}}$$

or rate of effusion $\times \sqrt{MW} = t_0$ a constant

Hence, when two gases effuse from the same apparatus at the same conditions:

$$\frac{\text{rate}_A}{\text{rate}_B} = \frac{\sqrt{MW_B}}{\sqrt{MW_A}}$$

Substituting the molecular weight for N_2 and H_2:

$$\frac{\text{rate } H_2}{\text{rate } N_2} = \frac{\sqrt{28}}{\sqrt{2}} = \frac{5.29}{1.41} = 3.8$$

117. **(C)** Normality is defined as the number of equivalent weights of solute per liter of solution.

$$N = \frac{\text{Number of equivalent weights}}{\text{liter}}$$

To solve this problem we must first determine the number of equivalent weights there are in 23.2 g of H_2SO_4. For acids the equivalent weight is defined as the mass of the acid that will furnish 1 mole of hydrogen ions. Since 1 mole of H_2SO_4 (98.0 g) produces 2 moles of H^+ ions,

$$H_2SO_4 \rightarrow 2H^+ + SO_4^-$$

its equivalent weight is 1/2 the molecular weight or 49.0 g. The number of equivalent weights in 23.2 g of H_2SO_4 will be:

$$\text{The number of equivalent weights} = \frac{\text{g present}}{\text{equivalent weight of } H_2SO_4}$$

$$= \frac{23.2 \text{ g}}{49.0 \text{ g/eq wt}} = 0.47$$

and the normality is then calculated by

$$N = \frac{\text{Number of equivalent weight}}{\text{liter}}$$

$$= \frac{0.47 \text{ eq wt}}{0.40 \text{ l}} = 1.2 \text{ N}$$

118. **(A)** Charles' Law states that the volume is directly proportional to temperature at constant pressure. Therefore,

$$\frac{V}{T} = k$$

in this problem:

$$V_1 = 200 \text{ ml}$$

$$T_1 = 25°C + 273°C = 298 \text{ K}$$

$$V_2 = \text{unknown}$$

$$T_2 = 40°C + 273°C = 313 \text{ K}$$

Thus,

$$\frac{200 \text{ ml}}{298 \text{ K}} = \frac{V_2}{313 \text{ K}}$$

and

$$V_2 = \frac{200 \text{ ml} \times 313 \text{ K}}{298 \text{ K}} = 210 \text{ ml}$$

Note: In all problems involving the gas laws the temperature must be expressed in degrees Kelvin (K).

119. **(A)** The electron configuration of He is $1s^2$. In He_2^+ the only orbitals available for molecular orbital formation are the 1 s. The 1 s from each He will interact to form a 1s bonding orbital and a 1s antibonding orbital.

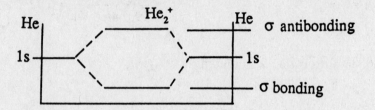

Placing the three electrons in the He_2^+ ion in the molecular orbital diagram, we have

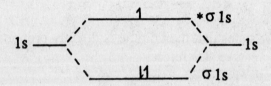

The bond order is then equal to

$$\text{Bond order} = \frac{\text{\# of e in bonding MO} - \text{\# of e in antibonding MO}}{2}$$

by substitution,

$$= \frac{2-1}{2} = \frac{1}{2}$$

120. **(B)** When MnO_4^- reacts with Fe^{2+} in acid solution, the following reaction occurs

$$MnO_4^- + Fe^{2+} + H^+ \rightarrow Fe^{3+}\ Mn^{2+} + H_2O$$

The Mn in MnO_4^-, which is in the +7 oxidation state, is reduced to Mn^{2+} which is almost colorless. The Fe^{2+} is oxidized by the MnO_4^- ion to Fe^{3+} and in turn the MnO_4^- is reduced to Mn^{2+}.

CHAPTER 5
SOCIAL SCIENCES AND HISTORY

PRACTICE
TEST 1

CLEP SOCIAL SCIENCES AND HISTORY
Test 1

(Answer sheets appear in the back of the book.)

Section 1

TIME: 45 Minutes
65 Questions

DIRECTIONS: Each of the questions or incomplete statements below is followed by five possible answers or completions. Select the best choice in each case and fill in the corresponding oval on the answer sheet.

---

1. In 1804, Aaron Burr killed Alexander Hamilton in a duel which was fought because

    (A) Hamilton had formally accused Burr of treason and Burr felt he had to defend his honor.

    (B) Burr blamed his loss of the 1804 election for governor of New York on Hamilton's charges that Burr was dangerous and untrustworthy.

    (C) Hamilton had uncovered Burr's plan to form an independent republic comprised of American territories west of the Appalachians.

    (D) Burr had caught his wife in a sexual liaison with Hamilton and felt that he had to defend his honor.

    (E) Burr believed that Hamilton had financially destroyed him in a real estate deal in which Burr lost nearly all of his wealth.

2. The following cartoon refers to the results of which war?

President McKinley (the tailor) measures Uncle Sam for a new suit to fit the fattening results of his imperial appetite.

(A) War of 1812   (D) World War I

(B) Civil War   (E) World War II

(C) Spanish-American War

3. "…there is no place for industry… no arts; no letters; no society; and which is the worst of all, continual fear, and danger of violent death; and the life of man, solitary, poor, nasty, brutish, and short." This quotation from Thomas Hobbes' *Leviathan* (1651) described the concept known as

(A) natural rights.   (D) reason of state (raison d'état).

(B) state of nature.   (E) nationalism.

(C) social contract.

4. Which one of the following would most likely oppose *laissez-faire* policies in nineteenth century Europe?

(A) A factory owner   (D) A socialist

(B) A liberal   (E) A middle-class businessman

(C) A free trader

5. The first time the Japanese people heard the voice of Emperor Hirohit on the radio was

    (A) during his coronation.

    (B) when he announced his wedding.

    (C) when he announced that Japanese troops were moving into Manchuria.

    (D) when he announced Japan's surrender to the Allied Powers.

    (E) when he declared war on the United States.

6. Which was the first European power to seize control of African territories?

    (A) Portugal   (D) France

    (B) Belgium   (E) Germany

    (C) England

7. Sociology is best defined as the scientific study of

    (A) social problems.   (D) human development.

    (B) human personality.   (E) attitudes and values.

    (C) social interaction.

8. Sociology developed as a separate discipline in the nineteenth century in response to

    (A) the growth of socialism.

    (B) the spread of colonialism.

    (C) a desire to promote greater equality.

    (D) the growth of industrial society.

    (E) disenchantment with psychology.

9. The German sociologist Max Weber is best known for his study

    (A) *Street Corner Society.*

    (B) *The Division of Labor in Society.*

    (C) *The Human Group.*

(D) *The Protestant Ethic and the Spirit of Capitalism.*

(E) *The Theory of the Leisure Class.*

10. In his writing, the French sociologist Emile Durkheim placed great emphasis on the concept of

(A) class conflict.

(B) social solidarity.

(C) rationalization.

(D) social mobility.

(E) reference groups.

11. In his theory, Karl Marx explained that conflict between industrial workers and the owners of industry was

(A) likely to decline in future years.

(B) usually harmful to social institutions.

(C) an inevitable consequence of capitalism.

(D) of little importance to social change.

(E) a rare occurrence in modern societies.

12. The research method that relies on interviews with a randomly selected sample of people is known as

(A) survey research.

(B) participant observation.

(C) content analysis.

(D) experimentation.

(E) exploratory research.

13. Organization theory uses theories of reinforcement to increase worker efficiency and satisfaction. According to reinforcement theory, the best time to reward a worker is

(A) at the end of the year in the form of a bonus.

(B) never.

(C) when he first begins work in the company.

(D) immediately before a task is performed.

(E) immediately after a task has been performed.

14. Which of the following is used to effect the release of a person from improper imprisonment?

(A) A writ of mandamus

(B) A writ of habeas corpus

(C) The Fourth Amendment requirement that police have probable cause in order to obtain a search warrant

(D) The Supreme Court's decision in *Roe v. Wade*

(E) The constitutional prohibition against *ex post facto* laws

15. When a member of the House of Representatives helps a citizen from his or her district receive some federal aid to which that citizen is entitled, the representative's action is referred to as

(A) casework.

(D) logrolling.

(B) pork barrel legislation.

(E) filibustering.

(C) lobbying.

16. One advantage incumbent members of Congress have over challengers in election campaigns is the use of

(A) unlimited campaign funds.

(B) national party employees as campaign workers.

(C) the franking privilege.

(D) unlimited contributions from "fat cat" supporters.

(E) government-financed air time for commercials.

QUESTIONS 17 to 19 refer to the tables below.

GRAIN PRODUCERS				GRAIN IMPORTERS			
Grain	1st	2nd	3rd	Grain	1st	2nd	3rd
Corn	USA	China	Brazil	Corn	CIS*	Japan	Spain
Wheat	CIS*	USA	China	Wheat	China	CIS*	Japan
Rice	China	India	Indonesia	Rice	Indonesia	Iran	CIS*

*Confederation of Independent States, the former U.S.S.R.

17. Which nation — or group of nations — seems to have the LEAST efficient agricultural system?

    (A) Brazil   (D) India

    (B) Indonesia   (E) China

    (C) CIS

18. Which nation seems to have the MOST productive agricultural system?

    (A) USA   (D) Indonesia

    (B) China   (E) India

    (C) Brazil

19. Which is NOT a characteristic of American agriculture?

    (A) The rich ecosystem of North America

    (B) The use of mechanization

    (C) The diversity of climate and soil

    (D) Total free market capitalism

    (E) The trend toward agribusiness

20. All of the following are true of the Confederate war effort during the Civil War EXCEPT

    (A) Confederate industry was never able to adequately supply Confederate soldiers with the armaments they needed to successfully fight the war.

    (B) Confederate agriculture was never able to adequately supply the people of the South with the food they needed.

    (C) inflation became a major problem in the South as the Confederate government was forced to print more paper currency than it could support with gold or other tangible assets.

    (D) the inadequate railroad system of the South hindered movement of soldiers, supplies, and food from the places where they were stationed (or produced) to the places where they were most needed.

(E) tremendous resentment at the military draft developed among poor and middle-class Southerners because wealthy Southern males could pay to have a substitute take their place in the army.

21. What was the OVERALL U.S. unemployment rate during the worst periods of the depression?

(A) 10%

(D) 60%

(B) 25%

(E) 90%

(C) 40%

QUESTION 22 refers to the following.

22. The painting by François Dubois, an eyewitness, describes the massacre on St. Bartholomew's Day of 1572 of

(A) Dutch nobility.

(D) Spanish Catholics.

(B) German peasants.

(E) English merchants.

(C) French Calvinists.

23. Which one of the following was a characteristic of the peace settlements at the end of World War I?

    (A) Division of Germany into two parts

    (B) Expansion of the territory of the Ottoman Empire

    (C) The emergence of the Soviet Union as a significant part of the European diplomatic system

    (D) The long-term stationing of American troops in Europe

    (E) Germany was not required to pay reparations.

24. Which of the following has NOT been a leader of an African country?

    (A) Kwame Nkrumah   (D) Julius Nyerere

    (B) Jomo Kenyatta   (E) Patrice Lumumba

    (C) Aime Cesaire

25. When Chinese students held a protest in Beijing's Tiananmen Square on May 4, 1989, they were commemorating the May 4 Movement of what year?

    (A) 1919   (D) 1895

    (B) 1911   (E) 1969

    (C) 1901

26. "Birth rates are lower in nations with high levels of economic development." This statement is an example of a

    (A) positive correlation.   (D) negative correlation.

    (B) spurious correlation.   (E) reverse correlation.

    (C) circular correlation.

27. Which of the following concepts is most clearly at the core of the sociological theory known as functionalism?

    (A) Economic development   (D) Intellectual creativity

    (B) Class conflict   (E) Interdependence

    (C) Human communication

28. Which of the following is an example of upward social mobility?

    (A) A farm worker's son becomes president of the United States

    (B) A physician's daughter attends medical school

    (C) A college professor's son works as a truck driver

    (D) The daughter of an army officer joins the navy

    (E) The son of a banker becomes a poet

29. Which of the following is most frequently used by sociologists as a measure of a person's socioeconomic status in industrial societies?

    (A) The prestige of their occupation

    (B) The amount of leisure time they possess

    (C) The number of children they have

    (D) Their participation in politics

    (E) Their religious beliefs

30. For sociologists, the key feature of a middle-class family that distinguishes it from a working-class family is the

    (A) head of the middle-class family works at more than one job.

    (B) wife of the middle-class family is a full-time homemaker.

    (C) children in the middle-class family attend private schools.

    (D) workers in the middle-class family hold white-collar occupations.

    (E) middle-class family owns more cars and more expensive homes.

31. Sociological research in the United States has found all of the following EXCEPT

    (A) middle-class people attend church more often than lower-class people.

    (B) lower-class people are ill more frequently than middle-class people.

    (C) middle-class parents use physical punishment less often than lower-class parents.

(D) lower-class people are less involved in politics than middle-class people.

(E) lower-class families have fewer children than middle-class families.

32. The role of imitation in social learning was first systematically observed by

(A) Miller and Dollard.   (D) B. F. Skinner.

(B) Bandura and Walters.   (E) J. B. Watson.

(C) Stanley Milgram.

33. Major differences between procedures in the House of Representatives and the Senate would include:

I. In the House, time for debate is limited, while in the Senate it is usually unlimited.

II. In the House, the rules committee is very powerful, while in the Senate it is relatively weak.

III. In the House, debate must be germane, while in the Senate it need not be.

(A) I only.   (D) I and II only.

(B) II only.   (E) I, II, and III.

(C) III only.

34. In the case *McCulloch v. Maryland* (1819), the Supreme Court

(A) gave a broad interpretation to the First Amendment right of freedom of speech.

(B) claimed the power of judicial review.

(C) struck down a law of Congress for the first time.

(D) gave a broad interpretation to the "necessary and proper clause."

(E) denied that the president has the right of executive privilege.

35. Which of the following statements about the cabinet is FALSE?

    (A) It includes heads of the 14 executive departments.

    (B) It includes members of the House of Representatives.

    (C) Although not mentioned in the Constitution, the cabinet has been part of American government since the presidency of George Washington.

    (D) Presidents may appoint special advisors to the cabinet.

    (E) Senators may not serve in the cabinet.

QUESTIONS 36 to 38 refer to the following graph.

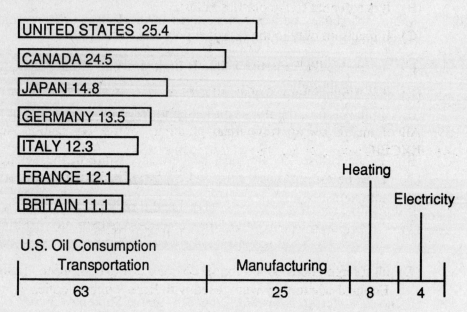

36. Which is NOT a conclusion that can be drawn from the graphs?

    (A) Transportation takes up too high a portion of U.S. oil usage.

    (B) U.S. per capita consumption is over twice that of most European nations.

    (C) North American oil demands are the highest.

    (D) Manufacturing is a major consumer of oil.

    (E) Heating needs take less than 10 percent of oil use.

37. Which would be LEAST likely to explain the statistics above?

    (A) The area size of a nation has a relationship to oil usage.

    (B) The European nations consume large quantities of oil.

    (C) The larger the population, the greater the usage.

    (D) Japan is the largest industrial power in Asia.

    (E) Industrial nations' people have lifestyles that use more oil.

38. Which is NOT true about the petroleum industry?

    (A) It is dealing with a nonrenewable resource.

    (B) It is essential to the plastics industry.

    (C) It reacts quickly to the law of supply and demand.

    (D) It is an example of a monopoly.

    (E) It is truly a multinational industry.

39. All of the following were main principles of the Navigation Acts EXCEPT

    (A) trade in the colonies was limited to only British or colonial merchants.

    (B) it prohibited the colonies from issuing their own paper currencies, greatly limiting their trading capabilities.

    (C) all foreign goods bound for the colonies had to be shipped through England where they were taxed with British import duties.

    (D) the colonists could not build or export products that directly competed with British export products.

    (E) colonial enumerated goods could only be sold in England.

40. The reason slavery flourished in the Southern English colonies and not in New England is

    (A) most New England farms were too small for slaves to be economically necessary or viable, whereas in the South the cultivation of staple crops such as rice and tobacco on large plantations necessitated the use of large numbers of indentured servants or slaves.

(B) blacks from the tropical climate of Africa could not adapt to the harsh New England winters. Their high death rates made their use as slave laborers unprofitable.

(C) a shortage of females in the Southern English colonies led to many female black Africans being imported as slaves and as potential wives for white planters in the region.

(D) whereas New England religious groups such as the Puritans forbade slavery on moral grounds, the Anglican church, which dominated the Southern English colonies, encouraged the belief that blacks were inferior, thus, not deserving of equal status.

(E) the Stono uprising in 1739 convinced New Englanders that the cost of controlling slaves was not worth their marginal economic benefits.

41. All of the following are characteristics of Renaissance humanism EXCEPT

(A) sanctity of the Latin texts of Scriptures.

(B) belief that ancient Latin and Greek writers were inferior to later authors.

(C) rejection of Christian principles.

(D) it functioned as a primary cause of the Reformation.

(E) accomplished scholarship in ancient languages.

42. The October Manifesto of Tsar Nicholas II promised all of the following EXCEPT

(A) a Duma.   (D) a fair, democratic voting system.

(B) political reforms.   (E) full civil liberties.

(C) a Russian parliament.

43. Which independent Asian nation did NOT exist before 1947?

(A) Thailand   (D) Korea

(B) Pakistan   (E) Vietnam

(C) India

44. All of the following were aspects of Britain's policy of indirect rule in colonial Africa EXCEPT

(A) subsidizing primary education for Africans.

(B) the expectation of eventual self-government.

(C) decentralized administration.

(D) uniform government policy throughout the colonized territories.

(E) incorporating traditional rulers into the government structure.

45. The Glorious Revolution of 1688-89 resulted in all of the following EXCEPT

(A) the flight and abdication of James II.

(B) an agreement that in the event of no heirs, the Hanover house would succeed the Stuarts.

(C) the elevation of William III and Mary as the monarchs.

(D) specification that all future monarchs must be members of the Church of England.

(E) the passage of the Bill of Rights.

46. Many young people around the world now wear American blue jeans and listen to American rock-and-roll music. This is an example of the concept of cultural

(A) decline.   (D) innovation.

(B) diffusion.   (E) disintegration.

(C) discovery.

47. Popular movies frequently portray young African-American men as gang members and drug dealers. This is an example of the sociological process known as

(A) affirmative action.   (D) status inconsistency.

(B) reverse racism.   (E) role conflict.

(C) stereotyping.

48. According to the functionalist theory of stratification developed by Kingsley Davis and Wilbert Moore, some occupations are more highly rewarded than others because they

    (A) have been held for a long time.

    (B) are organized into unions.

    (C) require physical labor.

    (D) appeal to widely shared values.

    (E) require long periods of training.

49. Demographers study all of the following aspects of human populations EXCEPT

    (A) growth.   (D) composition.

    (B) distribution.   (E) socialization.

    (C) migration.

50. Each of the following is an important agent of socialization EXCEPT

    (A) television.   (D) peers.

    (B) bankers.   (E) teachers.

    (C) parents.

51. In our society, money is an example of a

    (A) primary reinforcer.

    (B) secondary (conditioned) reinforcer.

    (C) socio/reinforcer.

    (D) negative reinforcer.

    (E) simple operant.

52. The major responsibility of the Federal Reserve Board is to

    (A) implement monetary policy.

    (B) control government spending.

    (C) regulate commodity prices.

(D) help the president run the executive branch.

(E) keep records of troop strength in army reserve units across the country.

53. Which of the following statements most accurately compares political parties in the United States with those in other Western democracies?

(A) Parties in the United States exert a greater influence over which candidates run for office.

(B) Parties are much more centralized in the United States.

(C) There are usually more political parties in other Western democracies.

(D) Party members in the national legislature are much freer to vote against the party line in other Western democracies.

(E) Party label is the principal criterion for voting for a candidate in the United States, whereas it is relatively unimportant in other Western democracies.

54. Which of the following is among the differences between a parliamentary and a presidential system?

I. In a parliamentary system, there is little or no separation of powers as in a presidential system.

II. In a parliamentary system, the chief executive officer is not chosen by a nationwide vote as in a presidential system.

III. In a presidential system, the chief executive officer may call elections for all members of the legislature at any time, unlike in a parliamentary system.

(A) I only.   (D) I and II only.

(B) II only.   (E) I, II, and III.

(C) III only.

QUESTIONS 55 to 57 refer to the following.

• We must develop the vision to see that in regard to the natural world private and corporate ownership should be so limited as to preserve the interest of society and the integrity of the environment.

- We need greater awareness of our enormous powers, the fragility of the earth, and the consequent responsibility of men and governments for its preservation.

- We must redefine "progress" toward an emphasis on long-term quality rather than immediate quantity.

"We, therefore, resolve to act. We propose a revolution in conduct toward an environment which is rising in revolt against us. Granted that ideas and institutions long established are not easily changed; yet today is the first day of the rest of our life on this planet. We will begin anew."

Source: U.S. Government statistics

55. Which group is not called upon to act in the statement?

    (A) Private and corporate ownership

    (B) Government

    (C) Individuals

    (D) Society

    (E) Communities

56. What makes this quote relevant to economics?

    (A) Ethical use of the environment

    (B) Man as a member of the "community of all living things"

    (C) Need for individual responsibility

    (D) References to man's machines and past abuses

    (E) Progress, in terms of quality of life

57. Which is NOT an example of how environmental concerns can become economic priorities?

    (A) Recycling

    (B) Reforestation

    (C) Strip-mining restoration

    (D) Greenhouse effect

    (E) Coal-generated electricity to replace imported oil

58. Which battle was the turning point in the Pacific war between Japan and the United States?

(A) Leyte Gulf

(D) Midway

(B) Pearl Harbor

(E) Guadalcanal

(C) Coral Sea

59. The United States Supreme Court Case of *Brown v. Board of Education of Topeka* was significant because it

(A) prohibited prayer in public schools on the grounds of separation of church and state.

(B) legally upheld the doctrine of "separate but equal" educational facilities for blacks and whites.

(C) clarified the constitutional rights of minors and restricted the rights of school administrators to set dress codes or otherwise infringe on students' rights.

(D) upheld school districts' rights to use aptitude and psychological tests to "track" students and segregate them into "college prep" and "vocational" programs.

(E) ordered the desegregation of public schools, prohibiting the practice of segregation via "separate but equal" schools for blacks and whites.

60. Ferdinand and Isabella's policies of Spanish nationalism led to the expulsion, from Spain, of large numbers of Spanish

(A) Protestants.

(D) Calvinists.

(B) Catholics.

(E) monks.

(C) Jews.

61. During the Thirty Years' War, the Lutheran movement was saved from extinction by the military intervention of which foreign monarch?

(A) The French king, Philip the Fair

(B) The English king, Henry VIII

(C) The Swedish king, Gustavus Adolphus

(D) The Austrian emperor, Charles V

(E) The Spanish king, Philip II

62. In 1898, the United States took control of the Philippines from which country?

(A) China

(B) Japan

(C) England

(D) Spain

(E) Portugal

63. The following pairs of names are the names of African countries before and after achieving independence EXCEPT

(A) Bechuanaland – Botswana.

(B) Dahomey – Benin.

(C) Gold Coast – Ghana.

(D) Swaziland – Malawi.

(E) Angola – Angola.

64. Emile Durkheim found that suicide rates were higher for

(A) women than men.

(B) young people than old people.

(C) poor people than wealthy people.

(D) single people than married people.

(E) Jews than Protestants.

65. A soldier in combat sacrifices his life so his comrades may survive. This is an example of which of the following types of suicide identified by Durkheim?

(A) Egoistic

(B) Altruistic

(C) Intrinsic

(D) Anomic

(E) Euphoric

Section 2

TIME: 45 Minutes
65 Questions

DIRECTIONS: Each of the questions or incomplete statements below is followed by five possible answers or completions. Select the best choice in each case and fill in the corresponding oval on the answer sheet.

66. The research method which involves a social scientist living among and interacting with the people being studied is known as

    (A) survey research.

    (B) experimentation.

    (C) content analysis.

    (D) participant observation.

    (E) stategic engagement.

67. "Female college athletes will have higher academic averages than male college athletes." In this hypothesis, which is the independent variable?

    (A) Athletic participation

    (B) College attendance

    (C) Academic achievement

    (D) Gender

    (E) Study habits

68. The concept of culture includes all of the following EXCEPT

    (A) personal values.

    (B) religious beliefs.

    (C) styles of dress.

    (D) family organization.

    (E) individual intelligence.

69. The concept of ethnocentrism refers to the tendency for members of a group to

    (A) speak the same language.

    (B) work for common goals.

    (C) show respect for the elderly.

    (D) teach children to practice religious rituals.

    (E) place a high value on their own culture.

70. An important function of rehearsal in verbal learning is

    (A) mediation.

    (B) transference of material from short-term to long-term memory.

    (C) acclimation to the meaning of the material.

    (D) Both (A) and (B).

    (E) All of the above.

71. The statement "America has a pluralistic political system" means

    (A) there are many subcultures within American society.

    (B) political power is divided between national and state governments.

    (C) many interest groups compete in the political arena to influence public policy.

    (D) rural interests are overrepresented in the national legislature.

    (E) candidates for national office are usually elected by plurality vote.

72. Which of the following best describes the relationship between educational background and participation in politics?

    (A) The more schooling one has, the more likely one is to vote.

    (B) The less schooling one has, the more likely one is to run for public office.

    (C) There is no relationship between educational background and participation in politics.

(D) People with a high school education are more likely to vote than either those who did not finish high school or those with a college degree.

(E) Those with no formal schooling have a greater personal interest in policy and tend to vote more often than those with high school diplomas.

73. All of the following are recognized functions of the major political parties EXCEPT

(A) recruiting candidates for public office.

(B) aggregating interests into electoral alliances.

(C) establishing channels of communication between public and government.

(D) providing personnel to staff elections and run the government.

(E) articulating interests.

QUESTIONS 74 and 75 refer to the diagram below.

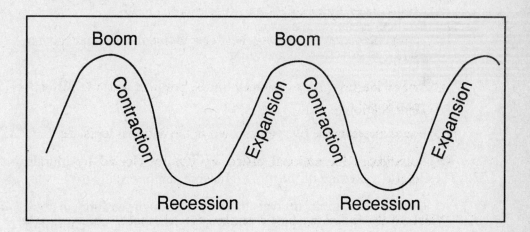

74. Which is the best title for the diagram above?

    (A) Boom and Bust

    (B) Causes of Economic Change

    (C) The Business Cycle

    (D) Causes of Recession

    (E) The History of Business Activity

75. In referring to the stages of the cycle, on the previous page, which would not be a factor considered by economists?

    (A) Unemployment figures

    (B) Manufacturing production

    (C) Income levels

    (D) War or peace

    (E) Retail sales

76. Which is not a method used to encourage expansion during a recession?

    (A) Political crisis, such as war

    (B) Increased government spending

    (C) Increased taxation

    (D) Deregulation of industry

    (E) Restriction of imports

77. The Great Awakening of the mid-eighteenth century refers to

    (A) a series of religious revivals that swept through the English colonies spreading evangelistic fervor and challenging the control of traditional clerics over their congregations.

    (B) the intellectual revolution which served as a precursor to the Enlightenment and challenged orthodox religion's claims to knowledge of humankind and the universe.

    (C) the beginnings of the Industrial Revolution in England and its New World colonies.

(D) the growing realization among English colonists that independence from England was only a matter of time and was the key to their future success.

(E) the sudden awareness among North American Indians that their only chance for survival against the rapidly growing number of European colonists was to fight them before the Europeans grew any stronger.

78. One of the major effects of the Industrial Revolution of the late nineteenth century in the United States was

(A) an increased emphasis on worker health and safety issues.

(B) an increased emphasis on speed rather than quality of work.

(C) an increased emphasis on high-quality, error-free work.

(D) an increase in the number of small industrial facilities, which could operate more efficiently than larger, more costly industrial plants.

(E) a decrease in worker productivity as a result of continuous clashes between unions and management.

79. All of the following were significant economic trends in Germany during the 1920s EXCEPT

(A) large amounts of money leaving the country to pay reparations.

(B) periods of high inflation.

(C) a very stable currency (the mark).

(D) periods of high unemployment.

(E) the German government placed large amounts of paper money in circulation.

QUESTION 80 refers to the following.

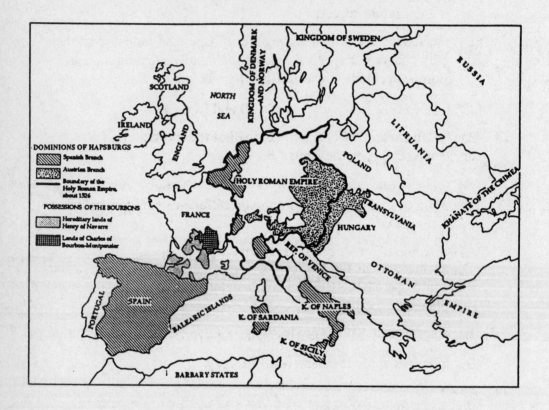

80. The map depicts Europe around

(A) 1800.   (D) 1950.

(B) 1500.   (E) 1900.

(C) 1700.

81. By 1914 which of the following countries was still an independent state not under colonial control?

(A) Algeria   (D) Egypt

(B) Congo   (E) Ethiopia

(C) Angola

82. Thailand is bordered by which of the following countries?

    I.   Burma

    II. Laos

    III. Vietnam

    IV. Cambodia

    (A) I, II, and III.   (D) II and III only.

    (B) I, II, and IV.   (E) All of the above.

    (C) I and II only.

83. According to sociologists, an important difference between folkways and mores is that

    (A) violation of a folkway leads to severe punishment.

    (B) mores are found among the upper classes only.

    (C) folkways include customary behaviors.

    (D) violations of mores are not considered crimes.

    (E) folkways apply to sexual behavior only.

84. Deviant behavior is the term used by sociologists to describe behaviors which a group defines as

    (A) violating basic norms.

    (B) uncommonly brave or heroic.

    (C) the standard for others to follow.

    (D) very rare or unusual.

    (E) based on personal motives.

85. Which of the following behaviors would NOT be considered an example of deviance in contemporary American society?

    (A) Eating spaghetti with one's fingers

    (B) Running naked down a main street of a city

    (C) A man regularly dressing in women's clothing

(D) College students drinking beer on Saturday night

(E) A person talking to himself in public places

86. According to the symbolic interactionist theory of George Herbert Mead, which of the following processes is central to the development of a self-concept by young children?

(A) Pretending to be other people

(B) Memorizing songs and poems

(C) Learning how to read in school

(D) Listening to bedtime stories

(E) Saying prayers in church

87. Studies of children who have been raised with limited contact with other humans during their first years have shown that they

(A) develop intellectually at a normal rate.

(B) have better coordination than other children.

(C) have great difficulty adjusting to society.

(D) easily learn to distinguish right and wrong.

(E) often show considerable artistic talent.

88. All of the following are basic assumptions of sociology EXCEPT

(A) most human behavior follows predictable patterns.

(B) scientific methods can be used to study human behavior.

(C) inherited genetic traits shape much human behavior.

(D) human beliefs and values can be studied objectively.

(E) human values are acquired through socialization.

89. Stanley Milgram, in his landmark study on obedience to authority, found that when subjects were asked to shock a confederate in increasing amounts in order to teach him a word matching task,

(A) 65 percent of the subjects administered shocks throughout the experiment and gave the maximum 450-volt shock.

(B) 75 percent of the subjects refused to participate in the experiment.

(C) 30 percent of the subjects administered shocks throughout the experiment and gave the maximum 450-volt shock.

(D) people of low intelligence were more likely to apply the maximum 450-volt shock.

(E) Both (A) and (D).

QUESTION 90 refers to the following.

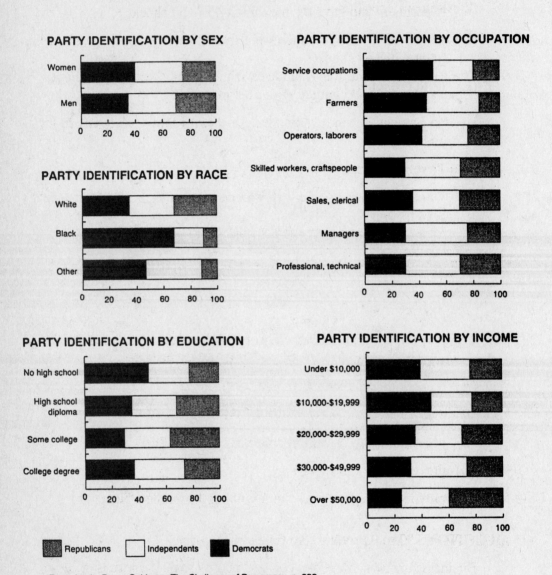

PARTY IDENTIFICATION BY SEX

PARTY IDENTIFICATION BY OCCUPATION

PARTY IDENTIFICATION BY RACE

PARTY IDENTIFICATION BY EDUCATION

PARTY IDENTIFICATION BY INCOME

Republicans   Independents   Democrats

From Janda, Berry, Goldman, *The Challenge of Democracy*, p. 286

90. Based on the graph above, which of the following were LEAST likely to have voted for Franklin Roosevelt in 1940?

(A) Southerners

(B) White northern business leaders

(C) Blue-collar workers

(D) Racial minorities

(E) Union members

91. The federal Constitution guarantees which of the following rights to persons arrested and charged with a serious crime?

I. To have an attorney appointed for them if they cannot afford to hire one

II. To remain silent

III. To compel witnesses in their favor to appear to testify if the case goes to court

(A) I only.   (D) I and II only.

(B) II only.   (E) I, II, and III.

(C) III only.

92. The purpose of grandfather clauses and literacy tests, used in the southern states in the late 1800s and early 1900s, was to

(A) prevent illiterate whites from voting.

(B) prevent recent immigrants from voting.

(C) prevent Hispanics from running for public office.

(D) prevent blacks from voting.

(E) prevent "carpetbaggers" from running for public office.

QUESTIONS 93 to 95 refer to the following passage.

Business functions by public consent, and its basic purpose is to serve constructively the needs of society – to the satisfaction of society.

"Historically, business has discharged this obligation mainly by supplying the needs and wants of people for goods and services, by providing jobs and purchasing power, and by producing most of the wealth of the nation. This has been what American society required of business, and business on the whole has done its job remarkably well...

"In generating... economic growth, American business has provided increasing employment, rising wages and salaries, employee benefit plans, and expanding career opportunities for a labor force....

"Most important, the rising standard of living of the average American family has enabled more and more citizens to develop their lives as they wish with less and less constraint imposed on them by economic need. Thus, most Americans have been able to afford better health, food, clothing, shelter, and education than the citizens of any other nation have ever achieved on such a large scale...."

Source: U.S. Government report

93. Which statement best summarizes the attitude of the quote?

    (A) Business has successfully met all the needs of society.

    (B) Business has done a good job supplying the economic needs of society.

    (C) Americans are best off with the least government.

    (D) All Americans have benefited from the rising living standard.

    (E) Government and business, in partnership, have created prosperity.

94. Which organization would be most likely to endorse this quote?

    (A) Chamber of Commerce   (D) Socialist Labor party

    (B) Department of Labor   (E) AFL/CIO

    (C) General Accounting Office

95. Which of the following economic goals is not addressed by the quote?

    (A) Economic growth   (D) Economic justice

    (B) Economic stability   (E) Economic freedom

    (C) Economic security

96. Which is NOT one of the four basic economic activities of capitalism?

    (A) Production   (D) Service

    (B) Distribution   (E) Labor

    (C) Manufacturing

97. The key event that guaranteed Lincoln's reelection in 1864 was

    (A) the fall of Vicksburg to General Grant.

    (B) the capture of New Orleans by Admiral Farragut.

    (C) the defeat of Lee's army by General Meade at Gettysburg.

    (D) the fall of Atlanta to General Sherman.

    (E) the successful defense of Nashville by General Thomas against repeated Confederate counterattacks.

98. The American Hostage Crisis in Iran was precipitated by

    (A) the American government allowing the deposed Shah of Iran to come to the United States for cancer treatment.

    (B) Jimmy Carter's involvement in arranging the Camp David accords between the Egyptians and the Israelis.

    (C) American air strikes against Iran's ally, Libya.

    (D) American support for Israel's 1980 invasion of southern Lebanon.

    (E) American attempts to overthrow the newly emplaced government of Ayatollah Khomeini.

99. During the era of European imperialism in Africa, 1870-1914, a "Cape to Cairo railway" was a project envisioned by

    (A) Italy.   (D) Germany.

    (B) Britain.   (E) Spain.

    (C) France.

100. Which European nation failed to establish an African colony when its expeditionary force was overwhelmingly defeated by a native force at Adowa, Ethiopia, in 1896?

    (A) Italy   (D) Britain

    (B) Belgium   (E) Austria

    (C) Portugal

101. The Himalayan mountain range runs through which of the following Asian countries?

    I.   China

    II.   Nepal

    III. India

    IV.   Bangladesh

    (A) I and II only.   (D) I, III, and IV only.

    (B) II and III only.   (E) All of the above.

    (C) I, II, and III only.

102. Which of the following was the first European country to make illegal the slave trade?

    (A) Holland   (D) Spain

    (B) Britain   (E) Portugal

    (C) France

103. "Working-class mothers will place a higher value on obedience in raising their children than will middle-class mothers." In this hypothesis, which is the dependent variable?

    (A) Social class of mothers

    (B) Gender of children

    (C) Value placed on obedience

    (D) Education of parents

    (E) Social status of mothers

104. Which of the following is NOT a method of social control?

    (A) Ridicule   (D) Praise

    (B) Insults   (E) Imitation

    (C) Spanking

105. George is a college student. He also works 25 hours a week to support his wife and small child. He is having a hard time pleasing his

boss and keeping his grades up. A sociologist would say that George is suffering from

(A) role ambiguity.   (D) role performance.

(B) role conflict.   (E) role playing.

(C) role strain.

106. Social mobility refers to the ability to

(A) gain a college education.

(B) enter any occupation one chooses.

(C) travel freely across national borders.

(D) change one's social class position.

(E) marry a person of another religion.

107. When sociologists discuss the working class, they are referring to people who

(A) work for a living.

(B) live below the poverty line.

(C) have not attended college.

(D) work in blue-collar occupations.

(E) live near factories.

QUESTIONS 108-110 refer to the following passage.

Many psychologists believe that aggression is a behavior which is learned through operant conditioning, in which rewards and punishments shape a person's behavior. Modeling, or vicarious conditioning, is also thought to contribute to the development of aggressive behavior. In contrast with this predominant school of thought is the school that believes that aggression is an inborn tendency, and that because humans use their intelligence to aggress, they have never developed natural controls on aggression against their own species, as have other animals.

108. The belief that aggression is learned is held by

(A) social learning theorists.

(B) phenomenological theorists.

(C) psychodynamic theorists.

(D) experimental theorists.

(E) All of the above.

109. Which of the following statements is false?

(A) If a child is rewarded for random, aggressive behavior, chances are good that the behavior will be repeated.

(B) If a child is punished for acting aggressively, the likelihood of that behavior recurring is lessened.

(C) If aggression is reinforced irregularly, the aggressive behavior is gradually discouraged.

(D) Both (B) and (C).

(E) None of the above.

110. The approach in which it is believed that aggression is an inborn tendency has been most supported by the work of

(A) Sigmund Freud.   (D) Albert Bandura.

(B) Konrad Lorenz.   (E) B. F. Skinner.

(C) Carl Rogers.

QUESTION 111 refers to the following excerpt from a Supreme Court decision.

It is emphatically the province and duty of the courts to say what the law is... If two laws conflict with each other, the courts must decide on the operation of each... If, then, the courts are to regard the Constitution, and the Constitution is superior to any ordinary act of the legislature, the Constitution and not such ordinary act, must govern the case to which they both apply.

111. This decision of the Supreme Court upheld the principle that

(A) a law contrary to the Constitution cannot be enforced by the courts.

(B) Congress has the power to pass laws to carry out its constitutional duties.

(C) interpretation of laws is a legislative function.

(D) a law passed by Congress overrides a constitutional provision with which it conflicts.

(E) courts are not equipped to decide questions of constitutional law.

112. "Mark-up sessions," where revisions and additions are made to proposed legislation in Congress, usually occur in which setting?

(A) The majority leader's office

(B) On the floor of the legislative chamber

(C) In party caucuses

(D) In joint conference committees

(E) In committees or subcommittees

113. Which of the following has chief responsibility for assembling and analyzing the figures in the presidential budget submitted to Congress each year?

(A) Department of Commerce

(B) Department of Treasury

(C) Federal Reserve Board

(D) Office of Management and Budget

(E) Cabinet

QUESTIONS 114 to 118 refer to the graphs below.

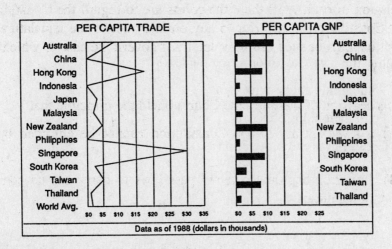

114. Comparing the two charts, the best conclusion is that

    (A) there is a direct relationship between GNP and trade.

    (B) the nations all have increased their GNP.

    (C) they all exceeded the world average in trade.

    (D) Japan is the leader in both GNP and trade.

    (E) China ranks lowest in both categories.

115. Which is NOT true about both charts?

    (A) Both are figured per person.

    (B) Both are in thousands of dollars.

    (C) Both compare the same nations.

    (D) Both are the same type of graph.

    (E) Both use the same year's data.

116. Which economic region of the world is reflected in the graphs?

    (A) East Asia   (D) All Pacific

    (B) All Asia   (E) All ex-British colonies

    (C) Northwest Asia

117. The nation that is increasing its prosperity the most is probably

    (A) Australia.   (D) Singapore.

    (B) Hong Kong.   (E) Taiwan.

    (C) Japan.

118. Which is the best way to describe the GNP?

    (A) Total goods and services

    (B) Total national production

    (C) Greater national production

    (D) Government natural production

    (E) Gross national resources

119. The Compromise of 1877 resulted in

    (A) the ascension of Republican Rutherford B. Hayes to the presidency in return for assurances that what was left of Reconstruction in the South would be ended.

    (B) the division of the Dakota Territory into North Dakota and South Dakota.

    (C) government financing for a Southern transcontinental railroad route in return for financial grants allowing the completion of the Great Northern Railroad from Minnesota to the Pacific Northwest.

    (D) the ascension of Republican Rutherford B. Hayes to the presidency in return for the passage of an Amnesty Act which would pardon former Confederate soldiers, allowing them to regain their voting rights.

    (E) the formal separation of Virginia and West Virginia and the official acceptance of statehood for West Virginia.

120. The Albany Congress of 1754 was convened for the major purpose of

    (A) adding New York to the Dominion of New England.

    (B) getting the colonies to form a "grand council" to coordinate their western expansion and their common defense against Indians.

    (C) uniting the colonies under a "grand council" to resist British economic sanctions and coordinate activities against British tax officials.

    (D) cooperating with the French in their efforts to rid western New York and southern Canada of raiding Indian tribes.

    (E) writing a proclamation to be sent to King George in protest of the Stamp Act.

121. "Sturm und Drang" was a significant period in the career of

    (A) Rousseau.   (D) Stendahl.

    (B) Goethe.   (E) Kant.

    (C) Mill.

122. All of the following were characteristics of the Positivism of Auguste Comte EXCEPT

(A) belief in a three-stage view of history.

(B) belief that all knowledge must be scientifically verified.

(C) achievement of Progress and Order through a government of major scientists and philosophers.

(D) a new Religion of Science.

(E) admiration for science and technology.

123. All of the pairs listed below represent the names of modern African countries and their capitals EXCEPT

(A) Angola – Luanda.   (D) Liberia – Monrovia.

(B) Somalia – Mogadishu. (E) Sierra Leone – Dakar.

(C) Nigeria – Lagos.

124. All of the following countries were colonized by a European power in the nineteenth century EXCEPT

(A) Cambodia.   (D) India.

(B) Laos.   (E) Thailand.

(C) Burma.

125. Which of the following is an ascribed status?

(A) College president   (D) White female

(B) Nobel prize winner   (E) Opera singer

(C) Honor student

126. Which of the following is an achieved status?

(A) Television game show host

(B) Senior citizen

(C) Japanese-American teenager

(D) Accident victim

(E) Seven feet tall

127. If a group is considered a subculture by sociologists, then the people in that group would be most likely to have similar

(A) values.

(D) ages.

(B) incomes.

(E) genders.

(C) educations.

128. "Our self-concept is based largely on the ways in which we see other people reacting to us." This statement reflects

(A) George Herbert Mead's theory of self-development.

(B) Charles Cooley's theory of the "looking-glass-self."

(C) Sigmund Freud's theory of ego development.

(D) Jean Piaget's theory of intellectual development.

(E) Lawrence Kohlberg's theory of moral development.

129. Sociologists have identified at least five different types of societies based on their level of sociocultural evolution. Hunting and gathering societies differ from other types of societies in that they have

(A) more rigid social stratification.

(B) greater occupational specialization.

(C) extensive inequality of wealth.

(D) stronger consensus on basic values.

(E) highly centralized government.

130. Which one of the following statements about poverty in the United States is correct?

(A) The majority of African-Americans are poor.

(B) The majority of elderly are poor.

(C) The majority of the poor are whites.

(D) The majority of the poor are African-Americans.

(E) The majority of the poor are single mothers.

CLEP SOCIAL SCIENCES AND HISTORY
TEST 1

ANSWER KEY

Section 1

1. (B)	14. (B)	27. (E)	40. (A)	53. (C)
2. (C)	15. (A)	28. (A)	41. (E)	54. (D)
3. (B)	16. (C)	29. (A)	42. (D)	55. (A)
4. (D)	17. (C)	30. (D)	43. (B)	56. (D)
5. (D)	18. (A)	31. (E)	44. (B)	57. (E)
6. (A)	19. (D)	32. (A)	45. (B)	58. (D)
7. (C)	20. (A)	33. (E)	46. (B)	59. (E)
8. (D)	21. (B)	34. (D)	47. (C)	60. (C)
9. (D)	22. (C)	35. (B)	48. (E)	61. (C)
10. (B)	23. (A)	36. (A)	49. (E)	62. (D)
11. (C)	24. (C)	37. (C)	50. (B)	63. (D)
12. (A)	25. (A)	38. (D)	51. (B)	64. (D)
13. (E)	26. (D)	39. (B)	52. (A)	65. (B)

Section 2

66. (D)	79. (C)	92. (D)	105. (B)	118. (A)
67. (D)	80. (B)	93. (B)	106. (D)	119. (A)
68. (E)	81. (E)	94. (A)	107. (D)	120. (B)
69. (E)	82. (B)	95. (D)	108. (A)	121. (B)
70. (B)	83. (C)	96. (E)	109. (C)	122. (D)
71. (C)	84. (A)	97. (D)	110. (B)	123. (E)
72. (A)	85. (D)	98. (A)	111. (A)	124. (E)
73. (E)	86. (A)	99. (B)	112. (E)	125. (D)
74. (C)	87. (C)	100. (A)	113. (D)	126. (A)
75. (D)	88. (C)	101. (C)	114. (E)	127. (A)
76. (C)	89. (A)	102. (B)	115. (D)	128. (B)
77. (A)	90. (B)	103. (C)	116. (A)	129. (D)
78. (B)	91. (E)	104. (E)	117. (D)	130. (C)

DETAILED EXPLANATIONS
OF ANSWERS
TEST 1

Section 1

1. **(B)** Burr and Hamilton had never been close friends, and Hamilton made no secret of the fact that he did not trust Burr. During the congressional voting to resolve the outcome of the presidential election of 1800, when Burr might have become the third president of the United States, Hamilton had made attacks against Burr's personal character. In 1804, as Burr ran for governor of New York, Hamilton repeated and expanded those charges. When Burr lost the election, he blamed Hamilton, although there is no clear evidence that Hamilton's charges led to Burr's defeat. Burr demanded "satisfaction" through a duel and Hamilton accepted. Hamilton's death not only deprived the young nation of one of its premier thinkers and statesmen, but it ruined Burr's political career. He was charged with murder and forced to flee to avoid arrest. It was after this disaster that he began formulating his plan for an independent Western empire. Thus, choice (C) is incorrect.

2. **(C)** The question deals with the growth of the United States during President McKinley's tenure. President Madison was in office during the War of 1812. President Lincoln headed the government during the Civil War. President Wilson led the country in World War I. President F. D. Roosevelt was the leader in World War II. Thus, the correct answer is (C).

3. **(B)** Although "quotation" questions may ask the name of the author or the book title, this question requests more than factual recall. It requires an ability to recognize the main idea of the passage – to read the quotation and understand its philosophic implications. Knowledge of the terminology of seventeenth-century writers is also helpful. Hobbes' *Leviathan* described early human society (the "state of nature") as an anarchic "war of all against all." For self-protection, citizens agreed among themselves to form the first government, an agreement termed by Hobbes the

"social contract." It is especially important to read the quotation carefully, since two of the answers, (B) and (C), are from the *Leviathan*; you may be misled into choosing (C) because you have studied the *Leviathan* in a class and the "social contract" sounds familiar. If the correct answer is not apparent after a second reading of the quotation, it may at least be possible to eliminate the other two answers. The concept of natural rights, incorporated into the French Declaration of the Rights of Man and the Bill of Rights to the United States Constitution, was summarized by John Locke as the idea that human beings are born "free, equal, and independent." "Reason of state" was the justification used by French statesmen such as Cardinal Richelieu to defend measures to create a centralized absolute monarchy in France. Choice (E), nationalism, is not only incorrect but also irrelevant to this question.

4.   **(D)** *Laissez-faire* (from the French *laissez-nous faire,* leave us alone) described the economic outlook of nineteenth-century liberals, many of whom were businessmen or industrialists who sought an end to government regulation of business. Proponents of *laissez-faire* envisioned an era of free economic activity in Europe without tariff barriers ("free trade"). Thus factory owners, liberals, and free traders were all supporters of *laissez-faire*. Not so with nineteenth-century socialists, who saw *laissez-faire* as an obstacle to even minimal measures to help the working class, such as government safety inspections of factories. This question tests both your knowledge and your analytical skills. It requires that you draw inferences or conclusions from the information given. It also requires an understanding of terminology (liberals, free traders, and middle-class businessmen), as well as an ability to analyze the implications of *laissez-faire* for groups such as factory owners and socialists. If you realize that at least two of the answers are virtually the same (for example, liberals and free traders), these answers may be eliminated. Since only (A) and (D) are left as possible answers, the chances of a successful guess have increased to 50 percent. Guessing is recommended when one, and especially two, of the answers may be eliminated.

5.   **(D)** On August 15, 1945, traffic came to a halt in Japan, as the nation listened to a prerecorded message in which Emperor Hirohito declared his acceptance of the Potsdam Declaration and Japan's defeat in the Second World War. This was the first time that the country had heard the emperor's voice. In the past, the emperor was considered to hold god-like status, and to allow his subjects to hear his voice, even for events and announcements like his coronation (A), his wedding (B), and declarations of war C) and (E), would bring him down to the level of a human being.

The fact that the emperor himself read the notice of surrender reinforced the completeness of Japan's defeat. They were no longer an imperial power, and their emperor was no longer a deity.

6.   **(A)** In 1415 the Portuguese captured Ceuta, one of the first of a series of bases they were to take along the African coast. This marks the first incident of European colonial aggression on the African continent. Portugal's interests in Africa were to find a sea route to India, to explore trade possibilities in the continent (which later developed into a trans-Atlantic trade in slaves), to convert the people of Africa to Catholicism, and to assess the strength of the Moslem enemy. By 1640, when Ceuta passed to the Spanish, other European powers had already entered Africa for the same reasons as Portugal. While Belgium (B), England (C), France (D), and Germany (E) all eventually had colonial holdings in Africa, the door was opened up by Portugal (A).

7.   **(C)** Sociology studies human interaction, both in small groups and in larger settings, and the results of that interaction such as groups, organizations, institutions, and nations. Social problems (A) are only a part of the subject matter of sociology. Human personality (B) and human development (D) are more often studied by psychologists. Attitudes and values (E) are only a part of the subject matter of sociology.

8.   **(D)** The Industrial Revolution in Europe brought about the decline of traditional agricultural societies and the rapid growth of cities. The social dislocations that resulted from this change stimulated thinkers to consider the nature of social order and social change, and the outcome was the emergence of sociology as a separate discipline. Socialism (A) was another result of this change, but socialism as a movement for political change was separate from the discipline of sociology. (B) is incorrect because early sociologists were little concerned about the spread of colonialism during this period. While the founders of sociology were interested in the study of social inequality, they did little to promote greater equality; therefore, (C) is incorrect. (E) is incorrect because psychology developed as a separate discipline somewhat later than sociology.

9.   **(D)** In *The Protestant Ethic and the Spirit of Capitalism* Weber studied the influence of the religious changes of the Reformation on the growth of capitalism in Europe. *Street Corner Society* (A) is by William F. Whyte. *The Division of Labor in Society* (B) is by Emile Durkheim. *The*

Human Group (C) is by George C. Homans. *The Theory of the Leisure Class* (E) is by Thorstein Veblen.

10. **(B)** In his study of suicide, Durkheim explained how the decline of social solidarity in modern society has led to the growth of anomie (normlessness) and associated social problems such as suicide. Class conflict (A) is most closely associated with the work of Karl Marx. Rationalization (C) is most closely associated with the work of Max Weber. (D) is incorrect because Durkheim devoted relatively little attention to social mobility. The theory of reference groups (E) was developed long after Durkheim's death.

11. **(C)** Marx concluded that conflict between workers and owners was an intrinsic feature of capitalist societies. Since Marx saw this conflict as the principal reason for social change, (D) is incorrect. He also believed this conflict would intensify over time and result in a socialist revolution, so (A) is also incorrect. (B) is incorrect because Marx felt this conflict would ultimately benefit society instead of harming it.

12. **(A)** Survey research is based on data gathered by personal interviews or written questionnaires administered to a random sample of a larger population. Participant observation (B) involves observing people interacting in natural settings. Content analysis (C) involves the analysis of the content of communications such as television, advertising, letters, or textbooks. Experimentation (D) involves manipulation of an experimental stimulus on an experimental group and withholding that stimulus from a control group. Exploratory research (E) employs no specific methodology.

13. **(E)** Reinforcement theory has proven that reinforcement is most effective if it occurs immediately after a task has been performed. End-of-the-year bonuses or quarterly reviews may not be as effective as immediate bonuses. Investigation of optimal schedules of reinforcement is ongoing and diverse; both negative and positive reinforcement schedules have been shown to be quite effective on worker productivity and satisfaction.

14. **(B)** A writ of habeas corpus is a court order which directs an official who is detaining someone to produce the person before the court so that the legality of the detention may be determined. The primary function of the writ is to effect the release of someone who has been imprisoned without due process of law. For example, if the police detained a suspect for an unreasonable time without officially charging the person

with a crime, the person could seek relief from a court in the form of a writ of habeas corpus. (A) is incorrect because a writ of mandamus is a court order commanding an official to perform a legal duty of his or her office. It is not used to prevent persons from being improperly imprisoned. The Fourth Amendment requirement that police have probable cause in order to obtain a search warrant regulates police procedure. It is not itself a mechanism for effecting release of a person for improper imprisonment, so (C) is incorrect. Choice (D) is incorrect since the decision in *Roe v. Wade* dealt with a woman's right to have an abortion. It had nothing to do with improper imprisonment. Choice (E) is incorrect since the prohibition against ex post facto laws is not a mechanism for effecting the release of someone who is improperly imprisoned. Rather, it declares that changing the legal implications of an act, after the act has been committed, is improper.

15.   **(A)**   is the best answer since the term "casework" is used by political scientists to describe the activities of congressmen on behalf of individual constituents. These activities might include helping an elderly person secure Social Security benefits, or helping a veteran obtain medical services. Most casework is actually done by congressional staff and may take as much as a third of the staff's time. Congressmen supply this type of assistance for the good public relations it provides. Choice (B) fails because pork barrel legislation is rarely, if ever, intended to help individual citizens. Pork barrel legislation authorizes federal spending for special projects, such as airports, roads, or dams, in the home state or district of a congressman. It is meant to help the entire district or state. Also, there is no legal entitlement on the part of a citizen to a pork barrel project, such as there is with Social Security benefits. (C) is not the answer because lobbying is an activity directed toward congressmen, not one done by congressmen. A lobbyist attempts to get congressmen to support legislation that will benefit the group which the lobbyist represents. Logrolling (D) is incorrect because it does not refer to congressional service for constituents. It refers instead to the congressional practice of trading votes on different bills. Congressman A will vote for congressman B's pork barrel project and in return B will vote for A's pork barrel project. Filibustering (E) is incorrect. It is a technique used in the Senate to postpone a vote on a piece of legislation. The Senate has a tradition of unlimited debate and nongermane debate. This means that a senator may hold the floor for as long as (s)he likes and need not confine his/her remarks to the bill under consideration. Senators opposing a bill might get control of the floor and talk until the supporters agree to withdraw the bill from consideration.

16.　**(C)**　The franking privilege is the right of congressmen to send mail to constituents at public expense. Challengers do not enjoy this privilege. Observers have noticed that the amount of free congressional mail increases during election years, as members try to keep their names before their constituents. Choice (A) is incorrect since incumbent congressmen certainly do not have access to unlimited campaign funds. Congressmen may spend as much of their own money as they wish, and they are free to raise money from contributors. But no candidate has unlimited personal funds, nor can incumbents raise unlimited funds from contributions. Choice (B) is incorrect because incumbents and challengers may both have access to national party employees as campaign workers. Both political parties have campaign committees for the House and Senate. All of the committees supply campaign managers, communications directors, and fund-raising experts to challengers and incumbents during election campaigns. (D) is incorrect because the Federal Election Campaign Act of 1974 placed a limit of $1,000 per election on individual contributions to political candidates. This put an end to so-called "fat cat" contributors who used to contribute vast sums to candidates. (E) is incorrect because the federal government does not finance any aspect of congressional campaigns.

17.　**(C)**　is correct. Despite the fact that it comprises leading wheat-producing regions, the former Soviet Union, or CIS, is the only entity that is in the top three in having to *import* extra grain in all three categories, including wheat.

18.　**(A)**　The United States is the only nation listed that is not only an importer but also listed in two categories as a top producer.

19.　**(D)**　is least correct. The American farmer has traditionally had government assistance available in the form of loan programs, subsidies, price supports, and tariff protection. (A) and (C) are natural assets that American farmers have enjoyed. (B) and (E) have made American farms more efficient and cost effective.

20.　**(A)**　Contrary to myth, Confederate industry did a masterful job in producing weapons and ammunition for the Confederate military during the war. While it is true that the Confederates never had the abundance of weapons possessed by Union forces, particularly in artillery, it was only near the end of the war, when Union forces had overrun many production centers and totally destroyed the South's transportation network, that severe shortages of ammunition and weapons developed. It is also true that at the start of the war, Confederate industry could not arm everyone who volunteered for military service; the Union had that same problem. Most Southerners had their own weapons so that despite the lack of government-produced weapons, there was no shortage of available weapons for soldiers. The biggest problem faced by the Confederate armies in regard to weapons and ammunition was a lack of uniformity for the vast array of "home grown" weapons and ammunition used by their soldiers, not a shortage of weapons themselves.

21.   **(B)** The national unemployment rate soared to approximately 25 percent of the work force in early 1933. This meant that approximately 13 million workers were unemployed. While 25 percent was the national unemployment rate, in some cities the number of unemployed approached 90 percent. This was at a time when there were no welfare benefits or unemployment funds in most areas of the country. What made things worse was the sheer amount of time workers remained unemployed. By early 1937, unemployment had fallen to 14.3 percent, still representing 8 million unemployed workers. Then the recession of 1937 put an additional 2 million workers out of work again. The suffering of being unemployed as long as many of these workers is beyond description. Hobo camps and "Hoovervilles" popped up in virtually every American city.

   Worse, even for those who kept their jobs, poverty became widespread. Crop prices for farmers dropped by 60 percent. Wages, for workers who still had jobs, dropped 40 percent. Banks continued to collapse, taking the personal savings of depositors down with them, leaving depositors with no savings to help them through this period. So, while 25 percent may not sound catastrophic at first, combined with the collapse of wages and crop prices, as well as the collapse of banks and the sheer amount of time many people were out of work, the nation's economy was close to total collapse.

22.   **(C)** The St. Bartholomew's Day Massacre in Paris of French Calvinists, often termed "Huguenots," led to a civil war in France (the War of the Three Henries) and the first Bourbon monarch (Henry IV). When dealing with questions based on illustrations (paintings or drawings), it is important to look for explicit details or other information in the question and in the illustration itself, since it is usually not possible to arrive at a correct answer by eliminating answers. The clues in this case are in the question rather than in the painting. If the primary clue is not sufficient ("St. Bartholomew's Day"), there is a secondary clue in the obviously French name of the painter. Do not be misled by the use of the term "French Calvinists" instead of the name "Huguenots," which is the term

usually used by textbook writers; the use of the term "French Calvinists" is another detail testing your knowledge and understanding of European history.

23.   **(A)**   At first glance this question appears to test only the memorization of facts, but another look will show that it also requires understanding of the diplomatic situation in Europe around 1920. The correct answer may require some thought, since there was no political division of Germany into two governments, as happened at the end of World War II. The "division of Germany into two parts" refers to the "Polish Corridor," created by the peacemakers in order to give Poland an "outlet to the sea." The "Polish Corridor," a strip of formerly German land ceded to Poland in order to provide access to the port city of Danzig, isolated eastern Prussia from the remainder of Germany. It may be possible to arrive at the correct answer by analyzing the other four answers and eliminating them; each is untrue. The end of World War I brought the final collapse of the Ottoman Empire and its reduction to the borders of modern Turkey. The newly Communist government of Russia, which came to power in 1917, was ostracized by the other great powers when the war ended. Choice (D) may be tempting because the United States left large numbers of troops in Europe after World War II. This question refers to World War I, however. The United States withdrew from Europe both militarily and diplomatically after that war, preferring to return to "normalcy." Under the terms of the Treaty of Versailles, Germany was required to pay reparations.

24.   **(C)**   Aime Cesaire was a poet from Martinique (in the West Indies). Although poetry and political writing have been widely influential for writers and thinkers like Franz Fanon, Cesaire has never been the leader of an African country. (A) Kwame Nkrumah was the prime minister of Ghana, (B) Jomo Kenyatta was president of Kenya, (D) Julius Nyerere was president of Tanzania, and (E) Patrice Lumumba was prime minister of the Congo.

25.   **(A)**   When Beijing students chose to hold a protest for the democracy movement in Tiananmen Square, they were making reference to the May 4 Movement of 1919. On this day, students in Beijing demonstrated in Tiananmen Square in protest of the Treaty of Versailles, ending World War I, which denied China all of its demands for return of territory held by foreigners. The demonstrations led to strikes by students and workers, and as a result, the Chinese delegation at Versailles refused to sign the treaty.

26. **(D)** A statistical relationship in which high values in one variable (economic development) are associated with low values in another variable (birth rate) is known as a negative or inverse correlation. Plotting the data points on a graph would produce a line with a downward (negative) slope. A positive correlation (A) is one in which high values in one variable are associated with high values in another variable. A spurious correlation (B) is one in which the apparent relationship between two variables is really due to a third variable. There is no such thing as a circular correlation (C) or a reverse correlation (E).

27. **(E)** Functionalism stresses the interdependence among parts of a society, pointing out how changes in one part of a social system will have consequences for other parts of that system. Economic development (A), class conflict (B), human communication (C), and intellectual creativity (D) are found in all human societies, but are not especially stressed in functionalist theory.

28. **(A)** Upward social mobility involves an individual improving his or her social status, i.e., moving from a lower class to a higher class. Going from a farm worker's home to the White House involves considerable upward mobility. The other examples involve children staying at the same status as their parents' or, in the case of the professor's son, downward mobility.

29. **(A)** The prestige of one's occupation is one of the most valid and reliable indicators of a person's status in industrial societies. Of course, there are exceptions, e.g., retired persons. The other answers may have some relation to social status, but none are as consistently or as strongly linked to a person's socioeconomic status.

30. **(D)** For sociologists, occupation is an essential feature that distinguishes the social classes. Working-class individuals hold blue-collar jobs. Middle-class individuals hold white-collar jobs. The other answers may be true of some middle-class families, but they would not be true of all.

31. **(E)** Birth rates tend to be higher in lower-class families than in other social classes. All of the other statements are supported by research findings.

32. **(A)** Experiments with children, in which they were rewarded for imitating a model, formed the basis of Miller and Dollard's conclusions

concerning learning from model imitation. They concluded that imitation of social behavior probably derives strength from the fact that conformist behavior is rewarded in many situations, whereas nonconformist behavior often results in punishment.

33.   **(E)**   The correct response is (E), since major differences between procedures in the House and Senate include all three of the features mentioned. Because the size of the House is fairly large, with 435 members, time for debate must be limited. If each member was allowed to speak as long as (s)he wanted on every bill, the House could not complete all of its business. Also, debate in the House must be germane. That is, when a member rises to speak, his/her comments must be related to the subject under consideration. This is another time-saving mechanism. The Senate has only 100 members and is not as rushed for time as the House. The Senate has traditionally allowed members to speak as long as they wish and does not force them to confine their remarks to the subject at hand. In the House, the rules committee is very powerful. No bill may get to the House floor without a rule from the rules committee. The rule gives the conditions for debate. The rule sets the time limit for debate and states whether and on what conditions the bill can be amended. The rules committee in the Senate has no such powers.

34.   **(D)**   In *McCulloch v. Maryland* (1819), the Supreme Court struck down a Maryland law which levied a tax on the Baltimore branch of the Bank of the United States. The Court's ruling was based on its interpretation of the "necessary and proper clause" of the Constitution. This clause may be found in Article I, section 8, of the Constitution. The Court ruled that the necessary and proper clause gives to Congress all powers which make it more convenient for Congress to carry out the enumerated powers of Article I, section 8. (Enumerated powers are those which are specifically mentioned.) The clause is also known as the "elastic clause" since the Court ruled that it gives unspecified powers to Congress. The Court's ruling gave the broadest possible interpretation to the clause, making it possible for Congress to do many things which are not specifically mentioned in the Constitution. By contrast, the Court could have ruled that the clause gave Congress only those powers which are absolutely indispensable to carrying out the enumerated powers. Such a narrow interpretation of the clause would have limited Congress to those activities without which it could not possibly carry out the enumerated powers. (A) is incorrect since *McCulloch v. Maryland* did not deal with freedom of speech. Choice (B) fails because the power of judicial review (the right of the

Court to strike down laws of Congress and to review the actions of the executive) was claimed by the Court in *Marbury v. Madison,* 1803. (C) is incorrect since the Court had previously struck down a law of Congress in *Marbury v. Madison.* Finally, (E) is incorrect because *McCulloch v. Maryland* had nothing to do with the question of executive privilege.

35.　**(B)**　The question asks which statement about the cabinet is false. Choice (B) is false, and, therefore, the correct answer. The Constitution states in Article I, section 6, that no person holding any office under the United States may be a member of Congress. Since cabinet positions are offices under the United States, cabinet officials may not be members of Congress. Choices (A) and (D) are true. The cabinet includes the heads of each of the 14 executive departments (State, Treasury, Interior, etc.) as stated in (A). In addition, the president may appoint any other high ranking official whom he wishes to the cabinet, as stated in (D). Choice (C) is true. President Washington was the first to hold cabinet meetings. Every president since Washington has used the cabinet as a tool for managing the federal bureaucracy. So choice (C) is not the correct answer. Choice (E) is not the correct choice. As we saw in the explanation for choice (B), the Constitution states that no one holding office under the United States may be a member of Congress. This means that senators may not be members of the cabinet.

36.　**(A)**　is not a proper conclusion because it is an opinion. The facts from the graph may be used to try to prove the need to cut transportation oil consumption, but the graph itself makes no conclusions. (B) This is true if the average of Germany, Italy, France, and Great Britain is used. (C) Since the United States and Canada top the chart, this is true. (D) This is true, with 25 percent. (E) is true with about 8 percent.

37.　**(C)**　This cannot be a conclusion from the graphs, which are per person. Also, Canada, ranking second, has the smallest population on the list. (A) This could be a conclusion because the two largest nations are also the top two consumers. (B) Since four of the top seven consumers are European, this is true. (D) Japan is the only Asian nation listed. (E) This is a probable conclusion, especially when the quantity used for manufacturing in the United States is used as an indicator.

38.　**(D)**　This is no longer true. Today's industry is divided between many private and nationalized companies. (A) The supply of petroleum is limited and exhaustible. (B) Oil is the key ingredient in plastics. (C) Prices and supply are very sensitive to many conditions. (E) Oil supplies and prices are affected by conditions all over the world with many producers.

39.   **(B)** The Navigation Acts were designed to force the colonies to trade exclusively with England and to give the British government extensive regulatory control over all colonial trade. All of the choices except choice (B) were major principles of these acts. The prohibition of the colonies from issuing paper currencies, while also having a major impact on colonial trade, was the focal point of the Currency Act of 1764 (approximately 100 years later than the Navigation Acts).

40.   **(A)** Slavery never effectively established itself in New England, in large part because the economic system of the New England colonies and the large population of New England, which provided a large pool of workers, rendered the need for large numbers of slaves unnecessary. Most New England farms were relatively small, self-sufficient farms, and the members of farming communities depended on each other to keep their communities economically viable. In the Southern English colonies, there was less community cohesion among the colonists, there were fewer people, and there was a constant demand for laborers to cultivate the cash crops necessary to keep the colonies economically afloat. At first this demand was met by the use of indentured servants, but after the 1660s the supply of potential servants dwindled and the only immediate replacement labor pool was imported slave labor.

41.   **(E)** This question is partly knowledge-based, but it also requires an understanding of the principles of Christian Humanism and an ability to analyze what ideas they would disapprove, (A) and (C), and approve, (E). Renaissance Humanism, also known as Christian Humanism, combined studies of ancient languages with a zeal to make the Scriptures available in the local languages. Virtually all Christian Humanists translated portions of the Scriptures into European languages, using the Latin text which was the sole version available during the Middle Ages. Very few Christian Humanists were connected with the Reformation; the most famous of them, Erasmus of Rotterdam, criticized laxness within the Catholic church but refused to join with the Protestant reformers.

42.   **(D)** Although the tsar's manifesto succeeded in calming and ending the Revolution of 1905, the document's promises of reforms contained a loophole: no mention was made of election procedures for the promised Duma, or parliament. When Nicholas II called the Duma into session after the revolution of 1905, he instituted voting procedures which gave consid-

erably heavier representation to the wealthy and to districts around Moscow, which were considered the most loyal to the government.

43.   **(B)** Pakistan, which includes parts of the Punjab, was carved from India in 1947. All of the other choices, Thailand (A), India (C), Korea (D), and Vietnam (E), existed as independent countries before 1947, though because of the partition, India's borders and political situation changed significantly after 1947. It is worthwhile to note that Pakistan, as created in 1947, was later split apart by the secession of Bangladesh in 1971.

44.   **(B)** The British policy of indirect rule in Africa was designed to reduce tensions and minimize financial costs. It included flexibility and a minimum of direct British intervention. For this reason, the British tried to adapt their colonial policies to fit the wide variety of native systems in and between countries, and they did not want a tribal uniform policy (D), which would have been more rigid. Instead they modified the role of traditional rulers in local areas (E) and relied on a decentralized administration (C). The goal for these colonies was eventual self-rule (B), and for this reason they supported basic primary education for Africans which would equip them for this eventuality (A).

45.   **(B)** The Glorious Revolution of 1688-89 did not result in an agreement that in the event of no heirs, the Hanover house would succeed the Stuarts. Such an arrangement was specified in the Act of Succession of 1701, a year before William III's death and the succession of Queen Anne. She outlived all her children. Upon her death in 1714, George I became the first Hanoverian King of England.

46.   **(B)** Cultural diffusion is the spread of an idea, a fashion, or a technology from one culture to another. Blue jeans and rock-and-roll music originated in the United States and have now spread to most other nations of the world. Cultural discovery (C) and cultural innovation (D) imply the appearance of something unique or original. Cultural decline (A) and cultural disintegration (E) imply the destruction of previous cultural traits.

47.   **(C)** A stereotype is a simplified image of personal characteristics (usually negative) which is applied to all members of a group. Affirmative action (A) involves giving preference or special consideration to members of minority groups. Reverse racism (B) involves discrimination against members of dominant or majority groups. Status inconsistency (D) refers to individuals who rank high in one measure of social status and low in

another (e.g., a Ph.D. who drives a taxi). Role conflict (E) refers to individuals who occupy multiple roles with contradictory expectations.

48. **(E)** Davis and Moore hypothesized that high rewards are necessary to motivate individuals to complete the long periods of training required for some occupations, such as physician. This theory does not consider factors such as seniority (A), unionization (B), physical labor (C), or appeal to values (D).

49. **(E)** Demography is the study of the growth (A), composition (D), distribution (B), and migration (C) of human populations. Socialization is not usually studied by demographers.

50. **(B)** Agents of socialization teach social norms and values to children and adults. Parents (C), peers (D), and teachers (E) impart social norms directly to young people. Television (A) is also an important medium for teaching norms and values. Occupations such as banking do not involve the teaching of norms and values as part of their primary responsibilities.

51. **(B)** Conditioned, or secondary, reinforcement occurs when the reinforcing stimulus is not inherently pleasing or reinforcing, but becomes so through association with other pleasant or reinforcing stimuli. Money is an example of a secondary (conditioned) reinforcer. Coins and paper currency are not in themselves pleasing, but the things they buy are pleasing. Therefore, an association is made between money and inherently pleasing primary reinforcers, such as food and drink. Hence, the term "conditioned reinforcer" is used.

52. **(A)** The Federal Reserve Board is a government agency consisting of seven members appointed for 14-year terms by the president, with the consent of the Senate. This board is at the head of the Federal Reserve System, which is comprised of member banks across the country. The primary function of the Federal Reserve Board is to implement monetary policy. The Federal Reserve Board has three methods of implementing monetary policy. First, it can change the reserve requirement, which is the amount of cash that member banks must keep on deposit in a regional Federal Reserve Bank. An increase in the requirement reduces the amount of cash a bank has on hand to loan. Second, the board can change the discount rate, which is the interest rate that member banks must pay to

borrow money from a Federal Reserve Bank. A higher rate discourages a member bank from borrowing and lending more money. Third, the board can buy and sell government securities. To increase the money supply, the board sells securities. To decrease the money supply, the board buys securities. Choice (B) is the most plausible alternative to (A), but fails because controlling government spending is a function of Congress and the president. Choice (C) is incorrect because the Federal Reserve Board has nothing to do with regulating commodity prices. Choice (D) is incorrect because the board does not help the president run the executive branch. Choice (E) is incorrect because the board does not keep records of troop strength in army reserve units.

53. **(C)** The three largest countries of Western Europe – the United Kingdom, France, and the Federal Republic of Germany – have either a multi-party system or a two-plus party system. A multi-party system is one in which three or more major parties compete for seats in the national legislature, while a two-plus party system has two large parties and one or more small parties. The United Kingdom has a two-plus party system. There are two large parties, the Conservatives and Labour. The Liberals are a smaller third party and there are even smaller regional parties in Scotland, Northern Ireland, and Wales. France has a multi-party system. The Socialists, Neo-Gaullists, and Republicans are major parties, while the Communists and the National Front are small parties with few seats in parliament. The Federal Republic of Germany has a two-plus party system. The major parties are the Christian Democratic Union and the Social Democratic party. At the fringes of public life are the Greens and the Neo-Nazis. The United States, by contrast, has only two parties, which successfully compete on a national basis from one election to the next. These are, of course, the Democrats and the Republicans. Choice (A) is incorrect. In Western European countries, party leaders determine which persons will run for office under the party banner. In the United States, on the other hand, candidates for office are selected by the voters in primary elections. Sometimes in the United States a candidate whom the party leadership detests wins the primary, and thus the right to run for office under the party banner. In most Western European countries, political parties are much more centralized than in the United States; therefore, (B) is false. Choice (D) is false. Because the parties are centralized in Western Europe, and because party leaders select candidates for national office, a party member in the national legislature seldom votes against the party. If one did, party leaders would remove his or her name from the ballot in future elections. Choice (E) is incorrect. Since party members vote the party line almost all of the time in Western Europe, voters tend to not focus on the

personalities of candidates, but rather on the party label. In the United States, where legislators vote their personal preference as often as the party line, party label is less important to voters. Voters in the United States tend to focus more on the personalities of candidates than European voters.

54.   **(D)**   In a parliamentary system the chief executive, normally called the prime minister, is a member of parliament, the legislative body. The majority party in the lower house of the parliament selects its leader to be prime minister. The prime minister then selects a cabinet from among the members of the lower house who are in his/her party. The prime minister and cabinet are the highest executive officers of the country and are usually referred to as the government. There is no strict separation of powers, since the executive branch is made up of members of the legislature. In a presidential system, by contrast, the president is not a member of the legislature and is selected by popular, not by legislative vote. Cabinet members may not sit in the legislature. There is, then, a strict separation of powers, and Statement I is true. In a presidential system, the voters choose the president either by direct popular vote or through an electoral college. In a parliamentary system, the majority party in the lower house of parliament chooses one of its members as prime minister. The general public does not participate in choosing the prime minister. So Statement II is also true. In a parliamentary system the prime minister may call special elections for the lower house of the legislature whenever (s)he wants. In a presidential system the president may not call a special election for members of the legislature, so III is false. The answer, then, is (D), I and II only.

55.   **(A)**   is taken to task and it is stated that they should be limited. All other groups are called upon to band together to help the environment.

56.   **(D)**   These are obvious references to the past use of the environment for economic purposes rather than environmental concerns. (A) and (B) are moral statements, not economic ones. (C) This is a call to action. (E) This tries to redefine society's values.

57.   **(E)**   This is a political, cost concern. Coal is more polluting than oil. (A) This is now used to sell products, changing packaging, and is becoming profitable. (B) This is an attempt to replace trees as a renewable resource. (C) Repair and replacement of topsoil, erosion control, and replanting are attempts to reuse mined areas for agriculture. (D) Concern

over this has changed products' chemical contents and created new laws to reduce airborne pollution.

58.   **(D)**   In early 1942, the Japanese high command, angered at air raids from American aircraft carriers, decided to force what was left of the American Pacific fleet into a decisive battle in which the American Navy and its carriers would be destroyed. They decided on an invasion of the American-held island of Midway. Midway was a logical choice. It was 1,100 miles northwest of Hawaii. More importantly, it had a seaplane base and an airstrip. In American hands it provided the United States with an observation post to monitor Japanese actions throughout the central Pacific. In Japanese hands, it would provide them with an airbase from which they could launch continuous air attacks on Pearl Harbor, making it unusable as an American base. If Japan invaded Midway, the Americans would have to send their fleet to defend it or face the loss of Pearl Harbor and Hawaii.

On paper, the plan seemed ideal. The Japanese could throw up to 10 aircraft carriers into the operation. They believed the Americans had only two available aircraft carriers (actually, the Americans had three usable carriers because the USS *Yorktown,* which the Japanese thought they had sunk at the Battle of Coral Sea, had survived and was repaired in time to fight at Midway). The Japanese had dozens of battleships and heavy cruisers. The Americans had only two battleships available, which they chose not to use, and only eight heavy cruisers. On paper, there seemed to be no way the Americans could win.

Unfortunately for the Japanese, the battle was not fought on paper. American cryptographers deciphered enough Japanese messages to uncover the plan. In addition, the overconfident Japanese, expecting to surprise a scattered American fleet, didn't concentrate their forces into an overwhelming single attack force. Instead they divided their fleet into four separate attack forces, each of which was vulnerable to American attack if caught off guard. When the Japanese arrived at Midway, a well-prepared, tightly concentrated American fleet was waiting. Despite a series of nearly catastrophic errors, the Americans caught the Japanese by surprise, sinking four of their largest aircraft carriers and killing 600 of Japan's best pilots. Without adequate air protection, the invasion was cancelled and the Japanese fleet returned to base. Midway was saved. At the time, American analysts thought they had just bought the United States some additional time until the Japanese regrouped and attacked again. In reality, the Japanese were so stunned by the defeat that they readjusted their war plans, switching to defensive operations. They never returned to Midway. With the Japanese now on the defensive, the United States was able to seize the initiative at Guadalcanal, beginning an island-hopping campaign that took America to Japan's outer islands. Midway was undoubtedly the turning point as it marked the first significant American victory over the Japanese and the end of major Japanese offensive operations in the central Pacific.

59. **(E)** *Brown v. Board of Education of Topeka* was the first legal shot in the war to desegregate America's public schools. Up to this time, many school districts, particularly in the South, had segregated schools for black and white schoolchildren under the doctrine of "separate but equal" education. Sadly, most education facilities for black children were anything but equal. Blacks usually got dilapidated facilities, the worst teachers, and an inferior education. Frustrated black parents challenged the "separate but equal" doctrine in several states, and those challenges were consolidated into one case to be presented before the United States Supreme Court in 1954. Up until this case, previous civil rights cases had been heard before conservative Supreme Courts which had upheld the "separate but equal" doctrine. However, by 1954, the Court was a more liberal court, more sensitive to constitutional protections for all people.

60. **(C)** While this question calls for fact retention, it also requires an ability to analyze the implications of their policies – unless the answer is apparent upon first reading. The first monarchs of a united Spain, Ferdinand and Isabella, achieved that unity by gaining control of the remaining Muslim sections of southern Spain. In an effort to promote cultural unity and establish a national identity, they defined Spanish nationalism in terms of their understanding of orthodox Catholicism. Those not fitting their definition of orthodoxy were condemned as disloyal or subversive. Two particular groups, Jews and Muslims who had converted to Christianity but retained Muslim customs or dress, were forced into exile by Spanish authorities.

61. **(C)** The diversity of monarchs listed in the choices should indicate that guessing is a possibility. Two were devout Catholics (D) and (E), while a third (A) predates the Reformation by almost 200 years. During the Thirty Years' War, when Catholic forces from southern Germany and Austria were close to pushing Lutheran forces into the Baltic sea, the Lutheran convert Gustavus Adolphus intervened in Germany, saving the Lutheran cause. Adolphus was himself killed during a key battle.

62. **(D)** As a result of the Spanish-American War in 1898, the United States gained control of the Philippines from Spain. The Philippines re-

mained a U.S. territory until the Tydings-McDuffie Act of 1934 provided for its independence. This independence was not realized until 1945. Today, however, Spanish influence, mostly in the shape of religion, language, and culture, is still felt, as is America's presence in the form of military bases (just recently closed in the early 1990s) and popular culture.

63.   **(D)**   Swaziland, a former British colony, has been called Swaziland both before and after its independence. Malawi is a separate independent country, and the other choices, (A), (B), (C) and (E), are all the former and present names of countries in Africa.

64.   **(D)**   Durkheim found that people with few social attachments (i.e., single people) tend to commit suicide more frequently. Men (A), old people (B), wealthy people (C), and Protestants (E) all have higher suicide rates.

65.   **(B)**   Durkheim used the term altruistic suicide to refer to people who commit suicide because of their intense sense of loyalty to a group. Egoistic suicide (A) refers to people who kill themselves for selfish, personal reasons. Anomic suicide (D) refers to people killing themselves because they lack clear moral guidelines. Intrinsic suicide (C) and euphoric suicide (E) are not terms that Durkheim used.

Section 2

66.   **(D)**   Participant observation involves a researcher interacting with and observing the personal lives of the research subjects. Survey research (A) gathers data from subjects using questionnaires or interviews. Experimentation (B) involves a researcher manipulating an experimental stimulus, usually in a laboratory setting. Content analysis (C) involves the study of communication products such as books, letters, advertising, or television programs. Strategic engagement (E) is not a method used in social research.

67.   **(D)**   The independent variable produces an effect or change in the dependent variable. In this case, gender is hypothesized to cause a difference in academic averages. Athletic participation (A) and college attendance (B) are not variables in this hypothesis since they are the same for both groups. Academic achievement (C) is the dependent variable. Study habits (E) may help to explain the difference between men and women, but it has not been stated in this hypothesis.

68.   **(E)**   Culture consists of the shared products of human interaction, both material and nonmaterial. An individual's intelligence is the result of personal development and genetic inheritance. Because intelligence may vary greatly among individuals, it is not shared among members of a society.

69.   **(E)**   Ethnocentrism is the practice of placing a high value on one's own culture and demeaning all cultures that differ from it. Shared cultural traits such as language (A) and religion (D) do not constitute ethnocentrism. Working for common goals (B) and showing respect for the elderly (C) also have nothing to do with the concept ethnocentrism.

70.   **(B)**   Rehearsal serves two functions. It allows items in short-term memory to be retained. Also, it appears to facilitate material from the short-term to long-term memory. In transference of most contents, rehearsal is necessary for learning.

71.   **(C)**   Political scientists use the term "pluralistic" to describe a political system in which innumerable groups of people share cultural, economic, religious, or ethnic interests. These groups organize and spend great amounts of time and money competing to influence government policy-making. The pluralistic concept of democracy is in contrast to the elitist model, which states that policy-making is dominated by elites such as wealthy industrialists, military leaders, or organizations such as the Trilateral Commission. Therefore, the answer is (C). Choice (A) fails because pluralism stresses not only cultural groups but economic, religious, and other types of groups. Also important to pluralism is the idea that the different groups do not merely exist but compete to influence public policy-making. Choice (B) fails because the term to describe a system in which political power is divided between national and state governments is "federalism." Choice (D) fails because to say that one group is overrepresented is more like an elitist view than a pluralistic view of politics. It is true that candidates for national office are elected by a plurality vote method (E). "Plurality vote" means that the candidate who gets the most votes, even if less than a majority, wins the election. However, the term "pluralism" does not refer to this method of election, so choice (E) is wrong.

72.   **(A)**   As the graph on the next page shows, there is a direct correlation between voter turnout and educational level. Those with four years or more of college are more likely to vote than are those with one to three years of college. Those with one to three years of college are more likely

to vote than are high school graduates. High school graduates are, in turn, more likely to vote than are those with less than a high school education. The answer is (A), the more schooling one has, the more likely one is to vote. Voting is only one form of political participation. Other forms are running for office, working in political campaigns, and contributing to campaigns. While it is difficult to find statistics which show the correlation between educational status and running for office, we do know that most people who are completely inactive (that is, do not participate in politics in any way) typically have little education and low incomes and are relatively young. Therefore, it is safe to conclude that the less education one has (B), the LESS likely one is to run for office; so (B) is not the answer. Choice (C) is clearly wrong, since many studies have shown a direct correlation between advanced educational status and political participation by voting. Choice (D) is wrong, as is clear from the graph below. Those with a high school education are NOT more likely to vote than are those with a college degree. Choice (E) is wrong because, as the graph shows, the less education one has, the less likely one is to vote. It is logical to infer from this that those with no formal schooling are less likely to vote than are those with a high school education.

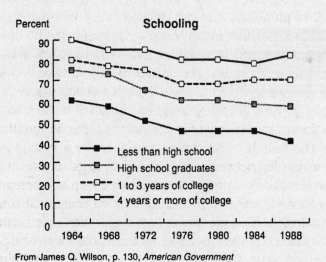

From James Q. Wilson, p. 130, *American Government*

73.   **(E)**   Articulating interests is generally thought of as the special task of interest groups. Parties, on the other hand, bring together or "aggregate" interests (B) in order to create a working majority to run government.

Parties also play a significant role in recruiting candidates (A), serving as channels of communication (C), and staffing elections (D).

74. **(C)** Although the chart can be used for several of the choices, it is a simplified version of the Business Cycle. (A) The chart does not refer to "bust" or depression. (B) and (D) Changes are shown, but not causes. (E) If you added data, such as dates, it could be used to track historical fluctuations, but doesn't in this form.

75. **(D)** This may influence the other factors, but can have a variety of effects and is not part of the purely economic picture. (A) The number of people employed is used to define whether we are in a recession or not. (B) Obviously directly related to (A), it also shows prosperity, if products are in demand. (C) Personal earnings rise with an economic boom and help sustain it with spending. (E) This is an important indicator of income, production, and consumer confidence in the economy.

76. **(C)** is the most counterproductive to economic growth because it takes money out of spending circulation and reduces sales. (A) is usually not planned, but has been credited with helping the economy as a side effect because of the increased need for services and products. (B) Keynesian economics calls for "pump-priming" of the economy through government spending to employ people and increase production. (D) Supply-side economics contends that reducing government regulation frees up capital to create products and jobs. (E) This is often used as a short-term solution to help specific industries, such as the auto industry in the early 1980s. Long-term use may trigger international retaliation and create worse problems.

77. **(A)** The Great Awakening was a series of religious awakenings, or rebirths, centered primarily in New England but spread throughout the colonies, which changed the lives of English colonists. It challenged the old hierarchical religious order in which ordained clergy were deferred to and were believed to have knowledge based on extensive formal learning that the average member of a congregation lacked. It brought a much broader sense of community to colonists making them aware of others with similar questions and beliefs who lived outside their village or town. In many ways, it was the first of a series of events that helped to forge distinctively American regional identities, separate from their European heritage, among the North American colonists.

78.   **(B)**   There were many major changes resulting from the rapid industrial development in the United States from 1860 through 1900. First, there was a shift to building larger and larger industrial facilities to accommodate the new machine technologies coming into existence. Small factories could not absorb the cost of much of the machinery and did not produce enough to make the machinery profitable. So contrary to choice (D), there was an increase in large industrial plants and a relative decline in small factories.

79.   **(C)**   Choices (B) and (C) are opposites; high inflation almost always affects the value of a country's currency. If you recognize this conflict, it will become apparent that one of these two answers is the correct answer. If necessary, it is worthwhile guessing, since your odds are 50 percent and only 0.25 point is deducted for an incorrect guess.

80.   **(B)**   On the map several areas of Europe are depicted with dark shading. These areas are the lands controlled by the Hapsburgs in the sixteenth century. Choice (C) is incorrect, since Spain was lost by the Hapsburgs in the 1600s. A further clue: the large size of the Ottoman Empire, covering the entire Balkan peninsula, precludes any answer after about 1870.

81.   **(E)**   In 1914 only Ethiopia, along with Liberia, remained an independent state. (A) Algeria belonged to France; (B) the Congo was Belgian; (C) Angola was occupied by the Portuguese; and (D) Egypt was under British control.

82.   **(B)**   Thailand is bordered by Burma on the northwest, Laos on the north and east, and Cambodia on the southeast. Vietnam borders Laos and Cambodia on the east with China to its north and the South China Sea to its east. The "Golden Triangle," where Burma, Laos, and Thailand meet, is a notorious area for the growing and trafficking of drugs.

83.   **(C)**   Folkways are social norms governing less important areas of behavior such as table manners or proper attire for events. Mores are social norms which concern more serious issues such as laws against murder or incest. (A) is incorrect since violations of folkways usually result in mild reprimands. (D) is incorrect because violations of mores are usually considered crimes and involve more drastic punishments. (B) and (E) are also incorrect because folkways and mores are found among all social groups and cover a wide range of behaviors.

84.　**(A)** Deviance refers to those behaviors that a group stigmatizes because they are seen as violating basic norms. Rape, child abuse, and incest are examples of behaviors which are seen as deviant by many groups in the United States. Acts that are rare or unusual (D) are not considered deviant if they involve praiseworthy or inoffensive behaviors.

85.　**(D)** In American society, social norms require that people eat spaghetti with a fork (A), wear gender appropriate clothing in public (B), and not talk to oneself (E). Beer drinking (D), however, is a normal activity among many American college students.

86.　**(A)** Mead's theory of social development emphasizes the importance of children's play. He maintains that they develop their self-concepts by imagining themselves in the roles of other people. "Taking the role of the other" is central to his theory.

87.　**(C)** Children who have been isolated from human contact do not learn basic social skills and values and, even with special help, have considerable difficulty functioning in society. Their intellectual (A) and moral development (D) lags behind other children of the same age. Unusual coordination (B) or artistic talents (E) have not been reported for these children.

88.　**(C)** Sociologists believe that social conditions and processes such as socialization (E), rather than genetic factors, are the basic explanatory variables in human behavior. They also assume human behavior follows predictable patterns (A) and that scientific methods (B) can be used to study these behaviors objectively (D).

89.　**(A)** In spite of the confederate's "desperate" screams and complaints of a heart condition, most of the subjects reluctantly complied with the orders of the experimenter – a "legitimate authority" – and eventually applied the maximum shock. Although intelligence of the subject had no effect on compliance, the status of the experimenter showed a strong effect. From this experiment, Milgram concluded that Nazi Germany could have occurred anywhere, even in small-town America, because of people's tendency to obey authority.

90.　**(B)** In 1932, Franklin Roosevelt was elected president in a landslide vote, ending a 12-year period of Republican domination of the presidency. This election is considered by political scientists a "realigning election." A realigning election is one in which a sharp, lasting change occurs in the coalition of voters which supports each of the parties. In the election of 1936, Roosevelt drew into the Democratic party a coalition of urban workers, blacks, southern whites, and Jews. Most of the urban workers were also union members. The coalition did not include large numbers of business interests, which continued to vote for the Republican party. This coalition continued to support the Democratic party until approximately 1968, when white southerners began to vote for the Republican candidate for president more often than for the Democratic candidate. The answer is (B), northern business leaders, since most of these voters supported the Republicans in each of the years Roosevelt ran for president (1932, 1936, 1940, and 1944). Choice (A) is wrong because most southerners, white and black alike, voted for Roosevelt each time he ran for president. Choice (C) is wrong because blue-collar workers heavily supported Roosevelt in each of his elections. Choice (D) is wrong because blacks and Jews, two prominent racial minorities, voted for Roosevelt. Choice (E) is false because union members, who were mostly blue-collar workers, heavily supported Roosevelt.

91.   **(E)**   The Fifth Amendment to the U.S. Constitution states "No person shall be compelled in any criminal case to be a witness against himself...." The Supreme Court held in *Miranda v. Arizona,* 1966, that "In order to...permit a full opportunity to exercise the privilege against self-incrimination, the accused must be adequately and effectively apprised of his rights and the exercise of those rights must be fully honored." This means that when police apprehend a suspect in a criminal case they must immediately tell the person that (s)he has a right to remain silent. The Sixth Amendment to the U.S. Constitution states "In all criminal prosecutions, the accused shall enjoy the right...to have compulsory process for obtaining witnesses in his favor, and to have Assistance of Counsel for his defense. The compulsory process clause means that the accused can subpoena witnesses in his/her favor to appear in court to testify for the defense. (A subpoena is a court order which commands a person to appear at a certain time and place to give testimony upon a certain matter.) The assistance of counsel clause of the Sixth Amendment was interpreted by the Supreme Court in *Argersinger v. Hamlin,* 1972, to mean that if the accused cannot afford an attorney, (s)he is entitled to have one appointed at government expense, in any felony or misdemeanor criminal case in which, if the accused is found guilty, (s)he may be sentenced to jail. It is clear from the above that the rights mentioned in statements I, II, and III are all guaranteed by the Constitution. Therefore, choice (E) is correct.

92.   **(D)** Before the Civil War most blacks in the South were slaves. They were not citizens and had no civil or political rights. After the war, the Fourteenth and Fifteenth Amendments were added to the Constitution. The Fourteenth Amendment extended citizenship to blacks. The Fifteenth Amendment stated that the "right of citizens of the United States to vote shall not be denied or abridged by the United States or by any state on account of race, color, or previous condition of servitude." Contrary to what one might assume, blacks did not immediately gain full voting rights. During the 1870s the Supreme Court held that the Fifteenth Amendment did not automatically confer the right to vote on anybody. States could not pass laws to prevent anyone from voting on the basis of race, but they could restrict persons from voting on other grounds. This interpretation of the Fifteenth Amendment allowed southern states to use several techniques to effectively exclude blacks from voting. Since most former slaves were illiterate, prospective voters were often required to pass literacy tests. Poll taxes were also levied, which kept blacks, who were mostly poor, from voting. Since many whites were also poor and illiterate, grandfather clauses were enacted to allow them to bypass the legal restrictions on voting. Grandfather clauses stated that if you or your ancestors had voted before 1867, you could vote without paying a poll tax or passing a literacy test. Choice (D) is correct because the purpose of grandfather clauses and literacy tests was to keep blacks from voting. Choice (A) is wrong because the purpose of the grandfather clause was to allow poor and illiterate whites to escape voting restrictions. Choice (B) is wrong because the intent of the restrictions was to prevent blacks, not immigrants, from voting. In addition, there was little immigration into the South during the time in question. Choices (C) and (E) are wrong because the measures were restrictions on the right to vote, not on the right to run for office.

93.   **(B)** is the most specific statement because, although the first paragraph refers to the "needs of society," those needs are specified as economic in the rest of the quote. (A) Many of society's needs – legal rights, social needs, poverty – are not addressed. (C) This is not discussed. (D) The terms "average," "more" and "more," and "most" are used, not "all". (E) The government role is not discussed.

94.   **(A)** The Chamber of Commerce represents U.S. businesspeople and this is definitely a pro-business statement. (B) The federal Department of Labor is not anti-business, but it is not its major concern to advocate pro-business stands. (C) The GAO is the auditing branch of the government and doesn't take a stand on pro- or anti-business statements. (D) The

Socialist belief would probably be the opposite of the quote. (E) The union position would probably credit workers more and business less.

95. **(D)** Justice means fair treatment for all, sometimes enforced by government regulation. (A) This is specifically referred to in relation to employment, wages, etc. (B) This is indirectly referred to through rising living standards and growth which also provides security (C). (E) This is implied throughout and referred to as "less constraint."

96. **(E)** Labor is a factor in creating all of the others, which are the basic activities.

97. **(D)** In the autumn of 1864, a war-weary North faced a presidential election that offered them a clear choice. Abraham Lincoln ran on a platform of continuing the Civil War until the South was totally defeated. His opponent, former general George McClellan, ran on a platform calling for an armistice and recognition of the South as a separate nation. Early in the campaign, Lincoln looked to be in trouble. Although the Union had made deep penetrations into the western half of the Confederacy and had complete control of the Mississippi River, the Confederate armies in the East still fought valiantly on. It looked as if the Union armies could never destroy them and many people were questioning if it was worth the cost to try. The war had now been raging for 3½ years. The cost in human lives, time, and money had far surpassed everyone's worst fears. Many Northerners just wanted it to be over. Both Lincoln and Confederate President Jefferson Davis realized this. Accordingly, the Confederate strategy was to just hold on and deny the North any major victories before the election. Lincoln realized he needed a decisive victory before the election, pointing to a rapid defeat of the Confederacy, if he was to win. That victory occurred in September 1864 when Union forces under the command of William T. Sherman occupied Atlanta and followed up on this victory with his infamous "march to the sea." This victory pointed to the imminent destruction of the Confederacy. Finally, people could see a "light at the end of the tunnel" and desire to completely defeat the Confederates rose again in the North. The capture of Atlanta guaranteed Lincoln's reelection and sealed the fate of the Confederate States of America.

98. **(A)** After he was overthrown by revolutionary forces in 1978, the Shah of Iran, now residing in Mexico, asked for permission to enter the United States to receive cancer treatment. President Carter was warned that admitting the Shah to the United States, for any reason, would look to

the Iranians like America still supported the Shah's regime and would lead to trouble. However, other advisors told Carter that the United States owed the Shah a large debt of gratitude for the favors he had done for America and also for the lack of decisive support from the United States when his government was overthrown. Carter had previously refused to grant the Shah exile in the United States, but when he was told of the Shah's need for cancer treatment, he decided to allow the Shah to enter the United States on humanitarian grounds. As predicted, the Iranians were infuriated by this. On November 4, 1979, young Iranian males, backed by their government and claiming to be students, seized the American embassy compound and took 76 hostages, 62 of whom were held for more than a year. It was the beginning of one of the worst nightmares in American foreign policy, and it helped ruin Carter's presidency.

99.   **(B)** Here is a question that may be answered correctly even if, upon first reading, you are tempted to pass it by. The correct answer must be a country which had some degree of control over land in both Egypt and South Africa. If no answer comes to mind, you still may be able to remember the fact that the British had the largest colonial empire. After wrestling control of the Suez Canal in Egypt from its French builders and the Egyptian Khedive, the British government planned construction of a rail line linking Egypt with its recent acquisition of largely Dutch-settled land in South Africa. Typically, other European nations successfully moved to block the railroad by making claims to central African land along the route.

100. **(A)** The mention of Ethiopia may bring Italy to mind. If not, a possible guess is indicated if you are able to remember Mussolini's invasion of Ethiopia during the 1930s. The sole European nation to have its plans to establish an African colony in the late nineteenth century blocked by a native African force, Italy for some time regarded the incident a national humiliation. The incident was one of several reasons the Italian dictator Mussolini gave for his successful military takeover of Ethiopia in 1935.

101. **(C)** The Himalayan mountain range, the highest in the world, runs 1,500 miles from the northernmost tip of India, through Nepal, and along the southwest border of China. The Himalayas include Mt. Everest (Qomolongma), the tallest mountain in the world, and India's tallest mountain, Nanda Devi, which rises 25,645 feet. Bangladesh is almost completely surrounded by the northeastern border of India, facing the Bay of Bengal. It does have a small border with Burma on its southeast side.

102. **(B)** When Britain, bowing to internal abolitionist pressure, declared the slave trade illegal for its people in 1807, only Denmark, which made illegal the slave trade in 1805, had already outlawed the practice. The next to follow suit was Holland (A) in 1814, France (C) in 1818, and Spain (D) and Portugal (E) which restricted their slave trade to the seas south of the equator in 1815 and 1817, respectively.

103. **(C)** The dependent variable (value placed on obedience) may be influenced by the independent variable – social class of mothers (E). Gender of children (B) and education of parents (D) are not mentioned in this hypothesis. Social class (A) is the independent variable in this hypothesis.

104. **(E)** Verbal and physical rewards (D) and punishments such as ridicule (A), insults (B), and spanking (C) are commonly used methods for enforcing conformity to social norms. (E) Imitation is not used to control the behavior of others.

105. **(B)** Role conflict is a situation where the multiple roles which an individual occupies place competing, and often contradictory, demands on his or her time and energy. Role ambiguity (A) implies that role expectations are not clearly understood. Role strain (C) refers to the excessive demands of a single role. Role performance (D) and role playing (E) refer to the process of carrying out the expectations of a role.

106. **(D)** Social mobility is movement to a higher (upward) or lower (downward) social status. Societies differ in the amount of social mobility that is possible for their members. The ability to gain an education (A) or enter an occupation (B) does not always lead to a change in status. Social mobility should not be confused with geographic mobility (C), moving across borders. It also has nothing to do with marriage to a person of another religion (E).

107. **(D)** The working class consists of people who hold manual, blue-collar jobs. Some may be highly skilled, such as electricians or tool makers, while others are unskilled laborers. Working-class status is not based on one's education (C), residence (E), or income level (B).

108. **(A)** The social learning theory of aggression holds that most aggression is learned through operant conditioning. Therefore, aggression results only after certain actions are reinforced by rewards and discour-

aged by punishments. Modeling is another form of social learning that contributes to the development of aggressive behavior.

109. **(C)** According to the social learning theory of aggression, if a child is rewarded for random aggressive behavior, it is highly probable that the behavior will occur again. On the other hand, if a child is punished for acting aggressively, the likelihood of that behavior occurring again is reduced. It has been found that the schedule of reinforcement is particularly important in the learning of aggressive responses. For example, if aggression is reinforced irregularly, the aggressive behavior will tend to last longer than if the reinforcement is continuous.

110. **(B)** The belief that aggression is an inborn tendency in all animals, including man, has been most supported by the work of Konrad Lorenz.

111. **(A)** The passage is taken from the landmark case *Marbury v. Madison,* 1803. What the passage means, in everyday language, is:

> 1. Interpreting laws is a judicial function. 2. When two laws conflict, the courts must decide which will be enforced. 3. The Constitution is superior to laws passed by Congress or state legislatures (called statutory law). 4. Therefore, if a statute conflicts with the Constitution, the statute cannot be enforced by the courts.

Choice (B) is incorrect because the passage says nothing about Congress's right to pass laws to carry out its duties. Rather, the passage deals with a conflict between statutory and Constitutional law. Choice (C) is incorrect because it contradicts the main thesis of the passage. The passage clearly says that it is the duty of COURTS, not legislatures, to "say what the law is," which means the same as "interpretation of laws." Choice (D) is incorrect because the passage says when an act of the legislature and the Constitution conflict, the Constitution governs the case. Choice (E) is incorrect because the passage states specifically that if two laws conflict, the courts must decide the operation of each. It then posits a case where the two laws in conflict are an act of the legislature and the Constitution. The clear implication is that, in such a case, the courts must decide on the operation of the Constitution, which means deciding questions of Constitutional law.

112. **(E)** After a bill is introduced into either house of Congress, it is referred to the appropriate committee. The bill will then usually be referred by the committee to a subcommittee. After holding a hearing on the bill, the subcommittee will then have a mark-up session where revisions and additions are made to the bill. The bill is then referred back to the full committee, which may also hold a hearing and have a mark-up session. Choices (A), (B), and (C) are incorrect because mark-up sessions do not occur in the majority leader's office, on the floor of the legislative chambers, or in party caucuses. Choice (D) is the most plausible alternative to (E), because a joint conference committee is, after all, a committee. However, proposed legislation goes to a joint conference committee only after it has passed both houses of Congress. The Constitution requires that before a piece of legislation can become law, it must pass both houses in identical form. The purpose of the joint conference committee is to iron out differences in a bill that has passed one house in a different form than in the other. It is true that changes are made to such a bill in a joint conference committee, to satisfy members of both houses. However, the term "mark-up session" refers only to the activity of standing committees and subcommittees in Congress, not to joint conference committees.

113. **(D)** The Office of Management and Budget is the chief presidential staff agency. Its primary responsibility is to put together the budget that the president submits to Congress. Each agency and office of the executive branch must have its budget requests cleared by OMB before it gets into the president's budget. The OMB also studies the organization and operations of the executive branch, to ensure that each office and agency is carrying out its appropriate duty, as assigned by law. Choice (A) is incorrect because the Department of Commerce does not help the president to draw up his annual budget. The Department of Commerce was created in 1903 to protect the interests of businesspeople at home and abroad. Choice (B) is incorrect because the Department of Treasury is not involved in drawing up the president's budget. The functions of the Treasury Department include collecting taxes through the Internal Revenue Service, an administrative unit of the Department, administering the public debt, and coining money. Choice (C) is incorrect because the main responsibility of the Federal Reserve Board is the implementation of monetary policy. It has nothing to do with drawing up the president's annual budget. Choice (E) is incorrect because the cabinet does not help the president draw up his budget. It advises the president on the administration of the executive departments.

114. **(E)** is correct. (A) is not correct, because there are some variances between nations high in GNP while not so high in trade. (B) is incorrect because there is no data comparing previous years. (C) is incorrect. Thailand, the Philippines, and Indonesia did not exceed the world average in trade. (D) is incorrect; Japan was not the leader in trade.

115. **(D)** is not true. The trade graph is a line graph, and the GNP is a bar graph. All the others are true. (A) Per capita means per person.

116. **(A)** is most accurate; all are on the eastern edge of Asia. (B) is incorrect because all of Asia is not represented, for example, India or the Persian Gulf. (C) is wrong; northwest Asia would be either the Persian Gulf area or Asian USSR. (D) is incorrect; Malaysia and Thailand are as close to the Indian Ocean as to the Pacific. (E) is wrong; only Australia, Hong Kong, Malaysia, New Zealand, and Singapore were ever British colonies. Japan and Thailand were never colonized by foreigners.

117. **(D)** Singapore shows the greatest growth rate because its per capita trade is not only highest but exceeds its GNP, which means its people are producing exportable products which bring money back into the nation. Hong Kong is second.

118. **(A)** GNP is the gross national product and is defined as the total goods and services produced by the nation in a given year. (B) is only partially correct because services are not specified. The others are not correct.

119. **(A)** In the presidential election of 1876, Samuel Tilden defeated his Republican opponent, Rutherford B. Hayes, in the popular vote by 250,000 votes. However, there were 20 contested votes in the electoral college. If Hayes received all the contested electoral votes, he would win the election by one vote in the Electoral College and he would gain the presidency. The matter was turned over to Congress, where a Republican-dominated commission awarded the disputed electoral votes to Hayes. The Senate ratified the commission's decision, but the Democrats in the House threatened to use political means to gain Tilden's victory through a House vote. Republicans negotiated the issue and the Compromise of 1877 was the result. Hayes got the presidency. Democrats received assurances that federal soldiers would be withdrawn from Southern states (effectively ending Reconstruction) and that blanket federal government support for Republicans in the South would end. This opened the door for Democrats to

regain control in all the Southern states (they had already effectively re-gained control in all but three). None of the other choices listed in the question were in any way involved in the Compromise of 1877.

120. **(B)** After the defeat of George Washington's Virginian forces at Fort Necessity by the French, it became clear that the colonies were too weak to individually tackle either the French or their various Indian allies. Benjamin Franklin perceived that united action by the colonies was the only hope of providing for their security. He called together the Albany Congress to discuss plans to enlist the aid of the various Iroquois tribes in colonial defense and to coordinate defense plans between the English colonies. It also called for the establishment of a "grand council" with representatives from each of the colonies to enact taxes and coordinate colonial economic activity. The plan is notable because it was the first plan calling for the individual colonies to act as a single, united entity. While the plan was visionary and ultimately necessary, the colonial legislatures ultimately rejected it.

121. **(B)** Knowledge-based questions such as this are not usually susceptible to successful guessing, since the other choices cannot be eliminated unless you know as least two or three of them well. As a young man, the German poet Goethe anticipated elements of Romanticism, and his youthful writings, such as *The Sorrows of the Young Werther* (1774), exhibited some Romantic characteristics. This period is often termed his "Sturm und Drang" (storm and stress) period.

122. **(D)** Comte, an early nineteenth-century writer, based his system of Positivism on the belief that history was entering a third, scientifically-oriented stage. In this new era, only statements that might be scientifically verified were to be considered knowledge. A committee of scientists and philosophers would govern, creating "Progress and Order." Religion would be considered outdated.

123. **(E)** The capital of Sierre Leone is Freetown, not Dakar, which is the capital of Senegal. All of the other capital cities in choices (A), (B), (C), and (D) correspond correctly to the country with which they are paired.

124. **(E)** In the nineteenth-century France and Britain were moving into most countries in South and Southeast Asia. In order to prevent them from taking control of Thailand (or Siam as it was known then), King Mongkut

(Rama IV) signed trade agreements with the two countries, granting them extraterritorial rights. Elsewhere in the region, the French, who were occupying southern Vietnam, made Cambodia (A) a protectorate in 1863 and Laos (B) a protectorate in the 1880s, ruling it as part of Indochina. By 1886 the British had made all of Burma (C) a province of India (D) which they had been occupying in various forms since the 1600s.

125. **(D)** An ascribed status is one which an individual gains through no effort on his or her part. Often one is born into an ascribed status. Becoming a college president (A), a Nobel prize winner (B), an honor student (C), or an opera singer (E) all require considerable effort by an individual. Being a white female is a condition over which one has no control.

126. **(A)** An achieved status is one which an individual receives through his or her own efforts. Categories based on age (B) or ethnic group (C) are ascribed, not achieved. Similarly, one has no control over one's height (E) or being an accident victim (D).

127. **(A)** A subculture is a distinctive lifestyle that exists within a larger culture. Members of the subculture share some values with the larger culture, but have other values that are unique to their group. People of the same income (B), education (C), age (D), or gender (E) do not necessarily share the same values.

128. **(B)** Cooley's theory of the "looking-glass-self" maintains that our perceptions of others' actions toward us are a key factor in developing our self-concepts. Mead (A), Freud (C), Piaget (D), and Kohlberg (E) do not place similar emphasis on the individual's perceptions of other's reactions.

129. **(D)** Hunting and gathering societies are characterized by small size, low level technology, equal status among adults, lack of strong authority figures, and consensus on values. There is little difference in wealth (C) or occupation (B) and there is no centralized government (E).

130. **(C)** While a higher percentage of African-Americans live in poverty, the largest number of poor people are white. While many single mothers (E) are poor, they are not a majority of poor Americans. The poverty rate for the elderly (B) is about the same as the national average – 13 percent.

PRACTICE
TEST 2

CLEP SOCIAL SCIENCES AND HISTORY
Test 2

(Answer sheets appear in the back of the book.)

Section 1

TIME: 45 Minutes
        65 Questions

DIRECTIONS: Each of the questions or incomplete statements below is followed by five possible answers or completions. Select the best choice in each case and fill in the corresponding oval on the answer sheet.

---

1.   The policy promoted by Theodore Roosevelt, most blatantly pursued in Central America, was the

   (A) "New Deal" policy.   (D) "Fair Deal" policy.

   (B) "Big Stick" policy.   (E) "Square Deal" policy.

   (C) "Good Neighbor" policy.

2.   The Newburgh Conspiracy resulted from

   (A) attempts to bring Kansas into the Union as a slave state.

   (B) a plot by the Nationalist faction to overthrow the Articles of Confederation and replace the Continental Congress with a strong central government headed by a European-style monarch.

   (C) fears, at the conclusion of the Revolutionary War, that the Continental Congress would disband the army without funding the soldiers' pensions.

   (D) plans by Aaron Burr to create a separate republic, with himself as the leader, in the American lands west of the Appalachians.

(E) schemes by France to regain dominance in the Mississippi Valley by enlisting the aid of several prominent Americans, promising them large tracts of land in the region in return for their assistance in the scheme.

3. All of the following inventions or processes were significant parts of the Industrial Revolution EXCEPT the

(A) spinning jenny.   (D) flying shuttle.

(B) steam engine.   (E) electric motor.

(C) Bessemer process.

4. Which one of the following individuals was an example of nineteenth-century liberalism?

(A) Proudhon   (D) Napoleon II

(B) Disraeli   (E) Mill

(C) Fourier

5. In 1956 Britain and France, with Israeli help, attacked Egypt over what issue?

(A) Egyptian resistance to decolonization

(B) Intervention in civil war

(C) Tariff reform

(D) Control over the Suez Canal

(E) Egyptian foreign policy in the Middle East

6. Which of the following is NOT one of Japan's islands?

(A) Honshu   (D) Shikoku

(B) Kyushu   (E) Yokohama

(C) Hokkaido

7. When sociologists use the term "ethnic group" they are referring to people who have

    (A) a shared cultural heritage.

    (B) low social status.

    (C) similar physical appearance.

    (D) common political views.

    (E) the same occupation.

8. The concept of prejudice is defined as

    (A) belief in the superiority of one's group.

    (B) negative attitudes toward another group.

    (C) harmful behavior toward minority groups.

    (D) blaming another group for one's problems.

    (E) inability to improve one's social status.

9. One distinctive feature of the Indian caste system is

    (A) women generally have higher status than men.

    (B) individual mobility between castes rarely occurs.

    (C) lower castes have considerable wealth.

    (D) status is based on one's level of education.

    (E) there is much intermarriage between castes.

10. A minority group is defined as a group of people who

    (A) usually vote for the same political party.

    (B) have high levels of income and education.

    (C) have experienced prejudice and discrimination.

    (D) practice the same religious rituals.

    (E) send their children to private schools.

11. Max Weber first discussed the essential characteristics of bureau-cracy. One of these is

    (A) equal authority among members of the organization.

    (B) group participation in important decisions.

    (C) workers develop skills at a variety of tasks.

    (D) a clearly defined chain of command.

    (E) maximum flexibility in interpreting rules.

12. When studying leadership in small groups, Robert Bales discovered that most groups have two types of leaders. These are

    (A) instrumental and expressive.

    (B) rigid and flexible.

    (C) forceful and timid.

    (D) participatory and consultative.

    (E) demonstrative and reserved.

13. Approach-avoidance conflicts are difficult to resolve because

    (A) the positive and negative aspects of a situation are equally strong.

    (B) a single goal possesses both positive and negative aspects.

    (C) one must choose the lesser of two evils.

    (D) they produce cognitive dissonance.

    (E) All of the above.

14. The term "executive privilege" refers to

    (A) the right of the president to veto legislation proposed by Con-gress.

    (B) the limited right of the president to withhold certain information from Congress and the public.

    (C) the right of the president to appoint and receive ambassadors.

    (D) the limited right of the president to pardon persons convicted of federal crimes.

    (E) the limited immunity of the president from prosecution for cer-tain misdemeanors.

15. Senator Pettifogger gets an item inserted into the federal budget which allocates $6,000,000 for building a ski lift at a resort in his home state. This is known as

(A) a filibuster.

(B) pork barrel legislation.

(C) logrolling.

(D) grease for the gears.

(E) senatorial courtesy.

16. Which of the following statements reflects an elitist view of American politics?

(A) American politics are dominated by the military-industrial complex.

(B) Thousands of competing interest groups influence public policy-making.

(C) Large states dominate public policy because of their overrepresentation in Congress.

(D) American politics are dominated by rural areas at the expense of urban areas.

(E) Since only one registered voter in three votes in off-year congressional races, Congress represents only the politically active.

QUESTIONS 17 to 21 refer to the following graphs.

TOP IMPORTERS FROM U.S. in billions of dollars, 1989		TOP EXPORTERS TO U.S. in billions of dollars, 1989		U.S. TRADE BALANCE with MEXICO in billions of dollars, 1989
$78.6	Canada	$93.6	Japan	25.0 27.2
$44.6	Japan	$88.2	Canada	Exports Imports
$25.0	Mexico	$27.2	Mexico	-2.2 Deficit
$20.9	Britain	$24.8	Germany	
$16.9	Germany	$24.3	Taiwan	

SOURCE: Commerce Dept.

17. Which nation is a top importer, but not a top exporter?

    (A) Britain   (D) Japan

    (B) Canada   (E) Mexico

    (C) Germany

18. Taken together, which area imports the most from the United States?

    (A) Northern North America   (D) Africa

    (B) Latin America   (E) Europe

    (C) Asia

19. Taken together, which area exports the most to the United States?

    (A) Northern North America   (D) Africa

    (B) Latin America   (E) Europe

    (C) Asia

20. Who has the most favorable trade balance with the United States?

    (A) Britain   (D) Japan

    (B) Canada   (E) Mexico

    (C) Germany

21. If exports exceed imports, it is called

    (A) favorable balance of payments.

    (B) unfavorable balance of payments.

    (C) favorable balance of trade.

    (D) unfavorable balance of trade.

    (E) deficit spending.

22. The thrust of Roosevelt's "Good Neighbor" policy was to

    (A) retreat from the military interventionism and blatant economic domination which had characterized previous American policy toward Latin America.

(B) guarantee the protection of Latin America and South America from European aggression by permanently stationing U.S. forces in the region.

(C) promote "Good Samaritanism" in the United States by encouraging people who still owned their own homes to provide temporary housing for their neighbors who had become homeless because of the Great Depression.

(D) force Latin American countries to cooperate peacefully with each other and end their petty border disputes or face United States military intervention.

(E) supply Britain with the food and nonmilitary essentials they needed to maintain their struggle against Nazi Germany.

23. Which of the following was NOT true of the Northwest Ordinance of 1787?

(A) It recognized the territorial claims of the various Indian tribes within the Northwest Territory.

(B) It guaranteed freedom of religion to settlers in the Northwest Territory.

(C) It guaranteed the right to a jury trial to settlers in the Northwest Territory.

(D) It prohibited slavery within the Northwest Territory.

(E) It specified procedures through which settlers could organize state governments and eventually apply for full statehood.

24. Which one of the following best characterizes the relationship between the Commercial Revolution and the Italian Renaissance?

(A) The Commercial Revolution caused Europeans to concentrate on their own continent, to the exclusion of the rest of the world.

(B) The Commercial Revolution was a result of the Italian Renaissance.

(C) The new merchant class of the Commercial Revolution was more interested in the secular world and less interested in religion.

(D) There is no connection.

(E) The Commercial Revolution enriched Italian farmers.

25. "Imperialism emerged as a development and direct continuation of the fundamental properties of capitalism...imperialism is the monopoly stage of capitalism."

   The writer quoted above would most likely accept which of the following statements as true?

   (A) Imperialism was caused by European advances in science and technology.

   (B) A desire for national prestige drove Europeans into a race to gain colonies.

   (C) Imperialism was a natural and predictable result of the growth of capitalism.

   (D) A country with an advanced capitalistic system might become the "colony" of another country.

   (E) Imperialism fed the egos of the smaller, less powerful nations of Europe.

26. The first All-African People's Conference, organized by Kwame Nkrumah, was held in what year?

   (A) 1949   (D) 1960

   (B) 1956   (E) 1963

   (C) 1958

27. What year did the revolution ending the last Chinese dynasty take place?

   (A) 1864   (D) 1911

   (B) 1900   (E) 1950

   (C) 1644

28. Sociologists who have studied industrial corporations in Japan have identified several differences between Japanese and American companies. One of these is

    (A) Japanese workers are better paid.

    (B) American workers work longer hours.

    (C) Japanese workers have less job security.

    (D) American workers are more loyal to their employers.

    (E) Japanese workers take part in more group activities.

29. Sociologists have identified several essential characteristics of social groups. All of the following are important characteristics of a group EXCEPT

    (A) regular interaction among members.

    (B) shared norms and values.

    (C) members identify with the group.

    (D) some specialization of roles.

    (E) absence of conflict among members.

30. Sociologists use the term voluntary association to refer to an organization which

    (A) is organized to make a profit.

    (B) engages in retail sales.

    (C) selects new members on the basis of merit.

    (D) has an authoritarian form of government.

    (E) members join to pursue common interests.

31. Which the following terms would be an accurate description of family and kinship practices that are most prominent in the United States today?

    I.   Matrilineal descent system

    II. Nuclear family

    III. Neolocal family

    IV. Matriarchal family

(A) I only.   (D) I and III only.

(B) I and II only.   (E) II and III only.

(C) I, II, and III only.

32. Which of the following sociological theorists argues that religion as a social institution tends to protect the status quo by encouraging less powerful groups toward a "false class consciousness," or a misunderstanding of what policies and practices would be in their true interests?

(A) Karl Marx   (D) Max Weber

(B) Robert Bellah   (E) Robert Michels

(C) Emile Durkheim

33. In studying schools in modern societies, conflict theorists point to a "hidden curriculum." This term refers to

(A) those parts of school budgets that are not made public.

(B) the passing on of values and norms in school that perpetuate the existing system of stratification.

(C) those parts of the curriculum that parents are not aware of.

(D) that proportion of the student body that drops out of school before graduating each year.

(E) those parts of the school budget that are used for things other than direct student instruction.

34. Stanley Schachter (1959), in his studies on the human affiliative need, found that

(A) highly fearful people are much more likely to affiliate than less fearful people.

(B) first-born children are more likely to affiliate than later-born children.

(C) when given a choice, highly fearful people preferred to affiliate only with those who were in the same experimental condition.

(D) people affiliate to reduce fear.

(E) All of the above.

35. All of the following are formal or informal sources of presidential power EXCEPT

   (A) the fact that the president is elected indirectly by the public, not by Congress.

   (B) Supreme Court decisions which have expanded the president's emergency powers.

   (C) high public approval ratings.

   (D) the veto power.

   (E) the ability to introduce legislation in either house of Congress.

36. Civil servants in the federal bureaucracy may sometimes successfully resist presidential initiatives because

   (A) they can go directly to Congress with their budget requests.

   (B) they have more opportunities to influence public opinion than the president does.

   (C) they are directly responsible to Congress, but not to the president.

   (D) they may not be removed from office for political reasons.

   (E) they have influence over the president through campaign contributions.

37. The 1985 Gramm-Rudman Act

   (A) outlawed the use of federal funds for abortions.

   (B) established a mechanism for balancing the federal budget.

   (C) prohibited the use of any federal funds for aiding the Contras in Nicaragua.

   (D) changed the tax code to eliminate loopholes for the wealthy.

   (E) provided for the destruction of intermediate range nuclear missiles in Europe.

QUESTIONS 38 to 42 refer to the following passage.

Hoover had been in office less than a year, stocks had been falling for over a month; they had lost, on the average, about one-sixth of their quoted value, and looked "cheap," according to the opinion of important bankers, economists, and government officials. Business was still good – the economic position of the country was "sound" and technically the stock market itself had been improved by a "healthy reaction." Almost everyone thought a rally must be close at hand.

The market opened steady with prices little changed from the previous day, though some rather large blocks, of 20,000 to 25,000 shares, came out at the start. It sagged easily for the first half hour, and then around eleven o'clock the deluge broke.

It came with a speed and ferocity that left men dazed. The bottom simply fell out of the market. From all over the country a torrent of selling orders poured onto the floor of the Stock Exchange and there were no buying orders to meet them. Quotations of representative active issues, like steel, telephone, and anaconda, began to fall two, three, five, and even ten points between sales. Less active stocks became unmarketable. Within a few moments the ticker service was hopelessly swamped and from then on no one knew what was really happening. By 1:30 the ticker tape was nearly two hours late; by 2:30 it was 147 minutes late. The last quotation was not printed on the tape until 7:08:05 p.m., four hours, eight and one-half minutes after the close. In the meantime, Wall Street had lived through an incredible nightmare.

38. What is the event the quote describes?

    (A) The Panic of 1837

    (B) The Great Depression

    (C) The Crash of 1929

    (D) Pearl Harbor Day

    (E) The assassination of John Kennedy

39. What compounded the problems of the day?

    (A) The ticker tape was running slow.

    (B) Business leaders were pessimistic.

    (C) Government leaders were pessimistic.

    (D) Major issues were not affected.

    (E) There was a lack of selling orders.

40. The stock prices were driven down by

    (A) lack of activity.

    (B) massive activity at the open of the market.

    (C) the market's rising trend over several months.

    (D) the general collapsing of businesses nationwide.

    (E) sell orders overwhelming buy orders.

41. The results of the Crash were partially blamed on the administration of

    (A) Woodrow Wilson.   (D) Herbert Hoover.

    (B) Warren Harding.   (E) Franklin Roosevelt.

    (C) Calvin Coolidge.

42. Which was not a reform created to try to prevent a repetition of 1929?

    (A) SEC

    (B) Margin restrictions

    (C) FDIC

    (D) Restrictions on corporations issuing stocks

    (E) Restrictions on insider trading

43. Reaganomics is most closely associated with

    (A) the "trickle-down" theory.

    (B) the "controlled growth" theory.

    (C) the "bubble up" theory.

    (D) New Deal reform economics.

    (E) Fair Deal progressivist economics.

44. The "White Man's Burden" referred to

    (A) the financial cost of running the huge European colonial empires.

(B) the cost in human lives of diseases, such as smallpox, to which only white people were susceptible.

(C) the duty of white laborers to rise up and overthrow the wealthy industrialists who were abusing their power and their workers.

(D) the cost of the wars that resulted from nineteenth-century militarism.

(E) the belief that it was the duty of whites to "civilize" nonwhite people through colonization or economic dominance of nonwhite lands.

45. "I think, therefore I am" was written by

(A) Locke.   (D) Diderot

(B) Descartes.   (E) Nietzsche.

(C) Leibniz.

46. "Intendants" were

(A) secret letters of arrest.

(B) courts where secret trials were held.

(C) censors employed by Louis XIV.

(D) secret emissaries of the pope.

(E) regional government agents in France.

47. The Swahili word "ujamaa," as used by Tanzanian president Julius Nyerere, stands for what political ideal?

(A) African socialism

(B) Pan-Africanism

(C) Economic modernization

(D) The independent nation-state

(E) Tanzanian national supremacy

48. Which of the following rivers is known as "China's Sorrow"?

    (A) Yellow River   (D) Wei River

    (B) Yangtze River   (E) Tarim River

    (C) Ganges River

49. Some parts of the political system in the United States utilize laws and bureaucratic rules to define who has what kind of power and authority over whom. These laws and rules exemplify which type of authority?

    (A) Traditional   (D) Institutionalized

    (B) Charismatic   (E) Corporate

    (C) Legal-rational

50. Which of the following statements best characterizes the trends in the economy of the United States over the past few decades?

    (A) The extent of corporate concentration has declined.

    (B) Market forces have become a less powerful determinant of the production and distribution of goods.

    (C) The power elite is now concentrated more in the political sphere than the economic.

    (D) Union membership has declined steadily as a percentage of the entire work force.

    (E) The industrial sector has grown as a proportion of the overall economy.

51. Which of the following would be considered characteristics of a caste stratification system?

    I.   Rigid boundaries between classes

    II. Rank based on heredity

    III. Achieved statuses predominate

    (A) I only.   (D) II and III only.

    (B) I and II only.   (E) I, II, and III.

    (C) II only.

52. Which of the following provides the best illustration of intra-generational social mobility?

    (A) Chris joined the ABC Publishing Corporation as a traveling sales representative and was promoted over the years to the position of senior vice president of the corporation.

    (B) Mary's mother is a neurosurgeon, and Mary goes to medical school and becomes a cardiac surgeon.

    (C) Fred works as a carpenter for the ABC Construction Company and then takes a job as a carpenter for the XYZ Construction Company because the pay is better.

    (D) Nancy worked as a nurse in a large hospital but quit so that she could stay at home and raise her new infant.

    (E) Tom's father is a grade school teacher, and Tom becomes a high school teacher after graduating from college.

53. Which of the following statements would be most consistent with the approach of conflict theory to the explanation of social stratification and social inequality?

    (A) Social inequality persists because it works to motivate people to make a contribution to society.

    (B) Social stratification persists because it benefits all groups in society by providing a wider distribution of resources.

    (C) Social inequality persists because the well-to-do use their monopoly over resources to dominate and exploit those with fewer resources.

    (D) Social inequality persists mostly because the poor will not expend the amount of work necessary to improve their circumstances.

    (E) Social stratification persists because it is a rational system for distributing resources.

54. In south Florida, Hispanics and Anglos live together but have each retained a distinct identity and lifestyle. The former continue to speak Spanish and keep much of their Caribbean, Cuban, or South American heritage while the latter speak English and retain their European heritage. This best illustrates

(A) Pluralism.   (D) Separatism.

(B) Assimilation.   (E) Submission.

(C) Segregation.

55. The Thematic Apperception Test supposedly reflects

(A) how one organizes ambiguous stimuli.

(B) one's overall level of introversion-extroversion.

(C) interpersonal conflicts and needs.

(D) one's relative ranking on several trait scales.

(E) one's possible latent psychosis.

56. In a single-member district, plurality vote system

(A) a runoff election is usually necessary to determine the winner.

(B) parties are assigned seats based on the proportion of votes they receive in a district.

(C) the candidate with the most votes represents the district.

(D) some votes count more than others in determining which candidate wins the election.

(E) third parties are more likely to win seats than in proportional representation systems.

57. The top official in the Department of Justice is the

(A) Solicitor-General.   (D) Attorney General.

(B) Secretary of Justice.   (E) Chief Justice.

(C) Secretary of State.

58. Which of the following is a FALSE statement about the Democratic party's national convention?

(A) It selects the state party chairmen.

(B) It determines the national party platform.

(C) It nominates the party's candidate for president.

(D) It has "super delegates" not chosen by state primaries and caucuses.

(E) It sets the time and place for the next national convention.

QUESTIONS 59 to 62 refer to the following graph.

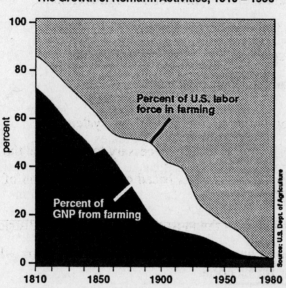

The Growth of Nonfarm Activities, 1810 – 1980

59. The graph most clearly shows

(A) the economic impact of farming was always more important
than the number of people working in the field.

(B) GNP and labor force maintained a constant relationship to each
other.

(C) farming remained the most important economic activity until
about 1900.

(D) the decline in the importance of farming finally reversed itself in
the 1970s.

(E) recently, the farming GNP and the farm labor force have more
accurately matched each other.

60. Which statement is most true about American agriculture and the graph?

    (A) Farming is no longer an important occupation.

    (B) It is not possible to make a good living from farming.

    (C) Farming is becoming more automated.

    (D) American agriculture's production is now possible with fewer workers.

    (E) There was never a time when either GNP or labor force actually increased.

61. Which does not apply to American agriculture?

    (A) Farmers usually have to borrow money to operate.

    (B) The U.S. farmer almost always creates a surplus.

    (C) Farming is one of the last areas to resist big corporations.

    (D) Modern farming still depends on weather conditions.

    (E) Modern farmers have depended heavily on government aid.

62. The best description of American agricultural problems in the near future is

    (A) increasing numbers of Americans will return to agriculture.

    (B) world food supplies will increase and the need for U.S. exports will diminish.

    (C) efficiency will increase and production will need fewer workers.

    (D) water supplies and chemical fertilizers will both increase.

    (E) Third World food-growing needs will diminish.

63. The paternalistic view of slavery held that

    (A) slavery was a necessary evil that should be phased out as soon as it was economically possible.

    (B) slavery was a totally unjustifiable abuse of humanity demanding immediate abolition.

    (C) slavery was an artifact of a more primitive past that would eventually fade out on its own.

(D) slavery was necessary to protect blacks from the mistreatment and abuse they would receive if they were freed.

(E) slavery was necessary to keep blacks from developing their superior potential and eventually dominating the white race.

64. Mark Twain's classic stories, such as *Tom Sawyer* and *Huckleberry Finn*, were primary examples of the _____ trend in turn-of-the-century American literature.

(A) romantic   (D) realistic

(B) gothic   (E) heroic

(C) fantasy

65. The early twentieth-century pacifist and winner of the Nobel Peace Prize for her book *Lay Down Your Arms* (1889) was

(A) Tirpitz.   (D) von Bethmann-Hollweg.

(B) Luxemberg.   (E) Cosima Wagner.

(C) von Suttner.

Section 2

TIME: 45 Minutes
65 Questions

DIRECTIONS: Each of the questions or incomplete statements below is followed by five possible answers or completions. Select the best choice in each case and fill in the corresponding oval on the answer sheet.

66. When the heir to the Austrian throne was assassinated in August 1914, and the Russian government responded to the ensuing crisis by mobilizing its troops, Germany followed its obligations under the Triple Alliance and declared war on Russia. Which of the following countries did Germany invade first?

    (A) Russia

    (B) Austria-Hungary

    (C) France

    (D) Britain

    (E) Italy

67. All of the following African countries were colonized by Britain EXCEPT

    (A) Nigeria.

    (B) Mozambique.

    (C) Kenya.

    (D) Northern Rhodesia.

    (E) Southern Rhodesia.

68. Which of the following countries would NOT appear on a 1965 map of Asia?

    (A) Bangladesh

    (B) Vietnam

    (C) Cambodia

    (D) Laos

    (E) North Korea

69. A group is called a minority group by sociologists when it

    (A) is denied access to power and resources available to other groups.

    (B) consists of less than one-half the total population in a society.

(C) consists of less than one-tenth the total population in a society.

(D) wields power in society even though it has few members.

(E) has recently immigrated to a particular society.

70. Generally speaking, prejudice and discrimination would be most likely to occur between two racial or ethnic groups under which of the following conditions?

(A) The two groups work together to achieve common goals.

(B) Contact between the two groups involves group members of roughly equal status getting to know one another.

(C) Members of the two groups compete for the same scarce jobs.

(D) One group has been completely assimilated into the other group.

(E) Members of both groups are able to find jobs that pay comparable wages.

71. Which of the following is a social policy aimed especially at reducing the disparities in income between men and women?

(A) Feminism   (D) Androgyny

(B) Sexism   (E) Separatism

(C) Comparable worth

72. Since 1900 in the United States, which occupational groups have been growing as a percentage of the work force?

I. White-collar workers

II. Blue-collar workers

III. Service workers

IV. Farm workers

(A) I only.   (D) I and III only.

(B) I and II only.   (E) II and III only.

(C) I, II, and III only.

73. In the study of population, the three elements that most directly determine the size, composition, and distribution of a population are

    (A) fertility, mortality, and migration.

    (B) fertility, mortality, and community.

    (C) fertility, migration, and fecundity.

    (D) mortality, migration, and segregation.

    (E) fertility, mortality, and ecology.

74. Which of the following psychoanalytic theorists proposed the need to move toward people, move against people, and move away from people?

    (A) Sullivan   (D) Anderson

    (B) Horney   (E) Adler

    (C) Fromm

75. All of the following statements represent positions the Supreme Court has taken on the First Amendment right to freedom of religion EXCEPT that

    (A) public school officials may write a nondenominational prayer for school children to recite at the beginning of each school day.

    (B) public school teachers may not conduct devotional readings of the Bible in class.

    (C) a copy of the Ten Commandments may not be posted on the walls of public school classrooms.

    (D) creation science may not be taught in public schools.

    (E) states may not outlaw the teaching of evolution in the public schools.

76. The Constitution, as ratified in 1788, provided for popular vote for

    (A) election of the president.

    (B) election of senators.

    (C) ratification of treaties.

(D) ratification of constitutional amendments.

(E) None of the above.

77. The Great Compromise of 1787

(A) resolved the controversy over the status of slaves under the Constitution.

(B) provided for an electoral college for selection of the president.

(C) provided for the direct election of senators.

(D) provided for equal representation of states in the Senate and representation based on population in the House.

(E) added a Bill of Rights to the Constitution.

QUESTIONS 78 to 80 refer to the following table.

**New York Stock Exchange Companies
With Largest Number of Stockholders, 1985**

Company	Stockholders
American Tel & Tel	2,927,000
General Motors	1,990,000
Bell South Corp.	1,685,000
Bell Atlantic	1,413,000
American Information Tech.	1,382,000
NYNEX Corp.	1,348,000
Southwestern Bell	1,320,000
Pacific Telesis Group	1,242,000
US WEST	1,156,000
International Business Machines	798,000
Exxon Corp.	785,000
General Electric	490,000
GTE Corp.	442,000
Bell Canada Enterprises	332,000
Sears Roebuck	326,000

From *1986 Fact Book,* copyright New York Stock Exchange, Inc., 1986.

78. Which is most true about the table?

(A) Telephone companies have the largest number of stockholders.

(B) Manufacturing companies have more stockholders than service companies.

(C) Retail merchandise companies have the largest number of stock-holders.

(D) Only domestic companies are represented.

(E) Oil companies do not have large numbers of stockholders.

79. Which company would you buy if you wanted the greatest voice in its management?

(A) AT&T

(B) Southwestern Bell

(C) Exxon Corp.

(D) GTE Corp.

(E) Sears Roebuck

80. Stockholders control a company through

(A) the chief executive officer.

(B) the chairperson of the board.

(C) the president of the company.

(D) the elected board of directors.

(E) stock options.

81. What proposal did President Woodrow Wilson make in 1918 that convinced the Germans they would be treated fairly if they surrendered?

(A) The Twenty-One demands

(B) The Fourteen Points

(C) The Versailles Proposals

(D) The Balfour Declaration

(E) The "New Freedom" policy

82. This engraving of the Nat Turner revolt takes what point of view?

HORRID MASSACRE IN VIRGINIA

The Scenes within the above plate are designed to represent —Fig. 1. a Mother intreating for the lives of her children —2. Mr. O'Reilly murdered by his own slaves.—3. Mr Barrow, who bravely defended himself until his wife escaped.—4. A comp. of mounted Dragoons in pursuit of the Blacks.   Library of Congress

(A) The revolt of the slaves was justified.

(B) Northern abolitionists were responsible for the revolt.

(C) The revolt was an attack upon innocent victims.

(D) The slaves were ineffective revolutionists.

(E) The slave revolt was successful.

QUESTION 83 refers to the following graph.

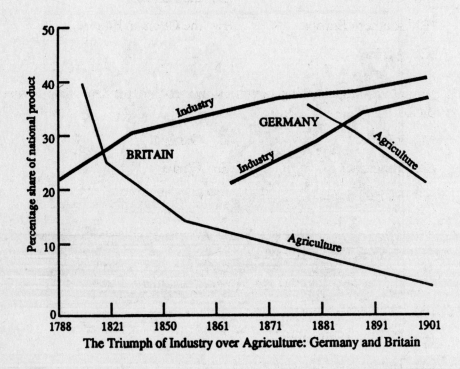

The Triumph of Industry over Agriculture: Germany and Britain

83. According to the graph, which one of the following statements is true?

(A) Industrial production had a greater impact than agricultural production in Britain in 1800.

(B) Agricultural production had a greater impact than industrial production in Germany in 1900.

(C) Agriculture became less significant in Britain and Germany by 1900.

(D) Britain produced fewer industrial products than Germany.

(E) During the period shown, industrial production was an insignificant part of the British economy.

84. The Fashoda crisis involved Britain and France in a dispute over land in

    (A) China.   (D) the Balkans.

    (B) southern Europe.   (E) the Ottoman Empire.

    (C) Africa.

85. Which of the following countries was an independent state before 1950?

    (A) Liberia   (D) Gambia

    (B) Tanzania   (E) Ghana

    (C) Sierre Leone

86. All of the following pairs represent the names of Asian countries and their capital cities EXCEPT

    (A) Indonesia – Jakarta.

    (B) Thailand – Siam.

    (C) Nepal – Kathmandu.

    (D) Bangladesh – Dacca.

    (E) Philippines – Manila.

87. In terms of controlling population growth in societies around the world, which of the following statements is true regarding the effects of various factors on birth rates?

    (A) Family planning programs actually lead to overall increases in birth rates.

    (B) Rising birth rates are associated with increases in urbanization.

    (C) Economic development results in declines in birth rates.

    (D) Greater gender equality results in a higher birth rate.

    (E) Patriarchal family systems have lower birth rates than egalitarian ones.

88. Which of the following terms would be most clearly linked with the kind of social life and social interaction found in cities rather than rural communities?

    (A) *Gemeinschaft*   (D) *Verstehen*

    (B) In-group   (E) *Gesellschaft*

    (C) Groupthink

89. Which of the following is the best example of a social aggregate?

    (A) Thirteen people riding in a subway car, each reading or staring out the window.

    (B) Twelve jurors listening to testimony in a courtroom.

    (C) Eleven members of a college football team executing a play on the field.

    (D) All African-American females attending a particular university.

    (E) The two parents and three children that constitute a particular nuclear family.

90. When a person interacts with his or her best friend, the group they form would most likely constitute which kind of group?

    (A) A secondary group   (D) A postindustrial group

    (B) An out-group   (E) A formal group

    (C) A primary group

91. John is introduced to Fred, and the two of them shake hands. This handshaking ritual is best characterized as a

    (A) more.   (D) folkway.

    (B) taboo.   (E) sanction.

    (C) law.

92. Which of the following theories of deviant behavior is based on the symbolic interactionist perspective in sociology?

    (A) Sutherland's differential association theory

    (B) Merton's anomie theory

    (C) Park's concentric-zone theory

    (D) Lombroso's body-type theory

    (E) Hoyt's sector theory

93. Fans at a rock concert respond to the music and mood by raucous shouting and screaming, dancing with one another in the aisle and in front of the stage, and throwing flowers onto the stage. These fans would be best characterized as

    (A) an acting crowd.   (D) a rioting crowd.

    (B) a casual crowd.   (E) mass hysteria.

    (C) an expressive crowd.

94. The repeated presentation of the CS without the UCS results in

    (A) spontaneous recovery.   (D) higher-order conditioning.

    (B) inhibition.   (E) negative reinforcement.

    (C) extinction.

95. Which of the following best defines the term "judicial restraint"?

    (A) A decision by judges to limit the number of cases they decide per year

    (B) Refusal by judges to lobby Congress for funds

    (C) A practice by which judges remove themselves from cases in which they have a personal interest

    (D) The tendency of judges to interpret the Constitution in light of the original intent of its framers

    (E) Willingness of judges to decline participation in partisan political campaigns

96. A bill introduced in the House or Senate will most likely

   (A) be passed by the first house but not the second.

   (B) be passed by both houses and become law.

   (C) be sent to the rules committee, then the full house.

   (D) die before it is referred to committee.

   (E) be referred to the appropriate committee, but never reach the floor of the house.

97. Which of the following is true of the president's veto power?

   I. A president may veto certain items in a bill but approve the rest.

   II. A president may pocket-veto a bill by refusing to sign it for 10 days while Congress is in session.

   III. A presidential veto may be overridden by a two-thirds vote of both houses of Congress.

   (A) I only.   (D) II and III only.

   (B) II only.   (E) I, II, and III.

   (C) III only.

QUESTIONS 98 to 100 refer to the following graph.

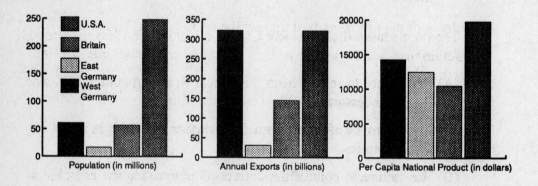

98. Under a unified Germany,

   (A) the United States continues to be the leading exporter.

   (B) Britain will export about 60 percent of Germany's total.

(C) the East will increase Germany's exports by nearly 10 percent.

(D) the United States and Germany will almost be tied in exports.

(E) British and German exports together will total nearly $600 billion.

99. The best indicator of people's standard of living is the

(A) per capita gross national product.

(B) the population divided into the annual exports.

(C) the annual exports.

(D) the per capita gross national product divided into the exports.

(E) the per capita national product multiplied by the population.

100. Which statement would be most true?

(A) The United States leads in productivity and GNP.

(B) Germany will go from fourth to second in GNP by unifying.

(C) For its population, the United States produced the fewest exports.

(D) For its population, Britain produced the most exports.

(E) Unified Germany's per capita income will surpass the United States.

101. The main reason that President Grant's administration is considered a failure is

(A) his failure to retreat from the radical Reconstruction policies of his predecessors.

(B) his failure to effectively quell the Indian uprisings in the Western territories.

(C) his failure to control the corruption permeating his administration.

(D) his attempts to destroy the Democratic party and return the country to a one-party system.

(E) his failure to be reelected after serving his first term in office.

102. "If your neighbor's house was on fire, and he didn't have a garden hose, wouldn't it make sense to let him use your hose to fight the fire so the fire could be put out before it spread to your house?" This question was raised by Franklin Roosevelt to justify

(A) the Neutrality Acts.

(D) the Good Neighbor policy.

(B) the Atlantic Charter.

(E) the Selective Service Act.

(C) the Lend-Lease Act.

103. During the Reformation, Anabaptism drew its membership mostly from the ranks of the

(A) nobility.

(D) businessmen.

(B) middle class.

(E) army officers.

(C) peasants.

104. All of the following were part of the Counter-Reformation EXCEPT

(A) the Index.

(D) the Council of Trent.

(B) the Augsburg Confession.

(E) the Society of Jesus.

(C) the Inquisition.

105. The Treaty of Nanjing ended which war in China?

(A) World War II

(B) Boxer Rebellion

(C) First Opium War (1839-42)

(D) Cultural Revolution

(E) Taipei Rebellion

106. When the explorer H. M. Stanley's plans for opening the Congo Basin were rejected by the British government in 1877, which European power, headed by King Leopold II, took him into its service?

(A) Germany

(D) Italy

(B) France

(E) Norway

(C) Belgium

107. When English and Spanish explorers in the 1500s found Indians in the Americas using tobacco, they brought the tobacco back to Europe. After this introduction, the use of tobacco spread throughout Europe. The beginning of the use of tobacco in Europe is most accurately an example of

    (A) invention.   (D) revolution.

    (B) diffusion.   (E) discovery.

    (C) cultural log.

108. Which of the following people is considered the founder of the field of sociology and is credited with first using the word "sociology"?

    (A) Emile Durkheim   (D) Auguste Comte

    (B) Talcott Parsons   (E) Herbert Spencer

    (C) Karl Marx

109. If a sociologist wished to collect data from a random sample of 1,500 people spread across the United States, it would be most feasible to use which type of research method?

    (A) A survey

    (B) Participant observation

    (C) Face-to-face interviews

    (D) Unobtrusive measures

    (E) A laboratory experiment

110. Which of the following statements would be most consistent with the social exchange theory in sociology?

    (A) Society consists of many interrelated and interdependent parts, each contributing to the maintenance of society.

    (B) People interpret reality and act on the basis of their definition of the situation.

    (C) People weigh the benefits and costs of various lines of action before deciding how to act in a situation.

    (D) Competition, conflict, and dominance and subordination are inherent features of the social system.

(E) A society tends toward a relative stability or dynamic equilibrium.

111. Which of the following is the best example of ethnocentrism?

(A) We travel to another country and realize their practice of worshiping many gods is both primitive and ignorant.

(B) We travel to a new society and find it difficult to adjust to the new food and language.

(C) We find the practice of eating raw fish by the Japanese unappealing.

(D) People move to a new state expecting to find more job opportunities. When they arrive and discover it does not work out that way, they become frustrated.

(E) John meets a student from Brazil and finds the student's culture fascinating.

112. Sally, who comes from a poor black family, finished college and graduate school to become a nuclear physicist. For Sally, being a nuclear physicist is a(n)

(A) master status.   (D) ascribed status.

(B) achieved status.   (E) status hierarchy.

(C) status attainment.

113. The classic social psychology experiments that demonstrated that most people would perform acts in direct contradiction to their morals and beliefs, if a legitimate authority figure accepted responsibility for those acts, was performed by

(A) B. F. Skinner.   (D) Leon Festinger.

(B) Sigmund Freud.   (E) Rollo May.

(C) Stanley Milgram.

114. Which of the following is true of independent regulatory commissions?

(A) They exercise quasi-legislative, quasi-judicial, and executive functions.

(B) They each form part of one of the 14 cabinet-level executive departments.

(C) They regulate certain parts of the federal bureaucracy.

(D) They are directly responsible to the president.

(E) They were created by the executive branch to help execute federal law.

QUESTION 115 refers to the following.

Source: *Guide to Congress*, 2nd ed. (Washington, D.C.: Congressional Quarterly Inc., 1976), p. 563.

115. The subject of the cartoon is most likely

(A) a gerrymandered congressional district.

(B) the influence of environmental issues on congressional behavior.

(C) the role of money in influencing the outcome of an election.

(D) the beastly effect of politics on the character of a congressman.

(E) "dinosaur bills" which congressmen sponsor for the folks back home.

116. The War Powers Resolution of 1973 may be invoked by Congress to accomplish which of the following?

(A) Prevent the president from deploying troops abroad

(B) Declare war

(C) Force the extradition of foreign ambassadors caught spying in the United States

(D) Limit the period for which the president may deploy troops abroad in hostile situations

(E) Force reductions in the defense budget in times of peace and stability

117. Consider a competitive industry composed of firms employing only the labor of their owners as inputs. Let this industry face a downward-sloping demand curve, and let the output price exceed the personal opportunity cost of the labor required to produce the marginal unit of output by the typical firm owner. What should the expected movement of price and market output be in the long run?

(A) Price up and quantity down

(B) Price up and quantity up

(C) Price down and quantity down

(D) Price down and quantity up

(E) Price and quantity remain unchanged

118. In general equilibrium and in a situation of perfect competition

(A) for each consumer, the marginal utility of each good consumed is equal to the price of that good.

(B) for each consumer, marginal utilities of all goods consumed are proportional to the marginal costs of those goods.

(C) the marginal physical product of each input is equal to the price of that input.

(D) the marginal revenue product of each input is equal to the price of the finished good it produces.

(E) the ratio of total expenditure on any good to its price equals marginal utility.

119. Consider an outside shock on the value of the dollar that causes it to depreciate. The Fed could defend the dollar by

(A) increasing the money supply, thereby lowering the LM curve and driving the interest rate up.

(B) increasing government spending, thereby raising the IS curve and driving the interest rate up.

(C) reducing the money supply, thereby raising the LM curve and driving the interest rate up.

(D) increasing taxes, thereby lowering the IS curve and driving the interest rate down.

(E) simultaneously increasing government spending and the money supply so that the GNP climbs with a fixed interest rate.

120. The most significant aspect of the Mexican-American War on the United States during the 20 years following the war was that it

(A) led to the development of the idea of "passive resistance" among those who opposed the war.

(B) ended years of hostility between the United States and Mexico.

(C) reignited the slavery conflict in regard to all the territories newly acquired from Mexico.

(D) gave America undisputed control over Mexican foreign policy for the next 20 years.

(E) revealed the shocking ineptitude of American military forces, leading to massive reforms in military training and procedures throughout the 1850s.

121. U.S. presidents between 1876 and 1900 were considered among the weakest in American history. A major reason for this was that

(A) none of them served more than one term in office.

(B) they considered themselves caretakers, not dynamic initiators of new legislation.

(C) Congress enacted several new laws restricting presidential power during this period.

(D) they were the products of machine politics, political followers who were typically incompetent leaders.

(E) they were limited in their actions by the overwhelming Populist sentiment of their time.

QUESTION 122 refers to the following.

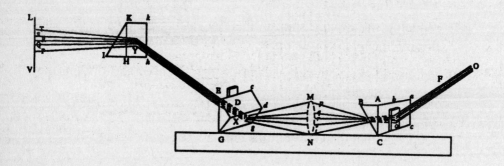

122. The drawing by Isaac Newton illustrates his experiments with

(A) fluids.   (D) gravity.

(B) energy.   (E) gases.

(C) light.

QUESTION 123 refers to the following.

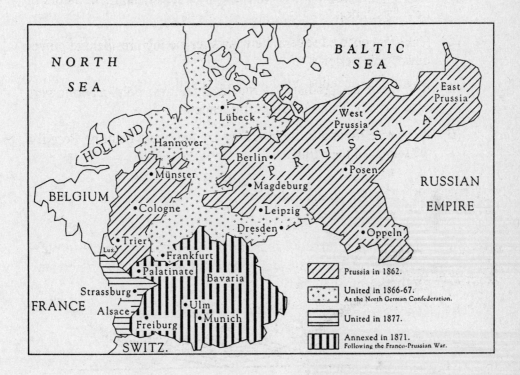

123. According to the map, Prussia

(A) held territory in both eastern and western Germany before 1870.

(B) assumed control of Alsace-Lorraine after 1866.

(C) annexed Bavaria to Prussia in 1866.

(D) was able to unite all of Germany in 1866.

(E) occupied more territory than the Austrian Empire.

124. Which of the following was NOT a feature of the French colonial policy of "association"?

    (A) Rapid economic development of the colonies

    (B) Granting of citizenship to all French West Africans

    (C) A centralized economy

    (D) No plans for independence of the colonies

    (E) All formal education conducted in French

125. What year did the Meiji era in Japan begin?

    (A) 1867   (D) 1945

    (B) 1910   (E) 1800

    (C) 1853

126. Stephanie, a plastic surgeon, finds time in her busy schedule to play on a soccer team and attend weekly church functions. Her church and soccer activities make up her

    (A) subordinate statuses.   (D) ascribed statuses.

    (B) master statuses.   (E) None of the above.

    (C) role inconsistencies.

127. Concerning the density of social networks, studies suggest that

    I.   dense social networks are positively related to mental and physical health.

    II. dense social networks are positively related to self-esteem.

    III. loose social networks are causally related to poor health.

    IV. gender is causally related to dense social networks.

    (A) I only.   (D) I and II only.

    (B) III only.   (E) I, II, and III only.

    (C) IV only.

128. The most radical and complete resocialization is achieved in

    (A) a total institution.

    (B) a bureaucracy.

    (C) late adolescence.

    (D) a subculture.

    (E) None of the above.

129. Which of the following is the best example of Durkheim's theory of anomic suicide?

    (A) After divorcing his wife and moving away from his family, feeling lonely and depressed, Tom decides to kill himself.

    (B) The massive political and economic changes accompanying the breakup of the Soviet Union has resulted in an increased number of suicides among Russian citizens.

    (C) Bob, a captured terrorist, chooses to commit suicide rather than reveal the secrets of his organization.

    (D) Feeling isolated and lonely her first year away at college, Jane decides to kill herself.

    (E) Susan, a member of the Branch Davidian cult, commits mass suicide with the other members of her organization.

130. Social learning theory was first proposed by

    (A) Bandura and Walters.

    (B) B. F. Skinner.

    (C) Miller and Dollard.

    (D) J. B. Watson.

    (E) Carl Rogers.

CLEP SOCIAL SCIENCES AND HISTORY
TEST 2

ANSWER KEY

Section 1

1. (B)	14. (B)	27. (D)	40. (E)	53. (C)
2. (C)	15. (B)	28. (E)	41. (D)	54. (A)
3. (E)	16. (A)	29. (E)	42. (C)	55. (C)
4. (E)	17. (A)	30. (E)	43. (A)	56. (C)
5. (D)	18. (A)	31. (E)	44. (E)	57. (D)
6. (E)	19. (C)	32. (A)	45. (B)	58. (A)
7. (A)	20. (D)	33. (B)	46. (E)	59. (E)
8. (B)	21. (C)	34. (E)	47. (A)	60. (D)
9. (B)	22. (A)	35. (E)	48. (A)	61. (C)
10. (C)	23. (A)	36. (D)	49. (C)	62. (C)
11. (D)	24. (C)	37. (B)	50. (D)	63. (D)
12. (A)	25. (C)	38. (C)	51. (B)	64. (D)
13. (B)	26. (C)	39. (A)	52. (A)	65. (C)

Section 2

66. (C)	79. (E)	92. (A)	105. (C)	118. (B)
67. (B)	80. (D)	93. (C)	106. (C)	119. (C)
68. (A)	81. (B)	94. (C)	107. (B)	120. (C)
69. (A)	82. (C)	95. (D)	108. (D)	121. (B)
70. (C)	83. (C)	96. (E)	109. (A)	122. (C)
71. (C)	84. (C)	97. (C)	110. (C)	123. (A)
72. (D)	85. (A)	98. (C)	111. (A)	124. (B)
73. (A)	86. (B)	99. (A)	112. (B)	125. (A)
74. (B)	87. (C)	100. (C)	113. (C)	126. (A)
75. (A)	88. (E)	101. (C)	114. (A)	127. (D)
76. (E)	89. (A)	102. (C)	115. (A)	128. (A)
77. (D)	90. (C)	103. (C)	116. (D)	129. (B)
78. (A)	91. (D)	104. (B)	117. (D)	130. (C)

DETAILED EXPLANATIONS
OF ANSWERS
TEST 2

Section 1

1.   **(B)** Roosevelt's most memorable line was also the underpinning of his foreign policy strategy in Central America: "Speak softly but carry a big stick." The thrust of this policy was that the United States wouldn't waste a lot of energy on words in settling issues in Central America. Instead, there would be a focus on action. This served to warn Central American countries to watch their behavior or they would face U.S. political and military intervention to insure that things were returned to "proper order." Basically, Roosevelt's policy was an expansion of the Monroe Doctrine and served notice that the United States intended to be the policeman of the Caribbean. Roosevelt, true to form, backed up his words with action. The United States sent troops into six different Latin American nations between 1900 and 1930. U.S. economic intervention was even more prevalent. Regrettably, while this policy allowed America to flex its muscles and solved many short-term problems, it ignored the sensitivities of Latin Americans, building deep resentments that linger today.

2.   **(C)** The Continental army had been poorly paid, when they were paid at all, throughout the war. As the war wound down after Yorktown, the army was camped at Newburgh, New York waiting for results of peace negotiations. Fears spread among the soldiers that the army might be disbanded without pay or pension. Nationalists fueled these fears, encouraging the belief that a military uprising might take place if the states refused to provide Congress with taxation powers to raise money to pay the soldiers' pensions, among other things. Only a personal appeal by Washington to his soldiers prevented the situation from exploding into a military crisis and perhaps an attempted military coup.

3.   **(E)**. Steam and waterpower drove the early machines and the mechanized looms of the Industrial Revolution, and so choice (B) is an important

part of that event. Choice (E) is unhistorical, since the electric motor was developed after the First Industrial Revolution; the electricity was often produced by a steam engine. The spinning jenny and flying shuttle were involved in the production of thread and cloth, while the Bessemer process was involved in the production of steel.

4.   **(E)** Although he was not typical of nineteenth-century liberalism in every respect – he favored the unions as a means of helping the working class, for example – John Stuart Mill wrote extensively on politics and is generally considered the most notable nineteenth-century liberal writer. His *On Liberty* (1859) is one of the most famous defenses of individual rights. The other choices may be quickly eliminated if the identity of the individuals involved is known. As the leader of the British Conservative party in the second half of the nineteenth century, Disraeli opposed many liberal programs. Napoleon III, emperor of France during the 1850s and 1860s, worked to limit one of the major liberal goals, the achievement of true parliamentary government in France. The other choices list lesser-known individuals but are also incorrect. Proudhon was the most famous anarchist of the first half of the nineteenth century, while Fourier was one of the best-known Utopian Socialists of the same period.

5.   **(D)** Of all the choices listed, the only conflict that applies to Egypt in the 1950s was control of the Suez Canal. The conflict began with a plan by Egypt's socialist president Nasser to build a huge dam across the Nile River at Aswan. When the United States withdrew its aid for the project, Nasser nationalized the Suez Canal, seizing control from the Anglo-French company that had been operating it since Britian withdrew its troops from the canal zone. His plan was to use the profits to finance the "high dam." The British and French invaded in an attempt to regain financial control of the canal, but U.N. pressure eventually forced them to withdraw, and the dam was finished with Russian aid.

6.   **(E)** Of all the choices, only Yokohama is not an island in Japan. It is actually a port city south of Tokyo on the island of Honshu (A). The largest of Japan's islands, Honshu is the home of about 80 percent of Japan's population and its capital city Tokyo. Kyushu (B) is the southern-most island and the next most heavily populated. Hokkaido (C) is at the northern tip of Japan and is the second largest island, and Shikoku (D), between Honshu and Kyushu, is the country's smallest island.

7. **(A)** An ethnic group consists of people who share a common culture and sense of identity. While some ethnic groups are also minorities, others are not. An ethnic group often includes people of *different* social classes (B), occupations (E), and political views (D). Some, like Puerto Ricans and Cubans, include people with a variety of skin colors (C).

8. **(B)** Prejudice refers to preconceived negative attitudes toward people with distinctive social characteristics. It should not be confused with (A) ethnocentrism (belief in the superiority of one's own group), (C) discrimination (harmful behavior toward members of a minority group), or (D) scapegoating (blaming another group for one's problems). Prejudice may make it difficult for members of a minority group to improve their position (E).

9. **(B)** In the caste system one's status is determined at birth. Members of the upper castes usually enjoy greater wealth (C), though there are many exceptions. No amount of individual accomplishment, such as education (D), can raise or lower this caste position. Women (A) do not enjoy a higher position than men. Marriage between castes (E) is usually forbidden.

10. **(C)** The concept of minority group refers to people who share a low status in society, hold relatively little power, and are the object of prejudicial attitudes and discriminatory treatment. High levels of income or education (B) usually are not found in minority groups. Political preference (A) and type of schooling (E) have nothing to do with minority group status. While some minority groups share the same religion (D), others do not.

11. **(D)** Weber identified a hierarchical authority structure as a distinctive characteristic of bureaucracy. There is a well-defined chain of command which identifies who has authority in every aspect of the organization. Some members of the bureaucracy have greater authority (A) than others. Group decision making (B) is not usually found in bureaucracies. (C) and (E) are incorrect because specialization of tasks and rigid adherence to rules and regulations are other essential characteristics of bureaucracies.

12. **(A)** Bales found that small groups typically have one leader who directs the group in accomplishing its goals (instrumental) and another who creates unity within the group and maintains harmony (expressive).

The other choices refer to personal characteristics which may or may not be present in group leaders.

13. **(B)** In an approach-avoidance conflict situation, one is both attracted to and repelled by the same goal. For example, one may want to go to college, but may also be fearful of the typical college workload.

14. **(B)** In 1974, in the case *United States v. Nixon,* the Supreme Court declared that the president has an executive privilege to protect military, diplomatic, and sensitive national security secrets from disclosure. However, the material may be successfully subpoenaed if needed by either the defense or the state in a criminal prosecution. (A) is incorrect since the right of the president to veto proposed legislation is called the veto power. It has nothing to do with the president's right to protect information from disclosure. (C) is incorrect because the right of the president to appoint and receive ambassadors is unrelated to the executive privilege of withholding certain information. (D) is incorrect because the president's power to pardon is unrelated to executive privilege. Also, the president has an unlimited, not a limited, right to pardon persons convicted of federal crimes. (E) is incorrect because the president enjoys no immunity from prosecution for misdemeanors or felonies.

15. **(B)** Special spending projects sponsored by members of Congress for their home states or districts are known as pork barrel legislation. (A) is incorrect because a filibuster is an attempt in the Senate to talk a bill to death by preventing it from coming up for a vote. (C) is incorrect because logrolling is the term used to designate vote-swapping by members of Congress for special projects. (D) is incorrect because "grease for the gears" is a fictitious term made up as a distractor for this question. (E) is incorrect because "senatorial courtesy" refers to an informal practice whereby the president seeks to have a judicial nominee approved by the senior senator from the state in which the nominee will sit.

16. **(A)** An elitist view of American politics stresses that the policy-making process is dominated by a small, unrepresentative minority. In *The Power Elite,* published in 1956, the American sociologist C. Wright Mills argued that corporate leaders, top military officers, and key political leaders dominated American politics. (B) is incorrect because the view that thousands of competing interest groups influence policy-making is called a "pluralistic" view of politics. (C) is incorrect because the view that large states dominate public policy, if such a view is held by anyone, has no

name. Such a view would be difficult to defend, since all states get two senators regardless of population. (D) is incorrect because such a view has no specific name. Again, such a view would be difficult to defend, since rural areas have such a small population relative to urban areas, and state legislators and U.S. representatives are chosen on the basis of population. (E) is plausible but incorrect. It is true that only about one-third of eligible voters turn out in off-year congressional races (the figure was 33 percent in 1986). However, this fact does not provide the basis for an elitist theory, since it is not clear that election outcomes would have been different if twice as many voters had voted. Also, low voter turnout does not necessarily mean that policy-making is insulated from public opinion and wishes, which is central to elitist theories.

17. **(A)** is correct. Britain is the only top importing nation that does not appear among the top five exporters.

18. **(A)** is correct. Canada is the largest importer. Even the two European nations, Britain and Germany, combined import less.

19. **(C)** is correct. Japan was the largest single exporter, and combining with Taiwan made it even larger. No other region had two exporters listed.

20. **(D)** is correct, with the difference between exports and imports being the greatest in Japan's favor. The others are relatively close, with no comparisons available for Britain.

21. **(C)** is correct. If your nation sells more exports than it buys imports, it creates a surplus of capital coming in or a profit. (A) and (B) refer to the payments made for many things, including trade. So they may reflect on trade balances, but are not the same. (D) is the opposite. In the graph, the United States's imports from Japan reflect a balance of trade unfavorable for the United States and favorable for Japan. (E) This can result from unfavorable trade balances, but reflects many other spending and revenue factors.

22. **(A)** The "Good Neighbor" policy sought to smooth over relations between the United States and Latin America by retreating from the blatant interventionism which dominated U.S. policy into the 1930s. The effects of interventionism had become increasingly costly to the point that the benefits derived were not worth the expense. In 1933, Franklin Roosevelt

officially consolidated many changes already under way in U.S. policy toward Latin America under the heading of the "Good Neighbor" policy. Under this plan, the United States would pull back from the nearly constant use of military intervention to control Latin American nations. The U.S. government would cease acting unilaterally in Latin American affairs and would attempt to consult with and seek the approval of Latin American governments before intervening in the region. In addition, the United States would support Latin American governments headed by strong, independent leaders and would help train Latin American military forces so they could defend themselves. U.S. banks would also provide loans and other economic assistance to help stabilize fragile Latin American economies.

While the United States still dominated many aspects of Latin American life, with the enactment of the "Good Neighbor" policy that domination was handled more diplomatically, with somewhat more respect for local authorities. Many of the leaders who emerged at this time were military dictators who were trained by American military personnel as part of the effort to train Latin American military forces. These dictators owed their power to the United States and often stayed in power only as a result of U.S. backing. So, while the days of the "Big Stick" effectively ended with the "Good Neighbor" policy, U.S. domination of the region continued, albeit at a somewhat reduced level of visibility.

23. **(A)** The Northwest Ordinance of 1787, like the previous ordinances of 1784 and 1785, ignored the Indian tribes' claims to the land contained within the Northwest Territory. The Shawnee, Delaware, and Miami, armed with weapons supplied by the British, attacked whites who settled north and west of the Ohio River and prevented settlement of the region for nearly 10 years. While the Northwest Ordinance was a progressive document for its time, it was meaningless until the Indian problem was resolved and settlement of the area was achieved. Contained within the Northwest Ordinance were the provisions listed in choices (B) through (E). The antislavery prohibition is particularly notable because it reflected a growing concern, particularly in the North, about the institution of slavery. It marked the first regional limitation of slavery in the United States beyond individual state boundaries.

24. **(C)** Here two different developments (the Commercial Revolution and Italian Renaissance) are tied, and you are asked to explain the connection. The correct answer requires memory retention, understanding of terminology, and an ability to analyze the social and economic connections between the two developments. The Commercial Revolution describes the

expansion of trade and the establishment of a broad system of joint-stock companies and banks in pre-Renaissance Italy. The new merchants of the Commercial Revolution held few ties to the earlier Middle Ages. They established new towns in Italy, such as Florence; they preferred "worldly" reading material on topics such as etiquette and politics; and for some time their new towns held no cathedrals or even smaller churches. In effect, the Commercial Revolution created a new, secular middle class which financed much of the artistic and literary work of the Italian Renaissance. The other choices are either incorrect or irrelevant.

25. **(C)** Although knowledge of terminology is a great help, in this question careful reading and analyzing of the implication of statements is essential. This quotation, from Vladimir Lenin, father of the Soviet Revolution of 1917, is part of his argument that capitalism held internal contradictions which would lead to its self-destruction; a major contradiction was the uncontrolled race for colonies.

[Source: Lenin, *Imperialism: The Highest Stage of Capitalism* (New York: International Publishers, 1934)]

26. **(C)** In December 1958, Kwame Nkrumah invited representatives from nationalist movements in 28 territories still under colonial rule to meet in Accra for the first All-African People's Conference. Nkrumah had often stated that once Ghana attained independence, it would be his goal to lead the rest of the African continent to freedom and unity. Ghana achieved independence on March 6, 1957, and he attempted to fulfill the second part of his objective the next year in 1958.

27. **(D)** On October 10, 1911, the revolutionary army near Hankow rebelled against the government. In January 1912, leaders of the revolt met in Nanjing and declared Sun Yat-Sen the new president of the republic, officially ending the rule of the last emperor and the Qing Dynasty.

28. **(E)** Several researchers have reported a heavy emphasis on group activities, both on and off the job, for employees of Japanese corporations. (A) and (B) are incorrect because Japanese workers typically work longer hours for lower wages than American workers. Japanese workers actually enjoy *greater* job security (C) and demonstrate more loyalty (D) to their employers than their American counterparts.

29. **(E)** A group consists of members who regularly interact with each other (A). This interaction creates shared values (B), a sense of identity (C), and specialization of roles (D). There may be conflict among group members, but as long as they continue to interact with each other the group exists.

30. **(E)** A voluntary association is an organization like the League of Women Voters, Lions Club, or American Legion. Members typically join the organization because they wish to participate in its activities, not to earn an income (B) or make a profit (A). Selection of members (C) and type of government (D) vary greatly among voluntary organizations.

31. **(E)** Most families in the United States today are nuclear (consisting of a married couple and their children) and neolocal (residence tends to be separate from the families of either spouse). Choices (A), (B), (C), and (D) include either Statement I or Statement IV, both of which do not describe families in the United States today. A matrilineal system reckons descent through both male and female lines (bilateral); a matriarchal family is one in which women hold power and authority, but the United States is either patriarchal (men hold power) or egalitarian.

32. **(A)** Central to Marx's analysis of religion was its role in protecting the status quo by discouraging people from realizing that changing society would alleviate their troubles. Bellah (B) was a theorist on religion, but he focused on the type of religious organization that is found in different societies. Durkheim (C) was also a theorist on religion, but he took a functionalist approach, rather than the conflict perspective which underlies Marx's approach. Weber (D) was best known for his analysis of how religious beliefs can support economic institutions, such as capitalism. Michels (E), best known for his "iron law of oligarchy," theorized about political and economic institutions, not religion.

33. **(B)** The "hidden curriculum" refers to the ways, sometimes subtle and indirect, that schools teach students to support the status quo and the school's system of inequalities. (A), (C), (D), and (E) refer to aspects of the school budget, the curriculum, or the student body that, while they may have implications for the hidden curriculum or be related to it, are not a statement of what the hidden curriculum is.

34. **(E)** All of these are characteristics of affiliation. Schachter had two conditions in his experiment: High versus low fear, in which he warned

subjects that they were going to receive a shock that was either extremely painful or just a tickle. After announcing a 10-minute delay before the shocks, he gave them a questionnaire that indicated their desire to affiliate. High-fear subjects wanted to affiliate much more than the low-fear subjects. He also found that first-born children affiliate more when fearful and that "misery only loves misery's company," that is, fearful subjects prefer to affiliate with others in the same situation.

35. **(E)** The president does not have the ability to personally introduce legislation in either house of Congress. To introduce legislation in either house, one must be a member of that house. (A) is incorrect because the fact that he is elected indirectly by the people, not by the legislature as in parliamentary systems, is a source of power and independence for the president. (B) is incorrect because the Supreme Court has expanded the president's emergency powers. See, for example, the Prize Cases, 1863; and *Korematsu v. U.S.,* 1944. (C) is incorrect because when the president has high public approval ratings, as measured in opinion polls, he is in a much better position to push his legislative proposals through Congress. (D) is incorrect because the veto power can be wielded very effectively by presidents to prevent the passage of legislation they don't like. President Bush had vetoed more than 20 bills by January 1992, and none of the vetoes had been overridden by Congress.

36. **(D)** Nearly all civil servants have jobs that are, practically speaking, beyond reach of the president. The only reasons for which a federal civil servant can be fired are misconduct or poor performance, and then only if the person's supervisor is willing to invest a great deal of time and effort. Civil servants cannot be fired for political reasons. This gives civil servants the opportunity to thwart or delay presidential initiatives by half-hearted compliance or passive noncompliance with presidential directives. (A) is incorrect because all agency budget requests must be submitted to and approved by the Office of Management and Budget before they can be sent to Congress. (B) is incorrect because the president has many more opportunities to influence public opinion than do civil servants. The presidency is a much more high-profile office than any civil service position, and the president has access to television and newspaper coverage that civil servants generally do not. (C) is incorrect because, technically, the federal bureaucracy is part of the executive branch, and is directly responsible to the president. (E) is incorrect because the Hatch Act, passed in 1939, made it illegal for civil servants to solicit campaign contributions.

37.   **(B)** In 1985, Congress passed the Gramm-Rudman Act with the intent to balance the federal budget by 1992. The law created a plan whereby the budget deficit for each year from 1986 through 1991 could not exceed a specified, declining amount. Therefore, the correct response is (B). (A) is incorrect because the Hyde Amendment of 1976 outlawed the use of federal funds for abortions, except where the life of the mother is at stake. (C) is incorrect because the Boland Amendments outlawed the use of federal funds to aid the Nicaraguan Contras. (D) is incorrect because the Gramm-Rudman Act did not change the tax code. (E) is incorrect because the INF Treaty of 1987 provided for the destruction of intermediate range missiles in Europe.

38.   **(C)** is correct because the event was obviously a stock market crash, with no outside event cited as a cause. Historical references, such as ticker tape and anaconda, help pinpoint the era. (A) is incorrect, because modern references, such as telephone, eliminate this era. (B) is incorrect. This will be a partial result of the crash, but no references to it are made. Pearl Harbor Day (D) is also incorrect. No reference to this is made, plus historically the attack occurred on a weekend when the market is closed. (E) is incorrect because there is no reference to point to this event, which occurred in the afternoon while the crash began in the morning.

39.   **(A)** The quote says that once the tape lost track no one knew what was happening. This lack of information would increase the panic. (B) and (C) are cited as being the opposite, with a sound economy waiting for a stock market rally. (D) is incorrect, because three major issues, steel, telephone, and anaconda (copper) were listed. (E) is incorrect. This is the opposite of what happened, there were "no buying orders...."

40.   **(E)** is most correct as cited, with sell orders coming in from all over the country, with no buy orders to meet them. (A) is wrong. The passage states that there was so much activity that the ticker tape was overwhelmed. (B) is incorrect. The quote says that the market opened "steady." (C) is incorrect. The opening sentence discusses the general falling market recently. (D) is incorrect. There is no evidence of this in the quote.

41.   **(D)** is correct, even though he had been in office for less than a year, and the economic conditions were already in place. (A), (B), and (C) were the three presidents before Hoover, and (E) was elected after Hoover to try to solve the depression that followed.

42.   **(C)**   is most correct. FDIC or federal bank account insurance was part of the New Deal to restore confidence in banks, not stocks. (A) is incorrect; the Securities and Exchange Commission was created to regulate the stock market after the crash. Among its reforms were (B), which reduced the percentage of stock that could be bought on credit (margin), tighter checks on the economic soundness of businesses issuing stocks (D), and checks on how people inside a company can buy and sell their own stocks (E).

43.   **(A)**   "Reaganomics" was the term coined for President Ronald Reagan's supply-side economic policies. Reagan believed that the way to repair the shattered economy he inherited from the Carter administration was to cut federal spending on domestic programs while at the same time cutting taxes for the wealthy and for corporations. The "supply-side" theory advocated by Reagan asserted that by cutting taxes to businesses and to the rich, money would be freed up for future investments and the creation of new jobs. This investment income would offset the initial loss of tax revenue caused by the tax cuts. Eventually, through the creation of new jobs and investments, the money freed up by tax cuts to the rich would "trickle down" to the middle classes and the poor. While this sounded good on paper, it never worked out quite as well in real life. Yes, the tax cuts did spur investment, but the investments often didn't translate into jobs that paid well. The "trickle-down" was uneven and often quite limited. Many wealthy people pocketed the money rather than investing it. Still, new jobs were created and the nation began an economic expansion that has lasted into the 1990s.

44.   **(E)**   Nineteenth-century Europeans and Americans fully believed in the superiority of their cultures, of the white race, and of Christianity. In their minds, it was perfectly acceptable to go into undeveloped nonwhite lands and do what they pleased with the lands and the natives. Since the natives of these lands were overwhelmingly nonwhite, non-Christian, and technologically undeveloped, Americans and Europeans rationalized their domination of these lands and the subjugation of the natives. They viewed their actions as a noble mission to "civilize" the "savages" and give them the benefits of Western culture. This "mission" was called the "white man's burden" because it was characterized as a burden that only the shoulders of the Western white male were big enough to handle.

45.   **(B)**   Here the emphasis is entirely upon memory retention; if the quotation is not known, and little is known about the other thinkers, a successful guess is unlikely and is not recommended. This much-quoted

passage by the French mathematician and philosopher René Descartes searches for absolute certainty by using a method of "systematic doubt." Rejecting the certainty of all knowledge but the knowledge that a thinking process was occurring, he believed that he had established one certain fact – his own existence.

46.   **(E)**   In their work to strengthen the French absolute monarchs, royal ministers Cardinals Mazarin and Richelieu placed government agents, or intendants, in areas throughout France, where they acted as both the "king's ears" and as collectors of revenue. The move established a "royal presence" in major areas of the country. Choices (A) (*lettres de cachet*) and (B) were other steps taken to strengthen absolutism in France.

47.   **(A)**   In Swahili "ujamaa" translates roughly into "brotherhood" or "friendship." Nyerere, the socialist president of Tanzania, developed this concept to represent his search for an ideal socialist society. The concept of "ujamaa" takes its model from traditional African societies in a pre-colonial past. In the words of Nyerere, it looks back to a society in which "nobody starved, whether of food or human dignity, because he lacked personal wealth; he could depend on the wealth possessed by the community of which he was a member. That was socialism. That *is* socialism." The equality inherent in ujamaa could be applied to all of Africa, not only Tanzania (E) or the nation-states created by colonialism (D). While Nyerere did support the pan-African movement (B), ujamaa stood for a specific kind of African socialism. Critics of ujamaa, such as Kwame Nkrumah, charged that it was too idealistic, depending on a mythical African past, as well as unrealistic. Nkrumah supported economic modernization (C) through the action of state-controlled corporations instead of the models of an outdated rural past.

48.   **(A)**   The Yellow River, about 2,700 miles long, runs west to east across China, bringing in the summer heavy deposits of yellow silt which give the river its name. The river enters the Pacific Ocean near the Shandong Peninsula. The nickname "China's Sorrow" came from the river's tendency to build up its own bed and flood hundreds of square miles of farmland. Since it may take years to recultivate flooded lands, many of the floods in China's history have led to periods of famine. While the Yangtze River (B) is longer than the Yellow River at about 3,200 miles, it has not had the same influence over the land. The Wei River (D) and the Tarim River (E) are both smaller rivers in the eastern and northwestern regions of China, respectively. The Ganges River (C) is in India.

49. **(C)** Legal-rational authority is the type of authority based on rules and laws. (A) and (B) are incorrect because they refer to other bases of authority, namely, authority based on customary and established ways of doing things and authority based on special and extraordinary powers or qualities, respectively. (D) is incorrect because all three types of authority can become institutionalized. (E) is incorrect because the question refers to political, not economic or corporate, authority.

50. **(D)** Union membership peaked in the 1950s at 25 percent of the work force and has declined steadily to about 15 percent today. (A) is wrong because corporate concentration has become even greater than a few decades ago. (B) is wrong because market forces are at least as powerful as a few decades ago. (C) is incorrect because the economic sphere is probably more important to the power elite than in the past. (E) is wrong because the industrial sector has been declining as a proportion of the economy.

51. **(B)** Caste stratification systems have both rigid boundaries between classes and ranking based on heredity. (A) and (C) are incorrect because they each only include one of the correct alternatives. (D) and (E) are incorrect because they include III (achieved statuses predominate) which is characteristic of an open or class stratification system, the opposite of a caste system. (D) also includes only one of the two correct choices.

52. **(A)** Intragenerational mobility refers to changes during a person's career. Chris has moved from a relatively low position in the corporation to a high position during his own career. (B) and (E) are incorrect because they refer to changes between a parent's occupational position and that of their offspring (*inter*generational mobility), and they also do not describe mobility, as the parent's position is relatively similar to that of their offspring. (C) is wrong because it shows no mobility, with the person moving from one carpentry position to another carpentry position. (D) is ambiguous as far as mobility is concerned, since it does not indicate anything about Nancy's occupational or economic position after quitting her nursing position.

53. **(C)** is correct because it is a direct statement of conflict theory's position that inequality results from the domination and exploitation of the less powerful by the more powerful. (A) is incorrect because it states the view of functionalism as to why inequality persists. (B) is wrong from all perspectives because stratification, by its nature, provides for a narrowing

of the distribution of resources. (D) is incorrect because conflict theory sees the source of inequality as stemming from social structures rather than individual inadequacies. (E) is wrong because conflict theory does not claim that stratification is a rational response but rather reflects an exercise of power.

54. **(A)** Pluralism refers to a situation in which racial or ethnic groups live side by side but retain a distinct identity and lifestyle. (B) is wrong because it refers to the opposite process, where different groups lose their distinctive identity and lifestyle. (C) is wrong because it refers to two groups living apart from one another. (D) is incorrect. Separatism refers to a minority taking steps to live apart from the majority. (E) is incorrect because it refers to a minority acquiescing to the demands of a majority.

55. **(C)** The Thematic Apperception Test was designed by Murray and Morgan in 1935, to determine the major themes of concern for a particular individual by allowing him to respond freely to the vague and ambiguous pictures presented on TAT cards. Theoretically, the themes expressed in the responses reflect the subject's present motivational, emotional, and conflicted condition.

56. **(C)** The "single member district" part of the term means that each district gets a single representative. The "plurality vote system" part means that the candidate with the most votes, even if less than a majority, wins the election. Therefore, (C) is the correct answer. (A) is incorrect because a runoff election is not necessary in a plurality voting system. If the candidate with the most votes wins, whether or not (s)he gets a majority, there is no need for a runoff. (B) is incorrect because each district gets only one representative in a single member district system. (D) is incorrect because there is no requirement that some votes count more than others in a single member district, plurality vote system. Members of the U.S. House of Representatives are chosen by the single member, plurality vote system. In elections for U.S. representatives, each person's vote counts the same as any other person's vote. (E) is incorrect because third parties are more likely to win seats in a multi-member district, proportional representation system. In such systems, each district gets several representatives, and each party gets a number of seats proportionate to its total vote in the district election. Third parties are more likely to gain seats, since it is possible for them to get 10 percent or 20 percent of the vote, and thus 10 percent or 20 percent of the seats for the district. In single member district, plurality vote systems, by contrast, the party with the plurality gets the one seat, and all others get nothing.

57.   **(D)**   The Attorney General is the cabinet official in charge of the Justice Department. (A) is incorrect because the Solicitor-General is the third-ranking official at the Justice Department. (B) is incorrect because there is no federal official designated Secretary of Justice. (C) is incorrect because the Secretary of State is in charge of the State Department. (E) is incorrect because the Chief Justice sits on the Supreme Court.

58.   **(A)**   The question asks which statement is false. (A) is a correct response because the state party conventions choose their respective state party chairmen. (B) is a true statement. The party platform is written at the national party convention. (C) is a true statement, since the convention does nominate the party's candidate for president. (D) is a true statement since the Democratic party, unlike the Republican party, has several hundred "super delegates" who are free to vote for the nominee of their choice at the convention. The super delegates are Democratic governors, congressmen, and other distinguished party members. (E) is a true statement because one of the functions of the convention is to set the time and place of the next convention.

59.   **(E)**   is most correct as the two line graphs have met in the 1970s. (A) The opposite has been true as the GNP line was almost always below that of the labor force. (B) is incorrect as the difference between the two lines widened and narrowed in different areas. (C) Farming had declined to below 50 percent well before 1900. (D) Even though the graphs' curves became more level in the 1970s, they still reflected a declining influence.

60.   **(D)**   is most correct. The closing of the gap between GNP and labor force reflect the increasing efficiency of each farmer. (A) is not an accurate conclusion because, with fewer farmers growing the food supply, their importance is great. (B) is not addressed by the graph. The range of farm incomes is wide. (C) Automation might be an explanation for the increased efficiency, but the graphs do not supply that information. (E) There was at least one period on each graph when the line went upward.

61.   **(C)**   is the correct answer. Farming has become increasingly agribusiness and the family farm has decreased in influence and number. (A) is a traditional problem as farmers have to borrow until crops are harvested and hope income is good. (B) The United States is usually a food exporter, using its surpluses to sell crops abroad. (D) Several years of severe weather, such as drought, in the 1980s illustrated how dependent agriculture still is on nature. (E) Government farm programs have been

very important for 70 years, helping by price supports, quotas, crop limits, and direct payments.

62.   **(C)** is most correct. Efficiency is not necessarily a problem, but the reduction of workers reduces both the earning power of agricultural workers and the political clout of agriculture as an occupation. (A) is the exact opposite of the trend which has continued for most of the twentieth century. (B) World food demands, not supplies, are increasing with population growth and all food exporters will be pressured to increase production. (D) Water supplies are decreasing in relation to the population worldwide. (E) Again, the world population growth will increase food needs.

63.   **(D)** The paternalistic view of slavery, held by most Southern plantation owners, held that blacks were inferior, mentally weak and ignorant, requiring "protection" from the evils that could befall them if they were left on their own. In this view, slaveowners were benevolent protectors who took care of their black slaves almost as parents take care of children. This was a comforting myth that most slaveholders really appear to have believed. It was comforting in that if they were really protectors of their poor black "children," then holding slaves wasn't sinful at all. It was, rather, a social service providing a good for everybody involved. Unfortunately, this twisted rationalization denied the fact that slaves were horribly mistreated and often abused or killed for little or no provocation. If they were ignorant or childlike, it is only because they were denied educational opportunities and many slaves learned that acting with childlike deference to their "master" often got them better treatment. In other words, their childishness was often an act based on a powerful instinct to survive rather than any limitations of mental capacity.

64.   **(D)** Mark Twain's writings pioneered a trend toward realism in American literature at the turn of the century. This trend portrayed the lives of real, flawed, and often quite colorful human beings. There was no effort to make the characters in these stories "larger than life" or pillars of virtue to be admired for their flawless character. These people struggled with the everyday issues of life as well as the bigger social and moral questions of the day, sometimes reaching successful resolutions to their quests, more often than not finding only partial answers to their problems. The focus of these stories was often on the temptations of sin, sexuality, and other of life's evils. The hero or heroine often faced difficult tests or questions regarding what was right or wrong in a particular situation. The realistic school of writing was in many ways a coming of age for Ameri-

can literature and bore its own unique stamp as a uniquely American contribution to the world of written fiction.

65.   **(C)**   The first woman to be awarded the Nobel Peace Prize, Bertha von Suttner, an Austrian, gained wide attention for her book, which contributed to the founding of Peace Societies in Austria and Germany. Admiral Tirpitz represented the opposite pole; he masterminded Germany's plans, beginning in the 1890s, to create a German navy to rival the British navy. Rosa Luxemberg, a German Marxist, was killed during a failed revolutionary attempt in Germany in 1919. Theobald von Bethmann-Hollweg was the chancellor of Germany during the early stages of World War I. Cosima Wagner was the influential wife of composer Richard Wagner.

Section 2

66.   **(C)**   This question deals with a complex situation at the start of the war. It requires analytical thinking, an understanding of a complex chain of events, and some knowledge of terminology (although the key term – "Schlieffen Plan" – does not appear in the question). Choice (A) may be eliminated, since such an obvious answer is unlikely to be the correct one on an advanced test. During frequent renewals of the Triple Alliance during the late nineteenth century, Germany was consistently pushed by Austria to make increasingly specific and secret promises of aid to Austria in the event of war. According to one German promise, a Russian mobilization was to lead to a German declaration of war. German military planners, however, were worried about a two-front war, to both the east (Russia) and west (France). A commission working under the German Count Alfred von Schlieffen produced the famous Schlieffen Plan, which required that Germany immediately invade the weaker country of the two in overwhelming numbers, with the goal of quickly defeating the weaker country. The writers of the Schlieffen Plan assumed the weaker nation was France.

67.   **(B)**   Mozambique, on the Southeast tip of the African continent above South Africa, was colonized by Portugal. All of the other countries (A), (C), (D), and (E) were occupied by the British.

68.   **(A)**   In 1971 India, led by Indira Gandhi, daughter of former Prime Minister Jawaharlal Nehru, joined East Pakistan in a war against West Pakistan. West Pakistan was eventually defeated and East Pakistan became the independent nation of Bangladesh. The countries of Vietnam (B), Cambodia (C), and Laos (D) were all independent countries in 1965 as was North Korea (E), which officially came into existence on September 9, 1948, when North Korean communists established the Democratic People's Republic of Korea.

69.   **(A)**   The amount of access to power and resources is one of the criteria that sociologists use to identify the minority status of a group. (B) and (C) are wrong because the concept of minority group does not depend on a group's relative numbers in a society. (D) is incorrect because a minority group, by definition, does not wield power. (E) is wrong because a minority may be recent immigrants, but immigrants are not minorities if they are not denied access to power.

70.   **(C)**   Research shows that prejudice and discrimination flourish when two groups must compete for scarce resources. Research shows that (A), (B), and (E) are situations in which prejudice and discrimination tend to be low: cooperative situations, equal-status contact, and the achievement of equivalent goals. (D) is wrong because, if complete assimilation has occurred, there are no longer two separate groups, so intergroup prejudice and discrimination occur.

71.   **(C)**   Comparable worth refers to programs to pay the same wages for jobs that have comparable responsibilities or require comparable skills. It is intended to change situations where men get paid more for doing jobs that are not the same, but are comparable to, jobs that women do. (A) is wrong because it refers to the general ideology of gender equality and does not focus especially on income equity. (B) is wrong because sexism refers to the beliefs that justify gender inequalities. (D) is incorrect because it refers to a situation where male and female traits are not rigidly assigned to people. (E) is wrong because it refers to a situation where a minority tries to separate from a dominant group.

72.   **(D)**   White-collar and service workers have been growing as a proportion of the work force while blue-collar and farm workers have been declining. (D) is the only choice that includes only these two occupational categories. (A) is wrong because it includes only one of those categories. (B), (C), and (E) include one of the job categories in decline.

73.   **(A)**   The three core population processes identified by demographers are fertility (births), mortality (deaths), and migration (movement into or out of an area). The other choices are wrong because they include only two of these and a third which is not one of the basic demographic processes. Community (B) refers to a place where people live rather than a demographic process; fecundity (C) refers to the potential number of children that can be born, but actual fertility is the key demographic process; segregation (D) refers to the isolating of people or activities in particular parts of a city; and ecology (E) refers to the field that studies population distributions rather than an element that determines population size and distribution.

74.   **(B)**   Karen Horney, an analyst who broke from classical psychoanalysis, developed a theory concerning the neurotic needs of the individual. She identified 10 neurotic needs which fall under three general categories: 1) moving toward people, 2) moving away from people, and 3) moving against people. She thought most people achieve an integration and balance of these forces, but the neurotic individual lacks this balance and integration.

75.   **(A)**   The question requires you to identify the false statement. The correct response is (A), since the Court declared in *Engel v. Vitale,* 1962, that a nondenominational prayer written by New York officials for recitation in public schools at the beginning of each school day was unconstitutional. (B) is a true statement because the Court declared in *Abbington School District v. Schempp,* 1963, that a Pennsylvania law which required daily Bible reading in public schools was unconstitutional. (C) is a true statement because in *Stone v. Graham,* 1980, the Court held unconstitutional a Kentucky statute which required the posting of a copy of the Ten Commandments, purchased with private funds, on the wall of every classroom in the state. (D) is a true statement because in *McLean v. Arkansas Board of Education,* 1982, the Court held unconstitutional a law requiring that creation science be taught in public schools. (E) is a true statement because in *Epperson v. Arkansas,* 1968, a law prohibiting the teaching of the theory of evolution in public schools was declared unconstitutional by the Court.

76.   **(E)**   The Constitution, as it came from the Constitutional Convention in 1788, provided for a direct popular vote for none of the items listed. Direct popular vote means that the general public votes on the item and that vote immediately determines the outcome of the election or issue. (A) is incorrect because the president is elected not by direct popular vote

but by the electoral college. Originally, state legislatures chose the electors who made up the electoral college. (B) is incorrect because senators were originally chosen by the state legislatures. The Seventeenth Amendment, adopted in 1913, provides for popular election of senators. (C) is incorrect because treaties are ratified by a two-thirds vote of the Senate. (D) is incorrect because constitutional amendments are ratified in one of two ways. The first is by three-fourths of the state legislatures. The second is by three-fourths of state ratifying conventions. Congress determines which method will be used.

77. **(D)** The Great Compromise, also known as the Connecticut Compromise, occurred at the Constitutional Convention of 1787. It was a compromise between two plans known as the Virginia, or Large State Plan, and the New Jersey, or Small State Plan. It provided for a Senate in which each state would receive two senators, and a House of Representatives in which representation would be based on population. (A) is incorrect because the Great Compromise had nothing to do with the slavery question. (B) is incorrect because the Great Compromise had nothing to do with the electoral college. (C) is incorrect because senators were selected by state legislatures until the passage of the Seventeenth Amendment. (E) is incorrect because the Great Compromise occurred during the Constitutional Convention, while the Bill of Rights was added to the Constitution after the Convention was over.

78. **(A)** is most true. Besides AT&T, the various Bell companies are all on the list. (B) Obvious manufacturing companies, such as General Motors and General Electric, are outnumbered by service companies, such as utilities. (C) Retailers, such as Sears, appear toward the bottom of the list. (D) Bell Canada obviously does foreign business, as do most of the others with their international branches, such as IBM. (E) Exxon appears on the list, with over three-quarters of a million stockholders.

79. **(E)** is correct because it has the least number of stockholders on the list, so, therefore, the fewest number of votes is required to make decisions. All of the others have more stockholders, so each share of stock is less important in a total vote. The reality is that the number of shares in any large company is so great that influence at the annual stockholders meeting is minimal for any one share of stock.

80. **(D)** is correct. The stockholders elect a board of directors and give them direction at the annual meeting. The board then directs the company for the rest of the year, appointing a chairperson and setting policy. (A)

The chief executive officer (CEO) is appointed or elected by the board of directors. (B) The board elects a chair, but controls its power. (C) The president (often the CEO) directs the day-to-day operations under board direction. (E) Stock options are opportunities for top employees to invest in the company, but do not give control unless the employees buy a large portion of the outstanding stock, thus gaining control.

81.   **(B)**   In January 1918, Woodrow Wilson proposed Fourteen Points which enunciated his goals for the peace that would follow World War I. These were idealistic goals based on notions of open diplomacy, the elimination of secret treaties, self-determination, arms reduction, open trade, and a League of Nations to serve as an international forum to prevent future wars. The thrust of the Fourteen Points emphasized fairness and openness in international relationships. By November 1918, the Germans faced military and political collapse, but they approached an armistice with the Allies convinced that the postwar treaty would be a fair one based upon Wilson's Fourteen Points. They reasoned that since the United States had turned the tide and saved France and Britain from almost certain defeat, the United States would dominate the peace negotiations. Unfortunately, they reasoned incorrectly and the Treaty of Versailles reflected British and French desires for vengeance more than it reflected the Wilsonian principles elucidated in his Fourteen Points.

82.   **(C)**   This engraving emphasizes the innocence and helplessness of the victims.

83.   **(C)**   Of the first three choices, the only one that is a correct interpretation of the graph is (C). Choice (D) may or may not be true, but the graph (which indicates percentage shares of national product) does not provide the kind of information required to decide.

84.   **(C)**   Attempting to guess the location on the basis of the name of the crisis will not be helpful, since "Fashoda" does not sound African. Another approach is recommended: try to remember the geographical areas where Britain and France clashed over colonial claims. This reasoning would eliminate choices (B), (D), and (E). Generally, the two nations acted in concert regarding the Balkans and Ottoman Empire, and they had no colonial claims in southern Europe. Only two answers remain; guessing is strongly recommended. The Fashoda crisis, which stands as an example of the danger that imperialist adventures might lead to a major European war, began when French and British army units contested ownership rights

to the village of Fashoda in the African Sudan during the 1890s. The potential for war became increasingly obvious when French and British cabinet debates over the crisis lasted three days; eventually both army units were ordered to withdraw peacefully.

85. **(A)** Liberia has been an independent state since its founding in 1847. Tanzania (B) achieved independence in 1964, Sierre Leone (C) in 1961, Gambia (D) in 1965, and Ghana (E) in 1957.

86. **(B)** The capital city of Thailand is Bangkok. Siam refers to the former name for Thailand. All of the other choices (A), (C), (D), and (E) match the countries with their capitals correctly.

87. **(C)** Research shows that, as economic development (industrialization, urbanization, higher levels of education) expands, birth rates tend to decline. (A) and (D) are wrong because, when women have a choice about how many children to have, they tend to have fewer children; family planning and gender equality give women that choice. (B) is incorrect because urbanization is a part of economic development which tends to reduce birth rates. (E) is wrong because patriarchy involves the subordination of women, which is associated with less choice for women and higher birth rates.

88. **(E)** *Gesellschaft* is the German word used by Ferdinand Tonnies to refer to the highly impersonal and individualistic social relationships that predominate in urban life. (A) is wrong because *gemeinschaft* is the word Tonnies used to describe the opposite: the personal, more collectively oriented relationships found in small towns and rural communities. (B), (C), and (D) are terms unrelated to distinguishing between social relations in urban and rural areas: in-groups are groups people belong to and identify with; groupthink refers to a form of decision making in groups; and *verstehen* is the German word for a research methodology in sociology.

89. **(A)** The subway riders exhibit no interaction or group awareness. A social aggregate is a collection of people who happen to be in the same place at the same time but with no interaction or group awareness. (B), (C), and (E) are wrong because these collections of people exhibit either interaction with one another or awareness of group membership. (D) is wrong because it describes a social category (all members share a social characteristic), but all members are not in the same place at the same time.

90. **(C)** Primary groups are close intimate groups such as friendships or families. (A) is wrong because it is the opposite of a primary group, namely a utilitarian and impersonal group. (B) is a group to which a person doesn't belong and feels neutral or negative toward – definitely not a friendship group. (D) is wrong because there is no such group as a postindustrial group. (E) is incorrect because friendship groups are informal.

91. **(D)** A folkway is a norm that is customary and popular but not required and involves no moral overtone. (A) is wrong because mores involve required, strong rules and have moral significance. Handshaking does not fit this. (B) is wrong because it refers to very strong mores. (C) is incorrect because handshaking is not required by law. (E) is wrong because sanctions are rewards and punishments, which are not involved in the handshaking ritual.

92. **(A)** Sutherland's theory is based on the assumption that deviance is learned through socialization and that the looking-glass self and significant others play an important part. (B) is wrong because Merton's theory is based on the assumption of the functionalist perspective that deviance arises from anomie, a condition where the arts of society are not well integrated. (C) and (E) are wrong because those are theories of urban development rather than deviance. (D) is incorrect because it is a biological theory of deviance.

93. **(C)** An expressive crowd is one whose primary purpose and activity is the release of emotions. (A) is wrong because an acting crowd is one that takes some action toward a target, which the fans are not doing. (B) is wrong because a casual crowd is one that shows some common focus of attention but relatively little emotional expression, interaction, or organization. (D) is incorrect because a rioting crowd refers to a type of acting crowd. (E) is wrong because mass hysteria refers to an emotional reaction to some anxiety-producing event, which is not the case for the fans whose reaction is more one of joy than anxiety.

94. **(C)** Extinction of conditioned respondent behavior occurs when the CS is presented without the UCS a number of times. The magnitude of the response elicited by the CS and the percentage of presentations of the CS which elicits responses, gradually decreases as the CS continues to be presented without the UCS. If CS presentation continues without the UCS,

the CR will decline to at least the level present before the classical conditioning was begun.

95. **(D)** There are two schools of thought on the proper method of constitutional interpretation by the judiciary. One is called "judicial activism." Advocates of this school believe that the intentions of those who wrote the Constitution should not be authoritative for the decision of controversial matters in the present. They say that judges should be free to adapt the Constitution to changing political and social circumstances. The other school is called "judicial restraint." Advocates of this school stress that the Constitution was a great contract by which the American people created a government. This contract laid the ground rules for the operation of the government, and it provided a formal process of amendment for changing those ground rules. In order to understand the ground rules, say advocates of restraint, one must determine the original intentions of those who wrote and ratified the Constitution. For unelected judges to assume to themselves the power to change the Constitution, according to this school, is for the judges to usurp a power that was not given them by the Constitution or the people. Therefore, the correct answer is (D). Choice (A) is incorrect because there is no general process by which judges limit the number of cases they hear in a year. Justices on the Supreme Court do have a lot of control over which cases they hear, through a process called "certiorari." When litigants appeal to the Court to have their cases heard, the justices vote on the merits of the cases. If four justices vote to hear a particular case, they issue a "writ of certiorari" to the lower court, ordering all documents relevant to the case to be sent up to the Supreme Court. Choice (B) is incorrect because judges do not lobby funds from Congress. Choice (C) is incorrect because when judges remove themselves from a case they are said to recuse themselves. Choice (E) is incorrect because judicial restraint refers to a method of interpreting the Constitution and has nothing to do with political campaigns.

96. **(E)** The vast majority of bills never make it out of committee to the floor of the chamber. Many are introduced by a member only to get publicity, or so the member can tell constituents that (s)he did something about the matter. (A) is incorrect since most bills die in committee. If a bill dies in committee, it cannot be considered, much less passed, by the whole house. There is a seldom-used procedure by which a bill can be forced out of committee in the house. First, 218 members must sign a discharge petition, then the petition must be approved by a majority vote of the full house. However, attempts to force a bill out of committee by discharge petition have succeeded only about 3 percent of the time in the twentieth

century. (B) is incorrect because only a fraction of all bills introduced in either house ever become law. (C) is incorrect because bills are sent to the rules committee only after being reported out of a standing committee. Since most die in standing committee, they never make it to the rules committee. (D) is incorrect because every bill introduced in either house is referred by the presiding officer to the appropriate committee.

97. **(C)** The correct response is (C) because I and II are false. A president may not veto particular items in a bill (I). Such a power is called a line-item veto, and is held by 43 governors in the United States. A president may not pocket-veto a bill by holding it 10 days while Congress is in session (II). In such a case the bill becomes law without the president's signature. If Congress adjourns during the 10-day period, the bill is pocket-vetoed. The only true statement is III, the president's veto can be overridden if two-thirds of both houses vote to pass the bill despite the veto.

98. **(C)** is the correct answer because East Germany's $31 billion is 10 percent of West Germany's $323 billion. (A) is incorrect because the United States was not the leading exporter ($322 billion vs. $323 billion for West Germany). (B) is wrong because Britain's $145 billion is less than half of Germany's total of $354 billion. (D) is not correct because with East Germany's $31 billion added to West Germany's $323 billion, the total gap will widen to $32 billion more than the United States (E) is wrong because the total will be almost $500 billion, not $600 billion.

99. **(A)** is correct. Per capita gross national product is one of the accepted economic figures to compare relative standards of living because it includes all (gross) goods and services produced by a nation. (B) relates to a nation's exporting production per capita only, not standard of living. (C) The annual exports alone do not show a relationship to the number of people who share those sales. (D) is incorrect because it compares an individual figure (per capita) with a total national figure. (E) creates the gross national product of a country, not individuals.

100. **(C)** is correct. The United States, with a population of 248 million, produced $322 billion in exports. Not worrying about the zeroes, the 248 is less than double 322. West Germany produced over five times its population, East Germany nearly double, and the British nearly three times. (A) is incorrect because the graphs do not show total productivity, only the products exported. (B) is wrong. Britain was fourth. It will go to third and the unified Germany will be second behind the United States. (D) is incor-

rect. As noted in explaining (C), the West Germans produced the most exports per capita. (E) is wrong. In a unified Germany, the East German lower GNP will temporarily create a figure for the total for the whole country somewhere between the two figures $12,480 and $14,260.

101. **(C)** Grant was an intensely loyal man who was, sadly, not the best judge of character in choosing his administrative appointees. During his first term in office, his administration was beset with financial scandals involving the vice president, Grant's brother-in-law, and a well-known financial entrepreneur named Jay Gould. In his second term, the "whiskey ring" scandal implicated Grant's private secretary. His secretary of war was implicated in a bribery scandal. While few believed Grant to be corrupt, Grant's loyalty to his corrupt associates tarnished his image in virtually everyone's eyes. It also crippled the effectiveness of his administration.

102. **(C)** While the United States was technically neutral in World War II until the Japanese attack on Pearl Harbor, Franklin Roosevelt made no secret of his distaste for Nazi Germany, Fascist Italy, and militaristic Japan. He openly sought repeal of the neutrality laws so the United States could sell weapons and supplies to Britain and France to help them stop Hitler in Europe. Congress finally agreed, in November 1939, to allow cash sales of goods to European belligerents, meaning France and Britain. When France fell to the Nazi *blitzkrieg*, England stood alone and quickly used up its cash reserves trying to replace its war losses and brace for the expected German invasion. Churchill told Roosevelt of the desperate British situation and predicted that without some means of obtaining American weapons Britain would quickly fall. Realizing that the British needed the help but could not pay for the weapons, Roosevelt proposed Lend-Lease, a policy through which Britain would be allowed to borrow the weapons it needed and would be expected to return the weapons when the war was over. Realizing that there was nothing subtle about this circumvention of the cash-and-carry law, Roosevelt used the analogy of the neighbor's burning house to justify Lend-Lease. Although critics attacked the proposal, it was passed by Congress and was critical in the eventual success of the Allied war effort.

103. **(C)** This question is a thorough test of your knowledge of the Reformation, since it asks about the social basis of a Protestant group. Some choices may be eliminated, if you already know the social bases of Calvinism and Lutheranism. Each of the three major Protestant groups – Lutheran, Calvinist, and Anabaptist – relied in major ways on particular

social elements. Although Lutheranism drew support from a broad social spectrum, Luther himself was forced to rely on sympathetic members of the nobility of the Holy Roman Empire in order to defend Lutheranism against the Holy Roman Emperor. Calvinism held special appeal for the new middle class, particularly business elements. Anabaptism drew most of its membership from the peasantry in western Germany and the Low Countries.

104. **(B)** If the "Augsburg Confession" is not recognized at first glance, attempt to eliminate the other choices. All of the other terms are part of the Counter-Reformation. Once again, terminology is important. Pope Paul III called the Council of Trent into session in 1545 as a means of revitalizing and reforming parts of the church. The Council approved restrictions on the reading material of ordinary Catholics (the Index), commissions to investigate the spread of Protestantism (which is what the Inquisition was originally designed to do), and a new group to combat the spread of Protestant ideas (the Society of Jesus, or Jesuits). The Augsburg Confession was a compromise confession of faith written by Luther's friend Philip Melanchthon in a vain attempt to reconcile Protestant and Catholic princes in the Holy Roman Empire.

105. **(C)** The first Opium War, which ran from 1839 to 1842, began when the Chinese government, in an attempt to stop the trade of opium with the British, seized millions of dollars worth of opium from traders in Canton. In 1839 the British declared war to regain the opium market and other lucrative trading rights. The Opium War ended in 1842 with the Treaty of Nanjing, the first of what China dubbed her "unequal treaties," which gave the British the colony of Hong Kong as well as trading rights at many ports. In addition, China had to pay Britain the cost of fighting the war and the value of the opium seized. The second Opium War raged from 1857-60.

106. **(C)** After his journey down the Congo River, Stanley approached the government in England with his plans for the geography and resources of the Congo Basin. When the British showed no interest, King Leopold II of Belgium employed Stanley in 1879 to open routes into what would become the Belgian Congo, initiating a brutal and exploitative colonization.

107. **(B)** Diffusion involves one group borrowing cultural items from another group. The Europeans borrowed tobacco from the New World

Indians. (A) and (E) are incorrect because they both involve the creation of something new or a new use, which was not the case with tobacco. (C) is wrong because it refers to the gap between technological developments and social practices. (D) is wrong because it refers to a social movement focusing on changing a political system, which is irrelevant to the case of tobacco.

108. **(D)** Comte is considered the first to formulate the idea of a separate field of study that tried to understand society from a scientific vantage point. (A) is wrong because Durkheim is better known for his functionalist approach to topics such as religion and suicide. (B) is wrong because Parsons is a much later figure best known for his development of the functionalist perspective. (C) is wrong because Marx was a little later than Comte and focused more on promoting political and economic change than on developing a scientific discipline. (E) is wrong because Spencer came later than Comte and built on his pioneering work.

109. **(A)** A survey could be done quickly and inexpensively over the phone or through the mail. (B) is normally used when a group is small and in a confined geographic location. (C) is wrong because it would be very expensive and time consuming. (D) is wrong because it would also require going to many locations to collect the data. (E) is wrong because laboratory experiments normally involve bringing all the people being studied to one location.

110. **(C)** Exchange theory is based on the assumption that people seek the best outcomes for themselves by weighing benefits and costs. (A) and (E) are incorrect because they address the functionalist assumptions of interrelatedness, interdependence, and stability. (B) is wrong because it states the symbolic interactionist concern with deriving meaning and interpreting reality. (D) is wrong because it addresses the conflict theory concerns with power and domination.

111. **(A)** Ethnocentric means to judge another culture by the standards of your own and to place yours as superior. Seeing another's practice of worshiping many gods as primitive and ignorant is judging the practice and seeing it as inferior. (B) is not an example of ethnocentrism because having difficulty adjusting to new food and a new language is not judging the practice as inferior. (C) is incorrect. One cannot find a practice unappealing without deeming it inferior. (D) is not an example of ethnocentrism because one does not encounter an entirely new culture when mov-

ing across states. (E) is incorrect. Rather than judging Brazilian culture as inferior, John demonstrates an enthusiasm and fascination with this culture.

112. **(B)** An achieved status is a social position based largely on one's merit. In this scenario, Sally has become a nuclear physicist, which requires individual merit to achieve. (A) is incorrect. A master status refers to one's central defining characteristic. Although this characteristic is often one's occupation, in our society, race is a more centrally defining characteristic. (C) Status attainment refers to the process by which individuals come to hold a certain position in the stratification system, which is unrelated to this example. (D) is incorrect. An ascribed status refers to a social position based on involuntary characteristics, such as sex, age, and race. In this example, being black and female are Sally's ascribed characteristics. (E) is incorrect, as status hierarchy is not a sociological term.

113. **(C)** Milgram designed an experiment where a subject (the teacher) would give electric shocks to another human (the learner) whenever the learner gave the wrong answer on a word association task. Each shock was stronger than the one before. Although the shock apparatus was labelled "WARNING – INTENSE SHOCK," and the learner begged the teacher to stop, 63 percent of the subjects continued the experiment because the researcher told them that he would take full responsibility for the results.

114. **(A)** When it created the independent regulatory commissions, Congress gave them the power to pass regulations (legislative), enforce the regulations (executive), and conduct hearings to determine the punishment for violators of the regulations (judicial). Choice (B) is incorrect because independent regulatory commissions, while nominally in the executive branch, are not included in any of the 14 executive departments. Choice (C) is incorrect because the regulatory commissions do not regulate the federal bureaucracy. Rather, some guard against unfair business practices, others police the side effects of business, such as pollution, and others protect consumers from unsafe products. Choice (D) is incorrect because the commissions were set up by Congress to be independent of the president. They are headed by commissioners who are appointed for fixed terms and are not removable by the president. The commissions must also be bipartisan in membership. Choice (E) is incorrect because the commissions were created by Congress.

115. **(A)** This is a famous political cartoon from 1812, when the Massachusetts state legislature created a misshapen district which would be a "safe district" for Congressman Elbridge Gerry. A safe district is one in which a particular political party, or in this case a particular person, is almost certain to win. When cartoonist John Gilbert saw the district he added a head, wings, and claws and called it a salamander. Newspaper editor Benjamin Russell replied that it should be called a "Gerrymander." The term has been used ever since to describe any congressional district of contorted boundaries which is created as a safe seat for a political party or candidate. Choice (B) is incorrect because the cartoon has nothing to do with environmental issues or congressional behavior. Choice (C) is incorrect because the cartoon has nothing to do with the influence of money on elections. Choice (D) is incorrect because the cartoon has nothing to do with the character of congressmen. Choice (E) is incorrect because the term "dinosaur bill" is a fictitious term concocted as a distractor for this question.

116. **(D)** The War Powers Resolution stipulates that the president can deploy troops abroad in situations where hostilities are imminent for only 60 days, unless Congress approves a longer deployment, declares war, or cannot meet because the nation is under attack. (A) is wrong because the War Powers Resolution does not authorize Congress to prevent the initial deployment of troops abroad by the president. Choice (B) is wrong because the Constitution gives Congress the power to declare war. The usual procedure begins with a request from the president for a declaration of war, which is then adopted by the Congress by joint resolution and signed by the president. The War Powers Resolution did nothing to change this procedure. Choice (C) is wrong because the War Powers Resolution has nothing to do with extradition of foreign ambassadors. Choice (E) is incorrect because the War Powers Resolution has no direct relation to the defense budget.

117. **(D)** Since the opportunity cost of providing more labor (and thus producing more output) is less than the price that can be received for that output, you should expect that each owner will increase his or her effort and thereby produce more output. This should cause industry output to climb, so the price must move down along the demand curve, At the same time, the opportunity cost of producing each unit of output should climb because of diminishing marginal productivity of labor and increasing marginal utility of leisure. Long run equilibrium can therefore be achieved at a lower price and a higher output.

118. **(B)** The conditions that define general equilibrium include only one of those listed in the question. In particular, every individual sets every marginal rate of substitution equal to every price ratio. For goods i and j, then, every person maximizes utility where

$$MRS = \frac{MU_i}{MU_j} = \frac{P_i}{P_j}$$

where MU_j represents marginal utility generated by consuming good i, P_i represents the price of good i, etc. Recalling that marginal cost equals price in competitive equilibrium, it is now clear that for every person and every good

$$\frac{MU_i}{MC_i} = \frac{MU_j}{MC_j} = \ldots = \text{some constant of proportionality.}$$

Choice (B) is thus correct. Choice (A) is incorrect because marginal utilities are not set equal to prices; ratios of marginal utilities are set equal to ratios of price (see above). Choices (C) and (D) are wrong because it is the marginal revenue products of all inputs that are set equal to prices of the inputs to maximize profits in any (including competitive) equilibrium. Choice (E) is just nonsense.

119. **(C)** When the value of the dollar falls, protecting the currency requires that the Fed consider doing something that will increase its demand overseas; i.e., it must somehow make some U.S. assets (whose purchase requires foreign nationals to obtain dollars) more attractive abroad. Restricting the money supply so that domestic interest rates climb is just the ticket. The real return to holding bonds denominated in dollars would then climb, making them more valuable to hold and increasing their demand. Since dollars would be required to purchase these bonds, the price of dollars (i.e., the exchange rate) would also climb according to nothing more mysterious than the simple fundamentals of supply and demand analysis.

120. **(C)** While the slavery issue had never died out, a series of compromises had smoothed over many of the underlying issues left unresolved throughout the 1830s and 1840s. With the acquisition of California, Texas, and the New Mexico Territory from Mexico, combined with the treaty

giving the United States complete control of southern Oregon Territory, the whole slavery issue resurfaced like an open wound. Fierce debates would dominate the political scene over which states should be "slave states" or "free states." Some people desired popular sovereignty in which residents of a territory could decide for themselves if they wanted to allow slavery. Others, primarily Southerners, argued that such popular sovereignty was unconstitutional. The debates often turned violent, as was notably true in Kansas in the 1850s. Eventually, the slavery debate, reopened by the Mexican-American War, would lead to the separationism and secessionism in the South that sparked the Civil War.

121. **(B)** The years between 1876-1900 were years of relative political equality between the Republicans and Democrats. It was also a time when most Americans were rejecting or resisting the cries for reform by political activists. Most people wanted the federal government to remain inactive and uninvolved as much as possible. The concept of laissez-faire leadership was flourishing. This resulted in little significant reform legislation from the Congress. It also led to the election of presidents who saw themselves as political caretakers of the office of the presidency, rather than advocates of social or political reform. The equality between the two parties at this time also made it difficult for any president to push for major changes, because the political base of support was too evenly divided to provide the necessary votes in Congress for effective action. While none of these presidents were incompetent (as asserted by choice (D)), they just didn't see the presidency as an office appropriate for taking strong initiatives. They believed their major job was to insure congressional legislation was effectively carried out and to veto any legislation in which they felt Congress had exceeded its powers. Such an attitude does not tend to lead to inspirational, dynamic leadership. Their style was such that they believed the LESS they were noticed, the better they were doing their job. This has left the long-term impression that they were "weak" presidents.

122. **(C)** In answering this question, study the drawing carefully. The prism-shaped objects are indeed prisms, splitting light entering from the right into a spectrum, recombining it, and splitting it again. Choice (D) may attract those who do not study the drawing, since Newton formulated laws of gravity and motion; carefully looking at the drawing should allow you to avoid this mistake.

123. **(A)** As shown by the variously marked areas of the map, Prussia was able to unite most of northern Germany in 1867 and combine it with

Prussian land in both eastern and western Germany. Choices (B), (C), (D) and (E) will be ruled out by a careful study of the map.

124. **(B)** Albert Sarraut, minister of the colonies from 1920-24 and 1932-33, developed the French policy of "association." While French West Africans would not be granted French citizenship (B) (with a few exceptions including black citizens from the four coastal communes of Senegal), all attempts would be made to assimilate the colonies into French culture, such as conducting all teaching in French (E). The colonies would then be "associated" with France, allowing it to take full advantage of their economic resources without granting independence from France (D). Sarraut declared that "our colonies must be centers of production, and no longer museums for specimens." This policy included the rapid economic development of the colonies (A) and a centralized economy (C) to provide France with raw materials and markets for French goods.

125. **(A)** The Tokugawa government, which preceded the Meiji era in Japan, had begun to weaken ever since Commodore Matthew Perry sailed his warships into Tokyo Bay in 1853 and forced Japan to open two ports to U.S. trade. Since that point, resentment had been growing over the government letting in Western "barbarians." In 1867 Emperor Mitsuhito announced that he was taking the traditional powers back from Shogun and moving the capital to Edo, now known as Tokyo. He took the reign name of Meiji, which means "Enlightenment Rule."

126. **(A)** Subordinate statuses refer to the statuses one occupies that are not the master status. For Stephanie, her status as a soccer player and churchgoer are secondary to her status as a plastic surgeon. (B) is incorrect. Her master status, or her central defining characteristic, is as a plastic surgeon. (C) is incorrect. Role inconsistency refers to the inconsistencies in the roles associated with a single status. In this example, Stephanie's numerous statuses are being addressed. (D) is incorrect. An ascribed status is an involuntary status, such as sex or race. Stephanie's statuses of churchgoer and soccer player are largely, if not entirely, voluntary statuses. Because a correct answer is provided, (E) is incorrect.

127. **(D)** Density of social networks has been shown to be health promoting, both mentally and physically, and a positive influence on self-concept. People reporting numerous close friends have better subjective and objective health ratings. (A) is incorrect as it only contains one of the correct responses. (B) and (E) are incorrect as they both include statement

III. Loose social networks are correlated with bad health, but the relationship has not been shown to be causal. We don't know if loose social networks lead to poor health, or if being in poor health leads to fewer social contacts. (C) is incorrect because we cannot ascertain whether the relationship between gender and social networks is causal.

128. **(A)** In a total institution, such as a prison or mental hospital, all aspects of an individual's life are controlled, in order to strip down and rebuild the self. (B) is incorrect. A bureaucracy is a large formal organization that does not have as its goal re-socialization and the rebuilding of the self. (C) This process does not occur only in late adolescence, but can occur at any age. People of all ages are resocialized in total institutions. (D) The term subculture refers to a culture within a culture and has no relevance to this example. Because a correct answer is provided, (E) is incorrect.

129. **(B)** Durkheim believed that anomic suicide resulted from normlessness. When the norms of a society are suddenly altered, it may result in people's being confused about the boundaries of their society. Only choice (B) addresses the large structural changes occurring in society that may impact the individual. (C) and (E) are examples of altruistic suicide where an individual overidentifies with a group and is willing to die for them. (A) and (D) are examples of egoistic suicide, which results from isolation and weak social ties.

130. **(C)** Social learning theory, first described by Miller and Dollard, is an attempt to combine the principles of social analysis of behavior with principles of learning taken from the behavior scientist's animal laboratory. In this respect, Miller and Dollard took important steps in integrating these two previously separate areas of inquiry in psychology. Based on this theory, Bandura and Walters created another social learning theory that emphasized the role of "modeling" in the acquisition of behavior.

PRACTICE
TEST 3

CLEP SOCIAL SCIENCES AND HISTORY
Test 3

(Answer sheets appear in the back of the book.)

Section 1

TIME: 45 Minutes
65 Questions

DIRECTIONS: Each of the questions or incomplete statements below is followed by five possible answers or completions. Select the best choice in each case and fill in the corresponding oval on the answer sheet.

---

1. The most active people in the religious revivals of the mid-nineteenth century were

   (A) Roman Catholics.

   (B) Jews.

   (C) mainstream Protestants.

   (D) Quakers.

   (E) Evangelical Christians.

2. The Bay of Pigs affair had what effect on John Kennedy's presidency?

   (A) It made Kennedy a national hero for his tough, uncompromising stand against Castro and Communist Cuba.

   (B) It forced Soviet Premier Khrushchev to schedule an early summit meeting with Kennedy to avoid future American-Soviet confrontations.

   (C) It had virtually no effect on Kennedy's presidency, as it was kept secret until after Kennedy's assassination.

   (D) It forced Kennedy to allow Soviet occupation of military bases in Cuba.

(E) It was a major embarrassment to Kennedy's administration and led to further crises in American-Cuban relations.

3. Which of the following forms of government would most likely win the approval of a *politique*?

    (A) A secular government in which religion plays no role

    (B) A theocracy

    (C) A parliamentary government

    (D) A Huguenot government

    (E) A government based on the ideas of Pope Innocent III

4. The first Swiss leader of the movement which became Calvinism was

    (A) Calvin.   (D) Menno Simons.

    (B) Zwingli.   (E) Cranmer.

    (C) Balthasar Hubmeier.

5. At the beginning of the nineteenth century, the North African continent to the west of Egypt was made up of the following four Muslim states.

    I.   Tripoli

    II. Tunis

    III. Algiers

    IV. Morocco

    Of these four, which one was an independent kingdom?

    (A) I.   (D) IV.

    (B) II.   (E) None of the above.

    (C) III.

6. Once a possession of Spain, Guam is now a territory of what country?

(A) Japan   (D) United States

(B) Philippines   (E) Australia

(C) Russia

7. The _____ perspective would probably try to understand a problem like drug abuse by looking to the power relations between those who abuse drugs and those who do not.

(A) conflict   (D) capitalist

(B) functionalist   (E) socialist

(C) sociological

8. In order to find out more about seat belt-wearing behavior, John stands unnoticed on a corner and marks down the sex and car type of those who do and do not wear seat belts. He is conducting

(A) a survey.

(B) obtrusive research.

(C) unobtrusive research.

(D) experimental research.

(E) participant-observation research.

9. Social stratification is a profoundly important subject because

I.   almost every aspect of our lives, from family size to occupational aspirations to eating habits, is linked to our position in the social hierarchy.

II. most societies are committed to the elimination of structured inequality.

III. a significant reduction in our life chances will occur if we are members of the social hierarchy.

IV. people in pre-industrial societies are less status-conscious than people in post-industrial societies.

(A) I only.   (D) II and IV only.

(B) II only.   (E) I, II, and IV only.

(C) I and III only.

10. In some groups where the practice of infanticide has resulted in a shortage of eligible female marriage partners, the practice of _____ is relatively common.

(A) polyandry   (D) polygyny

(B) polygamy   (E) monogamy

(C) exogamy

11. According to Paula, the norms and values of her culture are more rational and advanced than the norms and values of other cultures she has come into contact with. Paula is

(A) stereotyping another culture.

(B) expressing prejudice.

(C) being ethnocentric.

(D) expressing individual discrimination.

(E) selectively perceiving those events which reinforce her stereotype.

12. A lawyer whose client is convicted of selling marijuana argues against sending the first-time offender to prison because of the likelihood of his learning more about crime. Which theory of deviance best supports his argument?

(A) Strain theory   (D) Cultural transmission theory

(B) Labeling theory   (E) Deviance theory

(C) Control theory

13. The greater the deindividuation of any group the

(A) less anonymous the group members are.

(B) more irresponsibly its members behave.

(C) more responsibly its members behave.

(D) greater the chance for antisocial behavior.

(E) Both (B) and (D).

14. The concept of "dual federalism" is best characterized by which of the following statements?

(A) The states may exercise only those powers delegated to them by Congress.

(B) The states have reserved powers which Congress may regulate as it sees fit.

(C) The powers of the states and the federal government overlap to such a degree that it is impossible to distinguish the two in practice.

(D) The state and federal governments are each sovereign and independent within their respective spheres of influence.

(E) The states created the federal government and have the right to nullify laws which, in their opinion, violate the federal Constitution.

15. Which of the following issues was left by the Constitutional Convention for the states to decide?

(A) The method of electing the president

(B) Qualifications of the electorate for voting in federal elections

(C) The method of ratifying amendments to the Constitution

(D) Qualifications for members of the House and Senate

(E) Whether or not to levy protective tariffs on imported goods

16. Given the current method of electing the president, which of the following is NOT possible?

(A) The presidential candidate with the most electoral votes fails to be elected president

(B) A presidential candidate with a majority of the popular votes fails to be elected president

(C) A presidential candidate with less than a majority of the popular vote is elected president

(D) A presidential candidate with less than a majority of the electoral votes is elected president

(E) A presidential candidate with a majority of the electoral vote fails to be elected president

17. Which of the following statements is consistent with the new classical theory?

(A) If prices and wages are both flexible and expectations are rational, then policy is ineffective.

(B) If prices, but not necessarily wages, are flexible and expectations are rational, then policy is ineffective.

(C) If wages, but not necessarily prices, are flexible and expectations are rational, then policy is ineffective.

(D) If expectations are rational, then policy is ineffective regardless of wage and price behavior.

(E) If prices and wages are both flexible and expectations are rational, then monetary but not fiscal policy can be effective.

18. An economy operating at full employment enters a period of high anticipated inflation. Which of the following statements accurately describes the likely result?

(A) Most people increase saving to be better prepared for the higher prices that they know are coming, thereby increasing capital investment, stimulating the rate of economic growth, and supporting lower interest rates.

(B) Most people decrease saving to increase current consumption and capital investment, thereby stimulating economic growth and supporting lower interest rates.

(C) Most people decrease saving to increase current consumption, thereby slowing capital investment, slowing the rate of economic growth, and supporting lower interest rates.

(D) Most people increase saving to be better prepared for the higher prices that they know are coming, thereby reducing capital investment, slowing the rate of economic growth, and supporting lower interest rates.

(E) Most people decrease saving to increase current consumption, thereby slowing capital investment, slowing the rate of economic growth, and supporting higher interest rates.

19. One argument for tariffs is that they should be imposed to help a domestic producer to compete when the level of foreign wages is significantly below the level of domestic wages. This argument

   (A) is conceded by most economists to be correct, although sometimes exaggerated in order to justify some level of tariff protection.

   (B) is fallacious because there are almost no instances in which there is any real difference between the level of foreign and domestic wages.

   (C) ignores the fact that differences in relative costs constitute the principal basis for international trade.

   (D) may be correct with respect to money wages at home and abroad, but is not correct with respect to real wages.

   (E) is true only in terms of certainty equivalent quotas.

20. In what way did the muckrakers contribute to the rise of Progressivism in the early years of the twentieth century?

   (A) Their lurid stories of European abuses led directly to American isolationism until World War I.

   (B) Their stories glorifying the rich and famous led to the supremacy of laissez-faire economic theories during this period.

   (C) Their horror stories of Marxist infiltration into workers' unions led to public support for crackdowns against reform-minded unions and alliances.

   (D) Their exposés of government and business corruption, abuse, and mismanagement led to widely supported public demands for effective reform.

   (E) They created a repugnance for the national press that generalized into a distrust for all government and business institutions.

21. In the mid-eighteenth century, the first wave of non-English speaking immigrants (other than African slaves) arrived in the English colonies. They were ethnic

(A) Poles.

(D) Italians.

(B) Scandinavians.

(E) Russians.

(C) Germans.

22. The principle of *cuius regio, eius religio* – incorporated into the peace settlement at the close of the Thirty Years' War – signified

(A) a weakening of the authority of the Holy Roman Emperor.

(B) the power of monarchs to dictate the religion of their state or principality.

(C) an increase in papal authority in the Holy Roman Empire.

(D) increased authority for the nobility in religious controversies.

(E) that religion was a private matter to be decided by each individual.

23. Lorenzo Valla gained fame for

(A) becoming ruler of the Renaissance city of Florence.

(B) proving the Donation of Constantine a fraud.

(C) his inventions.

(D) challenging the authority of Voltaire.

(E) helping to unify Italy.

24. In 1958 General de Gaulle held a referendum among the colonies of French West and Equatorial Africa. The referendum offered them a choice between self-government as separate republics within a French community or immediate independence with the severing of all ties to France. All chose the first choice EXCEPT

(A) Senegal

(D) Cameroon

(B) Benin

(E) Guinea

(C) Ivory Coast

25. What country is the home of the Khmer Rouge?

    (A) Vietnam   (D) India

    (B) Laos   (E) Indonesia

    (C) Cambodia

26. The Sapir-Whorf hypothesis suggests that speakers of different languages

    (A) are predisposed to holding contrasting ideals and behaviors due to their divergent linguistic backgrounds.

    (B) can perceive the world in identical ways.

    (C) hold the same ideas and values due to the cognitive process of learning language.

    (D) are predisposed to certain attitudes and interpretations of reality through language.

    (E) None of the above.

27. Research on children in isolation suggests that

    (A) with little or no interaction, children can develop fairly normally.

    (B) socialization plays a role in human development.

    (C) continual human interaction is necessary for normal human development.

    (D) genetics is almost wholly responsible for human development.

    (E) None of the above.

28. According to Goffman, a professor presenting herself to her students as competent and knowledgeable is involved in

    (A) status inconsistency.

    (B) impression management activities.

    (C) skilled cooperation.

    (D) status performance.

    (E) None of the above.

29. According to sociologists, an important difference between folkways and mores is that

    (A) violation of a folkway leads to severe punishment.

    (B) mores are found only among the upper classes.

    (C) folkways include customary behaviors.

    (D) violations of mores are not considered crimes.

    (E) folkways apply only to sexual behavior.

30. During pre-modern times when agricultural societies prevailed, in order to increase the supply of labor, couples often had many children. Because today large families are an economic burden rather than an economic asset, couples have fewer children. This explanation of family size is most consistent with the _____ theory in sociology.

    (A) conflict   (D) micro

    (B) functional   (E) institutional

    (C) symbolic interaction

31. Studies show that as one's education level increases, prejudice decreases, illustrating a _____ relationship between education and prejudice.

    (A) spurious   (D) positive correlation

    (B) definitive   (E) negative correlation

    (C) causal

32. The phenomenon in which individuals lose their personal sense of responsibility when they are in a group is known as

    (A) adaptive conformity.   (D) impulsiveness.

    (B) disinhibition.   (E) None of the above.

    (C) deindividuation.

33. A discharge petition is used in the House of Representatives to

    (A) kill a bill that is under consideration on the House floor.

(B)   force the rules committee to discharge a bill back to a standing committee that has reported the bill out with unacceptable amendments.

(C)   force a discharge rule on a bill under consideration on the House floor so that amendments may be made to the bill.

(D)   force a bill out of a committee which has held it for 30 days without reporting it out.

(E)   send to the Senate a bill that has been approved by the House.

34.   Which of the following Supreme Court decisions involved the Fourth Amendment prohibition against unlawful search and seizure?

(A)   *Baker v. Carr,* 1962

(B)   *Roe v. Wade,* 1973

(C)   *Mapp v. Ohio,* 1961

(D)   *Korematsu v. United States,* 1944

(E)   *Gideon v. Wainwright,* 1963

35.   The Thirteenth, Fourteenth, and Fifteenth Amendments to the Constitution were intended primarily to

(A)   protect the rights of blacks against infringement by southern state governments.

(B)   expand the suffrage to women, blacks, and 18-year-olds.

(C)   protect freedom of speech, religion, and assembly.

(D)   increase the power of the federal government in order to prevent the outbreak of another civil war.

(E)   apply the Bill of Rights to the state governments.

36.   A monetary policy that tries to maintain fairly stable interest rates tends to make

(A)   random variation in the IS curve more harmful in terms of variation in interest rates.

(B)   random variation in the IS curve more harmful in terms of variation in the international capital account.

(C) random variation in the IS curve more harmful in terms of variation in GNP.

(D) random variation in the IS curve less harmful in terms of variation of GNP.

(E) random variation in the IS curve totally harmless in terms of variation in either interest rates or GNP.

37. A general sales tax, without any exempted commodities, is considered to be

(A) a progressive tax because it applies to luxuries as well as necessities.

(B) a regressive tax because wealthy people spend a smaller percentage of their total income on taxed commodities, and hence the proportion of tax payments to income is greater for poor people.

(C) a progressive tax because wealthy people spend more than poor people.

(D) a regressive tax because more money is collected from a poor person than from a rich one.

(E) a proportional tax because everybody pays the same tax percentage on each purchase.

38. An argument that is consistent with the statement that deficits caused by tax cuts should not cause interest rates to climb is

(A) consumption will not respond in anticipation of a counter-balancing increase in taxes sometime in the future.

(B) investment will increase in anticipation of a counterbalancing increase in corporate taxes sometime in the future.

(C) investment will not respond because of an impression that the tax cut is permanent.

(D) any increase in consumption will be matched by a corresponding decrease in net exports.

(E) any increase in the interest rate will be negated by an adjustment in the foreign exchange rate.

39. All of the following were characteristic of the 1920s EXCEPT

    (A) voting rights for women.

    (B) Prohibition and bootlegging.

    (C) consumerism and easy credit.

    (D) Progressivist reform and union growth.

    (E) Ku Klux Klan power and popularity.

40. Lincoln won the 1860 presidential election primarily because

    (A) there was overwhelming support throughout the country for the Republicans' antislavery platform.

    (B) he was seen as a moderate, by both Northerners and Southerners, who could possibly negotiate a compromise between abolitionists and slaveholders.

    (C) he gathered overwhelming support in the highly populated Northern states while his three opponents divided the anti-Lincoln vote in the West and South.

    (D) the Know-Nothing party gave Lincoln its endorsement, and combined with Republican support, the two parties were able to outpoll the politically isolated Democrats.

    (E) he was able to discredit his chief opponent, Stephen Douglas, as a "closet abolitionist."

41. The "commenda" was a commercial contract involving a merchant and

    (A) a serf.   (D) merchant-adventurers.

    (B) bankers.   (E) his local monarch.

    (C) an artisan.

42. The "Weber thesis" attempted to explain the connections between the rise of Calvinism and the rise of

    (A) absolute monarchies.   (D) Anglicanism.

    (B) capitalism.   (E) Lutheranism.

    (C) the nation-state.

43. Which of the following historical figures have been cited as intellectual influences of African nationalism?

    I.   Marcus Aurelius Garvey

    II. W. E. B. DuBois

    III. Karl Marx

    (A) I only.   (D) I and II only.

    (B) II only.   (E) All of the above.

    (C) III only.

44. The British East India Company, founded in 1600, was taken over by the British government in what year?

    (A) 1605   (D) 1901

    (B) 1757   (E) 1947

    (C) 1858

45. A researcher studying the diaries of Holocaust victims would be using which method to carry out her research?

    (A) A survey   (D) Content analysis

    (B) Participant observation   (E) None of the above.

    (C) Obtrusive research

46. Newpark is a diverse town, both ethnically and racially. The distribution of wealth and earnings among the town members tends to be similar, regardless of race or ethnicity. In Newpark prejudice is

    (A) likely to develop due to the competitive atmosphere.

    (B) likely to develop due to the presence of many racial and ethnic groups.

    (C) less likely to develop due to the inequality existing among groups.

    (D) less likely to develop due to the economic parity and equality among the groups.

    (E) None of the above.

47. After centuries of occupying a subordinate status and being exploited by the "Plorn," the "Zorn" attempt to form their own country, separate from the "Plorn." Their movement can be classified as

(A) pluralist.

(D) expulsion.

(B) assimilationist.

(E) None of the above.

(C) segregationist.

48. An informal sanction against shoplifting would be

(A) receiving a fine from the store.

(B) a judge requiring you to perform 20 hours of community service.

(C) your date Friday night canceling because he doesn't want to be seen with a thief.

(D) imprisonment for a week.

(E) All of the above.

49. Dr. Shaw is an expert on African religions. She finds the widespread religious practice of performing clitoridectomies on young girls to be disturbing, but believes it can be studied and understood, given the social norms and values of the society. Dr. Shaw is adopting an attitude of

(A) cultural relativism.

(D) ideal ritualism.

(B) multi-culturalism.

(E) None of the above.

(C) ethnocentrism.

50. A widespread desire to own toys and dolls based on a particular television show is an example of a

(A) social movement.

(D) fad.

(B) fashion.

(E) None of the above.

(C) mob.

51. Which of the following pairs of concepts are most closely related in social psychology?

(A) Cognitive dissonance – bystander effect

(B) Attribution bias – tragedy of the commons

(C) Internal locus of control – fundamental attribution error

(D) Risky shift – belief bias

(E) Anonymity – deindividuation

52. Federal courts have responded to disputes between the president and Congress by

(A) usually deciding in favor of Congress.

(B) usually deciding in favor of the president.

(C) terming the disputes "political questions" and generally refusing to hear or decide them.

(D) deciding in favor of the president on domestic policy disputes and in favor of Congress on foreign policy disputes.

(E) deciding against Congress only when it overrides a presidential veto and passes a law limiting the power of the president.

53. When the House rules committee issues a closed rule

(A) the House gallery is closed to the public during debate of a bill.

(B) a particular bill may not be amended during floor debate.

(C) vote on a bill is closed to those members who were not present during debate on the bill.

(D) a particular bill may not be calendared without going first to the rules committee.

(E) a bill passed in the House is closed to amendment in the Senate.

54. One of the major problems with national government under the Articles of Confederation was that

(A) the executive branch was too strong vis à vis the legislative branch.

(B) the government had no power to levy direct taxes.

(C) the national judiciary failed to exercise judicial review.

(D) the Articles of Confederation were amended too frequently.

(E) the bicameral legislature deadlocked frequently on controversial, but necessary, legislation.

55. If unemployment fell from 7.7 percent to 5.8 percent over the course of two years,

   (A) then inflationary concerns should be voiced, even if the natural rate of unemployment were 5.0 percent.

   (B) then inflationary concerns should be voiced if the natural rate of unemployment were 6.0 percent.

   (C) then concerns over a growth recession should be voiced, even if the natural rate were 6.0 percent.

   (D) then concerns over a growth recession should be voiced if the natural rate were 5.0 percent.

   (E) there would still be sufficient slack to reduce unemployment further without raising the specter of inflation even if the natural rate were 6.5 percent.

56. A difference between a tariff on an imported good and a quota on such a good is

   (A) that a quota can never be made to yield revenue for the government, whereas a tariff can.

   (B) that a tariff can never be made to yield revenue for the government, whereas a quota can.

   (C) that a quota can be used to shut off all, or virtually all, the inflow of the imported good, whereas a tariff cannot.

   (D) that a tariff can be used to shut off all, or virtually all, the inflow of the imported good, whereas a quota cannot.

   (E) that a quantity equivalent quota will only generate the same revenue if correctly priced (for example, by an auction for import licenses).

57. The idea of "consumer surplus" reflects the fact that

   (A) in some purchases, the gain consumers obtain from buying exceeds the gain suppliers obtain from selling.

   (B) the purchase of many goods is an immense bargain for consumers, because they would pay far more than they actually do in order to get them, if necessary.

   (C) the marginal utility of the first units of a product consumed may considerably exceed the total utility which this product supplies.

(D) total utility increases either when consumer incomes rise or when the prices they must pay for goods fall.

(E) when demand is inelastic with respect to price, buyers can obtain a larger quantity for an expenditure of less money.

58. Senator Joseph McCarthy was known for

(A) leading a "witch hunt" to expose Communists in the United States.

(B) recommending large-scale American intervention in Vietnam.

(C) helping to formulate a major economic aid plan for Western Europe in the late 1940s.

(D) leading the peace faction of the Democratic party in the 1968 presidential campaign.

(E) being the first American senator convicted of spying for the Soviet Union (in 1956).

59. The Saturday Night Massacre refers to

(A) Nixon's firing of Watergate special prosecutor, Archibald Cox, and his staff, in October 1973.

(B) the bombing of the Marine Corps barracks in Lebanon by a suicide truck bomber in October 1983.

(C) Reagan's bombing of military bases in Libya in April 1986.

(D) Oliver North's destruction of files related to the Iran-Contra scandal the day before his office was searched by the FBI.

(E) the slaughter of Vietnamese villagers in My Lai by American soldiers under the command of Lt. William Calley.

60. According to the graph below, which was the most urbanized part of Europe in the nineteenth century?

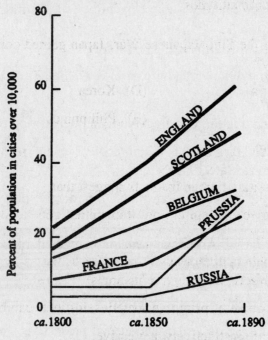

The Urbanization of Europe

(A) Eastern Europe   (D) Central Europe

(B) Prussia   (E) The British Isles

(C) France

61. The Fronde were directed primarily against

(A) the power of French landlords.

(B) the authority of the absolute monarchy.

(C) the influence of the nobility.

(D) the wealth of the church.

(E) the poverty of the peasants.

62. Which of the following best defines the principles of "Negritude"?

(A) An affirmation of the values of African culture

(B) The belief in the natural subjugation of African people by whites

(C) A system of separate but equal rights for Africans and whites

(D) The resettlement of freed American blacks in Africa

(E) A derogatory term, used by Europeans, to describe and condemn Afro-centric attitudes

63. As a result of the Sino-Japanese War, Japan gained control of which Asian country?

(A) Manchuria   (D) Korea

(B) Taiwan   (E) Philippines

(C) Singapore

64. Studies concerning human instincts suggest that

(A) many aspects of culture are transmitted genetically in the form of instincts.

(B) human beings do not inherit complex patterns of social behavior and, therefore, have no true instincts.

(C) among people of primitive societies, instincts can be observed.

(D) humans are instinctively aggressive.

(E) sexual behavior is the only genetically transmitted instinct.

65. Researchers decide to test the correlation between the effects of a film on race relations with students' level of prejudice. In this case, the level of prejudice is the _____ variable.

(A) dependent   (D) spurious

(B) independent   (E) None of the above.

(C) control

Section 2

TIME: 45 Minutes
           65 Questions

DIRECTIONS: Each of the questions or incomplete statements below is followed by five possible answers or completions. Select the best choice in each case and fill in the corresponding oval on the answer sheet.

66. In order to learn about a particular social phenomenon, Max Weber believed one needed to understand the point of view of the subject. The term used to describe this method is

(A) social view.

(D) *verstehen.*

(B) the looking-glass self.

(E) social statics.

(C) symbolic interaction.

67. Which of the following perspectives would focus on how the prosecution and defense interpret each other's actions in a criminal trial?

(A) Structural functionalism

(D) Socialization

(B) Social conflict

(E) Symbolic interactionism

(C) Ethnocentrism

68. Which of the following are forms of institutional discrimination?

I.   A geographic mismatch between workers and jobs following the move of a company from the inner-city

II.   A landlord's distaste for Latino tenants causes him to reject all applicants with Hispanic surnames.

III. During an economic downturn, a policy of "last hired = first fired" has resulted in a disproportionate layoff of women and minorities.

IV. The administration of IQ and other standardized tests

(A) I only.

(B) I and II only.

(C) II and III only.

(D) I, III, and IV only.

(E) I, II, III, and IV.

69. Which of the following is true of welfare recipients?

(A) The majority are women who have many children.

(B) Most are males who are unwilling to work.

(C) Most are children.

(D) Few ever get off welfare.

(E) None of the above.

70. Which of the following concepts is least related to prejudice?

(A) Cognitive dissonance

(B) Stereotypes

(C) Familiarity effect

(D) Racial differences in face recognition

(E) Socialization

71. Which of the following statements about the national media are FALSE?

I.   Magazines and newspapers need no license to publish in the United States.

II. It is more difficult for a public figure or official to win a libel suit against the media in the United States than in any other country.

III. The U.S. government can exercise restraint over the media to prevent the publication of sensitive government information.

(A) I only.

(B) II only.

(C) III only.

(D) I and II only.

(E) I and III only.

72. Which of the following statements is true about political action committees (PACs)?

(A) PACs have been an important part of American politics since the Great Depression.

(B) PACs gain influence over certain candidates by heavily subsidizing their campaigns.

(C) The number of PACs has grown dramatically between 1973 and the present.

(D) Formation of PACs is restricted to business and labor groups.

(E) The number of ideological PACs has increased much more slowly than the number of business or labor PACs.

73. Which of the following statements about the Equal Rights Amendment is FALSE?

(A) It passed both houses of Congress, but was never ratified by three-fourths of the states.

(B) Congress extended the time limit for ratification of the amendment.

(C) Some states that ratified the amendment later tried to rescind their ratification.

(D) The amendment was intended to restore certain rights to blacks and Hispanics that had been restricted by a series of Supreme Court decisions.

(E) It was endorsed by every president from Harry Truman to Jimmy Carter.

74. In a period of deflation (i.e., of generally falling prices), the "real" rate of interest obtained by a lender on money lent

(A) will exceed the nominal rate.

(B) will become a negative figure.

(C) will fall below the stated rate, although not to the extent of becoming a negative figure.

(D) will become a meaningless or incalculable figure.

(E) will be less than the nominal rate.

75. Net exports are most likely to be

    (A) positively correlated with both interest rates and GNP.

    (B) positively correlated with interest rates, but fairly independent of GNP.

    (C) positively correlated with GNP, but fairly independent of interest rates.

    (D) negatively correlated with GNP, but positively correlated with interest rates.

    (E) negatively correlated with both interest rates and GNP.

76. Consider a firm in a competitive market selling 10,000 units at a price of $2 per unit. Its total cost is $16,000, and it is producing at the minimum of its average cost curve. To maximize profits, this firm should

    (A) change nothing because it is already maximizing profits.

    (B) increase its price and output.

    (C) increase its output and sales.

    (D) reduce its output and sales.

    (E) shut down to maximize profits by minimizing losses.

77. All of the following "New Deal" agencies were created during the Great Depression to provide jobs for the unemployed EXCEPT

    (A) Farm Security Administration (FSA).

    (B) Civil Works Administration (CWA).

    (C) Civilian Conservation Corps (CCC).

    (D) Works Progress Adminstration (WPA).

    (E) National Youth Administration (NYA).

78. The most important factor in the destruction of the Plains Indians' societies by whites in the late nineteenth century was

    (A) the use of modern weapons by white soldiers and cavalrymen.

    (B) the destruction of the buffalo herds by whites.

    (C) the introduction of alcohol by whites to Indian society.

(D) the encroachment of railroads onto Indian lands.

(E) the use of reservations by whites to limit the movements of Indians.

79. "Anxiety, or the idea of anxiety, permeates modern thought in all its aspects. You find it almost everywhere you look: in Freudian psychology, in the philosophy of existentialism, in poetry and the novel, in the language of religion...and...of course, in contemporary political movements."

This passage is an example of writing in

(A) intellectual history.   (D) diplomatic history.

(B) social history.   (E) political history.

(C) economic history.

80. "The greatest good for the greatest number?" was a belief of

(A) Marx.   (D) Freud.

(B) Bentham.   (E) DeMaistre.

(C) Mill.

81. In the early 1950s the British government arrested Jomo Kenyatta and well-known Kikuyu leaders in Kenya in response to what event?

(A) Their participation in the United Gold Coast Convention

(B) The forming of an independent Kikuyu People's party

(C) The Mau Mau uprisings

(D) The formation of the African National Congress (ANC)

(E) The 1951 general elections

82. When the Manchus invaded northern China in 1644 and overthrew the Ming Dynasty, what dynasty did they establish?

(A) Shang Dynasty   (D) Sui Dynasty

(B) Qin Dynasty   (E) Qing Dynasty

(C) Han Dynasty

83. Regarding segregation, studies indicate that

    I.   blacks show a preference for segregation and prefer to live in predominantly black neighborhoods.

    II. whites prefer to maintain a segregated system in terms of public accommodations and housing.

    III. blacks, more than whites, prefer to live in integrated neighborhoods.

    IV. whites, more than blacks, prefer to live in integrated neighborhoods.

(A) I only.

(B) II only.

(C) III only.

(D) I and II only.

(E) None of the above.

84. Which of the following is best explained by the Strain theory?

(A) Voyeurism

(B) Marijuana use

(C) Robbery

(D) Speeding

(E) Jaywalking

85. One reason lower-class youth are more often arrested than individuals of other social classes is that

(A) they commit more dangerous crimes.

(B) there are greater numbers of police in their neighborhoods.

(C) police are guided by particular status cues such as demeanor, dress, and race.

(D) they are more likely to commit crimes that are reported.

(E) they commit more of all types of crimes.

86. A professor has certain rights and obligations associated with her status, such as meeting with her students and preparing lectures. These rights and obligations associated with a status are known as

(A) master statuses.

(B) ascribed statuses.

(C) achieved statuses.

(D) roles.

(E) impression management.

87. Cindy and Bobby, two siblings playing house, pretend they are their parents. According to George Herbert Mead, Cindy and Bobby are learning to internalize the values of their parents and are therefore taking on the role of the

(A) instinctual being.

(D) *verstehen.*

(B) socialized other.

(E) generalized other.

(C) looking-glass self.

88. A general difficulty confronted in doing social research is that

I. ethical considerations prevent certain types of research from taking place.

II. it deals with subjects who are self-aware and whose behavior is not always predictable.

III. social researchers are part of the phenomenon they study.

IV. the methods of social research are more advanced than those of other disciplines.

(A) II only.

(D) I and III only.

(B) III only.

(E) I, II, and III only.

(C) IV only.

89. When two people are introduced for the first time, an initial impression is formed. Which factor most powerfully affects this first impression?

(A) method of handshake

(D) external locus of control

(B) physical appearance

(E) speech mannerisms

(C) nonverbal communication

90. The Federalist Papers

I. were written by Washington, Madison, and Adams.

II. provided a theoretical justification for the Revolutionary War.

III. are considered an authoritative commentary on the U.S. Constitution.

(A) I only.   (D) I and II only.

(B) II only.   (E) I and III only.

(C) III only.

91. Which of the following statements about interest groups are accurate?

I.   Interest group activities, to influence public policy-making at the national level, are aimed almost entirely at Congress.

II. The influence of labor unions on public policy-making has declined since 1945.

III. Business organizations are the most numerous and powerful interest groups in America.

(A) I only.   (D) I and II only.

(B) II only.   (E) II and III only.

(C) III only.

92. During the past three decades, all of the following changes have occurred in political behavior and public opinion in the United States EXCEPT

(A) the declining importance of political ideology as a factor influencing presidential nominations to the Supreme Court.

(B) an increase in support for Republican presidential candidates in the South.

(C) an increase in the influence of the conservative wing on the Republican party.

(D) a drop in voter turnout for congressional and presidential elections.

(E) an increase in the number of voters who declare themselves to be independents.

93. The first party competition for public offices in the United States occurred between which parties?

(A) Federalists and Whigs

(B) Whigs and Jeffersonian Republicans

(C) Federalists and Jeffersonian Republicans

(D) Democrats and Whigs

(E) Democrats and Republicans

94. The term "gender gap" refers to

(A) the fact that women turn out to vote in larger numbers than men.

(B) differences in political opinions between men and women.

(C) the fact that women live longer than men.

(D) the fact that men hold a much larger proportion of elective political offices than women do.

(E) a general apathy among women regarding electoral politics, which is not observable among men.

95. In a certain plant, marginal cost is $2.00 at 400 units of output weekly, and it is $2.50 at 500 units of output. Referring to output increases within this 400-500 range, average cost

(A) must rise.

(B) must fall.

(C) must remain constant.

(D) may rise, or fall, or both, but cannot remain constant throughout this output range.

(E) may rise, then fall, with a net increase over the 100 unit range.

96. Real wages have, in the recent past, been

(A) positively correlated with changes in the international price of crude oil.

(B) negatively correlated with changes in the international price of crude oil.

(C) independent of changes in the international price of crude oil.

(D) indeterminately correlated with changes in the international price of crude oil – rising during the 1973-74 episode and falling during the 1978-79 price spike.

(E) indeterminately correlated with changes in the international price of crude oil – falling during the 1973-74 price spike and rising during the 1978-79 episode.

97. Let imports increase by $1 billion. If tax receipts are stable and private saving is fixed, which of the following adjustments is consistent with maintaining equilibrium?

    (A) Holdings of bonds and money both increase by $1 billion each

    (B) Holdings of bonds increase by $1 billion while holdings of money fall by an equal amount

    (C) Holdings of bonds increase by $1 billion while money holdings do not change

    (D) Holdings of money fall by $1 billion while bond holdings do not change

    (E) Holdings of bonds and money both fall by $ 1 billion each

98. When economists speak of investment, they are speaking of

    (A) the part of GNP used by households for current use.

    (B) the part of GNP, past and present, that has been set aside to add to productive capacity.

    (C) the part of GNP captured in the computation of the dollar value of goods but not services.

    (D) the part of GNP that the government devotes to the construction of roads, airports, and the like.

    (E) the part of current GNP used by business to add to productive capacity, and by households to add to their stock of new houses.

99. In which of the following circumstances would an excise tax be shifted entirely onto consumers?

    (A) Demand is relatively more price elastic than supply.

    (B) Supply displays unitary price elasticity.

    (C) Demand displays unitary price elasticity.

    (D) Supply is perfectly inelastic.

    (E) Demand is perfectly inelastic.

100. The first successful English colony in North America was located in

 (A) Roanoke, Virginia.

 (B) Plymouth, Massachusetts.

 (C) Jamestown, Virginia.

 (D) Salem, Massachusetts.

 (E) Manhattan, New York.

101. The sharecropping system in the South following Reconstruction had the effect of

 (A) allowing many former slaves and poor white tenant farmers, who could have never otherwise owned land, to buy their own farms.

 (B) moving many former slaves and poor white tenant farmers into the middle class.

 (C) pushing tenant farmers and poor independent farmers into deep levels of debt to large landowners and merchants.

 (D) helping to limit the power of former plantation owners and Northern business interests.

 (E) changing the basic attitudes of whites and blacks who were now forced to work side by side farming the same land.

102. The *Kulturkampf* of the German Chancellor Bismarck was directed against the

 (A) Social Democratic party.   (D) middle class.

 (B) Catholic church.   (E) nobility.

 (C) liberalism.

103. All of the following are true about the Nazi-Soviet pact of 1939 EXCEPT

 (A) it was also known as the Molotov-Ribbentrop Pact.

 (B) it was a nonaggression pact.

 (C) it was signed shortly before the beginning of World War II.

 (D) it protected the sovereignty of Poland.

(E) it was an agreement between governments which were thought to be ideological enemies.

104. All of the following African countries border on the Indian Ocean EXCEPT

(A) Madagascar.   (D) Somalia.

(B) Namibia.   (E) Tanzania.

(C) South Africa.

105. Of the following religions, which one has the largest number of followers in India?

(A) Islam   (D) Buddhism

(B) Hinduism   (E) Sikhism

(C) Christianity

106. In order to get a sample of Los Angeles residents for a survey on political attitudes, Carmen selects every 1,000th person from the Los Angeles city phone book. This is an example of _____ sampling.

(A) random   (D) stratified

(B) systematic   (E) nonrepresentative

(C) cluster

107. Sally, a social researcher studying education level and condom use, finds subjects who graduate from college are no more likely to use condoms than those who do not graduate from college. Her findings suggest that

(A) education and condom use are positively correlated.

(B) education and condom use are negatively correlated.

(C) a cause-and-effect relationship exists between education level and condom use.

(D) no apparent relationship exists between the two variables.

(E) a spurious relationship exists between the two variables.

108. The sociologist's interest in race is due to the fact that

    I.   race, as a biological fact, helps to determine and explain people's behavior.

    II.   stratification on the basis of race predates all other forms of stratification.

    III.   people attach meaning and values to real or imagined group differences.

    IV.   race is the basis for discrimination against all minority groups.

    (A) I only.   (D) II and IV only.

    (B) III only.   (E) None of the above.

    (C) I and II only.

109. The "Zorn," an ethnic group in the country of "Plorn," migrated voluntarily more than three centuries ago. Over time, they have completely adopted the norms, values, and language of the dominant group. Contact between the two groups, however, is still somewhat limited. "Zorns" have only some political representation, and economic inequality, though not drastic, still exists. Intermarriage between the two groups is remarkably low, and neighborhoods are not well integrated. "Zorn" assimilation can be characterized as

    (A) low cultural assimilation; low structural assimilation.

    (B) moderate cultural assimilation; moderate secondary structural assimilation; low primary structural assimilation.

    (C) moderate cultural assimilation; low structural assimilation.

    (D) high cultural assimilation; moderate secondary structural assimilation; low primary structural assimilation.

    (E) high cultural assimilation; moderate secondary structural assimilation; moderate primary structural assimilation.

110. The gap between male and female earnings is due to which of the following?

    I.   The failure of bosses to perceive women as competent and capable

    II.   Differences in how jobs are titled/labeled when filled by one sex rather than the other

III. The preference of all men to have their wives work in the home rather than in the labor market

IV. Women generally have less experience and skills, causing them to enter low-paying female-dominated occupations

(A) I only.

(D) II, III, and IV only.

(B) I and III only.

(E) I, II, and IV only.

(C) III and IV only.

111. As Tom's perpetual tardiness becomes disturbing to the class, the other students scorn him. The behavior of the students is an example of a(n)

(A) informal sanction.

(D) value.

(B) formal sanction.

(E) None of the above.

(C) norm.

112. Which of the following concepts is more physical than psychological?

(A) Crowding

(D) Loudness

(B) Noisiness

(E) Personal space

(C) Density

113. Of the following issues, which would be LEAST likely to be in the Republican national platforms of 1988 and 1992?

(A) Opposition to quotas to remedy past discrimination in housing, employment, and education

(B) Support for a reduction in the capital gains tax

(C) Support for a woman's right to choose on abortion

(D) Support for a balanced budget amendment

(E) Opposition to increasing the minimum wage

114. Most vice presidential candidates are selected

 I.   by the party's nominee for president.

 II. to balance the ticket.

 III. based on their qualifications to succeed to the presidency in case of the death of the president.

 (A) I only.   (D) I and II only.

 (B) II only.   (E) I, II, and III.

 (C) III only.

115. All of the following are tenets of Keynesian economics EXCEPT

 (A) an unregulated capitalist economy will inevitably go through boom and bust cycles.

 (B) in order to stimulate production, government should cut tax rates to give producers incentives to produce.

 (C) government should stimulate the economy by increased spending during times of high unemployment.

 (D) government should reduce spending during times of high inflation.

 (E) government should increase tax rates during times of high inflation.

116. Which of the following statements about public opinion polling is TRUE?

 (A) Straw polls are scientific polls usually conducted by newspapers.

 (B) The larger the population in question, the larger the sample size must be to maintain the same sampling error.

 (C) Requirements for randomness may be satisfied quite easily by having respondents phone answers in to a television station.

 (D) Overly technical questions may cause sampling error.

 (E) Telephone surveys are generally unreliable because they target only those who can afford telephones.

117. The federal tax system now allows individuals to write off some of their investment losses against their taxable income. The corporate income tax allows a similar deduction for financial setbacks. If those provisions were to lapse, you should expect

(A) risk-taking in the United States to rise if people display increasing or constant relative risk-aversion with respect to income, and fall if they display decreasing relative risk-aversion with respect to income.

(B) risk-taking in the United States to fall if people display increasing or constant relative risk-aversion with respect to income, and rise if they display decreasing relative risk-aversion with respect to income.

(C) risk-taking in the United States to fall if people display increasing or constant relative risk-aversion with respect to income, but you could not offer a prediction if they display decreasing relative risk-aversion with respect to income.

(D) risk-taking in the United States. to fall if people display decreasing or constant relative risk-aversion with respect to income, and rise if they display increasing relative risk-aversion with respect to income.

(E) risk-taking in the United States to fall if people display decreasing or constant relative risk-aversion with respect to income, but you could not offer a prediction if they display increasing relative risk-aversion with respect to income.

118. One reason that has been proposed to explain why housing is a leading indicator of economic activity is that

(A) the demand for housing depends upon real GNP, and declines in real GNP always precede the onset of recession.

(B) the demand for housing depends upon the real interest rate, and real interest rates generally climb as economies begin to turn down into recession.

(C) the demand for housing depends at least indirectly on the prices of construction materials, and those prices always accelerate during the inflationary booms that precede recessions.

(D) the demand for housing depends critically upon nominal GNP, which always falls during the inflation that precedes recession.

(E) the demand for housing is affected by changes in real GNP abroad – one harbinger of changes in domestic activity.

119. Starting with national income, which of the following procedures is included in the process that produces a value for disposable personal income?

(A) Subtracting excise and sales taxes

(B) Subtracting nonbusiness interest

(C) Subtracting transfer payments from government

(D) Subtracting income taxes

(E) Adding contributions for social insurance that will eventually be repaid

120. A current account deficit

(A) is never possible because the balance of payments must always balance.

(B) can seldom be larger than 50 percent of a capital account surplus.

(C) can be used to help finance a government deficit indefinitely.

(D) can be used to help finance a government deficit if foreign lenders accumulate government bonds.

(E) does not include investment earnings that are part of the capital account.

121. Assuming that nothing else changes, an increase in exports of $5 billion can

(A) allow both the money supply *and* bond issues to fall by $5 billion.

(B) allow bond issues *or* the money supply to fall by $5 billion.

(C) allow both the money supply *and* bond issues to fall by more than $2.5 billion.

(D) allow bond issues *or* the money supply to increase by $2.5 billion.

(E) allow bond issues to fall by more than the money supply increase of $5 billion.

122. If the share of real GNP paid to labor in the United States has been roughly 75 percent over the past 50 years, then

    (A) the real source of increase in the real wage has been productivity growth.

    (B) the real source of inflation has been wage settlement.

    (C) the real source of international trade instability has not been excessive wages in the United States.

    (D) real wages must have soared in the 1970s.

    (E) the real return to capital must have increased.

123. Recent studies suggest power over and subordination of another are most likely to be the motivations for which of the following crimes?

    I.   Car theft

    II.   Embezzlement

    III. Rape

    IV.   Jaywalking

    (A) I only.   (D) I, II, and III only.

    (B) III only.   (E) I, II, III, and IV.

    (C) I and II only.

124. The type of social cohesion that binds people who do similar work and have a similar world view is referred to by Durkheim as

    (A) organic solidarity.   (D) virtual solidarity.

    (B) mechanical solidarity.   (E) None of the above.

    (C) cohesive solidarity.

125. A sociologist is interested in studying American college students' opinions on euthanasia. What is the population of her study?

    (A) College students on her campus

    (B) The students randomly chosen for a response

    (C) All college students

(D) An individual student

(E) All people between the ages of 18-21

126. Research shows an inverse relationship between levels of education and extent of prejudice. As far as we know today, which of the following most likely accounts for at least some of that relationship?

    I.   People who are less educated have greater contact with people of various ethnic and racial groups, thereby making them less prejudiced.

    II. As people attain more education, they become more tolerant.

    III. People who are prejudiced are less likely to pursue a higher education.

    IV. As people become more educated, they are more careful about revealing their prejudices.

(A) I only.

(B) II only.

(C) IV only.

(D) I and II only.

(E) II and IV only.

127. Which of the following is a measure of variability in test scores?

(A) Standard error of the mean

(B) Central tendency

(C) Percentile score

(D) Mode

(E) Beta weight

128. The electoral college system is biased in favor of

(A) states that support the Republican party.

(B) states dominated by one political party.

(C) states with small populations.

(D) candidates with a college education.

(E) the industrial Northeast.

129. A successful candidate for president must receive

    (A) a majority of votes cast by the public.

    (B) a majority of votes cast by the electoral college.

    (C) a plurality of votes cast by the public.

    (D) a plurality of votes cast by the electoral college.

    (E) a majority vote of the public and of the electoral college.

130. The most important reason why George H.W. Bush was elected president in 1988 was

    (A) his forceful personality and public speaking ability.

    (B) the economy was in good condition.

    (C) his selection of Dan Quayle as a running mate.

    (D) his interest in education.

    (E) he was the incumbent.

CLEP SOCIAL SCIENCES AND HISTORY
TEST 3

ANSWER KEY

Section 1

1. (E)	14. (D)	27. (C)	40. (C)	53. (B)
2. (E)	15. (B)	28. (B)	41. (D)	54. (B)
3. (A)	16. (E)	29. (C)	42. (B)	55. (B)
4. (B)	17. (A)	30. (B)	43. (E)	56. (E)
5. (D)	18. (E)	31. (E)	44. (C)	57. (B)
6. (D)	19. (C)	32. (C)	45. (D)	58. (A)
7. (A)	20. (D)	33. (D)	46. (D)	59. (A)
8. (C)	21. (C)	34. (C)	47. (E)	60. (E)
9. (A)	22. (B)	35. (A)	48. (C)	61. (B)
10. (A)	23. (B)	36. (C)	49. (A)	62. (A)
11. (C)	24. (E)	37. (B)	50. (D)	63. (D)
12. (D)	25. (C)	38. (A)	51. (E)	64. (B)
13. (E)	26. (D)	39. (D)	52. (C)	65. (A)

Section 2

66. (D)	79. (A)	92. (A)	105. (B)	118. (B)
67. (E)	80. (B)	93. (C)	106. (B)	119. (D)
68. (D)	81. (C)	94. (B)	107. (D)	120. (D)
69. (C)	82. (E)	95. (D)	108. (B)	121. (B)
70. (A)	83. (C)	96. (B)	109. (D)	122. (A)
71. (D)	84. (C)	97. (C)	110. (E)	123. (B)
72. (C)	85. (C)	98. (E)	111. (A)	124. (B)
73. (D)	86. (D)	99. (E)	112. (C)	125. (C)
74. (A)	87. (E)	100. (C)	113. (C)	126. (E)
75. (E)	88. (E)	101. (C)	114. (D)	127. (A)
76. (C)	89. (B)	102. (B)	115. (B)	128. (C)
77. (A)	90. (C)	103. (D)	116. (D)	129. (B)
78. (B)	91. (E)	104. (B)	117. (E)	130. (B)

DETAILED EXPLANATIONS
OF ANSWERS
TEST 3

Section 1

1.   **(E)**   Soured by the liberalism and intellectualism of the mainstream churches, as well as the government's increasing separation from religion at both the federal and state levels, and the growing emphasis on secular, rather than religious education in state-funded schools, many people turned to religion to resolve their alienation. Their religious fervor led them to blame most of the country's problems on the decline of "living by the Good Book." They demanded reforms and believed that the reforms had better come quickly, for they fervently believed that the second coming of Christ was at hand. They pushed for political and economic reforms, as well as temperance, abolitionism, educational reform, and some even supported women's rights. Many of the utopian communities of this time period were radical outgrowths of this religious upwelling. Most of the major reform movements of the mid-nineteenth century were related to the religious revivals sparked by Evangelical Christians.

2.   **(E)**   When John Kennedy became president in January 1961, he inherited a program from President Eisenhower guaranteed to cause him headaches. Eisenhower had begun a CIA-backed program to train Cuban exiles to return to Cuba and militarily overthrow Fidel Castro and his Communist regime. The program was ready to begin operations when Kennedy assumed office. When Kennedy asked the CIA about the feasibility of an invasion by Cuban exiles and their chances of success, he was told that Castro was hated by the Cuban people; that most Cubans were waiting for the chance to rise up and overthrow Castro; and that the CIA-trained Cuban exiles would have an easy time swarming to victory if the United States just provided them with the transportation to Cuba to launch the invasion.

Kennedy, just two months into his first term of office (April 1960), put too much trust in the glowing CIA reports and decided to go ahead with the project. The Cuban exiles were ferried ashore at the Bay of Pigs in Cuba with American support and equipment, but once they got there the entire plan broke down. The Cuban people, most of whom in reality supported Castro, did not rise up in revolt. The Cuban military responded quickly and pinned the invaders to the beaches. For two days they remained trapped there. The CIA and some members of the military pushed Kennedy to launch air strikes to support the operation, but Kennedy refused, fearing active American involvement could lead to a full-scale and costly war, and could also lead to Soviet retaliation in Turkey or Europe. Besides, without the support of the Cuban people, no amount of American military intervention could change the long-term result. After the second day, the survivors, comprising only 20 percent of the original invasion force, were rescued from the beaches and returned to the United States.

The Bay of Pigs affair was a humiliating embarrassment to the new president. It also set the stage for further problems with Cuba. Partly because of the Bay of Pigs affair and other American attempts to overthrow or destabilize the Cuban government, the Cubans and the Soviets secretly conspired to install intermediate-range nuclear missiles in Cuba. Such missiles, if successfully installed, would provide a powerful deterrent to further American intervention in Cuban affairs. American discovery of the construction of missile launching sites in Cuba led to the Cuban Missile Crisis of 1962, perhaps the most difficult crisis in Kennedy's presidency.

3. **(A)** The *politiques*, who emerged from the French civil war of religion (the War of the Three Henries) as the leading political group in France, argued that government should be based purely on political principles. Religion in politics was seen as an obstacle to good government. Choices (B) (government by religious leaders), (D), and (E) might be eliminated, since they represent an opposite viewpoint. A *politique* might accept choice (C), but parliamentary government developed only later in France and was irrelevant to the central concerns of the *politiques*.

4. **(B)** The wording of the question ("first Swiss leader") indicates that the easy answer – Calvin – must be incorrect. If the correct answer is unknown, it may be possible to eliminate choice (D), who was the best-known Anabaptist leader. Choice (C) is a lesser-known Anabaptist and (E) is the name of the Archbishop of Canterbury who helped Henry VIII create the Church of England. Before the French lawyer John Calvin assumed the leadership of the movement which would bear his name, Cal-

vinism was known as "Zwinglism." Its leader, Ulrich Zwingli, created a religious community in Switzerland before his death in a battle with Swiss Catholic armies.

5.   **(D)**   Of the four Muslim states, only Morocco was an independent kingdom. Tripoli (A), Tunis (B), and Algiers (C) were still nominal dependencies of the Ottoman Empire, at least until the French invasion of Algeria in 1830.

6.   **(D)**   Guam became a possession of Spain in 1561 and was ceded to the United States in 1898 after the Spanish-American War, when it was placed under the administration of the U.S. Navy. Japan attacked Guam on December 7, 1941, and captured it on December 10. U.S. forces recaptured it on August 15, 1944. The United States declared Guam a territory on August 1, 1959, and transferred supervision from the Navy to the Department of the Interior. The people of Guam are U.S. citizens. They elect a one-house legislator, a governor, and a lieutenant governor.

7.   **(A)**   The conflict perspective views society as being unequal in terms of power. In this example, the power relations between groups and individuals are being questioned. (B) is incorrect. A functionalist perspective views society's systems as being interrelated and working together to maintain stability. (C), (D), and (E) are not sociological paradigms used to explain social phenomenon.

8.   **(C)**   In unobtrusive research, no interaction takes place between the researcher and the subject under study. The researcher in no way attempts to influence the behavior or response of the subject. In this case, John has absolutely no contact with his subjects. (A) A survey is a method used in which subjects respond to a series of questions on a questionnaire. John does not question his subjects directly. (B) Obtrusive research is exactly the opposite of what is being done in this example. It is when the researcher has extensive contact with his subject, potentially influencing the response. (D) Experimental research seeks to find cause-effect relationships and takes place under highly controlled conditions. Nothing in the question indicates an experimental design, so (D) is incorrect. (E) Participant-observation research is when the researcher becomes involved with the subject under study and actually participates in the same behaviors. John does not participate in his subjects' actions.

9. **(A)** Social stratification, or structured inequality, is so vital to understand because every aspect of our lives is influenced by where we fall in the hierarchical system. Our access to socially valued goods and rewards (i.e., money, education) is dependent upon our place in the stratification system. (B) is incorrect. Most societies do not seem committed to the elimination of structured inequality. All societies are stratified, whether by sex, age, or race. (C) is also incorrect. Every individual is born into a system of stratification. Our life chances will be reduced only if we occupy a subordinate position in that hierarchy. (D) and (E) are incorrect because they include Statement II, which is wrong.

10. **(A)** Polyandry is the practice of one woman marrying more than one man. In societies where there are fewer women than men, either through warfare or infanticide, the women will be shared by the men. (B) is incorrect. Polygamy refers only to one person marrying two or more other people. The term does not state whether it is the man or woman who has multiple marriages. (C) Exogamy refers to marriage outside one's group. For example, an African-American who marries an Asian is practicing exogamy. (D) Polygyny refers to one man marrying two or more women. This is opposite from the example. (E) Monogamy refers to a form of marriage where only two partners are involved.

11. **(C)** Ethnocentric means to judge another culture by the standards of one's own. By seeing all other cultures she has come into contact with as inferior, Paula is being ethnocentric. (A) is incorrect. Paula is not stereotyping any one culture, rather she is seeing all other cultures as inferior. (B) is incorrect. A prejudice is a judgment based on an individual's group membership, not his or her personal attributes. Paula is not judging an individual based on their group membership. Rather, she is making a judgment concerning an entire culture – her own. (D) Paula is not expressing individual discrimination. Discrimination is a behavior, while ethnocentrism is a belief. Paula does not behave unfairly toward another group. She merely holds opinions about many different groups and cultures. (E) Selective perception is selectively perceiving those cases which reinforce your stereotype of a certain group. Paula does not stereotype any single group and does not use any specific examples to reinforce her stereotype.

12. **(D)** Cultural transmission theory contends that crime is learned through cultural and subcultural norms. The lawyer is afraid his client will learn more about crime via the subcultural norms of prison. (A) is incorrect as strain theory does not include a component of learning. Strain theory suggests crime is the result of structural constraints placed on the

individual, blocking means for achievement. (B) is incorrect. Labeling theory does not rely on learning to commit crime. Rather, it focuses on the process by which one is labeled and defined as a criminal. (C) is incorrect. Control theory maintains that all of us deviate, and those who do not are more attached to their society. Since no theory termed "deviance theory" exists, (E) is wrong.

13.   **(E)** Deindividuation occurs when individuals lose their personal sense of responsibility when they are in a group. In a group, people feel more anonymous and thus less morally accountable for their actions. This loss of individuality has been found to be the cause of violent, antisocial behavior that is sometimes seen in large groups.

14.   **(D)** The concept of dual federalism was predominant in American government from the post-Civil War period until approximately the 1930s. A typical description of this concept was given by the Supreme Court in the Tarbells case, 1872:

> There are within the territorial limits of each state two governments (state and national), restricted in their spheres of action, but independent of each other, and supreme within their respective spheres. Each has its separate departments, each has its distinct laws, and each has its own tribunes for their enforcement. Neither government can intrude within the jurisdiction of the other or authorize any interference therein by its judicial officers with the action of the other.

(A) is incorrect because dual federalism held that the states had certain powers which were specifically reserved to them by the Tenth Amendment. These could be exercised regardless of congressional action. (B) is incorrect because it describes the current concept of federalism, which might be called one of national supremacy. In the case *Garcia v. San Antonio,* 1985, the Supreme Court declared that henceforth Congress should decide for itself to what extent it ought to regulate those powers that were originally reserved to the states by the Tenth Amendment to the Constitution. This means, in effect, that there are no longer any reserved powers of the states upon which Congress may not encroach. This concept is radically different from that of dual federalism. (C) is incorrect because the term for this concept of federalism is cooperative federalism. (E) is incorrect because it expresses a view typically referred to as the theory of nullification. This theory was held by many in the South before the Civil War. Perhaps the most famous advocate of this theory was John C. Calhoun.

15. **(B)** The original Constitution said nothing about what qualifications would be required for voting in federal elections. Article I, section 4, states:

> The times, places and manner of holding elections for Senators and Representatives, shall be prescribed in each state by the legislature thereof; but the Congress may at any time by law make or alter such regulations, except as to the places of choosing Senators.

The Fifteenth Amendment prevented the states from denying persons the right to vote on the basis of race; the Nineteenth Amendment extended the right to vote to women; the Twenty-Fourth Amendment outlawed the use of the poll tax by states; and the Twenty-Sixth Amendment extended the right to vote to persons 18 years of age or older. (C) is incorrect because two methods of ratifying amendments are given in Article V. Congress is given the power to decide which method will be used for any proposed amendment. (D) is incorrect because the qualifications for members of the House and Senate are stipulated in Article I. (E) is incorrect because Article I, section 10, of the Constitution says that a state cannot, without the consent of Congress, levy duties on imports or exports "except what shall be absolutely necessary for executing its inspection laws."

16. **(E)** The Constitution states in the Twelfth Amendment that "The person having the greatest number of [electoral] votes for President, shall be President, if such number be a majority of the whole number of Electors appointed...." (A) is incorrect because to win in the electoral college a candidate must receive a majority of the electoral votes, not merely a plurality. If three or more candidates received electoral votes, it would be possible that none received the necessary majority. In that case the decision would be made in the House of Representatives. In 1824, Andrew Jackson received 99 electoral votes, John Quincy Adams 84, William Crawford 41, and Henry Clay 37. The House of Representatives chose John Quincy Adams as president, despite the fact that Jackson had the most electoral votes. (B) is incorrect because the president is not elected directly by popular vote, but rather by the electoral college. Whichever candidate wins a plurality of the popular vote in a state wins that state's electoral vote. It is possible for a candidate to win a majority of the popular vote nationwide, but not win a majority of the electoral votes. This happened in 1876, when Samuel J. Tilden won 51 percent of the popular vote, but lost the presidency to Rutherford B. Hayes by an electoral vote of 184 to 185. (C) is not correct because several presidents have won less

than a majority of the popular vote, but a majority of the electoral vote. This happened in 1876, as explained above. It has also happened several times when three or more candidates split the popular vote, with the president-elect winning a majority of the electoral vote (1824, 1844, 1848, 1856, 1860, 1880, 1884, 1888, 1892, 1912, 1948, and 1968). (D) is incorrect because if no candidate wins a majority of the electoral vote, the House of Representatives selects the president from among the top three popular vote getters.

17. **(A)** The new classical theory requires both flexible prices and rational expectations. Flexible prices work to guarantee that aggregate supply is always set equal to potential GNP. Changes in aggregate demand, therefore, cause no change in actual GNP. Rational expectations undermine the ability of policy adjustments to change aggregate demand because people react to changes in a way that nullifies its effect. Changes in policy, therefore, leave real wage and output unchanged.

18. **(E)** In response to anticipated inflation, people should be expected to increase consumption expenditures to take advantage of low current prices. The result, given full employment, is a reduction in capital expenditure as the production mix moves toward supplying the consumption surge. Additionally, the reduced saving decreases the supply of financial capital, thereby increasing interest rates and contributing to the reduction in investment in physical capital. The rate of economic growth must therefore be reduced.

19. **(C)** This argument is certainly not totally acknowledged by economists. There are significant differences in labor costs (real and nominal) across national boundaries, but differences in relative (not absolute) costs are the foundation of mutually beneficial trade. Certainly equivalent quotas have nothing to do with it.

20. **(D)** Muckrakers got their name from Theodore Roosevelt who compared the sensationalistic exposés of high-level corruption to "raking muck." Their stories tended to focus on the very worst behaviors of industrial leaders and politicians. The stories were designed to arouse the public and play to their "baser instincts." They explored all of the flaws in American society and provided a method of airing the nation's "dirty laundry." While political and industrial leaders were horrified by the tone and focus of the stories, the general public couldn't get enough. The stories confirmed in many people's minds what they had long suspected: rather than protecting

the public interest, many public and private leaders were using their positions to further their own self-interest at the expense of everyone else. The stories led to an outcry for reform and provided Progressivists with just the ammunition and public support they needed to insure passage of legal reforms.

21. **(C)** The first wave of immigration to the English colonies by non-English speaking people was dominated by ethnic Germans fleeing from the Rhine region of what is now Germany. Most were farmers fleeing from war and starvation in their homeland. Some were seeking a respite from religious persecution. Many of them settled in western Pennsylvania and began successful farming communities where they were inaccurately labeled "the Pennsylvania Dutch." While the ethnic groups listed in the remaining choices were all involved in waves of immigration to the New World, they all came at later dates, mostly after the mid-nineteenth century.

22. **(B)** Questions such as this underline the importance of not only understanding terminology but also its implications. Short of knowing Latin, a reasonable approach to this question would be to identify which answers were not results of the Thirty Years' War. The Thirty Years' War ended with a compromise settlement which allowed local monarchs or princes in the Holy Roman Empire to dictate the religious denomination of their area. Dissenters among their subjects were expected to convert or to move to another territory.

23. **(B)** In this case, it is not enough to be able to name a Christian Humanist or explain the ideas of the Christian Humanist. This question tests the depth of your knowledge about Christian Humanism and the Renaissance. Even if you can identify Valla, the correct answer also requires that you know a particular term ("Donation of Constantine"). The Donation was a document which canon (church) lawyers used against Holy Roman emperors who challenged papal authority. Ostensibly a signed document in which the Roman emperor Constantine acknowledged papal superiority in both the religious and temporal (nonchurch) realms, the Donation was proved a fraud by Valla on the basis of Latin usage not appropriate for its date and for references to historical events which occurred at a later date.

24. **(E)** All of the colonies accepted de Gaulle's proposal except for Guinea, which was headed by the communist Sekou Toure, who demanded

immediate independence for his country. This was a risk that the other colonies were not yet willing to take because it meant giving up economic and political support from France. After the referendum, however, Ghana's Kwame Nkrumah offered his country's aid to Guinea and the two countries formed an alliance that would be copied by other African countries in the following years.

25.   **(C)** Cambodia, whose capital is Phnom Penh, changed systems from a monarchy to a republic in 1970. In 1975 Cambodian communists, called the Khmer Rouge, overthrew leaders of the republic. The Khmer is the name of the ethnic population of Cambodia and Rouge, meaning "Red" in French, symbolizes the principles of communism (as in the red flag of the Soviet Union and Mao's Red Book). The Cambodian monarchy has since been restored and is currently headed by King Norodom Sihanouk. His son, Prince Ranaridh, is prime minister.

26.   **(D)** The Sapir-Whorf hypothesis says that people think through language. Language is not just the vehicle through which we express ourselves; language also shapes our thoughts. (A) is incorrect. The Sapir-Whorf hypothesis makes no prediction of behavior of people who speak different languages. (B) states the opposite of the Sapir-Whorf hypothesis because speakers of different languages do not perceive the world in identical ways since perception and ideas vary across languages. (C) According to the Sapir-Whorf hypothesis, speakers of different languages would view the world differently because their language predisposes them to think and perceive in a particular way. Because a correct answer is provided, (E) is incorrect.

27.   **(C)** Research on children raised in isolation suggests that in order to develop and be fully human, people need continual interaction. (A) is incorrect as it states nearly the opposite. (B) and (D) are incorrect for the same reason. Both answers suggest that genetics (nature) is more powerful than social processes (nurture). To the contrary, studies show that social interaction is vital throughout the life course. Because a correct answer is provided, (E) is incorrect.

28.   **(B)** Impression management refers to the conscious manipulation of role performance. The professor in this example is manipulating her role performance in order to impress her students. (A) is incorrect. Status inconsistency is a condition in which a person holds a higher position on one dimension of stratification than on another. This example is not ad-

dressing different statuses, but the roles associated with a single status. (C) and (D) are both incorrect, as these terms have no sociological meaning. A correct answer is provided, so (E) is incorrect.

29.   **(C)**   Folkways are social norms governing less important areas of behavior such as table manners or proper attire for events. Mores are social norms which concern more serious issues such as laws against murder or incest. (A) is incorrect since violations of folkways usually result in mild reprimands. (D) is incorrect because violations of mores are usually considered crimes and involve more drastic punishments. (B) and (E) are also incorrect because folkways and mores are found among all social groups and cover a wide range of behaviors.

30.   **(B)**   A functionalist argument is based on the assumption that society's complex systems work together to maintain stability. In this example, family size is explained as part of a system that is maintaining its stability. (A) is incorrect. A conflict approach assumes conflict and in-equality underlie society. This explanation of family size does not discuss the tensions and inequalities that promote social change. (C) The symbolic interactionism approach assumes that society is the product of everyday interactions of people. In this example, individual interaction is never addressed. (D) is incorrect. Rather than being micro, or focusing at the individual level, this explanation is macro, and focuses on the structural level. (E) is incorrect because no sociological term "institutional argu-ment" exists.

31.   **(E)**   A negative correlation is an association between two variables so that as one increases the other decreases, as is the case with education and prejudice in this example. (A) A spurious relationship is an apparent association that can actually be explained by a third variable. Nothing from this example suggests that a third variable is explaining both preju-dice and education levels. (B) is incorrect as no sociological term "defini-tive" exists. (C) Nothing from this example suggests this relationship is causal. We cannot say definitively that education level causes prejudice. We only know that a relationship between the two exists. (D) is incorrect. The association would be positive if both variables increased or decreased together.

32.   **(C)**   Deindividuation is a state in which a person feels a lessened sense of personal identity and a decreased concern about what others think of him/her. This occurs when a person is part of a group and thus feels less responsible for his actions. This is also known as responsibility diffusion.

33. **(D)** A discharge petition is used to force a bill out of a standing committee which has refused to report the bill out to the full House. In the House, a bill cannot reach the floor unless reported out of a committee. A bill that has not been reported out within 30 days after referral to committee may be subject to discharge. The discharge petition must be signed by an absolute majority of House members (218). The motion to discharge is then voted on, and carries with a majority vote of those present and voting. The rules committee may be discharged of a bill after 7 days, rather than the 30 required for other committees. (A) is incorrect because the only way for a bill on the floor to be killed is by a negative vote by a majority of those present and voting. (B) is incorrect because a discharge petition cannot be used to force the rules committee to send a bill back to the committee to which the bill was originally referred. (C) is incorrect because a discharge petition is not used to open a bill up to amendments on the floor of the House. In the House, bills reported out of a standing committee go to the rules committee. The rules committee gives each bill a rule which specifies the time limit for debate on the bill, and whether or not the bill may be amended during floor debate. When the bill comes to the floor for debate, the first thing voted on is the rule assigned by the rules committee. Most of the time the rule is routinely approved. If it is rejected, its opponents may substitute a rule more to their liking. This process does not involve a discharge petition. (E) is incorrect because a bill approved by the House is certified by the clerk, printed on blue paper, and automatically sent to the Senate for its consideration.

34. **(C)** Although the Fourth Amendment protects the public against unreasonable search and seizure, the precise way by which that protection is to be enforced is not stipulated in the Amendment. Before 1914, any person whose Fourth Amendment rights were violated by federal authorities had as their only recourse a civil suit for damages against the offending official. Any evidence gained through the illegal search was admissible in court. Persons whose Fourth Amendment rights were violated by state officials had no recourse whatsoever under the Fourth Amendment, since it did not originally apply to the states. In 1914, in *Weeks v. United States,* the Supreme Court established the exclusionary rule, which allowed evidence obtained illegally by federal officials to be excluded from trial in federal courts. In *Wolf v. Colorado,* 1949, the Court applied the Fourth Amendment to the states, but did not apply the exclusionary rule to the states. This meant that, while evidence seized illegally by a state official was still admissible in a state court, the person whose rights were violated could now sue the offending official for violation of the person's civil rights. In *Mapp v. Ohio,* 1961, the Court finally applied the exclu-

sionary rule to state officials and courts. (A) is incorrect because *Baker v. Carr* dealt with the reapportionment of the Tennessee State Assembly. (B) is incorrect because *Roe v. Wade,* 1973, dealt with a woman's right to an abortion. (D) is incorrect because *Korematsu v. United States,* 1944, dealt with the president's power to exclude Japanese-Americans from military districts during World War II. (E) is incorrect because *Gideon v. Wainwright,* 1963, dealt with the right of indigents accused of felonies to have lawyers appointed at state expense to defend them.

35.   **(A)** Amendments Thirteen (1865), Fourteen (1868), and Fifteen (1860) were adopted in order to protect the rights of former slaves after the Civil War. The Thirteenth Amendment forbids slavery or involuntary servitude anywhere in the United States or in any place subject to its jurisdiction. It therefore prevented the reimposition of slavery in the southern states. The Fourteenth Amendment restricts the powers of states; the most important provisions are those that forbid a state to deprive any person of life, liberty, or property without due process of law, or to deny any person equal protection of the law. The Fifteenth Amendment prohibits states from denying anyone the right to vote on the basis of race, color, or previous condition of servitude. This was clearly meant as a precaution against attempts by southern states to prevent blacks from voting. (B) is incorrect because the Nineteenth Amendment extended the suffrage to women, and the Twenty-Sixth Amendment extended it to 18 year olds. (C) is incorrect because the First Amendment provides protection for speech, religion, and assembly. (D) is incorrect because these amendments did not increase the power of the federal government in any way which could help prevent another civil war. The due process clause of the Fourteenth Amendment has been used by the Supreme Court to apply the Bill of Rights to the state governments. However, it is not at all clear from the debates which took place in Congress when the amendment was proposed that this use of the due process clause was intended by the authors of the amendment. In addition, it was not until *Gitlow v. New York,* 1925, that the Court thought to use the due process clause of the Fourteenth Amendment for that purpose. Therefore, (E) is incorrect.

36.   **(C)** Trying to set monetary policy to achieve stable interest rates tends to make the LM curve flatter. As a result, any variation in the IS curve is translated into more variation in GNP but less variation in interest rates. Only choice (C) notes this change. The answer about the international capital account is also incorrect because those accounts are more sensitive to changes in interest rates than they are to changes in GNP.

37.   **(B)**   A general sales tax is proportional on consumption expenditures. Tax revenue collected, therefore, is

$$T = [t \times C] = t \times [Y - S],$$

where t equals the tax rate, C represents consumption, Y represents (national) income, and S represents saving. To the extent that wealthier people save more (and poorer people save less), wealthier people avoid more tax and pay a smaller proportion of their incomes to the government. In fact, the average tax rate equals $[t - (S/Y)]$ falls directly as S climbs. The general sales tax is therefore thought to be regressive.

38.   **(A)**   The only choice given that would not allow interest rates to rise is (A). This is because a decrease in taxes, all else equal, implies that consumers have more disposable income to use for additional consumption and savings. If it is not used for consumption, then the tax cuts must have been saved. This addition to private savings then finances the reduction in public savings. Thus, there is no required change in interest rates to attract additional sources of financing. This argument of tax cuts being ineffectual in changing consumption is known as the Barro-Ricardian equivalence theorem.

39.   **(D)**   The 1920s were a mixture of both conservative and liberal trends. On the liberal side, women were granted the right to vote with ratification in 1920 of the Nineteenth Amendment to the Constitution. With new forms of credit and advertising, combined with increases in wages and productivity, consumerism became the new American ethic.

On the conservative side, prohibition was enacted with the passage of the Eighteenth Amendment to the Constitution in 1919. Its enforcement began on a large scale in 1920, opening the door for bootlegging and the rise of organized crime in America. The Ku Klux Klan, using new advertising techniques to market itself, reached a peak membership of 5 million people in 1925, before sex scandals, corruption, poor leadership, and public revulsion at Klan activities broke its power base and discredited it as a major political force. Throughout the mid-1920s, however, the Klan was a force to be feared and accommodated, and Klan activities had a very intimidating effect on local and regional politics in the South, Midwest, and mid-Atlantic regions of the country.

The only choice not characteristic of the 1920s is choice (D). The Progressive movement, so forceful before World War I, was eclipsed by the pro-business economic growth philosophies of Harding, Coolidge,

Hoover, and the Republicans. Progressivist reforms were rolled back throughout the 1920s, negating many gains previously made in regulating businesses and securing labor rights. These gains were sacrificed on the altars of economic growth and laissez-faire capitalism. Progressivism would not return to the fore until the enactment of Franklin Roosevelt's "New Deal" in the 1930s, where Progressivist principles were carried far beyond anything hoped for at the turn of the century.

40.   **(C)**   In the election of 1860, Abraham Lincoln only received 40 percent of the national vote. But his three opponents divided the anti-Lincoln vote in such a way that Lincoln still received the largest vote total of any single candidate. Lincoln's closest opponent was Stephen Douglas, who received about 30 percent of the popular vote. Furthermore, Lincoln's popular support was concentrated in the North, the most populous region of the country where most of the electoral college votes were. He did not even appear on the ballot of some Southern states. By concentrating on the North and winning decisively there, he gathered so many electoral votes that even had his opponents combined their popular votes, which would have totaled 60 percent of the national vote, they would have lost the election in the electoral college.

41.   **(D)**   Italian economic success during the Renaissance was partly the result of ingenious devices which Italian merchants created to lessen the risks involved in long-distance travel and trade on the treacherous and frequently stormy Mediterranean Sea. The commenda freed the merchant himself from dangerous journeys; it was a contract between the merchant who furnished goods for sale and a "merchant-adventurer" who agreed to take the goods to distant locations and return with the proceeds. The merchant-adventurer was generally paid one-third of the resulting profits. If the term "commenda" is unknown, the clue "Italian Renaissance" may lead to the realization that choice (A) is unlikely. If you are unable to eliminate more answers, however, guessing may not prove profitable.

42.   **(B)**   Answering this question requires more than terminology, since it also asks for an understanding of the implications of the Weber thesis. Note, however, that some choices appear unlikely. Choices (A) and (C) were in development before the rise of Calvinism. Anglicanism should seem an unlikely choice, since it was restricted to only one part of Europe and was a result of the political and personal desires of King Henry VIII. Weber, an early twentieth century German sociologist, theorized that a mutually helpful relationship existed between Calvinism and capitalism

because they both were based on common virtues such as industriousness, thrift, etc. Choice (E) is simply incorrect.

43. **(E)** All three of the historical figures mentioned have provided important intellectual and political influences for the Pan-African movement. The nineteenth-century Jamaican Marcus Aurelius Garvey developed the concepts of a "Negro Empire" and of "Africa for the Africans," and he supported a plan to transport American blacks back to Africa, a plan which was, unfortunately, also espoused by racist white Americans after the Civil War. The American-born, German-educated, black philosopher and writer W. E. B. DuBois, writing in the 1920s and 30s, attended the original Pan-African congresses. And finally, since many African leaders of the Pan-African movement had been educated in Europe, they were exposed to the writings of Karl Marx (1818-1883) and the European models of socialism and communism he inspired, which became important elements of the Pan-Africanist ideology.

44. **(C)** The British East India Company, a trading company, was formed in 1600 with a royal charter from Queen Elizabeth I. By the 1700s there was no longer a strong central government in India, and the East India Company became a leading power in 1757. Between 1800 and 1857 the company waged wars against Afghanistan, Burma and Nepal, but unrest and rebellions like the 1857 Sepoy Rebellion convinced the British government that it needed to take over control of the company in 1858. By 1833 the company had lost its monopoly on East Asian trade, and in 1858 was replaced with a functional Indian government.

45. **(D)** Content analysis is a method in which the researcher uses artifacts and existing data. In this example, the researcher uses a diary to understand more about social behavior. Other examples might be the use of newspapers or song lyrics. (A) A survey is a method in which a subject is asked to respond to a series of questions. (B) and (C) are incorrect. The researcher is not participating or interacting in any way with the subject. Because a correct response is provided, (E) is incorrect.

46. **(D)** Research on prejudice suggests that in a noncompetitive atmosphere, when individuals from different ethnic backgrounds come together, there is likely to be little conflict. In an economically competitive atmosphere, conflict is likely to ensue. (A) is incorrect because in Newpark the distribution of goods is fairly equal. (B) and (C) are incorrect. Diversity leads to conflict when there are dramatic inequalities between groups. In

this example, there is economic parity, regardless of race and ethnicity. (E) is incorrect since a correct answer has been provided.

47.   **(E)** By attempting to create their own country, the "Zorn" movement can be classified as secessionist, which is not an answer choice. (A) is incorrect. In a pluralist movement, minority groups attempt to maintain their own distinctive cultural features, while still operating within the larger society. An example would be an Irish-American neighborhood. (B) An assimilationist movement is when the minority completely adopts the culture and way of life of the majority. (C) is incorrect. A segregationist movement is when separate public accommodations (schools, houses, parks, buses, etc.) are set up for minorities, within the same society. Minority groups still function within the larger society and are still subject to the majority's laws and political system. (D) is incorrect. Expulsion is the process whereby the dominant group attempts to force an unwanted population out of their borders. This differs from secession in that in the latter movement, the subordinate group attempts to leave or separate from the dominant group.

48.   **(C)** An informal sanction is direct social pressure from those around us to conform. The term "informal" suggests that the pressure is not coming from a formal or legal institution such as the criminal justice system. Instead the pressure to conform may be coming from our family or peer group. If your date cancels, the pressure to conform is informal. All of the other choices, (A), (B), and (D), show the role of formal institution in pressuring one to conform, either through fines, imprisonment, or community service. Because (A), (B), and (D) refer to formal sanctions, (E) is incorrect.

49.   **(A)** Cultural relativism is the attempt on the part of researchers to not judge another culture by the standards of one's own. By trying to understand the practice of performing clitoridectomies, without judging the practice as bad, or the culture as inferior, Dr. Smith is adopting an attitude of cultural relativism. (B) Multi-culturalism refers to a variety of cultures living in the same society. Dr. Smith is not studying a culture within her society; therefore, (B) is incorrect. (C) is incorrect. Ethnocentrism refers to the judgment of another culture seeing yours as superior. Dr. Smith is adopting the opposite approach. (D) is incorrect. No sociological term "ideal ritualism" exists. Because a correct answer has been provided, (E) is incorrect.

50.   **(D)**   A fad is an unconventional social pattern that people engaged briefly but enthusiastically. (A) is incorrect. A social movement is an organized activity that seeks social change. The interest in such toys and dolls is not organized, and there is no goal of social change. (B) A fashion is a social pattern favored for a long period of time by large numbers of people. The interest is quickly fleeting and therefore does not qualify as a fashion. (C) is incorrect. A mob is a highly emotional crowd that is pursuing a destructive goal. Because a correct answer is provided, (E) is incorrect.

51.   **(E)**   Anonymity is one condition that leads to deindividuation. This means a person loses a sense of individual identity and responsibility. Being an anonymous member of a large crowd, losing one's self in the group, illustrates deindividuation.

52.   **(C)**   The Supreme Court has generally been very reluctant to intervene in disputes between the executive and legislative branches over the extent of their respective powers. Such disputes have traditionally been termed "political questions," which the Court finds to be outside the scope of its jurisdiction. The settlement of political questions, according to the Court, is left to the voters through the electoral process. In *Goldwater v. Carter,* 1979, the Court invoked the political questions doctrine to avoid ruling on whether or not President Jimmy Carter could unilaterally terminate the United States' mutual defense treaty with Taiwan, which Senator Barry Goldwater held that he could not do. In 1987, a federal district court dismissed as a political question a lawsuit brought by Democratic congressmen, charging President Reagan with violating the War Powers Resolution by deploying the American navy in the Persian Gulf without notifying Congress. (A), (B), and (D) are incorrect because the Court usually declines to decide disputes between the two branches. (E) is incorrect for the same reason; in addition, the War Powers suit discussed above adds an additional gloss on this point. The War Powers Resolution was passed in 1973, over the veto of President Richard Nixon. The federal district court threw out the 1987 case as a federal question, even though the resolution limited the powers of the presidency and was passed over Nixon's veto. The court did not decide against Congress, it simply refused to hear the case at all.

53.   **(B)**   A bill's route to the floor of the House lies through the House rules committee. First, a bill is introduced by a member. The presiding officer refers the bill to a standing committee, which often sends it to a subcommittee. After being referred out of committee, the bill goes on one

of the calendars. Next, the bill goes to the rules committee. The bill's sponsor and the chairman of the committee which reported the bill will appear before the rules committee to request a rule on the bill. The rules committee will issue either a closed or open rule on the bill. A closed rule means that no amendments, or only those proposed by the committee that reported the bill, can be considered during floor debate. An open rule means that amendments may be proposed by any participant in the debate on the floor. Choice (A) is incorrect because the rules committee does not have the power to close the gallery to the public. Choice (C) is incorrect because there is no House procedure to prevent members from voting on a bill if they miss all or part of the debate on the bill. Choice (D) is incorrect because bills are calendared after being reported out of committee, before going to the rules committee. Choice (E) is incorrect since one house of Congress cannot prevent the other from amending any bill passed by the first house.

54.   **(B)** The Continental Congress was not given the right to levy direct taxes on individual citizens. Instead, the Articles of Confederation only allowed the Congress to requisition money from the state governments. A requisition amounted to the same thing as a request. When the state governments fell behind in making their requisition payments, Congress was unable to force payment of the money. For this reason, the continental treasury was constantly empty. (A) is incorrect because there was no separation of powers under the Articles of Confederation. The government consisted of a Congress alone, made up of delegates from each of the states. (C) is incorrect since there was no national judiciary under the Articles of Confederation. (D) is incorrect because the Articles of Confederation were very difficult to amend. Amendment required unanimous consent of the 13 states, and Rhode Island always refused to go along with any proposed amendments (for which it came to be known as Rogue Island). (E) is incorrect because the Continental Congress was a unicameral body.

55.   **(B)** Inflation, by definition, becomes a potential concern as the actual unemployment rate approaches the natural rate from above. If the natural rate were 6 percent, then inflation should be a concern with unemployment falling so quickly from 7.7 percent to 5.8 percent < 6 percent. A growth recession refers to an economy that is growing, but not quickly enough to keep the unemployment rate from climbing over time; it does not apply to this question. Only choice (B) correctly applies the definition of the natural rate.

56.   **(E)**   The equivalence of tariffs and quotas is widely known. Surely, there exists a quota that will achieve the same restricted level of imports or exports as any tariff. Which one? The one that matches the level of trade that would occur given the tariff. If, in addition, licenses are auctioned to importers equal to the level of trade allowed by the quota, then those licenses will command a price equal to the difference between the world price of the import and the price that the domestic market will bear. This is precisely the value of the quantity equivalent tariff, so price times quota will certainly raise exactly the same level of revenue.

57.   **(B)**   Choice (B) is essentially the definition of consumer surplus. The other statements are true and are implications of using the tool of consumer surplus, but they are not the reflections of the idea.

58.   **(A)**   Joseph McCarthy, the junior senator from Wisconsin, set the tone for the early 1950s in America with his relentless attacks on the "Communist menace" in America. McCarthy used American fears of Communist subversion to catapult himself out of obscurity in the United States Senate and into national prominence. He made his initial charges in a Lincoln's Birthday speech in Wheeling, West Virginia, claiming that the U.S. State Department was infested with Communists. Although he was lying, his charges struck a chord in the national psyche and within days people were clamoring for the ouster of the alleged Communists. He used these charges to build a political base of support from which he went on to blame virtually all of America's failures since World War II on wealthy intellectuals supposedly selling out the country to the Communists. His attacks played upon latent bigotry, racism, and anti-Semitism, but the Korean War and the arrest of alleged spies, such as the Rosenbergs, convinced enough people that he was probably correct in his allegations, that few attempted to stop him. President Eisenhower tried to ignore McCarthy and hoped he would undercut himself with his reckless allegations and unfounded charges.

Eventually, McCarthy did ruin his own career. His charges became more and more spectacular and more and more unprovable. Finally, when he charged that the Army officer corps was a hotbed of Communist activity, Eisenhower decided enough was enough. Senate hearings were called in 1954 to investigate McCarthy's charges, and they were nationally televised. McCarthy was as bullying and overbearing as ever, attempting to ruin the reputation of virtually anyone who stood up to him. In the end, these tactics disgusted the American public and fellow senators. McCarthy's popularity plummeted and the Senate condemned him. He remained a senator but finished his career a broken man. He died of alcohol-related causes in 1957.

59.   **(A)** When stories of White House involvement in the Watergate break-in began surfacing in 1973, President Richard Nixon came under increasing pressure to formally investigate the entire affair. Nixon denied any involvement in the Watergate caper, but during the trial of one of the Watergate burglars, a White House aide revealed that Nixon had a taping system which had recorded virtually all conversations in the Oval Office during the period in question. Investigators demanded the tapes. Nixon refused on the grounds of "executive privilege." Investigators smelled a cover-up.

To quiet his critics, Nixon appointed a special prosecutor, Archibald Cox, to investigate any White House involvement in Watergate. Cox also requested the tapes. When Nixon refused, Cox went to court to obtain a court order forcing Nixon to relinquish the tapes. When Nixon realized what Cox had done and also realized that Cox might succeed in getting the court order, he ordered Cox to be fired. Nixon's attorney general and his assistant both refused to carry out the order. Instead, they resigned in protest. Nixon finally got another Justice Department official to carry out the order. Cox and his staff were duly fired on Saturday night, October 20, 1973, thus the name "Saturday Night Massacre."

The press, the public, and Nixon's political opposition (even some of his supporters) were outraged. The demand for continued investigation forced Nixon to name a new special prosecutor, Leon Jaworski. Jaworski also sought, and eventually got, custody of the complete tapes. Those tapes proved to be the "smoking gun" which ruined the little credibility Nixon had left and finished his presidency.

60.   **(E)** This question requires that you not only interpret the graph correctly but also use your knowledge of history and geography. The two most urbanized areas (England and Scotland) are major parts of the British Isles.

61.   **(B)** Beginning with terminology ("identify the Fronde"), this question asks for an analysis of the purpose of these periodic revolts by the nobility of France. A phenomenon of largely the sixteenth and seventeenth centuries, they were regarded as threats to royal authority by monarchical ministers Mazarin and Richelieu, who suppressed them ruthlessly. Most ended when Louis XIV involved the most powerful members of the nobility in sterile and useless ceremonial lives at his palace of Versailles.

62.   **(A)**   The concept of "Negritude" was developed by the Senegalese writer Leopold Senghor and poet Aime Cesaire from Martinique to celebrate the artistic and cultural heritage of Africa. Unlike choices (B), (C), (D), and (E), "Negritude" was neither a derogatory term, a system of government, nor a political plan or policy. While the "Negritude" movement had implications for African independence and self-determination at home, its cultural center was in Paris where Senghor and fellow Senegalese Alioune Diop founded the journal *Presence Africaine* in 1947. The movement was able to capitalize on and contribute to an appreciation and incorporation of African forms and rhythms by European artists like Picasso.

63.   **(D)**   In 1876 Japan forced Korea to open its ports of trade, and in the 1880s Korea signed treaties with the United States, Russia, and other European countries. Japan gained control of Korea as a result of the 1894-95 Sino-Japanese War (which forced China out of Korea), and it took complete control of the country in 1910. Japan's occupation of Korea ended with Japan's defeat in World War II, after which the United States and Russia moved into the country, eventually dividing it up into North and South Korea.

64.   **(B)**   The variation in behavior cross-culturally suggests that culture and patterns of behavior are not instinctual or transmitted genetically. Most researchers agree that humans have drives (sex, hunger), but no true instincts, making (A) incorrect. (C) Instincts have never been observed in either primitive societies or developed societies. (D) and (E) are incorrect. While drives do exist, how they are played out varies immensely cross-culturally.

65.   **(A)**   The dependent variable is the one we are trying to explain. In this question, we are trying to explain the level of prejudice; therefore, it is the dependent variable. (B) is incorrect because the independent variable is the variable doing the explaining (the cause). Since the film is seen as explaining the level of prejudice, it is the independent variable. (C) is incorrect. The control variable is the variable being held constant so that one can assess the relationship among the other variables. Since level of prejudice is not being held constant in this example, it is not a control variable. A spurious relationship is one where the variables appear to be related, but are actually related to a third variable which explains both of them. Nothing from this example would suggest that the relationship between prejudice and the film is being caused by a third variable. Therefore, (D) is incorrect. Because a correct choice is provided, (E) is incorrect.

Section 2

66.   **(D)**   *Verstehen* was the term Weber used to describe his method for analyzing a particular social phenomenon. (A) "Social view" is not a sociological term. (B) The looking-glass self is a concept made popular by Charles Horton Cooley, which refers to how the self is formed in response to others. (C) is correct. Symbolic interaction is the paradigm which views society as the product of individuals' interactions. (E) is correct. Social statics is a term made popular by Herbert Spencer.

67.   **(E)**   The symbolic interaction perspective looks to individual inter-action and interpretation to explain social behavior. In the example, indi-vidual lawyers for the prosecution and defense interpret each other's ac-tions and reactions. (A) is incorrect. The structural functionalist perspec-tive views society on a macro level, looking not to individual interaction, but how society's parts fit together to maintain stability. (B) is incorrect. Social conflict perspective looks to the friction and conflict underlying society's institutions and groups in explaining particular phenomenon. (C) is incorrect. Ethnocentrism refers to judging of another culture, seeing yours as superior. (D) is incorrect. Socialization refers to the process by which an individual becomes human and acquires a "self." It is a process studied in sociology and does not refer to any of the three major perspec-tives, or paradigms, covered in sociology (functionalism, social conflict, and symbolic interactionism).

68.   **(D)**   Institutional discrimination occurs when inequalities are built into institutions and disproportionately disadvantage an entire category of people based on nothing more than their group membership. Institutional discrimination is unintended and carried out by institutions, not individu-als. (B) and (C) are incorrect as they include the incorrect statement II. A landlord's distaste for Latino applicants is a form of individual discrimina-tion, where the intentional discriminatory behavior is carried out by an individual. (A) is incorrect because it only includes one of the three cor-rect responses. Because a correct answer is provided, (E) is incorrect.

69.   **(C)**   The majority of welfare dollars go to children, who are the biggest group falling below the poverty line. (A) is incorrect. Statistics show that women who receive welfare do not have more children on the average than those who do not collect welfare. (B) Males have more difficulty getting public assistance and are not the primary recipients of

aid. Less than five percent of those on welfare are males who are able to work. (D) is incorrect. Every year, about one-third of welfare recipients climb out of welfare, while that same number or more fall into welfare. (E) is incorrect, since a correct response has been provided.

70. **(A)** Prejudice is a product of social upbringing and draws on stereotypes (B) of the stigmatized groups. The familiarity effect (C) is also relevant; the less familiar another group is, the more we fear that group. The lack of familiarity across different racial groups also makes face recognition (D) more difficult between groups compared to within a single group. This, too, feeds prejudice. Cognitive dissonance, in contrast, has no clear connection.

71. **(D)** Whereas television and radio stations must be licensed to operate in the United States, newspapers and magazines need not be. Therefore, statement I is true. It is more difficult for a public figure or official to win a libel suit against the media in the United States than in any other country, so statement II is true. The Supreme Court has held that before the news media can be found guilty of libeling a public figure or official, the person must show not only that what was published was false and damaging to his/her reputation, but also that it was published with "actual malice," a rule not used in other countries. The legal definition of actual malice is reckless disregard for the truth or falsity of the story. Since reckless disregard is difficult to prove, winning libel suits is difficult for public officials and figures in the United States.

72. **(C)** The Campaign Finance Reform law of 1973 made it legal for corporations and labor unions to form PACs. PACs quadrupled in number between 1975 and 1982, and are still forming. (A) is incorrect because PACs were unimportant in American politics before the campaign reform law of 1973. Indeed, one well-known dictionary of American politics, copyrighted in 1972, does not even have an entry for political action committee. (B) is incorrect for two reasons. First, by law a PAC can contribute no more than $5,000 to a candidate for a primary campaign, and no more than $5,000 during a general election campaign. A total contribution of $10,000 is not likely to buy a PAC a great deal of influence these days, when campaigns for Congress cost in the hundreds of thousands of dollars. Secondly, there are literally thousands of PACs, so there is PAC money available on every side of every issue. Candidates can accept PAC money and still decide for themselves how to vote on the issues. (D) is incorrect because PACs may be formed by a variety of groups, or even by an individual. When Representative Charles Rangel was running for whip

of the Democratic party in the House, he set up a PAC that made campaign contributions to other representatives' campaigns, hoping they would then vote for him as whip. (E) is incorrect because the number of ideological PACs has increased at a faster rate than business or labor PACs in recent years. In the 1988 election there were nearly 600 ideological PACs. Ideological PACs now raise more money than business or labor PACs, although they contribute less to candidates. This is due to the fact that they spend more than other PACs on advertising per dollar raised.

73.   **(D)**   The question asks which statement is false. The correct answer is (D) since the purpose of the equal rights amendment was to protect and enlarge the rights of women, not of blacks and Hispanics. The operative clause read "Equality of rights under the law shall not be denied or disparaged by the United States or any State on account of sex." (A) is not a false statement because both houses of Congress passed the amendment in 1972 and sent it to the states for ratification. The necessary three-fourths of the state legislatures never ratified the amendment, so it died in 1982. (B) is not a false statement because Congress did extend the time limit for ratification. The original time limit expired in 1979, but before that date arrived Congress extended the time limit to 1982. (C) is not a false statement because Nebraska and Tennessee, which had ratified the amendment, tried to rescind their ratification. (E) is not a false statement because every president from Truman to Carter, and both political parties, did endorse the amendment.

74.   **(A)**   The real rate of interest is, by definition, the arithmetic difference between the nominal rate of interest and the rate of inflation. Notationally, if r represents the real rate of interest, i the nominal rate of interest, and π represents the rate of inflation, then

$$r = 1 - \pi$$

In a period of inflation, $\pi < 0$ so that r equals i plus some positive number; it must be, therefore, that $r > i$.

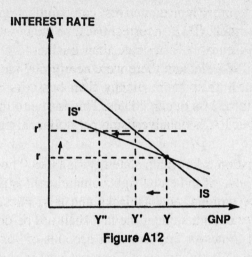

INTEREST RATE

Figure A12

75. **(E)** Net exports represent the difference between exports and imports. Imports climb with GNP, so net exports should be negatively correlated with income. An increase (a reduction) in the interest rate meanwhile causes capital to flow into (out of) the country and that puts downward (upward) pressure on net exports. For the United States, for example, higher interest rates make U.S. assets more attractive, increase the demand for the dollar, increase the value of the dollar, and thus make exports more expensive and imports less expensive. As a result, a negative correlation between the interest rate and net exports should also be expected.

76. **(C)** The average cost of this firm is $1.60 because the total cost of producing 10,000 units of output is $16,000. Since it is producing at the minimum of the average cost curve, marginal cost is also $1.60. Since price therefore exceeds marginal cost, the firm should expand its output and sales beyond 10,000 units until price equals marginal cost. It has no power over price, since it is in a competitive market; but the only direction price could go, with output climbing, is down.

77. **(A)** The Farm Security Administration was created to help restore faith in America by sending photojournalists around the country to photograph Americans and American life. The focus of the resulting publications was on how people had survived, rather than succumbed to, the Great Depression. This program was designed as a public relations program, not as a jobs creation program.

78.   **(B)** The Plains Indians depended upon buffalo for almost every aspect of their survival. When they killed a buffalo, they used virtually every part of it, from the hide to the bones. In 1850, over 13 million Buffalo meandered along their migration routes in the Great Plains. By 1890, fewer than 1,000 remained. Without the buffalo, the Plains Indians could not live according to their traditional ways. They were forced to either adapt to white rules (usually on reservations) or fight for their survival, as the Sioux and Cheyenne did in the 1870s. Fighting the whites was hopeless, but to many Indians, it was more honorable than dying in subjugation. While they managed a few victories such as at Little Big Horn, they were too badly outmanned and outgunned to have a long-term chance at victory. Without the buffalo, the entire Indian way of life was undermined and it led directly to the destruction of the Plains Indians' societies in a much broader way than any of the other choices listed in the question.

79.   **(A)** Intellectual historians study the role of ideas and intellectuals in history. Do not let the quotation intimidate you; read the quotation and note what kind of subject matter is involved. For a careful reader, the answer is not difficult.

80.   **(B)** Jeremy Bentham, who used this slogan to describe his philosophy of Utilitarianism, believed that one of the unsettled tasks remaining from the Enlightenment was the creation of a new, nonreligious system of morality that would be socially beneficial. His "moral calculus" sought to create a system of morality and laws that would reward the obedient with pleasure and criminals with painful emotions. Note that choice (A) is an attempt to mislead you; it seems a plausible answer, but is not the correct one. DeMaistre was an early nineteenth-century French conservative writer and a Romantic.

81.   **(C)** By 1951 tensions between the Kikuyu people and the occupying British, caused largely by increasing shortages of land due to British settler occupation, came to a head when the Kikuyu staged a violent insurrection, now known as Mau Mau. The government arrested Kenyatta and prominent Kikuyu leaders in an attempt to curb the uprisings, but the uprising developed into a civil war between insurgents and collaborators. When the crisis ended in 1955, several hundred British had been killed but the majority of casualties resulted from the civil war. At least 3,000 Kikuyu were killed, and some estimate that it was at least 10 times as many. The other choices are unrelated to Mau Mau. Nkrumah's United Gold Coast

Convention (A) took place in 1947 and the ANC (D) had been around since 1912. The other two choices (B) and (E) never occurred.

82. **(E)** The Qing Dynasty lasted from 1644 until the Republic of China in 1912. The dynasty was actually first proclaimed in Manchuria before the Conquest in 1636. The Shang Dynasty (A) has been estimated at about 1500 B.C. until 1027 B.C. The Qin Dynasty (B) has been estimated at 221 B.C. until 206 B.C. The Han Dynasty (C) lasted from 202 B.C. until 220 A.D., and the Sui Dynasty (D) from 589 A.D. until 618 A.D.

83. **(C)** Interviews with both blacks and whites suggest that blacks, more than whites, desire integrated neighborhoods. Blacks prefer to live in neighborhoods that are racially mixed, although most express a fear of being the first black family in a white neighborhood. (A) is incorrect, as blacks express the exact opposite preference. (B) and (D) are incorrect. Whites do not prefer to maintain a segregated system in terms of public accommodations and housing, although they did express a preference to live in all-white neighborhoods. In one survey, 25 percent of whites said they would move to a new neighborhood if more than one black family bought a house in the area. A correct answer is provided, so (E) is incorrect.

84. **(C)** Strain theory asserts that people commit crimes when their means for achievement are obstructed. According to this theory, all of us desire the "American Dream" but only some of us are put in positions to achieve that dream. The consequence is that those people blocked from achievement find illegitimate means to succeed. This theory, therefore, is best at explaining crime among the less advantaged. Committing robbery, according to this theory, suggests that a disadvantaged individual is stealing because he may acquire goods and possessions that we all desire. (A) is incorrect. Voyeurism is not a crime that reaps a material reward and is not necessarily committed by disadvantaged individuals. (B), (D), and (E) are incorrect for the same reasons. Smoking marijuana, jaywalking, and speeding are not usually done to reap a material reward, nor are they committed primarily by disadvantaged individuals.

85. **(C)** Studies suggest that police take race and class cues into account in the arrest process. (A) is incorrect. No evidence suggests that lower-class youth commit more dangerous crimes; rather they commit different crimes. While a dangerous crime like robbery is more often committed by lower-class individuals, other dangerous crimes, such as

arson, are more likely to be committed by middle-class youth. (B) is incorrect. There are not more police in lower-class neighborhoods. Often there are fewer. Areas with high poverty values (i.e., middle-class neighborhoods) usually have the tax base to support a large police force. (D) and (E) are incorrect. Youth of all social classes are equally likely to commit crimes; they simply commit different types of crimes. Lower-class youth are only more likely to be arrested for the crimes they commit.

86. **(D)** A role is a behavior expected of a certain status. The expected behaviors of a professor are to meet with her students and prepare lectures. (A) is incorrect. A master status is the central defining status. This example is not addressing the status of professors, but the roles associated with that status. (B) is incorrect. An ascribed status refers to a social position based on involuntary characteristics, such as age, sex, and race. (C) is incorrect. An achieved status is a social position based largely on one's own merit. This question asks for the obligations associated with a status, but doesn't ask which type of status. (B) and (C) refer to a type of status. (E) is incorrect. Impression management refers to the manipulation of one's role.

87. **(E)** The generalized other is Mead's term for the cultural norms and values we use as references when evaluating ourselves. That the children are able to internalize these norms and values suggests they are capable of understanding another's position. (A) and (B) are incorrect as no such sociological terms exist. (C) The looking-glass self concept comes from Cooley, Mead's predecessor, and refers to the process of forming our self on the basis of others' responses to us. (D) is incorrect. *Verstehen* means the developing of a subjective understanding of a particular social phenomenon. Mead did not popularize or expand on this term.

88. **(E)** Social research is more difficult to perform than other forms of research for a variety of reasons. Firstly, objectivity is impossible because social researchers are studying the same species as themselves. Secondly, humans, as opposed to other animals, are self-aware and are capable of manipulating their behavior under study conditions. For example, an individual may give a researcher the answer she thinks is desired. Finally, operations performed on animals or molecules cannot be performed on humans for ethical reasons. (A), (B), and (D) are incorrect as they contain only parts of the entire answer. (C) is incorrect. The methods of social research are no more advanced than other methods of research.

89.   **(B)**   Research in social psychology indicates that physical appearance is the most important determinant of first impressions. It is also relevant in social attraction and effectiveness in persuading others to change their beliefs.

90.   **(C)**   Only statement III is correct. James Madison has long been considered the Father of the Constitution, since he wrote the Virginia Plan, which was introduced at the Constitutional Convention, and which greatly influenced the content of the Constitution. His authorship of several of the *Federalist Papers*, which explain the Constitution in great detail, lends great weight to their analysis. Alexander Hamilton, author of several of the Federalist Papers, also attended the Constitutional Convention. Statement I is false since Washington and Adams were not contributors to the Federalist Papers. The three authors were Madison, Hamilton, and John Jay. Statement II is false since the Federalist Papers did not provide a theoretical justification for the Revolutionary War. That war ended in 1783, and the Federalist Papers were written in 1787-1788. The primary purpose of the Federalist Papers was to persuade the voters of the state of New York to elect delegates to their state ratifying convention who would vote to ratify the Constitution. They provided a detailed commentary on the Constitution to satisfy New Yorkers that it was a well-written document. Therefore (C), III only, is correct.

91.   **(E)**   Statements II and III are both accurate. Statement I is inaccurate because interest groups spend a lot of time and effort lobbying executive agencies and courts, as well as legislatures. Since Congress often merely sets general guidelines for the federal bureaucracy to follow, executive agencies must write specific regulations to guide the implementation of the laws. After a law is passed, then, lobbyists try to influence rule making by the bureaucrats who implement policy. Interest groups also spend a great deal of time trying to influence the courts. Some groups file civil suits on behalf of persons or causes they support. Others might write an amicus brief (a statement of how the case should be decided, offered by someone not a party to the suit) to influence the decision of a court case. Statement II is accurate because union membership in the United States peaked in 1945, when nearly 36 percent of all workers were unionized. Since then, union membership has fallen steadily. By 1984, only about 19 percent of workers were unionized. Declining membership in unions reflects changes in the economy, with fewer jobs being created in the manufacturing sector and more in the service sector. Also contributing to loss of union clout was President Reagan's unfriendliness to union demands, as evidenced by the wholesale firing of the striking airline traffic controllers

during his first term. Statement III is accurate because of the nearly 7,000 groups represented in Washington over half are corporations. Among the largest business organizations are the Chamber of Commerce, the National Association of Manufacturers, and the National Federation of Independent Businesses.

92.   **(A)** Presidents Reagan and Bush have emphasized political ideology as a factor in choosing their nominees to the Supreme Court. The single most important issue has been a potential candidate's stand on *Roe v. Wade,* 1973. In that case, the Supreme Court held that the right to privacy included a woman's right to choose an abortion, at least in the first trimester of pregnancy. Roe is perhaps the most controversial decision of the Court in the last 30 years. Republican presidents have tried to nominate justices who would vote to overturn Roe, while Democratic senators have done their best to thwart those nominations. (B) is incorrect because there has, in fact, been an increase in support for Republican presidential candidates in the South in the last 30 years. From the end of Reconstruction until the 1950s, the Democratic candidate for president could count on solid support from the states of the old Confederacy. However, that began to change in the 1960s. In the six elections since 1964, the Democratic candidate for president has won a majority of the southern states only once, in 1976. The Democratic candidate has not won Virginia and has won Mississippi, Alabama, Florida, South Carolina, and North Carolina only once each, since 1964. (C) is incorrect because the conservative wing of the Republican party has increased in influence in the past 30 years. After a bitter battle at the 1964 Republican National Convention, conservative Republicans managed to nominate Barry Goldwater as the party's candidate for president. This was the beginning of the takeover of the party by its conservative wing. In 1968, the party nominated Richard Nixon, a strongly anti-Communist conservative. In 1980 and 1984, the party nominated Ronald Reagan, long a conservative influence within the party. The conservative wing of the party has also managed to dominate the party's platform at most of the last seven party conventions. (D) is incorrect because voter turnout has decreased in the last 30 years. In 1960, about 62 percent of the voting age population voted in the presidential election. In 1988, less than 50 percent did. (E) is incorrect because the number of people declaring themselves to be independents has increased from about 21 percent in 1962 to 33 percent in 1986.

93.   **(C)** The first political parties to compete for public office in the United States were the Federalists and Jeffersonian Republicans, some-

times called the Democratic Republicans. An earlier alignment of political sentiment took place between the Federalists and Antifederalists. Of these two groups, the former supported ratification of the Constitution, while the latter opposed ratification. These two groups did not compete against each other for public office, because the Antifederalist organization ceased to exist after the Constitution was ratified. After the Constitution was ratified, the Federalists won most of the offices in the new government. Many former Antifederalists joined the Jeffersonian Republicans, who began to organize in the early 1790s in opposition to Federalist policies. The Jeffersonian Republicans won control of Congress and the presidency in the election of 1800. The Federalists soon faded from the scene and were almost nonexistent by 1820. (A) is incorrect because the Whigs organized in the 1830s, after the Federalists had passed from the political scene. (B) is incorrect because the Whigs appeared after the Jeffersonian Republicans had lost power. (D) is incorrect because the Whigs and Democrats competed in the 1830s, after the initial competition between the Federalists and Jeffersonian Republicans had occurred. (E) is incorrect because the Democrats and Republicans began to compete in the 1850s, long after the initial competition between the Federalists and Jeffersonian Republicans had occurred.

94.   **(B)** The term gender gap refers to the fact that women and men have noticeably different views on a variety of political questions. According to a poll taken in 1990, women support gun control by 85 percent, compared to men's 72 percent; they support more spending for Social Security by 60 percent to men's 50 percent; they support less military spending by 40 percent to men's 49 percent; and they support more spending for the homeless by 80 percent to men's 68 percent. In addition, women tend to vote Democrat in larger numbers than men do. In the 1984 presidential election, 57 percent of women voted for Reagan, compared to 61 percent of men. (A) is incorrect because although women do turn out to vote in larger numbers than men, the term gender gap does not describe this fact. (C) is incorrect because although women do have a longer life expectancy than men, the term gender gap designates measurable differences in political views between men and women. (D) is incorrect because although men do hold a higher percentage of elective offices than women, the term gender gap refers to measurable differences in political views between men and women. (E) is incorrect because women are not more apathetic than men regarding electoral politics. They turn out to vote in higher numbers than men.

95. **(D)** Average costs are U-shaped, so choice (E) is clearly incorrect. The question is whether or not rising marginal costs guarantee that average costs are moving in only one direction. Since marginal cost is rising when it intersects average cost at its minimum, the answer is no. Slightly to the left of the minimum, marginal costs are rising and average costs are falling. Slightly to the right, marginal costs are still rising and average costs are rising. At the minimum, average costs are constant even as marginal costs climb. Furthermore, average cost cannot remain constant because marginal costs would also have to be constant, and that condition is violated by the information given in the question.

96. **(B)** In the past, dramatic increases in the international price of crude oil have resulted in large increases in the rate of inflation. In the short run, this happens because energy consumption is a primary component of all price indices. Over the long run, higher energy costs translate into higher prices for almost every good whose manufacture and/or delivery involves energy. Since wages do not usually keep up with prices in periods of high inflation, the real wage should be expected to fall in these circumstances. A negative correlation between changes in the international price of crude oil and real wages should therefore be expected, and that expectation has been satisfied by experience over the past several decades of energy price volatility.

97. **(C)** Equilibrium requires that investment equal savings – the sum of private saving (disposable income minus consumption), public saving (total government revenues minus expenditures), and foreign saving (imports minus exports). In this question, foreign saving increases by $1 billion and private saving is fixed. To maintain equilibrium, therefore, government saving must fall by $1 billion. Since a change in government saving can be accomplished only by changes in either government debt or the total money supply, this reduction in saving must be associated with an increase in bond holdings or money supply equal to $1 billion. Choice (A) shows a $2 billion increase in bonds and money; choice (E) a $2 billion reduction. Choice (B) shows no change in bonds plus money. Choice (D) shows a $1 billion reduction. Only (C) combines to yield the requisite $1 billion increase in bonds and money.

98. **(E)** This is a question of definition. When economists speak of investment, they are talking about activity that adds the capital stock of an economy – additions to the economy's stock of (new) housing, factories, equipment, and inventories. It is generally not for current use, but it is a current flow of new assets that add to productive capacity.

99. **(E)** Of the cases indicated, only the last will have the entire tax borne by consumers; shift a supply curve against a vertical demand curve and the price changes by the full amount of the shift while the quantity demanded is fixed. In all of the other cases, quantity adjusts and moves the after-tax price received by suppliers down the supply curve; i.e., they pay at least part of the tax.

100. **(C)** While the Roanoke colony (1587) actually preceded the Jamestown colony (1607), the Roanoke colony was not successful. A supply ship sent to Roanoke in 1590 could find no survivors at the colony. The word "Croatoan," which referred to a nearby island, carved into a tree was the only clue left behind. No other sign of the colonists was ever found.

101. **(C)** The sharecropping system allowed poor tenant farmers and poor independent farmers to borrow seed, equipment, and supplies for planting and harvesting a crop. In return, sharecroppers had to pledge their crop, or a portion of their crop, as collateral. While this arrangement allowed sharecroppers to continue to farm the land and squeeze out a minimal survival, the costs charged to farmers for supplies and equipment as well as the exorbitant interest rates charged for loaning those supplies effectively kept sharecroppers in permanent debt. Interest rates ranged as high as 200 percent. Most sharecroppers never accumulated enough cash to work their way out from under the tremendous debt load they incurred trying to work their small plots of lands. The only ones who got wealthy from this system were the landowners and the merchants who controlled the sharecroppers. This system did nothing to bring poor farmers into the middle class. Neither did it expand the number of independently owned farms in the South. It had no restrictive effect on the power of former plantation owners or Northern business interests. Finally, it did nothing to enhance the relationship between blacks and whites as it did not force them to work side by side. In fact, in many ways it was used by Southern ruling elites to maintain the old social and racial order.

102. **(B)** Successful in his plans to unite Germany by 1870, Bismarck, who served as chancellor of the new German Empire until 1890, was obsessed with perceived threats to the unity of the new nation. During the 1870s, he believed the greatest threat to be the Catholic church in Germany. He persuaded the German Reichstag to pass legislation restricting and regulating Catholic publications, education, and orders. This *Kulturkampf* was replaced in the late 1870s when Bismarck decided that the Marxist Social Democratic party was a greater threat to his political

creation. Ironically, the title of the *Kulturkampf* ("struggle for civilization") was coined by the anti-Bismarckian German liberal Rudolf Virchow.

103. **(D)** When the Soviet dictator Joseph Stalin changed policies and decided to seek accommodation with Hitler's Germany in 1939, a Nazi-Soviet nonaggression pact was negotiated by foreign ministers Ribbentrop and Molotov. It contained a secret provision providing for invasion of Poland by both countries and partition of Poland between them. This question demands a detailed knowledge of the pact, even if the answer is to be arrived at by elimination. If you are able to eliminate two or three of the answers, guessing is indicated.

104. **(B)** Namibia, on the west coast of Africa, borders on the South Atlantic Ocean. Madagascar (A) is an island off the southeast coast of the African continent with the Mozambique Channel running along its west coast and the Indian Ocean on its east coast. South Africa (C) is the southernmost country on the continent with the Indian Ocean on its eastern shore and the Atlantic to the west. Both Somalia (D) and Tanzania (E) are on Africa's east coast, bordering the Indian Ocean.

105. **(B)** Of all of India's population, approximately 83 percent are Hindu. The next largest religion in India is Islam (A) with Muslims comprising about 11 percent of population. All of the other choices, Christianity (C), Buddhism (D), and Sikhism (E) are represented in India in smaller numbers.

106. **(B)** A systematic sample is when the researcher selects every element for the sample. (A) is incorrect. A random sample simply means that every observation has an equal chance of being selected for the sample. Although this example is an illustration of a random sample, a systematic sample is the specific type of random sample. (C) is incorrect. A cluster sample is a sampling method used where the units are clustered together and selected in stages. (D) A stratified sample is one that is first divided into strata before the researcher randomly selects her cases. (E) is incorrect. All of the previous sampling methods are representative, meaning that the results can be generalized to a larger population. Nonrepresentative implies that the sampling is not random.

107. **(D)** That education level has no bearing on whether or not someone uses condoms suggests that no relationship exists between these two variables. (A) and (B) are incorrect since they suggest education level influences condom use. If a correlation did exist between the two vari-

ables, we would see one increasing as the other decreases, or we would see them both increasing/decreasing together. Nothing in this example implies that a causal relationship exists between these two variables. (E) is incorrect. A spurious relationship is when a third variable is able to explain the movement of the other two. No third variable is brought into this example.

108. **(B)** Race is not a biological fact, but social construction. The sociologist's interest in race, then, is how meaning and value are attached to differences, both real and perceived, between groups. (A) is incorrect because race is a social fact, not a biological fact. Biologically, there is no basis for a relationship between race and behavior. Stratification on the basis of race is actually one of the most recent forms of stratification; sex and age are the oldest. (C) and (D) are therefore incorrect. Because a correct answer is provided, (E) is incorrect.

109. **(D)** Cultural assimilation refers to how well a group has adopted the norms, values, customs, and language of the dominant group. Because the "Zorn" have completely done so, their cultural assimilation has been high. Secondary assimilation refers to how well integrated the group is on a macro institutional level; that is, how equal they are in terms of money and political representation. The "Zorn" have some political representation, but because inequality still exists, they are only moderately assimilated. Primary structural assimilation refers to integration on a micro institutional level such as the family. In this example, neighborhoods are not well integrated and intermarriage is remarkably low, so primary structural assimilation is low. Only (D) answers in the correct order. (A), (B), and (C) place the cultural assimilation as low, or only moderate, making these incorrect choices. (E) is incorrect because it characterizes primary structural assimilation as moderate, when it is actually very low.

110. **(E)** Women earn 60 percent of what men do for a variety of reasons. Firstly, bosses continue to see women as less capable than male workers and promote them less frequently. Secondly, jobs are titled differently depending on who fills it. The Equal Pay Act states that men and women filling the same position must be paid the same. Employers are getting around this by hiring a male as an "administrative assistant" and a woman as a "secretary." They are entitled to pay the "administrative assistant" more than the "secretary," in spite of the fact their job roles and tasks are the same. Finally, women are paid less because they often have less labor market experience. In the process of child-bearing and rearing, many

women do not have continuous labor market experience, which enables employers to pay them less. Only choice (E) includes all of these reasons.

111. **(A)** An informal sanction is direct social pressure from those around us to conform. By scorning him, Tom's classmates are putting social pressure on him to come to class on time. (B) is incorrect. A formal sanction is pressure to conform that is enforced by a formal institution, such as the criminal justice system. (C) and (D) are incorrect. Norms are rules of behavior and values are ideals and goals. The other students scorning Tom is not an example of either of these concepts. (E) is incorrect since a correct response has been provided.

112. **(C)** Density refers to the number of people occupying a certain size of space, such as a square mile. In contrast to this physical concept, crowding (A) is a psychological concept referring to subjective reactions to high density. Personal space (E), loudness (D), and noisiness (B) are also psychological concepts.

113. **(C)** The Republican national platform for all three presidential election years in the 1980s contained clauses supporting the anti-abortion position. President Bush took a strong right to life position, and the Republican position in general was expressed in the Hyde Amendment, which forbids the use of federal funds to pay for abortions. It was highly unlikely that the 1992 Republican platform would contain a clause supporting a woman's right to choice. (A) is incorrect because both the 1984 and 1988 Republican platforms contained clauses opposing quotas to remedy past discrimination. (B) is incorrect because the 1988 Republican platform contained a clause calling for a reduction of the capital gains tax to 15 percent. President Bush long favored a reduction of the tax. (D) is incorrect because the 1988 Republican platform called for a balanced budget amendment. It was quite likely that this support for a balanced budget amendment would be repeated in the 1992 platform. (E) is incorrect because the 1988 Republican platform opposed increasing the minimum wage. It was likely that this position would also be taken in the 1992 platform.

114. **(D)** The correct answer is (D), I and II. Statement I is true because each of the major parties allows great discretion to its nominee for president in choosing his or her running mate. Statement II is correct because balancing the ticket is a major consideration for a presidential candidate in selecting a running mate. Geographical balance is very important. In 1988, George Bush, from Texas, chose Dan Quayle from Indiana. Michael

Dukakis, from Massachusetts, chose Lloyd Bentsen from Texas. In 1980 and 1984, Ronald Reagan, from California, chose George Bush from Texas. In 1984, Walter Mondale, from Minnesota, chose Geraldine Ferraro from New York. Statement III is not necessarily true. Many presidential candidates apparently do not take the qualifications of their running mates into consideration. Many people thought that Dan Quayle was not well-qualified to be president. Franklin Roosevelt thought so little of his vice president, Harry Truman, that he did not even bother to inform him that the United States was building an atomic bomb near the end of World War II.

115. **(B)** Keynesian economics was based on the idea that an unregulated capitalist economy will inevitably go through a boom and bust cycle (A). As employment increases, more money will be available to consumers, and spending for consumer goods will then increase. This stimulates inflation, as more money purchases available goods. Producers will produce more and more goods, until overproduction occurs. This is the boom part of the cycle. As overproduction occurs, producers will cut back on production, laying off workers. As workers are laid off, less money will be available for consumers to spend on goods. Demand for consumer goods will decline. As demand declines, producers cut back on production even more. This is the bust side of the cycle. Keynes taught that government should step in to regulate the boom and bust cycle. During times of high unemployment, government should engage in deficit spending to create jobs, (C). This will put money in consumers' pockets, which will stimulate demand. Increased demand will cause producers to hire more workers in order to increase output to meet the increased demand. During times of high inflation, government should raise taxes, (D). It should also increase taxes, (E). These policies will take money out of circulation and prevent the economy from heating up too much and going into a boom period. Keynesian economic theory stresses the demand side, as opposed to the supply side of the economy. Keynesian policies attempt to either stimulate or reduce demand in order to regulate the business cycle. Supply-side economics, on the other hand, stresses the supply side of the economy. Supply-siders rejected much of the Keynesian analysis in the late 1970s, when the economy went into a period of so-called stagflation. The economy was experiencing inflation and stagnation – two conditions which Keynesian economics said could not happen at the same time. Supply-siders said that the stagflation could be explained by the fact that government had placed too many disincentives on producers in the form of high taxes. The way to get the economy going was to focus on the supply side instead of the demand side. By cutting tax rates (B), the government would remove disincentives from producers, who were currently disinclined to produce

because government was taking too much of the profit in the form of taxes. If producers were allowed to keep more profit, they would increase production, pulling the economy out of recession. Since cutting tax rates was a feature of supply side economics, but not of Keynesian economics, the correct answer is (B).

116. **(D)** Overly technical questions ask about subjects that the general public has little or no knowledge of. This can cause sampling error, because when people answer questions they do not understand, their answers are unreliable. (A) is incorrect because straw polls are unscientific. They are usually conducted by newspapers and magazines. In the typical straw poll, reporters ask questions at shopping malls and other locations, and report the results back to the newspaper or magazine. The problem with straw polls is that there is no way to ensure that the sample of individuals giving answers is representative of the larger population. (B) is incorrect because one surprising feature of sampling error is that its magnitude depends on sample size and not on population size. Population size refers to the total number of people in the group in question. Sample size refers to the total number of people in the population who are sampled. A random sample of 1,500 residents of New York City will be as reliable an indicator of what New York City residents think on an issue as a random sample of 1,500 residents of the State of New York will be of what residents of the State of New York think on an issue. (C) is incorrect because having people phone in answers to a poll does not satisfy the requirements for randomness. The sample would be biased since only those who felt strongly about the issue in question would bother to phone in their response. This group would not be representative of the overall population. (E) is incorrect because almost everybody can afford a telephone. Since this is the case, a random telephone survey produces a representative sample group.

117. **(E)** The substitution effect caused by the lapse of the provisions must cause substitution from risky assets to more certain assets. This would cause the risky assets certainty equivalent price to increase, and this substitution effect is perfectly clear (people substitute out of the more expensive goods, keeping everything else, including utility, held constant). Meanwhile, relative risk-aversion can also be defined in terms of the income effect. As real income falls (as would be the case if the loss-offset provisions were removed from the tax codes), individuals displaying increasing, constant, or decreasing relative risk-aversion will increase, stay the same, or decrease their risk-taking, respectively. In the last case, the income effect would amplify the substitution effect, and there would be an

unambiguous reduction in risk taking. In the second case, the income effect would be neutral, and the substitution effect would still dominate, thus risk-taking behavior will also be reduced in the case. However, in the first case, increasing relative risk-aversion would work to increase risk-taking while the substitution will work to reduce it. Since there is no way of telling which effect dominates, the effect is ambiguous. Thus, only (E) reflects each possibility.

118. **(B)** Increases in real interest rates are, as a matter of record, closely associated with downward turns in economic activity. Major components of aggregate demand, mostly captured within investment through inventories and housing, are strongly and negatively correlated with changes in the real interest rate. Higher real rates, therefore, work to reduce aggregate demand (shift the IS curve in) and slow the growth of real GNP. The workings of interest rates in housing demand are not mysterious. Most people borrow to purchase housing. When interest rates climb, the monthly cost of carrying a mortgage climbs, and the amount of money that people can comfortably borrow falls. They buy cheaper houses or no houses at all.

119. **(D)** Only the subtraction of income taxes is listed among the alternatives with the correct sign; they are subtracted in the calculation that produces DI from NI. Excise and sales taxes, nonbusiness interest, and transfer payments from government are added to NI in the process; contributions for social insurance are subtracted.

120. **(D)** A current account deficit indicates a domestic economy's need for borrowing from abroad to finance excessive consumption (imports in excess of exports). Part of domestic consumption is a government component that may or may not indicate a government spending greater than the tax receipts. If a government is spending more than its receipts, then the government must borrow from someone by issuing bonds. If those bonds are purchased by foreigners as part of the balancing of a current account deficit, then foreign lenders are, in fact, helping to finance a domestic government deficit. This is what happened in the United States in the first half of the 1980s.

121. **(B)** An increase in exports of $5 billion reduces capital account borrowing from abroad by the same $5 billion. Since that works just like an increase in the money supply (because it represents dollars that do not

leave the country), it can be balanced, *ceteris paribus,* by any reduction in domestic bond issues and/or money supply equaling to $5 billion.

122. **(A)** A constant share of GNP paid to labor implies that the real wage paid to labor has been maintained, even though the size of the labor force has been increasing. Since an increase in the labor force should have resulted in a reduction in the marginal product of labor, a general increase in labor productivity caused by technological innovation and capital deepening must have occurred simultaneously. Since labor's share has been stable, its contributions to inflation and international trade instability must have been nil. Finally, real wages did not soar in the 1970s.

123. **(B)** Studies interviewing rapists suggest that the motive for rape is not the desire for sex, as one might think, but rather power and domination. Rapists are looking not for sex, but for control, which is evidenced by the fact that most are married or have sexual partners. The crimes of embezzlement, car theft, and jaywalking show motives other than power, such as financial reward and material gain.

124. **(B)** Mechanical solidarity is Durkheim's term for social bonds that are based on shared moral sentiments. Usually these types of bonds were found among people living in pre-industrial societies. (A) is incorrect. Organic solidarity is the term Durkheim used to describe the bonds that unite members of industrialized nations. (C) and (D) are incorrect, as no such sociological terms exist. Because a correct answer is provided, (E) is incorrect.

125. **(C)** The population of the study is the people who are the focus of the research; the group to whom you are trying to generalize. In this case, the researcher is trying to find out something about all college students. (A) is incorrect. The students only on her campus are not representative of all American students. (B) The students randomly chosen for a response are the actual study sample. (D) An individual student who was surveyed would be the unit of analysis, not the population. (E) All people between the ages of 18-21 are not necessarily the population because many people within this age range are not college students.

126. **(E)** Two opposing views have dominated discussion concerning the inverse relationship between level of education and prejudice. It has long been noted that as the level of education increases, the level of prejudice decreases. One view suggests that as the level of education

increases, individuals become more critical thinkers and no longer accept things at face value. The result is that they are less likely to endorse stereotypes because they become more tolerant. Another view, however, suggests that educated people are no less prejudiced, but are only more careful about revealing it. (B) includes only one of the correct responses, as does (C), therefore, they are both incorrect. (A) is incorrect. Evidence suggests that less educated people are more likely to be prejudiced regardless of their level of contact with various racial/ethnic groups, thus, (D) is incorrect.

127. **(A)** The standard error of the mean is calculated by dividing the standard deviation by the square root of the sample size. Thus, it is closely related to standard deviation and variance, both measures of variability.

128. **(C)** The electoral college system does not directly favor the Republican party (A), states dominated by one political party (B), or northeast as a region (E), but instead favors states with small populations (C) because each state is given electoral college votes equal to the number of representatives and senators from that state. Small states are overrepresented by this formula since all states, regardless of population, have two senators. The electoral college selection process has nothing directly to do with the education of candidates (D).

129. **(B)** To be elected president, a person must receive a majority of electoral college votes. To win the presidency a candidate need have neither a majority (A) nor a plurality (C) of the popular vote. Since that is so, (E) is also incorrect. Although unlikely, it is possible to obtain a majority of the electoral votes without winning the popular vote. In the absence of an absolute majority of the electoral college vote (D), the election is thrown into the House of Representatives, where the plurality winner in the electoral college could lose.

130. **(B)** Any selection of "the most important" reason is open to challenge, but (B) is clearly the best choice. Traditionally, it is difficult to defeat the party in office when economic conditions are regarded as favorable, as they were during most of 1988. Bush is not known for having either a forceful personality or strong public speaking skills (A). His running mate (C) was widely regarded as a liability, and education (D) was only a peripheral issue in the campaign. Although he had served as vice president, Bush was not the incumbent (E) president when he ran for office.

ANSWER
SHEETS

CLEP ENGLISH COMPOSITION

Section 1

1. Ⓐ Ⓑ Ⓒ Ⓓ Ⓔ
2. Ⓐ Ⓑ Ⓒ Ⓓ Ⓔ
3. Ⓐ Ⓑ Ⓒ Ⓓ Ⓔ
4. Ⓐ Ⓑ Ⓒ Ⓓ Ⓔ
5. Ⓐ Ⓑ Ⓒ Ⓓ Ⓔ
6. Ⓐ Ⓑ Ⓒ Ⓓ Ⓔ
7. Ⓐ Ⓑ Ⓒ Ⓓ Ⓔ
8. Ⓐ Ⓑ Ⓒ Ⓓ Ⓔ
9. Ⓐ Ⓑ Ⓒ Ⓓ Ⓔ
10. Ⓐ Ⓑ Ⓒ Ⓓ Ⓔ
11. Ⓐ Ⓑ Ⓒ Ⓓ Ⓔ
12. Ⓐ Ⓑ Ⓒ Ⓓ Ⓔ
13. Ⓐ Ⓑ Ⓒ Ⓓ Ⓔ
14. Ⓐ Ⓑ Ⓒ Ⓓ Ⓔ
15. Ⓐ Ⓑ Ⓒ Ⓓ Ⓔ
16. Ⓐ Ⓑ Ⓒ Ⓓ Ⓔ
17. Ⓐ Ⓑ Ⓒ Ⓓ Ⓔ
18. Ⓐ Ⓑ Ⓒ Ⓓ Ⓔ
19. Ⓐ Ⓑ Ⓒ Ⓓ Ⓔ
20. Ⓐ Ⓑ Ⓒ Ⓓ Ⓔ
21. Ⓐ Ⓑ Ⓒ Ⓓ Ⓔ
22. Ⓐ Ⓑ Ⓒ Ⓓ Ⓔ
23. Ⓐ Ⓑ Ⓒ Ⓓ Ⓔ
24. Ⓐ Ⓑ Ⓒ Ⓓ Ⓔ
25. Ⓐ Ⓑ Ⓒ Ⓓ Ⓔ
26. Ⓐ Ⓑ Ⓒ Ⓓ Ⓔ
27. Ⓐ Ⓑ Ⓒ Ⓓ Ⓔ
28. Ⓐ Ⓑ Ⓒ Ⓓ Ⓔ
29. Ⓐ Ⓑ Ⓒ Ⓓ Ⓔ
30. Ⓐ Ⓑ Ⓒ Ⓓ Ⓔ
31. Ⓐ Ⓑ Ⓒ Ⓓ Ⓔ
32. Ⓐ Ⓑ Ⓒ Ⓓ Ⓔ
33. Ⓐ Ⓑ Ⓒ Ⓓ Ⓔ
34. Ⓐ Ⓑ Ⓒ Ⓓ Ⓔ
35. Ⓐ Ⓑ Ⓒ Ⓓ Ⓔ
36. Ⓐ Ⓑ Ⓒ Ⓓ Ⓔ
37. Ⓐ Ⓑ Ⓒ Ⓓ Ⓔ
38. Ⓐ Ⓑ Ⓒ Ⓓ Ⓔ
39. Ⓐ Ⓑ Ⓒ Ⓓ Ⓔ
40. Ⓐ Ⓑ Ⓒ Ⓓ Ⓔ
41. Ⓐ Ⓑ Ⓒ Ⓓ Ⓔ
42. Ⓐ Ⓑ Ⓒ Ⓓ Ⓔ
43. Ⓐ Ⓑ Ⓒ Ⓓ Ⓔ
44. Ⓐ Ⓑ Ⓒ Ⓓ Ⓔ
45. Ⓐ Ⓑ Ⓒ Ⓓ Ⓔ
46. Ⓐ Ⓑ Ⓒ Ⓓ Ⓔ
47. Ⓐ Ⓑ Ⓒ Ⓓ Ⓔ
48. Ⓐ Ⓑ Ⓒ Ⓓ Ⓔ
49. Ⓐ Ⓑ Ⓒ Ⓓ Ⓔ
50. Ⓐ Ⓑ Ⓒ Ⓓ Ⓔ

Section 2

51. Ⓐ Ⓑ Ⓒ Ⓓ Ⓔ
52. Ⓐ Ⓑ Ⓒ Ⓓ Ⓔ
53. Ⓐ Ⓑ Ⓒ Ⓓ Ⓔ
54. Ⓐ Ⓑ Ⓒ Ⓓ Ⓔ
55. Ⓐ Ⓑ Ⓒ Ⓓ Ⓔ
56. Ⓐ Ⓑ Ⓒ Ⓓ Ⓔ
57. Ⓐ Ⓑ Ⓒ Ⓓ Ⓔ
58. Ⓐ Ⓑ Ⓒ Ⓓ Ⓔ
59. Ⓐ Ⓑ Ⓒ Ⓓ Ⓔ
60. Ⓐ Ⓑ Ⓒ Ⓓ Ⓔ
61. Ⓐ Ⓑ Ⓒ Ⓓ Ⓔ
62. Ⓐ Ⓑ Ⓒ Ⓓ Ⓔ
63. Ⓐ Ⓑ Ⓒ Ⓓ Ⓔ
64. Ⓐ Ⓑ Ⓒ Ⓓ Ⓔ
65. Ⓐ Ⓑ Ⓒ Ⓓ Ⓔ
66. Ⓐ Ⓑ Ⓒ Ⓓ Ⓔ
67. Ⓐ Ⓑ Ⓒ Ⓓ Ⓔ
68. Ⓐ Ⓑ Ⓒ Ⓓ Ⓔ
69. Ⓐ Ⓑ Ⓒ Ⓓ Ⓔ
70. Ⓐ Ⓑ Ⓒ Ⓓ Ⓔ
71. Ⓐ Ⓑ Ⓒ Ⓓ Ⓔ
72. Ⓐ Ⓑ Ⓒ Ⓓ Ⓔ
73. Ⓐ Ⓑ Ⓒ Ⓓ Ⓔ
74. Ⓐ Ⓑ Ⓒ Ⓓ Ⓔ
75. Ⓐ Ⓑ Ⓒ Ⓓ Ⓔ
76. Ⓐ Ⓑ Ⓒ Ⓓ Ⓔ
77. Ⓐ Ⓑ Ⓒ Ⓓ Ⓔ
78. Ⓐ Ⓑ Ⓒ Ⓓ Ⓔ
79. Ⓐ Ⓑ Ⓒ Ⓓ Ⓔ
80. Ⓐ Ⓑ Ⓒ Ⓓ Ⓔ
81. Ⓐ Ⓑ Ⓒ Ⓓ Ⓔ
82. Ⓐ Ⓑ Ⓒ Ⓓ Ⓔ
83. Ⓐ Ⓑ Ⓒ Ⓓ Ⓔ
84. Ⓐ Ⓑ Ⓒ Ⓓ Ⓔ
85. Ⓐ Ⓑ Ⓒ Ⓓ Ⓔ
86. Ⓐ Ⓑ Ⓒ Ⓓ Ⓔ
87. Ⓐ Ⓑ Ⓒ Ⓓ Ⓔ
88. Ⓐ Ⓑ Ⓒ Ⓓ Ⓔ
89. Ⓐ Ⓑ Ⓒ Ⓓ Ⓔ
90. Ⓐ Ⓑ Ⓒ Ⓓ Ⓔ
91. Ⓐ Ⓑ Ⓒ Ⓓ Ⓔ
92. Ⓐ Ⓑ Ⓒ Ⓓ Ⓔ
93. Ⓐ Ⓑ Ⓒ Ⓓ Ⓔ
94. Ⓐ Ⓑ Ⓒ Ⓓ Ⓔ
95. Ⓐ Ⓑ Ⓒ Ⓓ Ⓔ
96. Ⓐ Ⓑ Ⓒ Ⓓ Ⓔ
97. Ⓐ Ⓑ Ⓒ Ⓓ Ⓔ
98. Ⓐ Ⓑ Ⓒ Ⓓ Ⓔ
99. Ⓐ Ⓑ Ⓒ Ⓓ Ⓔ
100. Ⓐ Ⓑ Ⓒ Ⓓ Ⓔ

NOTE: Please make a photocopy of this answer sheet to use for English Composition Practice Test 2.

CLEP ENGLISH COMPOSITION
With Essay Question

Section 1

1. Ⓐ Ⓑ Ⓒ Ⓓ Ⓔ	19. Ⓐ Ⓑ Ⓒ Ⓓ Ⓔ	38. Ⓐ Ⓑ Ⓒ Ⓓ Ⓔ
2. Ⓐ Ⓑ Ⓒ Ⓓ Ⓔ	20. Ⓐ Ⓑ Ⓒ Ⓓ Ⓔ	39. Ⓐ Ⓑ Ⓒ Ⓓ Ⓔ
3. Ⓐ Ⓑ Ⓒ Ⓓ Ⓔ	21. Ⓐ Ⓑ Ⓒ Ⓓ Ⓔ	40. Ⓐ Ⓑ Ⓒ Ⓓ Ⓔ
4. Ⓐ Ⓑ Ⓒ Ⓓ Ⓔ	22. Ⓐ Ⓑ Ⓒ Ⓓ Ⓔ	41. Ⓐ Ⓑ Ⓒ Ⓓ Ⓔ
5. Ⓐ Ⓑ Ⓒ Ⓓ Ⓔ	23. Ⓐ Ⓑ Ⓒ Ⓓ Ⓔ	42. Ⓐ Ⓑ Ⓒ Ⓓ Ⓔ
6. Ⓐ Ⓑ Ⓒ Ⓓ Ⓔ	24. Ⓐ Ⓑ Ⓒ Ⓓ Ⓔ	43. Ⓐ Ⓑ Ⓒ Ⓓ Ⓔ
7. Ⓐ Ⓑ Ⓒ Ⓓ Ⓔ	25. Ⓐ Ⓑ Ⓒ Ⓓ Ⓔ	44. Ⓐ Ⓑ Ⓒ Ⓓ Ⓔ
8. Ⓐ Ⓑ Ⓒ Ⓓ Ⓔ	26. Ⓐ Ⓑ Ⓒ Ⓓ Ⓔ	45. Ⓐ Ⓑ Ⓒ Ⓓ Ⓔ
9. Ⓐ Ⓑ Ⓒ Ⓓ Ⓔ	27. Ⓐ Ⓑ Ⓒ Ⓓ Ⓔ	46. Ⓐ Ⓑ Ⓒ Ⓓ Ⓔ
10. Ⓐ Ⓑ Ⓒ Ⓓ Ⓔ	28. Ⓐ Ⓑ Ⓒ Ⓓ Ⓔ	47. Ⓐ Ⓑ Ⓒ Ⓓ Ⓔ
11. Ⓐ Ⓑ Ⓒ Ⓓ Ⓔ	29. Ⓐ Ⓑ Ⓒ Ⓓ Ⓔ	48. Ⓐ Ⓑ Ⓒ Ⓓ Ⓔ
12. Ⓐ Ⓑ Ⓒ Ⓓ Ⓔ	30. Ⓐ Ⓑ Ⓒ Ⓓ Ⓔ	49. Ⓐ Ⓑ Ⓒ Ⓓ Ⓔ
13. Ⓐ Ⓑ Ⓒ Ⓓ Ⓔ	31. Ⓐ Ⓑ Ⓒ Ⓓ Ⓔ	50. Ⓐ Ⓑ Ⓒ Ⓓ Ⓔ
14. Ⓐ Ⓑ Ⓒ Ⓓ Ⓔ	32. Ⓐ Ⓑ Ⓒ Ⓓ Ⓔ	51. Ⓐ Ⓑ Ⓒ Ⓓ Ⓔ
15. Ⓐ Ⓑ Ⓒ Ⓓ Ⓔ	33. Ⓐ Ⓑ Ⓒ Ⓓ Ⓔ	52. Ⓐ Ⓑ Ⓒ Ⓓ Ⓔ
16. Ⓐ Ⓑ Ⓒ Ⓓ Ⓔ	34. Ⓐ Ⓑ Ⓒ Ⓓ Ⓔ	53. Ⓐ Ⓑ Ⓒ Ⓓ Ⓔ
17. Ⓐ Ⓑ Ⓒ Ⓓ Ⓔ	35. Ⓐ Ⓑ Ⓒ Ⓓ Ⓔ	54. Ⓐ Ⓑ Ⓒ Ⓓ Ⓔ
18. Ⓐ Ⓑ Ⓒ Ⓓ Ⓔ	36. Ⓐ Ⓑ Ⓒ Ⓓ Ⓔ	55. Ⓐ Ⓑ Ⓒ Ⓓ Ⓔ
	37. Ⓐ Ⓑ Ⓒ Ⓓ Ⓔ	

NOTE: Please make a photocopy of this answer sheet to use for English Composition with Essay Question Practice Test 4.

CLEP HUMANITIES

Section 1

1. Ⓐ Ⓑ Ⓒ Ⓓ Ⓔ
2. Ⓐ Ⓑ Ⓒ Ⓓ Ⓔ
3. Ⓐ Ⓑ Ⓒ Ⓓ Ⓔ
4. Ⓐ Ⓑ Ⓒ Ⓓ Ⓔ
5. Ⓐ Ⓑ Ⓒ Ⓓ Ⓔ
6. Ⓐ Ⓑ Ⓒ Ⓓ Ⓔ
7. Ⓐ Ⓑ Ⓒ Ⓓ Ⓔ
8. Ⓐ Ⓑ Ⓒ Ⓓ Ⓔ
9. Ⓐ Ⓑ Ⓒ Ⓓ Ⓔ
10. Ⓐ Ⓑ Ⓒ Ⓓ Ⓔ
11. Ⓐ Ⓑ Ⓒ Ⓓ Ⓔ
12. Ⓐ Ⓑ Ⓒ Ⓓ Ⓔ
13. Ⓐ Ⓑ Ⓒ Ⓓ Ⓔ
14. Ⓐ Ⓑ Ⓒ Ⓓ Ⓔ
15. Ⓐ Ⓑ Ⓒ Ⓓ Ⓔ
16. Ⓐ Ⓑ Ⓒ Ⓓ Ⓔ
17. Ⓐ Ⓑ Ⓒ Ⓓ Ⓔ
18. Ⓐ Ⓑ Ⓒ Ⓓ Ⓔ
19. Ⓐ Ⓑ Ⓒ Ⓓ Ⓔ
20. Ⓐ Ⓑ Ⓒ Ⓓ Ⓔ
21. Ⓐ Ⓑ Ⓒ Ⓓ Ⓔ
22. Ⓐ Ⓑ Ⓒ Ⓓ Ⓔ
23. Ⓐ Ⓑ Ⓒ Ⓓ Ⓔ
24. Ⓐ Ⓑ Ⓒ Ⓓ Ⓔ
25. Ⓐ Ⓑ Ⓒ Ⓓ Ⓔ

26. Ⓐ Ⓑ Ⓒ Ⓓ Ⓔ
27. Ⓐ Ⓑ Ⓒ Ⓓ Ⓔ
28. Ⓐ Ⓑ Ⓒ Ⓓ Ⓔ
29. Ⓐ Ⓑ Ⓒ Ⓓ Ⓔ
30. Ⓐ Ⓑ Ⓒ Ⓓ Ⓔ
31. Ⓐ Ⓑ Ⓒ Ⓓ Ⓔ
32. Ⓐ Ⓑ Ⓒ Ⓓ Ⓔ
33. Ⓐ Ⓑ Ⓒ Ⓓ Ⓔ
34. Ⓐ Ⓑ Ⓒ Ⓓ Ⓔ
35. Ⓐ Ⓑ Ⓒ Ⓓ Ⓔ
36. Ⓐ Ⓑ Ⓒ Ⓓ Ⓔ
37. Ⓐ Ⓑ Ⓒ Ⓓ Ⓔ
38. Ⓐ Ⓑ Ⓒ Ⓓ Ⓔ
39. Ⓐ Ⓑ Ⓒ Ⓓ Ⓔ
40. Ⓐ Ⓑ Ⓒ Ⓓ Ⓔ
41. Ⓐ Ⓑ Ⓒ Ⓓ Ⓔ
42. Ⓐ Ⓑ Ⓒ Ⓓ Ⓔ
43. Ⓐ Ⓑ Ⓒ Ⓓ Ⓔ
44. Ⓐ Ⓑ Ⓒ Ⓓ Ⓔ
45. Ⓐ Ⓑ Ⓒ Ⓓ Ⓔ
46. Ⓐ Ⓑ Ⓒ Ⓓ Ⓔ
47. Ⓐ Ⓑ Ⓒ Ⓓ Ⓔ
48. Ⓐ Ⓑ Ⓒ Ⓓ Ⓔ
49. Ⓐ Ⓑ Ⓒ Ⓓ Ⓔ
50. Ⓐ Ⓑ Ⓒ Ⓓ Ⓔ

51. Ⓐ Ⓑ Ⓒ Ⓓ Ⓔ
52. Ⓐ Ⓑ Ⓒ Ⓓ Ⓔ
53. Ⓐ Ⓑ Ⓒ Ⓓ Ⓔ
54. Ⓐ Ⓑ Ⓒ Ⓓ Ⓔ
55. Ⓐ Ⓑ Ⓒ Ⓓ Ⓔ
56. Ⓐ Ⓑ Ⓒ Ⓓ Ⓔ
57. Ⓐ Ⓑ Ⓒ Ⓓ Ⓔ
58. Ⓐ Ⓑ Ⓒ Ⓓ Ⓔ
59. Ⓐ Ⓑ Ⓒ Ⓓ Ⓔ
60. Ⓐ Ⓑ Ⓒ Ⓓ Ⓔ
61. Ⓐ Ⓑ Ⓒ Ⓓ Ⓔ
62. Ⓐ Ⓑ Ⓒ Ⓓ Ⓔ
63. Ⓐ Ⓑ Ⓒ Ⓓ Ⓔ
64. Ⓐ Ⓑ Ⓒ Ⓓ Ⓔ
65. Ⓐ Ⓑ Ⓒ Ⓓ Ⓔ
66. Ⓐ Ⓑ Ⓒ Ⓓ Ⓔ
67. Ⓐ Ⓑ Ⓒ Ⓓ Ⓔ
68. Ⓐ Ⓑ Ⓒ Ⓓ Ⓔ
69. Ⓐ Ⓑ Ⓒ Ⓓ Ⓔ
70. Ⓐ Ⓑ Ⓒ Ⓓ Ⓔ
71. Ⓐ Ⓑ Ⓒ Ⓓ Ⓔ
72. Ⓐ Ⓑ Ⓒ Ⓓ Ⓔ
73. Ⓐ Ⓑ Ⓒ Ⓓ Ⓔ
74. Ⓐ Ⓑ Ⓒ Ⓓ Ⓔ
75. Ⓐ Ⓑ Ⓒ Ⓓ Ⓔ

Section 2

76. Ⓐ Ⓑ Ⓒ Ⓓ Ⓔ	101. Ⓐ Ⓑ Ⓒ Ⓓ Ⓔ	126. Ⓐ Ⓑ Ⓒ Ⓓ Ⓔ
77. Ⓐ Ⓑ Ⓒ Ⓓ Ⓔ	102. Ⓐ Ⓑ Ⓒ Ⓓ Ⓔ	127. Ⓐ Ⓑ Ⓒ Ⓓ Ⓔ
78. Ⓐ Ⓑ Ⓒ Ⓓ Ⓔ	103. Ⓐ Ⓑ Ⓒ Ⓓ Ⓔ	128. Ⓐ Ⓑ Ⓒ Ⓓ Ⓔ
79. Ⓐ Ⓑ Ⓒ Ⓓ Ⓔ	104. Ⓐ Ⓑ Ⓒ Ⓓ Ⓔ	129. Ⓐ Ⓑ Ⓒ Ⓓ Ⓔ
80. Ⓐ Ⓑ Ⓒ Ⓓ Ⓔ	105. Ⓐ Ⓑ Ⓒ Ⓓ Ⓔ	130. Ⓐ Ⓑ Ⓒ Ⓓ Ⓔ
81. Ⓐ Ⓑ Ⓒ Ⓓ Ⓔ	106. Ⓐ Ⓑ Ⓒ Ⓓ Ⓔ	131. Ⓐ Ⓑ Ⓒ Ⓓ Ⓔ
82. Ⓐ Ⓑ Ⓒ Ⓓ Ⓔ	107. Ⓐ Ⓑ Ⓒ Ⓓ Ⓔ	132. Ⓐ Ⓑ Ⓒ Ⓓ Ⓔ
83. Ⓐ Ⓑ Ⓒ Ⓓ Ⓔ	108. Ⓐ Ⓑ Ⓒ Ⓓ Ⓔ	133. Ⓐ Ⓑ Ⓒ Ⓓ Ⓔ
84. Ⓐ Ⓑ Ⓒ Ⓓ Ⓔ	109. Ⓐ Ⓑ Ⓒ Ⓓ Ⓔ	134. Ⓐ Ⓑ Ⓒ Ⓓ Ⓔ
85. Ⓐ Ⓑ Ⓒ Ⓓ Ⓔ	110. Ⓐ Ⓑ Ⓒ Ⓓ Ⓔ	135. Ⓐ Ⓑ Ⓒ Ⓓ Ⓔ
86. Ⓐ Ⓑ Ⓒ Ⓓ Ⓔ	111. Ⓐ Ⓑ Ⓒ Ⓓ Ⓔ	136. Ⓐ Ⓑ Ⓒ Ⓓ Ⓔ
87. Ⓐ Ⓑ Ⓒ Ⓓ Ⓔ	112. Ⓐ Ⓑ Ⓒ Ⓓ Ⓔ	137. Ⓐ Ⓑ Ⓒ Ⓓ Ⓔ
88. Ⓐ Ⓑ Ⓒ Ⓓ Ⓔ	113. Ⓐ Ⓑ Ⓒ Ⓓ Ⓔ	138. Ⓐ Ⓑ Ⓒ Ⓓ Ⓔ
89. Ⓐ Ⓑ Ⓒ Ⓓ Ⓔ	114. Ⓐ Ⓑ Ⓒ Ⓓ Ⓔ	139. Ⓐ Ⓑ Ⓒ Ⓓ Ⓔ
90. Ⓐ Ⓑ Ⓒ Ⓓ Ⓔ	115. Ⓐ Ⓑ Ⓒ Ⓓ Ⓔ	140. Ⓐ Ⓑ Ⓒ Ⓓ Ⓔ
91. Ⓐ Ⓑ Ⓒ Ⓓ Ⓔ	116. Ⓐ Ⓑ Ⓒ Ⓓ Ⓔ	141. Ⓐ Ⓑ Ⓒ Ⓓ Ⓔ
92. Ⓐ Ⓑ Ⓒ Ⓓ Ⓔ	117. Ⓐ Ⓑ Ⓒ Ⓓ Ⓔ	142. Ⓐ Ⓑ Ⓒ Ⓓ Ⓔ
93. Ⓐ Ⓑ Ⓒ Ⓓ Ⓔ	118. Ⓐ Ⓑ Ⓒ Ⓓ Ⓔ	143. Ⓐ Ⓑ Ⓒ Ⓓ Ⓔ
94. Ⓐ Ⓑ Ⓒ Ⓓ Ⓔ	119. Ⓐ Ⓑ Ⓒ Ⓓ Ⓔ	144. Ⓐ Ⓑ Ⓒ Ⓓ Ⓔ
95. Ⓐ Ⓑ Ⓒ Ⓓ Ⓔ	120. Ⓐ Ⓑ Ⓒ Ⓓ Ⓔ	145. Ⓐ Ⓑ Ⓒ Ⓓ Ⓔ
96. Ⓐ Ⓑ Ⓒ Ⓓ Ⓔ	121. Ⓐ Ⓑ Ⓒ Ⓓ Ⓔ	146. Ⓐ Ⓑ Ⓒ Ⓓ Ⓔ
97. Ⓐ Ⓑ Ⓒ Ⓓ Ⓔ	122. Ⓐ Ⓑ Ⓒ Ⓓ Ⓔ	147. Ⓐ Ⓑ Ⓒ Ⓓ Ⓔ
98. Ⓐ Ⓑ Ⓒ Ⓓ Ⓔ	123. Ⓐ Ⓑ Ⓒ Ⓓ Ⓔ	148. Ⓐ Ⓑ Ⓒ Ⓓ Ⓔ
99. Ⓐ Ⓑ Ⓒ Ⓓ Ⓔ	124. Ⓐ Ⓑ Ⓒ Ⓓ Ⓔ	149. Ⓐ Ⓑ Ⓒ Ⓓ Ⓔ
100. Ⓐ Ⓑ Ⓒ Ⓓ Ⓔ	125. Ⓐ Ⓑ Ⓒ Ⓓ Ⓔ	150. Ⓐ Ⓑ Ⓒ Ⓓ Ⓔ

NOTE: Please make two photocopies of this answer sheet to use for Humanities Practice Tests 2 and 3.

CLEP COLLEGE MATHEMATICS

Section 1

1. Ⓐ Ⓑ Ⓒ Ⓓ Ⓔ
2. Ⓐ Ⓑ Ⓒ Ⓓ Ⓔ
3. Ⓐ Ⓑ Ⓒ Ⓓ Ⓔ
4. Ⓐ Ⓑ Ⓒ Ⓓ Ⓔ
5. Ⓐ Ⓑ Ⓒ Ⓓ Ⓔ
6. Ⓐ Ⓑ Ⓒ Ⓓ Ⓔ
7. Ⓐ Ⓑ Ⓒ Ⓓ Ⓔ
8. Ⓐ Ⓑ Ⓒ Ⓓ Ⓔ
9. Ⓐ Ⓑ Ⓒ Ⓓ Ⓔ
10. Ⓐ Ⓑ Ⓒ Ⓓ Ⓔ
11. Ⓐ Ⓑ Ⓒ Ⓓ Ⓔ
12. Ⓐ Ⓑ Ⓒ Ⓓ Ⓔ
13. Ⓐ Ⓑ Ⓒ Ⓓ Ⓔ
14. Ⓐ Ⓑ Ⓒ Ⓓ Ⓔ
15. Ⓐ Ⓑ Ⓒ Ⓓ Ⓔ
16. Ⓐ Ⓑ Ⓒ Ⓓ Ⓔ
17. Ⓐ Ⓑ Ⓒ Ⓓ Ⓔ
18. Ⓐ Ⓑ Ⓒ Ⓓ Ⓔ
19. Ⓐ Ⓑ Ⓒ Ⓓ Ⓔ
20. Ⓐ Ⓑ Ⓒ Ⓓ Ⓔ
21. Ⓐ Ⓑ Ⓒ Ⓓ Ⓔ
22. Ⓐ Ⓑ Ⓒ Ⓓ Ⓔ
23. Ⓐ Ⓑ Ⓒ Ⓓ Ⓔ
24. Ⓐ Ⓑ Ⓒ Ⓓ Ⓔ
25. Ⓐ Ⓑ Ⓒ Ⓓ Ⓔ
26. Ⓐ Ⓑ Ⓒ Ⓓ Ⓔ
27. Ⓐ Ⓑ Ⓒ Ⓓ Ⓔ
28. Ⓐ Ⓑ Ⓒ Ⓓ Ⓔ
29. Ⓐ Ⓑ Ⓒ Ⓓ Ⓔ
30. Ⓐ Ⓑ Ⓒ Ⓓ Ⓔ

31. Ⓐ Ⓑ Ⓒ Ⓓ Ⓔ
32. Ⓐ Ⓑ Ⓒ Ⓓ Ⓔ
33. Ⓐ Ⓑ Ⓒ Ⓓ Ⓔ
34. Ⓐ Ⓑ Ⓒ Ⓓ Ⓔ
35. Ⓐ Ⓑ Ⓒ Ⓓ Ⓔ
36. Ⓐ Ⓑ Ⓒ Ⓓ Ⓔ
37. Ⓐ Ⓑ Ⓒ Ⓓ Ⓔ
38. Ⓐ Ⓑ Ⓒ Ⓓ Ⓔ
39. Ⓐ Ⓑ Ⓒ Ⓓ Ⓔ
40. Ⓐ Ⓑ Ⓒ Ⓓ Ⓔ
41. Ⓐ Ⓑ Ⓒ Ⓓ Ⓔ
42. Ⓐ Ⓑ Ⓒ Ⓓ Ⓔ
43. Ⓐ Ⓑ Ⓒ Ⓓ Ⓔ
44. Ⓐ Ⓑ Ⓒ Ⓓ Ⓔ
45. Ⓐ Ⓑ Ⓒ Ⓓ Ⓔ

Section 2

46. Ⓐ Ⓑ Ⓒ Ⓓ Ⓔ
47. Ⓐ Ⓑ Ⓒ Ⓓ Ⓔ
48. Ⓐ Ⓑ Ⓒ Ⓓ Ⓔ
49. Ⓐ Ⓑ Ⓒ Ⓓ Ⓔ
50. Ⓐ Ⓑ Ⓒ Ⓓ Ⓔ
51. Ⓐ Ⓑ Ⓒ Ⓓ Ⓔ
52. Ⓐ Ⓑ Ⓒ Ⓓ Ⓔ
53. Ⓐ Ⓑ Ⓒ Ⓓ Ⓔ
54. Ⓐ Ⓑ Ⓒ Ⓓ Ⓔ
55. Ⓐ Ⓑ Ⓒ Ⓓ Ⓔ
56. Ⓐ Ⓑ Ⓒ Ⓓ Ⓔ
57. Ⓐ Ⓑ Ⓒ Ⓓ Ⓔ
58. Ⓐ Ⓑ Ⓒ Ⓓ Ⓔ
59. Ⓐ Ⓑ Ⓒ Ⓓ Ⓔ
60. Ⓐ Ⓑ Ⓒ Ⓓ Ⓔ

61. Ⓐ Ⓑ Ⓒ Ⓓ Ⓔ
62. Ⓐ Ⓑ Ⓒ Ⓓ Ⓔ
63. Ⓐ Ⓑ Ⓒ Ⓓ Ⓔ
64. Ⓐ Ⓑ Ⓒ Ⓓ Ⓔ
65. Ⓐ Ⓑ Ⓒ Ⓓ Ⓔ
66. Ⓐ Ⓑ Ⓒ Ⓓ Ⓔ
67. Ⓐ Ⓑ Ⓒ Ⓓ Ⓔ
68. Ⓐ Ⓑ Ⓒ Ⓓ Ⓔ
69. Ⓐ Ⓑ Ⓒ Ⓓ Ⓔ
70. Ⓐ Ⓑ Ⓒ Ⓓ Ⓔ
71. Ⓐ Ⓑ Ⓒ Ⓓ Ⓔ
72. Ⓐ Ⓑ Ⓒ Ⓓ Ⓔ
73. Ⓐ Ⓑ Ⓒ Ⓓ Ⓔ
74. Ⓐ Ⓑ Ⓒ Ⓓ Ⓔ
75. Ⓐ Ⓑ Ⓒ Ⓓ Ⓔ
76. Ⓐ Ⓑ Ⓒ Ⓓ Ⓔ
77. Ⓐ Ⓑ Ⓒ Ⓓ Ⓔ
78. Ⓐ Ⓑ Ⓒ Ⓓ Ⓔ
79. Ⓐ Ⓑ Ⓒ Ⓓ Ⓔ
80. Ⓐ Ⓑ Ⓒ Ⓓ Ⓔ
81. Ⓐ Ⓑ Ⓒ Ⓓ Ⓔ
82. Ⓐ Ⓑ Ⓒ Ⓓ Ⓔ
83. Ⓐ Ⓑ Ⓒ Ⓓ Ⓔ
84. Ⓐ Ⓑ Ⓒ Ⓓ Ⓔ
85. Ⓐ Ⓑ Ⓒ Ⓓ Ⓔ
86. Ⓐ Ⓑ Ⓒ Ⓓ Ⓔ
87. Ⓐ Ⓑ Ⓒ Ⓓ Ⓔ
88. Ⓐ Ⓑ Ⓒ Ⓓ Ⓔ
89. Ⓐ Ⓑ Ⓒ Ⓓ Ⓔ
90. Ⓐ Ⓑ Ⓒ Ⓓ Ⓔ

NOTE: Please make two photocopies of this answer sheet to use for College Mathematics Practice Tests 2 and 3.

CLEP NATURAL SCIENCES

Section 1

1. Ⓐ Ⓑ Ⓒ Ⓓ Ⓔ
2. Ⓐ Ⓑ Ⓒ Ⓓ Ⓔ
3. Ⓐ Ⓑ Ⓒ Ⓓ Ⓔ
4. Ⓐ Ⓑ Ⓒ Ⓓ Ⓔ
5. Ⓐ Ⓑ Ⓒ Ⓓ Ⓔ
6. Ⓐ Ⓑ Ⓒ Ⓓ Ⓔ
7. Ⓐ Ⓑ Ⓒ Ⓓ Ⓔ
8. Ⓐ Ⓑ Ⓒ Ⓓ Ⓔ
9. Ⓐ Ⓑ Ⓒ Ⓓ Ⓔ
10. Ⓐ Ⓑ Ⓒ Ⓓ Ⓔ
11. Ⓐ Ⓑ Ⓒ Ⓓ Ⓔ
12. Ⓐ Ⓑ Ⓒ Ⓓ Ⓔ
13. Ⓐ Ⓑ Ⓒ Ⓓ Ⓔ
14. Ⓐ Ⓑ Ⓒ Ⓓ Ⓔ
15. Ⓐ Ⓑ Ⓒ Ⓓ Ⓔ
16. Ⓐ Ⓑ Ⓒ Ⓓ Ⓔ
17. Ⓐ Ⓑ Ⓒ Ⓓ Ⓔ
18. Ⓐ Ⓑ Ⓒ Ⓓ Ⓔ
19. Ⓐ Ⓑ Ⓒ Ⓓ Ⓔ
20. Ⓐ Ⓑ Ⓒ Ⓓ Ⓔ
21. Ⓐ Ⓑ Ⓒ Ⓓ Ⓔ
22. Ⓐ Ⓑ Ⓒ Ⓓ Ⓔ
23. Ⓐ Ⓑ Ⓒ Ⓓ Ⓔ
24. Ⓐ Ⓑ Ⓒ Ⓓ Ⓔ
25. Ⓐ Ⓑ Ⓒ Ⓓ Ⓔ
26. Ⓐ Ⓑ Ⓒ Ⓓ Ⓔ
27. Ⓐ Ⓑ Ⓒ Ⓓ Ⓔ
28. Ⓐ Ⓑ Ⓒ Ⓓ Ⓔ
29. Ⓐ Ⓑ Ⓒ Ⓓ Ⓔ
30. Ⓐ Ⓑ Ⓒ Ⓓ Ⓔ
31. Ⓐ Ⓑ Ⓒ Ⓓ Ⓔ
32. Ⓐ Ⓑ Ⓒ Ⓓ Ⓔ
33. Ⓐ Ⓑ Ⓒ Ⓓ Ⓔ
34. Ⓐ Ⓑ Ⓒ Ⓓ Ⓔ
35. Ⓐ Ⓑ Ⓒ Ⓓ Ⓔ
36. Ⓐ Ⓑ Ⓒ Ⓓ Ⓔ
37. Ⓐ Ⓑ Ⓒ Ⓓ Ⓔ
38. Ⓐ Ⓑ Ⓒ Ⓓ Ⓔ
39. Ⓐ Ⓑ Ⓒ Ⓓ Ⓔ
40. Ⓐ Ⓑ Ⓒ Ⓓ Ⓔ

41. Ⓐ Ⓑ Ⓒ Ⓓ Ⓔ
42. Ⓐ Ⓑ Ⓒ Ⓓ Ⓔ
43. Ⓐ Ⓑ Ⓒ Ⓓ Ⓔ
44. Ⓐ Ⓑ Ⓒ Ⓓ Ⓔ
45. Ⓐ Ⓑ Ⓒ Ⓓ Ⓔ
46. Ⓐ Ⓑ Ⓒ Ⓓ Ⓔ
47. Ⓐ Ⓑ Ⓒ Ⓓ Ⓔ
48. Ⓐ Ⓑ Ⓒ Ⓓ Ⓔ
49. Ⓐ Ⓑ Ⓒ Ⓓ Ⓔ
50. Ⓐ Ⓑ Ⓒ Ⓓ Ⓔ
51. Ⓐ Ⓑ Ⓒ Ⓓ Ⓔ
52. Ⓐ Ⓑ Ⓒ Ⓓ Ⓔ
53. Ⓐ Ⓑ Ⓒ Ⓓ Ⓔ
54. Ⓐ Ⓑ Ⓒ Ⓓ Ⓔ
55. Ⓐ Ⓑ Ⓒ Ⓓ Ⓔ
56. Ⓐ Ⓑ Ⓒ Ⓓ Ⓔ
57. Ⓐ Ⓑ Ⓒ Ⓓ Ⓔ
58. Ⓐ Ⓑ Ⓒ Ⓓ Ⓔ
59. Ⓐ Ⓑ Ⓒ Ⓓ Ⓔ
60. Ⓐ Ⓑ Ⓒ Ⓓ Ⓔ

Section 2

61. Ⓐ Ⓑ Ⓒ Ⓓ Ⓔ
62. Ⓐ Ⓑ Ⓒ Ⓓ Ⓔ
63. Ⓐ Ⓑ Ⓒ Ⓓ Ⓔ
64. Ⓐ Ⓑ Ⓒ Ⓓ Ⓔ
65. Ⓐ Ⓑ Ⓒ Ⓓ Ⓔ
66. Ⓐ Ⓑ Ⓒ Ⓓ Ⓔ
67. Ⓐ Ⓑ Ⓒ Ⓓ Ⓔ
68. Ⓐ Ⓑ Ⓒ Ⓓ Ⓔ
69. Ⓐ Ⓑ Ⓒ Ⓓ Ⓔ
70. Ⓐ Ⓑ Ⓒ Ⓓ Ⓔ
71. Ⓐ Ⓑ Ⓒ Ⓓ Ⓔ
72. Ⓐ Ⓑ Ⓒ Ⓓ Ⓔ
73. Ⓐ Ⓑ Ⓒ Ⓓ Ⓔ
74. Ⓐ Ⓑ Ⓒ Ⓓ Ⓔ
75. Ⓐ Ⓑ Ⓒ Ⓓ Ⓔ
76. Ⓐ Ⓑ Ⓒ Ⓓ Ⓔ
77. Ⓐ Ⓑ Ⓒ Ⓓ Ⓔ
78. Ⓐ Ⓑ Ⓒ Ⓓ Ⓔ
79. Ⓐ Ⓑ Ⓒ Ⓓ Ⓔ

80. Ⓐ Ⓑ Ⓒ Ⓓ Ⓔ
81. Ⓐ Ⓑ Ⓒ Ⓓ Ⓔ
82. Ⓐ Ⓑ Ⓒ Ⓓ Ⓔ
83. Ⓐ Ⓑ Ⓒ Ⓓ Ⓔ
84. Ⓐ Ⓑ Ⓒ Ⓓ Ⓔ
85. Ⓐ Ⓑ Ⓒ Ⓓ Ⓔ
86. Ⓐ Ⓑ Ⓒ Ⓓ Ⓔ
87. Ⓐ Ⓑ Ⓒ Ⓓ Ⓔ
88. Ⓐ Ⓑ Ⓒ Ⓓ Ⓔ
89. Ⓐ Ⓑ Ⓒ Ⓓ Ⓔ
90. Ⓐ Ⓑ Ⓒ Ⓓ Ⓔ
91. Ⓐ Ⓑ Ⓒ Ⓓ Ⓔ
92. Ⓐ Ⓑ Ⓒ Ⓓ Ⓔ
93. Ⓐ Ⓑ Ⓒ Ⓓ Ⓔ
94. Ⓐ Ⓑ Ⓒ Ⓓ Ⓔ
95. Ⓐ Ⓑ Ⓒ Ⓓ Ⓔ
96. Ⓐ Ⓑ Ⓒ Ⓓ Ⓔ
97. Ⓐ Ⓑ Ⓒ Ⓓ Ⓔ
98. Ⓐ Ⓑ Ⓒ Ⓓ Ⓔ
99. Ⓐ Ⓑ Ⓒ Ⓓ Ⓔ
100. Ⓐ Ⓑ Ⓒ Ⓓ Ⓔ
101. Ⓐ Ⓑ Ⓒ Ⓓ Ⓔ
102. Ⓐ Ⓑ Ⓒ Ⓓ Ⓔ
103. Ⓐ Ⓑ Ⓒ Ⓓ Ⓔ
104. Ⓐ Ⓑ Ⓒ Ⓓ Ⓔ
105. Ⓐ Ⓑ Ⓒ Ⓓ Ⓔ
106. Ⓐ Ⓑ Ⓒ Ⓓ Ⓔ
107. Ⓐ Ⓑ Ⓒ Ⓓ Ⓔ
108. Ⓐ Ⓑ Ⓒ Ⓓ Ⓔ
109. Ⓐ Ⓑ Ⓒ Ⓓ Ⓔ
110. Ⓐ Ⓑ Ⓒ Ⓓ Ⓔ
111. Ⓐ Ⓑ Ⓒ Ⓓ Ⓔ
112. Ⓐ Ⓑ Ⓒ Ⓓ Ⓔ
113. Ⓐ Ⓑ Ⓒ Ⓓ Ⓔ
114. Ⓐ Ⓑ Ⓒ Ⓓ Ⓔ
115. Ⓐ Ⓑ Ⓒ Ⓓ Ⓔ
116. Ⓐ Ⓑ Ⓒ Ⓓ Ⓔ
117. Ⓐ Ⓑ Ⓒ Ⓓ Ⓔ
118. Ⓐ Ⓑ Ⓒ Ⓓ Ⓔ
119. Ⓐ Ⓑ Ⓒ Ⓓ Ⓔ
120. Ⓐ Ⓑ Ⓒ Ⓓ Ⓔ

NOTE: Please make two photocopies of this answer sheet to use for Natural Sciences Practice Tests 2 and 3.

CLEP SOCIAL SCIENCES AND HISTORY

Section 1

1. Ⓐ Ⓑ Ⓒ Ⓓ Ⓔ
2. Ⓐ Ⓑ Ⓒ Ⓓ Ⓔ
3. Ⓐ Ⓑ Ⓒ Ⓓ Ⓔ
4. Ⓐ Ⓑ Ⓒ Ⓓ Ⓔ
5. Ⓐ Ⓑ Ⓒ Ⓓ Ⓔ
6. Ⓐ Ⓑ Ⓒ Ⓓ Ⓔ
7. Ⓐ Ⓑ Ⓒ Ⓓ Ⓔ
8. Ⓐ Ⓑ Ⓒ Ⓓ Ⓔ
9. Ⓐ Ⓑ Ⓒ Ⓓ Ⓔ
10. Ⓐ Ⓑ Ⓒ Ⓓ Ⓔ
11. Ⓐ Ⓑ Ⓒ Ⓓ Ⓔ
12. Ⓐ Ⓑ Ⓒ Ⓓ Ⓔ
13. Ⓐ Ⓑ Ⓒ Ⓓ Ⓔ
14. Ⓐ Ⓑ Ⓒ Ⓓ Ⓔ
15. Ⓐ Ⓑ Ⓒ Ⓓ Ⓔ
16. Ⓐ Ⓑ Ⓒ Ⓓ Ⓔ
17. Ⓐ Ⓑ Ⓒ Ⓓ Ⓔ
18. Ⓐ Ⓑ Ⓒ Ⓓ Ⓔ
19. Ⓐ Ⓑ Ⓒ Ⓓ Ⓔ
20. Ⓐ Ⓑ Ⓒ Ⓓ Ⓔ
21. Ⓐ Ⓑ Ⓒ Ⓓ Ⓔ

22. Ⓐ Ⓑ Ⓒ Ⓓ Ⓔ
23. Ⓐ Ⓑ Ⓒ Ⓓ Ⓔ
24. Ⓐ Ⓑ Ⓒ Ⓓ Ⓔ
25. Ⓐ Ⓑ Ⓒ Ⓓ Ⓔ
26. Ⓐ Ⓑ Ⓒ Ⓓ Ⓔ
27. Ⓐ Ⓑ Ⓒ Ⓓ Ⓔ
28. Ⓐ Ⓑ Ⓒ Ⓓ Ⓔ
29. Ⓐ Ⓑ Ⓒ Ⓓ Ⓔ
30. Ⓐ Ⓑ Ⓒ Ⓓ Ⓔ
31. Ⓐ Ⓑ Ⓒ Ⓓ Ⓔ
32. Ⓐ Ⓑ Ⓒ Ⓓ Ⓔ
33. Ⓐ Ⓑ Ⓒ Ⓓ Ⓔ
34. Ⓐ Ⓑ Ⓒ Ⓓ Ⓔ
35. Ⓐ Ⓑ Ⓒ Ⓓ Ⓔ
36. Ⓐ Ⓑ Ⓒ Ⓓ Ⓔ
37. Ⓐ Ⓑ Ⓒ Ⓓ Ⓔ
38. Ⓐ Ⓑ Ⓒ Ⓓ Ⓔ
39. Ⓐ Ⓑ Ⓒ Ⓓ Ⓔ
40. Ⓐ Ⓑ Ⓒ Ⓓ Ⓔ
41. Ⓐ Ⓑ Ⓒ Ⓓ Ⓔ
42. Ⓐ Ⓑ Ⓒ Ⓓ Ⓔ
43. Ⓐ Ⓑ Ⓒ Ⓓ Ⓔ

44. Ⓐ Ⓑ Ⓒ Ⓓ Ⓔ
45. Ⓐ Ⓑ Ⓒ Ⓓ Ⓔ
46. Ⓐ Ⓑ Ⓒ Ⓓ Ⓔ
47. Ⓐ Ⓑ Ⓒ Ⓓ Ⓔ
48. Ⓐ Ⓑ Ⓒ Ⓓ Ⓔ
49. Ⓐ Ⓑ Ⓒ Ⓓ Ⓔ
50. Ⓐ Ⓑ Ⓒ Ⓓ Ⓔ
51. Ⓐ Ⓑ Ⓒ Ⓓ Ⓔ
52. Ⓐ Ⓑ Ⓒ Ⓓ Ⓔ
53. Ⓐ Ⓑ Ⓒ Ⓓ Ⓔ
54. Ⓐ Ⓑ Ⓒ Ⓓ Ⓔ
55. Ⓐ Ⓑ Ⓒ Ⓓ Ⓔ
56. Ⓐ Ⓑ Ⓒ Ⓓ Ⓔ
57. Ⓐ Ⓑ Ⓒ Ⓓ Ⓔ
58. Ⓐ Ⓑ Ⓒ Ⓓ Ⓔ
59. Ⓐ Ⓑ Ⓒ Ⓓ Ⓔ
60. Ⓐ Ⓑ Ⓒ Ⓓ Ⓔ
61. Ⓐ Ⓑ Ⓒ Ⓓ Ⓔ
62. Ⓐ Ⓑ Ⓒ Ⓓ Ⓔ
63. Ⓐ Ⓑ Ⓒ Ⓓ Ⓔ
64. Ⓐ Ⓑ Ⓒ Ⓓ Ⓔ
65. Ⓐ Ⓑ Ⓒ Ⓓ Ⓔ

Section 2

66. Ⓐ Ⓑ Ⓒ Ⓓ Ⓔ	87. Ⓐ Ⓑ Ⓒ Ⓓ Ⓔ	109. Ⓐ Ⓑ Ⓒ Ⓓ Ⓔ
67. Ⓐ Ⓑ Ⓒ Ⓓ Ⓔ	88. Ⓐ Ⓑ Ⓒ Ⓓ Ⓔ	110. Ⓐ Ⓑ Ⓒ Ⓓ Ⓔ
68. Ⓐ Ⓑ Ⓒ Ⓓ Ⓔ	89. Ⓐ Ⓑ Ⓒ Ⓓ Ⓔ	111. Ⓐ Ⓑ Ⓒ Ⓓ Ⓔ
69. Ⓐ Ⓑ Ⓒ Ⓓ Ⓔ	90. Ⓐ Ⓑ Ⓒ Ⓓ Ⓔ	112. Ⓐ Ⓑ Ⓒ Ⓓ Ⓔ
70. Ⓐ Ⓑ Ⓒ Ⓓ Ⓔ	91. Ⓐ Ⓑ Ⓒ Ⓓ Ⓔ	113. Ⓐ Ⓑ Ⓒ Ⓓ Ⓔ
71. Ⓐ Ⓑ Ⓒ Ⓓ Ⓔ	92. Ⓐ Ⓑ Ⓒ Ⓓ Ⓔ	114. Ⓐ Ⓑ Ⓒ Ⓓ Ⓔ
72. Ⓐ Ⓑ Ⓒ Ⓓ Ⓔ	93. Ⓐ Ⓑ Ⓒ Ⓓ Ⓔ	115. Ⓐ Ⓑ Ⓒ Ⓓ Ⓔ
73. Ⓐ Ⓑ Ⓒ Ⓓ Ⓔ	94. Ⓐ Ⓑ Ⓒ Ⓓ Ⓔ	116. Ⓐ Ⓑ Ⓒ Ⓓ Ⓔ
74. Ⓐ Ⓑ Ⓒ Ⓓ Ⓔ	95. Ⓐ Ⓑ Ⓒ Ⓓ Ⓔ	117. Ⓐ Ⓑ Ⓒ Ⓓ Ⓔ
75. Ⓐ Ⓑ Ⓒ Ⓓ Ⓔ	96. Ⓐ Ⓑ Ⓒ Ⓓ Ⓔ	118. Ⓐ Ⓑ Ⓒ Ⓓ Ⓔ
76. Ⓐ Ⓑ Ⓒ Ⓓ Ⓔ	97. Ⓐ Ⓑ Ⓒ Ⓓ Ⓔ	119. Ⓐ Ⓑ Ⓒ Ⓓ Ⓔ
77. Ⓐ Ⓑ Ⓒ Ⓓ Ⓔ	98. Ⓐ Ⓑ Ⓒ Ⓓ Ⓔ	120. Ⓐ Ⓑ Ⓒ Ⓓ Ⓔ
78. Ⓐ Ⓑ Ⓒ Ⓓ Ⓔ	99. Ⓐ Ⓑ Ⓒ Ⓓ Ⓔ	121. Ⓐ Ⓑ Ⓒ Ⓓ Ⓔ
79. Ⓐ Ⓑ Ⓒ Ⓓ Ⓔ	100. Ⓐ Ⓑ Ⓒ Ⓓ Ⓔ	122. Ⓐ Ⓑ Ⓒ Ⓓ Ⓔ
80. Ⓐ Ⓑ Ⓒ Ⓓ Ⓔ	101. Ⓐ Ⓑ Ⓒ Ⓓ Ⓔ	123. Ⓐ Ⓑ Ⓒ Ⓓ Ⓔ
81. Ⓐ Ⓑ Ⓒ Ⓓ Ⓔ	102. Ⓐ Ⓑ Ⓒ Ⓓ Ⓔ	124. Ⓐ Ⓑ Ⓒ Ⓓ Ⓔ
82. Ⓐ Ⓑ Ⓒ Ⓓ Ⓔ	103. Ⓐ Ⓑ Ⓒ Ⓓ Ⓔ	125. Ⓐ Ⓑ Ⓒ Ⓓ Ⓔ
83. Ⓐ Ⓑ Ⓒ Ⓓ Ⓔ	104. Ⓐ Ⓑ Ⓒ Ⓓ Ⓔ	126. Ⓐ Ⓑ Ⓒ Ⓓ Ⓔ
84. Ⓐ Ⓑ Ⓒ Ⓓ Ⓔ	105. Ⓐ Ⓑ Ⓒ Ⓓ Ⓔ	127. Ⓐ Ⓑ Ⓒ Ⓓ Ⓔ
85. Ⓐ Ⓑ Ⓒ Ⓓ Ⓔ	106. Ⓐ Ⓑ Ⓒ Ⓓ Ⓔ	128. Ⓐ Ⓑ Ⓒ Ⓓ Ⓔ
86. Ⓐ Ⓑ Ⓒ Ⓓ Ⓔ	107. Ⓐ Ⓑ Ⓒ Ⓓ Ⓔ	129. Ⓐ Ⓑ Ⓒ Ⓓ Ⓔ
	108. Ⓐ Ⓑ Ⓒ Ⓓ Ⓔ	130. Ⓐ Ⓑ Ⓒ Ⓓ Ⓔ

NOTE: Please make two photocopies of this answer sheet to use for Social Sciences and History Practice Tests 2 and 3.

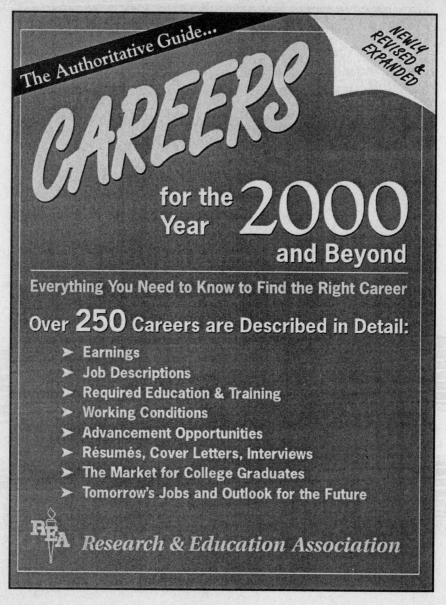

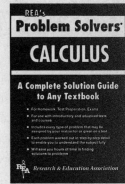

REA's Test Preps
The Best in Test Preparation

- REA "Test Preps" are **far more** comprehensive than any other test preparation series
- Each book contains up to **eight** full-length practice tests based on the most recent exams
- **Every** type of question likely to be given on the exams is included
- Answers are accompanied by **full** and **detailed** explanations

REA has published over 60 Test Preparation volumes in several series. They include:

Advanced Placement Exams (APs)
Biology
Calculus AB & Calculus BC
Chemistry
Computer Science
English Language & Composition
English Literature & Composition
European History
Government & Politics
Physics
Psychology
Statistics
Spanish Language
United States History

College-Level Examination Program (CLEP)
Analyzing and Interpreting Literature
College Algebra
Freshman College Composition
General Examinations
General Examinations Review
History of the United States I
Human Growth and Development
Introductory Sociology
Principles of Marketing
Spanish

SAT II: Subject Tests
American History
Biology E/M
Chemistry
English Language Proficiency Test
French
German

SAT II: Subject Tests (cont'd)
Literature
Mathematics Level IC, IIC
Physics
Spanish
Writing

Graduate Record Exams (GREs)
Biology
Chemistry
Computer Science
Economics
Engineering
General
History
Literature in English
Mathematics
Physics
Psychology
Sociology

ACT - ACT Assessment

ASVAB - Armed Services Vocational Aptitude Battery

CBEST - California Basic Educational Skills Test

CDL - Commercial Driver License Exam

CLAST - College Level Academic Skills Test

ELM - Entry Level Mathematics

ExCET - Exam for the Certification of Educators in Texas

FE (EIT) - Fundamentals of Engineering Exam

FE Review - Fundamentals of Engineering Review

GED - High School Equivalency Diploma Exam (U.S. & Canadian editions)

GMAT - Graduate Management Admission Test

LSAT - Law School Admission Test

MAT - Miller Analogies Test

MCAT - Medical College Admission Test

MSAT - Multiple Subjects Assessment for Teachers

NJ HSPT- New Jersey High School Proficiency Test

PPST - Pre-Professional Skills Tests

PRAXIS II/NTE - Core Battery

PSAT - Preliminary Scholastic Assessment Test

SAT I - Reasoning Test

SAT I - Quick Study & Review

TASP - Texas Academic Skills Program

TOEFL - Test of English as a Foreign Language

TOEIC - Test of English for International Communication

RESEARCH & EDUCATION ASSOCIATION
61 Ethel Road W. • Piscataway, New Jersey 08854
Phone: (732) 819-8880   **website: www.rea.com**

Please send me more information about your Test Prep books

Name _____

Address _____

City _____ State _____ Zip _____

MAXnotes®

REA's Literature Study Guides

MAXnotes® are student-friendly. They offer a fresh look at masterpieces of literature, presented in a lively and interesting fashion. **MAXnotes®** offer the essentials of what you should know about the work, including outlines, explanations and discussions of the plot, character lists, analyses, and historical context. **MAXnotes®** are designed to help you think independently about literary works by raising various issues and thought-provoking ideas and questions. Written by literary experts who currently teach the subject, **MAXnotes®** enhance your understanding and enjoyment of the work.

Available **MAXnotes®** include the following:

Absalom, Absalom!
The Aeneid of Virgil
Animal Farm
Antony and Cleopatra
As I Lay Dying
As You Like It
The Autobiography of
   Malcolm X
The Awakening
Beloved
Beowulf
Billy Budd
The Bluest Eye, A Novel
Brave New World
The Canterbury Tales
The Catcher in the Rye
The Color Purple
The Crucible
Death in Venice
Death of a Salesman
The Divine Comedy I: Inferno
Dubliners
The Edible Woman
Emma
Euripides' Medea & Electra
Frankenstein
Gone with the Wind
The Grapes of Wrath
Great Expectations
The Great Gatsby
Gulliver's Travels
Handmaid's Tale
Hamlet
Hard Times
Heart of Darkness

Henry IV, Part I
Henry V
The House on Mango Street
Huckleberry Finn
I Know Why the Caged
   Bird Sings
The Iliad
Invisible Man
Jane Eyre
Jazz
The Joy Luck Club
Jude the Obscure
Julius Caesar
King Lear
Leaves of Grass
Les Misérables
Lord of the Flies
Macbeth
The Merchant of Venice
Metamorphoses of Ovid
Metamorphosis
Middlemarch
A Midsummer Night's Dream
Moby-Dick
Moll Flanders
Mrs. Dalloway
Much Ado About Nothing
Mules and Men
My Antonia
Native Son
1984
The Odyssey
Oedipus Trilogy
Of Mice and Men
On the Road

Othello
Paradise
Paradise Lost
A Passage to India
Plato's Republic
Portrait of a Lady
A Portrait of the Artist
   as a Young Man
Pride and Prejudice
A Raisin in the Sun
Richard II
Romeo and Juliet
The Scarlet Letter
Sir Gawain and the
   Green Knight
Slaughterhouse-Five
Song of Solomon
The Sound and the Fury
The Stranger
Sula
The Sun Also Rises
A Tale of Two Cities
The Taming of the Shrew
Tar Baby
The Tempest
Tess of the D'Urbervilles
Their Eyes Were Watching God
Things Fall Apart
To Kill a Mockingbird
To the Lighthouse
Twelfth Night
Uncle Tom's Cabin
Waiting for Godot
Wuthering Heights
Guide to Literary Terms

RESEARCH & EDUCATION ASSOCIATION
61 Ethel Road W. • Piscataway, New Jersey 08854
Phone: (732) 819-8880   **website: www.rea.com**

Please send me more information about MAXnotes®.

Name _____

Address _____

City _____ State _____ Zip _____

REA's Test Prep Books Are The Best!

(a sample of the <u>hundreds of letters</u> REA receives each year)

" I am writing to congratulate you on preparing an exceptional study guide. In five years of teaching this course I have never encountered a more thorough, comprehensive, concise and realistic preparation for this examination. "

Teacher, Davie, FL

" I have found your publications, *The Best Test Preparation...*, to be exactly that. "

Teacher, Aptos, CA

" I used your *CLEP Introductory Sociology* book and rank it 99% – thank you! "

Student, Jerusalem, Israel

" Your GMAT book greatly helped me on the test. Thank you. "

Student, Oxford, OH

" I recently got the French SAT II Exam book from REA. I congratulate you on first-rate French practice tests."

Instructor, Los Angeles, CA

" Your AP English Literature and Composition book is most impressive."

Student, Montgomery, AL

" The REA LSAT Test Preparation guide is a winner! "

Instructor, Spartanburg, SC

(more on front page)